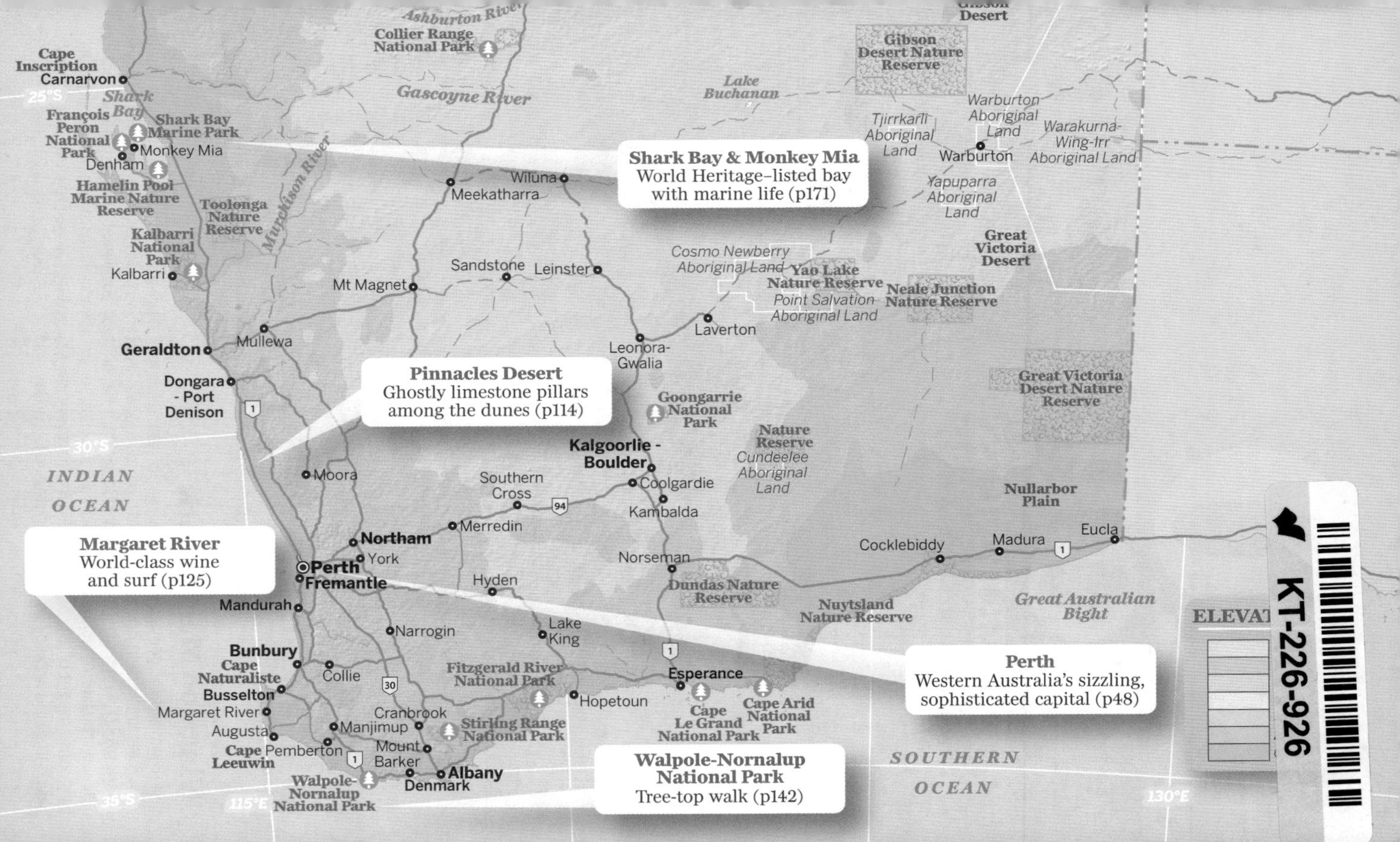

Shark Bay & Monkey Mia
World Heritage–listed bay with marine life (p171)
Pinnacles Desert
Ghostly limestone pillars among the dunes (p114)
Margaret River
World-class wine and surf (p125)
Perth
Western Australia's sizzling, sophisticated capital (p48)
Walpole-Nornalup National Park
Tree-top walk (p142)
Cape Inscription
Carnarvon
Shark Bay
François Peron National Park
Shark Bay Marine Park
Monkey Mia
Denham
Hamelin Pool Marine Nature Reserve
Toolonga Nature Reserve
Kalbarri National Park
Kalbarri
Murchison River
Ashburton River
Collier Range National Park
Gascoyne River
Meekatharra
Wiluna
Lake Buchanan
Gibson Desert Nature Reserve
Tjirrkarli Aboriginal Land
Warburton Aboriginal Land
Warburton
Warakurna-Wing-Irr Aboriginal Land
Yapuparra Aboriginal Land
Great Victoria Desert
Sandstone
Leinster
Mt Magnet
Cosmo Newberry Aboriginal Land
Yao Lake Nature Reserve
Point Salvation Aboriginal Land
Neale Junction Nature Reserve
Laverton
Leonora-Gwalia
Geraldton
Mullewa
Dongara - Port Denison
Great Victoria Desert Nature Reserve
Goongarrie National Park
Nature Reserve
Cundeelee Aboriginal Land
Kalgoorlie - Boulder
Coolgardie
Kambalda
Southern Cross
Moora
INDIAN OCEAN
30°S
Nullarbor Plain
Merredin
Northam
York
Perth
Fremantle
Mandurah
Hyden
Norseman
Dundas Nature Reserve
Cocklebiddy
Madura
Eucla
Nuytsland Nature Reserve
Great Australian Bight
Narrogin
Lake King
Bunbury
Cape Naturaliste
Collie
Busselton
Margaret River
Augusta
Cape Leeuwin
Pemberton
Manjimup
Cranbrook
Mount Barker
Albany
Denmark
Walpole-Nornalup National Park
Fitzgerald River National Park
Stirling Range National Park
Hopetoun
Esperance
Cape Le Grand National Park
Cape Arid National Park
SOUTHERN OCEAN
25°S
35°S
115°E
130°E
ELEVAT
KT-226-926

10 TOP EXPERIENCES

Ningaloo Marine Park

1 Swim beside 'gentle giant' whale sharks, snorkel amongst pristine coral, surf off seldom-visited reefs and dive at one of the world's premier locations at this World Heritage–nominated marine park (p187), which sits off North West Cape on the Coral Coast. Rivalling the Great Barrier Reef for beauty, Ningaloo's wonders are much more accessible; great snorkelling can be had in turquoise lagoons straight off the beach. Development is very low-key, so be prepared to camp or take day trips from the access towns of Exmouth and Coral Bay.

PAGE 46

ON THE ROAD

YOUR COMPLETE DESTINATION GUIDE
In-depth reviews, detailed listings and insider tips

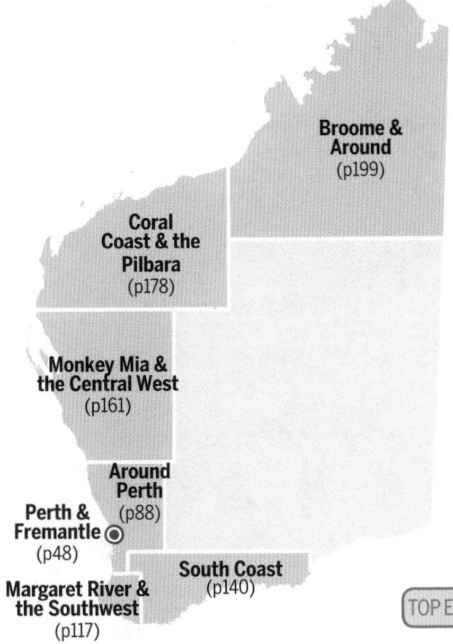

TOP EXPERIENCES MAP NEXT PAGE

PAGE 245

SURVIVAL GUIDE

YOUR AT-A-GLANCE REFERENCE
How to get around, get a room, stay safe, say hello

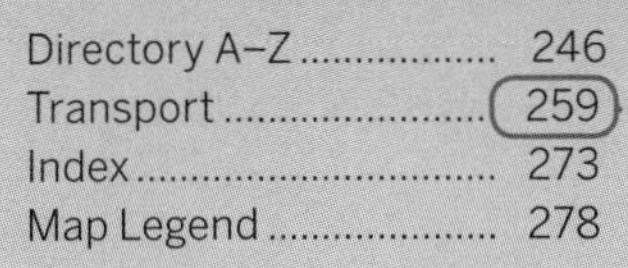

THIS EDITION WRITTEN AND RESEARCHED BY

Peter Dragicevich,
Rebecca Chau, Steve Waters

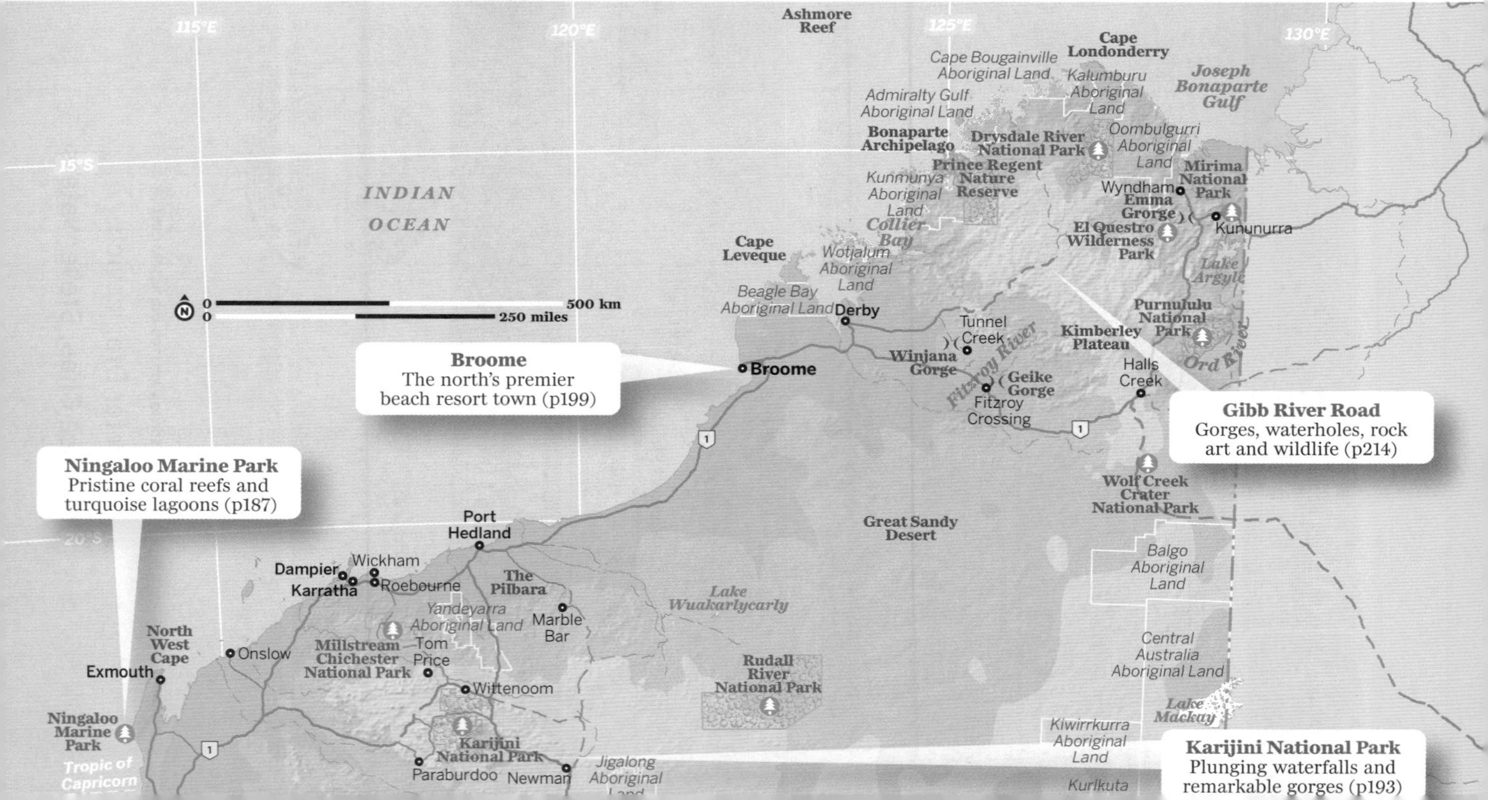
Broome
The north's premier beach resort town (p199)
Ningaloo Marine Park
Pristine coral reefs and turquoise lagoons (p187)
Gibb River Road
Gorges, waterholes, rock art and wildlife (p214)
Karijini National Park
Plunging waterfalls and remarkable gorges (p193)
INDIAN
OCEAN
0
500 km
0
250 miles
115°E
120°E
125°E
130°E
15°S
20°S
Ashmore Reef
Cape Londonderry
Cape Bougainville Aboriginal Land
Kalumburu Aboriginal Land
Joseph Bonaparte Gulf
Admiralty Gulf Aboriginal Land
Bonaparte Archipelago
Drysdale River National Park
Oombulgurri Aboriginal Land
Prince Regent Nature Reserve
Kunmunya Aboriginal Land
Mirima National Park
Wyndham
Emma Grorge
Kununurra
Collier Bay
El Questro Wilderness Park
Cape Leveque
Wotjalum Aboriginal Land
Lake Argyle
Beagle Bay Aboriginal Land
Derby
Tunnel Creek
Purnululu National Park
Kimberley Plateau
Winjana Gorge
Fitzroy River
Geike Gorge
Fitzroy Crossing
Halls Creek
Ord River
Broome
Wolf Creek Crater National Park
Great Sandy Desert
Port Hedland
Wickham
Dampier
Karratha
Roebourne
The Pilbara
Lake Wuakarlycarly
Balgo Aboriginal Land
Yandeyarra Aboriginal Land
Marble Bar
North West Cape
Onslow
Millstream Chichester National Park
Tom Price
Central Australia Aboriginal Land
Exmouth
Wittenoom
Rudall River National Park
Ningaloo Marine Park
Karijini National Park
Lake Mackay
Kiwirrkurra Aboriginal Land
Tropic of Capricorn
Paraburdoo
Newman
Jigalong Aboriginal Land
Kurlkuta

Margaret River Wine Region

2 The joy of drifting from winery to winery along country roads shaded by tall gum trees is just one of the delights of Australia's most beautiful wine region (p125). Right on its doorstep are the white sands of Geographe Bay, and even closer to the vines are the world-famous surf breaks of Yallingup and Margaret River Mouth. And then there are the caves – magical subterranean palaces of limestone, scattered along the main wine-tasting route. Sup, swim, surf, descend – the only difficulty is picking the order. Margaret River Mouth

Shark Bay & Monkey Mia

3 The aquamarine waters of World Heritage–listed Shark Bay (p171) teem with an incredible diversity of marine life, from the world famous dolphins of Monkey Mia (p174) to the ancient stromatolites of Hamelin Pool (p171). National parks provide simple coastal camping, and excellent Indigenous cultural tours explain how to care for and understand country. Explore remote Edel Land (p174), Australia's westernmost tip, and cross over to historically rich Dirk Hartog Island (p175), or sail after the elusive, sea-grass-munching dugong. Dolphins, Monkey Mia

Broome

4 Like no other town in the country, Broome (p202) is a kinetic, postmodern pastiche of bars, resorts, beaches, nature, locals and every type of traveller. Turquoise waters melt with tourists while red pindan earth blows into spa resorts. A cruel pearling past lies incongruously against the achingly beautiful curved sands of Cable Beach. Crowds at sunset watch camels wander by imported palms, and cavorting whales remain unnoticed just offshore. Galleries stock Indigenous art from across the Kimberley, while an Estonian backpacker serves up your evening meal. Camel-riding, Cable Beach

Perth & Fremantle

5 Perth (p49) may be isolated but it's far from being a backwater. Scattered across the city are sophisticated restaurants that fly the flag for modern Australian cuisine, while a new crop of chic cocktail bars lurks down unlikely laneways. In contrast to the flashy face that Perth presents to the river, charmingly grungy inner suburbs echo with the thrum of guitars and the sizzle of woks. Just downstream, the lively port of Fremantle (p77) has a pub on every corner that doesn't have a hostel on it, and a wealth of colonial buildings. Brass Monkey, Perth

Karijini National Park

6 Hidden deep in the heart of the Pilbara, Karijini (p193) offers pools and plunging waterfalls in its remarkable gorges, a cool respite from the oppressive heat of the surrounding ironstone country. Book an adventure trip to abseil, swim, dive, climb and paddle through the gorges in order to appreciate fully this sublime, special environment. Up top, witness the amazing spring transformation as wildflowers carpet the plains, and get some altitude on the state's highest peaks, including the most excellent Mt Bruce (1235m).

HOLGER LEUE / LONELY PLANET IMAGES ©

Pinnacles Desert

7 Thousands of ghostly limestone pillars, like a petrified ancient army, stand sentinel, scattered among the dunes of Nambung National Park (p114). One of the West's most iconic landscapes, the Pinnacles attract thousands of visitors each year. Although they are easily visited as a day trip from Perth, a much richer experience awaits those who elect to stay overnight in nearby Cervantes. Make multiple trips and observe the rich colour changes that occur at dawn, sunset and full moon, when most tourists are back in their hotels.

Bushwalking

8 Western Australia has 96 national parks, not counting dozens of other nature reserves and regional parks. These special places present oodles of opportunities to go walkabout on the many waymarked trails and camp in isolated spots. The Bibbulmun Track (p36), the mother of them all, starts on the outskirts of Perth and heads nearly 1000km to Albany on the south coast, sheltered by the cooling giant eucalypts of the southern forests. At the Valley of the Giants you can walk through the canopy on the 40m-high Tree Top Walk (p142).

Water Adventures

9 If you can't catch a wave on WA's 12,000km of coastline, mate, you're doing it wrong. In which case, head straight to one of the many surf schools and leave Margaret River and Gnaraloo to the pros, where breaks with nicknames like 'suicides' and 'tombstones' beckon the fearless. Diving and snorkelling is excellent in many spots and WA is the place to swim with [insert name of favourite marine animal here]. Windsurfers breeze off to gusty Lancelin and Gnaraloo, while paddlers splash their way along the many rivers.

Snorkelling, Coral Bay

Gibb River Road

10 Launch yourself into Australia's last frontier on a wild drive down this old cattle road (p214) into the heart of the Kimberley. This is not for the faint-hearted; you'll need a serious 4WD, good planning and plenty of fuel, spares, food and water. Bring big doses of self-reliance, flexibility and humour. The rewards are fantastic gorges, hidden waterholes, incredible rock art and amazing wildlife, and you'll gain a first-hand insight into life in the outback. Did we mention there are also flies, dust and relentless heat?

West Coast Escapes

Wineries & Food »
Art & Culture »
Outdoors »
Wildflowers & Wildlife »

Twilight Cove, Esperance

Wineries & Food

Unless you're a wine aficionado, Western Australia's epicurean delights might come as a complete surprise. Yet even devotees of the divine vine might find the southwest's cuisine, shaped by access to wonderful seafood and waves of migration, a pleasant revelation.

Perth

1 Welcome to the boom town, where top chefs vie for the attention of mining magnates with world-class cuisine (p65). Generations of Mediterranean migration have left a mark, as has the state capital's proximity to Southeast Asia.

Margaret River

2 The state's premier wine region (p125) satisfies lovers of wine, food, surf and natural beauty in equal measure. Enjoy a long lunch between the vines, with tastings and beaches slotted in on either side.

Bushtucker

3 While many Indigenous foodstuffs like kangaroo and emu have well and truly crossed into the mainstream, Aboriginal-led bushtucker tours offer an opportunity to sample the lesser known edible elements of WA's native flora and fauna.

The Sunday Session

4 A WA institution that consists of a long, lazy afternoon at the pub. It reaches its zenith on the coast, where you can watch the weekend sun sink into the sea, but it's equally honoured anywhere with a beer garden.

Great Southern Wine Region

5 Whether at the foot of the Porongurup Range (p153) or near Denmark's beaches (p143) these vines have got it good. The cooler southern climes produce sophisticated wines.

Clockwise from top left
1. Rialto's, Perth **2.** Grape vines, Margaret River **3.** Edible witchety grubs **4.** Red Teapot, Perth

1

4

2

OLIVER STREWE / LONELY PLANET IMAGES ©

3

Art & Culture

WA may be isolated, but it's certainly no cultural desert – not even in the desert. A tradition of artistic expression stretches back many millennia, with ancient Aboriginal rock art still visible in the Kimberley.

Galleries throughout the state feature the work of Aboriginal artists, with traditional dot forms, once inscribed directly onto the body or the desert itself, translated onto canvas or wood. Today, Indigenous artists continue to push boundaries, experimenting with form, style and media in cutting-edge spaces such as the Perth Institute of Contemporary Arts (p55) and the Fremantle Arts Centre (p80).

The state's premier art collection is held at the wonderful Art Gallery of Western Australia (p54) in Perth. The capital is also home to cultural heavyweights such as the West Australian Opera, West Australian Ballet and West Australian Symphony Orchestra. Yet other centres aren't left behind. Albany has sprouted a new multimillion-dollar concert hall on its waterfront, while Broome plays host to one of the state's most blissful classical music events, Opera Under the Stars (p206).

Major arts events take place all over the state in summer, or in the case of the far north, in the Dry. Big music festivals range from the cobweb-clearing Big Day Out (p62) to the spirit-soothing York Jazz & Soul Festival (p106).

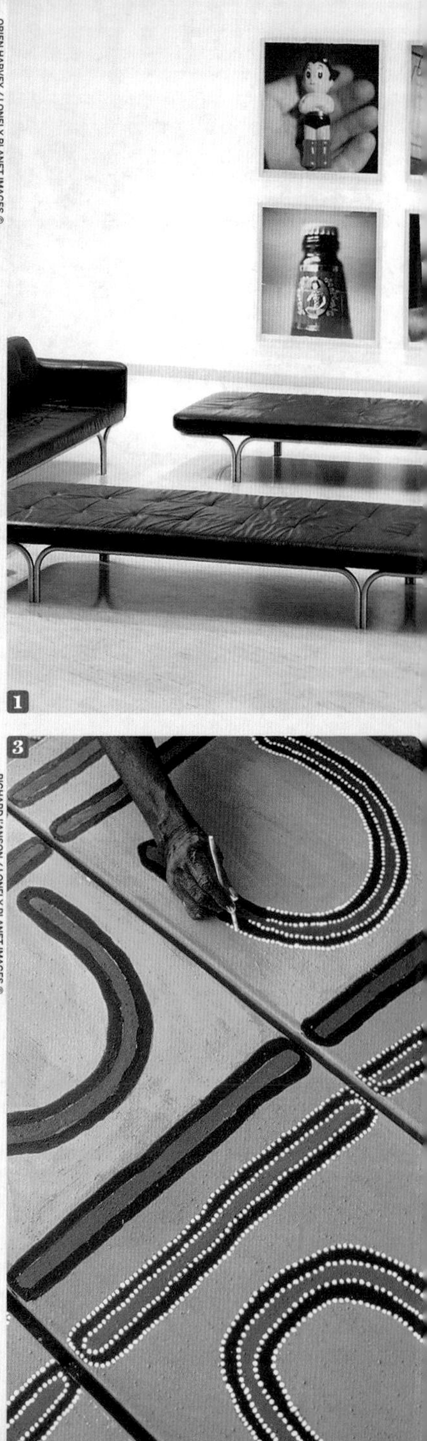

ORIEN HARVEY / LONELY PLANET IMAGES ©

RICHARD I'ANSON / LONELY PLANET IMAGES ©

Clockwise from top left

1. Art Gallery of Western Australia, Perth **2.** Street parade, Fremantle Festival, Fremantle **3.** Aboriginal artist painting, Kimberley

2

FREMANTLE ARTS FESTIVAL
AND FLASHCUBE PRESENT
THE GRAND FINALE
TONIGHT 8PM
METROPOLIS FREMANTLE
ANIMUSICATE
TURNTABLISM &
INSTRUMENTAL EXPLORATION
PUB BREWERY

Outdoors

There's an awful lot of outdoors to explore along this vast coastline. Active types will find myriad pursuits to keep them busy, both in and out of the water.

Surfing

1 Them's the breaks: down there in Margaret River, up there in Gnaraloo Station and in numerous other places along WA's 12,000km of coastline. Put simply, this is one of the world's great destinations for surfing (p37).

Bushwalking

2 Whether you walk the entire 963km Bibbulmun Track (p36) or take a short stroll through Kings Park (p55), WA's unique landscape won't disappoint. And with all this space, it's not hard to find a place to yourself.

Sporting Events

3 Not everything outdoors requires exertion; let others work up a sweat while you knock back a beer. Check out an Aussie Rules game at Subiaco Oval or cricket at the WACA (p73).

Diving & Snorkelling

4 Crystal-clear waters provide the perfect conditions to enjoy the underwater flora and fauna that lives on the state's numerous reefs and wrecks. Ningaloo Marine Park's huge fringing reef (p187) is the highlight.

Cultural Tours

5 What better way to understand the land than with Indigenous guides, descendents of people who have treasured it for thousands of years. There are many such opportunities available throughout the state.

PAUL KENNEDY / LONELY PLANET IMAGES ©

1

SLATTERY MEDIA GROUP

3

Clockwise from top left

1. Cottesloe Beach, Perth **2.** Cape to Cape Track, Leeuwin-Naturaliste National Park **3.** Fremantle Dockers, football match, Subiaco Oval, Perth

2

Wildflowers & Wildlife

A highlight of visiting Australia is the opportunity to come face-to-face with the island nation's distinct fauna in the wild. Kangaroos are a given, even on the outskirts of Perth. So are colourful parrots and cockatoos. You'll have to try a little harder to spot some of the smaller marsupials, although quokkas are a certainty on Rottnest.

If you're on the right part of the shoreline at the right time of the year, you're guaranteed to see whales – 30,000 follow the coastal 'Humpback Highway' on their annual migration in early summer. Organised cruises will get you nearer, but for a really close encounter with an aquatic mammal, there are opportunities to swim or paddle with wild dolphins in Rockingham (p95), Bunbury (p119) and, most famously, Monkey Mia (p174). There are sea lions at Green Head (p116) and dugongs at Ningaloo (p187), but nothing beats swimming with the world's biggest fish, the huge but harmless whale shark (see p187).

While the big beasties are the main drawcard for backpackers, small armies of nature-lovers descend in minibus battalions during spring for wildflower season. The state's usually sober native flora puts on its glad rags and parties from August to November, in a staggering display of diversity.

Right

1. Quokka, Rottnest Island **2.** Wildflowers, Kalbarri National Park

welcome to Perth & West Coast Australia

If you subscribe to the 'life's a beach' school of thought, you'll fall in love with Western Australia (WA) and its 12,500km of spectacular coastline.

An Immense, Sparsely Populated Land

WA is beyond huge. It takes up a third of the island continent, and if it were a separate country, as some of its denizens would prefer it to be, it would be the 10th largest country in the world. Despite this, it averages less than one person per square kilometre, and the majority of those cling like limpets to the coast. You can wander along a beach for hours without seeing a footprint in the sand, be one of a handful of campers stargazing in a national park, or bushwalk for days without seeing a soul.

The south is a playground of white-sand beaches, expanses of springtime wildflowers and lush green forests that teem with life. At the other end of the state, up north in the Kimberley, you'll encounter wide open spaces that shrewdly conceal striking gorges, waterfalls and ancient rock formations.

All Creatures Great & Small

What WA lacks in people it more than makes up for with its abundant and unique fauna. Kangaroos are a frequent sight, as are emus and colourful parrots. Then there are all the cute little critters you've probably never even heard of: quokkas, bilbies, potoroos and the like. Over the course of the WA coast's lengthy dalliance with two oceans, the Indian and the Southern, the wildlife-watching is also extraordinary. Each year about 30,000 whales cruise the so-called 'Humpback Highway', which hugs the coast; if you're travelling during the last half of the year, you're bound to spot them. At Ningaloo Marine Park you can dive with the world's largest fish, the whale shark, and at Rockingham, Bunbury and Monkey Mia you can interact with wild dolphins.

The Finer Things

WA is not all animals and landscapes. Perth and neighbouring Fremantle are cosmopolitan cities, yet both retain a languorously laid-back feel, perhaps inspired by having so many fantastic beaches and parks at their doorstep. The mining boom has sprinkled Perth's streets with figurative gold dust, adding a glitzy sheen to everything in the shadow of its skyscrapers. Earlier boom times have left a grand architectural legacy in charming towns such as Fremantle, Albany, Guildford and York – where, these days, a decent coffee is never hard to find.

At Margaret River, surfers carve world-class waves, while vignerons craft world-class wines, complemented by the inventive gourmet grub of the region's restaurants. Truffles are grown down south and dominate menus throughout the state in August. And, of course, the seafood is sublime.

need to know

Currency

» Australian dollar ($)

Language

» English

When to Go

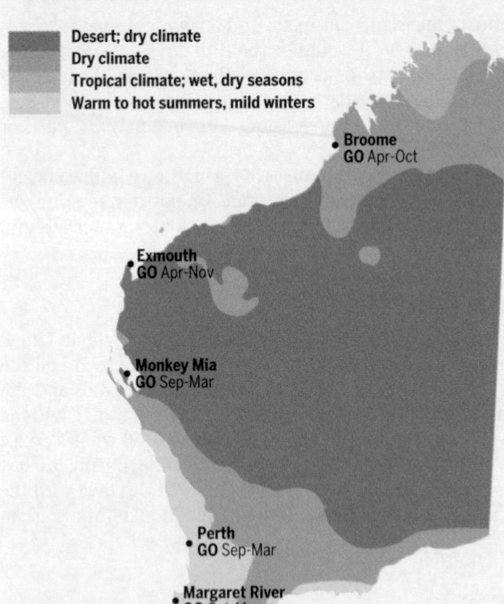

High Season (Dec–Mar)

» In the south, this is when the weather is at its hottest and driest.

» The season peaks from Christmas to the end of January school-holidays.

» In the north, this is the wet season (hence the low season).

Shoulder (Apr, May & Sep–Nov)

» Wildflowers are in bloom from September, bringing busloads of admirers to the southern half of the state.

» These are also popular months to visit the north.

Low Season (Jun–Aug)

» This is the wettest and coolest time in Perth and the south.

» Lows in the south are usually over 10°C.

» The high season in Broome and the Kimberleys; highs rarely dip below 30°C and there's barely any rainfall.

Your Daily Budget

Budget up to

$150

» Dorm bed: $23–35

» Private room in hostel: $60–85

» Stock up at the supermarket and cook in hostel kitchens

Midrange

$150–$250

» Double room in a midrange hotel: $100–200

» Lunch and dinner in decent cafes and restaurants

» Car hire: around $40 per day

Top end over

$250

» Mains in top restaurants: over $35

» Double room in a top hotel: from $200

Money

» ATMs widely available. Credit cards accepted in most hotels and restaurants.

Visas

» All visitors require a visa, although New Zealanders receive one on arrival. Residents of Canada, the US, many European and some Asian countries can apply online.

Mobile Phones

» Australia's network is compatible with most European phones, but generally not with the US or Japanese systems. The main service providers offer prepaid SIMs.

Driving

» Drive on the left; the steering wheel is on the right side of the car.

Websites

» **Lonely Planet** (www.lonelyplanet.com/australia) Destination information, traveller forum and more.

» **Tourism Western Australia** (www.westernaustralia.com) Official tourist site.

» **Tourism Australia** (www.australia.com) Transport, event and destination information.

» **West Australian** (www.thewest.com.au) Online version of the newspaper.

» **Department of Environment & Conservation** (www.dec.wa.gov.au) Details on the state's national parks.

Exchange Rates

Canada	C$1	$1
Euro	€1	$1.37
Japan	¥100	$1.22
New Zealand	NZ$1	$0.77
UK	£1	$1.59
USA	US$1	$1

For current exchange rates see www.xe.com.

Important Numbers

Drop the zero from the area code when calling from outside Australia (ie +61-8).

International access code	0011
Country code	61
WA area code	08
Emergency (police, fire, ambulance)	000
Directory assistance	12455

Arriving in Perth & West Coast Australia

» **Perth Airport** (p259)

Connect Shuttle: every 50 minutes to Perth ($18), less frequently to Fremantle ($33)

Taxi: about $35 to central Perth and $60 to Fremantle

Bus: every 10 to 30 minutes for the city, hourly after 7pm; journey time 44 minutes

For more in-depth information, see p75

Transport within Western Australia

By far the easiest way to get around the state is by car. Hire cars are readily available in Perth and other major centres. Distances are huge, so consider flying in at least one direction if you plan on travelling widely throughout the state – for instance, fly to Broome or Esperance and take out a one-way hire to drive back to Perth. You can sometimes pick up better deals doing it this way, as most one-way hires depart from Perth.

You can get by without a car in Perth and Fremantle, and many of the short trips in our Around Perth chapter (p88) can be undertaken on public transport. You could easily fill up a week or two in this area alone. The train system is only useful for a few destinations around Perth but buses ply the coastal routes north and south from the capital.

if you like...

Beaches

You're in luck. Western Australia (WA) has some of Australia's finest, which makes them among the finest in the world. And you'll have many of them completely to yourself.

Cottesloe Perth's most iconic beach, with cafes and bars close at hand (p57)

Rottnest Island Cycle to your own private slice of paradise (p90)

Bunker Bay Brilliant white sand edged by bushland; you'll have to look hard to spot the few houses scattered about (p124)

Hellfire Bay Sand like talcum powder in the middle of Cape Le Grand National Park, which is precisely in the middle of nowhere (p160)

Shark Bay 1500km of remote beaches and towering limestone cliffs (p171)

Turquoise Bay A beautiful bay in Ningaloo Marine Park, with wonderful snorkelling (p189)

Eighty Mile Beach You're guaranteed at least 79 miles of solitude on this remote, white-sand beach (p202)

Dampier Peninsula Deserted white-sand beaches with turquoise waters (p211)

Diving & Snorkelling

Reefs and wrecks are plentiful around WA and the marine life is lush, providing a smorgasbord of options for geared-up diving pros or gung-ho first-time snorkellers.

Mettams Pool Excellent snorkelling within Perth's city limits (p57)

Rottnest Island Over a dozen wrecks and two underwater snorkelling trails make this an excellent option (p91)

Busselton Lots to see around the Southern Hemisphere's longest timber jetty, plus the wreck of a decommissioned Navy destroyer not far away (p122)

Albany Look for sea dragons among the coral reefs and the wreck of the *HMAS Perth* (p148)

Ningaloo Marine Park The ultimate – Australia's largest fringing reef, where you can snorkel and dive with the world's largest fish, the whale shark, along with turtles, dolphins and dugongs (p187)

Surfing & Windsurfing

Wax the board and fire up the Kombi van: WA's surfing is legendary.

Trigg Beach Perth's surfers come here straight from work to catch a few waves (p57)

Lancelin A mecca for windsurfers and a great spot to learn to surf (p113)

Yallingup/Margaret River 'Yals' and 'Margs' are the hub of the WA surf scene – with a major pro competition held there every year (p31)

Ocean Beach, Denmark You might find yourself sharing this beautiful bay with whales (p143)

Geraldton The surrounding beaches are thrilling for both wind- and wave-powered surfers (p164)

Gnaraloo Surfers flock here in winter to try their luck at the famous Tombstones break; in summer the windsurfers take their place (p177)

North West Cape Big swells hit the west of the cape from July to October (p189)

»Punamii-unpuu (Mitchell Falls), Kimberley (p216)

FEARGUS COONEY / LONELYPLANET IMAGES ©

Trees

If you've never been here you might be forgiven for thinking that WA was all about white sand and red dirt. While there is an awful lot of both, the state's arboreal delights are an attraction in their own right.

Lesueur National Park A huge diversity of flora with many rare and endemic trees (p114)

Karri Forest Explorer This shady circuit passes through three national parks surrounding Pemberton (p138)

Valley of the Giants Tree Top Walk A wobbly walkway arches through the lofty canopy of the tingle forest (p142)

Karijini National Park Native figs cling to the sides of the vertiginous gorges (p193)

Derby With its bloated trunk and often bare, scrawny branches, the alien-looking boab tree is emblematic of this Kimberley town, where there's even a festival in its honour (p212)

Mitchell River National Park The rough road to this remote park passes through a forest of livistona palms (p216)

Bushwalking

The state's dozens of national parks are criss-crossed with hundreds of walking tracks, heading along the coast, beneath forests, through gorges and up mountains.

Bibbulmun Track The big one – stretching nearly 1000km from the edge of Perth through the southern forests to Albany (p36)

Walyunga National Park Explore the trails in this beautiful park, where the Avon River cuts through the Darling Range (p103)

Cape to Cape Track Enjoy Indian Ocean views on this 135km trail from Cape Naturaliste to Cape Leeuwin (p131)

Stirling Range National Park Climb every mountain...or maybe just one or two, in this luscious range, known for its flora and chameleon-like ability to change colour (p154)

Punurrunha (Mt Bruce), Karijini National Park Tackle WA's second-highest peak and enjoy wonderful views along the ridge (p193)

Punamii-unpuu (Mitchell Falls) The 8.6km track heads through spinifex, woodlands and gorges, passing Aboriginal rock art on the way (p216)

Marine Mammals

It's extraordinarily easy to come close to the great creatures of the deep along WA's coast.

Perth & Fremantle Thirty-thousand whales cruise past between mid-September and early December, and boat trips will take you out to cheer them on (p58)

Rottnest Island The sharp-of-eye may spot New Zealand fur seals, dolphins and whales (p90)

Rockingham Wild Encounters Cruise out to swim with dolphins and spot seals (p95)

Sea Lion Charters, Green Head Splash around with sea lions in the shallows (p116)

Dolphin Discovery Centre, Bunbury Wade next to the wild dolphins that regularly drop by, or take a boat trip to swim with them (p121)

Albany Between July and mid-October the bay turns into a whale nursery, with mothers and calves easily spotted from the beach and cruises to take you a little closer (p148)

Monkey Mia Watch dolphins feeding in the shallows and take a dugong-spotting cruise (p174)

If you like...mountains
Karijini National Park contains the state's three highest peaks (p193)

Wineries

While mining gets most of the glory, WA's wine industry is another of the state's major successes.

Swan Valley Within Perth's eastern reaches, this semirural stretch provides lots of wine and food stops to amuse the weekend hordes from the city (p103)

Margaret River The state's heavy-hitter, known for its Bordeaux-style red varietals, as well as Chardonnay and Sauvignon Blanc. The shady lanes and dramatic beaches make it our pick of Australia's wine regions (p125)

Pemberton Another esteemed wine area, producing extremely good Pinot Noir, Chardonnay and Sauvignon Blanc (p138)

Denmark Part of the cool-climate Great Southern Wine Region; several notable wineries are within champagne-cork-range of the town (p143)

Mt Barker & Porongurup Regarded as the most significant part of the Great Southern, the cool climes suit Riesling, Pinot Noir and Cabernet Sauvignon (p153)

Fine Food

Although people don't necessarily travel to WA for the cuisine, once they're there they may be pleasantly surprised by the sophisticated fare on offer – if not around the whole state, at least in some gastronomic hotspots.

Perth No longer the poor cousin to the eastern capitals, Perth's restaurants are the state's finest (p65)

Swan Valley Dubbed the 'Valley of Taste', with excellent restaurants and providores scattered along the main wine-tasting routes (p104)

Margaret River Wine Region Second only to Perth in the culinary stakes, Margaret River's restaurants turn up the heat, and serve beautiful meals in bucolic settings (p128)

Manjimup Foodies shouldn't resist a visit to the Wine & Truffle Co, where you can take part in a truffle hunt and dine from a menu enamoured with the pungent fungus (p136)

Broome Mango Festival Held in November, the harvest is celebrated with the Great Chefs of Broome Cook-Off (p206)

Aboriginal Art & Culture

Around 59,000 Aborigines still call WA home, comprising many different indigenous peoples, speaking many distinct languages.

Art Gallery of Western Australia A treasure trove of indigenous art (p54)

Yanchep National Park Didgeridoo and dance performances, and history and cultural tours with Noongar guides (p112)

Wardan Cultural Centre Learn about Wardandi beliefs and way of life, and try your hand at stone-tool making, and boomerang and spear throwing (p127)

Kepa Kurl Eco Cultural Discovery Tours Day tours to visit rock art and waterholes, sample bush food and hear ancient stories (p158)

Wula Guda Nyinda Aboriginal Cultural Tours Offers bushwalks and kayak tours, where you'll learn some of the local Malgana language, and how to identify bushtucker (p174)

Dampier Peninsula Interact with remote communities and learn how to spear fish and catch mud crabs (p211)

The Kimberley View ancient rock art and take a cultural tour (p212)

month by month

Top Events

1. **Southbound Festival**, January
2. **Perth International Arts Festival**, February
3. **Drug Aware Pro**, March
4. **Blues 'n' Roots Festival**, April
5. **Royal Perth Show**, October

January

The peak of the summer school holidays sees families head to the beach en masse. Days are hot and dry, except in the far north where the wet season is in full force.

Busselton's Big Music Festival

The Southbound Festival (www.southboundfestival.com.au) starts off the new year with three days of alternative music and camping in Busselton. Featuring big name international artists, it's Western Australia's equivalent of Glastonbury (but with less mud).

Lancelin's Windsurfing Challenge

In early January, tiny Lancelin's renowned blustery conditions attract thousands for its world-famous windsurfing event, the Lancelin Ocean Classic (www.lanceli noceanclassic.com.au). Held over four days, the event starts with wave sailing on the Thursday and Friday, followed by the marathon on Saturday and the Sunday slalom.

February

The kids head back to school, freeing up some room at the beach and taking some of the pressure off coastal accommodation. It's still hot and dry (and soggy in the north).

Alternative Music Festival, Perth

The Big Day Out (www.bigdayout.com) is Australasia's biggest touring music festival, attracting leading alternative artists and lots of local up-and-comers. It comes to Claremont Showground in early February.

Perth International Arts Festival

Held over 25 days from mid-February, Perth's festival (www.perthfestival.com.au) attracts an international line-up, spanning theatre, classical music, jazz, visual arts, dance, film, literature – the whole gamut. It's worth scheduling your trip around.

Leeuwin Concert Series

The fabulous Leeuwin Estate winery (www.leeuwinestate.com.au) in Margaret River hosts world-class performers of popular music, opera and the stage (Roxy Music, Dame Kiri Te Kanawa, Sting) during its annual event in mid-February; other concerts run from January to April.

Boyup Brook Country Music Festival

Good ol' boys and gals descend on a tiny southern forest town for five days of country music, bush poetry, markets and the annual 'Ute & Truck Muster' (www.countrymusicwa.com.au).

March

It's still beach weather but it's not quite as swelteringly hot in the south. It's hot and steamy in the north, however, with the rain still bucketing down. Prices shoot up at Easter.

Margaret River Wine Region Festival

This five-day festival (www.margaretriverfestival.com) titillates the tastebuds with the best of the southwest's wine, food, art, music and outdoor adventures. It includes carnivals, master classes, the Slow Food Long Table Feast and a cricket match at Cowaramup Oval.

Margaret River Surfing Pro

Officially called the Drug Aware Pro (www.drugawarepro.com), this World Qualifying Series (WQS) event, held over six days in mid-March, sees the world's best up-and-coming surfers battle it out in the epic surf at Margaret River.

April

Another pleasant month in Perth, with the temperatures dropping to the mid-20s and a little more rainfall. Up north, they're finally starting to dry out and it's a great time for a Kimberley flyover.

Blues 'n' Roots Festival

Held in April in Fremantle Park, the West Coast Blues 'n' Roots Festival (www.westcoastbluesnroots.com.au) interprets its remit widely: the 2011 line-up featured the likes of Bob Dylan, Elvis Costello, Toots & the Maytals and Grace Jones.

May

Temperatures creep down and Broome and Exmouth both finally drop below the 30s, making them particularly appealing – especially now the box jellyfish have retreated. Autumn showers are more common in the south.

Ord Valley Muster

For two weeks every May, Kununurra hits overdrive during the annual Ord Valley Muster (www.ordvalleymuster.com), a collection of various sporting, charity and cultural events leading up to a large outdoor concert under the full moon on the banks of the Ord River.

June

Winter hits Perth, with plenty of rain and possibly some snow on the Stirling Range further south. The warm, dry north, however, heads into peak season. Whale-watching commences in Augusta.

Denmark Festival of Voice

Rousing choruses blow away the cobwebs from the south-coast town of Denmark during the Festival of Voice (www.dfov.org.au), held over the June long weekend. The town is flooded with soloists, duos, choristers and their admirers. It's accompanied by a workshop program.

July

It's still wet and cold in the south and beautiful in the north – sparking a winter-break exodus from Perth. Whales congregate in the bays around Albany.

Indigenous Cultural Celebrations

Indigenous art exhibitions and performances take place throughout WA during National Aboriginal & Islander Day Observance Committee (NAIDOC; www.naidoc.org.au) week, which celebrates the history, culture and achievements of Indigenous people.

August

Much the same as July, climate-wise, although temperatures start to edge up. Manjimup truffles come into season, to the delight of Perth's chefs and their customers; whales continue to hang out on the south coast.

Avon River Festivities

Northam and Toodyay both turn on festivals the day before the Avon Descent (www.avondescent.com.au), a gruelling 133km white-water rafting event for powerboats, kayaks and canoes between the two towns. Northam hosts the Avon River Festival while Toodyay has a Festival of Food.

Broome Opera Under the Stars

World-class opera performers sing under clear Kimberley night skies at the Cable Beach Amphitheatre, their vocal pyrotechnics accompanied by a fireworks display. The event (www.operaunderthestars.com.au) is now preceded by the Oper-Arte fundraising art auction.

September

Spring brings a flurry of excitement, with wildflowers blooming and whales heading up the west coast. Broome pops back into the 30s and the tourists start to head south again.

Multicultural Celebrations in Broome

Starting either in late August or early September, Broome's Shinju Matsuri (www.shinjumatsuri.com) celebrates the town's pearl industry and multicultural heritage with a carnival of nations, film festival, art exhibitions, food, concerts, fireworks and dragon boat races.

Perth's Wildflower Festival

In September and early October, Kings Park and the Botanic Garden are filled with colourful wildflower displays in the annual Kings Park Festival (www.kingsparkfestival.com.au), which celebrates WA's unique and spectacular flora. Events include guided walks, talks and live music every Sunday.

Geraldton Greenough Sunshine Festival

It started in 1959 as a tomato festival but now Geraldton's solar celebrations (www.sunshinefestival.com.au) include dragon-boat races, parades, sand sculptures and parties. It's held over two weeks from late September to early October. Sunshine guaranteed.

October

The last of the whales depart the south coast and hit the west-coast leg of the Humpback Highway. The weather's noticeably warmer and drier, and the wildflowers are still wonderful.

Blessing of the Fleet, Fremantle & Geraldton

Popular traditional Catholic festival (www.gfcblessing.com) introduced to Fremantle by young Italian fishermen in 1948. It includes the procession of statues from St Patrick's Basilica to Fishing Boat Harbour, where the blessing takes place. Geraldton's version includes a family fun day with bouncy castles and bands.

Perth Royal Show

The country comes to the city for the west's biggest agriculture, food and wine show (www.perthroyalshow.com.au) in late September. For Perth's kids it's a week of fun-fair rides, spun sugar and showbags full of plastic junk.

York Jazz & Soul Festival

In late October jazz and soul aficionados flock to the historic Avon Valley town of York for concerts, busking and jamming. The music covers everything from traditional jazz to Dixieland, bebop, soul, modern jazz, gospel and funk.

November

A great time to be in Fremantle, with temperatures in the mid-20s, very little rain and a convoy of whales passing by. In the far north, it's the start of the box jellyfish season.

Fremantle Festival

Ten days of parades, performances, music, dance, comedy, visual arts, street theatre and workshops. Founded in 1905, it's Australia's longest running festival (www.fremantlefestivals.com). Highlights include the Kite Extravaganza on South Beach and the Wardarnji Indigenous Festival.

Broome Mango Festival

Broome celebrates the mango harvest with four days of mango-themed everything (www.broome.wa.au/events/mango-festival). So how exactly do you celebrate mangos? With a quiz night, fashion parade and a Great Chefs of Broome Cook-Off, apparently. If you don't come away with sweet, sticky fingers, you're doing it wrong.

itineraries

Whether you've got six days or 60, these itineraries provide a starting point for the trip of a lifetime. Want more inspiration? Head online to www.lonelyplanet.com/thorntree to chat with other travellers.

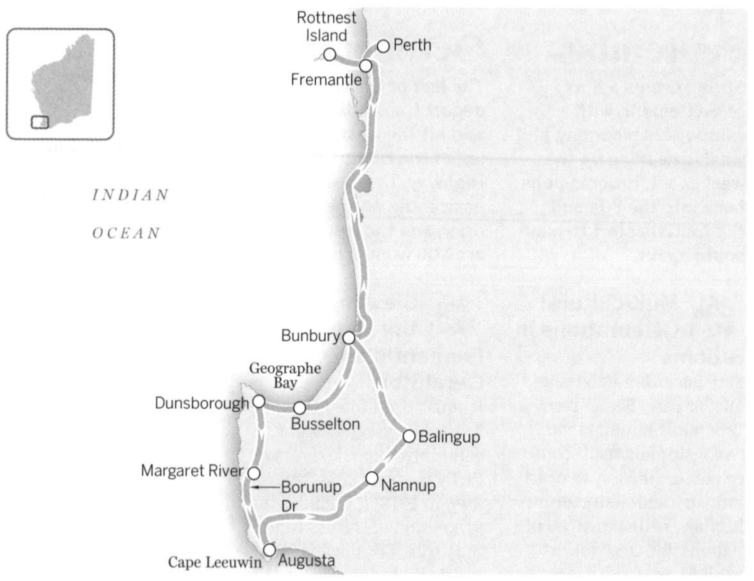

One Week

A Southwest Short Circuit

If you've got limited time, this itinerary offers a taster of the best the state has to offer – city life, colonial history, beaches, wildlife, wine, forests and rural roads. Base yourself in either **Perth** or **Fremantle** and spend three days exploring the conjoined cities and one day on **Rottnest Island**. Hire a car and head south, stopping first at **Bunbury** for lunch and a visit to the Dolphin Encounter Centre. Continue on to **Geographe Bay**, basing yourself in either **Busselton** or **Dunsborough**, and use the rest of the day to explore the beaches. Pick up a wine region map and spend day six checking out the wineries, surf beaches and caves, all of which are in close proximity. Base yourself in the **Margaret River** township that night and head to the local pub. The next morning, head to **Augusta** via Caves Rd and take the scenic detour through the karri forest along unsealed **Borunup Drive**. Visit **Cape Leeuwin**, where the Indian and Southern Oceans meet, before heading back to Bunbury on a picturesque rural drive through **Nannup** and **Balingup**. From here it's a two-hour drive back to Perth.

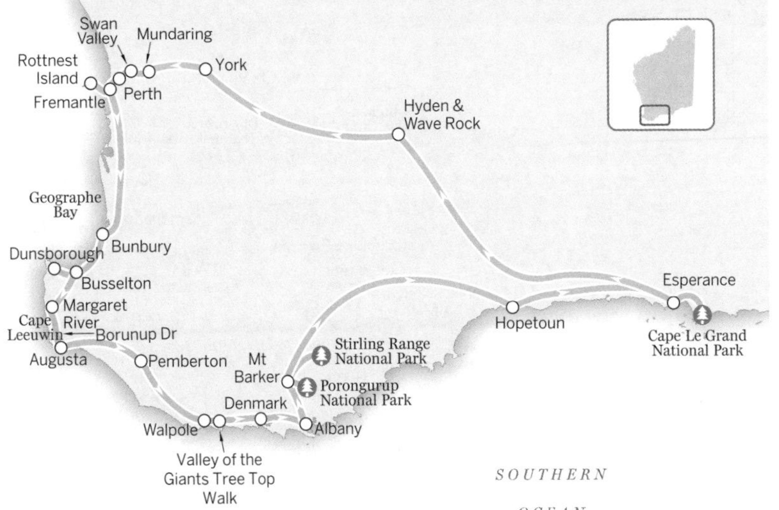

Three Weeks

The Southwest Uncut

Australia's southwest corner is a magical part of the continent and this itinerary covers its main highlights; bump it up by another week to really relax into it. Start by following the previous itinerary as far as **Cape Leeuwin**, but spend a second night in **Margaret River** for more winery and beach time.

Continue on to **Pemberton**, set amid three heavily forested national parks, for more wineries and the Karri Forest Explorer scenic drive. The next day, continue through **Walpole** to the extraordinary **Valley of the Giants Tree Top Walk**, then press on to **Denmark**. Check out the beaches and still more wineries before making the short hop to **Albany** on the following day. Base yourself there for two days of swimming (in summer), whale-watching (in winter) and exploring the beautiful coastal national parks that surround it.

Head north for a quick look at **Mt Barker** (more wineries) before scuttling east to spend the night at the foot of **Porongurup National Park**. Spend the next day (or two) tackling the mountainous tracks either here or at **Stirling Range National Park** further north.

From here the driving distances get longer. Continue through Ongerup and Jerramungup to the South Coast Hwy and at Ravensthorpe hop down to **Hopetoun** to spend the night. This will take about three hours from the Stirling Range, so you'll have the afternoon to hang out on the beach. The following day, head back to the South Coast Hwy and continue east to **Esperance**, a drive of around 2½ hours. Base yourself there for at least two days – spending one of them exploring gorgeous **Cape Le Grand National Park**.

Head back on the South Coast Hwy and turn north just past Ravensthorpe for the road to **Hyden** and extraordinary **Wave Rock** (allow four hours driving). The following day, head west on Hwy 40 to Brookton and then turn north on the Great Southern Hwy and follow the Avon Valley to quaintly colonial **York** (allow 3½ hours). For your last day, take a leisurely drive back to Perth via **Mundaring**, stopping at the **Swan Valley** wineries en route.

You could easily make this itinerary shorter by heading straight to Hyden from the Stirling Range, or by taking the Albany Hwy directly to Perth from Mt Barker.

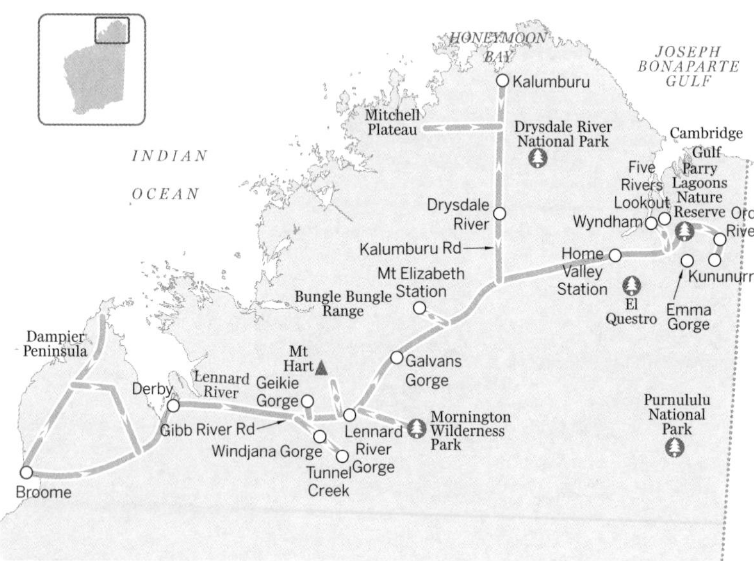

One Month
Kimberley Outback

The biggest adventure in the west leaves **Broome** during the Dry and traverses the heart of the rugged **Kimberley** by 4WD. First stop is the **Dampier Peninsula**, with its Aboriginal communities, beautiful beaches and mud crabs, and your last salt water swim. Take the back road to **Derby**, with its boabs, then onto the **Gibb River Rd** where **Lennard River** is the first of many inviting gorges. Explore wildlife and gorges at **Mt Hart** and remote **Mornington Wilderness Camp** and look for Wandjina at **Galvans Gorge** and **Mt Elizabeth Station**. Turn off onto the **Kalumburu Rd**, check the road conditions at **Drysdale River** and drive onto the **Mitchell Plateau**, with its forests of *livistona* and mind-blowing falls. Marvel at the area's rock art before hitting the northern coast and excellent fishing at **Honeymoon Bay**, just beyond the mission community of **Kalumburu**.

It's all downhill from here as you retrace your route back to the Gibb, then turn left for wonderful **Home Valley Station**, where someone else can do the cooking and the soft beds make a pleasant change to camping. Nearby **El Questro** has gorges a plenty, none more beautiful than **Emma Gorge**. Soon you're back on asphalt, but not for long as you take in the amazing birdlife of **Parry Lagoons Nature Reserve**. Let Wyndham's **Five Rivers Lookout** blow your mind with its view of **Cambridge Gulf**, before heading for the civility of **Kununurra**, with its excellent food and supplies. You can look for fruit-picking work, ride a canoe down the mighty **Ord River**, or jump back behind the wheel for the wonders of **Purnululu**, the orange-domed **Bungle Bungle Range**. Darwin and the Northern Territory are beckoning, or you can follow the Great Northern Hwy back to Broome, stopping in at beautiful **Geikie Gorge** for a relaxing boat cruise where you might spot freshwater crocs. If you don't see any, don't worry, as nearby **Windjana Gorge** has loads sunning on the river banks. Grab your torch and head for a cold wade through the icy waters of **Tunnel Creek**, with its bats and rock art, before planting the pedal back to Broome, where you won't care how much that beer costs anymore.

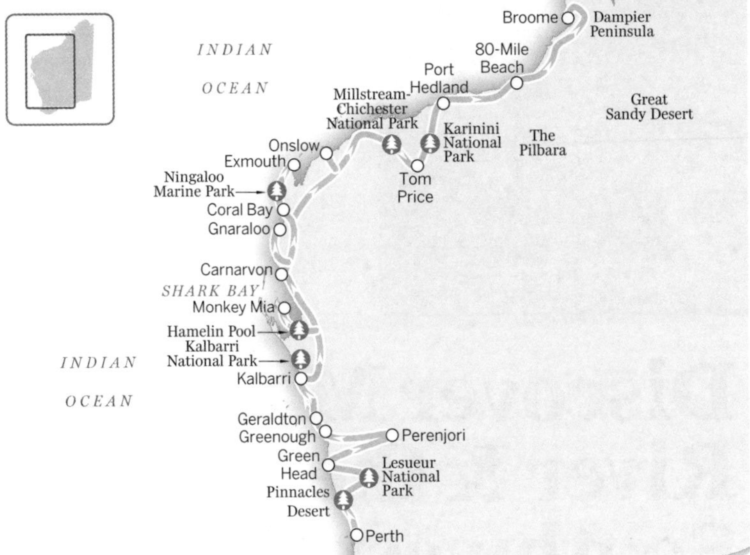

Two Weeks

Indian Ocean Dreaming

Beautiful beaches, spectacular sunsets and diverse wildlife are constant companions on this coastal cruise. Take Indian Ocean Dr north from **Perth** to Cervantes for sunset on the otherwordly **Pinnacles Desert**. Cruise the wildflower-laden Kwongan backroads and marvel at **Lesueur National Park's** flora before snorkelling with sea lions at **Green Head**. Follow the flowers out to **Perenjori**, then hit the cafes and museums of **Geraldton**. Have a surf on a kiteboard, then move onto the wonderful coastline of **Kalbarri**. Enjoy a canoe in the gorges before sampling the outback on the long drive to World Heritage–listed **Shark Bay**. Watch dolphins at **Monkey Mia**, go sailing with dugongs and learn about 'country' on an **Indigenous** cultural tour. Check out the stromatolites of **Hamelin Pool**, before putting in more 'road time' on the stretch to **Carnarvon**, with its huge NASA dish. Drop into **Gnaraloo** for world-class waves and searing sunsets, before arriving at tiny **Coral Bay** and **Exmouth**, where whale sharks, manta rays and turtles inhabit the exquisite **Ningaloo Marine Park**. You can fly out of Exmouth, drive back to Perth in two days (overnighting in historic **Greenough**), or push onto the gorges of **Karijini**.

One Week

Pilbara Jewels

You'll camp most of the way on this link between Ningaloo and Broome, with long empty beaches, shady pools and surprisingly good food. From **Exmouth**, take Burkett Rd back to the highway, and head north, turning off to salty **Onslow** for the excellent **Nikkis** restaurant and the aptly named **Sunrise** and **Sunset** beaches. Go back to the highway then continue north and turnoff via Pannawonica to the restful, shady **Crossing Pool** in **Millstream National Park**. Admire the mesas and breakaways of the **Chichester Range** before dropping in on **Tom Price** for fuel, internet and supplies. Spend the next few days camped in **Karijini National Park**, exploring the sublime gorges and indulging in a spot of peak-bagging among the state's highest mountains. Take the Great Northern Hwy directly to **Port Hedland**, and scoff some wonderful coffee and cake in the air-conditioned **Zephyr** railcar, before camping at pristine **80-mile Beach**, where you might spot nesting turtles. Your last leg is a long stretch of nothing as you skirt the **Great Sandy Desert** to arrive in tropical **Broome**. You can bail out here or tool-up for the Kimberley. Alternatively, skip the country on a direct Bali flight from Port Hedland.

Discover Margaret River & the Southwest Coast

Best Wineries

Vasse Felix Regional pioneer leads the way with its Heytesbury Cabernet blend and Heytesbury Chardonnay.

Cullen Wines Another pioneer, with the best Chardonnay in the world, according to the 2010 Decanter World Wine Awards.

Leeuwin Estate Wonderful wines, especially its Art Series Chardonnay and Sauvignon Blanc.

Brookland Valley Once again it's Chardonnay that impresses here, as well as the reserve Cabernet Sauvignon.

Ashbrook Great quality, good value; try the Cabernet Merlot.

Four Things You Wouldn't Expect

Works by Arthur Boyd and Sidney Nolan are hanging in the **Bunbury Regional Art Gallery**.

A highly rated French/Australian film festival, **CinéfestOZ**, is held annually in beachy Busselton.

A colony of **red-tailed tropicbirds** roosts off Cape Naturaliste.

Most of the best restaurants aren't open in the evenings.

What's the Big Deal?

In a nutshell: family-friendly beaches, brilliant surfing, caves full of fascinating limestone formations and, most famously, world-class wines – all in a relatively compact geographical area.

With its blissful country roads shaded by mature trees, its crashing surf beaches, and, of course, its excellent Chardonnays and Bordeaux-style reds, Margaret River is our favourite Australian wine region and a highlight of any trip to WA. Of course, where there's fine wine, fancy restaurants surely follow – and cheese shops, chocolate shops, art galleries and craft stores. Margaret River has all of the predictable trappings of gentrification yet it still seems to remember that it's in the country, rather than some swanky corner of Subiaco. The local pub keeps it real and, for the most part, wineries here don't charge for tastings.

The limestone cliffs that make their jagged way along the coastline between Cape Naturaliste (in the north) and Cape Leeuwin (in the south) give an inkling of what lies beneath. Limestone helps the formation of caves, as water seeps through the porous substance dissolving calcium carbonate, which is later deposited to create stalactites and other formations. There are perhaps as many as 350 limestone caves dotted throughout the Leeuwin-Naturaliste Ridge between the capes.

Plan Your Attack

What's the Layout?

The sheltered white sands of Geographe Bay start south of Bunbury and arch along to Cape Naturaliste. Busselton and Dunsborough are the bay's main towns. At Cape Naturaliste the coastline pirouettes and runs nearly due south to Cape Leeuwin. The wine region runs parallel to this coast with the Margaret River itself cutting roughly east to west through the centre, passing through the town of the same name. Wineries are scattered all around but the biggest concentration is north of the river.

Where to Stay

For a beach holiday Busselton or Dunsborough
For surfing Yallingup, Prevelly or Margaret River
For wineries Yallingup, Margaret River or anywhere in between
For caves Anywhere between Yallingup and Augusta
For peace and quiet Augusta

When to Go

For a beach holiday December to March
For surfing Anytime, but the big surf pro is in March
For wineries and caves Anytime
For whale-watching June to September from Augusta, September to December from Dunsborough
For French films August

When to Avoid

» January in Busselton, unless you're going to the Southbound music festival or have booked well in advance

» November in Dunsborough, when the place is overrun by end-of-school revellers

» Weekends in Margaret River – the accommodation prices are higher and there are always loads of people – but at least you can be sure that everything will be open

BEST FAMILY ACTIVITIES

» Dolphin Discovery Centre (p121), Bunbury

» Big Swamp Wildlife Park (p119), Bunbury

» Busselton Drive-in Outdoor Cinema (p123)

» Yallingup Maze (p127)

» Margaret River Chocolate Company (p128)

What to Do

Surfing the Wineries

The two main north–south routes are the Bussell Hwy (passing through Cowaramup, Margaret River and Augusta) and leafy Caves Rd (running south from Dunsborough). Numerous bucolic back roads link the two. You're best to pick up one of the excellent free maps that are widely available, squabble over who's going to be the nondrinking driver, and dive right in. The other alternative is to take a tour, of which there are many, as public transport is not a workable option.

Most of the wineries offer tastings between 10am and 5pm daily. At busy times (this includes every weekend), consider booking ahead for lunch before you set out.

Tasting the Waves

Known to surfers as 'Yals' (around Yallingup) and 'Margs' (around the mouth of the Margaret River), the beaches between Capes Naturaliste and Leeuwin offer powerful reef breaks, mainly left-handers (the direction you take after catching a wave). The surf at Margs has been described by surfing supremo Nat Young as 'epic', and by world surfing champ Mark Richards as 'one of the world's finest'.

As is the way with such hot spots, surfers can be quite territorial, so respect the etiquette and defer to locals if you're unsure. If you're planning on spending a lot of time on the breaks, call into the surf shops and get to know some of the old guns.

Around Dunsborough, the better locations include Rocky Point (short left-hander) and the Farm and Bone Yards (right-handers), which are between Eagle and Bunker Bay. Near Yallingup there's the Three Bears

(Papa, Mama and Baby, of course), Rabbits (a beach break towards the north of Yallingup Beach), Yallingup (reef with breaks left and right), and Injidup Car Park and Injidup Point (right-hand tube on a heavy swell; left-hander). You'll need a 4WD to access Guillotine/Gallows (right-hander), north of Gracetown. Also around Gracetown are Huzza's (an easy break within the beach), South Point (popular break) and Lefthanders (the name says it all). The annual surfer pro (p24) is held around Margaret River Mouth and Southside ('Suicides') in March.

Pick up a surfing map ($5.25) from one of the visitor centres on the way through.

Surfing is never without its risks. Two people have been killed by sharks in the vicinity of Gracetown in the last six years.

Going Underground

The main cave complexes are spread, perhaps unsurprisingly, along Caves Rd. Ngilgi Cave sits by itself near Yallingup, but the other main complexes are between Margaret River township and Augusta, and are split between those run by the Department of Environment & Conservation (Calgardup Cave and Giants Caves) and the more commercialised Caveworks caves (Lake Cave, Jewel Cave and Mammoth Cave). Caveworks offers a combined ticket for its three.

Other Attractions

» **Beaches** – and lots of them; they're particularly beautiful between Dunsborough and Cape Naturaliste.

» **Walking** – there are excellent tracks around Cape Naturaliste and between the capes.

» **Diving** – trips leave from Busselton and Dunsborough to explore local wrecks and reefs.

» **Whale-watching** – cruises leave from Augusta (starting in June) and Dunsborough (starting in September).

» **Lighthouses** – both capes have them and both can be visited. From Cape Leeuwin you can watch the Indian and Southern Oceans collide.

West Coast Australia Outdoors

Best for Daredevils

Karijini National Park Scramble, abseil, slide and dive through the gorges on an adventure tour

Horizontal Waterfalls, Derby Riding the surge in a speedboat

Best Wildlife Encounters

Whales Anywhere on the coast; whale-watching boats leave from Perth, Fremantle, Dunsborough, Augusta, Albany, Coral Bay, Broome and the Dampier Peninsula

Whale sharks & manta rays Ningaloo Marine Park

Dolphins Rockingham, Bunbury, Monkey Mia

Sea lions Rockingham, Green Head

Seals Rottnest Island

Dugongs Monkey Mia

Cute little marsupials Rottnest Island, Dryandra Woodland

Huge lizards Anywhere in the Kimberley

Kangaroos & parrots Everywhere

With incredible landscapes and seascapes, intriguing wildlife, and all of that brilliant sunshine, Western Australia (WA) is the perfect playground for outdoor enthusiasts, with numerous tracks to follow, waves to surf and reefs to explore.

Bushwalking

WA is blessed with plenty of wonderful bushwalking terrain, from the cool fertile forests of the southwest and the seemingly endless Bibbulmun Track, to the national parks of the north in the rugged, tropical Kimberley.

Get in touch with like-minded souls through the numerous bushwalking clubs around the state; for a list of clubs and some useful links, contact **Bushwalking Australia** (www.bushwalkingaustralia.org).

Perth & Surrounds

What better way to start than with WA's first national park, the John Forrest National Park (p102), where there's plenty of hiking as well as camping and picnicking facilities. There's an easy 15km walk that takes in waterfalls and has excellent views or, for a tougher walk, head to the rugged Walyunga National Park (p103), where there's a medium-to-hard 18km walk (and some easier variations) that fords the Avon River and has excellent wildlife-viewing. If you're heading north, the Yanchep National Park (p112) offers an excellent array of walks

RESPONSIBLE BUSHWALKING

To help preserve the ecology and beauty of West Coast Australia, consider the following tips when bushwalking.

Rubbish

» Carry out all your rubbish. Don't overlook easily forgotten items, such as silver paper, cigarette butts and plastic wrappers. Empty packaging should be stored in a dedicated rubbish bag. Make an effort to carry out rubbish left by others.

» Never bury your rubbish: digging disturbs soil and ground cover, and encourages erosion. Buried rubbish will likely be dug up by animals, which may be injured or poisoned by it. It may also take years to decompose.

» Minimise waste by taking minimal packaging and no more food than you will need. Take reusable containers or stuff sacks.

» Sanitary napkins, tampons, condoms and toilet paper should be carried out, despite the inconvenience. They burn and decompose poorly.

Human Waste Disposal

» Contamination of water sources by human faeces can lead to the transmission of all sorts of nasties. Where there is a toilet, use it. Where there are none, bury your waste. Dig a small hole 15cm deep and at least 100m from any watercourse. Cover the waste with soil and a rock.

Washing

» Don't use detergents or toothpaste in or near watercourses, even if they are biodegradable.

» For personal washing, use biodegradable soap and a water container (or even a lightweight, portable basin) at least 50m away from the watercourse. Disperse the waste water widely to allow the soil to filter it fully.

» Wash cooking utensils 50m from watercourses using a scourer or sand instead of detergent.

ranging from short, easy strolls to challenging full-day walks such as the Yaberoo Budjara walk trail, which follows an Aboriginal walking trail.

Down South

Serious walkers gravitate to the rugged craggy beauty of the Stirling Range National Park (p155) north of Albany, one of the state's prime bushwalking areas. The popular Bluff Knoll climb (6km, three to four hours) will take your breath away – and so will the park's 1500 different species of wildflowers. Time your trip in late spring or early summer (September to November) to capture the park in all its flowering glory and be prepared for wind chill and rain (and sometimes snow) in winter.

Also north of Albany is the smaller Porongurup National Park (p153), with its signature granite rocks and pocket of dense karri forest. It offers a range of trails for bushwalkers, from the easy 10-minute Tree in the Rock stroll to the medium-grade Hayward and Nancy Peaks (three hours) and challenging three-hour Marmabup Rock hike. Wildflowers and a flurry of bird activity make springtime the peak season for Porongurup, but the park can be visited at any time of year.

WA has long stretches of spectacular coastline punctuated by interesting walks. Highlights are walks through Walpole (p142), Fitzgerald River (p156) and Cape Le Grand (p160) national parks.

For travellers with stamina and time on their hands, the Cape to Cape Track (p131) follows the coastline 135km from Cape Naturaliste to Cape Leeuwin, takes five to seven days, and has four wild camp sites en route.

Up North

Summer's no picnic in the sweltering, remote national parks of the north, and high season for many is late autumn, winter and early spring (April to October). Terrain in

Erosion

» Hillsides and mountain slopes, especially at high altitudes, are prone to erosion. Stick to existing tracks and avoid short cuts.

» If a well-used track passes through a mud patch, walk through the mud so as not to increase the size of the patch.

» Avoid removing the plant life that keeps topsoils in place.

Fires & Low-Impact Cooking

» Don't depend on open fires for cooking. The cutting of wood for fires in popular trekking areas can cause rapid deforestation. Cook on a light-weight kerosene, alcohol or Shellite (white gas) stove and avoid those powered by disposable butane gas canisters.

» Fires may be acceptable below the tree line in areas that get very few visitors. If you light a fire, use an existing fireplace. Use only dead, fallen wood. Remember the adage 'the bigger the fool, the bigger the fire'. Use minimal wood, just what you need for cooking. In huts, leave wood for the next person.

» Total fire bans are declared in parts of the state during summer due to extreme fire risk. Obey all such directions; check with the local Department of Environment & Conservation (DEC) office if you're unsure.

» Fully extinguish a fire after use. Spread the embers and flood them with water.

Conservation

» Do not feed the wildlife as this can lead to animals becoming dependent on hand-outs, to unbalanced populations and to diseases. Don't leave food scraps behind you. Place gear out of reach and tie packs to rafters or trees.

» Bushwalking in much of the state's bushland is restricted because of the risk of spreading dieback, a nasty fungal disease that attacks the roots of plants and causes them to rot. Its spread can be prevented by observing 'no go' road signs and by cleaning soil from your boots before and after each hike.

these arid regions can be treacherous, so always do your homework, be prepared with water and supplies, and check in with the ranger's office before setting out.

Kalbarri National Park (p168) draws hikers with a seductive mix of scenic gorges, thick bushland and rugged coastal cliffs. The popular six-hour loop takes advantage of the dramatic seascapes and features a series of lookouts, including Nature's Window, a favourite with photographers.

Rugged, sometimes hazardous treks can be taken into the dramatic gorges of the Karijini National Park (p193) and are popular with experienced bushwalkers – especially the walk to Mt Bruce summit (9km, five hours).

Visitors to the Kimberley's Purnululu National Park (p219) come to see one of Australia's most amazing sights – the striped beehive-shaped domes of the World Heritage-listed Bungle Bungles. Walks include the easy Cathedral Gorge walk, and the more difficult overnight trek to Piccaninny Gorge. The park is only open from April to December.

Camping

Most people go camping to 'get away from it all', and this enormous state provides that in spades. This is especially the case in the national parks, where sleeping in a swag under the stars is almost obligatory. The weather is the major concern for campers; it can be uncomfortable in the north during summer due to the heat and flash flooding, and pretty miserable and cold in the south during winter. Note that school holidays are not a good time for solitude in WA. See p246 for practical details.

Cycling

WA has excellent day, weekend or even multiweek cycling routes. Perth has an ever-growing network of bike tracks, and you'll

THE BIBBULMUN TRACK

If you've got eight spare weeks up your sleeve, consider trekking the entire **Bibbulmun Track** (www.bibbulmuntrack.org.au), a long-distance walking trail that winds its way south from Kalamunda, about 20km east of Perth, through virtually unbroken natural environment to Walpole and along the coast to Albany – a total of 963km.

Bushwalkers trek through magnificent southwest landscapes, including jarrah and marri forests, wandoo flats carpeted with wildflowers, rugged granite outcrops, coastal heath country and spectacular cliffs, headlands and beaches.

Camp sites are spaced at regular intervals, most with three-sided shelters that sleep eight to 16 people, plus a water tank and pit toilets. The best time for walking is from late winter to spring (August to October).

find the southwest region of WA good for cycle touring. While there are thousands of kilometres of good, virtually traffic-free roads in country areas, the distances between many towns makes it difficult to plan – even if the riding is virtually flat.

Perth is a relatively bike-friendly city, with a good recreational bike-path system, including routes that follow the Swan River all the way to Fremantle, and extensive paths through Kings Park overlooking the city.

Cyclists rule on virtually car-free Rottnest Island (p90). It's a liberating place to ride, with long stretches of empty roads circumnavigating the island that allow you to stop off at each beach for a swim. You can hire bikes on the island. Geraldton (p165) also has great cycle paths.

The most exciting initiative for mountain bikers is the **Munda Biddi Trail** (www.mundabiddi.org.au), which means 'path through the forest' in the Noongar Aboriginal language. When completed, it will be the mountain-biking equivalent of the Bibbulmun Track, taking off-road cyclists some 1000km from Mundaring on Perth's outskirts through the beautiful, scenic southwest to Albany on the south coast. The first half (to Nannup, 498km) had been completed at the time of research; camps with water, bike storage and bike repair facilities are situated a day's easy ride apart. Maps are available online and at visitor centres.

For practical advice on cycling around WA, see p261. For bike hire in Perth, see p58.

Diving & Snorkelling

With plenty of fascinating dives on offer throughout the state, including stunning marine parks and shipwrecks, WA is the perfect place to don a wetsuit and take the plunge. Local tourist offices can often help out with brochures and booklets on top regional diving or snorkelling spots.

Close to Perth, divers can explore shipwrecks and marine life off the beaches of Rottnest Island (p91), or head south to explore the submerged reefs and historic shipwrecks of the West Coast Dive Park (p95) within Shoalwater Islands Marine Park, near Rockingham. You can take a dive course in Geographe Bay with companies based in Dunsborough (p124) or Busselton (p122); the bay offers excellent dives under the Busselton jetty, on Four Mile Reef (a 40km limestone ledge about 6.5km off the coast) and the scuttled *HMAS Swan*.

Other wrecks popular with divers are the *HMAS Perth* (at 36m), which was deliberately sunk in 2001 in King George Sound near Albany (p145); and the *Sanko Harvest*, near Esperance (p157). Both wrecks teem with the marine life that has made the artificial reefs home.

Divers seeking warmer water should head north. A staggering amount of marine life can be found just 100m offshore within the Ningaloo Marine Park (p187), making this pristine piece of coastline fantastic for diving and snorkelling. In Turquoise Bay you can drift over the coral, get out down the beach, and do it again. If that whets your appetite, take in one of the most spectacular underwater experiences in the world – diving or snorkelling alongside the world's largest fish, the whale shark. Tours are available from Exmouth (p183) and Coral Bay (p179).

Fishing

From sailfish in the north to trout in the south there are all types of fishing on offer along WA's immense coastline. Fishing is the state's largest recreational activity and you'll find locals dropping a line just about anywhere there's water – and catching their dinner nearly every time.

Close to Perth, recreational fishers dangle a hook at Rottnest Island (p90), with king wrasse and Western Australian dhufish (previously called the jewfish) both plentiful around the island.

South of Perth, popular fishing hot spots include Mandurah (p96), with options for deep-sea fishing, catching tailor from the long golden stretches of beach or nabbing Mandurah's famed blue manna crabs and king prawns in the estuaries. You can scoot down to Augusta (p133) to chase salmon in the Blackwood River or whiting in the bay; or drop a line into the fish-rich waters underneath the famous jetty at Busselton (p122).

Sunny Geraldton (p164) is an excellent place to fish, with Sunset Beach and Drummond Cove popular spots, or you can take one of the excellent fishing charters out to the nearby Houtman Abrolhos Islands (p167). There's great fishing all along the coast from here and as you move up into the hotter, steamier northwest, the fishing charter operators start to multiply; there's a good chance to hook a monster fish at Exmouth (p183), the Dampier Archipelago (p191) and the game-fishing nirvana of Broome (p202). The northern Kimberley is also a popular spot for catching the tough-fighting and tasty barramundi.

You'll need a recreational fishing licence (RFL; $40) if you intend catching marron (freshwater crayfish) or rock lobsters; if you use a fishing net; or if you're freshwater angling in the southwest. If you're fishing from a motorised boat, someone on the boat will need to have a Recreational Fishing from Boat Licence (RFBL; $30) and you'll all need to stay within the licence's bag limits. Licences can be obtained online (www.fish.wa.gov.au) or from Australia Post offices. Note that there are strict bag and size limits – see the website for specific details.

Surfing & Windsurfing

If you're here to surf, WA is simply brilliant. Beginners, intermediates, wannabe pros and adventure surfers will all find excellent conditions to suit their skill levels along the coast. WA gets huge swells (often over 3m), so it's critical to align where you surf with your ability. Look out for strong currents, huge sharks and territorial local surfers (who can be far scarier than a hungry white pointer).

The state's traditional surfing home is the southwest, particularly the beaches from Yallingup to Margaret River (see p31). This stretch is perfect for a surf trip, with heaps of different breaks to explore.

Around Perth the surf is a lot smaller, but there are often good conditions at bodyboard-infested Trigg (p57) and Scarborough (p57). Don't despair if waves are small, simply head off to Rottnest Island (p91) where the surf is usually much bigger and better – check out Strickland Bay.

Heading north there are countless reef breaks waiting to be discovered on a surfing safari (hint: take a 4WD), with the best-known spots being the left-hand point breaks of Jakes Point near Kalbarri (p168); Gnaraloo Station, 150km north of Carnarvon (p177); as well as Surfers Beach at Exmouth (p187). Buy the locals a beer and they might share the location of some lesser-known world-class spots.

Windsurfers and kitesurfers have plenty of choice spots to try out as well, with excellent flat-water and wave-sailing. Kitesurfers in particular will appreciate the long, empty beaches and offshore reefs away from crowds.

After trying out Perth's city beaches, the next place to head is Lancelin (p113), which is home to a large population of surfers, especially in summer. Both flat-water and wave-sailing are excellent here. Further up the coast, Geraldton (p164) is another surfing

OUTDOOR EQUIPMENT

These suppliers can provide outdoor equipment and advice:

» **Kathmandu** (www.kathmandu.com.au); Perth (895 Hay St); Fremantle (30 Adelaide St)

» **Mountain Designs** (www.mountaindesigns.com.au); Perth (862 Hay St); Fremantle (Queensgate Centre, William St); Bunbury (21a Stephen Street) The Perth store is the headquarters for the Bibbulmun Track Foundation.

» **Paddy Pallin** (www.paddypallin.com.au; 884 Hay St, Perth)

hot spot – especially at the renowned Coronation Beach. The Shark Bay (p171) area has excellent flat-water sailing and Gnaraloo Station is also a world-renowned wave-sailing spot.

Wildlife-Watching

Whales

For most visitors to WA there's no better wildlife-watching than seeing the southern right and humpback whales make their way along the coast. There are so many (upwards of 30,000) that it's become known as the Humpback Highway. From June the gentle giants make their annual pilgrimage from Antarctica to the warm tropical waters of the northwest coast; they can then be seen on their slow southern migration in early summer. The whales regularly make themselves at home in the bays and coves of King George Sound in Albany (p145) from July to October, particularly mothers with calves.

In whale-watching season, whales can be spotted from cliff tops all along the coast – and often from the beach as well. Whale-watching tours leave from Perth (p58), Fremantle (p81), Dunsborough (p124), Augusta (p134), Albany (p148), Coral Bay (p179), Broome (p205) and the Dampier Peninsula (p211).

Dolphins

Dolphins can be seen up close year-round at several places in the west, including the Dolphin Discovery Centre at Bunbury (p121), on an interactive dolphin tour from Rockingham (p95), or at the beach resort of Monkey Mia (p174), famous for its friendly colony of bottlenose dolphins. Monkey Mia also has 10% of the world's dugong population.

Birds

WA is a birdwatcher's delight. The Broome Bird Observatory (p211) sits in the middle of a mudflats region which attracts a staggering 800,000 birds each year. Yalgorup National Park (p98), south of Mandurah, is another important habitat for a wide variety of water birds, and is a magnet for local birdwatchers. Another great spot is Lesueur National Park (p114), home to the endangered Carnaby's Cockatoo.

Travel with Children

Best Regions for Kids

Perth & Fremantle

See p82 and p82 in the Perth & Fremantle chapter.

Margaret River & the Southwest

Geographe Bay features family-friendly beaches, Yallingup has a surf school, and the Dolphin Discovery Centre and Big Swamp Wildlife Park are located in Bunbury. The region also features whale-watching.

Monkey Mia & the Central West

Beaches, of course, and lots of marine wildlife – especially the dolphins and dugongs at Monkey Mia, the pelicans at Kalbarri, and the Ocean Park aquarium at Denham.

Broome & Around

Kids will go crazy for the camel rides, crocodile parks and whale-watching, in and around Broome. There are also lots of opportunities to have fun while learning about Indigenous culture, especially on the Dampier Peninsula, while camping along the Gibb River Road is a treat.

With lots of sunshine, beaches and big open spaces, Western Australia (WA) is a wonderful destination for children of all ages. Australians are famously laid-back and their generally tolerant, 'no worries' attitude extends to children having a good time and perhaps being a little raucous.

West Coast Australia for Kids

Interacting with Australia's native fauna, whether in the wild or in the numerous wildlife parks, is likely to be a memory that your kids treasure for a lifetime. Although Australia's wildlife can be dangerous and the nightmare that lurks in the subconscious of any parent visiting Australia for the first time is Meryl Streep crying 'a dingo took my baby', in reality you're extremely unlikely to strike any problems if you take sensible precautions. See p253 for more information.

More of a concern is the harshness of the Australian sun. Don't underestimate how quickly you and your kids can get sunburnt, even on overcast days. A standard routine for most Australian parents is to lather their kids in high-protection sunscreen (SPF 30+) before they head outside for the day, and it's a habit that's worth adopting. It's best to avoid going to the beach in the middle of the day – head out in the morning or mid-afternoon instead.

On really hot days, dehydration can be a problem, especially for small children on the go. Carry some fluids with you, especially on long car journeys.

Babies & Toddlers

Perth and most major towns have centrally located public rooms where parents can go to nurse their baby or change nappies; check with the local visitor centre for details. While many Australians have a relaxed attitude about breastfeeding or nappy changing in public, some don't.

Many motels and the better-equipped caravan parks have playgrounds and swimming pools, and can supply cots and baby baths. Motels in the more touristy areas may also have in-house children's videos and child-minding services. Top-end hotels and many (but not all) midrange hotels are well versed in the needs of guests who have children. B&Bs, on the other hand, often market themselves as sanctuaries from all things child-related.

Many cafes and restaurants lack a specialised children's menu, but many others do have kids' meals, or will provide small serves from the main menu. Some also supply high chairs.

Medical services and facilities in Australia are of a high standard, and items such as baby food, formula and disposable nappies are widely available in urban centres. Major hire-car companies will supply and fit booster seats for you at a charge.

School-age Kids

The biggest challenge for parents of school-age children is a sudden attack of the are-we-there-yets. As we've stressed over and over in this book, distances in WA are vast – if WA was a separate country it would be the 10th biggest country in the world. Even adults find the long drives tedious; kids no less so. Come well stocked with distractions: books, pens and papers, rousing travelling songs and games, computer games, child-friendly CDs – whatever it takes. Another nifty trick is to hire a car with a backseat screen for playing DVDs.

It may sound obvious, but a handy supply of snacks is essential for those long journeys, where shops might be 200km or further apart. Toilet paper is also a blessing.

Have a word to the kids about the biting beasties, such as snakes and spiders, impressing on them to keep their distance. This is particularly important for any little ones with a penchant for prodding things with sticks. While bushwalking, make sure they wear socks with shoes or boots – no matter how uncool they think it is.

Children's Highlights

Beaches

Beaches are a big part of the WA experience. Ensure that the kids swim between the flags and ask the locals about the safer beaches.

Wildlife Parks & Zoos

Wildlife parks are always a big hit at any age; you'll get the obligatory kangaroo-petting snap to send to the grandparents. There are parks throughout the state, and most tourist areas have one. Many have walk-in aviaries – so prepare for a freak-out when an overfriendly parrot lands on little Jimmy's shoulder! And watch out for the emus: those beady eyes, long necks and pointy beaks are even more intimidating when they're attached to something that's double your height.

Whale-watching

If you're at the right part of the coast at the right time of year, you will definitely see whales from the shore. Organised whale-watching boat trips take you up close and personal; they depart from Perth, Fremantle, Dunsborough, Augusta, Albany, Coral Bay, Broome and the Dampier Peninsula.

Other Marine Mammals

» Rockingham Wild Encounters (p95) An opportunity for the over fives to swim with wild dolphins

» Dolphin Discovery Centre, Bunbury (p121) Wade into the shallows alongside the dolphins

» Monkey Mia (p174) Watch dolphins being fed in the bay or head out on a cruise to spot dolphins and dugongs

» Sea Lion Charters, Green Head (p116) Splash about with sea lions in the shallows

Surf Schools

» Surfschool, Perth (60) and Lancelin (p113) Lessons for 11 year olds and over

» Yallingup Surf School (127) 'Microgrom' lessons for the under 10s

Amusement Parks & Rides

» Adventure World, Perth (p60)

» Perth Royal Show, Perth (p62)

Planning

If you're booking accommodation and hire cars in advance, be sure to specify any requirements you might have regarding cots, car seats and the like. If you're travelling with an infant, it's good to have a mosquito net to drape over the cot. Bring rash tops for the beach and warm clothes if you're travelling south in winter. However, there's really no need to stress too much – anything you forget can be purchased when you arrive.

Discounts

Child concessions (and family rates) often apply for such things as accommodation, tours, admission fees, and air, bus and train transport, with some discounts 50% of the adult rate. In many cases, babies and infants will get into sights for free. However, the definition of 'child' can vary from under 12 to under 18 years. Accommodation concessions generally apply to children under 12 years sharing the same room as adults. On the major airlines, infants travel for free provided they don't occupy a seat – child fares usually apply between the ages of two and 11 years.

regions at a glance

Perth & Fremantle

Beaches ✓
Museums & Galleries ✓✓✓
Historic Buildings ✓✓

Beaches
They may not offer the solitude and pristine natural surroundings of those elsewhere in the state, but Perth and Fremantle's long sandy beaches provide a multifaceted playground for city dwellers. Some are popular with surfers and some with families, some for snorkelling and some for swimming. There's one that's predominantly gay (and nude), and others where part of the attraction is walking straight off the beach and into a pub.

Museums & Galleries
As the state's capital and biggest urban centre, Perth is well endowed with public institutions. At the top of the list is the Art Gallery of Western Australia, which houses a wonderful collection of traditional and contemporary art. Its neighbours within the Perth Cultural Centre include the edgy Perth Institute of Contemporary Art and a major outpost of the Western Australian Museum. Not to be outdone, Fremantle has two of the museum's other branches – the superb maritime museum and Shipwreck Galleries.

Historic Buildings
Relics of the colonial era and early gold rushes abound in these twin cities. In Fremantle, the concentration is much greater, providing a streetscape with a historic ambience that's often lacking in this state. The big drawcard is the old convict-built prison, its murky stories brought to life through excellent guided tours.

Around Perth

Beaches ✓✓
Wildlife ✓✓✓
Heritage Towns ✓

Beaches
Just a short boat ride from Perth, Rottnest Island is ringed by gorgeous beaches – and it's surprisingly easy to find a patch all to yourself. By contrast, Mandurah, Rockingham and Yanchep are built-up beach 'burbs that bustle with cafes and marinas. Up north, picturesque Guilderton sits on a lagoon formed around the mouth of a river, while the Turquoise Coast offers even more delights.

Wildlife
Whales, dolphins, sea lions, seals, penguins, kangaroos, possums, quokkas, bilbies, boodies, woylies – it's quite amazing how much wildlife lives in such close proximity to the city.

Heritage Towns
The quaint townships that are scattered in the forests, hills and river valleys surrounding Perth make perfect day trips. The best of them is York, its contiguous rows of historic buildings preserving a gold rush atmosphere.

Margaret River & the Southwest

Beaches ✓✓✓
Wineries ✓✓✓
Forests ✓✓✓

Beaches

The sandy beaches of Geographe Bay are perfect for a bucket-and-spade holiday with the kids. The most beautiful spots are at its western end, near Cape Naturaliste. The best surf in Western Australia (WA) crashes on the coast south of here.

Wineries

Not only is Margaret River Australia's most beautiful wine region, it also produces some of its best wine. The cool climate vineyards around Pemberton are also worth exploring.

Forests

Even if you can't tell a tuart from a karri, you'll find the forests of tall trees an impressive sight. Some of the larger specimens are rigged with spikes, allowing the fit and fearless to climb up to 68m into the canopy.

South Coast

Beaches ✓✓✓
Wineries ✓✓
National Parks ✓✓✓

Beaches

Glorious, isolated bays of powdery white sand are spread all along this long stretch of coast. On many you'll be more likely to spot a whale than another person.

Wineries

Although not as tourist-oriented or as well known as Margaret River, the wineries of the Great Southern region are constantly growing in stature. Sup your way from Denmark to Mt Barker and on to Porongurup.

National Parks

WA isn't short on national parks, but this region has some of the best, starting with the dramatic Tree Top Walk in Walpole-Nornalup and ending with the superfine sands of Cape Arid. In between, don't miss the mysterious, mountainous Porongurup and Stirling Range national parks, or the vast wild heath of Fitzgerald River.

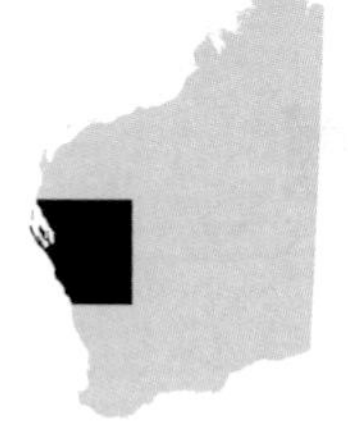

Monkey Mia & the Central West

Beaches ✓✓✓
Adventure ✓✓✓
History ✓✓✓

Beaches

The incredibly white shell beaches of Shark Bay, fringed by turquoise waters that teem with marine life – including the famous dolphins of Monkey Mia – are just part of an incredible coastline that stretches from family-friendly Port Denison to the wilds of Gnaraloo Station.

Adventure

Surfers and windsurfers flock to Geraldton and Gnaraloo Station for the winter swells and summer winds while fisherfolk and explorers head way out west to Edel Land and Dirk Hartog Island. Bushwalkers prefer Kalbarri in winter for the epic four-day gorge traverse.

History

This rugged coastline is littered with historic artefacts, shipwrecks and 19th-century buildings, including the pioneer settlement of Greenough and the 1629 wreck of the *Batavia* off the Houtman Albrolhos Islands.

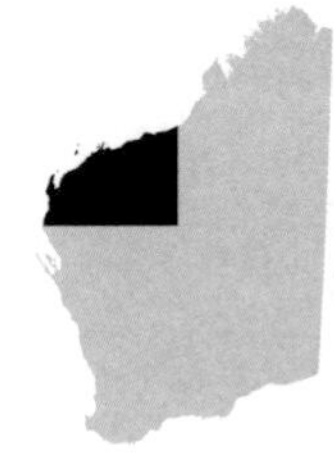

Coral Coast & the Pilbara

Beaches ✓✓✓
Adventure ✓✓✓
Wildlife ✓✓✓

Beaches
Superb isolated beaches lead down to shallow lagoons hemmed by World Heritage-nominated Ningaloo Marine Park. World-class snorkelling and diving is only a short wade from shore and camping is right behind the dunes. November sees turtles struggle ashore to lay their eggs.

Adventure
Karijini National Park is the Pilbara's adventure playground, with deep narrow gorges that invite exploration, and the state's highest peaks just begging to be climbed.

Wildlife
Whale sharks, manta rays, turtles and migrating whales are just a few of the marine creatures that visit Ningaloo, while inland birds flock to the oasis pools of Millstream-Chichester National Park, and pythons and rock wallabies hide in the shadows of Karijini.

Broome & Around

Beaches ✓✓✓
Indigenous Culture ✓✓
Adventure ✓✓✓

Beaches
Iconic Cable Beach with its sunset camel trains tops the list, but don't miss the pristine, seldom-visited beaches of the Dampier Peninsula and Coloumb Nature Reserve.

Indigenous Culture
Learn how to mudcrab, make a spear, hunt bushtucker and care for country with the Aboriginal communities of the Dampier Peninsula. Follow Broome's Lurujarri Dreaming Trail then explore the amazing Wandjina and Gwion Gwion images of the Kimberley.

Adventure
Bring it on! The Kimberley will provide the ride of your life along the bone-shaking Gibb River Road, with its many side roads and gorges, the exceptional Mitchell Falls, and remote Kalumburu. Jump a speedboat and head full throttle for the Horizontal Waterfalls, then grab a canoe and paddle down the mighty Ord River.

Look out for these icons:

Our author's recommendation

A green or sustainable option

FREE No payment required

See the Index for a full list of destinations covered in this book.

On the Road

Perth & Fremantle

Includes »

Best Places to Eat

» Balthazar (p66)
» Jackson's (p67)
» Must Winebar (p67)
» Namh Thai (p66)
» Divido (p67)

Best Places to Stay

» Richardson (p64)
» Emperor's Crown (p63)
» Durack House (p64)
» Pension of Perth (p63)
» Norfolk Hotel (p82)

Why Go?

Planted by a river and beneath an almost permanent canopy of blue sky, the city of Perth is a modern-day boomtown, stoking Australia's economy from its glitzy central business district. Yet it remains as relaxed as the sleepy Swan River – black swans bobbing atop – which winds past the skyscrapers and out to the Indian Ocean.

Even in its boardrooms, Perth's heart is down at the beach, tossing around in clear ocean surf and stretching out on the sand. The city's beaches trace the western edge of Australia for some 40km, and you can have one to yourself on any given day – for a city this size, Perth is sparsely populated.

Perth has sprawled to enfold Fremantle within its suburbs, yet the port city maintains its own distinct personality – proud of its nautical ties, working-class roots, bohemian reputation and, especially, its football team.

When to Go

Perth

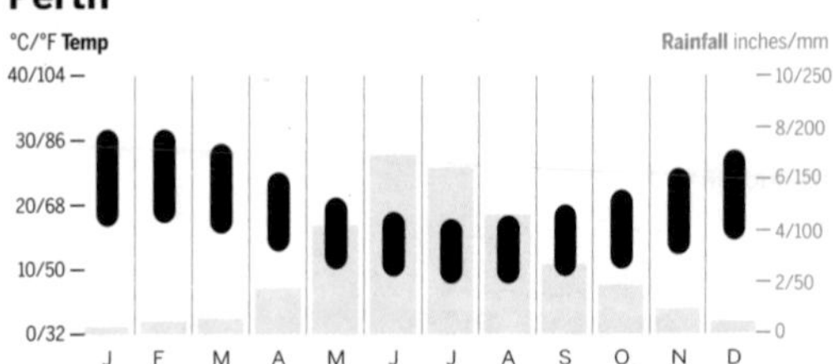

February
Perth's Arts Festival is on and school starts so the beaches are less crowded.

March
Warm and dry, so great weather for the beach, and not as swelteringly hot.

September
Kings Park wildflowers, the Perth Royal Show and the Parklife festival.

PERTH

POP 1.7 MILLION

Laid-back, liveable Perth has wonderful weather, beautiful beaches and an easygoing character. About as close to Bali as to some of Australia's eastern state capitals, Perth's combination of big-city attractions with relaxed and informal surrounds offers an appealing lifestyle for locals and a variety of things to do for visitors. It's a sophisticated, cosmopolitan city with myriad bars, restaurants and cultural activities all vying for attention. But the best bit is that when you want to chill out, it's easy to do so. Perth's pristine parkland, nearby bush, and river and ocean beaches – along with a good public transport system – allow its inhabitants to spread out and enjoy what's on offer.

Relaxed doesn't mean static, though. Western Australia's mining boom has seen Perth blossom like WA's wildflowers in spring. Those on the gravy train are out eating, socialising, spending money and flexing their muscles in the sun.

The city of Perth lies along a wide sweep of the Swan River. The river borders the city centre to the south and east, and links Perth to its neighbouring port city, Fremantle. Follow the river north from the city and you'll reach prosperous nooks such as Claisebrook Cove, lined with ostentatious houses, cafes and public sculpture.

Train tracks divide the city centre from the Northbridge entertainment enclave, immediately to the north. Here's where you'll find Perth's cultural institutions, most of its hostels and the lively Little Asia restaurant strip.

Continue northeast along Beaufort St and you'll reach the sophisticated suburbs of Highgate and Mt Lawley. Head west from here and there's Mt Hawthorn and hip little Leederville. To the west of the central city rises Kings Park, with well-heeled Subiaco beyond it. Go further west and you'll hit the beaches.

For the Swan Valley and other parts of Perth's eastern suburbs, see the Around Perth chapter.

History

The discovery of stone implements near the Swan River suggests that Mooro, the site on which the city of Perth now stands, has been occupied for around 40,000 years. The indigenous Wadjuk people, a subgroup of the Noongar, believed that the Swan River (Derbal Yaragan) and the landforms surrounding it were shaped by two Wargal (giant serpent-like creatures), which lived under present-day Kings Park.

In December 1696 three ships in the Dutch fleet commanded by Willem de Vlamingh anchored off what is now known as Rottnest Island. On 5 January 1697 a well-armed party landed near present-day Cottesloe Beach and then marched eastward to a river near Freshwater Bay. They tried to make contact with the local people to

PERTH & FREMANTLE IN...

Two Days

Book ahead for dinner in **Highgate** or **Mt Lawley** and then spend your first morning in the art galleries and museum of the **Perth Cultural Centre**. Grab lunch in **Northbridge** before following our walking tour to **Kings Park**. For your second day, catch the train to **Fremantle** and spend the whole day there, prioritising the world-heritage prison, maritime museum and Shipwreck Galleries. Grab a bite in **Fishing Boat Harbour** and then head to a **pub** to catch a band.

Four Days

Take the two-day itinerary but stretch it to a comfortable pace. Head to **Rottnest Island** for a day trip and spend any time left over on Perth's beaches. Allocate a night each to **Leederville** and the city's **cocktail bars**.

One Week

As for the four-day itinerary, but spend a day in **Guildford** and the **Swan Valley**, take a **whale-watching cruise** and head out to **Rockingham** to view penguins and sea lions and to swim with dolphins. Spend one of the extra evenings in **Subiaco** and another in **Northbridge**.

Perth & Fremantle Highlights

1. Stretch out on the lawn in **Kings Park** (p55) with the glittering river and city spread out below you
2. Do time with the ghosts of convicts past in World Heritage–listed **Fremantle Prison** (p77)
3. Delve into the depths of the state's maritime history within the Western Australian Museum's **Shipwreck Galleries** (p80)
4. Explore a wealth of local art, indigenous and otherwise, at the **Art Gallery of Western Australia** (p54)
5. Soak up the decaying gold rush grandeur of **Fremantle's historic streetscape** (p81)
6. Enjoy the sunset with a sundowner in hand after a hard day's beaching at **Cottesloe** (p57)
7. Hit **Fremantle's pubs** (p85) and let the bands of Bon Scott's hometown shake you all night long

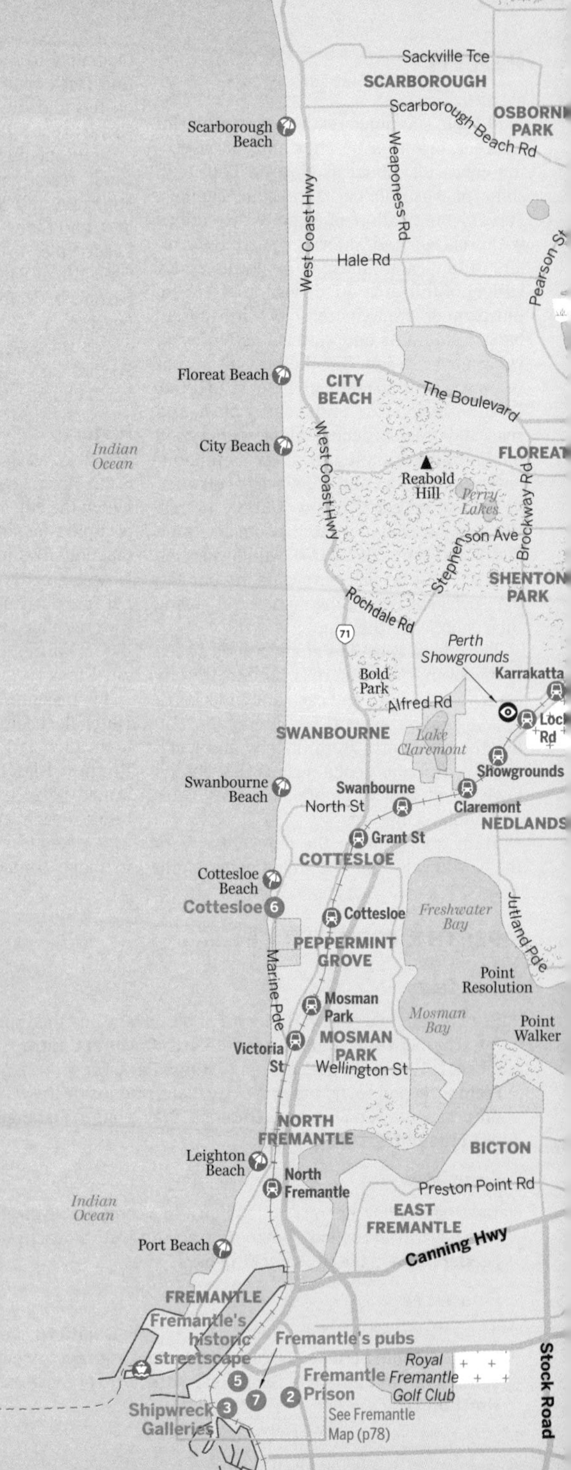

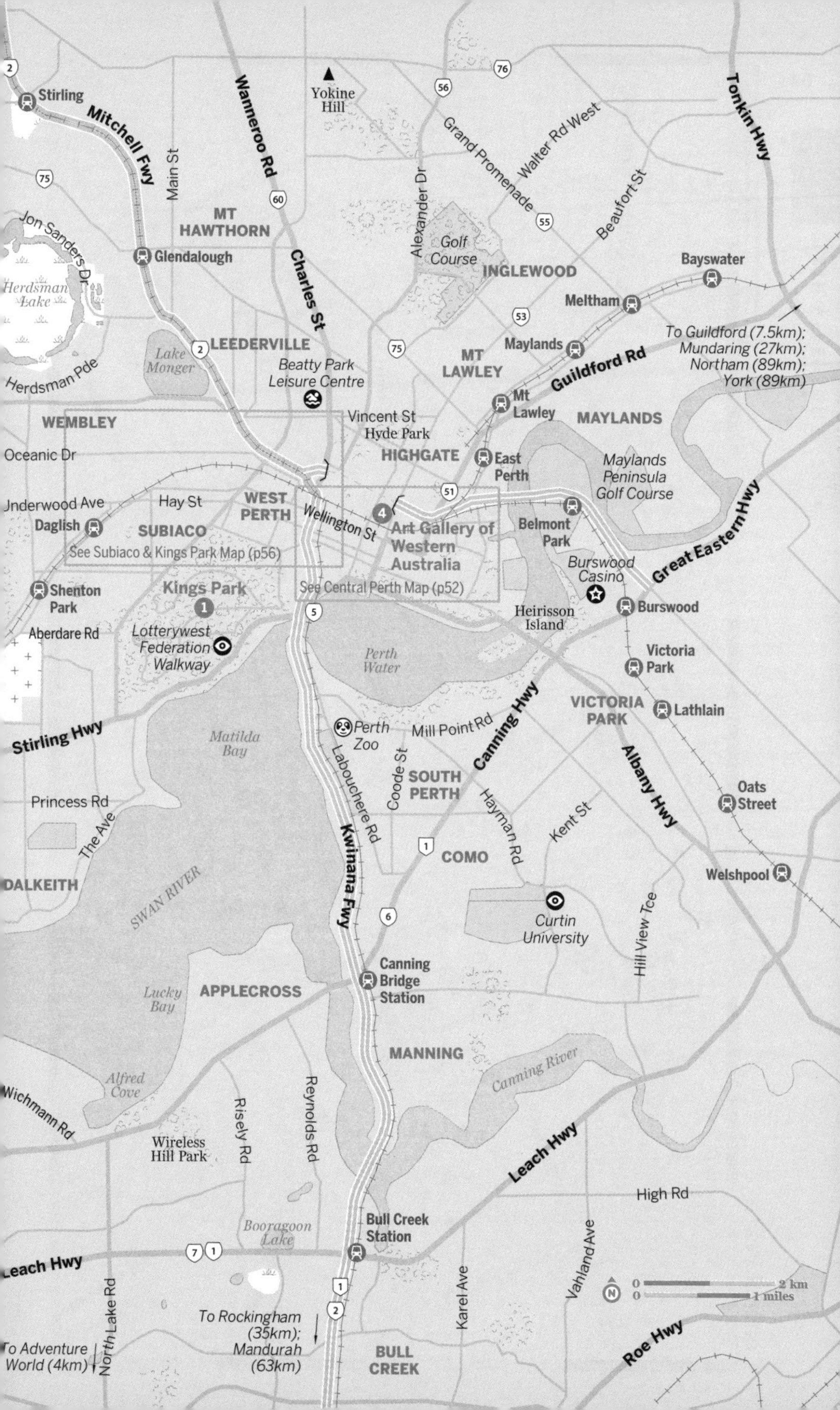

Stirling
Mitchell Fwy
Wanneroo Rd
Yokine Hill
Tonkin Hwy
Grand Promenade
Walter Rd West
Main St
MT HAWTHORN
Jon Sanders Dr
Glendalough
Herdsman Lake
Charles St
Alexander Dr
Golf Course
INGLEWOOD
Beaufort St
Bayswater
Meltham
LEEDERVILLE
Lake Monger
Beatty Park Leisure Centre
MT LAWLEY
Maylands
To Guildford (7.5km); Mundaring (27km); Northam (89km); York (89km)
Guildford Rd
Herdsman Pde
Mt Lawley
MAYLANDS
WEMBLEY
Vincent St
Hyde Park
HIGHGATE
East Perth
Maylands Peninsula Golf Course
Oceanic Dr
Hay St
WEST PERTH
Underwood Ave
Daglish
SUBIACO
Wellington St
Art Gallery of Western Australia
Belmont Park
Great Eastern Hwy
See Subiaco & Kings Park Map (p56)
Burswood Casino
Shenton Park
Kings Park
See Central Perth Map (p52)
Burswood
Heirisson Island
Aberdare Rd
Lotterywest Federation Walkway
Perth Water
Victoria Park
Canning Hwy
VICTORIA PARK
Lathlain
Stirling Hwy
Perth Zoo
Mill Point Rd
Matilda Bay
Labouchere Rd
Coode St
SOUTH PERTH
Albany Hwy
Hayman Rd
Oats Street
Princess Rd
Kent St
The Ave
COMO
Kwinana Fwy
Welshpool
DALKEITH
SWAN RIVER
Curtin University
Hill View Tce
Canning Bridge Station
Lucky Bay
APPLECROSS
MANNING
Canning River
Alfred Cove
Wichmann Rd
Risely Rd
Reynolds Rd
Leach Hwy
Wireless Hill Park
High Rd
Booragoon Lake
Bull Creek Station
Leach Hwy
Karel Ave
Vahland Ave
0 2 km
0 1 miles
To Rockingham (35km); Mandurah (63km)
North Lake Rd
To Adventure World (4km)
BULL CREEK
Roe Hwy

Central Perth

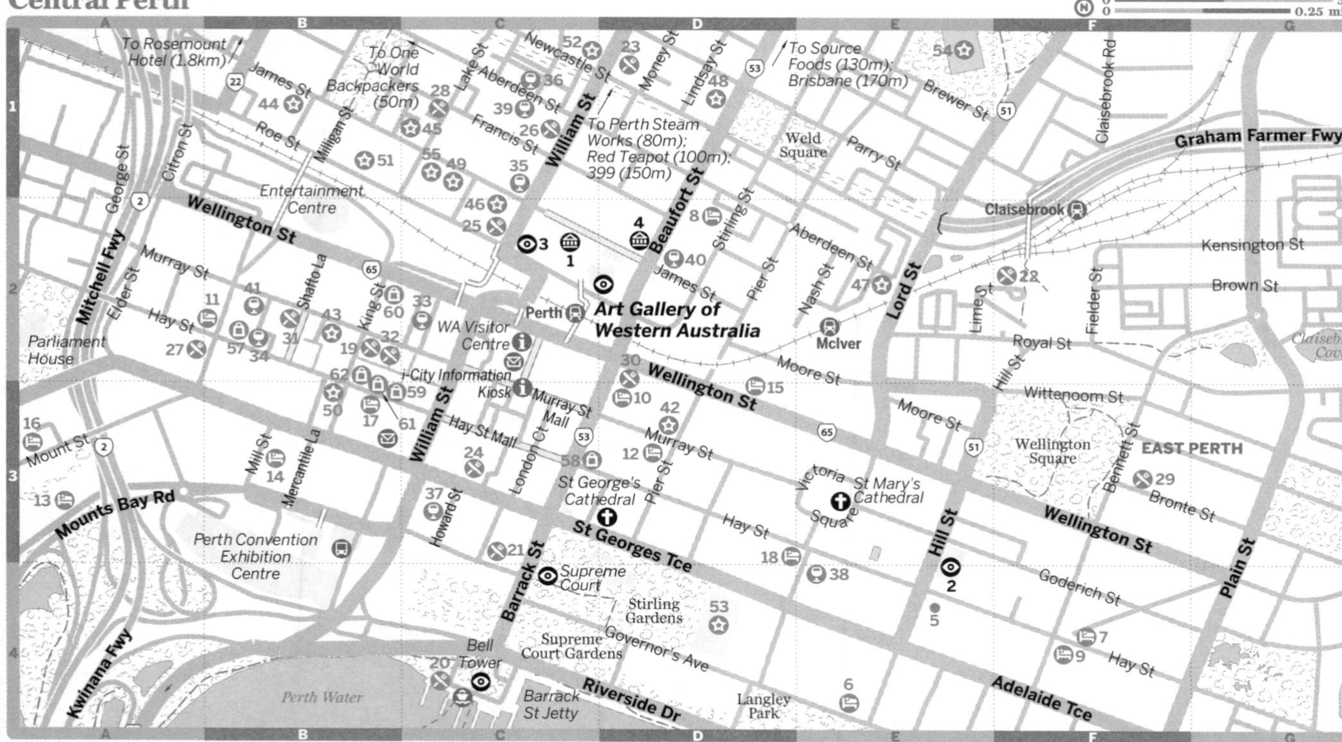

Central Perth

Top Sights
Art Gallery of Western Australia ... D2

Sights
1 Perth Institute of Contemporary Arts ... C2
2 Perth Mint ... E4
3 State Theatre Centre ... C2
4 Western Australian Museum – Perth ... D2

Activities, Courses & Tours
5 Cycle Centre ... E4

Sleeping
6 City Waters ... E4
7 Comfort Hotel Perth City ... F4
8 Emperor's Crown ... D2
9 Mantra on Hay ... F4
10 Medina Executive Barrack Plaza ... D3
11 Melbourne ... B2
12 Miss Maud ... D3
13 Mounts Bay Waters ... A3
14 Parmelia Hilton ... B3
15 Perth City YHA ... D3
16 Riverview on Mount St ... A3
17 Rydges Perth ... B3
18 Travelodge Perth ... D3

Eating
19 44 King St ... B2
20 Annalakshmi ... C4
21 Balthazar ... C3
22 City Farm Organic Growers Market ... F2
23 Good Fortune Roast Duck House ... D1
24 Greenhouse ... C3
25 Kakulas Bros ... C2
26 Little Willy's ... C1
27 Matsuri ... A2
28 Maya Masala ... C1
29 Restaurant Amusé ... F3
Secret Garden ... (see 32)
30 Taka Barrack St ... D2
31 Taka Shafto Lane ... B2
32 Tiger Tiger ... B2
Viet Hoa ... (see 52)

Drinking
33 1907 ... C2
Belgian Beer Cafe ... (see 19)
34 Box Deli ... B2
35 Brass Monkey ... C1
36 Deen ... C1
Ezra Pound ... (see 25)
Greenhouse ... (see 24)
37 Helvetica ... C3
38 Hula Bula Bar ... E4
39 Shed ... C1
40 The Court ... D2
41 Tiger Lil's ... B2

Entertainment
42 Ambar ... D3
43 Amplifier ... B2
44 Bakery ... B1
45 Cinema Paradiso ... C1
46 Connections ... C2
47 Devilles Pad ... E2
48 Ellington Jazz Club ... D1
49 Geisha ... C1
50 His Majesty's Theatre ... B3
51 Metro City ... B1
52 Moon ... C1
53 Perth Concert Hall ... D4
54 Perth Oval ... E1
55 Rise ... C1
Universal ... (see 35)
56 WACA ... G4

Shopping
57 78 Records ... B2
58 All Foreign Languages Bookshop ... C3
59 Boffins ... B3
60 Dilettante ... B2
61 Elizabeth's bookshop ... B3
Perth Map Centre ... (see 57)
62 Wheels & Doll Baby ... B2

enquire about survivors of the *Ridderschap van Hollant,* lost in 1694, but were unsuccessful, so they sailed north. It was De Vlamingh who bestowed the name Swan on the river.

Modern Perth was founded in 1829 when a hopeful Captain James Stirling established the Swan River Colony, and named the main settlement after the Scottish hometown of the British Secretary of State for the Colonies. The original settlers paid for their own passage and that of their servants and in return they received 200 acres for every labourer they brought with them.

At the time Mooro belonged to a Wadjuk leader called Yellagonga and his people, whose main camp was at Boorloo, near where the colony was founded. Relations were friendly at first, the Noongar believing the British to be the returned spirits of their dead, but competition for resources led to conflict. Yellagonga moved his camp first to Lake Monger and, by the time of his death in 1843, his people had been dispossessed of all of their lands around Perth's city centre and were forced to camp around the swamps and lakes to the city's north.

Midgegooroo, an elder from south of the Swan River, along with his son Yagan, led resistance to the British settlement. In 1833 Midgegooroo was caught and executed by firing squad, while Yagan was shot a few months later by teenage settlers whom he had befriended. Yagan's head was removed, smoked and sent to London where it was publically displayed as an anthropological curiosity.

Life for the settlers was much harder than they had expected it to be. The early settlement grew very slowly until 1850, when convicts alleviated the labour shortage and boosted the population. Convict labour was also responsible for constructing the city's substantial buildings such as Government House and the Town Hall. Even then, Perth's development lagged behind that of the cities in the eastern colonies. That is, until the discovery of gold inland in the 1890s increased Perth's population fourfold in a decade and initiated a building bonanza.

The mineral wealth of Western Australia (WA) has continued to drive Perth's growth. In the 1980s and '90s, though, the city's clean-cut, nouveau-riche image was tainted by a series of financial and political scandals. Today Perth is thriving once again, thanks to another mining boom.

Largely excluded from this race to riches are the Noongar people. In 2006, the Perth Federal Court recognised native title over the city of Perth and its surrounds, but this was appealed by the WA and Commonwealth governments. In December 2009 an agreement was signed in WA's Parliament, setting out a two-year time frame for negotiating settlement of native title claims across the southwest.

Sights

Many of Perth's main attractions are within walking distance of the inner city, with a clump of them in the Perth Cultural Centre precinct, just across the railway lines in Northbridge. Most of the further-flung sights, including the beaches, can be reached by public transport, although you'll find it easier to hop between them with a car. See also the Around Perth chapter for easy day trips from the city, including the Swan Valley.

CITY CENTRE

Bell Tower LANDMARK

(Map p52; www.thebelltower.com.au; adult/child $11/8; ⏲10am-4pm, ringing noon-1pm Mon, Tue, Thu, Sat & Sun) Close your eyes and think of England as you listen to the ringing of these bells. This pointy glass spire fronted by copper sails contains the royal bells of London's St Martin's-in-the-Fields, the oldest of which dates to 1550. They were given to WA by the British government in 1988, and are the only set known to have left England. Clamber to the top for 360-degree views of Perth by the river.

The tower sits on land that was reclaimed from the river in the 1920s and 1930s and now forms a green strip between the river and the city. Long, thin **Langley Park** is still occasionally used as an airstrip for light aircraft demonstrations. **Stirling Gardens** and **Supreme Court Gardens** have lovingly tended lawns and formal gardens which fill up with city workers at lunchtime.

Perth Mint HISTORIC BUILDING

(Map p52; www.perthmint.com.au; 310 Hay St; adult/child $15/5; ⏲9am-5pm Mon-Fri, 9am-1pm Sat & Sun) Dating from 1899, the oddly compelling mint displays a collection of coins, nuggets and gold bars. You can fondle a bar worth over $200,000, mint your own coins and watch gold pours (on the hour, starting 10am).

NORTHBRIDGE

FREE **Art Gallery of Western Australia** ART GALLERY

(Map p52; www.artgallery.wa.gov.au; Perth Cultural Centre, Northbridge; ⏲10am-5pm Wed-Mon) Founded in 1895, this excellent gallery houses the state's pre-eminent art collection. It contains important post-WWII works by Australian luminaries such as Arthur Boyd, Albert Tucker, Grace Cossington Smith, Russell Drysdale, Arthur Streeton and Sidney Nolan, but it's the indigenous galleries that provide the highlight. Here you'll find a large variety of work, from canvasses to bark paintings to sculpture, by the likes of Rover Thomas, Angilya Mitchell, Christopher

Pease and Phyllis Thomas. The annual WA Indigenous Art Awards entries are displayed here from August to December.

Free tours take place at 11am and 1pm on Sundays, Mondays, Wednesdays and Thursdays, at 12.30pm and 2pm on Fridays, and at 1pm on Saturdays.

FREE Perth Institute of Contemporary Arts ART GALLERY

(Map p52; www.pica.org.au; Perth Cultural Centre, Northbridge; 11am-6pm Tue-Sun) Commonly referred to by its acronym, PICA (pee-kah) may have a traditional wrapping (it's housed in an elegant 1896 red-brick former school) but inside it's anything but, being one of Australia's principal platforms for cutting-edge contemporary art – installations, performance, sculpture, video works and the like. It actively promotes new and experimental art, and exhibits graduate works annually.

FREE Western Australian Museum – Perth MUSEUM

(Map p52; www.museum.wa.gov.au; Perth Cultural Centre, Northbridge; 9.30am-5pm) The state's museum is a six-headed beast, with branches in Fremantle, Albany, Geraldton and Kalgoorlie. This one includes dinosaur, mammal, butterfly and bird galleries, a **children's discovery centre**, and an excellent **WA Land and People** display that covers indigenous and colonial history. In the courtyard, set in its own preservative bath, is **Megamouth**, a curious-looking species of shark with a soft, rounded head. Only about five of these benign creatures have ever been found; this one beached itself near Mandurah, south of Perth.

The museum complex includes Perth's original **gaol**, built in 1856 and used until 1888 – the site of many hangings.

Hyde Park PARK

(Map p50; William St, North Perth) One of Perth's most beautiful parks, suburban Hyde Park is a top spot for a picnic or lazy book-reading session on the lawn. A path traces the small lake, and mature palms, firs and Moreton Bay figs provide plenty of shade. It's within walking distance of Northbridge; continue northeast along William St.

SUBIACO & KINGS PARK

TOP CHOICE Kings Park & Botanic Garden PARK

(Map p56; www.bgpa.wa.gov.au) Rising above the Swan River on the western flank of the city, the 400-hectare bush-filled expanse of Kings Park is Perth's pride and joy. When the sun's shining (which isn't exactly a rare occurrence) the city's good burghers head here for a picnic under the trees or to let the kids off the leash in one of the playgrounds. Its numerous tracks are popular with walkers and joggers all year-round, while the steep stairs leading up from the river support a steady procession of masochistic middle-aged men, desperate to maintain those buns of steel for just a little longer. The exertion is rewarded by wonderful views from the top.

The Noongar people knew this area as Kaarta Gar-up and used it for thousands of years for hunting, food gathering, ceremonies, teaching and tool-making. A freshwater spring at the base of the escarpment, now known as Kennedy Fountain but before that as Goonininup, was a home of the Wargal, mystical snake-like creatures which created the Swan River and other waterways.

At the park's heart is the 17-hectare Botanic Garden, containing over 2000 plant species indigenous to WA. In spring there's an impressive display of the state's famed wildflowers. A highlight is the **Lotterywest Federation Walkway** (Map p50; 9am-5pm), a 620m path through the gardens that includes a beautifully designed, 222m-long, glass-and-steel bridge that passes through the canopy of a stand of eucalypts.

The main road leading into the park, Fraser Ave, is lined with towering lemon-scented gums which are dramatically lit at night. At its culmination are the **State War Memorial**, a cafe, gift shop, Frasers restaurant and the **Kings Park Visitor Centre** (9.30am-4pm). Free **guided walks** (10am & 2pm) leave from here.

To get here take bus 37 (39 on weekends), heading west along St Georges Tce (S-stand), to the visitor centre. You can also walk up (steep) Mount St from the city or climb Jacob's Ladder from Mounts Bay Rd, near the Adelphi Hotel, a stairway demanding enough to provide a sense of achievement at the top.

BEACHES

When the mercury rises the only sensible decision is to go west to one of Perth's many clean, sandy beaches. Most of them are comparatively undeveloped, which is just how the locals like it. Little wonder, if the clunky Observation City complex at Scarborough is the benchmark. There's certainly nothing as glitzy as, say, Sydney's Bondi – the most

Subiaco & Kings Park

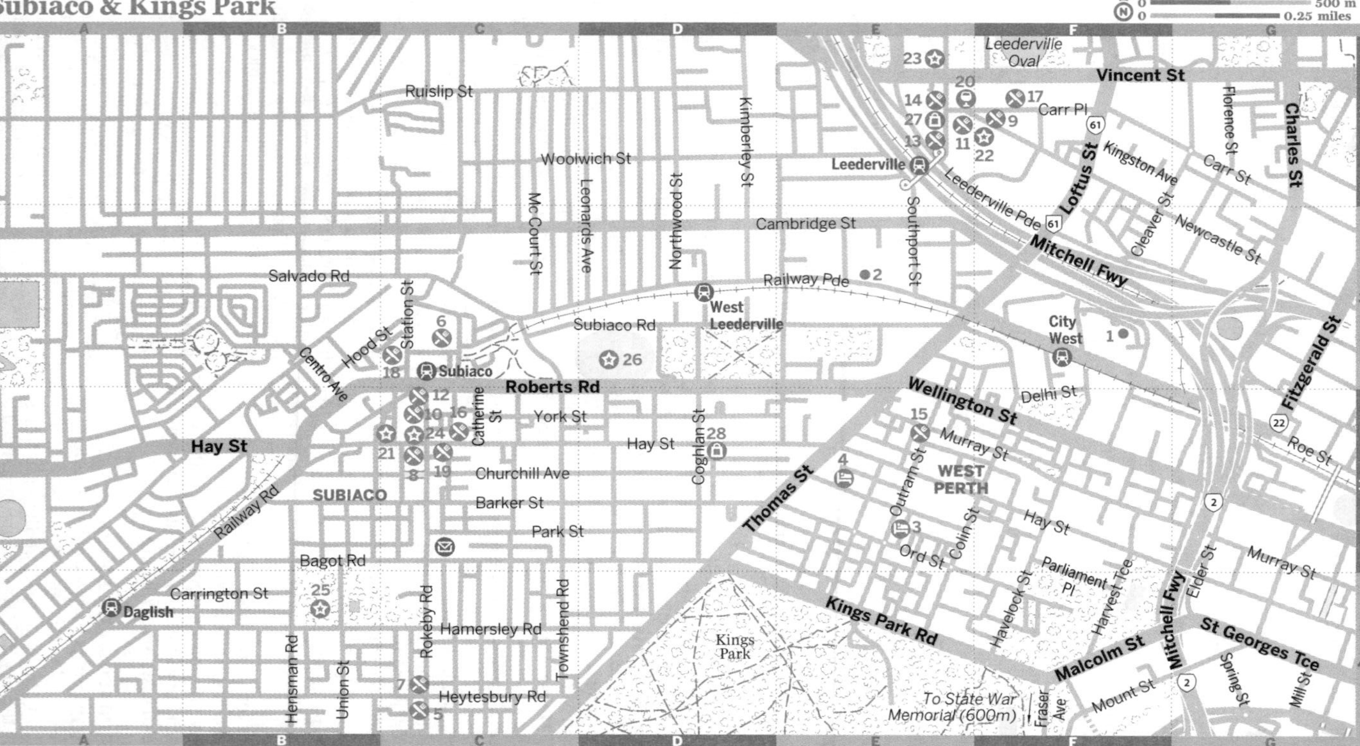

Subiaco & Kings Park

Activities, Courses & Tours
1 Scitech ... F2
2 Surf Sail Australia ... E2

Sleeping
3 Outram ... E3
4 Richardson ... E3

Eating
5 Boucla ... C4
6 Café Café ... C2
7 Chez Jean-Claude Patisserie ... C4
8 Chutney Mary's ... C3
9 Duende ... F1
10 Ecco ... C3
11 Jus Burgers Leederville ... E1
12 Jus Burgers Subiaco ... C3
13 Kailis Bros ... E1
14 Little Caesars ... E1
15 Perugino ... E3
16 Rialto's ... C3
17 Sayers ... F1
18 Station St Markets ... C2
19 Subiaco Hotel ... C3

Drinking
20 Leederville Hotel ... E1
Subiaco Hotel ... (see 19)

Entertainment
21 Ace Subiaco ... C3
Funk Club ... (see 20)
22 Hip-E Club ... F1
23 Luna ... E1
24 Regal Theatre ... C3
25 Subiaco Arts Centre ... B4
26 Subiaco Oval ... D2

Shopping
27 Atlas Divine ... E1
Elizabeth's Bookshop ... (see 10)
28 Indigenart ... D3
Oxford St Books ... (see 27)

famous of them, Cottesloe, gets by quite well with a beachside pavilion, a couple of giant pubs and a scattering of other businesses delineating the edge of suburbia.

Run by the Surf Life Saving Club of WA, the website www.mybeach.com.au has a profile of all the city beaches, including weather forecasts and information about buses, amenities and beach patrolling. Note that many can be rough, with strong undertows and rips – swim between the flags.

The following are the main beaches, listed from south to north:

Port & Leighton Beaches (Map p50) Popular for surfing; the Port (south) end is slightly better for swimming; some eateries. Leighton Beach is a short walk from North Fremantle station.

Cottesloe Beach (Map p50) The safest swimming; cafes; pubs; pine trees and fantastic sunsets. From Cottesloe station (on the Fremantle line) it's 1km to the beach.

Swanbourne Beach (Map p50) Safe swimming; unofficial nude and gay beach. From Grant Street station it's a 1.5km walk to the beach (2km from Swanbourne station).

City Beach (Map p50) Swimming, surfing, lawn and amenities. Take bus 84 (85 on weekends) from Wellington St (40 minutes, hourly).

Floreat Beach (Map p50) Less crowded but sometimes windy; swimming, surfing, cafes, playground. On public transport, take the bus to City Beach and walk north 800m.

Scarborough Beach (Map p50) Popular young surfers' spot; swim between flags as it can be dangerous; lots of shops and eateries. Take bus 400 from Wellington St (40 minutes, every 15 to 20 minutes).

Trigg Beach Better surf and a more hardcore group of locals who come out when the surf's up; dangerous when rough and prone to rips – always swim between the flags.

Mettams Pool Like a turquoise paddle pool; good snorkelling.

Hamersley Pool, North, Watermans & Sorrento Beaches Excellent swimming, picnic areas, BBQs, bike path through scrub.

Aquarium of Western Australia AQUARIUM
(AQWA; ☎9447 7500; www.aqwa.com.au; Hillarys Boat Harbour, Hillarys; adult/child $28/16; ⊙10am-5pm) Dividing WA's vast coastline into five distinct zones (Far North, Coral Coast, Shipwreck Coast, Perth and Great Southern), AQWA offers the chance to enjoy the

state's underwater treasures without getting wet. Or eaten, stung or otherwise poisoned (the displays of WA's most poisonous fish, octopi, shells and sea snakes is particularly interesting).

You can wander through a 98m underwater tunnel as gargantuan stingrays, turtles, fish and sharks stealthily glide over the top of you. Moon jellyfish billow iridescently through a giant cylinder lit up like a school disco, while sea horses and delicate sea dragons go about their gender-bending business, the males giving birth to the young. You can even practise not smiling at the infant saltwater crocodiles – living proof that not all baby critters are cute or cuddly.

The daring can snorkel or dive with the sharks in the giant aquarium with the help of the in-house dive master; book in advance ($159 with your own gear; hire snorkel/dive gear $20/40; 1pm and 3pm). Or you can simply dip your hands into the touch pool and get to know harmless guys like the Port Jackson shark, sea stars, sea cucumbers and the Western stingaree.

To get here on weekdays, take the Joondalup train to Warwick station and then transfer to bus 423. By car, take the Mitchell Fwy north and exit at Hepburn Ave, or take the coastal road north from Scarborough Beach. AQWA is by the water at Hillarys Boat Harbour, behind Hillarys shopping complex, where there are places to eat and drink.

OTHER AREAS

Perth Zoo ZOO

(Map p50; www.perthzoo.wa.gov.au; 20 Labouchere Rd, South Perth; adult/child $21/11; ⏲9am-5pm) Part of the fun of a day at the zoo is getting there – taking the ferry across the Swan River from Barrack St Jetty to Mends St Jetty (every half-hour) and walking up the hill. Zoo zones include Reptile Encounter, African Savannah (rhinos, cheetahs, zebras, giraffes and lions), Asian Rainforest (elephants, tigers, sun bears, orang-utans) and, of course, Australian Bushwalk (kangaroos, emus, koalas, dingos). If you don't fancy the ferry ride, catch bus 30 or 31 from the Esplanade Busport.

Lake Monger PARK

(Map p50; Lake Monger Dr, Wembley) In spring black swans and their signets plod about the grounds, something of a meeting place for the local birdlife, nonplussed by the joggers circling the lake on the flat 3.5km path. There's plenty of grass for cricket, football and picnics. It's walking distance from Leederville train station; exit on the side opposite the shops, turn right onto Southport St and veer left onto Lake Monger Dr.

Activities

Whale-watching

The whale-watching season runs from mid-September to early December, when 30,000 of them take the 'Humpback Highway' up the coast. Tour operators offer either a refund or a repeat trip in the unlikely event that whales aren't spotted. They're also fitted with hydrophones, which are like microphones that are dropped into the water, so that you can to listen to the whales singing.

Mills Charters WHALE-WATCHING

(☎9246 5334; www.millscharters.com.au; adult/child $80/55) Informative three- to four-hour trip departing from Hillarys Boat Harbour at 9am on Tuesdays, Thursdays, Saturdays and Sundays.

Oceanic Cruises WHALE-WATCHING

(☎9325 1191; www.oceaniccruises.com.au; adult/child $70/35) Departs Barrack St Jetty at 9.15am daily, returning at 5.45pm after spending the afternoon in Fremantle.

Cycling

Cycling is an excellent way to explore Perth. Kings Park has some good bike tracks and there are cycling routes along the Swan River, running all the way to Fremantle, and along the coast. Bikes can be taken free-of-charge on ferries at any time and on trains outside of weekday peak hours (7am to 9am and 4pm to 6.30pm) – with a bit of planning you can pedal as far as you like in one direction and return via public transport. They can't be taken on buses at any time, except some regional coaches (for a small charge). For route maps, see www.transport.wa.gov.au/cycling/or call into a bike shop.

To hire bikes, try:

About Bike Hire (☎9221 2665; www.aboutbikehire.com.au; Causeway Carpark, 1-7 Riverside Dr; per day/week from $36/80; ⏲9am-5pm) Also hires kayaks (per hour/day $16/65).

Cycle Centre (Map p52; ☎9325 1176; www.cyclecentre.com.au; 313 Hay St; per day/week $25/65; ⏲9am-5.30pm Mon-Fri, 9am-3pm Sat, 1-4pm Sun)

Scarborough Beach Cycles (☎9245 3887; www.scarboroughbeachcycles.com.au; 10-12 Scarborough Beach Rd, Scarborough; per day/week $40/150; ⏲9am-5pm)

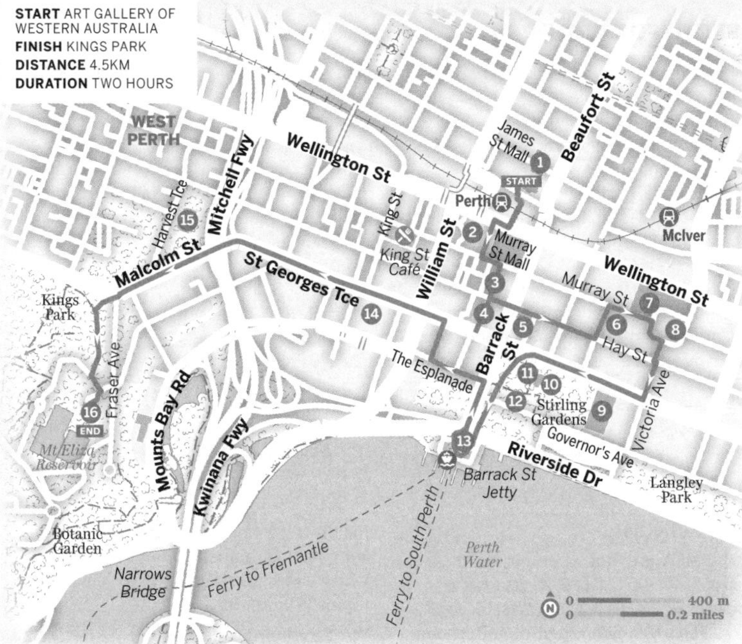

Walking Tour
Perth

This tour traces some old remnants of Perth. It also spans the new, and takes you to the best views of the city atop Kings Park. Start in the Cultural Centre, out the front of the 1 **Art Gallery of Western Australia**. Head over the walkbridge towards the train station. At the newsagency, head right down the last set of escalators (don't cross the second walkbridge). Take your first left, across Wellington St and into the square. The grand Beaux Arts–style 2 **post office** looms to your right.

Turn left onto Murray St Mall, the main shopping strip, and then cut through the art deco 3 **Plaza Arcade** to Hay St Mall. Directly opposite you'll see the wonderfully over-the-top 4 **London Court**, a mock Elizabethan arcade. At the corner of Hay and Barrack you'll find the beautifully restored 5 **Town Hall**.

Continue up Hay St, then turn left up Irwin St. At the corner of Irwin and Murray is the 6 **Old Central Fire Station**. Next you'll pass the red-brick buildings of 7 **Royal Perth Hospital**. At the end of the street is 8 **St Mary's Cathedral** (1863). Wander around Victoria Ave to 9 **Perth Concert Hall** – a fine auditorium and grand structure built in the early 1970s. Continue along St Georges Tce to 10 **Government House** and the impressive 11 **Council House**, then through Stirling Gardens to the 12 **courthouse** (1863), next to the Supreme Court.

Wind south of the Supreme Court and make for the river. Within moments the 13 **Bell Tower** will be in view. Double back up Barrack St, northwest along the Esplanade, and up Howard St. Back on St Georges Tce, look for the 14 **Old Perth Boys School**, a modest structure today dwarfed by office towers. At the end of St Georges Tce is Western Australia's 15 **Parliament House**.

Take Malcolm Ave up to Fraser Ave and enter 16 **Kings Park** through the processional avenue of gum trees and find a vantage point to look back over the city.

PERTH FOR CHILDREN

With a usually clement climate and plenty of open spaces and beaches to run around in, Perth is a great place to bring children. Of the beaches, Cottesloe is the safest and hence the family favourite. If the kids are old enough you can take advantage of the bike tracks that stretch along the river and the coast for a family expedition. Kings Park (p55) has playgrounds and walking tracks.

The Royal Perth Show, held late September, is an ever-popular family outing – all sideshow rides, showbags and proudly displayed poultry. Many of Perth's big attractions cater well for young audiences, especially the Aquarium of Western Australia, Perth Zoo, the Western Australian Museum and the Art Gallery of Western Australia.

Scitech (Map p56; www.scitech.org.au; City West Centre, Sutherland St, West Perth; adult/child $14/9; ⏲10am-4pm) is another option – especially if it's raining. It has over 160 hands-on, large-scale science and technology exhibits.

Adventure World (www.adventureworld.net.au; 179 Progress Dr, Bibra Lake; adult/child $47/39; ⏲10am-5pm Thu-Mon Oct-Apr) has all the palm-sweat-inducing rides such as 'Bounty's Revenge', a giant boat that swings around in an arc, as well as pools, water slides and a castle. It's open daily during school holidays and through December. From Perth, come off the Kwinana Fwy at Farrington Rd, turn right and follow the signs.

Other Activities

Surf Sail Australia WINDSURFING, KITESURFING
(Map p56; ☎1800 686 089; www.surfsailaustralia.com.au; 260 Railway Pde, West Leederville; ⏲10am-5pm Mon-Sat) When the afternoon sea breeze blusters in, windsurfers take to the Swan River, Leighton and beaches north of Perth. Here's where you can hire or buy your gear. Check wind speeds at the website www.seabreeze.com.au.

Australasian Diving Academy DIVING
(☎9389 5018; www.ausdiving.com.au; 142 Stirling Hwy, Nedlands) Hires diving gear (full set per day/week $70/180) and offers diving courses (four-day open-water $575). There are a variety of sites in the vicinity, including several around Rottnest Island and four wrecks.

Funcats SAILING
(☎0408 926 003; Coode St Jetty, South Perth; per hr $35; ⏲Oct-Apr) It'll take you five minutes to learn how to sail one of the catamarans for hire on the South Perth foreshore; each boat can hold up to three people.

Surfschool SURFING
(☎9444 5399; www.surfschool.com; 190 Scarborough Beach Rd, Mount Hawthorn; adult/child $55/50) Two-hour lessons at Scarborough Beach, including boards and wetsuits.

Beatty Park Leisure Centre SWIMMING
(Map /; ☎9273 6080; www.vincent.wa.gov.au/0/20/20/beatty_park_homepage.pm; 220 Vincent St, North Perth; adult/child $4/2.80) Built for the 1962 Commonwealth Games, this complex has indoor and outdoor pools, water slides and a gym. Turn left at the top of William St.

WA Skydiving Academy SKYDIVING
(☎1300 137 855; www.waskydiving.com.au; 458 William St, Northbridge; ⏲Mon-Thu) Tandem jumps from 8000/10,000/12,000ft for $450/490/530.

Tours

Indigenous Tours WA INDIGENOUS
(www.indigenouswa.com) See Perth through the eyes of the local Wadjuk people. Options include the **Indigenous Heritage Tour** (☎9483 1106; adult/child $25/15; ⏲1.30pm) – a 90-minute guided walk around Kings Park – and the **Swan River Dreaming Tour** (☎1300 467 688; adult/child $50/25; ⏲10am Tue & Wed), which is a 90-minute boat ride. A combined package is available (adult/child $75/40).

Perth Tram CITY
(☎9322 2006; www.perthtram.com.au; adult/child $30/12) This hop-on, hop-off bus, masquerading as a historic tram, takes you around some of Perth's main attractions – the city, Kings Park, Northbridge and Barrack St Jetty – in two interlinking loops. A live commentary is provided. It's possible to take just the Kings Park section of the route (adult/child $8/4).

City Sightseeing Perth Tour CITY
(☎9203 8882; www.citysightseeingperth.com; adult/child $28/10) Hop-on, hop-off double-

decker bus tour, with loop routes taking in the central city, Kings Park and the Burswood Entertainment Complex. Tickets are valid for two days. The Kings Park section can be purchased separately (adult/child $6/3).

Rockingham Wild Encounters WILDLIFE
(☎9591 1333; www.rockinghamwildencounters.com.au; departs Wellington St coach stand) Offers Perth CBD pick-ups for its various low-impact marine wildlife interaction tours (seals, penguins and dolphins) for around $20 above the usual prices, and an additional $30 for a hotel pick-up. See p95 for more details.

Planet Perth EXCURSIONS
(☎8132 8294; www.planettours.com.au) Runs a Pinnacles day tour ($165), which includes a wildlife park visit and sandboarding, and up to 15-day tours elsewhere in WA. Backpackers are in its sights – YHA/VIP discounts apply here.

Captain Cook Cruises CRUISES
(☎9325 3341; www.captaincookcruises.com.au) Takes the river to the Swan Valley or Fremantle, with an array of add-ons such as meals, wine tastings and tram rides.

Golden Sun Cruises CRUISES
(☎9325 9916; www.goldensuncruises.com.au) Cheaper and less-frills than Captain Cook.

Out & About WINE
(☎9377 3376; www.outandabouttours.com.au) A selection of wine-focused tours of the Swan Valley and historic Guildford. Some include river cruises, cheese and chocolate stops, or the opportunity to make your own wine blend.

Swan Valley Tours FOOD, WINE
(☎9274 1199; www.svtours.com.au) Food- and wine-driven tours that cruise up to and/or drive through the Swan Valley.

Big Sky Wine Tours WINE
(☎9454 2681; www.bigskytours.com.au; from $65) Tackles the Swan Valley in a minibus.

Rottnest Air Taxi SCENIC FLIGHT
(☎9292 5027; www.rottnest.de) Thirty-minute joy flights over the city, Kings Park and Fremantle ($85), leaving from Jandakot airport.

Festivals & Events

Perth Cup HORSE RACING
(www.perthracing.org.au) New Year's Day sees Perth's biggest day at the races, with the

GAY & LESBIAN PERTH

Perth is home to all of Western Australia's gay and lesbian venues. Before you get excited, let's clarify matters: it has precisely one bar, one club and one men's sauna. Many other bars, especially around Highgate and Mt Lawley, are somewhat gay friendly, but it's hardly what you'd call a bustling scene.

For a head's up on what's on, pick up the free monthly newspaper **Out In Perth** (www.outinperth.com) from one of the venues or log onto **GAYinWA** (www.gayinwa.com.au). **Perth Pride** (www.pridewa.asn.au) runs a three-week festival in October, starting with a fair day and culminating in the Pride Parade. There's also a Pride Ball held in August.

The Court BAR
(Map p52; www.thecourt.com.au; 50 Beaufort St, Northbridge; ⊙noon-midnight Sun-Thu, noon-2am Fri & Sat) A large, rambling complex consisting of an old corner pub and a big, partly covered courtyard with a clubby atmosphere. Wednesdays is amateur drag night, with kings and queens holding court in front of a young crowd.

Connections NIGHTCLUB
(Map p52; www.connectionsnightclub.com; 81 James St, Northbridge; ⊙10pm-late Wed, Fri & Sat) Reputedly the oldest surviving gay and lesbian venue in Australia, Connections keeps on keeping on, with DJs, drag shows and the occasional bit of lesbian mud wrestling. It's free on Wednesdays (therefore full of students) and before 11pm other nights, with cover charges ranging between $15 and $20 otherwise.

Perth Steam Works SAUNA
(www.perthsteamworks.com.au; 369 William St (entry on Forbes St), Northbridge; admission $21; ⊙noon-1am Sun-Thu, noon-3am Fri & Sat) Gay men's sauna.

party people heading to 'Tentland' for DJs and daiquiris.

Summadayze MUSIC
(www.summadayze.com) Electronic beeps and beats get booties shaking in Supreme Court Gardens in early January.

Australia Day Skyworks NATIONAL DAY
(www.perth.wa.gov.au/skyworks) On 26 January around 250,000 people come down to the riverside for a whole day of family entertainment, culminating in a 30-minute firework display at 8pm.

Big Day Out MUSIC
(www.bigdayout.com) Australasia's biggest music festival, attracting big-name alternative bands and lots of local up-and-comers, comes to Claremont Showground in early February.

Good Vibrations MUSIC
(www.goodvibrationsfestival.com.au) Later in February Claremont Showground hosts another one-day festival featuring international acts, this one with more of a party vibe.

Perth International Arts Festival ARTS
(www.perthfestival.com.au) Artists like Laurie Anderson, Antony Gormley (who once exhibited on a dry salt lake near Kalgoorlie) and Philip Glass (who once took to the desert, with his piano) perform, alongside the top local talent. Held over 25 days from mid-February, it spans theatre, classical music, jazz, visual arts, dance, film, literature – the whole gamut. It's worth scheduling your trip around the festival, particularly if you're nocturnal.

Kings Park Festival WILDFLOWERS
(www.kingsparkfestival.com.au) Held throughout September to coincide with the wildflower displays, it includes live music every Sunday, guided walks and talks.

Perth Royal Show AGRICULTURAL
(www.perthroyalshow.com.au; Claremont Showground) A week of fun-fair rides, spun sugar and showbags full of plastic junk. Oh, and farm animals. Late September.

Parklife MUSIC
(www.parklife.com.au; Wellington Sq) International indie bands of a more danceable bent take to the stage for this one-day festival in late September.

Awesome International Festival for Bright Young Things CHILDREN
(www.awesomearts.com) This 10-day contemporary arts festival in November celebrates young creativity with exhibitions, film, theatre, dance and wacky instruments. It strikes a balance between international performers and participation.

Sleeping

Perth is very spread out, so choose your location carefully. Northbridge is backpacker-/boozer-central, and is best for those unperturbed by noise. But the CBD and Northbridge are close to all forms of public transport, and hopping out to inner-city suburbs such as Leederville and Mt Lawley is simple. If you care most for the beach, consider staying there, as public transport to this part of town can be time-consuming.

CITY CENTRE

Riverview on Mount Street APARTMENTS $$
(Map p52; ☎9321 8963; www.riverviewperth.com.au; 42 Mount St; apt from $140; ❄@☎) There's a lot of brash new money up here on Mount St, but character-filled Riverview stands out as the best personality on the block. Its refurbished 1960s bachelor pads sit neatly atop a modern foyer and relaxed, minimalist cafe. Rooms are sunny and simple; the front ones have river views, while the back ones are quieter.

Medina Executive Barrack Plaza APARTMENTS $$$
(Map p52; ☎9267 0000; www.medina.com.au; 138 Barrack St; apt from $204; ❄≋) The Medina's meticulously decorated apartment-sized hotel rooms are minimalist yet welcoming. All one-bedrooms have balconies, and rooms on Barrack St tend to have more natural light (not always easy to obtain in central Perth).

Perth City YHA HOSTEL $
(Map p52; ☎9287 3333; www.yha.com.au; 300 Wellington St; dm $34, r without/with bathroom $70/85; ❄@☎≋) Occupying an impressive 1940s art-deco building by the train tracks, on the fringes of the central city, this large YHA has a slight boarding-school feel in the corridors, but the rooms are clean and the period features (polished floorboards, grand staircases) add a touch of class. Facilities are excellent; there's even a small gym.

Melbourne HOTEL $$
(Map p52; ☎9320 3333; www.melbournehotel.com.au; cnr Hay & Milligan Sts; r $165-290; ❄☎) Classic country charm wafts through this heritage-listed hotel. Built in the gold-rush era, its facade – particularly the deep corrugated-iron balcony that wraps around the building –

recalls the mining-town pub perched on the edges of the red-dust desert. Rooms are unpretentious and comfortable, though 1st-floor rooms facing Milligan St can be noisy.

Miss Maud HOTEL **$$**
(Map p52; ☎9325 3900; www.missmaud.com.au; 97 Murray St; s/d $169/189; ❄@📶) Anyone with a love of Scandinavia, kitsch or *The Sound of Music* will find a few of their favourite things in the alpine murals and dainty rooms. The Scandinavian rooms are best, as they're bigger and well maintained. The smorgasbords (lunch/dinner $32/43) are enough to feed a goat herd.

City Waters MOTEL **$$**
(Map p52; ☎9325 1566; www.citywaters.com.au; 118 Terrace Rd; s/d $105/120; ❄) Apricot-hued City Waters is one of a dying breed of old-fashioned Perth waterfront motels. Rooms are small, simple and face onto the car park, but they're clean, airy and the waterfront location is top-notch. Top-floor rooms are best; river views exist but are difficult to secure.

Mantra on Hay APARTMENTS **$$$**
(Map p52; ☎9267 4888; www.mantra.com.au; 201 Hay St; apt from $216; ❄@📶≋) Low-key but classy, Mantra's roomy apartments have laundries, dishwashers, good-sized benches and all the utensils you'll need.

Parmelia Hilton HOTEL **$$$**
(Map p52; ☎9215 2000; www.hilton.com; 14 Mill St; r midweek/weekend from $264/180; ❄@≋) The usual top-notch Hilton service and comfy beds, but could stand remodelling and no views to speak of.

Rydges HOTEL **$$$**
(Map p52; ☎9263 1800; www.rydges.com/perth; cnr King & Hay Sts; r midweek/weekend from $249/199; ❄) Double-glazed, comfortable, central city rooms, some with views.

Travelodge Perth HOTEL **$$**
(Map p52; ☎9238 1888; www.travelodge.com.au; 417 Hay St; r from $145; ❄📶) No surprises here, just unassuming well-kept rooms, some with views.

Comfort Hotel Perth City HOTEL **$$**
(Map p52; ☎9220 7000; www.comforthotelperthcity.com.au; 200 Hay St; r from $125; ❄@📶) Generic and outmoded, but rooms are large, staff friendly and the breakfast spread is excellent.

Mounts Bay Waters APARTMENTS **$$$**
(Map p52; ☎9213 5333; www.mounts-bay.com.au; 112 Mounts Bay Rd; apt $290-600; ❄≋) Giant apartment complex, where 165 out of 440 units are available for short-term lease.

NORTHBRIDGE

Most of Perth's hostels are in Northbridge. There are so many here, in fact, that it's possible to walk around and inspect rooms before putting your money down – some are not up to snuff. We've only listed the better ones.

TOP CHOICE **Emperor's Crown** HOSTEL **$**
(Map p52; ☎9227 1400; www.emperorscrown.com.au; 85 Stirling St; dm $32, r with/without bathroom $98/88; ❄@📶) The best of Perth's hostels has a great position (close to the Northbridge scene without being in the thick of it), friendly staff and high housekeeping standards. Granted, it's a bit pricier than most, but it's well worth it.

Pension of Perth B&B **$$**
(☎9228 9049; www.pensionperth.com.au; 3 Throssell St; s/d from $120/150; ❄@📶≋) Pension of Perth's French belle-époque style lays luxury on thick: chaise lounges, rich floral rugs, heavy brocade curtains, open fireplaces and gold-framed mirrors. Two doubles with bay windows (and small bathrooms) look out onto the park; the spa room is round the back. And it's across the road from gorgeous Hyde Park.

Witch's Hat HOSTEL **$**
(☎9228 4228; www.witchs-hat.com; 148 Palmerston St; dm/tw/d $30/70/80; ❄@📶) Witch's Hat is something out of a fairy tale. The 1897 building itself could be mistaken for a gingerbread house, and the witch's hat (an Edwardian turret) stands proudly out the front, beckoning the curious to step inside. Dorms are light and uncommonly spacious, and there's a red-brick barbecue area out the back.

Governor Robinsons HOSTEL **$**
(☎9328 3200; www.govrobinsons.com.au; 7 Robinson Ave; dm $30, d with/without bathroom $85/75; ❄@) On first impressions, the Guv seems too flash to be a hostel – occupying a conjoined pair of Federation-era homes with a modern kitchen/lounge area hollowed out of their centre. Dorms are fresh and clean, if a little snug, and the polished floorboards lend an upmarket feel. On the downside, when we visited the men's toilets sat under 2cm of water as soon as someone took a shower and there was no hand soap provided in the bathrooms. Robinson St heads

off William St, just north of the main Northbridge strip.

Coolibah Lodge HOSTEL $
(☎9328 9958; www.coolibahlodge.com.au; 194 Brisbane St; dm $25, r $60-70; ❄@📶) Built from two big old houses, Coolibah Lodge is comfortable and homely but nothing fancy. It's one of the oldest hostels on the block, actually, so there's a real backpackers vibe in here – no pretence. Dorms are tidy if a bit poky, and doubles are of a good standard. Brisbane St runs off William St, north of Northbridge.

One World Backpackers HOSTEL $
(☎9228 8206; www.oneworldbackpackers.com.au; 162 Aberdeen St; dm $27-30, d $80; @) One World is like a hippy backpackers on an inheritance: clean, green and beautifully maintained. Polished floorboards beam brightly in all the rooms of this nicely restored old house, and the dorms are big and sunny, if a little messy sometimes. The kitchen is large and functional, with everything provided, and the hostel tends to be quiet at night.

Hotel Northbridge HOTEL $$
(☎9328 5254; www.hotelnorthbridge.com.au; 210 Lake St; r $130-180; ❄@) Hotel Northbridge isn't the hippest kid in town, but a recent refurbishment has dropped a spa in every single room – and kept the prices down. The classic pub rooms in the budget wing ($65) face onto a broad verandah, but share shabby toilets.

HIGHGATE & MT LAWLEY

TOP CHOICE **Durack House** B&B $$
(☎9370 4305; www.durackhouse.com.au; 7 Almondbury Rd, Mt Lawley; s $160, d $175-190; 📶) It's hard to avoid words like 'delightful', enunciated in a slightly English accent, when describing this cottage, set on a peaceful suburban street behind a white picket fence swathed in climbing roses. The three rooms have plenty of old-world charm, paired with thoroughly modern bathrooms. It's only 250m from Mt Lawley station; turn left onto Railway Pde and then first right onto Almondbury Rd.

Billabong Backpackers Resort HOSTEL $
(☎9328 7720; www.billabongresort.com.au; 381 Beaufort St, Highgate; dm/r $28/82; ❄@📶🏊) This large, relaxed hostel (about 150 beds) has Australiana murals on its walls and a popular poolside. It's a basic set-up but there's a nice buzz about the place.

SUBIACO & KINGS PARK

TOP CHOICE **Richardson** HOTEL $$$
(Map p56; ☎9217 8888; www.therichardson.com.au; 32 Richardson St; r $450-550; 🏊) Ship-shaped and shipshape, the Richardson offers luxurious, thoughtfully designed rooms – some with sliding doors to divide them into pseudo suites. The whole complex has a breezy, summery feel, with pale marble tiles, creamy walls and interesting art. It's a bit pricier than you'd expect, but that's Perth for you. There's an in-house spa centre if you require additional pampering.

Outram HOTEL $$$
(Map p56; ☎9322 4888; www.wyndhamvrap.com.au; 32 Outram St, West Perth; r from $266; ❄📶) Discreet and understated, the Outram (now officially 'Wyndham Vacation Resorts Asia Pacific Perth' but – understandably – still known as the Outram) is super-stylish, with compact open-plan rooms, a bathroom with a walk-through shower, king-sized beds draped in white linens, flat-screen TVs and spas.

BEACHES

Swanbourne Guest House GUESTHOUSE $$
(☎9383 1981; www.swanbourneguesthouse.com.au; 5 Myera St, Swanbourne; s/d $90/120) Peace and solitude are the keys here. Off a leafy residential street, 20 minutes' walk from Swanbourne Beach, you'll hear nothing more than the birds twittering from your sun-filled room.

Trigg Retreat B&B $$
(☎9447 6726; www.triggretreat.com; 59 Kitchener St, Trigg; r $160; ❄@📶) Quietly classy, this three-room B&B offers attractive and supremely comfortable queen bedrooms in a modern house near the beach. Each has a fridge, TV, DVD player and tea- and coffee-making facilities. A full, cooked breakfast is included in the rates.

Sunmoon Resort HOTEL $$
(☎9245 8000; www.sunmoon.com.au; 200 West Coast Hwy, Scarborough; r from $145; ❄📶🏊) It's an unlikely spot for a Balinese-style resort, separated from Scarborough Beach by a busy road and a petrol station. Within the complex, wood-slatted pathways lead you under shady palms while bright-orange carp splash in ponds. Batik furnishings adorn large rooms with terracotta-tiled floors.

Ocean Beach Hotel HOTEL $$
(☎9384 2555; www.obh.com.au; cnr Marine Pde & Eric St, Cottesloe; r $130-200; ❄📶) A good

midrange option facing Cottesloe Beach, the accommodation is thankfully set at a slight remove from the popular pub of the same name, occupying an art-deco block that was renovated a few years back and is starting to look a little scuffed. Still, the rooms are large and reasonably good value.

Ocean Beach Backpackers HOSTEL $
(☎9384 5111; www.oceanbeachbackpackers.com; 1 Eric St, Cottesloe; dm/s/d $24/63/69; @ ᯤ) Offering (some) ocean views, this big, bright hostel right in the heart of Cottesloe is just a short skip from the sand. Rooms are basic but all have private bathrooms, and you'll probably just be here to sleep given the great location; hire a bike to get around locally. It's alcohol-free – which is no big deal, given the pub next door.

Western Beach Lodge HOSTEL $
(☎9245 1624; www.westernbeach.com; 6 Westborough St, Scarborough; dm $28, r with/without bathroom $85/75; @ ᯤ) A real surfer hang-out, this sociable, homely hostel has surfboards and boogie boards available, and a good, no-frills feel.

OTHER AREAS

Peninsula APARTMENTS $$
(☎9368 6688; www.thepeninsula.net; 53 South Perth Esplanade, South Perth; apt from $195; ❄ @ ᯤ) While only the front few apartments have full-on views, Peninsula's waterfront location lends itself to lazy ferry rides and sunset strolls along the river. It's a sprawling, older-style complex but it's kept in good knick. The apartments all have kitchenettes and there's a communal laundry room.

Discovery Holiday Parks – Perth CAMPGROUND $
(☎9453 6877; www.discoveryholidayparks.com.au; 186 Hale Rd, Forrestfield; powered sites for 2 $38-45, units $125-187; ❄ @ ᯤ ≋) This well-kept holiday park, 15km out of the city, has a wide range of cabins and smart-looking units, many with decks, TVs and DVD players.

Eating

While the rest of the world has been tightening their belts in the face of the global financial crisis, Perth still has plenty of grey-suited men loosening theirs at the end of long, lingering business lunches. Where many of Australia's other state capitals might have a handful of top restaurants charging over $40 a main, in Perth those prices are fast becoming the norm for any establishment that considers itself above average. Unfortunately, the experience doesn't always match the outlay. That said, Perth does have some truly exceptional restaurants, such as the ones we've included here.

It's still possible to eat cheaply, especially in the Little Asia section of William St, Northbridge. Many restaurants are BYO, meaning you can bring your own wine; check first. The better cafes are good places to go for a midrange meal and, thankfully, the standard of coffee has improved from

SELF-CATERING

Below we've listed the pick of the crop.

Boatshed Market (www.boatshedmarket.com.au; 40 Jarrad St, Cottesloe; ⏲6.30am-8pm) Upmarket shed stacked with fresh produce, meat, fish, delicatessen goods, pastries and bread.

Chez Jean-Claude Patisserie (Map p56; www.chezjeanclaudepatisserie.com.au; 333 Rokeby Rd; ⏲6am-6.30pm Mon-Fri) Line up with the locals for brioche and baguettes.

City Farm Organic Growers Market (Map p52; www.cityfarmperth.org.au; 1 City Farm Pl, East Perth; ⏲8am-noon Sat) Local organic producers sell eggs, fruit, vegetables and bread.

Kailis Bros (Map p56; www.kailisbrosleederville.com.au; 101 Oxford St, Leederville) Big, fresh seafood supplier with cafe attached.

Kakulas Bros (Map p52; www.kakulasbros.com.au; 183 William St; ⏲Mon-Sat) Provisions store overflowing with sacks and vats of legumes, nuts and olives, plus a deli counter, well stocked with cheese.

Station St Markets (Map p56; Station St, Subiaco; ⏲9am-5.30pm Fri-Sun) Covered market selling fresh produce.

the notorious 'western milkshake' days. Some have free wi-fi access.

CITY CENTRE

TOP CHOICE **Balthazar** MODERN AUSTRALIAN $$$
(Map p52; ☎9421 1206; 6 The Esplanade; mains $37-40; ⏰lunch Mon-Fri, dinner Mon-Sat) Low lit, discreet and sophisticated, with a hipster soundtrack and charming staff, Balthazar's informal cool vibe is matched by exquisite food and a famously excellent wine list. The menu here is refreshingly original, combining European and Asian flavours with not-at-all-reckless abandon.

Greenhouse TAPAS $$
(Map p52; ☎9481 8333; www.greenhouseperth.com; 100 St Georges Tce; tapas $10-18 ; ⏰7am-midnight Mon-Sat) The talk is shifting from the groundbreaking design (straw bales, plywood, corrugated iron and living exterior walls covered with 5000 individual pot plants – all grafted onto the side of a skyscraper) and onto the excellent food offered at this hip tapas-style eatery, awarded the Best New Restaurant gong in 2010's *Good Food Guide*. The low-impact ethos continues inside, with candles in jam jars and furniture that looks like it's been knocked up in Dad's shed.

Tiger, Tiger CAFE $
(Map p52; ☎9322 8055; Murray Mews; mains $8-19; ⏰breakfast & lunch; 📶) The small shabby-chic interior isn't as popular as the outdoor setting, in a lane leading off Murray St. The free wi-fi's a drawcard, but the food is also excellent – all the regular breakfast favourites, along with pasta, curry, tarts, soups and baguettes on the lunch menu. Table service kicks in at lunchtime; before that you'll need to order at the counter.

Annalakshmi INDIAN $
(Map p52; ☎9221 3003; www.annalakshmi.com.au; 1st fl, Western Pavilion; pay by donation; ⏰lunch Tue-Fri & Sun, dinner Tue-Sun; ✎) While the 360-degree views of the Swan River are worth a million dollars, the food's literally priceless. Run by volunteers (formidable baby-boomers, in the main), you pay by donation. An eclectic mix of hippies, Hindus and the just plain hungry line up for spicy vegetarian curries and fragrant dhal. Chilled coconut-milk and cardamom desserts cleanse the palate. It's all good fun.

Restaurant Amusé MODERN AUSTRALIAN $$$
(Map p52; ☎9325 4900; www.restaurantamuse.com.au; 64 Bronte St, East Perth; degustation $120; ⏰dinner Tue-Sat) The critics have certainly been amused by this degustation-only establishment, regularly rated as WA's finest. Book ahead and come prepared for a culinary adventure – preferably with an empty stomach.

Secret Garden CAFE $
(Map p52; www.secretgardencafe.com.au; Murray Mews; mains $7-17; ⏰7am-3pm Mon-Sat) Sharing the same tucked-away lane as Tiger, Tiger, Secret Garden has good coffee, enticing counter food and all-day breakfast for Saturday hangovers.

Taka JAPANESE $
(Map p52; www.takaskitchen.iinet.net.au; mains $7-10; ⏰11am-9pm Mon-Sat); Barrack St (150-152 Barrack St); Shafto Lane (shop 5 & 6 Shafto Lane) This straightforward Japanese eatery whips out standards like teriyaki, udon and sushi. Great for a quick bite if you're out drinking.

44 King Street CAFE $$
(Map p52; 44 King St; breakfast $5-19, mains $29-44; ⏰breakfast, lunch & dinner) A big Viennese-style cafe with a central wooden bar that was one of the trailblazers of the local coffee scene.

Matsuri JAPANESE $$
(Map p52; www.matsuri.com.au; 250 St Georges Tce; mains $16-24; ⏰lunch Mon-Fri, dinner Mon-Sat) You'll feel a bit like a carp in a fish tank here – floor-to-ceiling glass runs the perimeter of this large, long-standing Japanese restaurant.

NORTHBRIDGE

TOP CHOICE **Namh Thai** THAI $$
(☎9328 7500; 223 Bulwer St; mains $22-40; ⏰dinner Mon-Sat) Not your average Thai restaurant, Namh experiments with interesting taste combinations (duck with lychees is the speciality but we adore the soft-shell crab with watermelon) and serves them in an elegant candlelit dining room. Fridays and Saturdays are given over to banquet-style dining (per person $75). Bulwer St intersects William St, north of Northbridge.

Little Willy's CAFE $
(Map p52; 267 William St; mains $8-12; ⏰breakfast & lunch) It's tiny and it's on William St, so the name's probably got nothing to do with the tall dude driving the coffee machine who's universally known as Hot Rob (much to his obvious embarrassment). He works that baby like a pro and the food, while simple (bagels, wraps, cooked breakfasts), is delicious.

Viet Hoa VIETNAMESE $
(Map p52; 349 William St; mains $8-19; ⌚lunch & dinner) Don't be fooled by the bare-bones ambience of this corner Vietnamese restaurant – or you'll miss out on the fresh rice-paper rolls and top-notch *pho* (beef-and-rice-noodle soup). Greenery creeping up the beams gives the place an offbeat feel.

Tarts CAFE $
(www.tartscafe.com.au; 212 Lake St; mains $14-19; ⌚7am-5pm) Massive tarts piled with berries, apples or lime curd; rich scrambled eggs tumbling off thickly sliced sourdough; mini custard tarts stacked with glazed strawberries. Packed like a hamper on weekends.

Good Fortune Roast Duck House CHINESE $
(Map p52; www.goodfortuneduckhouse.com.au; 344 William St; mains $8-20; ⌚10am-10pm Wed-Mon) This is the real thing – just like being in China. Locals charge in for family-sized feeds of barbecue pork, roast duck and noodles – the front window is crammed with options. An entire boneless duck is $28, and you can ask for a half-serve.

Red Teapot CHINESE $
(413 William St; mains $7-18; ⌚lunch & dinner Mon-Sat) An intimate restaurant, always busy with diners enjoying stylishly executed Chinese favourites like fragrant prosperous chicken and chilli salt squid.

Source Foods CAFE $
(www.sourcefoods.com.au; 289 Beaufort St; mains $10-18; ⌚breakfast & lunch; 📶) Unassuming cafe committed to sustainable practices; free wi-fi also.

Maya Masala INDIAN $
(Map p52; ☎9328 5655; www.mayamasala.net.au; 64 Lake St; mains $10-26; ⌚10.30am-10.30pm; ✎) Lamb biryani and goat curry are the specialities at this Southern Indian cafe.

Sparrow INDONESIAN $
(434a William St; mains $7-10; ⌚lunch Fri & Sat, dinner Mon-Sat) Perfect for those on a sparrow-sized budget, this no-frills eatery serves traditional dishes.

HIGHGATE & MT LAWLEY

Jackson's MODERN AUSTRALIAN $$$
(☎9328 1177; 483 Beaufort St, Highgate; mains $44, degustation $125; ⌚dinner Mon-Sat) The finest of fine dining is offered in this upmarket dining room, where the wait staff don white gloves to present you with wonderfully creative treats from the kitchen of Neal Jackson, one of Perth's most established chefs. In the pampering stakes, it's the foodie equivalent of a day spa, minus the bikini wax.

Must Winebar FRENCH $$$
(☎9328 8255; www.must.com.au; 519 Beaufort St, Highgate; mains $36-44; ⌚noon-midnight) Not content with being Perth's best wine bar, Must is one of its best restaurants as well. The vibe's a little like Balthazar – hip, slick and a little cheeky – with added Frenchness. The menu marries classic bistro dishes with the best local produce and the baguettes alone are worth the visit, delivered gratis to your table just as they would be in Paris.

Soto Espresso CAFE $
(www.sotoespresso.com; 507 Beaufort St, Highgate; breakfast $5-19, lunch $10-20; ⌚7am-midnight; 📶) Modern Soto opens out onto the street, welcoming its inner-city crowd: stay-at-home dads, ladies who lunch and shop, bleary-eyed students. The banquette is a great spot to watch all the comings and goings, and the large, cooked breakfasts will tackle any hangover.

Cantina 663 MEDITERRANEAN $$
(☎9370 4883; www.cantina663.com; 663 Beaufort St, Mt Lawley; lunch $12-24, dinner $26-34; ⌚8am-late Mon-Sat, 8am-3pm Sun) It's a Spain v Italy showdown, from the dishes to the wine list, at this cool but casual cantina, with tables spilling into the arcade.

MT HAWTHORN

Divido ITALIAN $$
(☎9443 7373; www.divido.com.au; 170 Scarborough Beach Rd; mains $30-36; ⌚dinner Mon-Sat) Italian but not rigidly so (the chef's of Croatian extraction, so delicious Dalmatian-style doughnuts make it onto the dessert menu), this excellent, romantically inclined restaurant serves handmade pasta dishes and delicately flavoured mains. The service is first-rate. To get here turn left off Loftus St, which is the continuation of Thomas St, which runs alongside Kings Park.

New Norcia Bakery BAKERY, CAFE $
(www.newnorciabaker.com.au; 163 Scarborough Beach Rd; mains $11-17; ⌚7am-6pm) Perth's best bread, delicious pastries and a bright cafe as well. It gets crammed on the weekends.

LEEDERVILLE

Duende TAPAS $$
(Map p56; ☎9228 0123; www.duende.com.au; 662 Newcastle St; tapas $5-17; ⌚6pm-late Sat-Thu, noon-late Fri) Sleek Duende occupies a corner

site watching the comings and goings of Leederville after dark. Sit at a table, at the bar or, for the best people-watching, on the colourful outdoor furniture set up on the Astroturfed footpath. A long list of modern-twisted tapas is served; make a meal of it or call in for a late-night glass of dessert wine and *churros* (doughnuts served with hot chocolate sauce).

Sayers CAFE $

(Map p56; www.sayersfood.com.au; 224 Carr Pl; mains $10-29; ⏲7am-5pm) Nothing to do with Leo, as far as we know, this classy cafe has a counter groaning under the weight of an alluring cake selection. The breakfast menu includes surprising luxuries such as Wagyu beef baked eggs and Manjimup truffle scrambled eggs.

Jus Burgers BURGERS $

(Map p56; www.jusburgers.com.au; burgers $11-14; ⏲lunch & dinner); Leederville (743 Newcastle St); Subiaco (1 Rokeby Rd) Carbon-neutral gourmet burgers.

Little Caesars PIZZA $$

(Map p56; www.littlecaesarspizzeria.com.au; 127 Oxford St; pizza $15-20; ⏲5pm-late Mon-Sat, noon-late Sun) Highly rated pizzeria.

SUBIACO & KINGS PARK

Subiaco Hotel GASTROPUB $$

(Map p56; ☎9381 3069; www.subiacohotel.com.au; 465 Hay St; mains $19-32; ⏲breakfast, lunch & dinner) A legendary boozer that's been given a glitzy makeover, the Subi's buzzy dining room is the suburb's main place to see and be seen. The menu ranges from lighter fare like Caesar salads and vegetarian risottos to perfectly cooked steaks and excellent fish dishes.

Star Anise MODERN AUSTRALIAN $$$

(☎9381 9811; www.staraniserestaurant.com.au; 225 Onslow Rd, Shenton Park; mains $45-50; ⏲dinner Tue-Sat) Tucked down a quiet suburban street in Shenton Park (just west of King's Park), this elegant, intimate dining room is widely lauded as one of Perth's very best. Everything is set to impress, from the candle-light playing on the chocolate-brown walls to the giant wrought-iron whisk sculpture, and from the quiet professionalism of the staff to the sophisticated, sometimes challenging menu.

Fraser's MODERN AUSTRALIAN $$$

(Map p56; ☎9481 7100; www.frasersrestaurant.com.au; Fraser Ave, Kings Park; mains $38-44; ⏲breakfast, lunch & dinner) Atop Kings Park, overlooking the city and the glittering Swan River, Fraser's location is wonderful. Thankfully the food is also excellent, making it a popular spot for business lunches and romantic dinners on the terrace on balmy summer nights.

Old Brewery STEAKHOUSE $$

(Map p56; ☎9211 8910; www.theoldbrewery.com.au; 173 Mounts Bay Rd; mains $29-43; breakfast Sun, lunch & dinner daily) Perth's the kind of town where even the steakhouses are glamorous, as evidenced by this designer joint at the heart of the historic Swan Brewery building (1838). There are wonderful views over the river to the city, but hardcore carnivores can trade them for views of the beef aging gracefully in glass display cabinets – before splashing out on a 200g Wagyu eye fillet ($83).

Boucla CAFE $

(Map p56; 349 Rokeby Rd; mains $12-19; ⏲breakfast & lunch Mon-Sat, dinner Thu) A locals' secret, a little isolated from the thick of the Rokeby Rd action. Baklava and cakes tempt you from the corner, and huge tarts filled with blue-vein cheese and roast vegetables spill off plates. The salads are great too.

Chutney Mary's INDIAN $$

(Map p56; www.chutneymarys.com.au; 67 Rokeby Rd; mains $15-28; ⏲lunch Mon-Sat, dinner daily; ✎) The feisty, authentic Indian food here is much loved and a sizeable chunk of the large menu is devoted to vegetarian favourites. The vibe is colourful and casual, with wall-sized scenes of Indian life.

Ecco PIZZA $$

(Map p56; www.eccopizza.com.au; 23 Rokeby Rd; mains $18-29; ⏲11am-late Tue-Sun) With black-and-white prints of Italy slicked along the walls, small and rustic Ecco is all about the perfect pizza. Slip into a wooden table inside, or gaze at passers-by out front, and get busy munching.

Zafferano ITALIAN, SEAFOOD $$$

(Map p56; ☎9321 2588; www.zafferano.com.au; 173 Mounts Bay Rd; mains $39-56; ⏲breakfast Sat & Sun, lunch & dinner daily) You're mainly paying for the views (the perfect vista of the city over the river) but the food is very good. Breakfasts here are much better value ($10 to $20).

Café Café CAFE $

(Map p56; Subiaco Sq, 29 Station St; mains $5-17; ⏲breakfast & lunch) Metres from the Subiaco train station, this is a down-to-earth, unfussy spot where the focus is more on the Illy coffee than the food; the cakes always look delicious.

Rialto's ITALIAN $$

(Map p56; ☎9382 3292; www.rialtos.com.au; 424 Hay St; mains $25-35; ⏰lunch Mon-Fri, dinner Mon-Sat) Bold red leather, slick black stools, mirrored walls, and staff with attitude: Rialto's offers a consummate Euro-chic experience that extends to the Neapolitan-influenced menu.

Perugino ITALIAN $$

(Map p56; ☎9321 5420; www.perugino.com.au; 77 Outram St, West Perth; mains $27-41; ⏰lunch Tue-Fri, dinner Tue-Sat) Traditional, formal Italian restaurant; three-course lunch $49.

BEACHES

Peter's by the Sea KEBABS, BURGERS $

(128 The Esplanade, Scarborough; mains $7-20; ⏰lunch & dinner) A while back, the developers of the huge Observation City complex tried to buy out this Perth icon, but its owners refused to budge, and the complex was built around it. The bacon-and-egg burgers are oft-prescribed hangover cures and there's wonderful homemade baklava to follow them up with.

Dancing Goat CAFE $

(14 Railway St, Swanbourne; mains $8-12; ⏰6am-4pm Mon-Fri, 7.30am-12.30pm Sat) The hairy-legged parent of Northbridge's Little Willy's, and the best place in the beach suburbs for a coffee. It's near the Swanbourne train station.

John St Cafe CAFE $

(37 John St, Cottesloe; mains $10-25; ⏰7am-4pm) Tucked up a residential street, five minutes from the beach, John St is the definitive Cottesloe breakfast spot.

Naked Fig CAFE $$

(www.thefig.com.au; 278 Marine Pde, Swanbourne; breakfast & lunch $16-33, dinner $27-36; ⏰breakfast, lunch & dinner; 📶) It's all about the location here, especially the sublime ocean-gazing deck.

Drinking

Once upon a time, licences to sell alcohol in WA were tightly restricted and massively expensive. Venues therefore had to be built on a Ceausescu scale in order to recoup the investment, and big booze barns, such as those common in Northbridge and Cottesloe, became part of the culture.

A law change a few years back has given birth to a new breed of quirky little bars that are distinctly Melbourne-ish in their hipness and difficulty to locate. They're sprouting up all over the place, including in the formerly deserted-after-dark central city.

One of the by-products of the mining boom has been the rise of the Cashed-Up Bogan (CUB) – young men with plenty of cash to splash on muscle cars, beer and drugs. A spate of fights and glassings in bars has caused many venues, particularly around Northbridge, to step up security. Most pubs now have lockouts, so you'll need to be in before midnight in order to gain entry. You may need to present photo ID in order to obtain entry and it would pay to keep your wits about you in pubs and on the streets after dark.

CITY CENTRE

TOP CHOICE **Greenhouse** COCKTAIL BAR

(Map p52; www.greenhouseperth.com; 100 St Georges Tce; ⏰7am-midnight Mon-Sat) In a city so in love with the great outdoors, it's surprising that nobody's opened a rooftop bar in the central city before now. Hip, eco-conscious Greenhouse is leading the way, mixing up a storm amid the greenery above the award-winning restaurant.

Helvetica BAR

(Map p52; www.helveticabar.com; rear, 101 St Georges Tce; ⏰3pm-midnight Tue-Thu, noon-midnight Fri, 6pm-midnight Sat) Clever artsy types tap their toes to delicious alternative pop in this bar named after a typeface and specialising in whisky and cocktails. The concealed entry is off Howard St: look for the chandelier in the lane behind Andaluz tapas bar.

Hula Bula Bar COCKTAIL BAR

(Map p52; www.hulabulabar.com; 12 Victoria Ave; ⏰4pm-midnight Wed-Fri, 6pm-1am Sat) You'll feel like you're back on *Gilligan's Island* in this tiny Polynesian-themed bar, decked out in bamboo, palm leaves and tikis. A cool but relaxed crowd jams in here on weekends to sip ostentatious cocktails out of ceramic monkey's heads.

1907 COCKTAIL BAR

(Map p52; www.1907.com.au; 26 Queen St; ⏰4pm-midnight Wed-Sat) Hidden away down a lane, behind a gate and down the side of a building, this modern-day speakeasy has a backlit bar and Rat Pack photos on the walls.

Belgian Beer Cafe BAR

(Map p52; www.belgianbeer.com.au; 347 Murray St; ⏰11am-midnight) The Belgian Beer bar is a good spot to start your evening, with loads of imported beers on tap.

Tiger Lil's COCKTAIL BAR
(Map p52; www.tigerlils.com.au; 437 Murray St; ⌚11am-late Tue-Sat) DJs, Asian-inspired cocktails and over-the-top decor – lanterns, Buddhas, the works. It's also a restaurant.

Box Deli BAR
(Map p52; 918 Hay St; ⌚10am-late Mon-Fri, 4pm-2am Sat) This bar-cum-restaurant has a distinct club feel, with its deep bar and decks. A well-located spot for a pre-dancing drink.

NORTHBRIDGE

Northbridge is the rough-edged hub of Perth's nightlife, with dozens of pubs and clubs clustered mainly around William and James Sts. It's so popular, it even has its own website (www.onwilliam.com.au).

Brisbane PUB
(www.thebrisbanehotel.com.au; 292 Beaufort St; ⌚11.30am-late) It was a very clever architect indeed who converted this classic corner pub (1898) into a thoroughly modern venue, where each space seamlessly blends into the next. Best of all is the large courtyard where the phoenix palms and ponds provide a balmy holiday feel. Dining, shooting pool or lazing on a lounge are all options.

399 BAR
(www.399bar.com; 399 William St; ⌚10am-midnight Mon-Sat, 10am-10pm Sun) It doesn't look like much from the outside but this little local bar is an exemplar of the kind of personable establishment that the new licensing laws have brought to Perth. There are booths along one side and a long bar down the other, so you can interact with the engaging bar staff while they artfully mix you a cocktail or pour you a glass from the chalked-up wine list.

Ezra Pound BAR
(Map p52; 189 William St; ⌚1pm-midnight Thu-Tue) Down a much graffitied lane leading off William St, Ezra Pound is favoured by Northbridge's bohemian set. It's the kind of place where you can settle into a red velvet chair and sup a Tom Collins out of a jam jar. Earnest conversations about poetry are strictly optional.

Brass Monkey PUB
(Map p52; www.thebrassmonkey.com.au; cnr James & William Sts; ⌚11am-1am Wed-Sat, 11am-10pm Sun) A massive 1897 pub with several different component parts, each with its own vibe: sit up on a stool at the bar, lean back in the relaxed beer garden, or hunker down on a chesterfield by the fire (and sports screen). Semidetached GrapeSkin is the Monkey's somewhat upmarket wine and tapas bar.

Deen PUB
(Map p52; www.thedeen.com.au; 84 Aberdeen St; ⌚5pm-2am Mon & Thu-Sat) The Deen's popular with travellers, especially on Monday night's student and backpacker night (the covers band kicks off at 8.30pm). Thursday is for Latin lovers – just slug back some cheap beer and your salsa will improve in no time. Other nights see DJs, pool tables and big lines out the front ($5 queue jump).

Shed PUB
(Map p52; www.the-shed.com.au; 69-71 Aberdeen St; ⌚noon-late) Big indoor-outdoor venue with sports screens and live bands.

HIGHGATE & MT LAWLEY

Luxe COCKTAIL BAR
(www.luxebar.com; 446 Beaufort St, Highgate; ⌚8pm-late Wed-Sun) With retro wood panelling, big sexy lounge chairs and velvet curtains, Luxe is knowingly hip. It's also armed with turntables and the gregarious bar staff are good for a chat while they shake their stuff.

Must Winebar WINE BAR
(www.must.com.au; 519 Beaufort St, Highgate; ⌚noon-midnight) With cool French house music pulsing through the air and the perfect glass of wine in your hand (40 offerings by the glass, 500 on the list), Must is hard to beat. Upstairs is an exclusive, bookings-only Champagne bar.

Queens PUB
(www.thequeens.com.au; 520 Beaufort St, Highgate; ⌚10am-midnight Mon-Sat, 10am-10pm Sun) Big, nicely renovated Federation-style pub, popular on Sundays. A cold beer in the dappled courtyard is the standard routine.

Flying Scotsman PUB
(www.theflyingscotsman.com.au; 639 Beaufort St, Mt Lawley) Old-style pub that attracts an indie crowd; see also Velvet Lounge (p71).

LEEDERVILLE

Leederville Hotel PUB
(Map p56; www.leedervillehotel.com; 742 Newcastle St; ⌚noon-midnight Wed-Sun) The good old Leederville has been turning out beers and Midori shakers for many generations. The something-for-everyone philosophy

is etched out in the sports screens, dance floors, pool tables and, on Fridays, the very-fun Funk Club upstairs. Wednesdays are big with the younger folk.

SUBIACO & KINGS PARK

Subiaco Hotel PUB

(Map p56; www.subiacohotel.com.au; 465 Hay St) The Subi's the locals' institution of choice for a morning coffee with the papers or a pre-footy beer. Middie-clutching men perch themselves for hours in the side bar, friends banter in lounges by the central bar and the Sunday sundowner crowd settle into the sun-speckled courtyard to squeeze the last drops out of the weekend.

Old Brewery MICROBREWERY

(Map p56; www.theoldbrewery.com.au; 173 Mounts Bay Rd) Cowhide stools gather around the bar, gazing towards the shiny copper vats making the magic (ales and wheat beers, actually), carrying on the tradition of the Swan Brewery, which opened on this site in 1879. It's the perfect place for a riverside sundowner.

BEACHES

Elba BAR

(www.elbacottesloe.com.au; 29 Napoleon St, Cottesloe; ⏲noon-midnight Mon-Sat, noon-10pm Sun) In the swanky part of Cottesloe, not the chilled-out beach strip, Elba has taken its street name as inspiration and produced a slick little Napoleonic bar complete with shiny black walls, sparkly chandeliers and a gilt-framed portrait of the little man. Come dressed for cocktails, although perhaps in flats out of deference. Napoleon St is one of the shopping streets running off the Stirling Hwy.

Ocean Beach Hotel PUB

(www.obh.com.au; cnr Marine Pde & Eric St, Cottesloe; ⏲11am-midnight Mon-Sat, 11am-10pm Sun) Backpackers and locals drink up the beer and soak up the sun at this rambling beachside pub, especially on Sundays.

Cottesloe Beach Hotel PUB

(www.cottesloebeachhotel.com.au; 104 Marine Pde; ⏲11am-midnight Mon-Sat, 11am-10pm Sun) Grab a spot on the lawn in the massive beer garden, or watch the sun set from the balcony. Sundays are big.

☆ Entertainment

Nightclubs

Hip-E Club NIGHTCLUB

(Map p56; www.hipeclub.com.au; 663 Newcastle St, Leederville; ⏲Tue-Sat) Thrust about to *Tainted Love* all night long. Tuesday is backpackers night.

Ambar NIGHTCLUB

(Map p52; www.boomtick.com.au/ambar; 104 Murray St) Perth's premier club for breakbeat, drum'n'bass and visiting international DJs.

Geisha NIGHTCLUB

(Map p52; www.geishabar.com.au; 135a James St, Northbridge; ⏲11pm-6am Fri & Sat) A small-and-pumping DJ-driven, gay-friendly club, the vibe's usually music-focused and chilled out.

Velvet Lounge PUB

(www.theflyingscotsman.com.au; 639 Beaufort St, Mt Lawley) Out the back of the Flying Scotsman is this small, red-velvet-clad lounge playing everything from hip-hop to ska.

Funk Club PUB

(Map p56; www.funkclub.com.au; 742 Newcastle St, Leederville; ⏲8pm-midnight Fri) Upstairs at the Leederville Hotel, a happy bunch bop away for hours up here, seemingly unaware of the entirely different vibe downstairs. Live bands and DJs.

Rise NIGHTCLUB

(Map p52; www.rise.net.au; 139 James St) Serious clubbers head here for nonstop techno and trance.

Metro City NIGHTCLUB

(Map p52; www.metrocity.com.au; 146 Roe St, Northbridge) Thumping super-club (capacity 2000), which doubles as a concert venue. R&B on Saturday nights.

Live Music

Ellington Jazz Club NIGHTCLUB

(Map p52; www.theellington.com.au; 191 Beaufort St, Northbridge; ⏲7pm-1am Mon-Thu, to 3am Fri & Sat, 5pm-midnight Sun) There's live jazz nightly in this handsome, intimate venue. Standing-only admission is $10, or you can book a table for tapas and pizza.

Bakery ARTS CENTRE

(Map p52; www.nowbaking.com.au; 233 James St, Northbridge; ⏲7pm-1am Thu-Sun) Run by Artrage, Perth's contemporary arts festival body, the Bakery draws an arty crowd. Popular indie gigs are held almost every weekend.

Amplifier BAR

(Map p52; www.amplifiercapitol.com.au; rear 383 Murray St, Perth) The good old Amplifier is one of the best places for live (mainly indie) bands.

Moon CAFE
(Map p52; www.themoon.com.au; 323 William St, Northbridge; ⏲6pm-12.30am Mon & Tue, 11am-1.30am Wed, Thu & Sun, 11am-3.30am Fri & Sat) Low-key, late-night cafe with singer-songwriters on Wednesdays, jazz on Thursdays, poetry slams on Saturday afternoons and '10 Minute Tuesdays', where it's guaranteed that 10 minutes of oddness will occur.

Universal PUB
(Map p52; www.universalbar.com.au; 221 William St; ⏲7am-late) The unpretentious Universal is one of Perth's oldest bars and much-loved by jazz and blues enthusiasts.

Rosemount Hotel PUB
(www.rosemounthotel.com.au; cnr Angove & Fitzgerald Sts, North Perth; ⏲noon-midnight Mon-Sat, noon-10pm Sun) Local and international bands play regularly in this spacious art-deco pub with a laid-back beer garden.

Charles Hotel PUB
(www.charleshotel.com.au; 509 Charles St, North Perth) Hosts lots of live music, including the Perth Jazz Society (www.perthjazz society.com) every Monday night and the Legendary Perth Blues Club on Tuesdays.

Jazz Cellar MUSIC VENUE
(cnr Scarborough Beach Rd & Buxton St, Mt Hawthorn; admission $20; ⏲from 7pm Fri) Step downstairs here to find an older crowd of jazz freaks revelling in swing. It's always been BYO-only, but at the time of writing licensing problems were threatening its future.

Astor THEATRE
(www.liveattheastor.com.au; 659 Beaufort St, Mt Lawley) The beautiful art-deco Astor still screens the odd film, but is mainly used for concerts these days.

Cabaret & Comedy

TOP CHOICE **Devilles Pad** CABARET
(Map p52; www.devillespad.com; 3 Aberdeen St, Northbridge; ⏲6pm-midnight Thu, to 2am Fri & Sat) The devil goes to Vegas disguised as a 1950s lounge lizard in this extremely kooky venue, hidden in a quiet-by-night part of town. You're encouraged to dress up to match the exceedingly camp interiors (complete with erupting volcano). A lively roster of burlesque dancers, magicians, live bands and assorted sideshow freaks provide the entertainment, and there's a full menu available.

Lazy Susan's Comedy Den COMEDY
(www.lazysusans.com.au; 292 Beaufort St, Highgate; ⏲8.30pm Tue, Fri & Sat) Above the Brisbane Hotel. Shapiro Tuesdays offers a mix of first-timers, seasoned amateurs and pros trying out new shtick (for a very reasonable $5). Friday is for more grown-up stand-ups, including some interstaters. Saturday is the Big Hoohaa – a team-based comedy wrassle.

Theatre & Classical Music

Check the *West Australian* newspaper for what's on. Most tickets can be booked through **BOCS Ticketing** (☎9484 1133; www.bocsticketing.com.au).

His Majesty's Theatre THEATRE
(Map p52; www.hismajestystheatre.com.au; 825 Hay St) The majestic home to the West Australian Ballet (www.waballet.com.au) and West Australian Opera (www.waopera.asn.au), as well as lots of theatre, comedy and cabaret.

Perth Concert Hall CONCERT HALL
(Map p52; www.perthconcerthall.com.au; 5 St Georges Tce) Home to the Western Australian Symphony Orchestra (WASO; www.waso.com.au).

Subiaco Arts Centre THEATRES
(Map p56; www.subiacoartscentre.com.au; 180 Hamersley Rd, Subiaco) Indoor and outdoor theatres used for drama and concerts; home to Barking Gecko young people's theatre (www.barkinggecko.com.au).

Regal Theatre THEATRE
(Map p56; www.regaltheatre.com.au; 474 Hay St, Subiaco)

Cinema

Somerville Auditorium OUTDOOR FILM FESTIVAL
(www.perthfestival.com.au; UWA, 35 Stirling Hwy, Crawley; ⏲Dec-Mar) A quintessential Perth experience, the Perth Festival's film program is held here on beautiful grounds surrounded by pines. Picnicking before the film is a must.

Luna CINEMA
(Map p56; www.lunapalace.com.au; 155 Oxford St, Leederville) Art-house cinema with Monday double features ($9.50) and a bar. Screens outdoor movies in summer.

Cinema Paradiso CINEMA
(Map p52; www.lunapalace.com.au; Galleria complex, 164 James St, Northbridge) Art-house cinema.

Ace Subiaco CINEMA
(Map p56; www.moviemasters.com.au; 500 Hay St) Four-screen multiplex screening Hollywood fare.

Moonlight Cinema OUTDOOR CINEMA
(Map p56; ☎1300 551 908; www.moonlight.com.au; Kings Park) Bring a picnic and blanket and enjoy a romantic moonlit movie; summer only.

Camelot Outdoor Cinema OUTDOOR CINEMA
(www.lunapalace.com.au; Memorial Hall, 16 Lochee St, Mosman Park) Seated open-air cinema, running from December to Easter.

Sport

In WA 'football' means Aussie Rules and during the Australian Football League (AFL) season it's hard to get locals to talk about anything but the two local teams – the **West Coast Eagles** (www.westcoasteagles.com.au) and the **Fremantle Dockers** (www.fremantlefc.com.au) – and the joy of beating 'the Vics' (any Victorian team is considered an arch-enemy). Rugby League (considered an east-coast game) doesn't get a look in, even during the finals season.

The *West Australian* has details of all sports games.

Subiaco Oval AUSTRALIAN RULES
(Map p56; ☎1300 135 915; www.subiacooval.com.au; 250 Roberts Rd, Subiaco) The home of Aussie Rules and huge concerts; you're guaranteed a great atmosphere.

WACA CRICKET
(Western Australian Cricket Association; Map p52; www.waca.com.au; Nelson Cres, East Perth) In summer, cricket fans while away lazy afternoons here watching a test or state match.

Perth Oval SOCCER, RUGBY
(NIB Stadium; Map p52; Lord St, Perth) Both the Perth Glory (www.perthglory.com.au) soccer (football) team and the Western Force (www.westernforce.com.au) Super 12 rugby union team have many obsessive fans. See them in action here. It's also the home of WA rugby league.

Challenge Stadium NETBALL, BASKETBALL
(www.venueswest.wa.gov.au; Stephenson Ave, Mt Claremont) Home to the West Coast Fever (netball; www.westcoastfever.com.au), the championship-winning Perth Wildcats (basketball; www.nbl.com.au/wildcats) and regular concerts.

Shopping

CITY CENTRE

Murray St and Hay St Malls are the city's shopping heartland, while King St is the place for swanky boutiques. London Court arcade has opals and souvenirs.

Wheels & Doll Baby CLOTHING
(Map p52; www.wheelsanddollbaby.com; 26 King St) Punky rock chick chic with a bit of baby doll mixed in. Perhaps Perth fashion's coolest export, being worn by the likes of Amy Winehouse and Debbie Harry.

Dilettante CLOTHING
(Map p52; www.dilettante.net); Femme (575 Wellington St); Homme (90 King St) Neighbouring boutiques stocking international designer labels including Helmut Lang and Vivienne Westwood.

78 Records MUSIC STORE
(Map p52; www.78records.com.au; 914 Hay St) Big, independent record shop with a massive range of CDs and lots of specials.

Boffins BOOKSTORE
(Map p52; www.boffinsbookshop.com.au; 806 Hay St) Boffins' technical and specialist range includes travel.

All Foreign Languages Bookshop BOOKSTORE
(Map p52; www.allforeignlanguages.com.au; 572 Hay St) Foreign-language books, phrasebooks and guidebooks.

Elizabeth's Bookshop BOOKSTORE
(Map p52; 820 Hay St) Fremantle institution's city-centre branch.

Perth Map Centre MAPS
(Map p52; www.mapworld.com.au; 900 Hay St) Full range of maps and travel guides.

NORTHBRIDGE, HIGHGATE & MT LAWLEY

William Topp DESIGN
(www.williamtopp.com; 452 William St, Northbridge) Lots of very cool knick-knacks.

Planet BOOKSTORE
(www.planetvideo.com.au; 636-638 Beaufort St, Mt Lawley) A big, polished-concrete shell decked out with leather lounges and a brazen chandelier. Stacked with books and lots of obscure movies.

LEEDERVILLE

Leederville's Oxford St is the place for groovy boutiques, eclectic music and bookshops.

Atlas Divine CLOTHING
(Map p56; www.atlasdivine.com; 121 Oxford St) Hip women's and men's clobber: jeans, quirky tees, dresses etc.

BUYING ABORIGINAL ART – ETHICALLY

Perth's Art Gallery of Western Australia houses an enormous and outstanding collection of indigenous art, and serves as a wonderful introduction. But the Aboriginal art industry's reputation has been marred by the carpetbagging ways of some art dealers and gallery owners. For this reason, who you buy from is an important consideration. A little bit of research can go a long way: the Association of West Australian Art Galleries (www.awaag.org.au) and the Australian Commercial Galleries Association (www.acga.com.au) lists galleries considered to observe ethical practices.

Oxford St Books BOOKSTORE
(Map p56; 119 Oxford St) Knowledgeable staff, great range of fiction and a travel section.

SUBIACO & KINGS PARK

Upmarket Rokeby Rd and Hay St boast fashion, art and classy gifts.

Indigenart INDIGENOUS ART
(Map p56; www.mossensongalleries.com.au; 115 Hay St, Subiaco) Reputable Indigenart carries art from around the country but with a particular focus on WA artists. Works include weavings, paintings on canvas, bark and paper, sculpture and limited edition prints.

Aboriginal Art & Craft Gallery INDIGENOUS ART
(Map p56; www.aboriginalgallery.com.au; Fraser Ave, Kings Park) Carries a mixture of work but tends to be less high-end than Indigenart.

Aspects of Kings Park ART, SOUVENIRS
(Map p56; www.bgpa.wa.gov.au; Fraser Ave, Kings Park) Run by the park authority and stocking a wide range of Australian art, craft and books.

Elizabeth's Bookshop BOOKSTORE
(Map p56; 29 Rokeby Rd) Fremantle institution's Subiaco branch.

OTHER AREAS

æ'lkemi CLOTHING
(www.aelkemi.com; Times Square Centre, 337 Stirling Hwy, Claremont) Top WA designer's signature store, showcasing his feminine frocks and distinctive prints.

Karrinyup MALL
(www.karrinyupcentre.com.au; 200 Karrinyup Rd, Karrinyup) Big mall, east of Trigg Beach.

Garden City MALL
(www.gardencity.com.au; 125 Riseley St, Booragoon) Another large shopping centre, south of the river.

Information

Emergency

Police station (13 14 44; www.police.wa.gov.au; 60 Beaufort St, Northbridge)

Sexual Assault Resource Centre (9340 1828; www.kemh.health.wa.gov.au/services/sarc; 24hr)

Internet Access

State Library of WA (www.slwa.wa.gov.au; Perth Cultural Centre, Northbridge; 9am-8pm Mon-Thu, 10am-5.30pm Fri-Sun) Offers both free wi-fi and hooked-up computer terminals. Look for the symbol in the Eating section for cafes offering free wi-fi access.

Media

Look for free listings booklets, such as *Your Guide to Perth & Fremantle*, available at hostels, hotels and tourist offices.

Drum Media In the same vein as *X-Press*.

Go West (www.gowesternaustralia.com.au) Backpacker magazine that has information on activities throughout WA, as well as seasonal work.

West Australian (www.thewest.com.au) Local newspaper with what's on, cinema times etc.

X-Press Magazine (www.xpressmag.com.au) Long-running street rag and a good source of live music information. Available in cafes, bars and music stores.

Medical Services

Lifecare Dental (9221 2777; www.dentistsinperth.com.au; Forrest Chase, 419 Wellington St; 8am-8pm)

Royal Perth Hospital (9224 2244; www.rph.wa.gov.au; Victoria Sq)

Travel Medicine Centre (9321 7888; www.travelmed.com.au; 5 Mill St; 8am-5pm Mon-Fri)

Money

Accessing Aussie dollars is straightforward; ATMs are plentiful. There are currency-exchange facilities at the airport and city banks, and branches of major banks in the CBD.

Post

Main Post Office (GPO; ☎13 13 18; 3 Forrest Pl; ⏱8.30am-5pm Mon-Fri, 9am-12.30pm Sat)

Tourist Information

i-City Information Kiosk (Map p52; Murray St Mall; ⏱9.30am-4.30pm Mon-Thu & Sat, 9.30am-8pm Fri, 11am-3.30pm Sun) Volunteers answer your questions and run walking tours.

WA Visitor Centre (Map p52; ☎9483 1111; www.wavisitorcentre.com; cnr Forrest Pl & Wellington St; ⏱9am-5.30pm Mon-Fri, 9.30am-4.30pm Sat, 11am-4pm Sun) A good resource for a trip anywhere in WA.

Websites

www.heatseeker.com.au Gig guide and ticketing.

www.perth.citysearch.com.au Entertainment and restaurants.

www.scoop.com.au Entertainment.

www.whatson.com.au Events and travel information.

Getting There & Away

Air

For details on flights to Perth from international and interstate destinations, see p259.

Airnorth (☎1800 627 474; www.airnorth.com.au) Flies between Perth and Kununurra.

Cobham (☎1800 105 503; www.cobham.com.au) Flies between Perth and Kambalda.

Qantas (☎13 13 13; www.qantas.com.au; 55 William St) WA destinations include Kalgoorlie, Paraburdoo, Newman, Exmouth, Karratha, Port Hedland and Broome.

Skippers Aviation (☎1300 729 924; www.skippers.com.au) Flies six routes in both directions: Perth–Carnarvon, Perth–Geraldton–Carnarvon, Perth–Kalbarri–Monkey Mia, Perth–Leonora–Laverton, Perth–Wiluna–Leinster and Perth–Mt Magnet–Meekatharra.

Skywest (☎1300 660 088; www.skywest.com.au) Flies to regional centres within WA: Albany, Esperance, Kalgoorlie, Geraldton, Exmouth, Karratha, Broome and Kununurra.

Strategic Airlines (☎13 53 20; www.flystrategic.com.au) Flies between Perth and Derby.

Tiger Airways (☎03-9335 3033; www.tigerairways.com) Cheapies between Perth and Melbourne.

Virgin Blue (☎13 67 89; www.virginblue.com.au) WA destinations are Newman, Karratha, Port Hedland and Broome.

Bus

Greyhound (☎1300 473 946; www.greyhound.com.au) Has services from the East Perth terminal to Broome ($240 to $438, 34 hours, thrice weekly) via Geraldton, Carnarvon, Karratha and Port Hedland.

Integrity Coach Lines (☎9574 6707; www.integritycoachlines.com.au; Wellington St Bus Station) Runs services between Perth and Port Hedland ($232, 22 hours, weekly) via Mt Magnet, Cue, Meekatharra and Newman.

South West Coach Lines (☎9261 7600; www.veoliatransportwa.com.au) Focuses on the southwestern corner of WA, running services from the Esplanade Busport (some stopping at the airport) to most towns in the region, including:

» Dunsborough (3½ hours, daily) via Mandurah, Bunbury and Busselton

» Augusta (4½ hours, daily) via Bunbury, Busselton, Cowaramup and Margaret River

» Manjimup (seven hours, daily except weekends) via Mandurah, Bunbury, Balingup and Bridgetown

Transwa (☎1300 662 205; www.transwa.wa.gov.au) Operates services from the bus terminal at East Perth train station to/from many destinations around the state. These include:

» SW1 to Augusta ($46, six hours, 12 per week) via Mandurah, Bunbury, Busselton and Dunsborough

» SW2 to Pemberton ($48, 5½ hours, thrice weekly) via Bunbury, Balingup and Bridgetown

» GS1 to Albany ($56, six hours, daily) via Mt Barker

» GE2 to Esperance ($83, 10 hours, thrice weekly) via Mundaring, York and Hyden

» N1 to Geraldton ($58, six hours, daily) and on to Northampton and Kalbarri ($72, 8½ hours, three weekly)

Train

See below for trains to Guildford, Fremantle, Rockingham and Mandurah. See p260 for details of the *Indian Pacific* to Adelaide and Sydney.

Transwa (☎1300 662 205; www.transwa.wa.gov.au) runs the following services:

» **Australind** (twice daily) Perth to Pinjarra ($16, 1¼ hours) and Bunbury ($29, 2½ hours)

» **AvonLink** (thrice weekly) East Perth to Toodyay ($16, 1¼ hours), Northam ($18, 1½ hours) and Merredin ($41, 3¼ hours)

» **Prospector** (daily) East Perth to Kalgoorlie–Boulder ($82, seven hours)

Getting Around

To/From the Airport

The domestic and international terminals of Perth's airport are 10km and 13km east of Perth respectively, near Guildford. Taxi fares to the city are around $25/35 from the domestic/

international terminal, and about $60 to Fremantle.

Connect (☎1300 666 806; www.perthairportconnect.com.au) runs shuttles to and from hotels and hostels in the city centre (one way/return $18/30, every 50 minutes) and in Fremantle (one way/return $33/58, every 2½ hours). Prices are slightly cheaper between Perth and the domestic terminal and substantially discounted for groups of two to four people (check the website for details). Bookings are essential for all services to the airport and are recommended for services to Fremantle. No bookings are taken for shuttles from the airport to Perth's city centre.

Transperth bus 37 travels to the domestic airport from St Georges Tce, near William St ($3.70, 44 minutes, every 10 to 30 minutes, hourly after 7pm).

Car & Motorcycle

Driving in the city takes a bit of practise, as some streets are one way and many aren't signed. There are plenty of car parking buildings in the central city but no free parks. For unmetered street parking you'll need to look well away from the main commercial strips and check the signs carefully.

See p262 for car-hire companies.

A fun way to gad about the city is on the back of a moped. **Scootamoré** (☎9380 6580; www.scootamore.com.au; 356a Rokeby Rd, Subiaco; per 4hr/day/week/month $29/45/200/400) hires 50cc scooters with helmets (compulsory) and insurance included (for over 21 year olds, $500 excess).

Public Transport

Transperth (☎13 62 13; www.transperth.wa.gov.au) operates Perth's public buses, trains and ferries. There are Transperth information offices at Perth station (Wellington St), Wellington St bus station, Perth underground station (off Murray St) and the Esplanade Busport (Mounts Bay Rd). There's also a journey planner on the website.

From the central city, the following fares apply for all public transport:

Free Transit Zone (FTZ) – covers the central commercial area, bounded (roughly) by Fraser Ave, Kings Park Rd, Thomas St, Newcastle St, Parry St, Lord St and the river (including the City West and Claisebrook train stations, to the west and east respectively)

Zone 1 – includes the city centre and the inner suburbs ($2.50)

Zone 2 – Fremantle, Guildford and the beaches as far north as Sorrento ($3.70)

Zone 3 – Hillarys Boat Harbour (AQWA), the Swan Valley and Kalamunda ($4.60)

Zone 5 – Rockingham ($6.60)

Zone 7 – Mandurah ($8.70)

DayRider – unlimited travel after 9am weekdays and all day on the weekend in any zone

FamilyRider – lets two adults and up to five children travel for a total of $9 on weekends, after 6pm weekdays and after 9am on weekdays during school holidays.

If you're in Perth for a while, it may be worth buying a SmartRider card, which covers you for bus, train and ferry travel. It's $10 to purchase, then you add value to your card. The technology deducts the fare as you go, as long as you tap-in and tap-out (touching your card on the electronic reader) every time you travel, including within the FTZ. The SmartRider works out 15% cheaper than buying single tickets and automatically caps itself at the DayRider rate if you're avoiding the morning rush hour.

BUS As well as regular buses the FTZ is well covered during the day by the three free Central Area Transit (CAT) services. The Yellow and Red CATs operate east–west routes, Yellow sticking mainly to Wellington St, and Red looping roughly east on Murray St and west on Hay St. The Blue Cat does a figure of 8 through Northbridge and the south end of the city; this is the only one to run late – until 1am on Friday and Saturday nights only. Pick up a copy of the free timetable (widely available on buses and elsewhere) for the exact routes and stops. Best of all, they run every five to eight minutes during weekdays and every 15 minutes on weekends; there are digital displays at the stops telling you when the next bus is due.

The metropolitan area is serviced by a wide network of Transperth buses. Pick up timetables from any of the Transperth information centres or use the 'journey planner' on its website.

FERRY The only ferry runs every 20 to 30 minutes between Barrack St Jetty and Mends St Jetty in South Perth – you'll probably only use it to get to the zoo.

TRAIN Transperth operates five train lines from around 5.20am to midnight weekdays and until about 2am Saturday and Sunday. Your rail ticket can also be used on Transperth buses and ferries within the ticket's zone. You're free to take your bike on the train in nonpeak times. The lines and useful stops include:

Armadale Thornlie Line – Perth, Burswood

Fremantle Line – Perth, City West, West Leederville, Subiaco, Shenton Park, Swanbourne, Cottesloe, North Fremantle, Fremantle

Joondalup Line – Esplanade, Perth Underground, Leederville

Mandurah Line – Perth Underground, Esplanade, Rockingham, Mandurah

Midland Line – Perth, East Perth, Mt Lawley, Guildford, Midland

Taxi

Perth has a decent system of metered taxis, though the distances in Perth makes frequent use costly and on busy nights you may have trouble flagging one down off the street. There are ranks throughout the city. The two main companies are **Swan Taxis** (☎13 13 30; www.swantaxis.com.au) and **Black & White** (☎13 10 08; www.bwtaxi.com.au), both of which have wheelchair-accessible cabs.

FREMANTLE

POP 28,100

Creative, relaxed, open-minded: Fremantle's spirit is entirely distinct from Perth's. Perhaps it has something to do with the port and the city's working-class roots. Or the hippies, who first set up home here a few decades ago and can still be seen casually bobbling down the street on old bicycles. Or perhaps it's just that a timely 20th-century economic slump meant that the city retained an almost complete set of formerly grand Victorian and Edwardian buildings, creating a heritage precinct that's unique among Australia's cities today.

Whatever, today's clean and green Freo makes a cosy home for performers, professionals, artists and more than a few eccentrics. There's a lot to enjoy here – fantastic museums, edgy galleries, pubs thrumming with live music and a thriving coffee culture. On weekend nights the city's residents vacate the main drag, leaving it to kids from the suburbs, who move in to party hard and loud.

History

This was an important area for the Wadjuk Noongar people, as it was a hub of trading paths. Some of these routes exist to this day in the form of modern roads. Before the harbour was altered, the mouth of the river was nearly covered by a sandbar and it was only a short swim from north to south. The confluence of the river and ocean, where Fremantle now stands, was known as Manjaree (sometimes translated as 'gathering place'). The Fremantle coast was called Booyeembara, while inland was Wallyalup, 'place of the eagle'.

Manjaree was mainly occupied in summer when the Wadjuk would base themselves here to fish. In winter they would head further inland, avoiding seasonal flooding.

Fremantle's European history began when the ship *HMS Challenger* landed in 1829. The ship's captain, Charles Fremantle, took possession of the whole of the west coast 'in the name of King George IV'. Like Perth, the settlement made little progress until convict labour was used. They constructed most of the town's earliest buildings; some of them, such as the Round House, Fremantle Prison and Fremantle Arts Centre, are now among the oldest in WA.

As a port, Fremantle wasn't up to much until the engineer CY O'Connor created an artificial harbour in the 1890s, destroying the Wadjuks' river crossing in the process. This caused such disruption to their traditional patterns of life that it's said that a curse was placed on O'Connor; some took his later suicide at Fremantle as evidence of its effectiveness.

The port blossomed during the gold rush and many of its distinctive buildings date from this period. Economic stagnation in the 1960s and 1970s spared the streetscape from the worst ravages of modernisation. It wasn't until 1987, when Fremantle hosted the America's Cup, that it transformed itself from a sleepy port town into today's vibrant, artsy city.

The cup was lost that year, but the legacy of a redeveloped waterfront remains. In 1995 the Fremantle Dockers played their first game, quickly developing one of the most fanatical fan bases in the AFL, boosted in 2010 by a semifinals berth.

⊙ Sights

Fremantle Prison HISTORIC BUILDING

(☎9336 9200; www.fremantleprison.com.au; 1 The Terrace; torchlight tours adult/child $25/21; ⊙9am-5.30pm) With its foreboding 5m-high walls enclosing a nearly 6-hectare site, the old convict-era prison still dominates present-day Fremantle, with its tales of adventure and hardship living on in the city's imagination. In 2010 its cultural status was recognised, along with 10 other penal buildings, as part of the Australian Convict Sites entry on the Unesco World Heritage list.

The first convicts were made to build their own prison, constructing it from beautiful pale limestone dug out of the hill on which it was built. From 1855 to 1991, 350,000 people were incarcerated here, although the highest numbers held at any one time were 1200

Fremantle

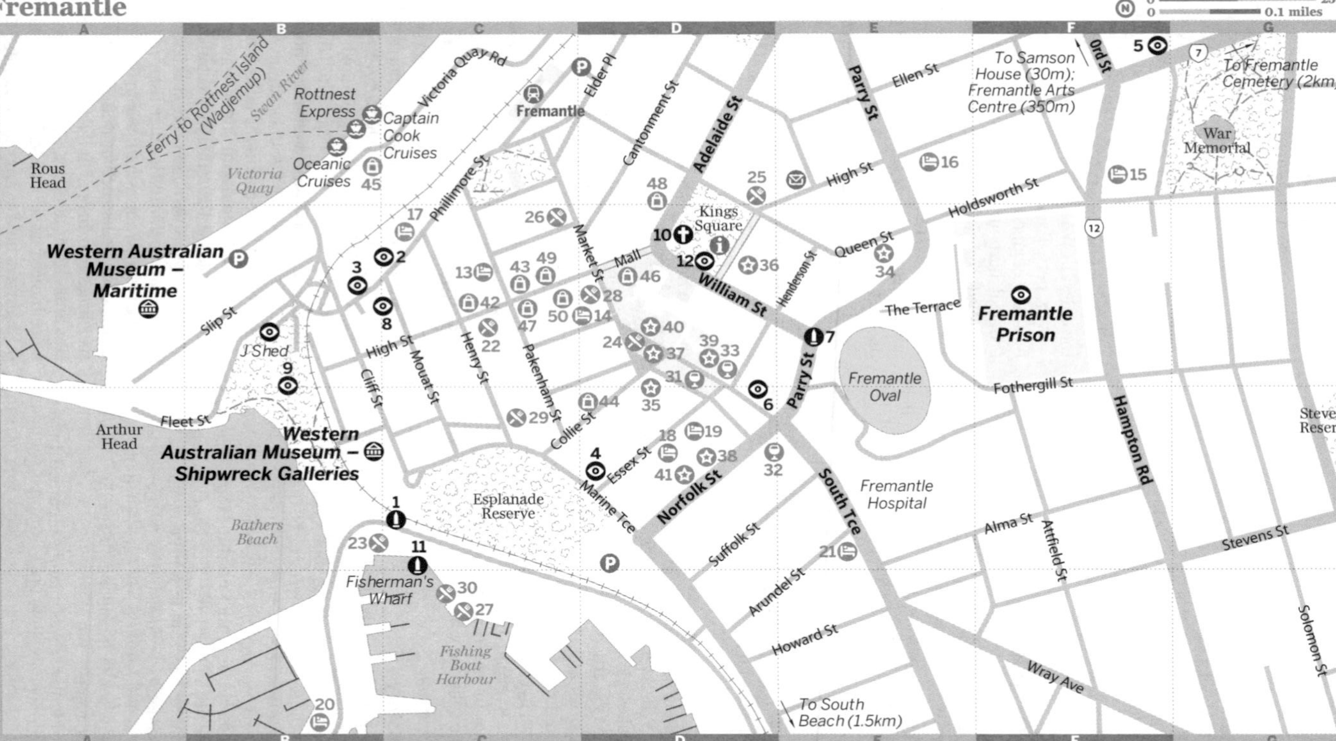
0 250 m
0 0.1 miles
Rous Head
Ferry to Rottnest Island (Wadjemup)
Swan River
Victoria Quay
Rottnest Express
Captain Cook Cruises
Oceanic Cruises
Victoria Quay Rd
Fremantle
Elder Pl
Cantonment St
Adelaide St
Parry St
Ellen St
To Samson House (30m); Fremantle Arts Centre (350m)
Ord St
To Fremantle Cemetery (2km)
War Memorial
Phillimore St
Western Australian Museum – Maritime
Slip St
J Shed
Market St
Mall
Kings Square
High St
Holdsworth St
Queen St
Henderson St
William St
The Terrace
Fremantle Prison
Cliff St
Mouat St
Henry St
Pakenham St
Collie St
Essex St
Norfolk St
Fremantle Oval
Fothergill St
Hampton Rd
Stevens Reserve
Arthur Head
Fleet St
Western Australian Museum – Shipwreck Galleries
Esplanade Reserve
Marine Tce
South Tce
Fremantle Hospital
Alma St
Attfield St
Stevens St
Bathers Beach
Fisherman's Wharf
Suffolk St
Arundel St
Howard St
Fishing Boat Harbour
Wray Ave
Solomon St
To South Beach (1.5km)

Fremantle

Top Sights
Fremantle Prison ... F2
Western Australian Museum – Maritime ... A2
Western Australian Museum – Shipwreck Galleries ... B3

Sights
1 Bon Scott Statue ... C3
2 Chamber of Commerce Building ... C2
3 Customs House ... B2
4 Esplanade Hotel ... D3
5 Fremantle Grammar School ... F1
6 Fremantle Markets ... D3
John Curtin Statue ... (see 12)
7 Mark of the Century ... E2
8 Old German Consulate ... C2
Pietro Porcelli Statue ... (see 10)
9 Round House ... B2
10 St John's Anglican Church ... D2
11 To The Fishermen Statue ... C3
12 Town Hall ... D2

Sleeping
13 Backpackers Inn Fremantle ... C2
14 Bannister Suites Fremantle ... D2
15 Fothergills of Fremantle ... F1
16 Fremantle Colonial Accommodation ... E1
Norfolk Hotel ... (see 32)
17 Old Firestation Backpackers ... C2
18 Pirates ... D3
19 Port Mill B&B ... D3
20 Quest Harbour Village ... B4
21 Terrace Central B&B Hotel ... E3

Eating
22 Cafe 55 ... C2
23 Cicerello's ... B3
24 Gino's ... D2
25 Juicy Beetroot ... D1
26 Kakulas Sister ... C2
27 Little Creatures ... C4
28 Maya ... D2
29 Moore & Moore ... C3
30 Mussel Bar ... C4

Drinking
Little Creatures ... (see 27)
31 Monk ... D2
32 Norfolk Hotel ... D3
33 Sail & Anchor ... D2

Entertainment
34 Fly by Night Musicians Club ... E2
35 Hoyts Millennium ... D3
36 Hoyts Queensgate ... D2
37 Kulcha ... D2
38 Luna on SX ... D3
39 Metropolis Fremantle ... D2
40 Newport Hotel ... D2
41 X-Wray Cafe ... D3

Shopping
42 Bill Campbell Secondhand Book Seller ... C2
43 Bodkin's Bootery ... C2
44 Chart & Map Shop ... D3
45 E Shed Markets ... B1
46 Elizabeth's Bookshop Fremantle ... D2
Elizabeth's Bookshop South Terrace ... (see 40)
Japingka ... (see 22)
47 Love In Tokyo ... C2
48 Mills Records ... D1
49 New Edition ... C2
50 Record Finder ... C2
Remedy ... (see 50)

men and 58 women. Of those, 43 men and one woman were executed on-site, the last of which was serial killer Eric Edgar Cooke in 1964.

Entry to the **gatehouse**, including the **Prison Gallery**, **gift shop** (where you can purchase fetching arrow-printed prisoner PJs) and **Convict Cafe** is free. To enter the prison proper, you'll need to take a tour. During the day there are two fascinating 1¼-hour tours on offer, timed so that you can take one after the other on a combined ticket (single tour adult/child $19/10, combined adult/child $25/17), although you can return for the second tour anytime in the next fortnight.

The **Doing Time Tour** (departs every 30 minutes, first 10am, last 5pm) takes in the kitchens, men's cells (the original 2.1m by 1.2m convict cells are smaller than modern toilets), the black-as-hell solitary confinement cells (the longest anyone did here was six months on bread and water), the exercise areas, the whipping post (people could be sentenced to up to 100 lashes of the cat o' nine tails, although most would die after

30), the gallows, an interesting display on the 1988 riot, and the big, light-filled chapel (daily attendance was compulsory).

The **Great Escapes Tour** (departs every hour, first 11.45am, last 4.45pm) introduces you to famous inmates such as bushranger and famed escape artist Moondyne Joe and bank robber Brenden Abbott, who escaped in a prison guard's uniform. It also takes in the women's prison and the rifle range.

Bookings are required for the two more intense experiences on offer. **Torchlight Tours** (90 minutes, adult/child $25/21, Wednesday and Friday evenings) are designed to chill, focusing on the creepy and unpleasant aspects of the prison's history. The 2½-hour **Tunnels Tour** (adult/child over 12yr $59/39) takes you 20m underground to tunnels built by prisoners sentenced to hard labour. You'll be kitted out in overalls and hardhats with headlamps for the descent, which includes an underground boat ride.

Western Australian Museum – Maritime MUSEUM

(www.museum.wa.gov.au; Victoria Quay; museum adult/child $10/3, submarine $8/3, museum & submarine $15/5; ⌚9.30am-5pm) Housed in an intriguing sail-shaped building on the harbour, just west of the city centre, this is a fascinating exploration of WA's relationship with the ocean. It faces out to the sea, which has shaped so much of the state's, and Fremantle's, destiny.

Various boats are on display, including **Australia II**, the famous winged-keel yacht that won the America's Cup yachting race in 1983 (ending 132 years of American domination of the competition – an achievement which is the source of much Sandgroper pride). Other boats on show include an **Aboriginal bark canoe**, an **Indonesian outrigger canoe**, introduced to the Kimberley and used by the Indigenous people, and a **pearl lugger** used in Broome. Even a classic **1970s panel van** (complete with fur lining) makes the cut – because of its status as the surfer's vehicle of choice.

Well-presented displays cover a wide range of topics, from Aboriginal fish traps to the sandalwood trade. If you're not claustrophobic, take an hour-long tour of the submarine **HMAS Ovens**. The vessel was part of the Australian Navy's fleet from 1969 to 1997. Tours leave every half-hour from 10am to 3.30pm.

FREE **Western Australian Museum – Shipwreck Galleries** MUSEUM

(www.museum.wa.gov.au; Cliff St; ⌚9.30am-5pm) Housed in an 1852 commissariat store, the Shipwreck Galleries are considered the finest display of maritime archaeology in the southern hemisphere. The highlight is the **Batavia Gallery**, where a section of the hull of Dutch merchant ship *Batavia,* wrecked in 1629, is displayed. Nearby is a large stone gate, intended as an entrance to Batavia Castle, which was being carried when it sank.

Other items of interest include the inscribed pewter plate left on Cape Inscription by Willem de Vlamingh in 1697, positioned next to a replica of the plate left by Dirk Hartog in 1616 during the first confirmed European landing in WA.

Round House HISTORIC BUILDING

(☎9336 6897; Arthur Head; admission by donation; ⌚10.30am-3.30pm) Commenced in 1830 and 1831, shortly after the founding of the colony, this odd 12-sided stone prison is the oldest surviving building in WA. It was the site of the colony's first hangings, including that of 15-year-old John Gavin (convicted of murdering his employer's son). Later, it was used for holding Aborigines before they were taken to Rottnest Island. To the Noongar people, it's a sacred site because of the number of their people killed while incarcerated here. Freedom fighter Yagan was held here briefly in 1832.

On the hilltop outside is the **Signal Station**, where at 1pm daily a time ball and cannon blast were used to alert seamen to the correct time. The ceremony is re-enacted daily; book ahead if you want to fire the cannon.

Beneath is an impressive 1837 **Whalers' Tunnel** carved through sandstone and used for accessing Bathers Beach, where whales were landed and processed.

FREE **Fremantle Arts Centre** GALLERY

(www.fac.org.au; 1 Finnerty St; ⌚9am-5pm) An impressive neo-Gothic building surrounded by lovely elm-shaded gardens, the Fremantle Arts Centre was constructed by convict labourers as a lunatic asylum in the 1860s. Saved from demolition in the late 1960s, it houses a changing roster of interesting exhibitions as well as a cafe and shop. During summer, it's a hive of cultural activity, with concerts, courses and workshops.

FREE **Fremantle Markets** MARKET

(www.fremantlemarkets.com.au; cnr South Tce & Henderson St; ⌚8am-8pm Fri, 8am-5pm Sat

& Sun) Originally opened in 1897, these colourful markets were reopened in 1975 and today draw slow-moving crowds, combing over souvenirs like plastic boomerangs and swan-shaped magnets. The fresh produce section is a good place to stock up on snacks.

Gold Rush Buildings HISTORIC BUILDINGS
Fremantle boomed during the WA gold rush in the late 19th century, and many wonderful buildings remain which were constructed during, or shortly before, this period. High St, particularly around the bottom end, has some excellent examples including several old hotels. The following are worth seeking out:

Chamber of Commerce Building (16 Phillimore St) In its original use since 1873.

St John's Anglican Church (Kings Sq) Built 1882.

Fremantle Grammar School (200 High St) Built as an Anglican public school in 1885.

Town Hall (Kings Sq) Opened on Queen Victoria's jubilee in 1887.

Samson House (Ellen & Ord Sts) A well-preserved 1888 colonial home, owned by the National Trust but not currently open to the public.

Esplanade Hotel (Marine Tce) Attractive colonnaded hotel (1896).

Old German Consulate (5 Mouat St) Built 1903; now a B&B.

Fremantle Train Station (Phillimore St) Built from Donnybrook sandstone in 1907; we're not sure why the swans are white rather than black.

Customs House (cnr Cliff & Phillimore Sts) Built in 1908 in a Georgian style.

Public Sculptures MONUMENTS
Enlivening Fremantle's streets are numerous bronze sculptures, many by local artist Greg James (www.gregjamessculpture.com). Perhaps the most popular, certainly with black-clad pilgrims, is the statue of **Bon Scott** (1946–80) strutting on a Marshall amplifier in Fishing Boat Harbour. The AC/DC singer moved to Fremantle with his family in 1956 and his ashes are interred in **Fremantle Cemetery** (Carrington St); it's reputedly the most-visited grave in Australia, with many travellers stopping in for 'a beer with Bon'.

Also in Fishing Boat Harbour is **To The Fishermen**, a cluster of bronze figures, unloading and carrying their catch up from the wharf. There's a lively statue of former Member for Fremantle and wartime Labor Prime Minister **John Curtin** (1885–1945) in Kings Sq, outside the Town Hall. Nearby is a Greg James sculpture of fellow sculptor **Pietro Porcelli** (1872–1943), in the act of making a bust.

Another quirky bronze is **Mark of the Century** (Parry St), outside Fremantle Oval. For those not au fait with AFL, a mark is where a player cleanly catches a kicked ball, and the mark in question was by South Fremantle's John Gerovich in 1956. Gerovich is depicted leaping and resting his knee on the shoulder of opposing player, Ray French, who from the rear looks like he's wearing high heels.

Beaches & Parks BEACHES
There are plenty of opportunities to partake in the great outdoors around Fremantle, including **Esplanade Reserve** (Marine Tce), a large park shaded by Norfolk Island pines between the city and Fishing Boat Harbour.

Although you could theoretically swim at neighbouring **Bathers Beach**, most people content themselves with wandering along the sand here and save the soaking for beaches further from the port. **South Beach** is sheltered, swimmable, only 1.5km from the city centre and on the free CAT bus route. The next major beach is **Coogee Beach**, 6km further south.

Army Museum of WA MUSEUM
(www.armymuseumwa.com.au; Burt St; adult/child $8/5; ⏲11am-4pm Wed-Sun) Situated within the imposing Artillery Barracks, this little museum pulls out the big guns, literally. Howitzers and tanks line up outside, while inside you'll find cabinets full of uniforms and medals.

Activities

Fremantle Trails WALKING
(www.fremantletrails.com.au) Pick up trailcards from the visitor centre or library for 11 self-guided walking tours: Art & Culture, Convict, CY O'Connor (a pioneering civil engineer), Discovery (a Fremantle once-over), Fishing Boat Harbour, Hotels & Breweries, Maritime Heritage, Manjaree Heritage (indigenous), Retail & Fashion, Waterfront and Writers.

Oceanic Cruises WHALE-WATCHING
(☎9325 1191; www.oceaniccruises.com.au; adult/child $50/25; ⏲mid-Sep–early Dec) Departs C Shed, Victoria Quay, at 10.30am daily for a two-hour tour, with an additional boat

FREMANTLE FOR CHILDREN

You can let the littlies off the leash at Esplanade Reserve, watch buskers at the market, make sand castles at Bathers Beach or have a proper splash about at South or Port Beaches. Older kids might appreciate the creepier aspects of the prison and the innards of the submarine at the Maritime museum, where they can also poke about on actual boats. Adventure World is nearby for funfair rides (see p60). Finish up with fish and chips at Fishing Boat Harbour.

at 1.30pm on weekends. See p58 for more details.

STS Leeuwin II SAILING
(☎9430 4105; www.sailleeuwin.com; Berth B, Victoria Quay; adult/child $95/60) Take a trip on a 55m, three-masted tall ship; see the website for details of breakfast, afternoon or twilight sails.

Tours

Fremantle Tram Tours CITY
(☎9433 6674; www.fremantletrams.com.au) Actually a bus that looks like an old-fashioned trolley car, departing from the Town Hall on an all-day hop-on, hop-off circuit around the city (adult/child $24/5). The **Ghostly Tour** (adult/child $60/45) runs 6.45pm to 10.30pm Fridays and visits the prison, Round House and Fremantle Arts Centre (former asylum) by torchlight. On Sundays at noon and 2pm, the **Highway to Hell Tour** (adult/child $25/10) takes in sites associated with Bon Scott.

Combos include:

Lunch & Tram (adult/child $80/48) – tram plus lunch cruise on river

Triple Tour (adult/child $68/25) – tram, river cruise and the Perth sightseeing bus

Tram & Prison (adult/child $41/13) – tram and prison tour

Captain Cook Cruises CRUISES
(☎9325 3341; www.captaincookcruises.com.au; C Shed, Victoria Quay) Cruises between Fremantle and Perth (one way/return $22/41), departing Fremantle at 11.15am, 12.45pm and 3.45pm (the last is one-way only). A three-hour lunch cruise departs at 12.45pm (adult/child $64/41).

Festivals & Events

West Coast Blues 'n' Roots Festival MUSIC
(www.westcoastbluesnroots.com.au; Fremantle Park) Held in April and interpreting its remit widely: the likes of Bob Dylan, Elvis Costello and Grace Jones were booked for 2011.

Blessing of the Fleet RELIGIOUS
(Esplanade Reserve) An October tradition since 1948, brought to Fremantle by immigrants from Molfetta, Italy. It includes the procession of the Molfettese Our Lady of Martyrs statue (carried by men) and the Sicilian Madonna di Capo d'Orlando (carried by women), from St Patrick's Basilica (47 Adelaide St) to Fishing Boat Harbour, where the blessing takes place.

Fremantle Festival CULTURAL
(www.fremantlefestivals.com) In November, the city's streets and concert venues come alive with parades and performances in Australia's longest-running festival.

Sleeping

TOP CHOICE **Norfolk Hotel** PUB $$
(☎9335 5405; www.norfolkhotel.com.au; 47 South Tce; s/d without bathroom $80/110, d with bathroom $150; ❄📶) While eucalypts and elms stand quietly in the sun-streaked beer garden, the old limestone Norfolk harbours a secret upstairs: its rooms. Far above your standard pub digs, they've all been tastefully decorated in muted tones and crisp white linen, and there's a communal sitting room. It can be noisy on weekends, but the bar closes at midnight and it's still good value.

Fothergills of Fremantle B&B $$
(☎9335 6784; www.fothergills.net.au; 18-22 Ord St; r $160-255; 📶) Naked bronze women sprout from the front garden, while a life-size floral cow shelters on the verandah of these neighbouring mansions on the hill. Inside, the decor is in keeping with their venerable age (built 1892), aside from the contemporary art scattered about – including some wonderful Aboriginal pieces. Breakfast is served in a sunny conservatory.

Terrace Central B&B Hotel B&B $$
(☎9335 6600; www.terracecentral.com.au; 79-85 South Tce; d $165; ❄@📶) Terrace Central may be a character-filled B&B at heart, but its larger size – there are about eight rooms here – gives it the feel of a boutique hotel. The main section is created from an 1888 bakery and an adjoined row of terraces, and

there are modern one- and two-bedroom apartments out the back. You'll find ample off-street parking – rare in Freo – and free wi-fi throughout.

Quest Harbour Village APARTMENTS **$$$**
(☎9430 3888; www.questharbourvillage.com.au; Mews Rd, Challenger Harbour; apt $223-595; ❄📶) At the end of a wharf, this attractive, two-storey, sandstone and brick block of one- to three-bedroom apartments makes the most of its nautical setting; one-bedroom units have views over the car park to the Fishing Boat Harbour, while the others directly front the marina. Downstairs the rooms are light and simple, if a little dated, and kitchens are fully equipped. Upstairs has a more spacious feel.

Bannister Suites Fremantle HOTEL **$$$**
(☎9435 1289; www.bannistersuitesfremantle.com.au; 22 Bannister St; r from $210; ❄) Modern and fresh, boutiquey Bannisters is a stylish new addition to the central city's accommodation scene. It's worth paying extra for one of the suites with the deep balconies, where you can enjoy views over the rooftops while lounging on the upmarket outdoor furniture.

Port Mill B&B B&B **$$**
(☎9433 3832; www.portmillbb.com.au; 3/17 Essex St; r $195-250) One of the most luxurious B&Bs in town, it's clearly the love child of Paris and Freo. Crafted from local limestone (built in 1862 as a mill), inside it's all modern Parisian style, with gleaming taps, contemporary French furniture and wrought-iron balconies. French doors open out to the sun-filled decks, where you can tinkle the china on your breakfast platter.

Old Firestation Backpackers HOSTEL **$**
(☎9430 5454; www.old-firestation.net; 18 Phillimore St; dm $26-28, r $70; @) The brawny firemen have long left the building, but there's still plenty of entertainment in this converted firestation: free internet, foosball, movies and a sunny courtyard. Dorms have natural light and the afternoon sea breeze fluttering in, and there's a female-only section. The hippy vibe culminates in late-night bongo- and guitar-led singalongs around the campfire; bring earplugs if you value sleep.

Backpackers Inn Fremantle HOSTEL **$**
(☎9431 7065; www.backpackersinnfreo.com.au; 11 Pakenham St; dm $23-28, s $55, d with/without bathroom $75/65; @) Large communal areas and a courtyard are the hallmark of this backpackers, housed in a gold rush-era heritage building in the central city. Rooms are high-ceilinged, bright and clean. Flicks are shown on a mini cinema screen.

Pirates HOSTEL **$**
(☎9335 6635; piratesbackpackers@westnet.com.au; 11 Essex St; dm $23-25, r $63; @) This cosy, sun- and fun-filled hostel in the thick of the Freo action is a top spot to socialise. Rooms are small and reasonably basic, but the bathrooms are fresh and clean. The kitchen area is well equipped, there's a shady courtyard and eye-catching marine murals remind you that an ocean swim is minutes away.

Fremantle Colonial Accommodation APARTMENTS **$$**
(☎9430 6568; www.fremantlecolonialaccommodation.com.au; 215 High St; d from $150; ❄@) Rambling two-storey terrace or historic prison cottage? Whichever you choose, both embrace the colonial theme with gusto. White-painted wrought-iron bed frames, floral quilt covers and dusty-pink walls open out onto lace-work balconies. The complex was for sale when we visited; we're hoping it remains a going concern.

Number Six APARTMENTS **$**
(☎9299 7107; www.numbersix.com.au; studio/1-bedroom apt from $75/130; ❄) Has self-contained and stylish studios, apartments and houses available for overnight to long-term stays in great locations around Freo.

Woodman Point Holiday Park CAMPGROUND **$**
(☎9434 1433; www.aspenparks.com.au; 132 Cockburn Rd, Munster; site for 2 people $41, d $118-253; ❄@🏊) A particularly pleasant spot, 10km south of Fremantle. It's usually quiet, and its location makes it feel more summer beach holiday than outer-Freo staging post.

Coogee Beach Holiday Park CARAVAN PARK **$$**
(☎9418 1810; www.aspenparks.com.au; 3 Powell Rd, off Cockburn Rd, Coogee Beach; d $102-172; ❄) There are no camp sites, only paved caravan spaces and a range of cabins, motel units and chalets at this large holiday park. It's popular with young families, and has a tennis court and cafe.

Pier 21 APARTMENTS **$$$**
(☎9336 2555; www.pier21.com.au; 9 John St, North Fremantle; apt from $215; ❄@🏊) Pier 21 is in a tucked-away spot on the riverside in North Freo. It's more like a motel than you'd expect for the price but there's a tennis court, pool and spa.

Eating

Although it doesn't have Perth's variety of fine-dining places (or thankfully, Perth's prices), eating and drinking your way around town are two of the great pleasures of Freo. The main areas to browse before you graze are around the town centre, Fishing Boat Harbour and East Freo's George St and riverbank. People-watching from outdoor tables on South Tce is a legitimate lifestyle choice. The Fremantle Markets are a good place to stock up on fruit and other picnic items.

CITY CENTRE

Maya INDIAN $$
(9335 2796; www.mayarestaurant.com.au; 77 Market St; mains $17-28; dinner Tue-Sun, lunch Fri) Maya's white tablecloths and wooden chairs signal classic style without the pomp. Its well-executed meals have made it a popular local spot for years, earning it the reputation of WA's best Indian restaurant. Try a regional banquet meal: Punjabi, Delhi or Bombay.

Moore & Moore CAFE $
(46 Henry St; mains $8-22; 8am-4pm;) An urban-chic cafe that spills into the adjoining art gallery and overflows into a flagstoned courtyard. Great coffee, good cooked breakfasts (including half serves for undersized appetites), pastries, wraps, free wi-fi.

Cafe 55 VIETNAMESE $
(55 High St; mains $7-11; 7.30am-3pm Mon-Fri, 9am-3pm Sat) Vietnamese food with a Freo feel, this bright cafe's fragrant soups – *pho, bun bo Hue* (spicy beef noodle soup) and laksa – are fantastic. Plus there are baguettes just like you'd get in the former French colony.

Juicy Beetroot VEGETARIAN $
(off 132 High St; mains $9-13; 10am-4pm Mon-Fri;) This popular meat-free zone serves tasty vego and vegan dishes of the wholefood variety (tofu burgers, curries etc), and zingy fresh juices. Look past the bad New Age art to the posters advertising Freo's more eclectic events. It's tucked up an alley off High St, with outdoor seating.

Gino's CAFE $
(www.ginoscafe.com.au; 1 South Tce; mains $13-17; breakfast, lunch & dinner;) Old-school Gino's is Freo's most famous cafe, and while it's become a tourist attraction in its own right, the locals still treat it as their second living room, only with better coffee. The potbellied Italian men, artsy types and other assorted regulars know the drill, but for the uninitiated, you need to order and pay at the till and collect your own coffee from the counter. Don't expect anyone to explain this to you.

Kakulas Sister DELI $
(29-31 Market St) This provedore – packed with nuts, quince paste and Italian rocket seeds – is a cook's dream, and an excellent spot to stock up on energy-filled snacks. If you've been to Kakulas Bros in Northbridge, you'll know the deal.

FISHING BOAT HARBOUR

TOP CHOICE **Little Creatures** PUB FARE $$
(www.littlecreatures.com.au; 40 Mews Rd; mains $16-34; 10am-midnight) Little Creatures is classic Freo: harbour views, fantastic brews (made on the premises) and excellent food. In a cavernous converted boatshed overlooking the harbour, it can get chaotic at times, but the home-brewed ales and wood-fired pizzas are well worth the wait. More substantial mains include kangaroo, scotch fillets or the ever-popular fish and chips. No bookings.

Mussel Bar SEAFOOD $$
(9433 1800; www.musselbar.com.au; 42 Mews Rd, Fishing Boat Harbour; mains $26-31; breakfast Sun, lunch & dinner daily) For a more formal Freo experience, Mussel Bar's large glass windows afford romantic views of the glittering harbour. Mussels, of course, are the go (including traditional *moule marinieres*) or you can knock back fresh oysters with a sunset glass of bubbly. The seafood-based pastas are excellent.

Cicerello's FISH AND CHIPS $
(www.cicerellos.com.au; 44 Mews Rd; mains $11-29; 9am-9pm) This busy fish and chippery has been around since 1903 and remains a quintessential Freo experience. Leave the kids staring at the large aquariums (filled with living coral, bright fish, an octopus and a hemmed-in shark – there are more in the toilets), choose your fish and chips, then pick a spot out on the boardwalk and soak up the sun – just watch those seagulls.

EAST & NORTH FREMANTLE

Harvest MODERN AUSTRALIAN $$
(9336 1831; www.harvestrestaurant.net.au; 1 Harvest Rd, North Fremantle; mains $32-39; breakfast & lunch Fri-Sun, dinner Tue-Sun) First you'll find a green-painted cottage, complete with picket fence, next to some fields. Swing

through the heavy, fuchsia-painted metal doors and into the dark-wood dining room lined with artworks and curios. Then settle down to comforting Mod Oz dishes cooked with a dash of panache.

Red Herring SEAFOOD $$
(☎9339 1611; www.redherring.com.au; 26 Riverside Rd, East Fremantle; mains $30-46; ⏰breakfast Sun, lunch & dinner daily) Set out on a pier with picture windows overlooking the Swan River, this restaurant offers (mainly) seafood with a view. Fresh and simple is the key, with Asian touches to some dishes. Book well ahead.

George St Bistro GERMAN $$
(☎9339 6352; 73 George St, East Fremantle; lunch $15-35, dinner $29-34; ⏰lunch Tue-Sun, dinner Wed-Sat) George St Bistro is something of a secret, nestled along quiet, leafy George St. Contemporary art takes pride of place along the walls, and the banquette and small tables lend a European feel.

Drinking & Entertainment

Most of Fremantle's big pubs are lined up along South Tce and there are some character-filled old taverns on High St. Freo's pubs have long been incubators for rock kids, turning out hairy progeny like the John Butler Trio and Eskimo Joe.

Little Creatures MICROBREWERY
(www.littlecreatures.com.au; 40 Mews Rd, Fishing Boat Harbour; mains $16-34; ⏰10am-midnight) In a huge old boatshed by the harbour, this brewery's four beers – Pale Ale, Pilsner, Rogers and Bright Ale – are a great source of WA pride. You can admire the brewery vats and spot bald patches from the mezzanine or almost nuzzle the boats from the boardwalk out the back. Creatures Loft (open Thursday to Sunday) is a lounge bar with regular live entertainment (bands, films) and a great selection of international beers and wine to accompany the view.

Norfolk Hotel PUB
(www.norfolkhotel.com.au; 47 South Tce; ⏰11am-midnight Mon-Sat, 11am-10pm Sun) Slow down to the Freo pace and take your time over one of the many beers on tap at this 1887 pub – Monteiths, Moo Brew, James Squire. The limestone courtyard, with the sun streaking in through the elms and eucalypts, is downright soporific sometimes. There's a big sports screen tucked around the side so you don't miss anything.

Monk MICROBREWERY
(www.themonk.com.au; 33 South Tce; ⏰11.30am-late) Park yourself at the voyeuristic front terrace or in the chic interior, partly fashioned from recycled railway sleepers, and enjoy the Monk's own brews (kolsch, mild, wheat, porter, rauch, pale ale) or a slap-up meal. It was formerly called the Mad Monk, but perhaps they were concerned about stealing the nickname of federal Opposition leader Tony Abbott.

Fly by Night Musicians Club CLUB, MUSIC
(www.flybynight.org; Parry St) Variety is the key at Fly by Night, a not-for-profit club that's been run by musos for musos for years. All kinds perform here, and many local bands made a start here. It's opposite the car park below the old Fremantle Prison.

Kulcha NIGHTCLUB, MUSIC
(☎9336 4544; www.kulcha.com.au; 1st fl, 13 South Tce) World music of all sorts is the focus here. At the time we researched the line-up included flamenco, belly-dancing, sitar, blues, Indonesian tribal music, salsa classes, an Indian music workshop and a Jamaican reggae party. Book ahead.

X-Wray Cafe CAFE, MUSIC
(3-13 Essex St) There's something on every night (live jazz, rock, open piano) at this hipster hang-out, comprising a smallish indoor area and a large canvas-covered terrace. Light meals are available ($13 to $28).

Mojo's PUB, MUSIC
(www.mojosbar.com.au; 237 Queen Victoria St, North Fremantle; ⏰7pm-late) Good old Mojo's is one of Freo's longstanding live music pubs – a real stalwart. Local and national bands (mainly Australian rock and roll and indie) and DJs play at this small venue, and there's a sociable beer garden out the back. First Friday of the month is reggae night; every Monday is open-mic night.

Sail & Anchor PUB, MUSIC
(www.sailandanchor.com.au; 64 South Tce; ⏰11am-midnight Mon-Sat, 11am-10pm Sun) Built in 1854, this Fremantle landmark has been impressively restored to recall much of its former glory. Downstairs is big and beer focused; it's more sedate upstairs, where there's a verandah and singer-songwriter nights on Wednesdays.

Metropolis Fremantle CLUB, MUSIC
(www.metropolisfremantle.com.au; 58 South Tce) A great space to watch a gig and a proper nightclub on the weekends. International

TOP 10 WA SONGS

If you're looking for a soundtrack for your trip, download these WA-centric songs to your MP3 player.

» **Empire of the Sun** – *Standing on the Shore* (2009) That's Lancelin in the video clip.

» **The Waifs** – *sundirtwater* (2006) Sun, dirt and water? Sounds like Broome to me.

» **The Jayco Brothers** – *Town Hall* (2006) Alt-country paean to the Fremantle Town Hall.

» **The Sleepy Jackson** – *You Won't Bring People Down in My Town* (2006) We presume that's Luke Steele's hometown of Perth?

» **Eskimo Joe** – *From the Sea* (2003) The hit from their Fremantle-inspired *A Song Is A City* album.

» **Kasey Chambers** – *Nullarbor Song* (2001) About the treeless plain where 'dingoes howl just to break the silence'.

» **Pavement** – *I Love Perth* (1996) American indie royalty's love letter to the Perth noise scene.

» **Midnight Oil** – *Blue Sky Mine* (1990) Ode to the Wittenoom blue asbestos mine in the Pilbara.

» **Midnight Oil** – *Warakurna* (1987) Set in the WA outback.

» **The Triffids** – *Wide Open Road* (1986) Homage to the Nullarbor-crossing Eyre Hwy.

and popular Australian bands and DJs perform here.

Left Bank PUB, MUSIC
(www.leftbank.com.au; 15 Riverside Rd, East Fremantle; ⏲7am-midnight Mon-Sat, 7am-10pm Sun) You could do a lot worse than gazing over the river, beer in hand, from this Edwardian inn. There's live music several nights of the week.

Newport Hotel PUB, MUSIC
(www.thenewport.com; 2 South Tce; ⏲noon-midnight Mon-Sat, noon-10pm Sun) Local bands play Saturdays and Sundays, with DJs other nights.

Swan Hotel PUB, MUSIC
(www.swanloungecafe.com; 201 Queen Victoria St, North Fremantle; ⏲11am-10pm Mon, to midnight Tue-Sat, noon-10pm Sun) DJs and bands perform in the basement of this rough-edged pub.

Luna on SX CINEMA
(www.lunapalace.com.au; Essex St) Art-house films; set back in a lane between Essex and Norfolk Sts.

Hoyts CINEMA
(www.hoyts.com.au); Millennium (Collie St); Queensgate (William St) Blockbusters.

Shopping

The bottom end of High St is the place for interesting and quirky shopping. Fashion stores run along Market St, towards the train station. Queen Victoria St in North Fremantle is the place to go for antiques. And don't forget Fremantle Markets for clothes, souvenirs and knick-knacks.

TOP CHOICE **Japingka** INDIGENOUS ART
(www.japingka.com.au; 47 High St; ⏲10am-5.30pm Mon-Fri, noon-5pm Sat & Sun) An excellent gallery specialising in Aboriginal fine art, from WA and beyond. Purchases come complete with extensive notes about the works and the artists that painted them.

Found ART
(www.fac.org.au; 1 Finnerty St; ⏲10am-5pm) The Fremantle Arts Centre shop stocks an inspiring range of WA art and craft.

Love in Tokyo CLOTHING
(www.loveintokyo.com.au; 61-63 High St) Local designer turning out gorgeously fashioned fabrics for women.

New Edition BOOKSTORE
(www.newedition.com.au; 82 High St; ⏲8.30am-9.30pm) A bookworm's dream with comfy armchairs for browsing, this excellent, well-stocked bookshop carries fiction as well as a range of local titles.

Elizabeth's Bookshop BOOKSTORES
(www.elizabethsbookshop.com.au); Fremantle (High St Mall); South Terrace (8 South Tce); Warehouse (23 Queen Victoria St) One of Aus-

tralia's biggest second-hand booksellers, with a staggering range. Elizabeth's is a Fremantle institution.

Record Finder MUSIC STORE
(87 High St) A treasure trove of old vinyl, including rarities and collectables.

Bodkin's Bootery SHOES
(www.bodkinsbootery.com; 72 High St) Men's and women's boots and hats.

Chart & Map Shop MAPS
(www.chartandmapshop.com.au; 14 Collie St) Great range of maps and travel guides.

Bill Campbell Secondhand Book Seller BOOKSTORE
(48 High St; ⏲10am-pm Mon-Fri, noon-5pm Sat & Sun) For those out-of-print Penguin classics you always meant to read.

Remedy GIFTS
(☎9431 7080; 95 High St) An eclectic collection of goodies, including kids' clothes, adults' tees, gifts and the Aesop range of toiletries.

Mills Records MUSIC STORE
(www.mills.com.au; 22 Adelaide St) Music, including some rarities, and tickets.

E Shed Markets MARKET
(www.eshedmarkets.com.au; Victoria Quay; ⏲9am-5pm, food court until 8pm; wi-fi) An old wharf shed with market stalls, a food court, cafes, bars and free wi-fi.

Information

For free wi-fi, try Gino's cafe, E Shed Markets or the library.

Fremantle City Library (☎9432 9766; www.frelibrary.wordpress.com; Town Hall, Kings Sq; ⏲9.30am-5.30pm Mon, Fri & Sat, 9.30am-8pm Tue-Thu; wi-fi) Free wi-fi and internet terminals.

Fremantle Hospital (☎9431 3333; www.fhhs.health.wa.gov.au; Alma St)

Post Office (☎13 13 18; 152 High St; ⏲8am-5pm Mon-Fri, 8am-1pm Sat)

TravelLounge (☎9335 8776; www.thetravellounge.com.au; 16 Market St; internet per hr $5) Private agency offering information, bookings and internet terminals.

Visitor Centre (☎9431 7878; www.fremantle.wa.com.au; Town Hall, Kings Sq; ⏲9am-5pm Mon-Fri, 10am-3pm Sat, 11.30am-2.30pm Sun) Helpful centre offering free maps and brochures, and bookings for accommodation, tours and hire cars. Check the website for what's on.

Getting There & Around

Fremantle sits within Zone 2 of the Perth public transport system (Transperth) and is only 30 minutes away by train. There are numerous buses between Perth's city centre and Fremantle, including routes 103, 106, 107, 111 and 158. For more details on Transperth and on the Connect airport shuttle, see p75.

Another very pleasant way to get here from Perth is by the 1¼-hour river cruise run by Captain Cook Cruises; see p61 for details.

There are numerous one-way streets and parking meters in Freo. It's easy enough to travel by foot or on the free CAT bus service, which takes in all the major sites on a continuous loop every 10 minutes from 7.30am to 6.30pm on weekdays, until 9pm on Fridays and 10am to 6.30pm on the weekend.

Around Perth

Includes »

Best Places to Eat

- » RiverBank Estate (p104)
- » Black Swan (p104)
- » Loose Box (p102)
- » Cervantes Country Club (p115)
- » Cafe Yasou (p108)

Best Places to Stay

- » Faversham House (p106)
- » Amble Inn (p114)
- » Kookaburra Dream (p106)
- » Rottnest Island Authority Cottages (p93)
- » Lancelin Lodge YHA (p113)

Why Go?

Although Western Australia (WA) is huge, you don't have to travel too far from the capital to treat yourself to a tantalising taste of what the state has to offer. A day trip could see you frolicking with wild dolphins, snorkelling with sea lions, scooping up brilliant-blue crabs or spotting bilbies in the bush. Active types can find themselves canoeing, rafting, surfing, windsurfing, sandboarding, diving, skydiving and ballooning. Those who prefer pursuits less likely to ruffle one's hair can tour vineyards, settle down for a culinary feast or explore historic towns classified by the National Trust.

We've designed this chapter so that the main headings can be tackled as day trips, or better still, overnighters. If you're heading on a longer trip, whether north, south or east, you'll find your first stops within these pages.

When to Go

Mandurah

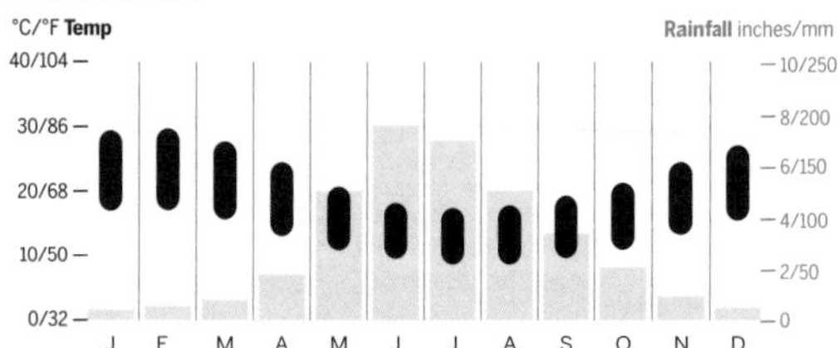

March
Good beach weather and a good time to spot thrombolites in Lake Clifton.

August
Wildflowers start to bloom, the Avon River Festival, and the Toodyay Festival of Food.

October
More wildflowers, Penguin Island reopens to visitors, and the York Jazz & Soul Festival.

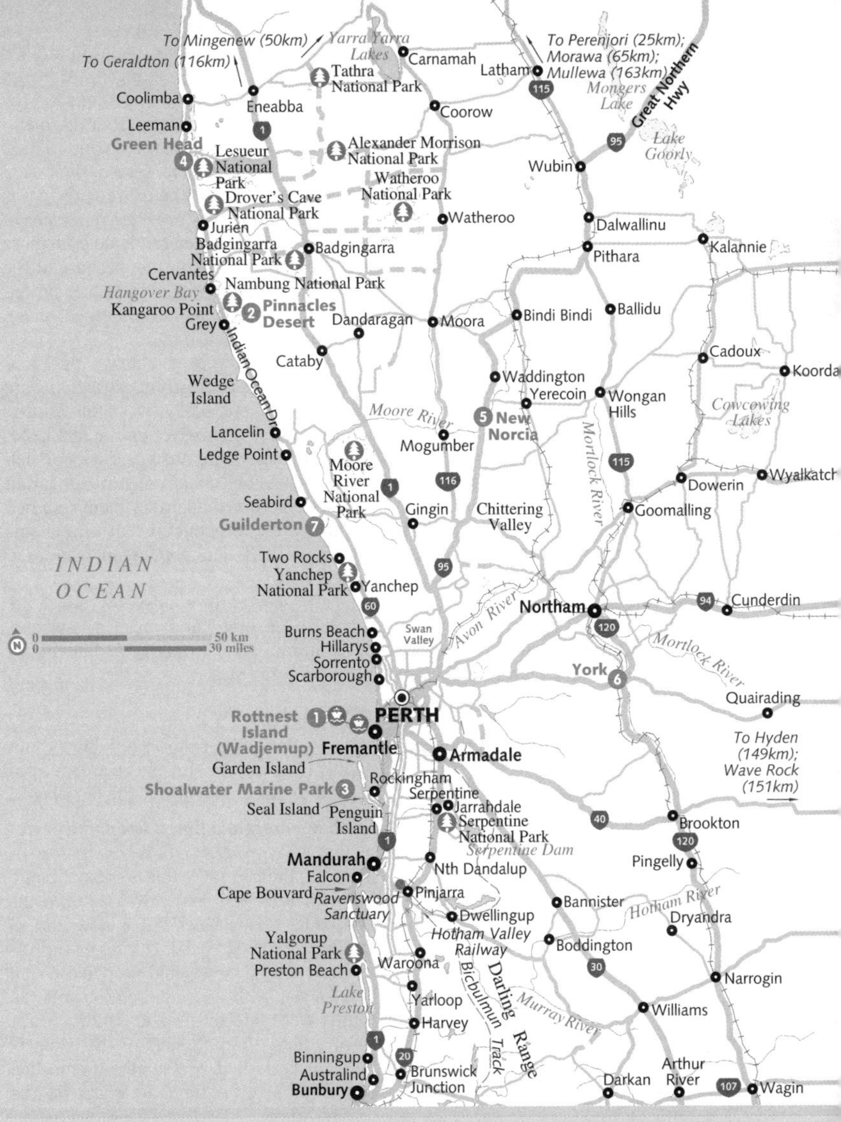

Around Perth Highlights

1. Cycle your way to a private slice of coastal paradise on **Rottnest Island** (Wadjemup; p90), then spend the afternoon swimming, sunning and snorkelling

2. Enjoy a sublime sunset over the other-worldly **Pinnacles Desert** (p114)

3. Get chipper with Flipper, palling about with scores of wild dolphins in **Shoalwater Marine Park** (p95) off Rockingham

4. Splash about with sea lions at **Green Head** (p116)

5. Explore the intriguing monastery town of **New Norcia** (p110)

6. Wander the quaint, atmospheric streets of historic **York** (p106)

7. Soothe your soul on the white sands of chilled out **Guilderton** (p112)

ROTTNEST ISLAND (WADJEMUP)

POP 475

'Rotto' has long been the family holiday playground of choice for Perth locals. Although it's only about 19km offshore from Fremantle, this car-free, off-the-grid slice of paradise, ringed by secluded beaches and bays, feels a million miles from the metropolis.

Cycling around the 11km-long, 4.5km-wide car-free island is a real pleasure; just ride around and pick your own bit of beach to spend the day on. You're bound to spot quokkas on your journey. These are the island's only native land mammals, but you might also spot New Zealand fur seals splashing around off magical **West End**; dolphins; and, in season, whales. King skinks are common, sunning themselves on the roads until you draw near – and then they're just as likely to scuttle into the path of your bike as they are to scuttle in the opposite direction.

If you fancy further diversions, snorkelling, fishing, surfing and diving are all excellent on the island. In fact, there's not a lot to do here that's not outdoors, so you're better off postponing your day trip if the weather is bad. It can be unpleasant when the wind really kicks up.

Rotto is also the site of annual school leavers' and end-of-uni-exams parties, a time when the island is overrun by kids 'getting blotto on Rotto'. Depending on your age, it's either going to be the best time you've ever had or the worst – check the calendar before proceeding.

History

Originally called Wadjemup (place across the water), Wadjuk oral history recalls the island being joined to the mainland before being cut off by rising waters. Modern scientists date that occurrence to before 6500 years ago, making these memories some of the world's oldest. Archaeological finds suggest that the island was inhabited 30,000 years ago, but not after it was separated from the mainland.

Dutch explorer Willem de Vlamingh claimed discovery of the island in 1696 and named it Rotte-nest ('rat's nest', in Dutch) because of the king-sized 'rats' (which were actually quokkas) he saw there.

From 1838 it was used as a prison for Aboriginal men and boys from all around the state. At least 3670 people were incarcerated here, in harsh conditions, with around 370 dying (at least five were hanged). Although there were no new prisoners after 1903 (by which time holiday-makers from the mainland had already discovered the island), some existing prisoners served their sentences until 1931. Even before the prison was built, Wadjemup was considered a 'place of the spirits', and it's been rendered even more sacred to Indigenous people because of the hundreds of their people, including prominent resistance leaders, who died there. Many avoid it to this day.

During WWI, approximately a thousand men of German or Austrian extraction were incarcerated here, their wives and children left to fend for themselves on the mainland. Ironically most of the 'Austrians' were actually Croats who objected to Austro-Hungarian rule of their homeland. Internment resumed during WWII, although at that time it was mainly WA's Italian population who were imprisoned.

There's currently a push to return the island to its original name. One suggested compromise is to adopt a dual name, Wadjemup/Rottnest.

Sights

Most of Rottnest's historic buildings, built mainly by Aboriginal prisoners, are grouped around Thomson Bay where the ferry lands.

Quod & Aboriginal Burial Ground HISTORIC SITE

(Kitson St) Built in 1864, this octagonal building with a central courtyard was once the Aboriginal prison block but is now part of the Rottnest Lodge hotel. During its time as a prison, several men would sleep in each 3m by 1.7m cell, with no sanitation (most of the deaths were due to disease). Unless you're staying here, the only part of the complex that can be visited is a small whitewashed chapel to the left of the main entrance. The cells have been redeveloped into hotel rooms.

Immediately adjacent to the Quod is a wooded area where hundreds of Aboriginal prisoners are buried in unmarked graves. Until relatively recently, this area was used as a camping ground but it's now fenced off with signs asking visitors to show respect to what is considered a sacred site. Plans are underway to convert the area into a memorial, in consultation with Aboriginal elders.

Rottnest Museum MUSEUM

(Kitson St; admission by gold coin donation; ⌚11am-3.30pm) Housed in the old hay-store build-

QUOKKAS

These cute little docile bundles of fur have suffered a number of indignities over the years. First Willem de Vlamingh's crew mistook them for rats as big as cats. Then the British settlers misheard and mangled their name (the Noongar word was probably *quak-a* or *gwaga*). But worst of all, a cruel trend of 'quokka soccer' by sadistic louts in the 1990s saw many kicked to death before a $10,000 fine was imposed; occasional cases are still reported.

These marsupials of the macropod family (relatives of kangaroos and wallabies) were once found throughout the southwest but are now confined to forest on the mainland and a population of 8000 to 10,000 on Rottnest Island. You will see plenty of them during your visit. Don't be surprised if one comes up to you looking for a titbit (don't oblige them, as human food isn't good for them) – many are almost tame, or, at least, fearless.

ing, this little museum tells the island's natural and human history, warts and all, including dark tales of shipwrecks and incarceration.

FREE **Salt Store** HISTORIC BUILDING
(Colebatch Ave) A photographic exhibition in this 19th-century building looks at a different chapter of local history: when the island's salt lakes provided all of WA's salt (between 1838 and 1950).

Vlamingh's Lookout LOOKOUT
(View Hill, off Digby Dr) Not far away from Thomson Bay (go up past the old European cemetery), this unsigned vantage point offers panoramic views of the island, including its salt lakes.

Activities

Beaches SWIMMING
Most visitors come for Rottnest's beaches and aquatic activities. The **Basin** is the most popular beach for family-friendly swimming as it's protected by a ring of reefs. Other popular spots are **Longreach Bay** and **Geordie Bay**, though there are many smaller secluded beaches such as **Little Parakeet Bay**.

Reefs & Wrecks SNORKELLING, DIVING
Excellent visibility in the temperate waters, coral reefs and shipwrecks makes Rottnest a top spot for **scuba diving** and **snorkelling**. There are **snorkel trails** with underwater plaques at **Little Salmon Bay** and **Parker Point**. The **Basin**, **Little Parakeet Bay**, **Longreach Bay**, **Geordie Bay** are also good. Rottnest Island Bike Hire (p94) has masks, snorkels and fins available, as well as kayaks.

Over a dozen boats have come a cropper on Rottnest's reefs, the earliest significant one being the schooner *Transit* in 1842. Marker plaques around the island tell the sad tales of how and when the ships sank. The only wreck that is accessible to snorkellers without a boat is at **Thomson Bay**. The Australasian Diving Academy (p58) takes diving trips to some of the wrecks.

Surfing SURFING
The best surf breaks are at **Strickland**, **Salmon** and **Stark Bays**, towards the western end of the island. Boards can be hired at Rottnest Island Bike Hire (see p94).

Birds BIRDWATCHING
Rottnest is ideal for twitchers because of the varied habitats: coast, lakes, swamps, heath, woodlands and settlements. Coastal birds include pelicans; gannets; cormorants; bar-tailed godwits; whimbrels; fairy, bridled and crested terns; oystercatchers; and majestic ospreys. For more, grab a copy of *A Bird's Eye View of Rottnest Island* from the visitor centre.

Tours

Check the times online, at the Salt Store or call the visitor centre.

FREE **Rottnest Voluntary Guides** WALKING
(☎9372 9757; www.rvga.asn.au) Free, themed walks leave from the Salt Store daily: History; Reefs, Wrecks & Daring Sailors; Vlamingh Lookout & Salt Lakes; and the Quokka Walk. They also run tours of Wadjemup Lighthouse (adult/child $7/3) and Oliver Hill Gun & Tunnels (adult/child $7/3); you'll need to make your own way there for the last two.

Oliver Hill Train & Tour TRAIN
(www.rottnestisland.com; adult/child $26/15) The Oliver Hill gun battery was built in the 1930s and played a major role in the defence of the WA coastline and Fremantle harbour. This trip takes you by train to

Rottnest Island (Wadjemup)

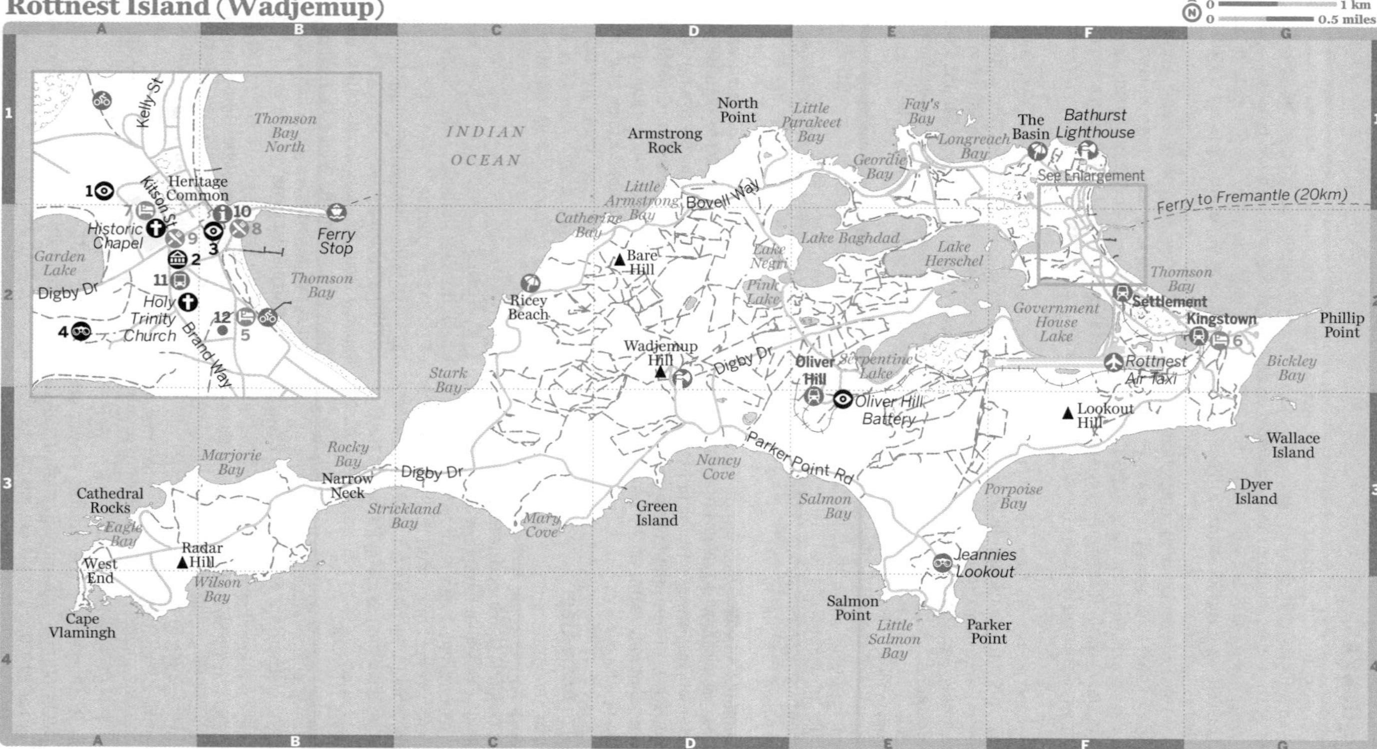

Rottnest Island

Sights

1 Aboriginal Burial Ground A1
Quod ..... (see 7)
2 Rottnest Museum A2
3 Salt Store B2
4 Vlamingh's Lookout A2

Sleeping

5 Hotel Rottnest B2
6 Kingston Barracks Youth Hostel G2
7 Rottnest Lodge A2

Eating

8 Aristos B2
Hotel Rottnest ..... (see 5)
Marlins ..... (see 7)
9 Rottnest Bakery A2

Information

10 Visitor Centre B2

Transport

11 Main Bus Stop A2
12 Rottnest Island Bike Hire B2

Oliver Hill (departing from the train station twice daily) and includes the Gun & Tunnels tour above.

Discovery Coach Tour COACH
(www.rottnestisland.com; adult/child $33/16) Leaves from Thomson Bay three times daily (book at the visitor centre); includes a commentary and a stop at West End.

Rottnest Adventure Tour BOAT
(www.rottnestexpress.com.au; adult/child $50/25) Ninety-minute cruises around the coast with a special emphasis on spotting wildlife, including whales in season. Packages available ex Perth (adult/child $130/65) and Fremantle ($115/57).

Rottnest Air Taxi SCENIC FLIGHT
(☎9292 5027; www.rottnest.de) Ten-minute joy flights over the island ($35).

Sleeping

Rotto is wildly popular in summer and school holidays, when accommodation is booked out months in advance. Prices can rise steeply at these times – low-season rates are given here.

Rottnest Island Authority Cottages RENTAL HOUSES $$
(☎9432 9111; www.rottnestisland.com; cottages $117-214) There are more than 250 villas and cottages for rent around the island. Some have magnificent beachfront positions and are palatial; others are more like beach shacks. Sizes range from four to eight beds. Prices rise by around $40 for Friday and Saturday nights, and they shoot up around $100 in peak season.

Hotel Rottnest HOTEL $$$
(☎9292 5011; www.hotelrottnest.com.au; 1 Bedford Ave; r $270-320; ❄) Based around the former summer holiday pad for the state's governors, which was built in 1864, the former Quokka Arms has been completely transformed by a stylish renovation. The whiter-than-white rooms are smart and modern, if a little pricy for what's offered – but that's island living for you. Some have beautiful sea views.

Rottnest Lodge HOTEL $$
(☎9292 5161; www.rottnestlodge.com.au; Kitson St; r $205-310; 🏊) It's claimed that there are ghosts in this comfortable complex, which is based around the former Quod and boys' reformatory school. If that worries you, ask for one of the cheery rooms in the new section, which look onto a salt lake.

Allison Tentland CAMPGROUND $
(☎9432 9111; www.rottnestisland.com; Thomson Bay; site per person $10) Camping on the island is restricted to this leafy camping ground, which has barbecues. Be vigilant about your belongings, especially your food – quokkas have been known to help themselves.

Kingston Barracks Youth Hostel HOSTEL $
(☎9432 9111; www.rottnestisland.com; dm/f $49/99) This hostel is located in old army barracks that still have a rather institutional feel, and few facilities. Check in at the visitor centre before you make the 1.8km walk, bike or bus trip to Kingston.

Eating & Drinking

Most visitors to Rotto self-cater. The general store is like a small supermarket (and also stocks liquor), but if you're staying a while, you're better to bring supplies with you. All of the following are in Thomson Bay.

Hotel Rottnest PUB $$
(www.hotelrottnest.com.au; 1 Bedford Ave; mains $18-27; ⏰lunch & dinner) It's hard to imagine

a more inviting place for a sunset Sauvignon Blanc than the astroturf 'lawn' of this newly remodelled waterfront hotel. The old building has had a big glass pavilion grafted onto it, creating a big, open, inviting space. Bistro-style food and pizza is served at quite reasonable rates, given the location and ambience. Bands play here during summer.

Aristos SEAFOOD **$$**
(www.aristosrottnest.com.au; Colebatch Ave; mains $16-30; ⏲lunch & dinner) An upmarket option for fish and chips, burgers, ice cream or excellent coffee, right on the waterfront near the main jetty. Grab a table on the deck for absolute sea views.

Rottnest Bakery BAKERY **$**
(Malley St; mains $5-12) Traditional Aussie bakery, with pies, soup and ice cream.

Marlins RESTAURANT **$$**
(Rottnest Lodge, Kitson St; mains $26-36; ⏲lunch & dinner) Does buffet lunches for tour groups, as well as a crowd-pleasing menu of pub-style evening meals – fish and chips, curry, pasta, fish, steak etc.

Information

At the Thomson Bay settlement, behind the main jetty, there's a shopping area with ATMs.

Ranger (☎9372 9788)

Visitor centre (www.rottnestisland.com); Thomson Bay (☎9372 9732; ⏲7.30am-5pm Sat-Thu, 7.30am-7pm Fri, extended in summer); Fremantle (☎9432 9300; E Shed, Victoria Quay) The Thomson Bay office, at the end of the main jetty, handles check-ins for all the island authority's accommodation. There's a bookings counter at the Fremantle office, near where the ferry departs.

Getting There & Away

Air

Rottnest Air-Taxi (☎9292 5027; www.rottnest.de) Flies from Jandakot airport in four-seater (one-way/same-day return/extended return $220/300/350) or six-seater planes (one-way/same-day return/extended return $300/400/480). Prices include up to three passengers in the four-seater and five passengers in the six-seater.

Boat

Rottnest Express (☎1300 467 688; www.rottnestexpress.com.au); Fremantle (☎9335 6406; C Shed, Victoria Quay; adult/child $60/36); Northport (⏲9430 4036; 1 Emma Pl, Rous Head, North Fremantle; adult/child $60/36); Perth (☎9421 5899; Pier 2, Barrack St Jetty; adult/child $80/46) The prices listed here are for return day trips and include the island admission fee; add $9 for an extended return. Ferry schedules are seasonal, though those listed here are roughly the minimum: Perth (1¾ hours, twice daily), Fremantle (30 minutes, five times daily) and North Fremantle (30 minutes, three times daily). Secure parking is available at Northport; the Perth and Fremantle departure points are handy to train stations. Various packages are available, which can add bike hire, snorkelling equipment, meals and tours. Rottnest Express also runs the **Mega Blast** (adult/child $69/36), a speed-boat service for thrill seekers, which departs Fremantle daily from September to May.

Rottnest Fast Ferries (☎9246 1039; www.rottnestfastferries.com.au; adult/child $82/43) Departs from Hillarys Boat Harbour (40 minutes; three times daily); add $3 for an extended return. Packages also available.

Getting Around

BIKE Bicycles are the time-honoured way of getting around the island. Rottnest is just big enough (and with enough hills) to make a day's ride good exercise.

Rottnest Island Bike Hire (☎9292 5105; www.rottnestisland.com; cnr Bedford Ave & Welch Way; single speed per 1/2/3/4/5 days $20/31/40/48/56, multigear per 1/2/3/4/5 days $27/43/54/65/76; ⏲8.30am-4pm, to 5.30pm in summer) is reputedly the biggest of its kind in the southern hemisphere. Bikes can be booked in advance online or on arrival. A $25 bond is required if you don't have photo ID. They're the only operator to have a pick-up service if you're unable to return to the office due to injury or damage to the bike.

The ferry companies also hire bikes. Rottnest Express has them waiting as you get off the boat (per 1/2/3 days $28/41/56). They don't provide locks but neither do they check them off when you return them. Bikes don't tend to be stolen per se (it would be hard to smuggle them off the island without the ferry companies noticing), but it's not unheard of for an unlocked bike to be grabbed and used by someone else.

BUS A free shuttle runs between Thomson Bay, the main accommodation areas and the airport, departing roughly every 35 minutes, with the last bus at 7pm. The Bayseeker (day pass adult/child $13/5.50) is a hop-on, hop-off service that does an hourly loop around the island with the first bus at 8.30am and the last at 3.30pm. Between Geordie Bay and Thomson Bay, it's free.

ROCKINGHAM

POP 100,000

Not as rocking as the name implies, this seaside city has some nice beaches and a noticeable British expat community. These characteristics probably wouldn't lure travellers 46km south from central Perth if it weren't for the Shoalwater Islands Marine Park, where you can observe dolphins, sea lions and penguins in the wild.

Rockingham was founded in 1872 as a port, although this function was taken over by Fremantle in the 1890s. There's still a substantial industrial complex to the north, at Kwinana.

Most places of interest are stretched along Rockingham Beach.

Sights & Activities

Shoalwater Islands Marine Park NATURE RESERVE

Just a few minutes' paddle, swim or boat ride from the mainland is tiny, fabulous and strictly protected **Penguin Island**. Home to about 600 breeding pairs of seriously cute little penguins, and several thousand pairs of ground-nesting and in-your-face silver gulls, the island also has an informal and informative feeding centre (for long-term injured or orphaned penguins), boardwalks, swimming beaches and picnic tables for day visitors. It's lovely, low-key and very ecoconscious; no food is sold on the island, toilets are composting, and the island is closed for nesting from June to mid-September. Apart from birdwatching (pied cormorants, pelicans, crested and bridled terns, oystercatchers), you can swim and snorkel in the crystal-clear waters. Nearby **Seal Island** is home to a colony of Australian sea lions and off-limits to the public. The naval base of Garden Island can be reached only by private boat.

The **Penguin Island ferry** (Mersey Point Jetty; ferry $12; hourly 9am-3pm Sep-May) is run by Rockingham Wild Encounters (p95). Tickets that combine the ferry with entry to the penguin feeding at the island's discovery centre (adult/child $18/15) are available.

At low tide it's possible to wade the few hundred metres to the island across the sandbar. However, take heed of warning signs as people have drowned here after being washed off the bar during strong winds and high tides.

West Coast Dive Park DIVING

(www.westcoastdivepark.com; permit per day/week $25/50) Diving within the marine park became even more interesting after the sinking of the *Saxon Ranger*, a supposedly jinxed 400-tonne fishing vessel. Permits to dive at this site are available from the visitor centre. **Bell Scuba** (9527 9211; www.bellscuba.com.au; 43 Rockingham Beach Rd) leads expeditions to this and the wrecks of three other boats, two planes and various reefs in the vicinity.

Tours

Rockingham Wild Encounters WILDLIFE

(9591 1333; www.rockinghamwildencounters.com.au) Long-standing and laden with ecotourism awards, these guys are the only operator licensed to take people to Penguin Island, and they also run a variety of low-impact tours. The most popular is the **dolphin swim tour** (departs Val St Jetty; tour $205; 7.30am Sep-May), which lets you interact with some of the 200 wild bottlenose dolphins in the marine park. The dolphins aren't bribed with food to perform tricks but some of them will play with small groups of swimmers just for the fun of it. If you don't fancy getting wet, there are two-hour **dolphin-watch tours** (departs Val St Jetty; adult/child $65/50; 8.30am Sep-May).

There's also a 45-minute **penguin and sea lion cruise** (departs Penguin Island; adult/child $35/26; 10.15am, 11.15am & 1.15pm, Sep-May), which heads around the islands in a glass-bottomed boat. The **dolphin, penguin and sea lion combo** (Val St Jetty; adult/child $108/84; 8.30am Sep-May) combines the dolphin-watch tour and cruise with ferry transfers to Penguin Island.

Capricorn Seakayaking KAYAKING

(6267 8059; www.capricornseakayaking.com.au; $149 from Perth, Fremantle or Rockingham) Runs full-day sea-kayaking tours around Penguin and Seal Islands between November and March.

Sleeping & Eating

Beachside Apartment Hotel APARTMENTS $$

(9529 3777; www.beachsideapartment.com.au; 58 Kent St; apt $190-275;) Right on the esplanade, these apartments are spacious, sunny and secure. The block's not super-modern but there's an up-to-date feel to the decor and discounts for stays longer than a week.

Bettyblue Bistro SEAFOOD $$

(9528 4228; www.bettybluebistro.com; 3-4 The Boardwalk; mains $18-34; breakfast, lunch & dinner) The vibe at this licensed bistro is

HEADING SOUTH

The fastest and simplest route south from Central Perth is to jump on the Kwinana Fwy. Rather than visiting Rockingham and the Peel Region as separate day trips, you could turn them into a 220km loop: Perth–Rockingham–Mandurah–Pinjarra–Dwellingup–Jarrahdale–Perth. In which case, you might like to consider stopping overnight in Mandurah, as that's a lot of driving for one day.

casual, with tables that allow you to gaze straight out to sea. Serves are large.

Sunsets CAFE $$
(☎9528 1910; www.sunsets.com.au; 1-2 The Boardwalk; mains $19-32; ⏲breakfast & lunch daily, dinner Thu-Tue) Shares the same views and vibe as its neighbour, Bettyblue, and a similar menu.

Information

Visitor centre (☎9592 3464; www.rockinghamvisitorcentre.com.au; 19 Kent St; ⏲9am-5pm; @)

Getting There & Around

Rockingham sits within Zone 5 of the Perth public transport system, **Transperth** (☎13 62 13; www.transperth.wa.gov.au). Regular trains depart, via the Mandurah line, to Perth Underground/Esplanade ($6.60, 34 minutes) and Mandurah ($4.60, 18 minutes).

Rockingham station is around 4km southeast of Rockingham Beach and around 6km east of Mersey Point, from where the Penguin Island ferries depart; catch bus 551 or 555 to the beach or stay on the 551 to Mersey Point.

PEEL REGION

Taking in swathes of jarrah forest, historic towns and the increasingly glitzy coastal resort of Mandurah, the Peel Region can easily be tackled as a day trip from Perth or as the first stopping point of a longer expedition down the South Western Hwy (Rte 1).

As you enter the Peel, you'll pass out of Wadjuk country and into that of their fellow Noongar neighbours, the Pinjarup (or Binjareb) people.

Mandurah

POP 68,300

Shrugging off its fusty retirement-haven image, Mandurah has made concerted efforts to reinvent itself as an upmarket beach resort, taking advantage of its new train link to Perth's public transport network. And, although its linked set of redeveloped 'precincts' and 'quarters' may sound a little pretentious, the overall effect is actually pretty cool. You can wander along the waterfront from the Ocean Marina (boats, cafes and the Dolphin Quay indoor market), past the Venetian Canals (glitzy apartments linked by Venetian-ish sandstone bridges), through the Boardwalk and Cultural Precinct (more eateries, visitor centre, cinema, arts centre), to the Bridge Quarter (still more restaurants and bars).

The bridge spans the Mandurah Estuary, which sits between the ocean and the large body of water known as the Peel Inlet. It's one of the best places in the region for fishing, crabbing, prawning (March and April) and dolphin-spotting.

Sights & Activities

Beaches SWIMMING
There are plenty of beautiful beaches within walking distance of the Mandurah waterfront. **Town Beach** is just across from the marina, at the southern end of **Silver Sands** – perhaps the best of the ocean beaches. There's a designated, boat-free swimming area on the far side of the estuary, just north of Mandurah Bridge. Here dolphins have been known to swim up to unwitting kids for a frolic. Facing the ocean, west of the mouth of the estuary is family-friendly **Doddi's Beach**.

Mandurah Ferry Cruises CRUISES
(☎9535 3324; www.mandurahferrycruises.com; Boardwalk) Take a one-hour **Dolphin & Mandurah Waterways Cruise** (adult/child $25/12, five to seven daily), a half-day **Murray River Lunch Cruise** (adult/child $72/47) and, through December, a one-hour **Christmas Lights Canal Cruise** (adult/child $25/15), that gawps at millionaires' mansions under the pretence of admiring their festive displays. Check the website for details of special dinner and Indigenous cruises.

Mandurah Boat & Bike Hire BOATING, CYCLING
(☎9535 5877; www.mandurahboatandbikehire.com.au; Ormsby Tce, on the Boardwalk; bike hire per hr/day $10/33) Chase the fish on a four-

seat dinghy or six-seat pontoon (per hour/day $50/320).

Australian Sailing Museum MUSEUM
(www.australiansailingmuseum.com.au; Ormsby Tce; adult/child $10/5; 9am-5pm) A very cool new building housing 200 model yachts and tall ships, as well as a replica of the America's Cup and a cafe.

Hall's Cottage HISTORIC HOUSE
(Leighton Pl, Halls Head; 10am-3pm Sun) An 1830s cottage and one of the first dwellings in the state; visits are by gold coin donation.

Sleeping

Sebel APARTMENTS $$
(9512 8300; www.mirvachotels.com/sebel-mandurah; 1 Marco Polo Dr; r/apt from $129/209;) If this was actually Venice, you'd have to be staying in the Doge's Palace for a better location. Clearly it's not – as the extremely reasonable prices attest. This big white apartment block offers well-appointed modern apartments and studio rooms, all with views. There's plenty of free parking plus a heated pool and small gymnasium.

Seashells Resort RESORT $$
(9550 3000; www.seashells.com.au; 16 Dolphin Dr; apt from $163;) While the apartments here are marginally less cool than the Sebel's, the great advantage of Seashells is the beach on its doorstep and the lovely infinity-lipped pool facing it. Check into the luxury beachfront villas and you may not want to leave.

Quest APARTMENTS $$
(9535 9599; www.questmandurah.com.au; 20 Apollo Pl; apt from $148;) With light-blue weatherboards and white-painted gutters, this self-contained apartment complex backs directly on to the estuary. Rooms are clean, spacious and bright; the three-bedroom apartments, numbers 51 and 52, which feature courtyards and estuary views, are the pick of the bunch.

Eating

Miami Bakehouse BAKERY $
(www.miamibakehouse.com.au; Boardwalk; pies $5-9; breakfast, lunch & dinner) This celebrity of a bakery is the winner of over 300 awards, mainly for its pies.

Han's Cafe ASIAN $
(www.hanscafemandurah.com.au; 41 Ormsby Tce, enter from the Boardwalk; mains $10-16; 11am-10pm;) Like the other branches of this WA chain, brightly lit Han's serves a tasty selection of classic Chinese, Vietnamese, Thai, Malaysian and Singaporean dishes.

Cafe Moka CAFE $
(www.cafemoka.com.au; Dolphin Quay; breakfast $8-16, lunch $13-23; breakfast & lunch daily, dinner Sat) Mandurah's best brekkie option is well positioned to soak up the morning sun from the edge of the marina.

Cicerello's FISH AND CHIPS $
(www.cicerellos.com.au; 73 Mandurah Tce; mains $12-27; 9.30am-11.30pm) A boardwalk-facing branch of the Fremantle institution.

Drinking & Entertainment

M on the Point BAR
(www.m-onthepoint.com.au; 1 Marco Polo Dr) Aside from the fact that its logo looks a bit like a McDonalds logo, the bar beneath the Sebel is actually quite classy. It's the place to be for a Sunday sundowner.

Brighton Hotel PUB
(www.brightonmandurah.com.au; 10-12 Mandurah Tce) Watch the sun set over the estuary with a glass of wine, and return after 9pm on the weekends for a jiggle to the DJs.

Mandurah Performing Arts Centre CONCERT HALL
(9550 3900; www.manpac.com.au; Ormsby Tce) The main regional centre for theatre, dance, concerts etc.

Reading Cinema CINEMA
(www.readingcinemas.com.au; 7 James Service Pl, off the boardwalk)

Information

Visitor centre (9550 3999; www.visitmandurah.com; 75 Mandurah Tce; 9am-5pm;)

Getting There & Away

Mandurah is 72km from central Perth; take the Kwinana Fwy and follow the signs. It sits within the outermost zone (7) of the Perth public transport system and is the terminus of Transperth's Mandurah line. There are direct trains from Mandurah to Perth Underground/Esplanade ($8.70, 50 minutes) and Rockingham ($4.60, 18 minutes).

Transwa (1300 662 205; www.transwa.wa.gov.au) coach routes include:

» SW1 (12 per week) to East Perth ($16, 1½ hours), Bunbury ($16, two hours), Busselton ($23, 2¾ hours), Margaret River ($31, four hours) and Augusta ($34, 4¾ hours).

PINJARRA: BATTLE OR MASSACRE?

The popular myth of Australia's Indigenous people sitting back passively while the British took their land doesn't fly in the Peel Region. From the outset, after Thomas Peel was 'granted' this land, its Pinjarup owners asserted their rights – spearing stock and destroying crops. An uneasy truce was reached, with the Pinjarup given regular rations of flour, which they probably viewed as a kind of rent.

In 1834 the cutting of flour rations led Pinjarup leader Calyute to stage a raid on a flour mill. Four of his men were arrested in Mandurah and taken to Perth, where they were publically flogged. Retribution was taken on a 19-year-old British servant (fair game under Noongar law as he was considered a member of the offending party's tribe), who was killed and then ritually mutilated.

This caused an uproar amongst the settlers, with Peel strongly urging Governor Stirling to take action. Stirling led a party of soldiers and settlers, including Peel, to Pinjarra, where they surprised Calyute's people and opened fire on their encampment. What happened then is contested. Stirling's official report put the death toll at 15 men, while the *Perth Gazette* reported 25 to 30 dead. The Pinjarup claim that the camp consisted mainly of women and children and that the death toll was far higher. There was only one British casualty.

Stirling's threat to the survivors, that 'if any other person should be killed by them, not one (of their people) would be allowed to remain alive on this side of the mountain', seemed to have had the desired effect, and curtailed any future resistance.

» SW2 (thrice weekly) to Balingup ($26, three hours), Bridgetown ($29, 3½ hours) and Pemberton ($39, 4½ hours);

» GS3 (weekly) to Denmark ($62, 7¼ hours) and Albany ($67, eight hours).

South West Coach Lines (☎9261 7600; www.veoliatransportwa.com.au) has services to/from Perth's Esplanade Busport (1¼ hours, twice daily), Bunbury (1¼ hours, twice daily), Busselton (2½ hours, daily), Dunsborough (3¼ hours, daily) and Bridgetown (3¼ hours, weekdays).

Yalgorup National Park

Fifty kilometres south of Mandurah is this beautiful 12,000-hectare coastal park, consisting of a succession of ten tranquil lakes (come armed with insect repellent) and their surrounding woodlands and sand dunes. The park is recognised as a wetland of international significance for seasonally migrating waterbirds, with 130 different species identified.

Amateur scientists can visit the distinctive **thrombolites** of Lake Clifton, which are descendants of the earliest living organisms on earth (they are the only life form known to have existed over 650 million years ago). These rocklike structures are most easily seen when the water is low, particularly during March and April. There's a viewing platform on Mt John Rd off Old Coast Rd; keep an eye out for long-neck tortoises below the boardwalk. A 5km **walking track** starts from here and loops around the lake.

The **Lake Pollard trail** (6km) begins about 8km down Preston Beach North Rd (not Preston Beach Rd, as marked on some maps). The pleasant Martins Tank Lake campground is just to the right of the trail's entrance. The trail takes in tuart, jarrah and bull banksia to the lake, which is also known for its black swans (October to March).

The **Heathlands trail** (4.5km) to Lake Preston starts at the information bay on Preston Beach Rd (before the turn-off to Preston Beach North Rd) and explores the tuart woodland. Further along Preston Beach Rd is **Preston Beach**.

Pinjarra

POP 3300

Stretching along the Murray River, genteel Pinjarra now seems the epitome of peace and quiet. Yet it's best known as the site of a bloody incident in 1834 that was once remembered as the Battle of Pinjarra and is now known as the Pinjarra Massacre.

Sights & Activities

Town Centre HISTORIC BUILDINGS

The South Western Hwy passes through Pinjarra's small historic precinct, immediately after crossing the Murray. It's a good place to stretch your legs, with a park that leads down to the river and a cluster of significant buildings. **St John's Church**, built in 1861 and 1862 from mud bricks, sits beside a heritage **rose garden** and the original 1860 **schoolhouse** (which now houses a quilt workshop). Across Henry St is the **Edenvale Complex**, with excellent **tearooms** (mains $6-15; ⏱9am-4pm) in the old homestead (1888), art and craft galleries and a machinery display in the outbuildings. On the other side of the highway, you can cross the river on foot via an old **suspension bridge**.

Peel Zoo ZOO
(www.peelzoo.com; Sanctuary Dr, off Pinjarra Rd; adult/child $15/7; ⏱10am-4pm) Peacocks strut while parrots issue wisecracks as you wander around this cute little zoo, which focuses on Australian wildlife: kangaroos, wallabies, Tasmanian devils, koalas, wombats, possums, quolls, snakes and lots of native birds.

Hotham Valley Railway HISTORIC TRAIN
(☎9221 4444; www.hothamvalleyrailway.com.au; adult/child $40/20; ⏱11am Sun & Wed, May-Oct) Runs six-hour steam-train trips from Pinjarra through jarrah forests and blooming wildflowers, stopping in Dwellingup for 2½ hours before returning.

Old Blythewood Homestead HISTORIC BUILDING
(www.ntwa.com.au; South Western Hwy; adult/child $4/3; ⏱10.30am-3.30pm Sat, 12.30-3.30pm Sun) An 1859 National Trust–owned farmhouse, furnished with antiques, located about 4km south of Pinjarra.

WA Skydiving Academy SKYDIVING
(☎1300 137 855; www.waskydiving.com.au) Tandem jumps from 6000/10,000/14,000ft for $240/320/400).

Information

Visitor centre (☎9531 1438; www.murray.wa.gov.au; Fimmel Lane; ⏱9.30am-4pm) Housed in the heritage train station.

Getting There & Away

Pinjarra is on the **Transwa** (☎1300 662 205; www.transwa.wa.gov.au) Australind train line, with twice-daily services to Perth ($16, 1¼ hours) and Bunbury ($16, 1¼ hours).

Dwellingup

POP 550

Dwellingup is a small, forest-shrouded township with character, 100km south of Perth. Its reputation as an activity hub has been enhanced by the hardy long-distance walkers and cyclists passing through on the Bibbulmun Track (p36) and the Munda Biddi Trail (p35), respectively.

Sights & Activities

Forest Heritage Centre NATURE RESERVE
(www.forestheritagecentre.com.au; 1 Acacia St; adult/family $5.50/11; ⏱10am-4pm) Set within the jarrah forest, this interesting rammed-earth building takes the shape of three interlinked gum leaves. Inside are displays about the forest's flora and fauna, and a woodwork school, complete with a shop that sells beautiful pieces crafted by the students. Short, marked trails lead into the forest, including an 11m-high canopy walk. Keep your eyes peeled for the resident flock of red-tailed black cockatoos, and feel free to invent some bloodsucking story about the giant insect (fake, but lifelike) above the canopy walkway to frighten your travelling companions with.

Hotham Valley Railway HISTORIC TRAIN
(☎9221 4444; www.hothamvalleyrailway.com.au) On weekends, the **Dwellingup Forest Train** (adult/child $18/9, departs 11am & 2pm) chugs along 8km of forest track on a 90-minute return trip. It's usually steam driven but in summer they revert to diesel engines, presumably due to the fire risk. There's a 30-minute stopover at the end where you can take a short bushwalk. Every Saturday night and some Fridays, the **Restaurant Train** ($75; ⏱7.45pm) follows the same route, serving up a five-course meal in a 1919 dining car. Dwellingup is the destination of the Steam Ranger service from Pinjarra.

Dwellingup Adventures KAYAKING, RAFTING
(☎9538 1127; www.dwellingupadventures.com.au; 1-person kayaks & 2-person canoes $37 per day; ⏱8.30am-5pm) Don't miss the opportunity to get out on the beautiful Murray River. This is the place to hire camping gear, bikes,

LANE POOLE RESERVE

Lane Poole Reserve, on the banks of the Murray River, is a wonderful place to stop for a barbecue, picnic, bushwalk or (in summer, when the waters are calmer) swim. The best spots for swimming are Island Pool and near the Baden-Powell water spout. To get here, head south of Dwellingup on 2WD-friendly River Rd for 10km. The reserve is vast, incorporating over 55,000 hectares of jarrah forest.

NATIONAL PARK PASSES

Thirty of WA's 96 national parks charge vehicle entry fees (per car/motorcycle $11/5), which are valid for any park visited that day. If you're camping within the park, the entry fee is only payable on the first day (camping fees are additional). If you plan to visit more than three chargeable parks in the state, which is quite likely if you're travelling outside of Perth for longer than a week, take advantage of the four-week Holiday Pass ($40). All Department of Environment & Conservation (DEC) offices sell them and if you've already paid a day-entry fee in the last week (and have the voucher to prove it), you can subtract it from the cost.

kayaks and canoes, or to take an assisted, self-guided paddling (full day, one-person kayak, $90) or cycling tour (full day, per one/two/three people $97/124/174). White-water rafting tours are available from June to October (per person $130).

Information

Visitor centre (☎9538 1108; www.murray.wa.gov.au; Marrinup St; ⊙9am-3pm) Has interesting displays about the 1961 bushfires that wiped out the town, destroying 75 houses but taking no lives. The centrepiece is a shiny Mack firetruck (1939).

Jarrahdale & Serpentine National Park

POP 956

Established in 1871, Jarrahdale is another old mill village reached by a leafy 6km drive east from the South Western Hwy. It's small and sleepy, and that's part of its charm. The **Old Post Office** (www.jarrahdale.com; walks $5; ⊙10am-4pm Sat & Sun), built in 1896, houses a small local museum. Guided walks run by volunteers from the heritage society depart from here.

Picturesque **Millbrook Winery** (☎9525 5796; www.millbrookwinery.com.au; Old Chestnut Lane, signed off Jarrahdale Rd; mains $36-42; ⊙lunch Wed-Sun) is an excellent lunch choice, with a tranquil setting overlooking a small lake. There's a lively Mod Oz (modern Australian) menu and you can taste wine from grapes grown here and in Margaret River.

Jarrahdale sits on the northern fringes of **Serpentine National Park** (www.dec.wa.gov.au; admission per car $11; ⊙8.30am-5pm), a forested area with walking tracks, picnic areas and a leisurely 15m slide of water known as the **Serpentine Falls** (Falls Rd, off South Western Hwy). If you're in no hurry you can take a pleasant detour through the park from Jarrahdale, following Kingsbury Dr to the **Serpentine Dam** before curving back to the highway.

There's no public transport to Jarrahdale but you can catch a train to the village of Serpentine on the Australind line (from Perth: $8.60, 55 minutes, twice daily), 3km from the Falls Rd park entrance.

DRYANDRA TO HYDEN

A beautiful forest, rare marsupials, ancient granite-rock formations, salt lakes, interesting back roads and the unique Wave Rock are the scattered highlights of this widespread farming region.

Dryandra Woodland

This superb, isolated remnant of eucalypt forest, 164km southeast of Perth, hints at what the Wheatbelt was like before large-scale land-clearing and feral predators wreaked havoc on the local ecosystems. It features thickets of white-barked wandoo, powderbark and rock she-oak, and small populations of threatened numbats, woylies and tammar wallabies, and makes a great weekend getaway from Perth.

There are great walking trails for wildlife spotting; the 5km **Ochre Trail**, which highlights Noongar culture; and even an 'audio drive' that uses solar-powered transmitters to supply a commentary via your car radio.

The excellent **Barna Mia Animal Sanctuary**, home to endangered bilbies, boodies, woylies and marla, conducts 90-min after-dark torchlight tours, which provide a rare opportunity to see these cute furry creatures up close. Book through the **Department of Environment & Conservation** (DEC; ☎weekdays/weekends 9881 9200/9881 2064; www.dec.gov.au; Hough St, Narrogin; ⊙9am-4pm; adult/child/family $13/7/35) for post-sunset tours on Mondays, Wednesdays, Fridays and Saturdays. Book early during peak periods.

Although you can hoist your tent at the pleasant **Congelin Camp Ground** (per person $7), Dryandra is one place you should splurge a little. The **Lions Dryandra Village** (☎9884 5231; www.dryandravillage.org.au; midweek adult/child $25/10, weekends & holidays 2-/4-/8-12-person cabins $60/75/100) is a 1920s forestry camp in the heart of the forest, offering fully self-contained, renovated woodcutters' cabins complete with fridge, stove, fireplace, en suite and nearby grazing wallabies. Coming from Perth, the woodland is a pleasant drive via the wineries of the Darling Range; turn-off at North Bannister. **Narrogin** (www.dryandratourism.org.au), serviced by Transwa buses, is 22km southeast, where you might find a **taxi** (☎9881 4381).

Hyden & Wave Rock

Large granite outcrops dot the area known as the Central and Southern Wheatbelts, and the most famous is the perfectly shaped, multicoloured **Wave Rock**. Formed 60 million years ago by weather and water erosion, Wave Rock's streaks of colour were created by run-off from local mineral springs. While the outcrop is massive, the 'wave' portion is rather small, no more than 15m high and 110m long.

To get the most out of Wave Rock, located 350km from Perth, you should wander around the many walking trails, especially the one across the top of the rock (marked 'Hyden Rock'). Grab the brochure *Walk Trails at Wave Rock and The Humps* from the **visitor centre** (☎9880 5182; www.waverock.com.au; ⌚9am-5pm) but avoid their expensive coffee. Drive to the **Hippos Yawn** car park, which doesn't require a $7 parking permit, and follow the shady track (1km) along the rock base to the rock itself. If you've never seen a salt lake before, consider the easy 3.5km **Wave Rock Circuit Walk** from either car park.

Better still is the superb **Mulkas Cave**, and **The Humps**, a further 16km from Wave Rock. Mulkas Cave is an important rock-art site with over 450 stencils and hand prints, and is an easy walk from the car park. The more adventurous can choose from two walking tracks, both with interpretative signage. The **Kalari Trail** (1.6km return) leads up to a huge granite outcrop (one of the Humps), which has excellent views that somehow manage to be wilder and more impressive than Wave Rock, while the **Gnamma Trail** (1.2km return) stays low and investigates natural waterholes; it also has panels explaining Noongar culture.

If you plan to stay at Wave Rock, phone ahead – accommodation can fill with tour groups. Camp near the rock amid the gum trees at **Wave Rock Cabins & Caravan Park** (☎9880 5022; www.waverock.com.au; unpowered/powered sites $28/35, cabin s/d $120/135; ❄☒).

In **Hyden** (population 190), 4km east of the rock, the 1970s brick **Wave Rock Motel** (☎9880 5052; hotelmotel@waverock.com.au; 2 Lynch St; d from $145; ❄☒) has well-equipped rooms, a comfy lounge with fireplace, and an indoor bush bistro.

Transwa runs a bus from Perth to Hyden ($48, five hours) and onto Esperance ($50, five hours) every Tuesday, which returns on Thursdays. If heading to/from the Nullarbor, you can take the unsealed but direct Hyden–Norseman Rd, which saves 100km or so. Look for the brochure *The Granite and Woodlands Discovery Trail*, available from Norseman or Wave Rock visitor centres.

ℹ Getting There & Away

This area is best seen with your own vehicle, ideally en route to somewhere else. **Transwa** (☎1300 662 205; www.transwa.wa.gov.au) runs sporadic buses between Perth and the south coast. **Western Travel Bug** (☎9486 4222; www.travelbug.com.au; tours $175) offers a one-day tour, or, alternativley, you could see it as part of a five-day southwest loop with **Western Xposure** (☎9414 8423; www.westernxposure.com.au; tours $750).

DARLING RANGE

Commonly known as the Perth Hills, this forest-covered escarpment provides the city with a green backdrop and offers great spots for picnicking, barbecues, bushwalking and

ROCK & ROLL

At 350km from Perth, Wave Rock is rather a long day trip, and some people are disappointed by what's really a one-trick gig. However, you can spice up this trip by hunting out other, lesser-known granite outcrops and curiosities. All you need is a map and a sense of adventure. (Hint: most of the granite outcrops end in 'Rock'.) To get you started try Kokerbin Rock, Jilakin Rock, Dragon Rocks, Yorkrakine Rock…get the picture? The visitor centres along the way can supply useful maps.

rubbing shoulders with wild kangaroos. Leafy suburbs nestle at their feet, along with a few dozen wineries.

Kalamunda

POP 54,700

Kalamunda is a well-heeled township on the crest of the Darling Range. The area began as a timber settlement, but it's since become a haven for those keen to enjoy the seclusion of the hills and still be close to the city (it's a 30-minute drive).

The main shopping area, centred on Haynes St, has some nice pubs and cafes, such as **Le Paris-Brest Café Patisserie** (9293 2752; 22 Haynes St; mains $17-24; breakfast & lunch Tue-Sun), where you can stock up on French pastries; look for the mini Eiffel Tower. Nearby is **Stirk Cottage** (Kalamunda Rd; admission free; 2-4pm Sun), which was built of mud, saplings and shingle in 1881.

For walkers, Kalamunda's main claim to fame is as the northern terminus of the **Bibbulmun Track** (p36), which starts near the shops and quickly heads up into the marri and jarrah forest of **Kalamunda National Park**.

From Zig-Zag Dr, just north of Kalamunda off Lascelles Pde, there are fantastic views over Perth to the coast. Even if you're just passing through, the trip up here is worth it. The drive through the forested hills to Mundaring via Mundaring Weir Rd is also wonderful, but watch out for kangaroos.

Getting There & Away

From Perth, buses 283, 295, 296, 298 and 299 all head to Kalamunda ($4.60, 47 minutes).

WORTH A TRIP

ARALUEN BOTANIC PARK

South of Kalamunda, just off Brookton Hwy, is **Araluen Botanic Park** (www.araluenbotanicpark.com.au; 362 Croyden Rd, Roleystone; adult/child $4/2; 9am-6pm). It's quite a gem. Constructed in the 1920s by the Young Australia League (YAL) as a bush retreat, the park was neglected for years and became overgrown. The state government purchased it in 1990 and have since restored its elaborate garden terraces, waterfalls and ornamental pool. The spring tulip displays are wonderful.

Mundaring

POP 38,300

Mundaring's a laid-back spot with a small artistic community, located 35km east of Perth. The township itself isn't particularly interesting, with the busy Great Eastern Hwy running through the centre of it, but it is worth calling into the **Mundaring Arts Centre** (www.mundaringartscentre.com; 7190 Great Eastern Hwy; 10am-5pm Mon-Fri, 11am-3pm Sat & Sun), which exhibits and sells the work of local artists.

The 16-sq-km **John Forrest National Park** (www.dec.wa.gov.au; admission per car $11), west of Mundaring, was the state's first national park. With protected areas of jarrah and marri trees, granite outcrops, waterfalls and a pool, it's long been a favourite.

Immediately south of Mundaring is lovely **Beelu National Park** (www.dec.wa.gov.au) part of a continuous swathe of forest that includes Kalamunda National Park. The **Perth Hills National Parks Centre** (9295 2244; www.dec.wa.gov/au/n2n; Allens Rd, off Mundaring Weir Rd) hosts a series of kids programs like 'flutter by butterfly' and 'funky fossils'. There's a well set-up campground here (per adult/child $8.80/6.60), which has showers; it's well positioned for the Bibbulmun Track, which passes nearby. A more secluded and primitive campground is available at Paten's Brook (per person $5).

From November to April, kick back in a deck chair and watch a movie at the open-air **Kookaburra Cinema** (9295 6190; Allen Rd), just across the road from the park centre. A little further south is **Mundaring Weir**, a dam built 100 years ago to supply water to the goldfields more than 500km to the east. The reservoir is a blissful spot, with walking trails and a well-positioned pub. Come dusk, the whole area swarms with kangaroos.

East from Mundaring and north of the Great Eastern Hwy, near Chidlow, is freshwater **Lake Leschenaultia** (8.30am-dusk), a picturesque former railway dam, complete with a swimming pontoon.

Sleeping & Eating

Loose Box RESTAURANT, COTTAGES $$$
(9295 1787; www.loosebox.com.au; 6825 Great Eastern Hwy; degustation $150; dinner Wed-Sat, lunch Sun) A French fine-dining restaurant with provincial decor, Loose Box has such a formidable reputation that it can maintain a strictly degustation-only policy and still

have people clambering to get in. Luxury cottages are available within the grounds, so you can splash out and make a night of it (B&B $400, with meal $650 to $750).

Mundaring Weir Hotel PUB $$
(☎9295 1106; www.mundaringweirhotel.com.au; Weir Village Rd; r Sun-Thu $110, Fri/Sat $125/135;) Overlooking the weir, this 1898 pub has bucketloads of ramshackle character. The accommodation is in a little terrace block at the back; rooms are simple but tidy, with DVD players and microwaves. The rooms open onto an amphitheatre, which mainly functions as a beer garden but occasionally hosts concerts. Once the pub closes, it couldn't be more peaceful.

Perth Hills Forest Lodge YHA HOSTEL $
(☎9295 1809; www.yha.com.au; Mundaring Weir Rd; dm $24-30, s $50-62, tw $62-72) It's very basic but this hostel has a quiet bush setting, close to the weir, about 8km south of town. If you've ever fancied hanging out with 'roos, this is your place.

Information

Visitor centre (☎9295 0202; www.mundaringtourism.com.au; 7225 Great Eastern Hwy; 9.30am-4pm Mon-Sat, 10.30am-2.30pm Sun)

Getting There & Away

You can reach Mundaring from Perth on public transport in just over an hour, by taking a train to Midland and then bus 320 ($5.40). From here it's still 6km to the weir.

Walyunga National Park

The Avon River cuts a narrow gorge through the Darling Range at **Walyunga National Park** (www.dec.wa.gov.au; admission per car $11; 8am-5pm) in Upper Swan. Walyunga is a great place for hiking and picnicking, the river is much like a handsome carpet python winding through the range. This 18-sq-km park is off the Great Northern Hwy (Rte 95), 40km northeast of Perth.

The bushwalks include a 5.2km-return walk to Syd's Rapids as well as a 1.2km Aboriginal Heritage Trail. The best trail is the 10.6km Echidna Loop, which has tremendous views over the Swan and Avon Valleys. The park has one of the largest known camp sites of the Noongar people; the camp site was still in use in the late 1800s. The area may well have been occupied by Aborigines for more than 6000 years.

GUILDFORD & THE SWAN VALLEY

Perthites love to swan around this semirural valley on the city's eastern fringe to partake in the finer things in life: booze, nosh and the great outdoors. Perhaps in a tacit acknowledgement that its wines will never compete with the state's more prestigious regions (it doesn't really have the ideal climate), the Swan Valley compensates with plenty of galleries, breweries, providores and restaurants.

The gateway to the valley is the National Trust–classified town of Guildford, established in 1829, around the same time as Perth and Fremantle. A clutch of interesting old buildings, one housing the visitor centre, make it the logical starting place for day trippers. Guildford is only 12km from central Perth and well served by suburban trains.

History

Guildford is built on the conjunction of three rivers and it is probably for this reason that it was an important meeting and ceremonial place for the Wadjuk people. When the British arrived and travelled up the Swan, it was the access to fresh water that led them to establish one of their first settlements here. In 1833, four years after the colony's founding, resistance leader Yagan was shot and decapitated in the Swan Valley.

The fertile valley land was soon turned to farming. Vines were first planted in the 1830s at Houghton's but it was after the arrival of Croatian settlers (from around 1916) that the farmland was increasingly transformed into wine production.

Sights & Activities

The centre of old Guildford is Stirling Sq, at the intersection of Swan and Meadow Sts. The cluster of buildings opposite the square includes the **Old Courthouse** (1866), which houses the visitor centre and has interesting historical displays. In the same grounds are the **gaol** (adult/child $2/free; 9am-3pm Wed, Fri & Sat) and **Taylor's Cottage** (1863; admission included with gaol entry). Various **heritage walks** start from here; get information from the visitor centre or download a trail card from their website. Two kilometres east is **Woodbridge House** (Ford St; adult/child

$5/3; ⏲1-4pm Thu-Sun), an 1885 colonial mansion overlooking the river.

FREE **Gomboc Gallery** ART GALLERY
(www.gomboc-gallery.com.au; 50 James Rd, Middle Swan; ⏲10am-5pm Wed-Sun) One of WA's best commercial galleries, surrounded by an intriguing sculpture park.

Whiteman Park PARK
(www.whitemanpark.com; enter from Lord St or Beechboro Rd, West Swan; ⏲8.30am-6pm) At 26-sq-km, this is Perth's biggest park, with over 30km of walkways and bike paths, and numerous picnic and barbecue spots. Within its ordered grounds are the following attractions:

Caversham Wildlife Park
(www.cavershamwildlife.com.au; adult/child $22/10; ⏲8.30am-5.30pm, last entry 4.30pm) Has creatures such as cassowaries, echidnas, kangaroos, koalas, echidnas, potoroos, quokkas and native birds, as well as farm shows.

Bennet Brook Railway
(www.bennettbrookrailway.org; adult/child $8/4; ⏲11am-1pm Wed, Thu, Sat & Sun) Train rides.

Tram Rides
(www.pets.org.au; adult/child $5/2.50; ⏲noon-2pm Tue & Fri-Sun)

Revolutions
(entry by gold coin donation; ⏲10am-4pm) An interesting museum collection celebrating transport in WA: horse-drawn wagons, camels, trains, boats and planes.

Motor Museum of WA
(www.motormuseumofwa.asn.au; adult/child $8/5; ⏲10am-4pm) Vintage cars and motorbikes.

Eating & Drinking

In this 'Valley of Taste' eating and drinking tend to go hand-in-hand as many of the wineries and breweries have restaurants attached. In the following reviews, we've listed each establishment's best attribute first, right next to their name.

The Swan Valley vibe is more low-key and relaxed than, say, Margaret River – don't come expecting grand estates. There are more than 40 vineyards, concentrated mainly along busy West Swan Rd (the road leading north from the visitor centre) and the Great Northern Hwy (which runs parallel to the east). There's a map in the free *Food & Wine Trail Guide,* available from the visitor centre. Tastings are usually free.

TOP CHOICE **RiverBank Estate** RESTAURANT, WINERY $$
(☎9377 1805; www.riverbankestate.com.au; 126 Hamersley Rd, Caversham; mains $32-38; ⏲tastings 10am-5pm, lunch) Our pick of the valley's restaurants, RiverBank is a thoroughly pleasant place to while away a few hours over excellent Mod Oz cuisine. It's a little more dressed up than most other places and they charge for tastings ($3 for six, if you're not dining in the restaurant) but we're willing to let that go when the food's this good. There's live jazz played on the first Saturday of the month.

Black Swan RESTAURANT, WINERY $$
(☎9296 6090; www.blackswanwines.com.au; 8600 West Swan Rd, Henley Brook; mains $28-33; ⏲tastings 11am-3pm, lunch daily, dinner Wed-Sat) It's slightly ugly duckling from the outside, but inside Black Swan has an upmarket dining room with views looking over the vines to the ranges. The food is sophisticated and delicious, ranging from delicate seafood pastas to top quality wagyu steaks (the latter around $50).

Rose & Crown PUB $$
(www.rosecrown.com.au; 105 Swan St, Guildford; mains $25-38) WA's oldest still-operating pub (1841) has a wonderful, leafy beer garden and lots of different spaces to explore inside. Have a beer in the cellar bar, where there's a convict-built well, and, while you're there, check out the sealed-off tunnel which used to connect the hotel with the river.

Sandalford WINERY, RESTAURANT $$
(www.sandalford.com; 3210 West Swan Rd, Caversham; mains $32-40; ⏲tastings 10am-5pm, lunch) Sandalford has the nicest surrounds of any of the wineries, and plays host to weddings and major concerts. Along with Houghton, it's one of the valley's big-time, long-term operators.

Houghton WINERY, CAFE $$
(www.houghton-wines.com.au; Dale Rd, Middle Swan; ⏲10am-5pm) The Swan's oldest and best-known winery is surrounded by pleasant grounds, including a jacaranda grove. There's a gallery in the cellar where bushranger Moondyne Joe was caught, and a small display of old winemaking equipment.

Lamont's WINERY, TAPAS $$
(www.lamonts.com.au; 85 Bisdee Rd, Millendon; tapas $9-18; ⏲10am-5pm Fri-Mon) Now that Lamont's fine-dining efforts are focused in East Perth, it's just lazy tastings and tapas up here under the open sky. The wine's very good, much of it grown in their Margaret River vineyard.

Mash BREWERY, RESTAURANT **$$**
(www.mashbrewing.com.au; 10250 West Swan Rd, Henley Brook; mains $20-28; ⏲lunch daily, dinner Wed-Sun) A lively bar-like atmosphere and a selection of homemade lager, ales, wheat beer and cider.

Duckstein BREWERY, RESTAURANT **$$**
(www.duckstein.com.au; 9270 West Swan Rd, Henley Brook; mains $18-32; ⏲lunch & dinner Wed-Sun) This brewery turns out well-executed German classics like grilled bratwurst and wheat beer.

Margaret River Chocolate Company CHOCOLATES, CAFE **$**
(www.chocolatefactory.com.au; 5123 West Swan Rd, West Swan; ⏲9am-5pm) Unsurprisingly, this chocolate shop is often mobbed by families and tour groups.

Information

Visitor centre (☎9379 9400; www.swanvalley.com.au; Old Courthouse, cnr Swan & Meadow Sts, Guildford; ⏲9am-4pm) Well-stocked with information and maps, plus an interesting display on local history.

Getting There & Away

Guildford falls within Zone 2 of Perth's public transport system, meaning that it's only $3.70 to get here by one of the many buses or by a train on the Midland Line from Perth, East Perth or Mt Lawley station. It's only 12km from the centre, so you could easily cycle here.

To get around the Swan Valley you'll need to drive or take one of the many tours (see p60). Bikes can be hired from **Swan Valley Bike Hire** (☎0488 160 770; www.swanvalleybikehire.net.au; Meadow St, Guildford; per hr/day $10/30; ⏲9am-6pm), next to the visitor centre.

For Whiteman Park you can take bus 60 from the Esplanade Busport in Perth to Morley and change to the Ellenbrook-bound bus 336; allow at least 1½ hours.

AVON VALLEY

The lush green Avon Valley – with its atmospheric homesteads with big verandahs, rickety wooden wagons and moss-covered rocks – was 'discovered' by European settlers in early 1830 after food shortages forced Governor Stirling to dispatch Ensign Dale to search the Darling Range for arable land. What he found was the upper reaches of the Swan River, but he presumed it was a separate river – which is why its name changes from the Swan to the Avon in Walyunga National Park. The valley was very soon settled, just a year after Perth was founded, and many historic stone buildings still stand proudly in the towns and countryside in the

Avon Valley

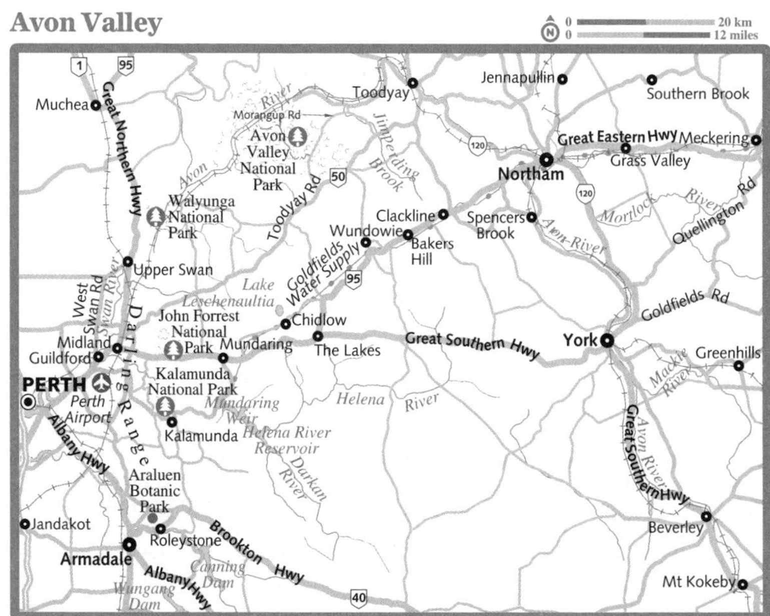

area. The picturesque Avon River is popular for picnics.

This country traditionally belongs to the Balardung, another of the Noongar peoples.

York

POP 2100

Unrelentingly quaint, York is the most atmospheric spot in the Avon Valley and a wonderful place to while away a couple of hours on a Sunday, when it's at its liveliest. A stroll down the main street, Avon Tce, with its restored old buildings, is a real step back in time – so much so that the whole town has been classified by the National Trust.

Only 97km from Perth, York is the oldest inland town in WA, first settled in 1831, just two years after the Swan River Colony. The settlers here saw similarities in the Avon Valley and their native Yorkshire, so Governor Stirling bestowed the name York on the region's first town.

Convicts were brought to the region in 1851 and contributed to the development of the district; the ticket-of-leave hiring depot was not closed until 1872, four years after transportation of convicts to WA ceased. During the gold rush, York prospered as a commercial centre, servicing miners who were heading to Southern Cross, a goldfields town 273km to the east. Most of its buildings date from this time.

Sights & Activities

Avon Tce is lined with significant buildings, such as the **town hall**, **Castle Hotel**, **police station**, **Old Gaol & Courthouse** and **Settlers House**. **Holy Trinity Church** (Pool St), by the Avon River, was completed in 1854 and features stained-glass windows designed by WA artist Robert Juniper, and a rare pipe organ. The **suspension bridge** across the Avon was built in 1906.

York Mill MARKET, GALLERY
(www.theyorkmill.com.au; 13 Broome St; ⏲10am-4pm Thu-Tue) Built in 1892, York's four-storey flour mill now houses the **Mill Cafe** (lunch $15-19, dinner $23-30; ⏲lunch Thu-Tue, dinner Fri & Sat) and an excellent gallery selling jarrah furniture, art, and craft by local artisans. The weekend markets (from 9am) have proved a huge success, with a target of 80% WA-made goods and produce. It's well worth visiting for the chocolates alone.

Residency Museum MUSEUM
(Brook St; adult/child $3.50/1.50; ⏲1-3pm Tue, Wed & Thu, 11am-3.30pm Sat & Sun) Built in 1858, this museum houses some intriguing historic exhibits, which range from an antique egg rack and a butter churn, to beautiful old black-and-white photos of York.

Motor Museum MUSEUM
(116 Avon Tce; adult/child $8.50/3.50; ⏲9.30am-3pm) A must for vintage-car enthusiasts.

Skydive Express SKYDIVING
(☎1800 355 833; www.skydive.com.au; tandem jumps 8000/10,000/14,000ft $299/339/429) The Avon Valley has earned a reputation as the state's skydiving centre; the drop zone is about 3km from town.

Festivals & Events

See the visitor centre's website for exact dates.

York Racing HORSE RACING
(York Racecourse; Spencers Brook Rd) York boasts the oldest jockey club in Australia and the monthly race meets are still popular. There's harness racing also.

Antique and Collectables Fair ANTIQUES
Long-running event held in the Masonic Hall in September.

York Jazz & Soul Festival MUSIC
(www.yorkjazz.com.au) Held over a weekend in late October.

Sleeping & Eating

York is a popular weekend destination for charm-chasing Perthites, so prices rise on the weekends.

TOP CHOICE **Faversham House** B&B $$
(☎9641 1366; www.favershamhouse.com.au; 24 Grey St; r $110-265; ❄📶) If you've ever wished you were 'to the manor born', indulge your fantasies in this grand stone mansion (1840). The rooms in the main house are large, TV-free and strewn with antiques; some have four-poster beds. All have private bathrooms but these tend to be smallish. The cheaper rooms are in the old servants' quarters, naturally.

Kookaburra Dream HOSTEL $
(☎9641 2936; www.kookaburradream.com.au; 152 Avon Tce; dm/s/d $35/70/90; ❄@) Rustic in that well-considered, posh way, this excellent, centrally located backpackers' hostel occupies a lovingly cared-for 1890 building.

Guests love the laid-back vibe, barbecue facilities and free continental breakfasts (including farm-fresh eggs).

York BOUTIQUE HOTEL **$$**
(☎9641 2188; www.theyork.com.au; 145 Avon Tce; r/ste from $195/255; ❄) The grand old York has huge heritage suites that open on to the wraparound balcony upstairs, and elegantly decorated rooms in a terrace block at the rear. Downstairs, the upmarket Mod Oz–style **restaurant** (breakfast $11-19, lunch $17-30, dinner $27-30; ⏲breakfast Sat & Sun, lunch Wed-Sun, dinner Wed-Sat) serves the town's best food. Striking art from locally based artist John Feeney is a feature throughout.

Settlers House HOTEL **$$**
(☎9641 1096; www.settlershouse.com.au; 125 Avon Tce; d $95-130; ❄) Built in 1845 as a staging post and guesthouse for goldfields travellers, Settlers has old-fashioned but charming rooms that face onto a leafy courtyard. At the time of research a new block was in the process of being built. There's an English pub feel to the downstairs **restaurant** (mains $33-32; ⏲lunch & dinner) which extends to the hearty menu.

Imperial Inn BOUTIQUE HOTEL **$$**
(☎9641 1255; www.imperialhotelyork.com.au; 83 Avon Tce; r $100-240; 📶) Located in a beautiful stone building on the main street, the Imperial offers zooshed-up rooms across the lawn in what might well have been the old stables. There are no TVs but there are iPod docks.

York Caravan Park CARAVAN PARK **$**
(☎9641 1421; www.yorkwacaravanpark.com; Eighth Rd; site per s/d $25/30) You can pitch your tent in a bush setting in this small park on the edge of town.

ℹ Information

Visitor centre (☎9641 1301; www.yorkwa.org; Town Hall, 81 Avon Tce; ⏲10am-4pm)

ℹ Getting There & Away

Transwa (☎1300 662 205; www.transwa.wa.gov.au) coach routes include:

» GE2 (three per week) to East Perth ($16, 1½ hours), Mundaring ($13, 47 minutes), Hyden ($36, 3¼ hours) and Esperance ($74, 8½ hours)

» GS2 to Northam ($8, 33 minutes, six per week), Mt Barker ($51, 5¼ hours, four per week) and Albany ($56, six hours, four per week)

Northam

POP 6000

This busy commercial centre is the major town of the Avon Valley. It's is a likeable place with some fine heritage buildings and pleasant cafes but there's little here to justify a longer stay. The railway line from Perth once ended here and miners had to make the rest of the weary trek to the goldfields by road; it now continues all the way to Sydney.

The major event on the calendar is August's **Avon River Festival** (street parade, market, fireworks) followed the next day by the **Avon Descent**, a gruelling 133km whitewater-rafting event for powerboats, kayaks and canoes.

Sights & Activities

Burlong Pool RIVERSIDE POOL
Apart from being a nice spot for a picnic, this natural pool on the Avon River is a very significant Noongar site. It is believed to be the summer home of the Wargal, the giant snakelike creature that created the waterways, and brought life to the land. It's customary to throw a handful of sand into the water out of respect. If the water stirs, keep out; otherwise all's well. A very interesting set of information boards have been erected to recount this story and some of the site's history.

Burlong can be reached by following the river southwest from the visitor centre for 3.5km. This is part of an 18km path along the river called Dorntj Koorliny (Walking Together). Otherwise, take Fitzgerald Rd, which becomes Burlong Rd, and follow it to the end.

Morby Cottage HISTORIC BUILDING
(Katrine Rd; adult/child $2/1; ⏲10.30am-4pm Sun) Built in 1836 as the home of John Morrell (founder of Northam), it now houses various Morrell family heirlooms and other early Northam memorabilia.

Old Railway Station Museum MUSEUM
(Fitzgerald St; adult/child $2/0.50; ⏲10am-4pm Sun) Housed in a National Trust–registered building (1886), this museum has a large collection of railway memorabilia.

Windward Adventures BALLOONING
(☎9621 2000; www.windwardballooning.com; weekday/weekend flight $270/320; ⏲Apr-Oct) Sunset flights followed by a champagne breakfast.

Avon Valley Ballooning BALLOONING
(☎9622 8805; www.avb.net.au; 100 Fitzgerald St; weekday/weekend flight $270/315) Another sunset/champagne combo.

Sleeping & Eating

Shamrock Hotel PUB $$
(☎9622 1092, www.shamrockhotelnortham.com.au; 112 Fitzgerald St; r $132-220;) An imposing country hotel (1866), the Shamrock offers better-than-average pub accommodation in spacious, renovated rooms. The pub downstairs is a good place for a quiet drink (and has free wi-fi) and you needn't worry about noise – it's usually all over by about 10pm. Meals are also available.

TOP CHOICE **Cafe Yasou** CAFE $
(www.cafeyasou.com.au; 175 Fitzgerald St; mains $11-16; 8am-4pm Mon-Fri, 8am-noon Sat) Greek gods frolic on the pea-green walls of this wonderful Cypriot cafe, which serves excellent coffee, wonderful mezze plates, lamb souvlaki and proper home-made Turkish delight. If you're not in a Med mood, there's a selection of sandwiches and cakes.

Mon Petit CAFE $
(100 Fitzgerald St; breakfast & lunch $12-19, dinner $15-32; 8am-5pm Sun-Wed, 8am-10pm Thu-Sat) Run by the same folks as Avon Valley Balloons (hence the prominent ballooning basket), this little cafe has a distinctly French feel. It transforms into a bistro in the evenings.

Riversedge Cafe CAFE $
(☎9622 8500; 1 Grey St; breakfast $10-19, lunch $15-21; Tue-Sun) The verandahs of this big corrugated-iron building on the river are a wonderful place to soak up the sun and river views over a slice of scrumptious cake.

Information

Visitor centre (☎9622 2100; www.visitnorthamwa.com.au; 2 Grey St; 9am-5pm Mon-Fri, 9am-4pm Sat & Sun) An excellent centre, that overlooks a picturesque portion of river, with fountains and a little island. Pick up the *Experience the Avon Valley* brochure, which has lots of info and maps.

Getting There & Away

BUS Transwa (☎1300 662 205; www.transwa.wa.gov.au) coach GS2 heads to East Perth ($18, 1½ hours, six per week), York ($8, 33 minutes, six per week), Mt Barker ($53, 5¾ hours, four per week) and Albany ($60, 6½ hours, four per week).

TRAIN Northam is a stop on the AvonLink and Prospector lines, with trains to East Perth ($19, 1½ hours, 12 per week), Toodyay ($8, 20 minutes, 12 per week) and Kalgoorlie ($71, 5¼ hours, nine per week).

Toodyay

POP 1100

Historic Toodyay, only 85km northeast of Perth, is a popular weekend destination for city folk who like to while away an hour or so browsing the bric-a-brac shops and having a beer on the verandah of an old pub. As you'd expect of a town classified by the National Trust, it has plenty of heritage buildings, and charm oozes from their old stone bricks. Originally known by the name Newcastle, Toodyay (pronounced '2J'), came from the Aboriginal word *duidgee* (place of plenty); the name was adopted around 1910.

Sights & Activities

Connor's Mill MUSEUM
(Stirling Tce; admission $3; 9am-4pm) Start at the top of this aged flour mill (1870) and work your way down through three floors of chugging machinery and explanatory displays that cover the milling process, along with local history. Entry is through the neighbouring visitor centre. **St Stephen's Church** (1862), directly across the road, is also worth a look.

Newcastle Gaol MUSEUM
(17 Clinton St; admission $3; 10am-3pm) Built in the 1860s using convict labour, the goal complex includes a courtroom, cells and stables. A gallery tells the story of bushranger Joseph Bolitho Johns.

Coorinja WINERY
(Toodyay Rd; 10am-5pm Mon-Sat) Operating continuously since the 1870s, this winery specialises in fortified wines such as port, sherry, muscat and Marsala. It's 6km out of town, on the road to Perth.

Festivals & Events

Moondyne Festival HERITAGE
Costumed high jinks in honour of the outlaw; first Sunday of May.

Toodyay Festival of Food FOOD
Held on the first weekend in August on the day before the Avon Descent (see p107).

Toodyay Agricultural Show AGRICULTURAL SHOW
Early October.

THE MYTHOLOGY OF MOONDYNE JOE

The state of Victoria's most famous outlaw, Ned Kelly, is known for his gun battles with the law, but Western Australia's most illustrious bushranger, Moondyne Joe, is famous for escaping. Over and over again.

Joseph Bolitho Johns (1828–1900), sent to Western Australia for larceny, arrived in Fremantle in 1853 and was granted an immediate ticket of leave for good behaviour. This good behaviour lasted until 1861 when he was arrested on a charge of horse stealing, however, he escaped that night from Toodyay jail on the horse he rode in on, sitting snugly on the magistrate's new saddle. He was recaptured and sentenced to three years imprisonment. Between November 1865 and March 1867 he made four attempts to escape, three of them successful. When eventually captured he was placed in a special reinforced cell with triple-barred windows in Fremantle, but in 1867 he managed to escape from the prison yard while breaking rocks. He served more time in Fremantle prison when recaptured and was conditionally pardoned in 1873. After release he worked in the Vasse district and kept his nose relatively clean, but suffered from poor mental health later in life until his death in 1900. You can see his grave at Fremantle cemetery.

While Moondyne Joe was a criminal, these days it pays to be in the 'Moondyne Joe' business. Three books, including the latest, a prize-winning juvenile-fiction novel called *The Legend of Moondyne Joe* (Mark Greenwood), have been written about him; a Moondyne festival is held in Toodyay on the first Sunday of May; a cave in Margaret River is named after him; as well as a pub, a caravan park and who knows what else. Let's hope he doesn't escape his final resting place and start asking for royalties...

Sleeping & Eating

Avalon Homestead GUESTHOUSE $$
(☎9574 5050; www.avalonhomestead.com.au; 381 Julimar Rd; r $130) Popular with discerning oldies, Avalon has tidy, somewhat chintzy rooms in a peaceful spot 4km out of town. The gardens are lovely.

Top of the Terrace CAFE $$
(www.topoftheterrace.com.au; 1st fl, 123 Stirling Tce; breakfast & lunch $12-18, dinner $21-35; ⏱breakfast & lunch Wed-Sun, dinner Wed-Sat; wi-fi) The entrance through an uninspiring bakery makes this upmarket, upstairs cafe a very pleasant surprise. The terrace is great for daytime people-watching. Return in the evening for a substantial fusion-style meal but be sure to save room for the chef's homemade ice cream.

Cola Café & Museum CAFE $
(www.colacafe.com.au; 128 Stirling Tce; snacks $8-18; ⏱9am-4.30pm) Coca-Cola memorabilia runs amok here. Order a cola spider (coke with a scoop of ice-cream) and a big burger and play 'guess the 1950s tune'.

Information

Ye Olde Lolly Shoppe (☎9574 2435; www.toodyay.com; 7 Piesse St; ⏱9am-4pm) WA's tastiest visitor centre. Stock up on information and fudge at the same time.

Getting There & Away

Toodyay is a stop on the **Transwa** (☎1300 662 205; www.transwa.wa.gov.au) AvonLink and Prospector lines, with trains to East Perth ($16, 1¼ hours, seven per week), Northam ($8, 20 minutes, 12 per week) and Kalgoorlie ($74, 5½ hours, four per week).

Avon Valley National Park

Featuring granite outcrops, forests and wonderful fauna, this **national park** (www.dec.wa.gov.au; admission per car $11; ⏱8am-4pm) is accessed from Toodyay and Morangup Rds. The Avon River flows through the centre of the park in winter and spring, but is usually dry at other times.

The park is the northern limit of the jarrah forests, and the jarrah and marri are mixed with wandoo woodland. Bird species that make use of the forests include rainbow bee-eaters, honeyeaters, kingfishers and rufous treecreepers. Animals and reptiles live in the understorey: honey possums and western pygmy-possums hide among the dead leaves, and skinks and geckos are everywhere.

There are **camp sites** (☎9574 2540; per adult/child $7/2) with basic facilities (eg pit toilets and barbecues).

NEW NORCIA

POP 70

The idyllic monastery settlement of New Norcia, 132km from Perth, consists of a cluster of ornate, Spanish-style buildings set incongruously in the Australian bush. Founded in 1846 by Spanish Benedictine monks as an Aboriginal mission, the working monastery today holds prayers and retreats, alongside a business producing boutique breads and gourmet goodies.

New Norcia Museum & Art Gallery (☎9654 8056; www.newnorcia.com; Great Northern Hwy; combined museum & town tour adult/family $25/60; ⊙9am-4.30pm) traces the history of the monastery and houses impressive art, including contemporary exhibitions and one of the country's largest collections of post-Renaissance religious art. The gift shop sells souvenirs, honeys, preserves and breads baked in the monks' wood-fired oven.

Inside **abbey church**, try to spot the native wildlife in the sgraffito artworks that depict the stations of the Cross. Look hard, as there's also an astronaut.

Guided two-hour **town tours** (⊙11am & 1.30pm) offer a look inside the monks' private chapel within the monastery, the abbey chapel and the frescoed college chapels; purchase tickets from the museum. **Meet a Monk** (⊙10.30am Mon-Fri, 4.30pm Sat) gives you the chance to find out what it's like to be a monk. Choral concerts and organ recitals are also held.

New Norcia Hotel (☎9654 8034; www.newnorcia.com; Great Northern Hwy; s/d $75/95) harks back to a more genteel time, with sweeping staircases, high ceilings, understated rooms (with shared bathrooms) and wide verandahs. An international menu ($15 to $30) is available at the bar or in the elegant dining room (where you can also nab a cooked breakfast). Sit outside on the terrace and sample the delicious but deadly New Norcia Abbey Ale, a golden, hand-crafted, Belgian-style ale brewed especially for the abbey.

The abbey also offers full lodging in the **Monastery Guesthouse** (☎9654 8002; www.newnorcia.com; full board, suggested donation $75) within the walls of the southern cloister. Guests can also join in prayers with the monks (and males can dine with them).

Getting There & Away

Transwa coaches run from Perth ($21, 2hrs) on Tuesdays, Thursdays, Saturdays and Sundays, and return on Sundays, Tuesday and Thursdays. Integrity Coach Lines has a weekly service along the Great Northern Hwy that leaves Perth on Wednesdays and returns on Saturdays ($24, two hours).

THE WILDFLOWER WAY

Away from the coast, there are four other common routes that head north, with three running to Geraldton and the fourth, the Great Northern Hwy, disappearing into the outback and re-emerging 1600km later at Port Hedland. The Brand Hwy (Rte 1) is the least interesting for travellers, and its wildflowers can be sampled in daytrips from the Turquoise Coast (see p115). Midlands Rd (Rte 116) and The Wildflower Way (Rte 115) are home to wheat silos, wildflowers and little one-pub towns; the towns are a hive of activity between August and September as minibuses full of pensioners zoom around like frantic bees hunting blossoms. Whatever the time of year, the wheat farmers have one eye on the weather and one on their crop, no doubt wondering if it will ever rain again.

Getting There & Away

Transwa (☎1300 662 205; www.transwa.wa.gov.au) run bus services along Rte 116 on Tuesdays, Thursdays, Saturdays and Sundays, and twice weekly (to/from Geraldton on Mondays and Thursdays/Tuesdays and Fridays) on Rte 115.

Integrity (☎1800 226 339; www.integritycoachlines.com.au; to/from Perth Sat/Wed) runs buses weekly up the Great Northern Hwy (Rte 95).

Moora

POP 2574

Tall gums, wide streets, a pub with a wide verandah, a couple of galleries, a few B&Bs and a railway line (wheat trains only) define this agricultural service centre, all of which make it a good base to explore the surrounding area.

The excellent **visitor centre** (☎9653 1053; www.moora.wa.gov.au; Moora Railway Stn; ⊙8.30am-4pm Mon-Fri; @) can supply a map of the local wildflowers and other sites including **Jingemia Cave** in **Watheroo National Park**. There's also an interesting town walk that takes in Moora's heritage buildings and murals.

Moora Caravan Park (☎0409 511 400, 9651 1401; Dandaragan St; unpowered/powered site $18/25) offers basic, shady sites. Pay at the Gull service station. If you're after more comfort, the visitor centre can arrange accommodation at some well-maintained B&Bs but you'll need a car as most are slightly out of town. Try **Manning on Moore** (☎9651 1279; 302 Dandaragan Rd; d $100) or **Green Willows** (☎9653 1176; 209 Riley Rd; d $95; 📶).

Right in the centre of town, the **Drovers Inn** (☎9651 1108; cnr Dandaragan & Padbury Sts; mains $20-30, d $95; ⏲dinner) is a classic Aussie pub that offers standard rooms and typical counter meals.

Moora's **Pioneer Bakery & Restaurant** (☎9651 1277; 50 Padbury St; meals $5-20; ⏲7.30am-4pm Mon-Fri) is a great place for brekkie, and the fresh pies are delicious. The best coffee (and muffins!) in town is at the **Wheatbelt Gallery** (Padbury St, opp visitors centre; ⏲9am-5pm Tue-Sat), while art nobs can cross the tracks to **Moora Art Gallery** (☎0447 997 423; 95 Gardiner St;⏲11am-4pm Thu-Sat).

There's a supermarket, newsagency and ATMs on Dandaragan and Padbury Sts.

Transwa buses run to Perth ($28, three hours) and Geraldton ($43, four hours) along Rte 116.

Wongan Hills

POP 1462

If you're coming from the direction of New Norcia, take the back road via Yerecoin and you'll pass by the intriguing **Lake Ninan**, a huge saltpan. Wongan Hills, with its gently undulating country and myriad verticordias, makes a pleasant change from the flat Wheatbelt towns, and there are plenty of trails here to excite bushwalkers.

The friendly **visitor centre** (☎9671 1973; www.wongantourism.com.au; Railway Station, Wongan Rd; ⏲9am-5pm, closed Sun Nov-Easter) has maps (and guides) for popular wildflower haunts such as **Mt Matilda** (8km return), 12km west of Wongan Hills and **Christmas Rock** (behind the caravan park; 2km return). **Reynoldson Nature Reserve** (1km one-way), 29km north of Wongan Hills, has spectacular verticordias, and you can drive to the top of **Mt O'Brien**, 11km west of Wongan Hills.

Wongan Hills Caravan Park (☎9671 1009; Wongan Rd; unpowered/powered site $17/22, chalet $90) has shady sites and a good kitchen.

Art deco **Wongan Hills Hotel** (☎9671 1022; www.wonganhillshotel.com.au; 5 Fenton Pl; hotel s/d $55/75, motel d $100, meals $15-35) offers classic hotel rooms, some opening onto the upstairs verandah, and modern motel rooms in a separate building. Meals are typical pub fare.

There's an excellent, well-stocked supermarket and a bakery on Fenton Place.

Transwa has services to Perth ($28, three hours), and Perenjori ($28, three hours) via Rte 115.

Perenjori

POP 573

Perenjori, 360km from Perth, is a pretty little town surrounded by abundant wildlife and, from July to November, stunning wildflowers, making it a pleasant stopover. The **visitor centre** (☎9973 1105; www.perenjori.wa.gov.au; Fowler St; ⏲9am-4pm Mon-Fri Jul-Oct), also home to the **pioneer museum** (adult/child $2/0.50), has handy self-drive tour brochures called *The Way of the Wildflowers* and *Monsignor Hawes Heritage Trail,* and can provide access to the beautiful **St Joseph's Church**, designed by the prolific Monsignor John Hawes.

Shady **Perenjori Caravan Park** (☎9973 1193; Crossing Rd; unpowered/powered site $15/25, cabin $100) offers grassy tent sites and decent facilities, including a camper's kitchen with a beautiful mosaic table.

The friendly, family-owned **Perenjori Hotel** (☎9973 1020; Fowler St; d $65; mains $18-24) has basic pub rooms including breakfast, and possibly the cheapest reef and beef (steak with seafood sauce) in the state ($24).

Transwa has services to Perth ($50, six hours) and Geraldton ($34, three hours) via Rte 115.

Morawa, Mingenew & Mullewa

The 'three Ms' form a triangle that buzzes during wildflower season, but offers limited appeal to travellers outside this time; most of the visitor centres close, and the attractions of Port Denison-Dongara and Geraldton are only an hour away.

All three towns have a basic caravan park with tent sites, a local pub that does standard counter meals and rooms, a supermarket or general store, and a Transwa bus that passes through several times a week. In wildflower season, the shire may run minibuses from the visitor centres to the best sites.

Morawa and Mullewa both have distinctive churches designed by Monsignor John Hawes.

Coalseam Conservation Park (camping per person $7), 34km northeast of Mingenew on the Irwin River, has a variety of everlastings (paper daisies), a short loop walk with interpretive signs, and ancient fossil shells embedded in the cliffs. There are dusty, unpowered campsites at Miners, with toilets and picnic tables.

Mullewa is famous for its wreath flower, *Lechenaultia macrantha,* and the visitor centre has a good map of self-guided walks on which you'll hopefully spot it. The town holds an annual wildflower show at the end of August.

In season, the roads heading east to Yalgoo are normally carpeted in everlastings.

Information

Mingenew visitor centre (☎9928 1081; Mingenew post office; ⌚9am-5pm Jul-Sep)

Morawa visitor centre (☎9971 1421; 34 Winfield St; ⌚8.30am-4.30pm May-Oct)

Mullewa visitor centre (☎9961 1500; www.mullewatourism.com.au; cnr Jose St & Maitland Rd; ⌚8.30am-4.30pm, closed Sat & Sun Oct-Jun; @)

SUNSET COAST

The coast road north of Perth leads to some popular spots, each with its own unique drawcard. Within an hour's drive of the city centre, Perth's outer suburbs give way to the bushland oasis of Yanchep National Park, which has plenty of wonderful wildlife and walking trails.

The coastline ranges from tranquil bays at Guilderton, which are good for swimming and fishing, to windswept beaches at Lancelin, with excellent conditions for windsurfing and kite-surfing.

Yanchep

POP 2482

Yanchep and its close neighbour Two Rocks are effectively Perth's northernmost suburbs. The town was developed extensively during the 1980s by convicted fraudster Alan Bond, and the legacy of this era includes a large marina and some dubious bits of sculpture (dolphins, a dragon and a giant King Neptune).

Apart from some nice beaches, the big drawcard here is the woodlands and wetlands of **Yanchep National Park** (www.dec.wa.gov.au/yanchep; Wanneroo Rd; admission per car $11; ⌚visitors centre 9.15am-4.30pm), home to hundreds of species of fauna and flora, including koalas, kangaroos, emus and cockatoos. The free *Wild About Walking* brochure outlines nine walking trails, which range from the 20-minute Dwerta Mia walk to the four-day Coastal Plain walk; register with the park centre for longer walks.

The park features splendid caves, which can be viewed on 45-minute tours (adult/child $10/5; five per day). On weekends, local Noongar guides run excellent tours on Indigenous history, lifestyle and culture (adult/child $10/5), and didgeridoo and dance performances (adult/child $10/5). There's also a free koala talk at 3pm daily and a free history tour on Saturdays.

Within the national park, **Yanchep Inn** (☎9561 1001; hotel s/d from $45/70, old motel s/d $80/105, new motel s $140-160, d $170-210; ❄) is much more attractive from the outside than inside. The inn itself has basic rooms with ageing shared facilities and a cafe downstairs. It's much more comfortable in the newer of the two motel blocks (which has lake views and rammed earth walls), but perhaps a little overpriced. Prices jump up by around $20 on weekends.

To get to Yanchep by public transport, catch a train on the Joondalup line from Perth's Esplanade station to Clarkson, then catch bus 490.

Guilderton

POP 150

Some 43km north of Yanchep, Guilderton is a popular and staggeringly beautiful family-holiday spot. Children paddle safely near the mouth of the Moore River, while adults enjoy the excellent fishing and surfing on the ocean beach.

The name comes from the wreck of the *Vergulde Draeck,* part of the Dutch East India Company fleet, which ran aground nearby in 1656 reputedly carrying a treasure in guilders. Its original name was Gabbadah, meaning 'mouth of water', although many older Perthites still refer to it as Moore River.

The wonderfully positioned **Guilderton Caravan Park** (☎9577 1021; www.guildertoncaravanpark.com.au; 2 Dewar St; sites per 2 people $24-32, chalets $100-175;) is the holidaymakers' hub in this laid-back town. Chalets are self-contained, but you'll need your own linen. The park has a cafe and a general store that sells essentials, and there's a little volunteer-run **visitor centre** (which has erratic hours) next door.

Lancelin

POP 670

What do you do when the beach is windy? Harness yourself to a sail and strap yourself to a surfboard, of course! Afternoon offshore winds and shallows, protected by an outlying reef, make for perfect windsurfing and kitesurfing conditions, attracting action-seekers from around the world. In January it's a veritable festival of wind-worshippers during the **Lancelin Ocean Classic** (www.lancelinoceanclassic.com.au) windsurfer race, which starts at Ledge Point.

Lancelin's attractions aren't all blowin' in the wind. The coral and limestone reef, no-fishing zone and dazzling white sands make it a great snorkelling spot, while the mountainous, soft, white dunes on the edge of town are a playground for sandboarders.

Activities

Surfschool SURFING
(☎9444 5399; www.surfschool.com; lessons adult/child $55/50, 2-/3-/4-day surf camps $330/460/585) The gentle waves at the main beach make it a good place for beginners to learn to surf and there are bigger breaks nearby for more experienced surfers. Two-hour lessons include boards and wetsuits. They also run surf-camp packages, which include transfers from Perth, accommodation and five hours of lessons per day.

Desert Storm Adventures DUNE RIDES
(☎9655 2550; www.desertstorm.com.au; adult/child $55/35) This shiny yellow vampiric American school bus on steroids, billed as 'the world's largest 4WD tour coach', takes delighted (sometimes shrieking) travellers on a wild ride daily through the dunes.

Werner's Hot Spot WINDSURFING
(☎9655 1448; www.wernershotspot.blogspot.com) Werner offers windsurfing lessons and hires out gear from his Kombi parked at the beach between October and March (phone at other times and he'll meet you).

Have a Chat General Store SANDBOARDING
(☎9655 1054; 104 Gingin Rd; ⏰7am-7pm) Hires sandboards for $10 per two hours.

Sleeping & Eating

TOP CHOICE **Lancelin Lodge YHA** HOSTEL $
(☎9655 2020; www.lancelinlodge.com.au; 10 Hopkins St; dm $27-30, r $70; @🛜🏊) This laid-back hostel is well equipped and welcoming, with wide verandahs and lots of communal spaces to hang about in. The excellent facilities include a big kitchen, barbecue, wood-fire pizza oven, decent-sized swimming pool, ping-pong table, volleyball court and free use of bikes and boogie boards.

Windsurfer Beach Chalets APARTMENTS $$
(☎9655 1454; www.lancelinaccommodation.com.au; 1 Hopkins St; d $150, plus $35 per additional person) These simple, self-contained two-bedroom chalets are the closest accommodation to the windsurfing beach and are a good choice for groups of friends and families (each chalet sleeps up to six). They're functional and well equipped, and have a sun terrace that backs onto a grassy area.

Lancelin Caravan Park CARAVAN PARK $
(☎9655 1056; Hopkins St; site per person $14; on-site vans $70) Sailboarders love camping out at this neat park – not for the facilities and amenities, which are rudimentary, but for the beachfront location.

Endeavour Tavern PUB $$
(58 Gingin Rd; mains $15-34) A classic beachfront Aussie pub with a beer garden that overlooks the ocean, and a pool table, darts and a TAB (betting agency). The casual eatery serves decent seafood, pub grub classics and a tasty Mediterranean platter.

Getting There & Away

Lancelin is 130km north of Perth. **Greyhound** (☎1300 473 946; www.greyhound.com.au) has coaches to and from East Perth ($26, 1¾ hours), Cervantes ($26, 1½ hours), Geraldton ($50, 4¼ hours) and Carnarvon ($142, 9½ hours).

TURQUOISE COAST

Stretching north of Lancelin to Leeman, the Turquoise Coast contains sleepy fishing villages, stunning beaches, extraordinary geological formations, rugged national parks and incredibly diverse flora. The area was once considered somewhat out of the way, however, the completion of the final section of Indian Ocean Dr between Lancelin and Cervantes has brought the whole area within easy grasp of Perth.

Getting There & Away

Greyhound (☎1300 473 946; www.greyhound.com.au) runs services to and from Perth along Indian Ocean Drive three times per week.

Cervantes & Pinnacles Desert

POP 500

Heading north from Lancelin on the new road, you will pass the tiny fishing-shack villages of **Wedge Island** and **Grey**, where access was previously only via 4WD along the beach. The future of these shack villages is uncertain, and although there are no facilities for tourists, you're welcome to wander.

The laid-back crayfishing town of **Cervantes**, 198km north of Perth, makes a pleasant overnight stop for enjoying the **Pinnacles Desert** and a good base for exploring the flora of the Kwongan, the inland heathland of **Lesueur National Park** and **Badgingarra National Park**. There are also some lovely beaches on which to while away the time.

Grab a copy of the *Turquoise Coast Self Drive Map* from Cervantes' combined **post office and visitor centre** (☎9652 7700; www.visitpinnaclescountry.com.au; Cadiz St; ⊙7.30am-5pm) which also supplies accommodation and tours information. The town's general store, liquor shop, internet access and takeaway store are also along this small strip.

Sights & Activities

Nambung National Park NATURE RESERVE

(per car $11) This national park, 19km from Cervantes, is home to the spectacular **Pinnacles Desert**, where an army of petrified aliens lies scattered across the surface of Mars – or so it seems. Thousands of limestone pillars rise up from the desert floor, their lime-rich sand originating from seashells that have compacted with rain and subsequently eroded. A loop-road runs through the formations, but it's more fun to wander among them, especially at sunset, full moon or dawn when the light is sublime and the crowds evaporate. Nearby **Kangaroo Point** and **Hangover Bay** both make nice picnic spots with BBQs and tables. The latter has the better swimming.

Just before town, turn-off for **Lake Thetis**, where living stromatolites – the world's oldest organisms – inhabit the shoreline. Nearby **Hansen Bay Lookout** has excellent views across the coast. In town, walkways wend along the coastline and provide beach access.

Lesueur National Park NATURE RESERVE

(per car $11) About 50km north of Cervantes is the botanical paradise of Lesueur National Park, which has a staggering 820 different plant species, many of them rare and endemic, such as the pine banksia and Mt Lesueur grevillea; the heath erupts into a mass of colour in late winter. The park also provides a habitat for the endangered Carnaby's Cockatoo. There's an 18km circuit drive on a good road, with lookouts and picnic areas. Don't miss the walk to the trig on flat-topped **Mt Lesueur** (4km return) with its panoramic view of the coast.

Tours

Lots of Perth-based companies offer day trips to the Pinnacles. One excellent local company is **Turquoise Coast Enviro Tours** (☎9652 7047; www.thepinnacles.com.au; 59 Seville St; 3hr Pinnacles tour $60, full-day Kwongan tour $170). Ex-ranger Mike Newton runs three-hour Pinnacles trips in the morning (8am) and evening (2½ hours before sunset), as well as a full-day Kwongan tour which includes Lesueur National Park and the coast up to Leeman.

Sleeping & Eating

Some accommodation prices increase over school holidays.

TOP CHOICE **Cervantes Lodge & Pinnacles Beach Backpackers** HOSTEL $

(☎1800 245 232; www.cervanteslodge.com.au; 91 Seville St; dm $30, d with/without bathroom $120/80; @) In a great location behind the dunes, this relaxing hostel has a wide verandah, small and tidy dorms, a nice communal kitchen and cosy lounge area. Bright, spacious en-suite rooms, some with ocean or heath views, are next door in the lodge.

TOP CHOICE **Amble Inn** B&B $$

(☎0429 652 401; 2150 Cadda Rd, Hill River; d spa/non-spa $150/135; ❄) High up on the heathland, about 25km east of Cervantes, is this hidden gem of a B&B with beautiful

WORTH A TRIP

KWONGAN WILDFLOWERS

Take any road that heads inland from the Turquoise Coast and you'll soon be into the Kwongan heathlands, where, depending on the season, the roadside verges burst with native wildflowers: banksia, grevillea, hakea, calothamnus, kangaroo paw and smokebush are just a few. While Lesueur National Park is the obvious choice for wildflower spotters, consider some of the following options.

» **Badgingarra National Park** Three and a half kilometres of walking trails, kangaroo paws, banksias, grass trees, verticordia and a rare mallee. The back road linking Badgingarra to Lesueur is particularly rich in flora. Obtain details from the Badgingarra Roadhouse. There's also a picnic area on Bibby Rd.

» **Alexander Morrison National Park** Named after WA's first botanist. There are no trails, but you can drive through slowly on the Coorow Green Head Rd, which has loads of flora along its verge all the way from Lesueur. Expect to see dryandra, banksia, grevillea, smokebush, leschenaultia and honey myrtle.

» **Tathra National Park** Tathra has similar flora to Alexander Morrison National Park and the drive between the two is rich with banksia, kangaroo paw and grevillea.

» **Brand Highway (Rte 1)** Not exactly conducive to slow meandering, however, the highway verges are surprisingly rich in wildflowers, especially either side of Eneabba.

If you're getting overwhelmed and frustrated by not being able to identify all these strange new plants, consider staying at **Western Flora Caravan Park** (☎9955 2030; wfloracp@activ8.net.au; Brand Hwy, North Eneabba; unpowered/powered sites $23/25, d $65, on-site vans $75; chalets $110) where the passionate owners run free two-hour wildflower walks across their 65-hectare property every day at 4.30pm.

thick stone walls, cool, wide verandahs and superbly styled rooms. Watch the sunset over the coast from the nearby hill with a glass of your complimentary wine.

Pinnacles Caravan Park CARAVAN PARK $
(☎9652 7060; www.pinnaclespark.com.au; 35 Aragon St; unpowered/powered sites from $15/26, on-site vans/cabins $50/75; wi-fi) There are plenty of shady, grassy sites right behind the beach at this excellent park. **Seashells Cafe** (⊙8am-5pm) does a super coffee and cake with the best view in town.

Cervantes Country Club SEAFOOD $$
(☎9652 7123; Aragon St; seafood platters $55) Shorts and sandals are fine at this humble sporting club, which does incredible seafood platters for two, which include crays (in season), prawns, oysters, fish, calamari, salad and a mountain of chips.

Cervantes Holiday Homes APARTMENTS $$
(☎9652 7115; www.cervantesholidayhomes.com.au; cnr Malaga Ct & Valencia Rd; cottage from $120; air-con) These well-equipped, fully self-contained cottages are great value, especially if there are a few of you needing group accommodation.

Pinnacles Edge Resort RESORT $$$
(☎9652 7788; www.pinnaclesedgeresort.com.au; 7 Aragon St; studio/spa/2-bedroom $205/255/330; air-con, pool, wi-fi) Beautifully appointed luxury rooms, the more expensive with spas and balconies, are arranged around a central pool. There's an in-house restaurant and bar, and the adjoining motel has older-style doubles from $145.

Getting There & Away

Greyhound has services to Perth ($34, three hours) and Dongara ($39, two hours), continuing to Broome ($350, 31 hours). The bus stops locally at Jurien (10 minutes), Green Head (30 minutes) and Leeman (40 minutes).

Jurien Bay

POP 1500

The largest town on the Turquoise Coast is home to a hefty fishing fleet and lots of big houses. It's rather spread out, and has a nice long swimming beach and a choice of jetties for fishing. There's a pleasant seaside walk and park near the Old Jetty.

Book ahead for the popular **Jurien Bay Tourist Park** (☎9652 1595; www.jurienbay

touristpark.com.au; Roberts St; unpowered/powered site $26/35; on-site van $75-105; 1-/2-bedroom chalet $130/165), with its comfortable chalets right behind the beach, although the tent sites are set back against the main road. Next door, the **Jetty Cafe** (☎9652 1999; meals $5-17; ⏰7.30am-5pm) has a great position and does all-day brekkies as well as grilled fish and burgers.

The friendly **Sandpiper Tavern** (☎9652 1229; cnr Roberts & Sandpiper Sts; mains $18-38; ⏰lunch & dinner) has a relaxed beer garden and does all the usual pub faves. There are several takeaway shops strung along Bashford St, as well as a supermarket and ATM.

Green Head & Leeman

On the way to Green Head, stop at **Grigson Lookout** for a panoramic view of the coast and Kwongan. Tiny **Green Head** (pop 300) has several beautiful bays; the horseshoe-shaped **Dynamite Bay** is the most spectacular and sheltered for swimmers. There's good fishing, surfing and windsurfing here and at nearby **Leeman** (population 680), where the annual summer 'Screaming Leeman' windsurfing tournament is held.

Sea Lion Charters (☎9953 1012; http://sealioncharters.biz; 24 Bryant St, Green Head; half-day tours adult/child $120/60) offers a truly magical experience by allowing you to interact with sea lions in their own environment. These ever-curious creatures approach in shallow water, playing with each other while checking you out, and then mimic your movements. It helps to be a good snorkeller. Wetsuits are $10 extra.

Green Head has a couple of nice B&Bs with views – **Seaview** (☎9953 1487; 25 Whiteman St; per person $75) and **Maccas** (☎9953 1461; 1 Farley St; d $140). The **Green Head Caravan Park** (☎9953 1131; 9 Green Head Rd, Green Head; unpowered/powered site $18/21, on-site van from $47) is relaxed and shady, though it seems to run on autopilot most of the time.

Leafy **Leeman Caravan Park** (☎9953 1080; 43 Thomas St, Leeman; unpowered/powered site $20/25, on-site van $60, cabin $70-90) has lots of shade, grassy sites and a good camp kitchen all just behind the beach.

Green Head has a general store and **Cool Combination Cafe** (Dynamite Bay; ⏰9.30am-4pm Mon-Sat); Leeman has a supermarket, service station, internet and the **Snack Shack** (☎9953 1110; Spencer St; snacks $3-11; ⏰7am-8pm, to 3pm Mon).

If you have a 4WD, **Stockyard Gully Caves** are 30km away, off the Coorow Green Head Rd, and you can explore the underground creek and caverns with a torch. Watch out for bees and bats.

Margaret River & the Southwest

Includes »

Best Places to Eat

- » Vasse Felix (p128)
- » Knee Deep in Margaret River (p128)
- » McHenry's Farm Shop (p133)
- » Xanadu (p133)
- » Lamont's (p128)

Best Places to Stay

- » Injidup Spa Retreat (p127)
- » Baywatch Manor YHA (p134)
- » Old Picture Theatre Holiday Apartments (p137)
- » Margaret River Lodge YHA (p129)
- » Smiths Beach Resort (p127)

Why Go?

The farmland, forests, rivers and coast of the lush, green southwestern corner of Western Australia (WA) contrast vividly with the stark, sunburnt terrain of much of the state. On land, world-class wineries beckon and tall trees provide shade for walking trails and scenic drives, while offshore, bottlenose dolphins and whales frolic, and devoted surfers search for – and often find – their perfect break.

Unusually for WA, distances between the many attractions are short, and driving time is mercifully limited, making it a fantastic area to explore for a few days – you will get much more out of your stay here if you have your own wheels. Summer brings hordes of visitors, but in the wintry months from July to September the cosy pot-bellied stove rules and visitors are scarce, and while opening hours can be somewhat erratic, prices are much more reasonable.

When to Go

Margaret River

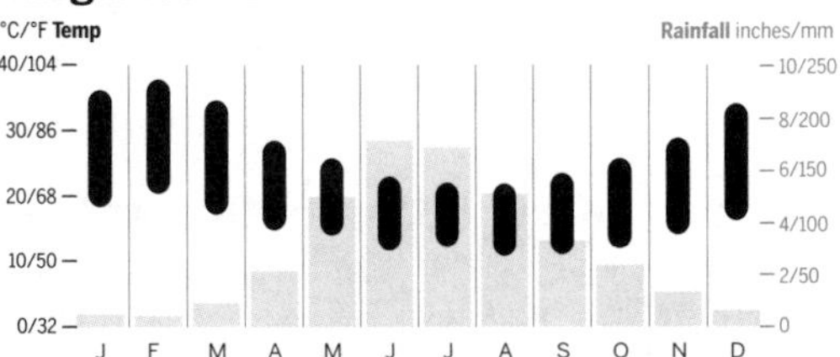

January Follow the party crowds from the Southbound festival to the beach.

March Catch surf and wine festivals in Margaret River, and the Nannup music festival.

August Head to empty beaches, Margaret River wineries and Busselton's film festival.

Margaret River & the Southwest Highlights

1. Sample the first-class wine, food and architecture of the **Margaret River wine region** (p125)
2. Explore the labyrinthine limestone caverns along Caves Rd, especially beautiful **Lake Cave** (p132)
3. Front-up to the impressive coastline at Augusta's **Cape Leeuwin lighthouse** (p133), at the confluence of the Indian and Southern Oceans
4. Sink into the depths of the tall trees surrounding **Pemberton** (p137)
5. Revel in the wild beauty of **Cape Naturaliste** and **Bunker Bay** (p124)
6. Canoe from the forest to the sea along the Blackwood River, starting at **Nannup** (p134)
7. Get all your blues out in the charming little town of **Bridgetown** (p135)

GEOGRAPHE BAY

Turquoise waters and white sands are the defining features of this gorgeous bay, lined with 30km of excellent swimming beaches. Positioned between the Indian Ocean and a sea of wine, the beachside towns of Busselton and Dunsborough attract hordes of holidaymakers seeking to spend their vacations with sand between their toes and a glass between their lips. It may be 230km from Perth, but once you get here the attractions are close together, certainly by WA standards. Unsurprisingly, it gets *very* busy during summer and at holiday times when prices may rise 30% on those given here.

For 55,000 years the area from Geographe Bay to Augusta belonged to the Wardandi, one of the Noongar peoples. They lived a nomadic life linked to the seasons, heading to the coast in summer to fish and journeying inland during the wet winter months.

The French connection to many of the current place names dates from the early 19th-century expedition by the ships *Le Géographe* and *Naturaliste,* after which the bay and the cape were named. Thomas Vasse, a crewman who was lost at sea, is remembered in the name of a village, river, inlet, Busselton bar and Margaret River winery. The latter two are particularly fitting as it's quite possible he was drunk when he was washed away. According to local Wardandi, who found and fed him, he made it to shore but later died on the beach waiting for his ship to return.

Bunbury

POP 66,100

The southwest's only city is struggling to remake its image from that of an industrial port into a seaside holiday destination. It still isn't particularly interesting or attractive, but it is an important gateway to the area. It's here where the main route south from Perth branches off into the Bussell Hwy (to the Margaret River wine region) and the South Western Hwy (Rte 1, to the southern forests and south coast). It's also the southmost stop on the train network and a hub for regional buses.

If you've just travelled 170km from Perth by car, it's a logical spot to stretch your legs, with plenty of eateries and a few things to do. The town centre has basically one main street (Victoria) with a little commercial area on either side of it and then, suddenly, houses and, within a few blocks to the west, the beach. The port area, immediately to the north, has been redeveloped, with waterside restaurants and silos converted into a hotel.

The city lies at the western end of Leschenault Inlet; the area was named Port Leschenault after the botanist on Nicolas Baudin's ship *Le Géographe* in 1803, but in a classic case of colonial one-upmanship, Governor James Stirling renamed it Bunbury in honour of the lieutenant that he placed in charge of the original military outpost. The first British settlers arrived in 1838.

Sights

Big Swamp Wildlife Park ZOO
(Prince Philip Dr; adult/child $8/5; 10am-5pm) A parrot with the broadest Aussie accent greets you with a cheery 'Hullo, how ya goin', while in the big walk-through aviary his inquisitive cousins swoop onto shoulders, making cartoon pirates out of unwary visitors. There are also kangaroos, wallabies, possums, owls and emus. Across the road, the **Big Swamp** has good walking tracks around the wetlands and seats to hang out and birdwatch from. To get here, head south on Ocean Dr, turn left at Hayward St and continue through the roundabout to Prince Philip Dr.

FREE **Bunbury Regional Art Galleries** ART GALLERY
(www.brag.org.au; 64 Wittenoom St; 10am-4pm) Housed in a restored pink-painted convent (1897), this excellent gallery has a collection, which includes works by Australian art luminaries Arthur Boyd and Sir Sidney Nolan.

St Mark's (Old Picton) Church CHURCH
(cnr Charterhouse Close & Flynn St, East Bunbury) Built in 1842 using wattle and daub construction, this is WA's second-oldest church. If you can't get inside, you can always peer through the windows and check out the old wooden grave markers.

King Cottage MUSEUM
(77 Forrest Ave; adult/child $5/3; 2-4pm) A family house (1880) with a small collection of tools and knick-knacks. To find it, head south on Spencer St and veer left onto Forrest Ave.

Activities

Walking Tracks WALKING
Mangrove Boardwalk (enter off Koombana Dr) allows you to explore the most southerly mangroves in WA, rich with more than 70 species of birds. Helpful interpretive signs

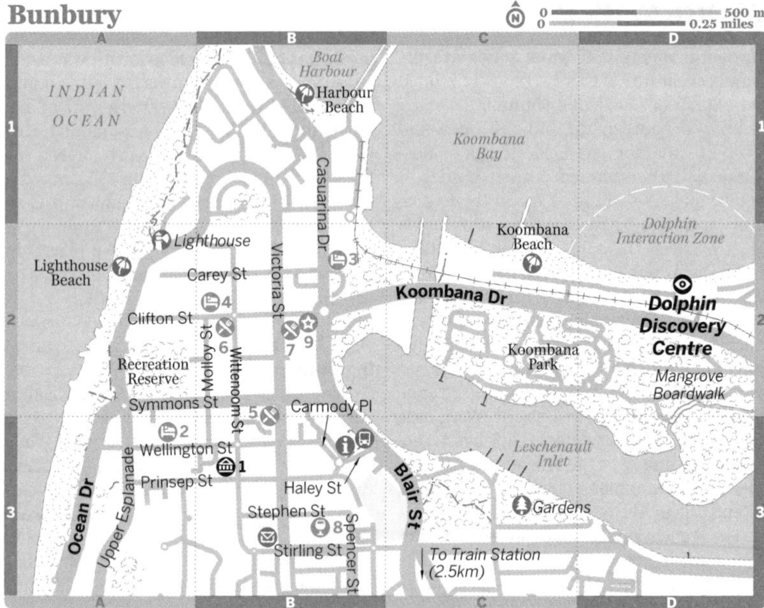

Bunbury

Top Sights

Dolphin Discovery Centre....D2

Sights

1 Bunbury Regional Art Galleries....B3

Sleeping

2 Dolphin Retreat YHA....A3
3 Mantra....B2
4 Wander Inn Backpackers....B2

Eating

5 Benesse....B2
6 L'Amour de la Femme....B2
7 Mojo's....B2

Drinking

Fitzgerald's....(see 7)
8 Prince of Wales....B3

Entertainment

9 Bunbury Regional Entertainment Centre....B2
Grand Cinemas....(see 7)

provide information about this ancient ecosystem, thought to be about 2500 years old. In contrast, a stretch of tall **Tuart Forest** runs along the southern end of Ocean Dr.

Pick up the *Walk-it Bunbury* brochure from the visitor centre.

Dekked Out Adventures KAYAKING
(☎9796 1000; www.dekkedout.com.au; Grand Canals boat ramp, Riviera Way, Eaton; adult/student $70/50; ⏰8.30am) Runs four-hour dolphin-spotting tours in the Collie River, Leschenault Estuary and bay. It also hires kayaks (single per half-/full-day $45/55) and sandboards (per half-/full-day $15/25).

Sleeping

Mantra APARTMENTS $$
(☎9721 0100; www.mantra.com.au; 1 Holman St; apt from $179;) One of the most unusual heritage conversions we've seen, the Mantra has sculpted a set of modern studios and apartments out of four grain silos by the harbour. Deluxe rooms have spa baths and full kitchens.

Bunbury Glade Caravan Park CARAVAN PARK $
(☎9721 3800; www.glade.com.au; Timperley Rd; 2-person sites $25-33, cabins $70-140;) Hidden behind high hedges, this spotless park is a five-minute drive from the centre of town on Blair St, the main road heading south.

Dolphin Retreat YHA HOSTEL $
(☎9792 4690; www.dolphinretreatbunbury.com.au; 14 Wellington St; dm/s/d $27/47/68; @)

DON'T MISS

DOLPHIN DISCOVERY CENTRE

Around 60 bottlenose dolphins live in Bunbury's Koombana Bay year-round, their numbers increasing to 260 in summer. The **Dolphin Discovery Centre** (☎9791 3088; www.dolphindiscovery.com.au; Koombana Beach; adult/child $10/5; ⊙9am-2pm Jun-Sep, 8am-4pm Oct-May) has a beachside zone where dolphins regularly come to interact with people in the shallows and you can wade in alongside them, under the supervision of trained volunteers. There are no guarantees of a close encounter but they are more likely in the early mornings between November and April, although they can happen at any time. Entry tickets are valid to the end of the calendar month, so you can try your luck as often as you like within that time.

If you want to up your chances, there are **Eco Cruises** (1½-hr cruise adult/child $53/35; ⊙11am year-round, plus 1pm Oct & May, 3pm Nov-Apr) and **Swim Encounter Cruises** (3-hr cruise $185; ⊙8am Oct-Apr & noon Nov-May).

The centre also has lots of dolphin information and tanks with lobsters and seahorses. A new digital theatre is being planned along with more aquariums. If you fancy volunteering, there's a minimum commitment of six weeks full-time.

Just around the corner from the beach, this small hostel is well located in a rabbit warren of an old house, with hammocks and a barbecue on the back verandah.

Wander Inn Backpackers HOSTEL $
(☎1800 039 032; www.bunburybackpackers.com.au; 16 Clifton St; dm $27-29, s $40-47, d $68; @) Occupying a cheerful, old blue-and-yellow house down a quiet side street between the beach and the main strip, this friendly hostel offers free basic breakfasts.

Eating

Benesse CAFE $
(83 Victoria St; mains $10-18; ⊙7.30am-5.30pm) Chic and petite, Benesse is the best of Bunbury's cafes, serving tasty toasties, salads, pizza and all-day breakfasts.

Mojo's CAFE $$
(www.mojosrestaurant.com.au; Victoria St; breakfast $7-22, lunch $17-25, dinner $21-38; ⊙breakfast, lunch & dinner) Stylish Mojo's sunny outdoor tables are the place to watch the world go by and agonise over what you'll order from the local-produce-focused menu.

L'Amour de la Femme MODERN AUSTRALIAN $$$
(www.lamourrestaurant.com.au; 18 Wittenoom St; 2-/3-courses $65/75; ⊙lunch Fri & Sun, dinner Wed-Sat) Passionate cooking nuzzles up to quality ingredients in this oddly positioned restaurant, in a residential street near the centre.

Drinking & Entertainment

Fitzgerald's PUB
(Victoria St; ⊙6pm-3am Thu-Sun) With a big beer garden and an easy, laid-back vibe, Fitzie's is popular for a Sunday session. And, yes, it's an Irish bar.

Prince of Wales PUB
(41 Stephen St) Longstanding live music venue.

Grand Cinemas CINEMA
(www.moviemasters.com.au; cnr Victoria & Clifton Sts)

Bunbury Regional Entertainment Centre CONCERT HALL
(www.bunburyentertainment.com; Blair St) The region's main cultural centre, attracting local and international acts.

Information

Visitor Centre (☎9792 7205; www.visitbunbury.com.au; Carmody Pl; ⊙9am-5pm Mon-Sat, 9.30am-4.30pm Sun) Located in the historic train station (1904).

Getting There & Around

Bus

Central Bus Station (☎9722 7800; Carmody Pl) Coaches stop at the central bus station, next to the visitor centre, or at the **train station** (Picton Rd, Woolaston).

Transwa (☎1300 662 205; www.transwa.wa.gov.au) Routes include the following:

» SW1 (12 weekly) to East Perth ($29, 3¼ hours), Mandurah ($16, two hours), Busselton ($9, 43 minutes), Margaret River ($16, two hours) and Augusta ($24, 2½ hours)

» SW2 (three weekly) to Balingup ($13, 53 minutes), Bridgetown ($16, 1¼ hours) and Pemberton ($26, 2¼ hours)

» GS3 (daily) to Walpole ($41, 4½ hours), Denmark ($46, 5½ hours) and Albany ($53, six hours)

WORTH A TRIP

GEOGRAPHE WINE REGION

If it's wine that's lured you to the southwest, the **Geographe wine region** (www.geographewine.com.au) is the perfect primer for the glories to come. You may not have heard of it, but Geographe has 1200 hectares under vines, producing 11% of the state's output in 46 different wineries. The region's best-known brand is conveniently located halfway between Bunbury and Busselton. **Capel Vale** (www.capelvale.com; Mallokup Rd; ⊙10am-4pm) offers free tastings and a restaurant overlooking the vines, serving morning and afternoon tea and lunch. It's located off the Bussell Hwy on the opposite side of the highway from Capel village.

South West Coach Lines (☎9261 7600; www.veoliatransportwa.com.au) Runs services to/from Perth's Esplanade Busport (2½ hours, three daily), Mandurah (1¼ hours, daily), Busselton (1¼ hours, five daily), Dunsborough (1¾ hours, daily) and Bridgetown (1¾ hours, daily).

Bunbury City Transit (☎9791 1955; www.bct.com.au).Runs buses 101 (20 minutes, seven daily) and 103 (30 minutes, five daily) between the central bus station and train station (both routes $2.50; no Sunday service).

Train

Bunbury is the terminus of the **Transwa** (☎1300 662 205; www.transwa.wa.gov.au) Australind train line, with two daily services to Perth ($29, 2½ hours) and Pinjarra ($16, 1¼ hours).

Tuart Forest National Park

The tuart is a type of eucalypt that only grows on coastal limestone, 200km either side of Perth, and this 20-sq-km strip squeezed between the Bussell Hwy and the Indian Ocean is the last pure tuart forest left. An alternative route to Busselton from Bunbury leads through the shade cast by these giants, some more than 33m tall.

Turn off the highway at Tuart Dr, 4km southwest of Capel. After driving 11km through the forest, turn right onto Layman Rd, where you'll find **Wonnerup House** (www.ntwa.com.au; 935 Layman Rd; adult/child $5/3; ⊙10am-4pm Thu-Mon), a whitewashed colonial homestead (1859) which has been lovingly restored by the National Trust. Continue on this road as it curves past the seaside village of Wonnerup and then follows the coast to Busselton.

Busselton

POP 15,400

Unpretentious, uncomplicated and with a slightly faded charm, Busselton is what passes for the big smoke in these parts. Surrounded by calm waters and white-sand beaches, its outlandishly long jetty is its most famous attraction. Family-friendly Busselton has plenty of diversionary activities for lively kids, including playgrounds on the foreshore, sheltered beaches, waterslides, animal farms and even a classic drive-in cinema. During school holidays, it really bustles – the population increases fourfold and accommodation prices soar.

⊙ Sights & Activities

Busselton Jetty JETTY
(☎9754 0900; www.busseltonjetty.com.au; adult/child $2.50/free) Busselton's 1865 timber-piled jetty, which holds the distinction of being the longest of its kind in the southern hemisphere (1841m), reopened to the public in early 2011 following a $27 million refurbishment. Its little **train** (adult/child $10/5) chugs along to the **Underwater Observatory** (adult/child incl train $28/14; ⊙9am-4.25pm), where tours take place 8m below the surface; bookings essential. There's also an **Interpretive Centre** (admission free; ⊙9am-5pm), an attractive building in the style of 1930s bathing sheds, about 50m along the jetty.

ArtGeo Cultural Complex ART GALLERY
(www.artgeo.com.au; 6 Queen St) Grouped around the old courthouse (1856), this complex includes tearooms, woodturners, an artist-in-residence and the Busselton Art Society's gallery, selling works by local artists of varying degrees of proficiency.

Dive Shed DIVING
(☎9754 1615; www.diveshed.com.au; 21 Queen St) Runs regular dive charters along the jetty, to Four Mile Reef (a 40km limestone ledge about 6.5km off the coast) and to the scuttled navy vessel HMAS *Swan* (off Dunsborough).

Old Butter Factory Museum MUSEUM
(Peel Tce; adult/child $6/2; ⊙10am-4pm Wed-Mon) Local history.

Festivals & Events

Southbound MUSIC
(www.southboundfestival.com.au) Start off the new year with three days of alternative music and camping; it's WA's Glastonbury but with less mud.

CinéfestOZ CINEMA
(www.cinefestoz.com.au) Busselton briefly morphs into St-Tropez with this oddly glamorous festival of French and Australian cinema, including lots of Australian premieres and the odd Aussie starlet; held late August.

Sleeping

Busselton is packed in the holidays and pretty much deserted come low season. Accommodation sprawls along the beach for several kilometres either side of the town, so make sure you check the location if you don't have your own wheels.

Beachlands Holiday Park CARAVAN PARK $
(1800 622 107; www.beachlands.net; 10 Earnshaw Rd, West Busselton; 2-person sites $42, chalets from $130;) Part of the Big4 chain, this excellent family-friendly park offers a wide range of accommodation, in amongst the shady trees, palms and flax bushes. Deluxe spa villas ($170) have corner spas, huge TVs, DVD players and full kitchens.

Observatory Guesthouse B&B $$
(9751 3336; www.observatory-guesthouse.com; 7 Brown St; s/d $110/135) A five-minute walk from the jetty, this friendly B&B rents four bright, cheerful rooms. They're not overly big but you can spread out on the communal sea-facing balcony and front courtyard.

Grand Mercure RESORT $$$
(9754 9800; www.mercure.com; 553 Bussell Hwy, Broadwater; apt from $213;) You'll find everything you need for an active family holiday at this large complex of 87 flash apartments and villas, set among native vegetation, 6km from town. There's an exhausting array of tennis and squash courts, indoor and outdoor pools, and a small gym – or you can just lie around on the beach at the foot of the property.

Blue Bay Apartments APARTMENTS $$
(08-9751 1796; www.bluebayapartments.com; 66 Adelaide St; apt from $95;) Close to the beach, these good-value, self-contained apartments are bright and cheery, each with private courtyard and barbecue.

Eating & Drinking

Newtown House MODERN AUSTRALIAN $$$
(www.newtownhouse.com.au; 737 Bussell Hwy, Abbey; mains $40-44; breakfast Sat & Sun, lunch & dinner Wed-Sat) Set amid green lawns and gardens, this early settler residence (1851), 10km west of town, has a hefty reputation for serving the best-quality regional ingredients. There's also B&B accommodation ($225). You will need to bring your own (BYO) wine.

Goose CAFE $$
(www.thegoose.com.au; Geographe Bay Rd; breakfast $14-24, lunch $20-38, dinner $29-39; breakfast, lunch & dinner Wed-Sun;) Near the jetty, this stylish cafe offers an eclectic, interesting menu and views out to sea. Between meals it's open for coffee, wine and tapas (from $15 to $18).

Coco's Thai THAI $$
(55 Queen St; mains $15-17; dinner Tue-Sun;) A little place serving tasty Thai favourites and more adventurous dishes such as a delicious fish curry with apple.

Vasse BAR, CAFE $
(www.vassebarcafe.com.au; 44 Queen St; mains $13-35; 9am-late;) The menu mainstays of this slick bar are pizza and pasta, but it also turns out more eclectic fare, including a special French menu for CinéfestOZ in August.

Equinox Cafe CAFE $$
(www.theequinox.com.au; Queen St; mains $24-34; breakfast, lunch & dinner) Lower-key and somewhat more relaxed than its goosy neighbour, this is a fine waterfront hang-out near the jetty.

Entertainment

Busselton Drive-In Outdoor Cinema CINEMA
(9752 3655; www.busseltondrive-in.com.au; 500 Bussell Hwy, Broadwater; adult/child $14/7) Double-features, under the stars. Season starts mid-September.

Information

Visitor Centre (9752 1288; www.geographebay.com; 38 Peel Tce; 9am-5pm Mon-Fri, 9am-4pm Sat & Sun)

Getting There & Around

Transwa (1300 662 205; www.transwa.wa.gov.au) Coach SW1 (12 weekly) stops at the visitor centre, heading to/from East Perth ($34, 4¼ hours), Bunbury ($9, 43 minutes),

Dunsborough ($7.15, 28 minutes), Margaret River ($13, 1½ hours) and Augusta ($16, 1¾ hours).

South West Coach Lines (☎9261 7600; www.veoliatransportwa.com.au) Runs services to/from Perth's Esplanade Busport (3¾ hours, three daily), Bunbury (1¼ hours, five daily), Dunsborough (24 minutes, three daily), Margaret River (38 minutes, three daily) and Augusta (1¼ hours, three daily).

TransBusselton (☎9754 1666; 39 Albert St) The most useful bus is the 903 that follows the coast to Dunsborough (four daily, Monday to Saturday).

Dunsborough

POP 3400

Smaller and less sprawling than Busselton, Dunsborough is a relaxed, beach-worshipping town that goes bonkers towards the end of November when about 7000 'schoolies' descend. When it's not inundated with drunken, squealing teenagers, it's a thoroughly pleasant place to be. The beaches are better than Busselton's but accommodation is more limited.

The name Dunsborough first appeared on maps in the 1830s but to the Wardandi people it was always Quedjinup, meaning 'place of women'.

Activities

Cape Dive DIVING
(☎9756 8778; www.capediveexperience.com; 222 Naturaliste Tce) There is excellent diving in Geographe Bay, especially since decommissioned Navy destroyer HMAS *Swan* was purposely scuttled in 1997 for use as a dive wreck. Marine life has colonised the ship, which lies at a depth of 30m, 2.5km offshore.

Naturaliste Charters WHALE-WATCHING
(☎9725 8511; www.whales-australia.com; adult/child $75/45; ⊙10am Sep-Dec) Two-hour whale-watching cruises.

Sleeping

There are many, many options for self-contained rentals in town depending on the season; the visitor centre has current listings.

Dunsborough Beachouse YHA HOSTEL $
(☎9755 3107; www.dunsboroughbeachouse.com.au; 205 Geographe Bay Rd; dm $30-32, s/d $53/76; @📶) On the Quindalup beachfront, this friendly hostel has lawns stretching languidly to the water's edge; it's an easy 2km cycle from the town centre.

Eating & Drinking

Food Farmacy FUSION $$$
(www.thefoodfarmacy.com.au; Dunn Bay Rd; mains $35-47; ⊙dinner Thu-Mon) Chef Simon Beaton dispenses innovative fare from this cool little restaurant. Asian flavours are to the fore, combined with the best of local produce. The pharmacy theme plays out in tasters and drinks served in flasks and test tubes.

Malt Market BISTRO, BAR $$
(www.maltmarket.com.au; 26 Dunn Bay Rd; mains $18-28; ⊙4pm-late) Malt ticks all the boxes for what you'd want in a beach town bar: cool but not pretentious, comfy couches, board games, regular live bands, a fireplace for winter and an upstairs terrace for summer. The pizzas are excellent.

Cape Wine Bar WINE BAR $$
(www.thecapewinebar.com; 239 Naturaliste Tce; mains $20-38; ⊙dinner Mon-Thu, tapas Fri & Sat) Buzzing most nights, the wine bar has a well-deserved reputation for fresh seasonal food.

ArtéZen CAFE $
(234 Naturaliste Tce; mains $14-21; ⊙7am-5pm) Funky wallpaper and good breakfasts.

Information

Visitor Centre (☎9755 3517; www.geographebay.com; Seymour Blvd; ⊙9am-5pm) In the same building as the post office.

Getting There & Around

Transwa (☎1300 662 205; www.transwa.wa.gov.au) Coach SW1 (12 weekly) stops at the visitor centre, heading to/from East Perth ($36, 4½ hours), Bunbury ($13, 1¼ hours), Busselton ($7.15, 28 minutes), Margaret River ($13, 49 minutes) and Augusta ($16, 1¼ hours).

South West Coach Lines (☎9261 7600; www.veoliatransportwa.com.au) Runs services to/from Perth's Esplanade Busport (6½ hours, daily), Mandurah (3¼ hours, daily), Bunbury (1¾ hours, daily) and Busselton (24 minutes, three daily).

TransBusselton (☎9754 1666; 39 Albert St, Busselton) Runs services between Dunsborough and Busselton (four daily, Monday to Saturday).

Cape Naturaliste

Northwest of Dunsborough, Cape Naturaliste Rd leads to the excellent beaches of **Meelup**, **Eagle Bay** and **Bunker Bay**, and on to Cape Naturaliste. There are walks and lookouts along the way; pick up brochures from the visitor centre before heading out. Whales and hammerhead sharks like to hang out on the edge of Bunker Bay where the continental shelf drops 75m. There's excellent snorkelling right on the edge of the shelf at Shelley Cove.

Bunker Bay is also home to **Bunkers Beach Cafe** (www.bunkersbeachcafe.com.au; Farm Break Lane; breakfast $12-19, lunch $16-36; ⌚breakfast & lunch Thu-Mon, daily summer) which serves an adventurous menu from a blissful spot which is only metres from the sand.

The **Cape Naturaliste lighthouse** (adult/child $12/6), built in 1903, can be visited on tours which leave every 30 minutes from 9.30am to 4pm. There's also a two-room free museum here. Above and Below (adult/child $27/14) packages are available, combined with entry to Ngilgi Cave near Yallingup.

The southernmost nesting colony of the red-tailed tropicbird is at scenic **Sugarloaf Rock**, to the south of the cape; the viewpoint can be reached by a 3.5km boardwalk from the lighthouse or by Sugarloaf Rd.

RED TAILS IN THE SUNSET

The coast between Cape Naturaliste and Cape Leeuwin is anything but the tropics, yet this stretch is home to the most southerly breeding colony of the red-tailed tropicbird *(Phaethon rubricauda)* in Australia, reliably seen here between September and May. Look for it soaring above Sugarloaf Rock, south of Cape Naturaliste.

The tropicbird is distinguished by its two long, red tail streamers – almost twice its body length. It has a bill like a tern's and, from a distance, could easily be mistaken for a Caspian tern. Bring binoculars to watch this small colony soar, glide, dive and then swim with their disproportionately long tail feathers cocked up. They are ungainly on land and have to descend almost to the spot where they wish to nest.

MARGARET RIVER WINE REGION

We've introduced this magical region in depth in the Discover Margaret River & the Southwest Coast planning chapter (p30), so rather than repeating ourselves here, we'll launch straight into the guts of it. You should refer to that chapter for tips on how to tackle the wineries, surf breaks and caves. To make it more manageable, we've divided our coverage here into sections based on proximity to the main towns and villages.

Festivals & Events

Drug Aware Pro SURFING
(www.drugawarepro.com) Six-day pro surfing competition, with associated concerts and fashion shows; held mid-March.

Margaret River Wine Region Festival WINE, FOOD
(www.margaretriverfestival.com) Five days of street carnivals, slow food and master classes; held mid-March.

Tours

There are a huge number of tour companies operating in Margaret River; see the visitor centre for all options.

Bushtucker Tours CANOEING, WINE
(☎9757 9084; www.bushtuckertours.com; adult/child $85/40) The four-hour trip combines walking and canoeing up the Margaret River, and features aspects of Aboriginal culture along with uses of flora, and a bush-tucker lunch. Also runs a Winery & Brewery Tour (adult/child $85/40).

Wine for Dudes WINE
(☎0427 774 994; www.winefordudes.com; tours $85) Slacker-friendly tour, including the chocolate factory, three wineries, a wine-blending experience and lunch.

Dirty Detours MOUNTAIN BIKING
(☎9758 8312; www.dirtydetours.com; tours $80) Runs guided mountain-bike rides, including through the magnificent Boranup Forest, as well as a Sip n' Cycle cellar door tour.

Margaret River Tours WINE, SIGHTSEEING
(☎0419 917 166; www.margaretrivertours.com) One of the longest-standing local operators; runs winery and sightseeing tours (half-/full-day $75/125) or can arrange charters.

Lifestyle Margaret River WINE, FOOD
(☎9757 9111; www.lifestylemargaretriver.com.au) For something totally indulgent, you can be chauffeured in a Rolls-Royce Silver Shadow or a 1955 Bentley around the vineyards.

Margaret River Wine Region

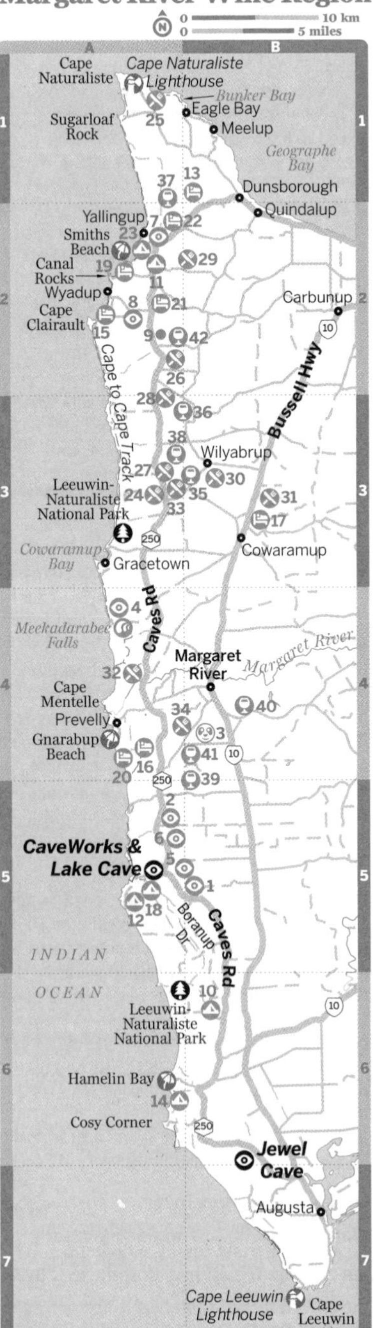

Margaret River Wine Region

Top Sights

- CaveWorks & Lake Cave A5
- Jewel Cave B6

Sights

1. Boranup Gallery B5
2. Calgardup Cave A5
3. Eagles Heritage B4
4. Ellensbrook Homestead A4
5. Giants Cave A5
6. Mammoth Cave A5
7. Ngilgi Cave A2
8. Wardan Aboriginal Centre A2

Activities, Courses & Tours

9. Yallingup Maze A2

Sleeping

10. Boranup Campground B6
11. Caves Caravan Park A2
12. Conto Campground A5
13. Empire Retreat B1
14. Hamelin Bay Holiday Park A6
15. Injidup Spa Retreat A2
16. Llewellin's A4
17. Noble Grape Guesthouse B3
18. Point Road Campground A5
- Seashells Yallingup .... (see 7)
19. Smiths Beach Resort A2
20. Surfpoint A4
21. Wildwood Valley A2
22. Windmills Break A2
23. Yallingup Beach Holiday Park A2

Eating

24. Brookland Valley & Flutes Restaurant A3
25. Bunkers Beach Cafe A1
26. Clairault A2
27. Cullen Wines A3
28. Knee Deep in Margaret River A3
29. Lamont's B2
30. Margaret River Chocolate Company B3
31. Margaret River Dairy Company B3
32. McHenry's Farm Shop A4
33. Vasse Felix A3
34. Xanadu A4

Drinking

35. Ashbrook B3
36. Bootleg Brewery A3
37. Bush Shack Brewery A1
38. Evans & Tate A3
39. Leeuwin Estate B4
40. Stella Bella B4
- Thompson Estate .... (see 35)
41. Voyager Estate B4
42. Wills Domain A2

Margies Big Day Out WINE, BEER
(☎0416 180 493; www.margaretrivertourswa.com.au; tours $80) Offers a more balanced beverage diet (three wineries, two breweries), pick-ups and lunch.

Getting There & Away

Transwa (☎1300 662 205; www.transwa.wa.gov.au) Coach SW1 (12 weekly) from Perth to Augusta stops at Yallingup and Margaret River, with three coaches weekly continuing to Pemberton.

South West Coach Lines (☎9261 7600; www.veoliatransportwa.com.au) Buses between Busselton and Augusta (12 weekly) stop at Cowaramup and Margaret River, linking with Perth on the weekends.

Yallingup & Around

POP 1070

Beachside Yallingup is as much a mecca for salty-skinned surfers as it is for wine aficionados. You're permitted to let a 'wow' escape when the surf-battered coastline first comes into view. In fact, it's practically obligatory. Romantics may be encouraged to know that the name Yallingup means 'place of love' in the Wardandi Noongar tongue.

A set of beautiful walking trails follow the coast between here and **Smiths Beach**. **Canal Rocks**, a series of rocky outcrops forming a natural canal, are just past Smiths Beach.

Sights & Activities

FREE **Wardan Aboriginal Centre** INDIGENOUS CULTURE
(Map p126; ☎9756 6566; www.wardan.com.au; Injidup Springs Rd; ⌚10am-4pm daily 15 Oct-15 Mar, closed Tue & Sat 15 Mar-15 Oct, closed 15 Jun-15 Aug) Offers a window into the lives of the local Wardandi people. There's a gallery, an interpretive display on the six seasons which govern the Wardandi calendar (admission $5) and the opportunity to take part in various **experiences** (adult/child $15/8; ⌚Sun, Mon, Wed & Fri): stone tool-making; boomerang and spear throwing; or a guided bushwalk exploring Wardandi spirituality and the uses of various plants for food, medicine and shelter.

Ngilgi Cave CAVE
(Map p126; ☎9755 2152; www.geographebay.com; Caves Rd; adult/child $19/10; ⌚9.30am-4.30pm) Between Dunsborough and Yallingup, this 500,000-year-old cave is associated in Wardandi spirituality with the victory of the good spirit Ngilgi over the evil spirit Wolgine. To the Wardandi people it became a kind of honeymoon location. A European man first stumbled upon it in 1899 while looking for his horse. Formations include the white **Mother of Pearl Shawl** and the equally beautiful **Arab's Tent** and **Oriental Shawl**. Entry is by semiguided tours, which depart every half hour.

More adventurous caving options include the two-hour Ancient Riverbed Tour (adult/child $42/21), 2½-hour Explorer Tour (adult/child $65/42), three-hour Crystal Crawl Tour (adults-only $95) and the four-hour Ultimate Ngilgi Adventure (adults-only $135).

A series of well-marked bushwalks start from here.

Yallingup Surf School SURFING
(☎9755 2755; www.yallingupsurfschool.com) Offers 90-minute lessons for beginners ($50/125 for one/three lessons) and private coaching ($110).

Yallingup Maze LABYRINTH
(Map p126; www.yallingupmaze.com.au; 3059 Caves Rd; adult/child $12.50/10; ⌚9am-5pm) If you can complete this wooden outdoor maze in 35 minutes, you're up with the best.

Sleeping

TOP CHOICE **Injidup Spa Retreat** BOUTIQUE HOTEL $$$
(Map p126; ☎9750 1300; www.injidupsparetreat.com.au; Cape Clairault Rd, off Wyadup Rd; ste from $650; ❄) The most stylish and luxurious accommodation in the region, Injidup perches atop an isolated cliff, south of Yallingup. A striking carved concrete and iron facade fronts the car park, while inside there are heated polished concrete floors, 'eco' fires and absolute sea views. Each of the 10 suites has its own plunge pool.

Smiths Beach Resort RESORT $$$
(Map p126; ☎9750 1200; www.smithsbeachresort.com.au; Smiths Beach Rd; apt from $220; ❄ ≋) Injidup's sister property is a large complex of tastefully plush one- to four-bedroom apartments by a very beautiful beach – which it nearly has all to itself. There's a restaurant, cafe, deli and bottle shop on site but the apartments also have full kitchens.

Yallingup Beach Holiday Park CARAVAN PARK $
(Map p126; ☎9755 2164; www.yallingupbeach.com.au; Valley Rd; 2-person sites $32, cabins $100-150; ☎) You'll sleep to the sound of the surf here, with the beach just across the road from the rolling lawns.

TOP FIVE SURF SPOTS

For more information about these breaks, see p31.

- Margaret River Mouth
- Southside
- Three Bears
- Yallingup
- Injidup Car Park

Empire Retreat BOUTIQUE HOTEL $$$
(Map p126; ☎9755 2065; www.empireretreat.com; Caves Rd; ste $260-550; ❄📶) Everything about the intimate Empire Retreat is stylish, from the Indonesian-inspired design to the attention to detail and service. A day spa is attached.

Windmills Break BOUTIQUE HOTEL $$$
(Map p126; ☎9755 2341; www.windmillsbreak.com.au; 2024 Caves Rd; r from $295; ❄@📶🏊) Enter through the clubby lounge, which opens onto a terrace and landscaped grounds spreading down to a lovely pool. Rooms are plush and contemporary.

Seashells Yallingup HOTEL, APARTMENTS $$
(Map p126; ☎9750 1500; www.seashells.com.au; Yallingup Beach Rd; r from $185; 📶) Located at Caves House (1938), which has been impeccably renovated, and a set of modern apartments has sprung up alongside. It's an atmospheric spot for a drink, with live bands on Sunday afternoons.

Caves Caravan Park CARAVAN PARK $
(Map p126; ☎9755 2196; www.cavescaravanpark.com.au; cnr Caves & Yallingup Beach Rds; 2-person sites $20-30, cabins $70-100) A leafy caravan park with clean cabins and friendly management.

Wildwood Valley B&B $$
(Map p126; ☎9755 2120; www.wildwoodvalley.com.au; 1481 Wildwood Rd; r $190-210; 📶) First-rate B&B looking through the gum trees out over a lush green valley. It's set on a farm, with an olive plantation and horses.

Eating & Drinking

Lamont's WINERY, RESTAURANT $$$
(Map p126; ☎9755 2434; www.lamonts.com.au; Gunyulgup Valley Dr; mains $39-41; ⏲lunch daily, dinner Sat) Raised on stilts over its own lake, Lamont's is an idyllic spot for lunch or tapas, with a glass of wine, naturally. The food is excellent. Afterwards you can wander next door to the **Gunyulgup Galleries** (www.gunyulgupgalleries.com.au; ⏲10am-5pm) showcasing exquisite contemporary WA art.

Bush Shack Brewery BREWERY
(Map p126; www.bushshackbrewery.com.au; Hemsley Rd; ⏲10am-5pm) A small-scale and eccentric brewery in a great bush setting.

Wills Domain WINERY
(Map p126; www.willsdomain.com.au; cnr Brash & Abbey Farm Rds; ⏲10am-5pm) Restaurant, gallery and wonderful hilltop views over vines.

Cowaramup & Wilyabrup

POP 988

Cowaramup (Cow Town to some) is little more than a couple of blocks of shops lining Bussell Hwy. That a significant percentage of those are devoted in one way or another to eating or drinking is a testament to its position at the heart of the wine region. The rustic area to the northwest, known as Wilyabrup, is where in the 1960s the Margaret River wine industry was born. This area has the highest concentration of wineries and the pioneers (Cullen Wines and Vasse Felix) are still leading the way.

Sleeping

Noble Grape Guesthouse B&B $$
(Map p126; ☎9755 5538; www.noblegrape.com.au; 29 Bussell Hwy, Cowaramup; s $130-150, d $150-165; ❄) Noble Grape is more like an upmarket motel than a traditional B&B – rooms offer a sense of privacy and each has a little courtyard as well as a microwave and DVD player. The charming owners clearly have green fingers – the gardens are wonderful.

Eating

Vasse Felix WINERY, RESTAURANT $$$
(Map p126; ☎9756 5050; www.vassefelix.com.au; cnr Caves Rd & Harmans Rd South; mains $35-39; ⏲lunch) Vasse Felix is considered by many to have the finest restaurant in the region, the big wooden dining room reminiscent of an extremely flash barn. The grounds are peppered with sculptures, while the gallery displaying works from the Holmes à Court collection is worth a trip in itself. And, of course, the much lauded and awarded wine is magnificent.

Knee Deep in Margaret River WINERY, RESTAURANT $$
(Map p126; ☎9755 6776; www.kneedeepwines.com.au; 61 Johnson Rd; mains $32-37; ⏲lunch) Small

and focused seems to be the motto here. Only a handful of mains are offered – with locally sourced, seasonal produce at the fore – and the open-sided pavilion among the vines provides a pleasantly intimate setting. The attention to detail is impressive, both in the flavours and in the service. Order your food then shuffle up to the tasting counter to select its liquid companion.

Cullen Wines WINERY, RESTAURANT **$$**
(Map p126; ☎9755 5277; www.cullenwines.com.au; 4323 Caves Rd; mains $32-36; lunch) Grapes were first planted here in 1966 and Cullen continues to break ground with a commitment to organic and biodynamic principles which extend from the winemaking to the restaurant. It's much less formal than its fancy neighbour Vasse Felix, but the food is excellent – fresh, local and very seasonal. Bright fabrics hang from the ceiling, or you can dine on the verandah under the shady trees. Cullen's Chardonnay was judged the world's best in the 2010 Decanter World Wine Awards.

Clairault WINERY, RESTAURANT **$$$**
(Map p126; ☎9755 6655; www.clairaultwines.com.au; 3277 Caves Rd; mains $35-39; lunch Thu-Mon Easter-Oct, daily Nov-Easter) A contemporary building of timber and corrugated iron amid vineyards and eucalypts, with an eclectic, appealing menu.

Brookland Valley & Flutes Restaurant WINERY, RESTAURANT **$$$**
(Map p126; ☎9755 6250; www.flutes.com.au; Caves Rd; mains $34-44; lunch Thu-Mon, daily summer) A large producer whose wines include the widely exported Verse 1 range. The restaurant sits over a pretty lake.

Margaret Riviera DELICATESSEN
(www.margaretriviera.com.au; Bottrill St, Cowaramup; 10am-5pm) Gourmet food store stocking local produce including olive oils, preserves and cheeses.

Margaret River Chocolate Company CHOCOLATE
(Map p126; www.chocolatefactory.com.au; Harmans Mill Rd; 9am-5pm) Perpetually frantic, you can watch truffles being made, sample chocolate buttons, grab a coffee or let the kids burn off their sugar rushes outside. The building itself looks edible.

Margaret River Dairy Company CHEESE
(Map p126; www.mrdc.com.au; Bussell Hwy; 9.30am-5pm) Offers cheese tastings at two sites on the Bussell Hwy north of Cowaramup.

Drinking

Margaret River Regional Wine Centre WINE SHOP
(www.mrwines.com; 9 Bussell Hwy, Cowaramup; 10am-7pm) A one-stop shop for Margaret River wine, this helpful store offers daily tastings rotating between a dozen or so smaller wineries that don't operate cellar doors.

Ashbrook WINERY
(Map p126; www.ashbrookwines.com.au; 448 Harmans Rd South) Here's to the little guys! Family-owned and -operated Ashbrook grows all of its grapes on site.

Thompson Estate WINERY
(Map p126; www.thompsonestate.com; 299 Harmans Rd South) Another small-scale producer, this one with an architectural award-winning concrete tastings/barrel room.

Evans & Tate WINERY
(Map p126; www.evansandtate.com.au; Metricup Rd) Now owned by wine giant McWilliam's, this is one of the region's oldest and most famous vineyards.

Bootleg Brewery BREWERY
(Map p126; www.bootlegbrewery.com.au; off Yelverton Rd; 11am-6pm) Bills itself as 'an oasis of beer in a desert of wine'. Serves food and hosts live bands on Saturdays.

Margaret River

POP 4500

Although tourists might outnumber locals much of the time, Margaret River still feels like a country town. The advantage of basing yourself here is that after 5pm, once the wineries shut up shop, it's one of the few places with any vital signs. Plus it's close to the incredible surf of Margaret River Mouth and Southside, and the swimming beaches at Prevelly and Gracetown.

Margaret River spills over with tourists every weekend and gets very, *very* busy at Easter and Christmas (when you should book weeks, if not months, ahead). Accommodation prices tend to be cheaper midweek.

Sleeping

TOP CHOICE **Margaret River Lodge YHA** HOSTEL **$**
(☎9757 9532; www.mrlodge.com.au; 220 Railway Tce; dm $25-29, r $62-74; @) About 1.5km southwest of the town centre, this is a

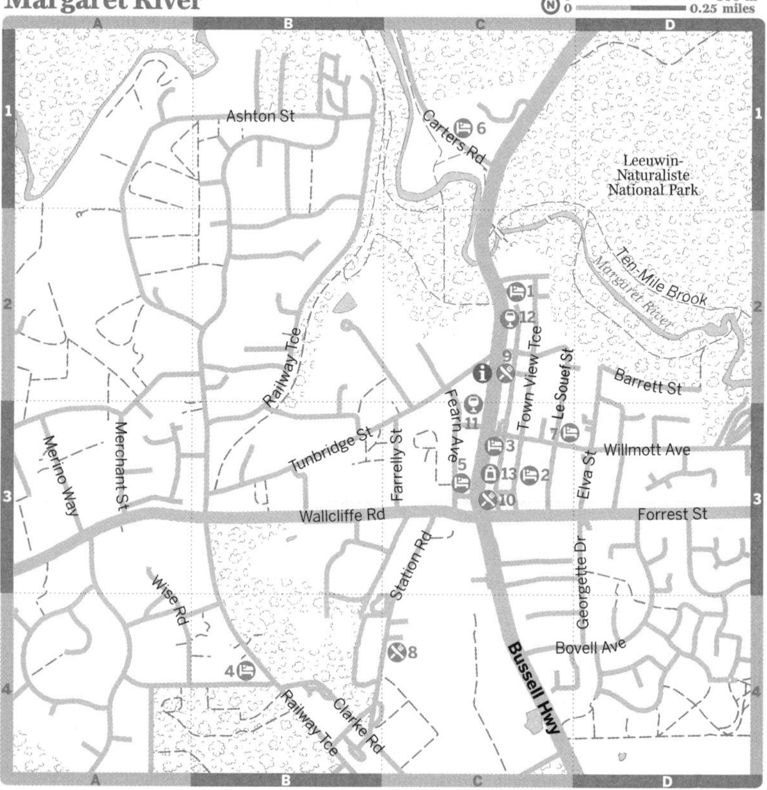

Margaret River

Sleeping

Eating

Drinking

Shopping

clean, well-run hostel with a pool, volleyball court and football field. It's divided into two distinct sections: one with dorms and a big communal kitchen, and a quieter space with private rooms and its own little kitchen and lounge.

Riverglen Chalets CHALETS **$$**
(☎9757 2101; www.riverglenchalets.com.au; Carters Rd; chalets $155-280; ❄📶) Just north of town, these good-value and very comfortable timber chalets are spacious and fully self-contained, with verandahs looking onto bushland; there's wheelchair access to a couple of them.

Prideau's MOTEL **$$**
(☎0438 587 180; www.prideaus.com.au; 31 Fearn Ave; r $145-185; ❄📶) At this price and in such a central location, you'd expect a fairly middling sort of motel, which, to be honest, is what Prideau's looks like from the outside. But step through the door and you'll find

sharp, newly renovated units opening on to little courtyards at the back. Some have spa baths.

Bridgefield B&B $$
(☎9757 3007; www.bridgefield.com.au; 73 Bussell Hwy; r $130-160;) A 19th-century coach house, this lovely higgledy-piggledy B&B is all wood panels, high ceilings, tiled floors and ancient clawfoot baths.

Vintages MOTEL $$
(☎9758 8333; www.vintagesmargaretriver.com.au; cnr Willmott Ave & Le Souef St; r $137-222;) Another swanky motel, this one set in tropical gardens. It's close to the centre of town but all windows are double-glazed, so noise won't be a problem.

Margaret River Backpackers HOSTEL $
(☎9757 9572; www.margaretriverbackpackers.com.au; 66 Town View Tce; dm $28-32;) The sister to Margaret River Lodge YHA caters mainly to working holiday makers. Dorms are a little spartan (there are no private rooms) but there's a nice big deck out back.

Margaret River Hotel PUB $$
(☎9757 2655; www.margaretriverhotel.com.au; 125 Bussell Hwy; r $105-170;) The rooms in this central, 1936 heritage building have been tastefully restored with loads of jarrah detail, though the bathrooms are already looking dated. The cheaper rooms are tiny.

Eating & Drinking

Settler's Tavern PUB $
(www.settlerstavern.com; 114 Bussell Hwy; 11am-midnight Mon-Sat, 11am-10pm Sun) There's live entertainment most nights at Settler's, so settle in for the evening with good pub grub (where else could you get a wagyu beef burger for $10?) and a beer or wine from the extensive list.

Must RESTAURANT, BAR $$
(☎9758 8877; www.must.com.au; 107 Bussell Hwy; mains $30-38, 2-/3-course lunch $33/44; lunch & dinner) The sister property to one of our favourite Perth restaurants (Must Winebar), Must Margaret River doesn't disappoint. True to its location, wine bottles line the Shiraz-coloured walls and dangle from the chandelier. The service is excellent and the charcuterie plates are legendary. If you can't bear the thought of leaving, there are four bedrooms upstairs (per night $180).

CAPE TO CAPE TRACK

Stretching from Cape Naturaliste to Cape Leeuwin, the 135km **Cape to Cape Track** (www.capetocapetrack.com.au) passes through the heath, forest and sand dunes of the **Leeuwin-Naturaliste National Park**, all the while providing Indian Ocean views. Most walkers take about seven days to complete the track, staying in a combination of national park camp sites and commercial caravan parks along the way, but you can walk it in five days or break up the route into day walks.

Blue Ginger CAFE, DELICATESSEN $
(www.bluegingerfinefoods.com; 31 Station Rd; mains $11-17; breakfast & lunch) Ease into the colourful, mismatched furniture on the enclosed terrace and tuck into hearty cafe fare with some adventurous twists.

Urban Bean CAFE $
(157 Bussell Hwy; mains $9-18; breakfast & lunch) A funky little place serving bleary-eyed locals their first daily brew, selling loose-leaf tea and coffee, and making good fresh things for lunch.

Wino's WINE BAR $$
(www.winos.com.au; 85 Bussell Hwy; tapas $3-26; 3pm-late Mon & Tue, 5pm-late Wed-Sun) Leather lounges, bentwood chairs, delicious tapas and local wines to sample make this modern bar very appealing. If they could just get the service sorted...

Shopping

Tunbridge Gallery INDIGENOUS ART
(www.tunbridgegallery.com.au; 1st fl, 139 Bussell Hwy; 10am-5pm Mon-Sat, 10am-3pm Sun) Excellent Aboriginal art gallery featuring mainly WA works.

Information

Visitor Centre (☎9780 5911; www.margaretriver.com; 100 Bussell Hwy; 9am-5pm) This sleek visitor centre has wads of information, plus displays on local wineries.

Getting Around

Margaret River Beach Bus (☎9757 9532; www.mrlodge.com.au) Minibus heading between the township and the beaches around Prevelly ($10, three daily); summer only, bookings essential.

Around Margaret River

West of the Margaret River township, the coastline provides spectacular surfing and walks. Prevelly is the main settlement, with a scattering of places to sleep and eat. Most of the sights are on Caves Rd or just off it.

Sights & Activities

CaveWorks & Lake Cave CAVE

(Map p126; www.margaretriver.com; Conto Rd; ⌚9am-5pm) Acting as the main ticket office for three of the region's most impressive caves (Lake, Mammoth and Jewel), CaveWorks also has excellent displays about caves, cave conservation and local fossil discoveries, as well as an authentic model cave and a 'cave crawl' experience.

Directly behind the centre is **Lake Cave** (adult/child $20/10; ⌚tours hourly 9.30am-3.30pm), the prettiest of them all, where limestone formations are reflected in the still waters of an underground stream. Creative lighting effects enhance the forms of the stalactites and stalagmites. The vegetated entrance to this cave is spectacular and includes a karri tree with a girth of 7m. Lake Cave is the deepest of all the caves open to the public. There are more than 300 steps down (a 62m drop) to the entrance.

Single cave tickets include entry to CaveWorks. The Grand Pass (adult/child $48/22), covering CaveWorks and all three caves, is valid for seven days, while the Ultimate Pass (adult/child $60/27) also includes Cape Leeuwin lighthouse.

CaveWorks is 20km south of Margaret River, off Caves Rd.

Mammoth Cave CAVE

(Map p126; Caves Rd; adult/child $20/10; ⌚9am-4pm) Mammoth Cave boasts a fossilised jawbone of *Zygomaturus trilobus,* a giant wombat-like creature, as well as other fossil remains and the impressive Mammoth Shawl formation. Visits are self-guided; an MP3 audio player is provided.

Calgardup & Giants Caves CAVES

These two self-guided caves are managed by the Department of Environment and Conservation (DEC), which provides helmets and torches. **Calgardup Cave** (Map p126; Caves Rd; adult/child $15/8; ⌚9am-4.15pm) has a seasonal underground lake and is an attractive illustration of the role of the caves in the ecosystem – a stream transports nutrients to the creatures living in the cave, while tree roots hang overhead. **Giants Cave** (Map p126; Caves Rd; adult/child $10/5; ⌚9.30am-3.30pm school & public holidays only), further south, is deeper and longer and has some steep ladders and scrambles.

Ellensbrook Homestead HISTORIC HOUSE

(Map p126; www.ntwa.com.au; Ellensbrook Rd; adult/child $4/2; ⌚10am-4pm Sat & Sun) An intriguing National Trust property 8km northwest of Margaret River, Ellensbrook (1857) was the first home of pioneer settlers Alfred and Ellen Bussell. The Wardandi people welcomed them, gave them Noongar names and led them to this sheltered but isolated site, with its supply of fresh water.

The house is basic and more than a little ramshackle, constructed of paperbark, driftwood, timber, lime, dung and hair. Between 1899 and 1917, Edith Bussell, who farmed the property alone for many years, established an Aboriginal mission here. The children were taught to read and write, and two of them were beneficiaries of Edith's will.

A short walk leads to **Meekadarabee** ('bathing place of the moon'), a beautiful grotto set below trickling rapids and surrounded by lush bush, associated with a pair of star-crossed Indigenous lovers. The grounds are open even when the house isn't.

Boranup Drive FOREST ROAD

(Map p126) If you're enjoying the tall trees of Caves Rd, you'll absolutely love this 14km diversion along an unsealed road through Leeuwin-Naturaliste National Park's beautiful karri forest. Near the south end there's a lookout offering sea views.

Eagles Heritage WILDLIFE CENTRE

(Map p126; ☎9757 2960; www.eaglesheritage.com.au; adult/child $13/6.50; ⌚10am-5pm) Housing Australia's largest collection of raptors, this centre, 5km south of Margaret River, rehabilitates many birds of prey each year. There are free-flight displays at 11am and 1.30pm.

Boranup Gallery ART & CRAFT

(Map p126; www.boranupgallery.com; 7981 Caves Rd; ⌚9am-5pm) Local arts and crafts, 22km south of Margaret River.

Sleeping

Surfpoint HOSTEL $

(Map p126; ☎9757 1777; www.surfpoint.com.au; Reidle Dr, Gnarabup; dm/d $25/80; @) This light and airy place offers the beach on a budget. The rooms are clean and well presented, and there's a very enticing little pool.

Llewellin's B&B $$
(Map p126; ☎9757 9516; www.llewellinsguesthouse.com.au; 64 Yates Rd; r $170-190;) It may be a Welsh name but the style's French provincial in the four upmarket yet homely guestrooms.

National Park Campgrounds CAMPGROUNDS $
(www.dec.wa.gov.au; sites per adult/child $7/2) The Department of Environment and Conservation (DEC) has three basic campgrounds within Leeuwin-Naturaliste National Park. **Conto Campground** (Map p126; Conto Rd) has gas BBQs, toilets and running water; **Boranup Campground** (Map p126), under the tall trees off the southern end of Boranup Dr, can get damp in winter; **Point Road Campground** is only accessible by foot or 4WD from the northern end of Boranup Dr.

Eating & Drinking

TOP CHOICE McHenry's Farm Shop BISTRO, BUTCHER $
(Map p126; www.mchv.com.au; 5962 Caves Rd; mains $9-19; lunch Thu-Sun) Our top pick for a delicious, affordable lunch, McHenry's serves French rustic food (terrines, soups, stews) on its terrace, accompanied by first-rate wine from the family's much acclaimed McHenry Hohnen label.

Xanadu WINERY, RESTAURANT $$
(Map p126; ☎9758 9531; www.xanaduwines.com; Boodjidup Rd; mains $32-38; lunch) No sign of Olivia Newton John on roller skates, although she could get some speed up circling the central stone hearth in this vast chic barn. Save room for the desserts, particularly the chocolate velouté: tangy raspberry sorbet meets velvety chocolate goo.

Voyager Estate WINERY
(Map p126; ☎9757 6354; www.voyagerestate.com.au; Stevens Rd; 10am-5pm) The formal gardens and Cape Dutch–style buildings at Voyager Estate, the grandest of Margaret River's wineries, are capped by a ludicrously oversized Australian flag, presumably to remind you that you're not actually in South Africa. Tours are available ($25 including tastings).

Leeuwin Estate WINERY
(Map p126; ☎9759 0000; www.leeuwinestate.com.au; Stevens Rd; 10am-5pm) Another impressive estate, with tall trees and lawns gently rolling down to the bush. Its Art Series Chardonnay is one of the best in the country. Behind-the-scenes wine tours and tastings take place at 11am, noon and 3pm (adult/child $12.50/4). Big open-air concerts are regularly held here.

Stella Bella WINERY
(Map p126; www.stellabella.com.au; 205 Rosabrook Rd; 10am-5pm) No bangs and whistles, just excellent wines with the prettiest labels in the region.

Information

National Park Information Centre (Map p126; ☎9757 7422; www.dec.wa.gov.au; Calgardup Cave, Caves Rd; 9am-4.15pm)

Augusta & Around

POP 1700

Augusta is positioned at the mouth of the magnificent Blackwood River, 5km north of Cape Leeuwin, at quite a remove from the rest of the wine region. There are a few vineyards scattered around but the vibe here is less epicurean, more languid.

Sights & Activities

Cape Leeuwin LIGHTHOUSE
(Map p126; adult/child $5/3; 8.45am-4.45pm) Cape Leeuwin, where the Indian and Southern Oceans meet, is the most southwesterly point in Australia and on a wild day you may fear being blown off the edge of the earth. It takes its name from a Dutch ship which passed here in 1622. The lighthouse (1896), WA's tallest, offers magnificent views of the coastline. Tours leave on the half-hour from 9am to 4.30pm (adult/child $15/7) and only 10 people at a time can enter, so be prepared to wait a while in holiday season.

Jewel Cave CAVE
(Map p126; Caves Rd; adult/child $20/10; tours hourly 9.30am-3.30pm) The most spectacular of the region's caves, it has an impressive 5.9m straw stalactite, so far the longest seen in a tourist cave. Fossil remains of a Tasmanian tiger (thylacine), believed to be 3500 years old, were discovered here. It's located near the south end of Caves Rd, 8km northwest of Augusta.

Blackwood River Houseboats HOUSEBOATS
(☎9758 0181; www.blackwoodriverhouseboats.com.au; Westbay) Take care of your accommodation, river cruise and fishing trip all at once with a houseboat holiday. They're easy to drive and available for two-night/three-day hire (weekend $950 to $1600, midweek $700 to $1150) or for weekly hire ($1900 to $2800).

Naturaliste Charters WHALE-WATCHING
(☎9725 8511; www.whales-australia.com; adult/child $75/45; ⊙10am Jun-Sep) Two-hour whale-watching cruises.

Blackwood River CRUISES
Operators running boat trips up the Blackwood River from October to May include **Absolutely Eco River Cruises** (☎9758 4003; cdragon@westnet.com.au; adult/child $30/10) and **Miss Flinders** (☎0409 377 809; adult/child $40/15).

Augusta Historical Museum MUSEUM
(Blackwood Ave; adult/child $3/1.50; ⊙1-3pm) Has interesting local exhibits.

Sleeping & Eating

TOP CHOICE **Baywatch Manor YHA** HOSTEL $
(☎9758 1290; www.baywatchmanor.com.au; 9 Heppingstone View; dm $25, d $60-85; @☎) No sign of David Hasselhoff, just clean, modern rooms with creamy brick walls and pieces of antique furniture. There is a bay view from the deck and, in winter, a roaring fire in the communal lounge.

Hamelin Bay Holiday Park CARAVAN PARK $
(Map p126; ☎9758 5540; www.mronline.com.au/accom/hamelin; Hamelin Bay West Rd; 2-person sites $20-25, cabins $80-180) Right on a beautiful beach, northwest of Augusta, this secluded gem of a place gets very busy during holiday times.

Best Western Georgiana Molloy MOTEL $$
(☎9758 1255; www.augustaaccommodation.com.au; 84 Blackwood Ave; r $105-160) The decor's a little dated but the spacious, self-contained units are stand-out value, each with a small garden area.

Deckchair Gourmet CAFE, DELICATESSEN $
(Blackwood Ave; mains $7-16; ⊙8.30am-4pm; ☎) Excellent coffee, delicious food and free wi-fi – what more could you want? Oh, and there are some watery views.

Information

Visitor Centre (☎9758 0166; www.margaretriver.com; cnr Blackwood Ave & Ellis St; ⊙9am-5pm)

SOUTHERN FORESTS

The tall forests of WA's southwest are simply magnificent, with towering gums (karri, jarrah, marri) sheltering cool undergrowth. Between the forests, small towns bear witness to the region's history of logging and mining. Many have redefined themselves as small-scale tourist centres where you can take walks, wine tours, canoe trips and trout- and marron-fishing expeditions.

Getting There & Away

Transwa (☎1300 662 205; www.transwa.wa.gov.au) Coach routes include the following:

» SW1 (three weekly) to Nannup and Pemberton from East Perth, Bunbury, Busselton, Margaret River and Augusta

» SW2 (three weekly) to Balingup, Bridgetown, Manjimup and Pemberton from East Perth, Mandurah and Bunbury

» GS3 (daily) to Balingup, Bridgetown, Manjimup and Pemberton from Perth, Bunbury, Walpole, Denmark and Albany

South West Coach Lines (☎9261 7600; www.veoliatransportwa.com.au) Runs services to:

» Nannup from Busselton (twice weekdays) and Bunbury (weekdays)

» Balingup, Bridgetown and Manjimup from Bunbury, Mandurah and Perth (daily)

Nannup

POP 500

Nannup's historic weatherboard buildings and cottage gardens have an idyllic bush setting on the Blackwood River. The Noongar-derived name means 'a place to stop and rest', which indeed it still is, although it's also a good base for bushwalkers and canoeists.

Sporadic but persistent stories of sightings of a striped wolf-like animal, dubbed the Nannup tiger, have led to hopes that a Tasmanian tiger may have survived in the surrounding bush (the last known Tasmanian Tiger, or thylacine, died in Hobart Zoo in 1936). Keep your camera handy and your eyes peeled!

Activities

Blackwood River Canoeing CANOEING
(☎9756 1209; www.blackwoodrivercanoeing.com; from $18) Provides equipment, basic instruction and transfers for canoeing paddles and longer expeditions. The best time to paddle is in late winter and early spring, when the water levels are up.

St John Brook Conservation Park PARK
(Barrabup Rd) A pretty spot to walk, cycle, swim and camp, 8km west of Nannup along an unsealed road.

ELVIS SIGHTED IN BOYUP BROOK

The pretty township of Boyup Brook (population 540), 31km northeast of Bridgetown, is the centre of country music in Western Australia (WA). The fantastically over-the-top **Harvey Dickson's Country Music Centre** (www.harveydickson.com.au; adult/child $5/2; ⏲9am-5pm) comes complete with a life-sized Elvis, an Elvis room and three 13.5m-tall guitar-playing men. It hosts regular rodeos (the big one's in October) and big-name country music events, as well as the **Boyup Brook Country Music Festival** (www.countrymusicwa.com.au) in February. Scenic but basic **bush camping** (per site $8) is always available.

If you'd like to combine your country music with country critters, stay at **Nature's Guest House** (dm/cottage $20/80); book through **Department of Environment and Conservation** (DEC; ☎9771 7988) in Manjimup. It's located in the heart of the 520-sq-km Perup Forest whose inhabitants include rare mammals such as the numbat, tammar wallaby and southern brown bandicoot. You'll find it south of Boyup Brook, off the Boyup Brook Cranbrook Rd.

Festivals & Events

Nannup Music Festival MUSIC
(www.nannupmusicfestival.org) Held in early March, focusing on folk and world music.

Sleeping & Eating

Holberry House B&B $$
(☎9756 1276; www.holberryhouse.com; 14 Grange Rd; r $110-190;) The decor might lean towards granny-chic but this large house on the hill has charming hosts and comfortable rooms. It's surrounded by large gardens dotted with quirky sculptures (open to non-guests for $4).

Caravan Park CARAVAN PARK $
(1-/2-person sites from $15/25, cabins $66-77) Run by the visitor centre, this caravan park is set on the river bank.

Nannup Bridge Cafe CAFE $$
(1 Warren Rd; lunch $16-27, dinner $25-37; ⏲lunch Tue-Sun, dinner Wed-Sat) Right opposite the tourist office, this cool-looking riverfront cafe morphs into a bistro at night.

Information

Visitor Centre (☎9756 1211; www.nannupwa.com; 4 Brockman St; ⏲10am-4pm) Check out the Nannup tiger press clippings at the visitor centre, housed in the 1922 police station.

Balingup & Greenbushes

It's like 1967 never ended in trippy **Balingup** (population 450), where coloured flags, scarecrows and murals of fairies and toadstools line the main street. The main reason to stop is to rummage around eclectic stores such as the **Old Cheese Factory** (Nannup Rd; ⏲9.30am-4pm), which sells more knick-knacks than you could poke a fridge magnet at, and the **Tinderbox** (www.cheekyherbs.com; South West Hwy; ⏲9am-5pm) herbal remedies shop. The **visitor centre** (☎9764 1818; www.balinguptourism.com.au; South West Hwy; ⏲10am-4pm) is on the main street.

Greenbushes (population 342) is a historic mining and timber township, 10km to the south of Balingup. Some splendid, decaying buildings from the boom days line the road, and heritage memorabilia is dotted through town. A series of walks loop around town and out to join the Bibbulmun track; the Balingup and Bridgetown visitor centres keep walking trail brochures.

Bridgetown

POP 2400

Spread around the Blackwood River and surrounded by karri forests and farmland, Bridgetown is one of the loveliest little towns in the southwest. Despite being busy most weekends, and overrun with visitors on the second weekend of November during its annual **Blues at Bridgetown Festival** (www.bluesatbridgetown.com), it retains a community feel.

Bridgetown's old buildings include **Bridgedale House** (Hampton St; admission gold coin; ⏲10am-2.30pm Sat & Sun), which was built of mud and clay by the area's first settler in 1862 and has been restored by the National Trust.

Sleeping & Eating

Bridgetown Hotel PUB $$
(☎9761 1034; www.bridgetownhotel.com.au; 157 Hampton St; r $165-265, mains $17-29; ❄) You don't expect quirky pizzas (lime and tequila, lamb and tzatziki) to be served in an Australian country pub and neither do you expect large modern bedrooms with spa baths, but a recent revamp has left this 1920s gem with both.

Bridgetown Riverside Chalets CHALETS $$
(☎9761 1040; www.bridgetownchalets.com.au; 1338 Brockman Hwy; chalets $115-175) On a peaceful riverside property with friendly cows wandering around, 5km up the road to Nannup, these four stand-alone wooden chalets (complete with pot-bellied stoves and washing machines) sleep up to six in two bedrooms.

Nelsons of Bridgetown MOTEL $$
(☎9761 1645; www.nelsonsofbridgetown.com.au; 38 Hampton St; s $95-135, d $115-195; ❄📶🏊) The central location is great, but go for the spacious new rooms built to the side of this 1898 Federation-style hotel.

Cidery BREWERY
(www.thecidery.com.au; 43 Gifford Rd; mains $10-25; ⏲11am-4pm Sat-Thu, 11am-7.30pm Fri) Brewing cider and beer and serving it, along with light lunches, on outdoor tables by the river.

Information

Visitor Centre (☎9761 1740; www.bridgetown.com.au; 154 Hampton St; ⏲9am-5pm Mon-Fri, 10am-3pm Sat, 10am-1pm Sun; @) Has a collection of apple-harvesting and cider memorabilia, and a curious jigsaw collection.

Manjimup

POP 4300

Surrounded by spectacular forest, Manjimup is at the very heart of WA's timber industry. Yet for foodies it's known for something very different: truffles. During August especially, Manjimup's black Périgord truffles make their way onto the menus of all of the state's top restaurants.

Sights & Activities

Wine & Truffle Co WINE, FOOD
(☎9777 2474; www.wineandtruffle.com.au; Seven Day Rd; mains $20-33; ⏲10am-4.30pm) If you want to learn more about how the world's most expensive produce is harvested, follow your snout to Wine & Truffle Co. You can join a 2½-hour truffle hunt (per person $95; book ahead), taste wines and end with a wonderful meal. The chefs here understand that when you're regularly pulling cricket balls of black gold out of the ground you can afford to put it in everything. And we're not just talking about subtle infusions – we're talking big slivers shaved over beef Wellington and confit duck. It's pure indulgence.

Timber & Heritage Park PARK
(cnr Rose & Edward Sts; ⏲9am-5pm) Located in the centre of town, this is a good place to stop, picnic and potter, with a little lake, free BBQs and bits of logging paraphernalia scattered about, including a replica of **One Tree Bridge**.

One Tree Bridge & Glenoran Pool POOL
(Graphite Rd) In a clearing in the forest some 22km from town are the remains of One Tree Bridge. It was constructed from a single karri log carefully felled to span the width of the river but rendered unusable after the floods of 1966. In its vicinity is gorgeous Glenoran Pool, a sizeable swimming hole.

Four Aces TREES
(Graphite Rd) The Four Aces are four superb 300-plus-year-old karri trees in a straight line; stand directly in front and they disappear into one. There's a short loop walk through the surrounding karri glade, or a 1½-hour loop bushwalking trail from the Four Aces to One Tree Bridge.

Equipark HORSE RIDING
(☎9771 8448; www.equipark.com.au; Perup Rd) If you fancy a 12km horseback forest trek ($60) or think the kids might like a pony ride ($30), head to Equipark, 24km east of Manjimup.

Diamond Tree Lookout LOOKOUT
Nine kilometres south of Manjimup along the South Western Hwy is the Diamond Tree Lookout. Metal spikes allow you to climb this 52m karri (not for the faint-hearted or vertigo sufferers) and there's a nature trail nearby.

Sleeping

Diamond Forest Cottages COTTAGES $$
(☎9772 3170; www.diamondforest.com.au; 29159 South Western Hwy; chalets $150-200; ❄) About halfway between the Diamond Tree Lookout and the Pemberton turn-off is a collection of well-equipped wooden chalets with decks, scattered around a farm. Turkeys and sheep wander around and there's a petting zoo and daily animal feeding for the kids to join in with.

Information

Visitor Centre (☎9771 1831; www.manjimup.wa.gov.au; Giblett St; ⏰9am-5pm)

Pemberton

POP 760

Hidden deep in the karri forests, drowsy Pemberton has also taken an epicurean turn, producing excellent wine that rivals Margaret River for quality if not for scale. If Margaret River is WA's Bordeaux, Pemberton is its Burgundy – producing excellent Chardonnay and Pinot Noir, among other varietals. Wine tourism isn't as developed here, with some of the better names only offering tastings by appointment; grab a free map listing opening hours from the visitor centre.

The national parks circling Pemberton are impressive. Aim to spend a day or two driving the well-marked Karri Forest Explorer tracks, walking the trails and picnicking in the green depths.

Sights & Activities

Salitage WINERY

(☎9776 1195; www.salitage.com.au; Vasse Hwy; ⏰10am-4pm) If you visit just one vineyard in the Pemberton region, make it this one. Its Pinot Noir has been rated the state's best, while its Chardonnay and Sauvignon Blanc are also very highly regarded. Hour-long vineyard tours leave at 11am; call ahead.

Pemberton Tramway SCENIC RIDE

(☎9776 1322; www.pemtram.com.au; adult/child $18/9; ⏰10.45am & 2pm) Built between 1929 and 1933, the route travels through lush karri and marri forests to Warren River, with occasional photo stops. A commentary is provided and it's a fun 1¾-hour return trip, if noisy.

King Trout Cafe & Marron Farm FISHING

(Map p139; ☎9776 1352; www.kingtroutcafe.com.au; cnr Northcliffe Rd & Old Vasse Rd; ⏰9.30am-5pm Fri-Tue) The menu at this cafe showcases trout and marron prepared in more ways than seems possible. A tour (adult/child $5/3; 11am weekdays) may whet your appetite to hire a rod and hook your own lunch; it can be cleaned and cooked on site for a small fee.

Mountford WINERY, CIDERY

(Map p139; www.mountfordwines.com.au; Bamess Rd) The wines and ciders produced here are all certified organic, plus there's a gallery on site. It's located north of Pemberton and easily incorporated into the Karri Forest Explorer circuit.

Pemberton Wine Centre WINE TASTING

(Map p139; www.marima.com.au; 388 Old Vasse Rd; ⏰noon-5pm) At the very heart of Warren National Park, this attractive centre offers tastings of most local wines and can put together a mixed case of your favourites.

FREE **Pemberton Pool** SWIMMING

(Swimming Pool Rd) Surrounded by karri trees, this natural pool is popular on a hot day – despite the warning sign (currents, venomous snakes). They breed them tough around here.

Tours

Pemberton Hiking & Canoeing HIKING, CANOEING

(☎9776 1559; www.hikingandcanoeing.com.au) Runs well-regarded (and environmentally sound) tours in Warren and D'Entrecasteaux National Parks and to the Yeagarup sand dunes. Specialist tours (wildflowers, frogs, rare fauna) are also available.

Pemberton Discovery Tours 4WD

(☎9776 0484; www.pembertondiscoverytours.com.au; adult/child $90/50) Operates half-day 4WD tours to the Yeagarup sand dunes and the Warren River mouth, and can tailor tours to suit.

Donnelly River Cruises BOAT

(☎9777 1018; www.donnellyrivercruises.com.au; adult/child $55/35) Runs cruises through 12km of D'Entrecasteaux National Park to the cliffs of the Southern Ocean.

Sleeping & Eating

Pemberton has some excellent accommodation choices but less in the way of eateries. The local specialities are trout and marron, which make their way onto most menus.

TOP CHOICE **Old Picture Theatre Holiday Apartments** APARTMENTS $$

(☎9776 1513; www.oldpicturetheatre.com.au; cnr Ellis & Guppy Sts; apt $150-300; ❄) The town's old cinema has been revamped into well-appointed, self-contained, spacious apartments with lots of jarrah detail and black-and-white movie photos. It offers terrific value for money and the guest laundry and spa are rare treats.

Pemberton Breakaway Cottages COTTAGES $$

(☎9776 1580; www.pembreak.com.au; Roberts Rd; cottages $130-300; ❄) Choose between very nice, simple karri cottages – which are already a step above the average at this price range – or leap to the top of the ladder with the luxury eco-chalets. The latter are light and airy, with elegant, contemporary decor, eco-conscious wastewater systems and a solar-passive design.

Pemberton Backpackers YHA HOSTEL $
(☎9776 1105; www.yha.com.au; 7 Brockman St; dm/s/d $27/42/65; @) The main hostel is given over to seasonal workers, but you'll need to check in here for a room in the separate cottage (8 Dean St) that's set aside for travellers. It's cute and cosy but book ahead as it only has three rooms, one of which is a six-person dorm.

Salitage Suites COTTAGES $$$
(☎9776 1195; www.salitagesuites.citysearch.com.au; Vasse Hwy; d/q $250/350) Hidden away amongst tall trees, these four modern wooden cottages offer supreme privacy and luxury. Their mirrored design, with two spacious bedrooms separated by a communal lounge, makes them perfect for two couples.

Marima Cottages COTTAGES $$$
(Map p139; ☎9776 1211; www.marima.com.au; 388 Old Vasse Rd; cottages from $215) Right in the middle of Warren National Park, these four country-style rammed-earth-and-cedar cottages with pot-bellied stoves and lots of privacy are luxurious getaways.

Pump Hill Farm Cottages COTTAGES $$
(Map p139; ☎9776 1379; www.pumphill.com.au; Pump Hill Rd; cottages $125-355) Families love this farm property, where kids are taken on a daily hay ride to feed the animals. Child-free folk will enjoy the ambience of the private, well-equipped cottages too.

Lavender & Berry Farm COTTAGES, CAFE $$
(Map p139; ☎9776 1661; www.lavenderberryfarm.com.au; Browns Rd; cottages $145-205, mains $13-22; ⏲9.30am-4.30pm) The four rammed-earth cottages and the charming cafe are set around a little duck-bothered lake. Berry pancakes come with homemade ice cream and local trout is also on the menu.

Best Western Pemberton Hotel HOTEL $$
(☎9776 1017; www.pembertonhotel.bestwestern.com.au; 66 Brockman St; r from $140; wi-fi) Attached to an old pub – which is an old-fashioned country local – the comfortable accommodation occupies a striking new rammed-earth and cedar extension.

Gloucester Motel MOTEL $
(☎9776 1266; www.gloucestermotel.com.au; Ellis St; r $80-150; a/c) The best of the town's motels, the Gloucester has its own perfectly respectable restaurant.

Fizz CAFE $
(40 Brockman St; mains $6-19; ⏲breakfast & lunch; wi-fi) Neither the food or the decor are anything special, but friendly staff and free wi-fi make it worth a look.

Millhouse Cafe CAFE $
(Brockman St; mains $10-29; ⏲breakfast & lunch) The breakfast menu's dull in this old cottage with wraparound verandahs, but you can feast on local marron and trout for lunch.

WORTH A TRIP

KARRI FOREST EXPLORER

Punctuated by glorious walks, magnificent trees, picnic areas and lots of interpretive signage, the Karri Forest Explorer (Map p139) tourist drive wends its way along 86km of scenic (partly unsealed) roads through three national parks (vehicle entry $11).

Its popular attractions include the **Gloucester Tree**, named after the Duke of Gloucester, who visited in 1946. It's a splendid fire-lookout tree, laddered with a spiral metal stairway; if you're feeling fit and fearless, make the 58m climb to the top. The **Dave Evans Bicentennial Tree**, tallest of the 'climbing trees' at 68m, is in Warren National Park, 11km southwest of Pemberton. Its tree-house cage weighs 2 tonnes and can sway up to 1.5m in either direction in strong winds. The Bicentennial Tree one-way loop leads via **Maiden Bush** to the **Heartbreak Trail**. It passes through 250-year-old karri stands, and nearby Drafty's Camp and Warren Campsite are great for overnighting (sites per adult/child $7/2).

The enchanting **Beedelup National Park**, 15km west of town on the Vasse Hwy (Rte 104), shouldn't be missed. There's a short, scenic walk that crosses Beedelup Brook near **Beedelup Falls**. There are numerous bird species to be found in and around the tall trees; at ground level the red-winged fairy wren is commonly seen in the undergrowth. North of town, **Big Brook Arboretum** (admission free) features 'big' trees from all over the world.

The track loops on and off the main roads, so you can drive short sections at a time. Pick up a brochure from Pemberton's visitor centre.

Karri Forest Explorer

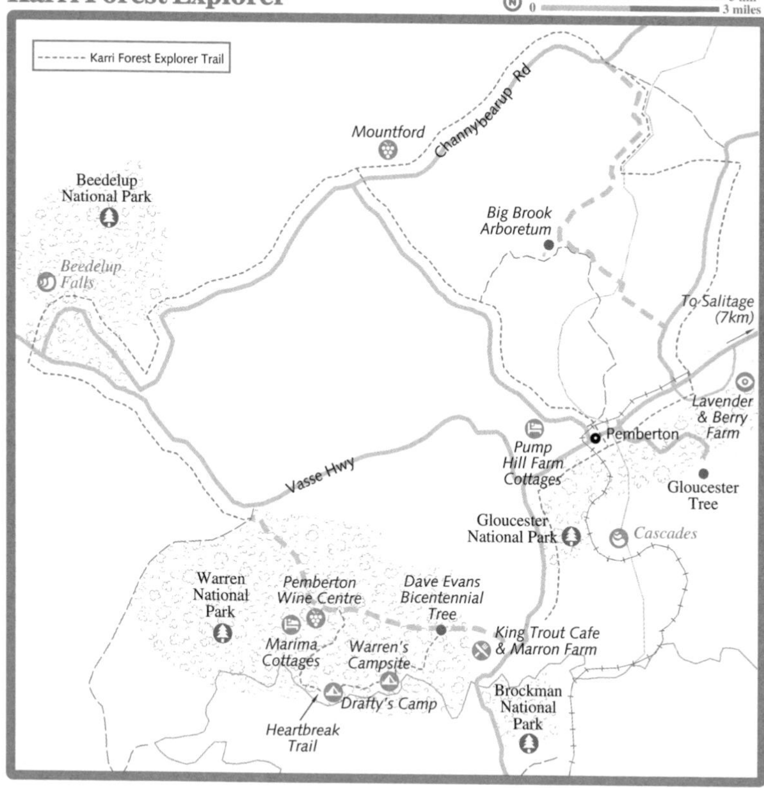

Information

DEC (☎9776 1207; www.dec.wa.gov.au; Kennedy St; ⏲8am-4.30pm) Has detailed information on the local parks and stocks the useful *Pemberton Bushwalks* brochure ($3.30).

Visitor Centre (☎9776 1133; www.pembertonvisitor.com.au; Brockman St; ⏲9am-5pm) Shares an old schoolhouse with an internet centre. Includes a pioneer museum and karri-forest discovery centre, and it's also the place for Transwa bookings.

Shannon National Park

The 535-sq-km **Shannon National Park** (entry per car/motorcycle $11/5) is on the South Western Hwy, 53km south of Manjimup. Until 1968 Shannon was the site of WA's biggest timber mill, and plants including deciduous trees from the northern hemisphere are some of the few reminders of the old settlement.

The 48km **Great Forest Trees Drive** is a one-way loop, split by the highway – tune in to 100FM for a commentary. Start at the park day-use area on the north of the highway. From here there's an easy 3.5km walk to the Shannon Dam and a steeper 5.5km loop to Mokare's Rock, with a boardwalk and great views. Further along, the 8km-return **Great Forest Trees Walk** crosses the Shannon River. Off the southern part of the drive, boardwalks look over stands of giant karri at **Snake Gully** and **Big Tree Grove**.

In the park's southwest, a 6km return walking track links Boorara Tree with a lookout point over Lane Poole Falls.

There is a sizeable **campground** (site per adult/child $9/2) with showers in the spot where the original timber-milling town used to be. A self-contained bunkhouse, **Shannon Lodge** (per night $66, bond $150), is available for groups of up to eight people; book this through DEC in Pemberton.

South Coast

Includes »

Best Places to Eat

» Wild Duck (p150)

» York Street Cafe (p150)

» Bay Merchants (p150)

» Vancouver Cafe & Store (p150)

Best Places to Stay

» Cape Howe Cottages (p144)

» Flinders Park Lodge (p148)

» Beach House at Bayside (p149)

» Esperance B&B by the Sea (p159)

Why Go?

Standing on the cliffs of the wild South Coast as the waves pound below is a truly exhilarating experience. And on calm days, when the sea is various shades of aquamarine and the glorious white-sand beaches lie pristine and welcoming, it's an altogether different type of magnificent. If you're seeking to get away from it all, even busy holiday periods here in the 'Great Southern' are relaxed; it's just that bit too far from Perth for the holiday hordes. Marine visitors come this way, though – the winter months bring a steady stream of migrating whales.

When you need a change from the great outdoors, Albany – the earliest European settlement in the state – has a wealth of colonial history, and towns such as Denmark and Esperance invite you to sit back with a glass of fine local wine and watch the world go by.

When to Go

Esperance

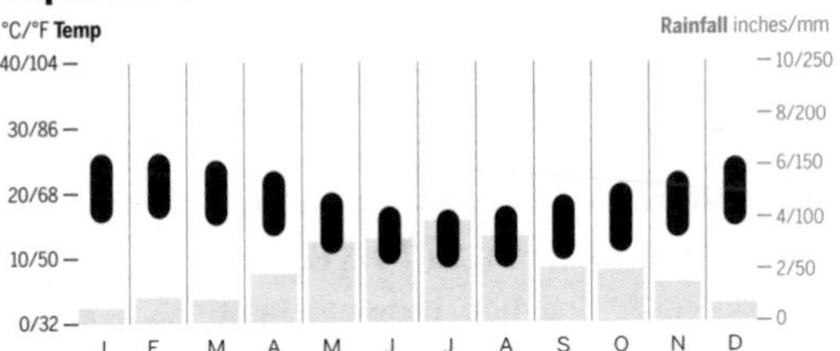

January The best beach weather – and it's not as hot or crowded as the west coast.

September Go wild for wildflowers and whales.

December Perfect weather for the Stirling Range and Porongurup National Parks.

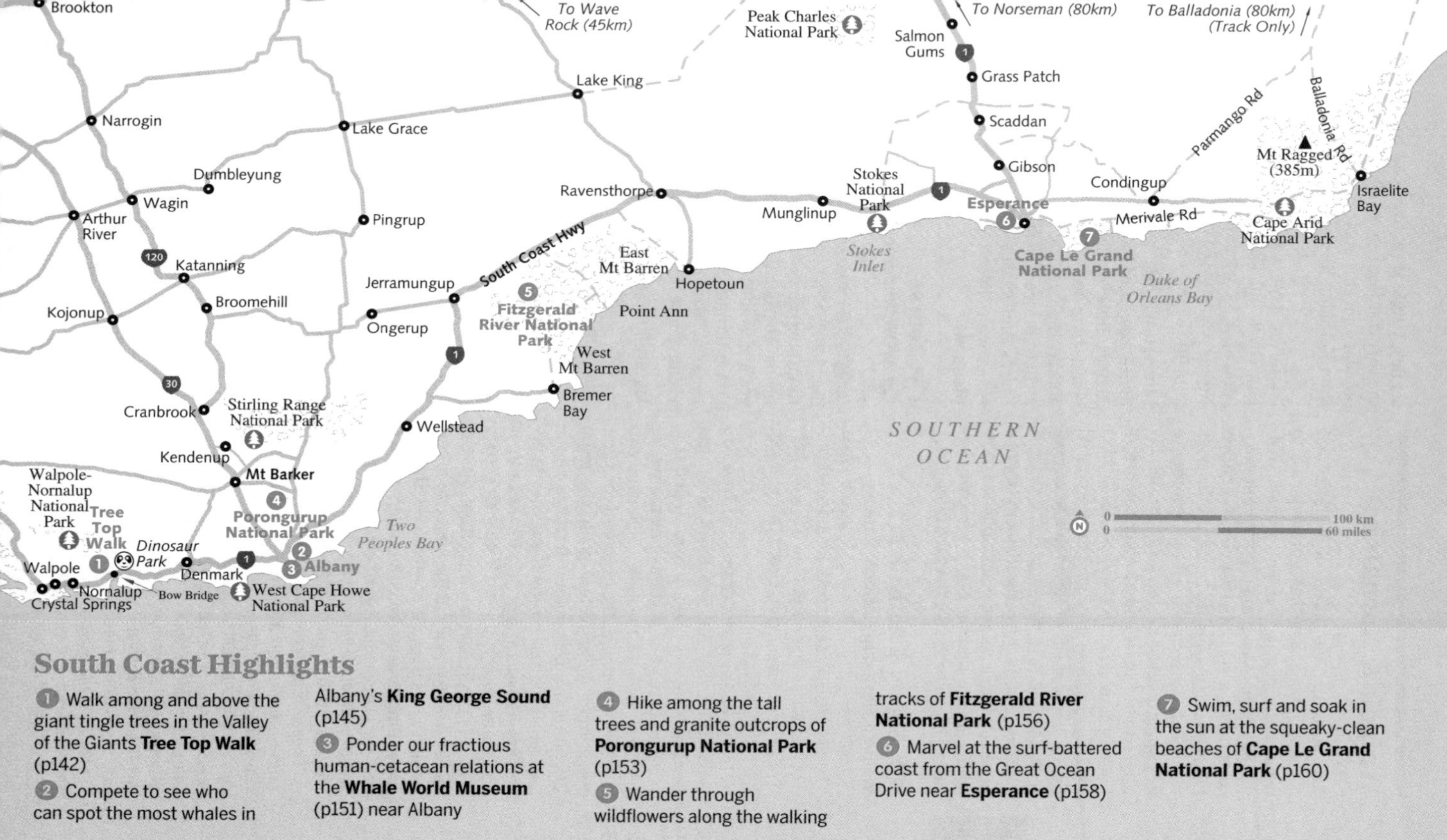

South Coast Highlights

1 Walk among and above the giant tingle trees in the Valley of the Giants **Tree Top Walk** (p142)

2 Compete to see who can spot the most whales in Albany's **King George Sound** (p145)

3 Ponder our fractious human-cetacean relations at the **Whale World Museum** (p151) near Albany

4 Hike among the tall trees and granite outcrops of **Porongurup National Park** (p153)

5 Wander through wildflowers along the walking tracks of **Fitzgerald River National Park** (p156)

6 Marvel at the surf-battered coast from the Great Ocean Drive near **Esperance** (p158)

7 Swim, surf and soak in the sun at the squeaky-clean beaches of **Cape Le Grand National Park** (p160)

Walpole & Nornalup

POP 320 & 50

The peaceful twin inlets of Walpole and Nornalup make good bases from which to explore the heavily forested Walpole Wilderness Area – an immense wilderness incorporating a rugged coastline, several national parks, marine parks, nature reserves and forest conservation areas – covering a whopping 3630-sq-km (an area considerably bigger than Samoa and 57 other countries). Look for *Exploring the Walpole Wilderness and Surrounding Area* pamphlet produced by the Department of Environment & Conservation (DEC).

Walpole is the bigger settlement (though not big enough to get mobile-phone coverage). It's here that the South Western Hwy (Rte 1) becomes the South Coast Hwy.

Sights & Activities

Walpole-Nornalup National Park NATURE RESERVE

The giant trees of this park include red, yellow and Rates tingle trees (all types of eucalypt or gum trees) and, closer to the coast, the red flowering gum.

In the **Valley of the Giants** the **Tree Top Walk** (adult/child $10/5; 9am-4.15pm) has become Walpole's main drawcard, and it is not hard to see why. A 600m-long ramp rises from the floor of the valley, allowing visitors access high into the canopy of the giant tingle trees. At its highest point, the ramp is 40m above the ground. It's on a gentle incline so it's easy to walk and is even accessible by assisted wheelchair. The ramp is an engineering feat in itself, though vertigo sufferers might have a few problems; it's designed to sway gently in the breeze to mimic life in the treetops. At ground level, the **Ancient Empire** boardwalk meanders around and through the base of veteran red tingles, some of which are 16m in circumference, including one that soars to 46m.

There are numerous good walking tracks around, including a section of the **Bibbulmun Track**, which passes through Walpole to Coalmine Beach. There are a number of scenic drives, including the **Knoll Drive**, 3km east of Walpole; the **Valley of the Giants Rd**; and through pastoral country to **Mt Frankland**, 29km north of Walpole. Here you can climb to the summit for panoramic views or walk around the trail at its base. Opposite Knoll Drive, Hilltop Rd leads to a **giant tingle tree**; this road continues to the **Circular Pool** on the Frankland River, a popular canoeing spot. You can hire canoes from Nornalup Riverside Chalets (see Sleeping).

Midway between Nornalup and Peaceful Bay, check out **Conspicuous Cliffs**. It's a great spot for whale-watching from July to November, with a boardwalk, hilltop lookout and steep-ish 800m walk to the beach.

Dinosaur World WILDLIFE PARK

(Bow Bridge; adult/child $12/6; 9.30am-4.30pm) Replica dinosaur skeletons and information boards have been added to spice up this bird and reptile park, off the South Coast Hwy at Bow Bridge. There are some kangaroos, lizards and snakes, but the many parrots (most with clipped wings) are the stars of the show.

Tours

WOW Wilderness Ecocruises RIVER CRUISE

(9840 1036; www.wowwilderness.com.au; adult/child $40/15) The magnificent landscape and its ecology are brought to life with anecdotes about Aboriginal settlement, salmon fishers and shipwrecked pirates. The 2½-hour cruise through the inlets and river systems leaves at 10am daily; make bookings at the visitor centre.

Naturally Walpole Eco Tours 4WD TOURS

(9840 1019; www.naturallywalpole.com.au) Offers half-day tours through the Walpole Wilderness (adult/child $75/40). Winery and wildflower tours can be customised on request.

Sleeping

For bush camping sites in the Walpole Wilderness Area (per adult/child $7/2), including at Crystal Springs and Fernhook Falls, use the honesty registration and fee boxes on site.

Riverside Retreat CHALETS $$

(9840 1255; www.riversideretreat.com.au; South Coast Hwy, Nornalup; chalets $140-260) Set up off the road and on the banks of the beautiful Frankland River, these well-equipped chalets are great value, with pot-bellied stoves for cosy winter warmth and tennis and canoeing as outdoor pursuits.

Nornalup Riverside Chalets CHALETS $

(9840 1107; www.walpole.org.au/nornaluperiversidechalets; Riverside Dr, Nornalup; chalets $85-170) Stay a night in sleepy Nornalup in these comfortable, colourful self-contained chalets, just a rod's throw from the fish in the Frankland River. The chalets are well spaced out, giving a feeling of privacy.

Coalmine Beach CARAVAN PARK $
(☎9840 1026; www.coalminebeach.com.au; Coalmine Beach Rd, Walpole; sites per 2 people $26-30, cabins from $72; ❄@) You couldn't get a better location than this, under shady trees above the sheltered waters of the inlet.

Walpole Lodge HOSTEL $
(☎9840 1244; www.walpolelodge.com.au; Pier St, Walpole; dm/s/d $26/45/55; @) This popular place is basic, open-plan and informal, with great info boards around the walls and casual, cheery owners.

Tingle All Over YHA HOSTEL $
(☎9840 1041; www.yha.com.au; 60 Nockolds St, Walpole; dm/s $29/51, d $67-79; @) Help yourself to lemons and chillies from the garden of this clean, basic option near the highway.

Rest Point Holiday Village CARAVAN PARK $
(☎9840 1032; www.restpoint.com.au; Rest Point; sites per 2 people $22, cabins $75-115) Set on wide lawns with direct water frontage, this spacious holiday park has shade for campers and a range of self-contained accommodation.

Eating

Thurlby Herb Farm CAFE $
(www.thurlbyherb.com.au; 3 Gardiner Rd; mains $13-18; ⏲9am-5pm Mon-Fri) Apart from distilling its own essential oils and making herb-based products including soap, Thurlby serves up tasty light lunches and cakes – accompanied by fresh-picked herbal teas ($4) – in a cafe overlooking the garden.

Flaming Hot Takeaways FAST FOOD $
(Vista St, Walpole; mains $8-15; lunch & dinner) The local chippie is a solid choice for burgers, pizza, some pasta dishes and, of course, fish and chips.

Bowbridge Roadhouse FAST FOOD $
(South Coast Hwy, Bow Bridge; mains $7-18) A reader alerted us to 'the best ever bacon sandwiches', served in a covered area by the forecourt, but we prefer the bacon and egg burgers.

Information

Visitor Centre (☎9840 1111; www.walpole.com.au; South Coast Hwy, Walpole; ⏲9am-5pm; @)

DEC (☎9840 0400; South Coast Hwy, Walpole; ⏲8am-4.30pm Mon-Fri) For national park and bushwalking information.

THE ROAD TO MANDALAY

About 13km west of Walpole, at Crystal Springs, is an 8km gravel road to **Mandalay Beach** where the *Mandalay*, a Norwegian barque, was wrecked in 1911. As the sand gradually erodes with storms, the wreck eerily appears every 10 years or so, in shallow water that is walkable at low tide (check out the photos at Walpole visitor centre). The beach is glorious, often deserted, and accessed by an impressive boardwalk across sand dunes and cliffs. It's now part of D'Entrecasteaux National Park.

Getting There & Away

Transwa (☎1300 662 205; www.transwa.wa.gov.au) bus GS3 heads daily to/from Bunbury ($41, 4½ hours), Bridgetown ($23, 3¼ hours), Pemberton ($18, 1¾ hours), Denmark ($13, 42 minutes) and Albany ($21, 1½ hours).

Denmark

POP 2800

Denmark's beaches and coastline, river and sheltered inlet, forested backdrop and hinterland have attracted a varied, creative and environmentally aware community. Farmers, ferals, fishers, families and folk of all sorts mingle during the town's four market days each year, when the population and accommodation prices soar.

Denmark was established to supply timber to the early goldfields. Known by the Minang Noongar people as Koorabup (place of the black swan), there's evidence of early Aboriginal settlement in the 3000-year-old fish traps found in Wilson Inlet.

Sights & Activities

The town is located in the cool climate Great Southern wine region and has some notable wineries, including **Howard Park** (www.howardparkwines.com.au; Scotsdale Rd; ⏲10am-4pm) and **Forest Hill** (www.foresthillwines.com.au; cnr South Coast Hwy & Myers Rd; ⏲10am-5pm). The latter has an architecturally impressive tasting room and restaurant.

Surfers and anglers usually waste no time in heading to ruggedly beautiful **Ocean Beach**. If you're keen to try surfing, accredited local instructor Mike Neunuebel gives **surf lessons** (☎0401 349 854; 2hr private lesson incl equipment $80) and hires boards and wetsuits (per hour $20).

To get your bearings, walk the **Mokare Heritage Trail** (3km circuit along the Denmark River) or the **Wilson Inlet Trail** (12km return, starting at the river mouth), which forms part of the longer **Nornalup Trail**. Put everything into perspective at **Mt Shadforth Lookout**, with its view of fine coastal scenery. The lush **Mt Shadforth Rd**, running from the centre of town and finishing up on the South Coast Hwy west of town makes a great scenic drive, as does the longer pastoral loop of **Scotsdale Rd**. Potter along these, taking your pick of attractions including alpaca farms, wineries, cheese farms, and art and craft galleries.

William Bay National Park, about 20km west of town, offers sheltered swimming in gorgeous **Greens Pool** and **Elephant Rocks**, and has good walking tracks. Swing by **Bartholomews Meadery** (www.honeywine.com.au; 2620 South Coast Hwy; ⏲9.30am-4.30pm) for a post-beach treat of mead (honey wine) or delicious homemade honey-rose-almond ice cream ($4).

Tours

Denmark Bike Adventures CYCLING
(☎9848 3300; www.denmarkbluewren.com.au) The local YHA offers drop-off/ride back cycling tours along a coastal or winery route; a great way to see the country at your own pace.

Out of Sight! NATURE, WINE
(☎9848 2814; www.outofsighttours.com) Nature trips into the Walpole Wilderness (three hours, adult/child $75/38), West Cape Howe (six hours, adult/child $120/60) or Stirling Range (eight hours, adult/child $150/75); sightseeing around Denmark (two hours); or sampling tours of the local wineries (half-/full day $75/95).

Denmark Wine Lovers Tour WINE
(☎0410 42 32 62; www.denmarkwinelovers.com.au) Full-day tours taking in Denmark wineries ($95), or further afield to Porongurup or Mt Barker (price on application).

Festivals & Events

Market Days MARKET
Four times a year (mid-December, early and late January and Easter) Denmark hosts a colourful market day on the parkland by the river, with an unusual range of high-quality craft stalls, music and food.

Festival of Voice MUSIC
(www.dfov.org.au) Performances and workshops, on the June long weekend.

Sleeping

TOP CHOICE **Cape Howe Cottages** COTTAGES $$
(☎9845 1295; www.capehowe.com.au; 322 Tennessee Rd South, off Lower Denmark Rd; cottages $160-270; ❄) If you fancy a remote getaway, these five cottages in bushland southeast of Denmark make the grade. They're all different but the best is only 1½km from dolphin-favoured Lowlands Beach and is properly plush – with a BBQ on the deck, a dishwasher in the kitchen and laundry facilities.

Sensational Heights B&B $$
(☎9840 9000; www.sensationalheightsbandb.com.au; 159 Suttons Rd; r $175-260; ❄📶) Yep, it's on top of a hill (off Scotsdale Rd) and, yes, the views are sensational. It's a new house, so expect contemporary decor, shiny new fixtures, luxurious linen and very comfy beds. The pricier rooms have spa baths.

Denmark Rivermouth Caravan Park CARAVAN PARK $
(☎9848 1262; www.denmarkrivermouthcaravanpark.com.au; Inlet Dr; sites per 2 people $27, cabins $65-240) Once again, the name tells the story. Ideally located for nautical pursuits, this caravan park sits along Wilson Inlet beside the boat ramp. Some of the units are properly flash, although they are quite tightly arranged. There's also a kids playground and kayaks for hire.

Denmark Ocean Beach Holiday Park CARAVAN PARK $
(☎9848 1106; www.denmarkobhp.com.au; Ocean Beach Rd; sites per 2 people $26-30; cabins $110-180; ❄) This large, long-standing complex was getting a new reception building, waterpark and set of stylish units when we visited. Once the dust settles we're sure it will be much improved. It's just about on the beach, after all.

Spring Bay Villas COTTAGES $$
(☎9848 1211; www.springbayvillas.com; Ocean Beach Rd; villas from $160) Perfectly peaceful, tidy brick villas near the beach. Some have spa baths.

Denmark Waterfront MOTEL $$
(☎9848 1147; www.denmarkwaterfront.com.au; 63 Inlet Dr; r $100-190) The rammed-earth units are light, airy and clean, and there are great views of the water through the gum trees.

Willowleigh B&B B&B $$
(☎9848 1089; www.denmarkbedandbreakfast.com.au; Kearsley Rd; r $140; ❄📶) Enjoy the two acres of gorgeous gardens from your conservatory or verandah at this B&B on the edge of town.

Aiyana Retreat APARTMENTS $$
(☎9848 3258; www.aiyanaretreat.com.au; 28 Anning Rd; apt $180-220) Three luxurious apartments, tucked down a quiet cul-de-sac; spa treatments available.

Riverbend Caravan Park CARAVAN PARK $
(☎9848 1107; rivabend@omninet.net.au; River bend Lane; sites per 1/2 people from $17/23, chalets from $90) About 2km from town on a quiet stretch of river, this lovely shaded site has well-equipped cabins with private verandahs and a veggie garden.

Chimes Spa Retreat RESORT $$$
(☎9848 2255; www.chimes.com.au; Mt Shadforth Rd; r $255-390; ❄📶) At the top end of the scale, this spa resort perched above town has a Balinese aesthetic and wonderful views.

Eating

Denmark Bakery BAKERY $
(Strickland St; pies $5-6; ⏰7am-5pm) Prize-winning and proud of it; this bakery is an institution, because of its pies – and the bread is also good.

Bibbulmun Cafe CAFE $
(cnr Strickland St & South Coast Hwy; mains $8-17; ⏰breakfast & lunch) Stop here to eavesdrop on the local gossip and eat great homemade cakes and sandwiches.

McSweeney's Gourmet CAFE $
(5B Strickland St; mains $6-17; ⏰breakfast & lunch) Beautiful gourmet sandwiches and rolls.

Drinking

Southern End BREWERY
(www.denmarkbrewery.com.au; 427 Mt Shadforth Rd; ⏰11.30am-4.30pm Thu-Mon) Home to Denmark Brews & Ales ('the brew with a view'), this new brewery is currently only producing one ale, bitter and stout but also serves a wide range of imported beers and local wines on their hilltop terrace. Lunch and dinner are also available.

Denmark Hotel PUB, LIVE MUSIC
(www.denmarkhotel.com.au; Hollings Rd) Overlooking the river, the local boozer is the hub of nocturnal activity, with live music every Friday night.

WORTH A TRIP

WEST CAPE HOWE NATIONAL PARK

Midway between Denmark and Albany, this 35-sq-km coastal park is a playground for naturalists, bushwalkers, rock climbers and anglers. Inland, there are areas of coastal heath, lakes, swamp and karri forest. With the exception of the road to Shelley Beach, access is restricted to 4WDs, mostly travelling through sand dunes, to explore the wild coast.

Camping is permitted at Shelley Beach, although campfires are banned.

Information

Visitor Centre (☎9848 2055; www.denmark.com.au; 73 South Coast Hwy; ⏰9am-5pm) Information, accommodation booking service, gift- and bookshop, gallery and the 'world's largest barometer' in its own custom-made tower. Despite the extensive scientific explanations, we still don't understand how the damn thing works – or indeed how it makes water 'boil' at 20 degrees.

Getting There & Away

A **Transwa** (☎1300 662 205; www.transwa.wa.gov.au) bus service GS3 heads daily to/from Bunbury ($46, 5½ hours), Bridgetown ($31, 4¾ hours), Pemberton ($26, 2¾ hours), Walpole ($13, 42 minutes) and Albany ($8.60, 42 minutes).

Albany

POP 25,200

Established shortly before Perth in 1826, the oldest European settlement in the state is now the bustling commercial centre of the southern region. Albany is a mixed bag comprising a stately and genteel decaying colonial quarter, a waterfront in the midst of sophisticated redevelopment and a hectic sprawl of malls and fast-food joints. Less ambivalent is its coastline, which is uniformly spectacular – from Torndirrup National Park's surf-pummelled cliffs to Middleton Beach's white-sands, to the calm waters of King George Sound.

Albany

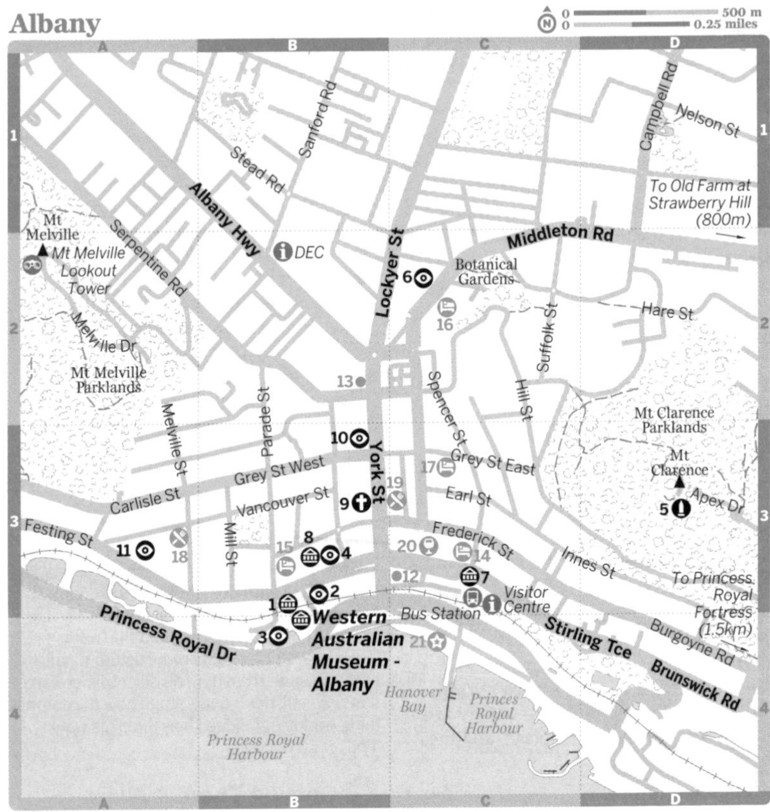

Albany

Top Sights
Western Australian Museum - Albany B4

Sights
1 Albany Convict Gaol B3
2 Alkoomi Wines B3
3 Brig Amity B4
4 Courthouse B3
5 Desert Mounted Corps Memorial D3
6 Dog Rock C2
7 Old Post Office C3
8 Patrick Taylor Cottage B3
9 St John's Anglican Church B3
10 Town Hall B3
11 Vancouver Arts Centre A3

Activities, Courses & Tours
Alkoomi Wines .... (see 2)
12 Dive Locker Albany C3
13 Southcoast Diving Supplies B2

Sleeping
14 Albany Backpackers C3
15 Bayview Backpackers YHA B3
16 Dog Rock Motel C2
17 My Place C3

Eating
18 Vancouver Cafe & Store A3
Wild Duck .... (see 12)
19 York Street Cafe C3

Drinking
20 White Star C3

Entertainment
21 Albany Entertainment Centre C4

The town is in an area that's seen the violence of weather and whaling. Whales are still a part of the Albany experience, but these days are viewed through a camera lens rather than at the business end of a harpoon.

The **Bibbulmun Track** (www.bibbulmuntrack.org.au) ends (or starts) here, just outside the visitor centre; the exhausted and/or exuberant comments in the walkers' log books make great reading.

History

The Minang Noongar people called this place Kinjarling (the place of rain) and believed that fighting Wargals (mystical giant serpents) created the fractured landscape. The Minang set up sophisticated fish traps on Oyster Harbour, the remains of which can still be seen.

Initial contacts with Europeans were friendly, with over 60 ships visiting between 1622 and 1826. The Minang traded crops with the early arrivals, in exchange for ship biscuits. The establishment of a British settlement here was welcomed as it regulated the behaviour of sealers and whalers, who had been responsible for kidnaps, rapes and murder of Minang people. Yet by the end of the 19th century, every shop in Albany refused entry to Aborigines, and control over every aspect of their lives (including the right to bring up their own children) had been lost.

For the British, Albany's raison d'être was its sheltered harbour, which made it a thriving whaling port. Later the city became a coaling station for British ships bound for the east coast and during WWI it was the mustering point for transport ships of the 1st Australian Imperial Force heading for Egypt and the Gallipoli campaign.

Sights

Middleton & Emu Beaches BEACHES

(Map p151) Just around the headland, east of the town centre, these beautiful beaches facing King George Sound share one stretch of sand and are perfect for families – both human and cetacean. In winter, you'll often see mother whales and their calves here – sometimes two or three sets at once. Head around Emu Point to Oyster Harbour and there are swimming pontoons and even calmer waters.

A clifftop walking track hugs much of the waterfront between the town centre and Middleton Beach. Boardwalks continue along Emu Beach.

Western Australian Museum – Albany MUSEUM

(Map p146; www.museum.wa.gov.au; Residency Rd; admission by donation; ⏲10am-4.30pm Thu-Tue) This branch of the state museum is split between two neighbouring buildings. The newer Eclipse building has a kid's discovery section, a lighthouse exhibition, a gallery for temporary exhibitions and a gift shop. More interesting for adults is the newly refitted 1850s home of the resident magistrate, where displays illuminate Minang Noongar history, local natural history and seafaring stories.

Brig Amity SHIP

(Map p146; www.historicalbany.com.au; adult/child $6/2; ⏲9.30am-4pm) Next to the museum is a full-scale replica of the brig which carried Albany's first British settlers from Sydney in 1826. It was completed for the city's 150th anniversary.

Town Centre HISTORIC BUILDINGS

(Map p146) Near the foreshore you'll see the buildings of the historic precinct. This area is relatively quiet, as if the town's boom years belong to another time. Take a stroll down Stirling Tce – noted for its Victorian shopfronts, **Courthouse** and **Old Post Office** – and up York St, where you'll see the lovely **St John's Anglican Church** and Albany's **Town Hall**. A guided walking-tour brochure of colonial buildings is available from the visitor centre.

Patrick Taylor Cottage MUSEUM

(Map p146; www.historicalbany.com.au; 39 Duke St; admission $2; ⏲11am-3pm) Believed to be the oldest colonial dwelling in WA, this 1832 wattle-and-daub cottage is packed with antiques, freaky mannequins and displays on its former residents.

Albany Convict Gaol MUSEUM

(Map p146; www.historicalbany.com.au; Stirling Tce; adult/child $5/2.50; ⏲10am-4pm) The old gaol was built in 1851 as a hiring depot for ticket-of-leave convicts but by 1855 most were in private employment. In 1872 the building was extended and reopened as a civil gaol. These days it's a folk museum.

Old Farm at Strawberry Hill HISTORIC BUILDING

(Map p151; www.ntwa.com.au; 174 Middleton Rd; adult/child $5/3; ⏲10am-4pm) National Trust-owned Strawberry Hill is one of the oldest farms in WA, established in 1827 as the town's government farm. The homestead (1836) features antiques and artefacts that belonged to the original owner.

Vancouver Arts Centre GALLERY
(Map p146; Vancouver St; admission free; ⌚9am-4pm) Housed in a former hospital (1887), this is the centre of the city's arts community, hosting regular touring exhibitions and cultural events.

Mt Melville & Mt Clarence LANDMARKS
There are more fine views over the coast and inland from the twin peaks, Mt Clarence and Mt Melville, which overlook the town. On top of Mt Clarence is the **Desert Mounted Corps Memorial** (Map p146), originally erected in Port Said as a WWI memorial. It was irreparably damaged during the Suez crisis in 1956, when colonial reminders were less than popular in Egypt. This copy was made from masonry salvaged from the original.

To climb Mt Clarence follow the track accessible from the end of Grey St East, turn left, take the first turn on the right and follow the path by the water tanks. The walk is tough but the views make it worthwhile; take a picnic and enjoy a well-earned rest at the top. By car, take Apex Dr.

Princess Royal Fortress HISTORIC SITE
(Map p151; www.forts.albany.wa.gov.au; Forts Rd, off Marine Dr; adult/child $11/2; ⌚9am-5pm) As Albany was a strategic port, its vulnerability to attack was seen as a potential threat to Australia's security. This fort was built in 1893 on Mt Adelaide, which is joined to Mt Clarence. The restored buildings, gun emplacements and views make a rewarding visit. Particularly poignant are the photos of the troop transports on their way to Gallipoli.

Dog Rock LANDMARK
(Map p146) On Middleton Rd you can't miss one of Albany's icons, which looks like a dog's head (the locals have even painted on a dog collar to reinforce the point). The Minang believed the dog had been decapitated by an angry Wargal.

Activities

Whale-watching WHALE-WATCHING
After whaling ended in 1978, whales slowly began returning to the waters of Albany. They're now here to the extent that it can sometimes be hard *not* to see southern right and humpback whales near the bays and coves of King George Sound from July to mid-October. You can usually spot them from the beach but if you fancy a closer look, both **Albany Dolphin & Whale Cruises** (☎0428 429 876; www.whales.com.au; adult/child $80/45) and **Albany Whale Tours** (☎9845 1068; www.albanywhaletours.com.au; adult/child $75/40) run regular whale-watching trips in season.

Diving DIVING
Albany's appeal as a top-class diving destination grew after the 2001 scuttling of the warship HMAS *Perth* to create an artificial reef for divers (visit www.hmasperth.com.au for live webcam images of the wreck). Its natural reefs feature temperate and tropical corals, and are home to the bizarre and wonderful leafy and weedy sea dragons. **Dive Locker Albany** (Map p146; ☎9842 6886; www.albanydive.com.au; 114 York St) and **Southcoast Diving Supplies** (Map p146; ☎9841 7176; www.divealbany.com.au; 84b Serpentine Rd) will show you the underwater world. Two-tank dives cost around $190, including equipment.

Fishing FISHING
Local anglers reckon you can throw a line anywhere in Albany and catch something. Beach fishing at Middleton and Emu Beaches is popular. **Spinners Charters** (☎9844 1906; www.spinnerscharters.com.au; Emu Point) runs deep-sea fishing trips. **Emu Point Boat Hire** (☎9844 1562; Emu Point; ⌚Sep-May) provides paddle boats, kayaks and motorised dinghies.

Alkoomi Wines WINE-TASTING
(Map p146; www.alkoomiwines.com.au; 225 Stirling Tce; ⌚11am-5pm) Just in case you were having withdrawals from wine-tasting, Frankland River's Alkoomi has set up a handy tasting room right in the middle of town.

Tours

Kalgan Queen RIVER CRUISE
(☎9844 3166; www.albanyaustralia.com; Emu Point; adult/child $65/35; ⌚9am Sep-Jun) Take a four-hour cruise up the Kalgan River in a glass-bottomed boat and learn about the history and wildlife of the area.

Down Under MOTORCYCLE TOUR
(☎9842 2468; www.harleytours.com.au; 30min/hour/half-day $60/110/300) Hop on a hog and see Albany from a Harley Davidson. In addition, 'Quick Thrills' are available from Middleton Beach during the Christmas and Easter school holidays ($10).

Sleeping

TOP CHOICE **Flinders Park Lodge** B&B $$
(Map p151; ☎9844 7062; www.parklodge.com.au; cnr Lower King & Harbour Rds, Bayonet Head; r $145-195; wi-fi) The restraint of this elegant 1930s white stucco building is com-

ALBANY'S WHALING BATTLEGROUND

Talk to some Western Australians about their childhood holidays in Albany and, as well as carefree days of fishing and swimming, they're also likely to recall an almighty stench in the air and sharks circling in bloody corners of Frenchman Bay. The local whales – whose blubber created the vile smell while being melted down in pressure cookers, and whose blood spilled into water around the then Cheynes Beach Whaling Station – also appear to remember this scene far too well. It took them well over a decade to return in full strength to the waters around Albany after the last whale was hunted on 20 November 1978.

The whaling industry was gruesome in a most public way – whales were hunted, harpooned and dragged back to shore to be cut up and boiled – which is perhaps why the environmental movement managed to make its closure one of their earlier successes. It became harder for the industry to make the smell, the blood and the sight of harpooned carcasses being towed into the harbour anything but unattractive. One of Tim Winton's earlier novels (*Shallows*,1984), set in Albany, where Winton lived for some time as an adolescent, describes how whaling became an emotional battleground for environmentalists and the many local employees of the industry, like the situation in timber towns throughout the southwest in recent years. This pressure from protesters, as well as dwindling whale numbers and a drop in world whale-oil prices, sounded the death knell for the industry.

But Albany has cleverly managed to turn this now-unacceptable industry into a quaint tourist attraction, with the fascinating Whale World Museum (see p151) and maritime festivals, which celebrate its rough-and-ready history on the seas. The whales who play in the surrounding waters are all the happier for it – as are the town's tourism-boosted coffers.

pletely thrown off with the exuberant decor of the bedrooms and a hostess that matches that exuberance measure for measure. Sip a gin on the lawn and imagine you've strolled into a scene from *The Great Gatsby*.

Beach House at Bayside BOUTIQUE HOTEL **$$$**
(Map p151; ☎9844 8844; www.thebeachhouseatbayside.com.au; 33 Barry Ct, Collingwood Park; r $243-328) Positioned right by the beach and the golf course in a quiet cul-de-sac, midway between Middleton Beach and Emu Point, this modern block distinguishes itself with absolutely wonderful service. Rates include breakfast, afternoon tea, and evening port and chocolates, engendering a relaxed clubbish vibe with plenty of opportunity for guest fraternisation.

My Place APARTMENTS **$$**
(Map p146; ☎9842 3242; www.myplace.com.au; 47-61 Grey St East; r $120-135; ❄📶) We love the (possibly) tongue-in-cheek nana-ish vibe to the studios, with floral duvets and a trio of flying ducks on the wall. The considerably larger one-bedroom options aren't as kooky but they're all clean, central and excellent value.

Discovery Inn HOSTEL **$**
(Map p151; ☎9842 5535; www.discoveryinn.com.au; 9 Middleton Rd, Middleton Beach; dm/s $30/55, d $75-80; @) Sitting somewhere between a hostel and a guesthouse, Discovery Inn offers great value and a convivial atmosphere, located close to the beach. Guests congregate amid the tropical plants in the central conservatory.

Emu Beach Holiday Park CARAVAN PARK **$**
(Map p151; ☎9844 1147; www.emubeach.com; 8 Medcalf Pde, Emu Point; sites for 2 people $32, chalets $85-200; ❄) Families love the Emu Beach area and this holiday park, close to the beach, has good facilities, including a BBQ area and a kids' playground.

Middleton Beach Holiday Park CARAVAN PARK **$**
(Map p151; ☎9841 3593; www.holidayalbany.com.au; 28 Flinders Pde, Middleton Beach; sites per 2 people $34, chalets $115-230; @🏊) This excellent beachfront caravan park is sheltered by high sand dunes (a good thing when a gale is raging). Book early – it's popular.

Albany Backpackers HOSTEL **$**
(Map p146; ☎9841 8848; www.albanybackpackers.com.au; cnr Stirling Tce & Spencer St; dm/r $27/63; @📶) With bright murals and a reputation for partying, this old hostel offers extras such as coffee and cake each evening, bike hire and limited free internet access.

Bayview Backpackers YHA HOSTEL $
(Map p146; ☎9842 3388; www.bayviewbackpackers.com.au; 49 Duke St; dm/s/d $24/45/60; @☎) In a quiet street 400m from the centre, this rambling backpackers has a lazy feel and is less frenzied than the hostel in town.

Dog Rock Motel MOTEL $$
(Map p146; ☎9841 4422; www.dogrockmotel.com.au; 303 Middleton Rd; s $105-169, d $125-189; ❄) The newly renovated 'delux' rooms in this large brick motel complex have a tasteful, contemporary feel, although we quite like the period-piece 1970s tiles in the older, cheaper rooms.

Eating & Drinking

TOP CHOICE **Wild Duck** FRENCH $$
(Map p146; ☎9842 2554; 112 York St; mains $30-40; ⊙dinner Wed-Sun) Sophisticated, clever without being overly modish, absolutely food focussed – Wild Duck is one of WA's best regional restaurants. Save room for dessert, which when we visited included witty takes on liquorice allsorts, Welsh cakes and a fried egg on toast.

York Street Cafe CAFE $$
(Map p146; 184 York St; lunch $16-25, dinner $25-33; ⊙breakfast & lunch Mon-Sat, dinner Wed-Sat) The food is wonderful at this bright new place on the main strip. Lunch includes pasta, focaccia, schnitzels and deliciously crisp fish balls, while for dinner it turns into more of a bistro.

Bay Merchants CAFE $
(Map p151; 18 Adelaide Cres, Middleton Beach; mains $9-17, ⊙6am-6pm) Just a sandy-footed stroll from the beach, this cafe-cum-providore makes good coffee, enticing cakes and to-die-for gourmet sandwiches.

Vancouver Cafe & Store CAFE $
(Map p146; ☎9841 2475; 65 Vancouver St; mains $10-19; ⊙7.30am-3.30pm daily) This great little cafe is perched above the coast, with balcony views and delicious home baking. It's open on Tuesday and Thursday evenings for pasta and pizza respectively.

Squid Shack FISH AND CHIPS $
(Map p151; Swarbrick St, Emu Point; mains $11-18; ⊙10am-7pm Wed-Sun) A local institution serving fish straight from the ocean from what is literally a shack at the marina; take a bottle of wine and have a picnic on the beach.

White Star MICROBREWERY, PUB $$
(Map p146; 72 Stirling Tce; mains $16-29; ⊙lunch & dinner) With 20 beers on tap (including their own brews), excellent pub grub, a beer garden and lots of live music, this old pub gets a gold star.

Entertainment

Albany Entertainment Centre CONCERT HALL
(Map p146; www.albanyentertainment.com.au; Princess Royal Dr) Supremely pointy and vaguely reminiscent of a scaled down Sydney Opera House in terms of its location and audaciousness, this $58-million, 600-seat venue was aiming for an August 2011 opening when we visited.

Town Hall THEATRE
(Map p146; www.albanytownhall.com.au; 217 York St) Has regular shows.

Orana Cinemas CINEMA
(Map p151; ☎9842 2210; www.oranacinemas.com.au; 451 Albany Hwy) For the latest snog-and-shoot blockbusters.

Information

DEC (☎9842 4500; 120 Albany Hwy; 8am-4.30pm Mon-Fri) For national park information.

Visitor Centre (☎9841 9290; www.amazingalbany.com; Proudlove Pde; ⊙9am-5pm) In the old train station.

Getting There & Away

AIR Albany Airport (ALH; Albany Hwy) is 11km northwest of the city centre. **Skywest** (☎1300 660 088; www.skywest.com.au) has 18 flights a week to and from Perth (70 minutes).

BUS **Transwa** (☎1300 662 205; www.transwa.wa.gov.au) services stop at the visitor centre. These include:

» GS1 to/from Perth ($56, six hours) and Mt Barker ($8.60; 39 minutes) daily;

» GS2 to/from Perth ($56, eight hours), Northam ($60, 6½ hours), York ($56, six hours) and Mt Barker ($8.60, 41 minutes) four times a week;

» GS3 to/from Bunbury ($53, six hours), Bridgetown ($41, 4¾ hours), Pemberton ($34, 3½ hours), Walpole ($21, 1½ hours) and Denmark ($8.60, 42 minutes) daily;

» GE4 to/from Esperance ($62, 6½ hours, twice weekly).

Getting Around

Loves (☎9841 1211) runs local bus services (adult/child $1.90/0.80) on weekdays and Saturday morning. The visitor centre has routes and timetables.

You can rent a car from **King Sound Vehicle Hire** (Map p146; ☎9841 8466; www.kingsoundcars.com; 6 Sanford Rd) and both **Avis** (☎9842

2833; www.avis.com.au) and **Budget** (☎9841 7799; www.budget.com.au) have agencies at the airport.

Around Albany

Whale World Museum MUSEUM
(Map p151; ☎9844 4019; www.whaleworld.org; Frenchman Bay Rd; adult/child $25/10; ⏰9am-5pm) When the Cheynes Beach Whaling Station ceased operations in November 1978, few could have guessed that its gore-covered decks would eventually be covered in tourists, craning to see whales passing within harpoon-shot of the slaughterhouse itself. The museum screens several films about marine life and whaling operations, and displays giant skeletons, harpoons, whaleboat models and scrimshaw (etchings on whalebone). Outside there's the rusting *Cheynes IV* whale chaser and station equipment to inspect. Free guided tours depart on the hour from 10am.

Attached to the complex is the Walk On The Wild Side (adult/child $10/5) wildlife park, which can also be visited as part of a nocturnal tour (adult/child $35/10; bookings essential).

FREE **Torndirrup National Park** NATIONAL PARK
(Frenchman Bay Rd) Covering much of the peninsula that encloses the southern reaches of Albany's Princess Royal Harbour and King George Sound, this national park is known for its windswept, ocean-bashed cliffs. Rocks in this area have been proved to be direct matches to those in Antarctica, to which they were once joined. This is a dangerous coastline so beware of freakish, large waves – many have lost their lives after being swept off the rocks. The **Gap** is a natural cleft in the rock, channelling blistering surf through giant walls of granite. Close by is the **Natural Bridge**, a self-explanatory landmark. Further east, the **Blowholes** can put

Around Albany

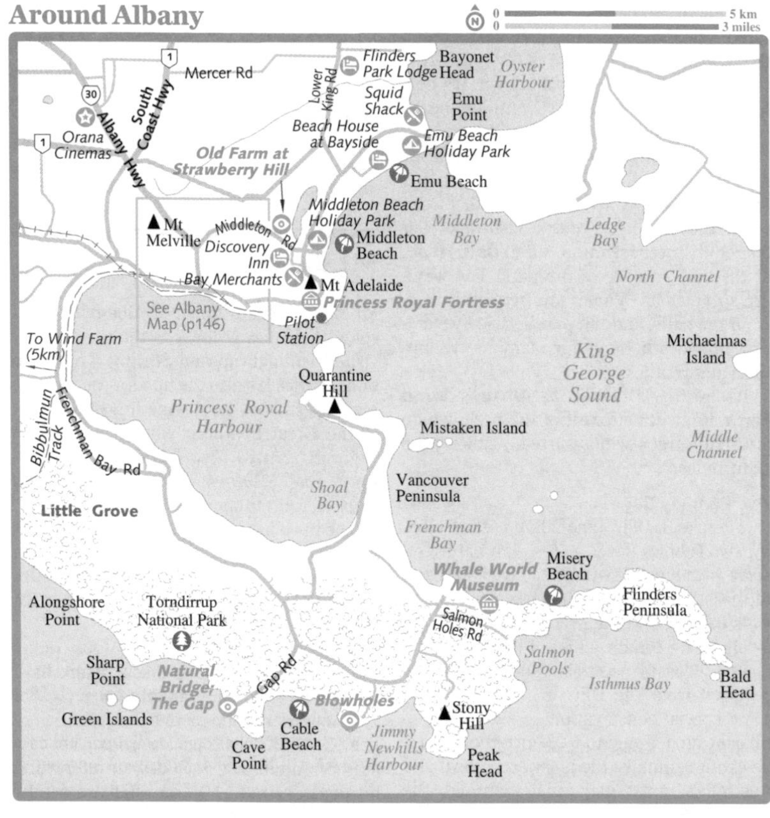

ALBANY TO ESPERANCE ALTERNATIVES

The 480km of South Coast Hwy (Rte 1) between Albany and Esperance is a pleasant enough rural drive but there's not an awful lot to tempt you out of the car en route on this relatively isolated and unpopulated stretch. You can break up the first leg by taking the Albany Hwy (Rte 30) to Mt Barker and heading east to Porongurup and then north through the Stirling Ranges before turning east again through Ongerup and rejoining the highway at Jerramungup. This route will add 57km to the trip.

At Ongerup, the excellent community-managed and volunteer-run **Yongergnow Malleefowl Centre** (☎9828 2325; www.yongergnow.com.au; adult/child $6/3; ⏲10am-4pm Sat-Mon, Wed & Thu) is worth a look. It's devoted to the conservation of a curious endangered bird that creates huge mounds to incubate its chicks.

Near Jerramungup is **Fitzgerald River National Park** (see p156), where you can perhaps base yourself at Hopetoun or Bremer Bay, the beautiful beaches which bookend it. However, Bremer Bay is best reached by taking the South Coast Hwy from Albany.

on a show when the surf is up, worth the 78 steps down and back up.

Where the cliffs give way to beach, the results are just as spectacular. Steep, rocky, green-water coves such as **Jimmy Newells Harbour** and **Salmon Holes** are popular with surfers but quite scary for swimmers. You're better to head to the peninsula's sheltered side, where beautiful **Misery Beach** (a contradiction in terms) is often deserted and is an easy drive in/walk down. It's next to **Frenchman Bay**, a fine swimming beach with a shady barbecue area.

At **Stony Hill**, a short heritage trail leads around the site of an observatory station from both World Wars. Keen walkers can tackle the hard 10km-return bushwalk (over five hours) over **Isthmus Hill** to **Bald Head**, at the eastern edge of the park. The views are spectacular. Whales are frequently seen from the cliffs, and the park's varied vegetation provides habitats for many native animals and reptiles.

It's worth a detour to Albany's **Wind Farm**, immediately west of the park, where a walking track winds surreally among the 12 turbines.

Two Peoples Bay NATURE RESERVE

(Two Peoples Bay Rd) Some 20km east of Albany, Two Peoples Bay is a 46-sq-km nature reserve with a good swimming beach and scenic coastline. From the main beach you can walk east around the headland (or drive) to lovely **Little Beach**. Little of the rest of the reserve is easily accessible and permits are required from the DEC in Albany to visit some special conservation zones. It's a significant area, home to two once-thought-to-be-extinct animals: the noisy scrub bird and Australia's rarest marsupial mammal, the Gilbert's potoroo. Find out more from the Albany **DEC Visitor Centre** (p150).

In case you're wondering whether the bay's name is a testimony to Aboriginal-Anglo race relations, it's not. It was named after a meeting of French and US ships here in 1803.

FREE **Waychinicup National Park** NATIONAL PARK

(Cheyne Beach Rd) Gilbert's potoroos and noisy scrub birds are also protected at this little national park, east of Two Peoples Bay. Unlike at the bay, DEC operates a **camp site** (adult/child $7/3) here. It's a beautiful spot, by the inlet of the Waychinicup River; vault toilets are provided but no fresh water is available.

Mt Barker

POP 1770

Mt Barker (50km north of Albany) has become the gateway town to the increasingly visited Porongurup and Stirling Range National Parks. It's also the hub for the increasingly prestigious local wine industry – part of the Great Southern wine region. **Plantagenet Wines** (www.plantagenetwines.com; Albany Hwy; ⏲10am-4.30pm) is conveniently situated right in the middle of town.

The town has been settled since the 1830s and the convict-built 1868 police station and gaol have been preserved as a **museum** (Albany Hwy; adult/child $5/free; ⏲10am-3pm Sat & Sun).

All 78 types and 24 subtypes of Australia's weird and wonderful Banksia plant have found a home at the **Banksia Farm** (☎9851 1770; www.banksiafarm.com.au; Pearce Rd; admission $11; ⏲9.30am-4.30pm Mon-Fri Mar-Jun, daily Aug-Nov); admission includes an interesting introductory talk. Also on offer are a fully guided tour ($25), morning and afternoon tea, and comfortable B&B accommodation (double $145).

It's well worth heading up **Mt Barker** itself, 5km south of town, for excellent views of the neighbouring ranges. Southwest of Mt Barker, on the rolling grounds of the Egerton-Warburton estate, is the exquisitely photogenic **Saint Werburgh's Chapel**, built between 1872 and 1873. The wrought-iron chancel screen and altar rail were shaped on the property. The grand old farmhouse can be spotted across the fields in the distance.

A surprising sight is the authentic Mongolian yurt (felt tent) and gallery of eclectic Mongolian and Chinese art in the grounds of **Nomads Guest House** (☎9851 2131; www.nomadsguesthousewa.com.au; 12 Morpeth St; s/d/yurt/chalet $70/90/100/110).

If you're stopping for lunch, try **Old Station Cafe** (11 Albany Hwy; mains $11-17; ⏱breakfast & lunch), which offers a big selection of cakes in a little cottage.

Getting There & Away

Transwa (☎1300 662 205; www.transwa.wa.gov.au) operates the following bus services:

» GS1 to/from Perth ($48, 5½ hours) and Albany ($8.60; 39 minutes) daily.

» GS2 to/from Perth ($48, 7¼ hours), Northam ($53, 5¾ hours), York ($51, 5¼ hours) and Albany ($8.60, 41 minutes) four times a week.

Porongurup National Park

The 24-sq-km, 12km-long **Porongurup National Park** (entry per car/motorcycle $11/5) has 1100-million-year-old granite outcrops, panoramic views, beautiful scenery, large karri trees and some excellent bushwalks.

Karris grow in the deep-red soil (known as karri loam) of the range's upper slopes; nurtured by run-off from the granite, this area is 100km east of their usual range. The rich forest also supports 65 species of orchid in spring and, in September and October, there are wildflowers among the trees.

Bushwalks range from the 100m **Tree-in-the-Rock** stroll (just what it sounds like) to the harder **Hayward and Nancy Peaks** (5.5km loop). The **Devil's Slide** (5km return) is a walk of contrasts that takes you through a pass of karri forest and onto the stumpy vegetation of the granite. These walks start from the main day-use area (Bolganup Rd). The **Castle Rock Trail to Balancing Rock** (3km return) starts further east, signposted off the Mt Barker–Porongurup Rd. A very lovely 6km **scenic drive** along the northern edge of the park offers great views towards the Stirling Range, which from this angle looks like a woman lying on her back. If you're driving anywhere around here near dusk, take it slow and watch out for kangaroos.

Porongurup is also part of the Great Southern wine region and there are 11 wineries in the immediate vicinity, some in blissfully bucolic settings.

Sleeping & Eating

There is no accommodation (not even a campground) within the national park itself but all of these options are right on its doorstep. Eating options are very limited.

Ty-Jarrah CHALETS **$$**
(☎9853 1255; www.tyjarrah.com; 3 Bolganup Rd; 1/2 bedroom from $110/140) Very nice and

Porongurup National Park

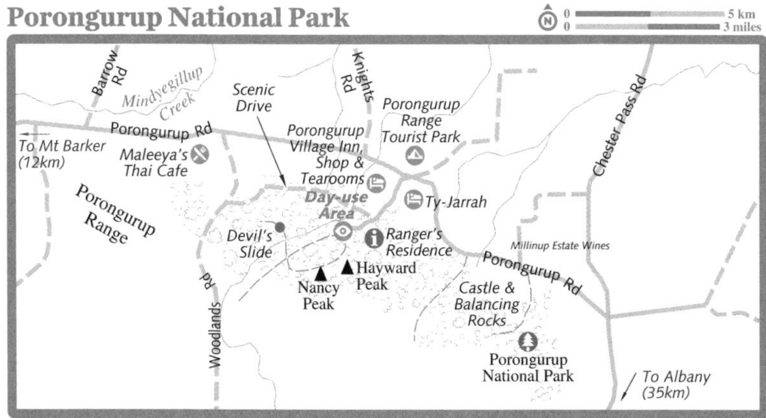

comfortable. A-frame chalets in a forest setting and, yes, there is a Welsh connection.

Porongurup Range Tourist Park CARAVAN PARK **$**

(☎9853 1057; www.porongurupangetouristpark.com.au; 1304 Porongurup Rd; sites per 2 people $26-29, cabins $85-99;) Tidy with good facilities; credit cards not accepted.

Porongurup Village Inn, Shop & Tearooms B&B, CAFE **$**

(☎9853 1110; www.porongurupinn.com.au; 1972 Porongurup Rd; s/d/cottages $30/60/100) This welcoming hostel-like place has grown higgledy-piggledy over the years to include home-cooked food (breakfast $5 to $14, lunch $16 to $18) with veggies from the organic garden.

Maleeya's Thai Cafe THAI **$$**

(☎9853 1123; www.maleeya.com.au; 1376 Porongurup Rd; mains $20; ⏲lunch & dinner, Fri-Sun). Authentic Thai food, plus crafts and a nursery.

Stirling Range National Park

Ever seen a Queen of Sheba orchid or a Stirling Bell? Here's your chance. Rising abruptly from the surrounding flat and sandy plains, Stirling Range's propensity to change colour through blues, reds and purples will captivate photographers during the spectacular wildflower season from late August to early December.

This 1156-sq-km national park consists of a single chain of peaks pushed up by plate tectonics to form a range 10km wide and 65km long. Running most of its length are isolated summits, some knobbly and some perfect pyramids, towering above broad valleys covered in shrubs and heath. Bluff Knoll (Bular Mai), at 1095m, is the highest point in the southwest.

Due to the altitude and climate there are many localised plants in the Stirlings. It is estimated that there are more than 1500 species of native plants, 80 of which are endemic. The most beautiful are the Darwinias or mountain bells, which occur only above 300m; one species may be seen in season on the Mt Talyuberlup walk.

The range was named after James Stirling, first governor of the Swan River Colony. For tens of thousands of years before that it was known as Koi Kyenunu-ruff, meaning 'mist moving around the mountains'. It's recognised by Noongar people as a place of special significance – a place where the spirits of the dead return. Every summit has an ancestral being associated with it – so it's

Stirling Range National Park

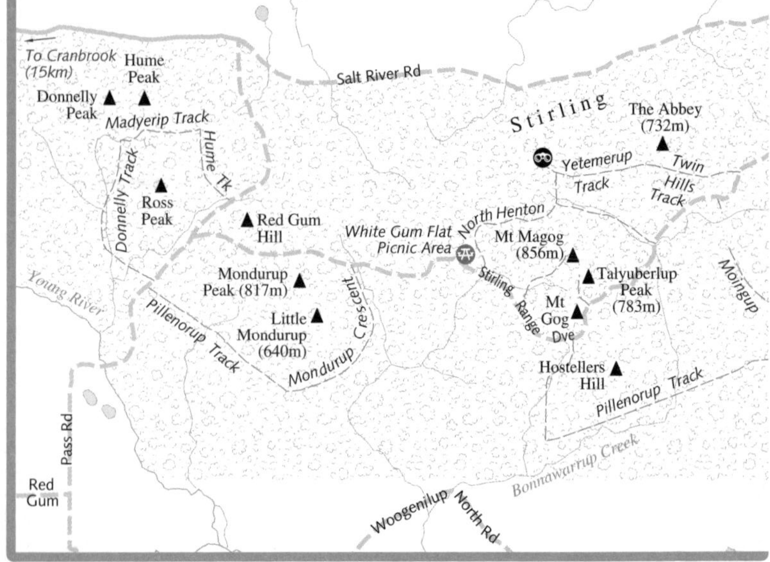

appropriate to show proper respect when visiting here.

Park fees are charged at the start of Bluff Knoll Rd (entry per car/motorcycle $11/5).

Activities

The Stirlings are renowned for serious **bushwalking**. Keen walkers can choose from a number of high points: Toolbrunup (for views and a good climb; 1052m, 4km return), Bluff Knoll (a well-graded tourist track; 1095m, 6km return), and Mt Hassell (827m, 3km return) and Talyuberlup (783m, 2.6km return) are popular half-day walks.

Challenging walks cross the eastern sector of the range from **Bluff Knoll to Ellen Peak**, which should take three days, or the shorter traverse from the **Arrows to Ellen Peak** (two days). The latter option is a loop but the former, from Bluff Knoll, will require a car shuttle. Walkers must be suitably experienced and equipped as the range is subject to sudden drops in temperature, driving rain and sometimes snow; register in and out of your walk with the rangers (☎9827 9230).

Sleeping & Eating

Options are limited in this remote area, so stock up on food in Mt Barker.

Lily COTTAGES $$
(☎9827 9205; www.thelily.com.au; Chester Pass Rd; cottages from $139) Looking like a 16th-century Dutch farm has been beamed directly into the WA landscape, 12km north of the park, this set of cottages is grouped around a working windmill. The cottages are all very comfortable and fully self-contained, and meals are available for guests at the neighbouring restaurant, housed in the 1924 railway station building. Non-guests can call to enquire about which nights the restaurant is open to the public (hours are haphazard and infrequent), as well as to organise tours of the flour mill (per person $10; minimum four).

Mount Trio Bush Camping & Caravan Park CARAVAN PARK $
(☎9827 9270; www.mounttrio.com.au; Salt River Rd; unpowered/powered sites per person $12/14) Rustic bush campground on a farm property close to the walking tracks, north of the centre of the park. It has hot showers, a kitchen, free gas BBQs and a campfire pit.

Stirling Range Retreat CARAVAN PARK $
(☎9827 9229; www.stirlingrange.com.au; 8639 Chester Pass Rd; sites per adult/child $13/8, dm/s $30/65, cabins from $70; ❄@) Also on the park's northern boundary. There's a wide range of accommodation, from

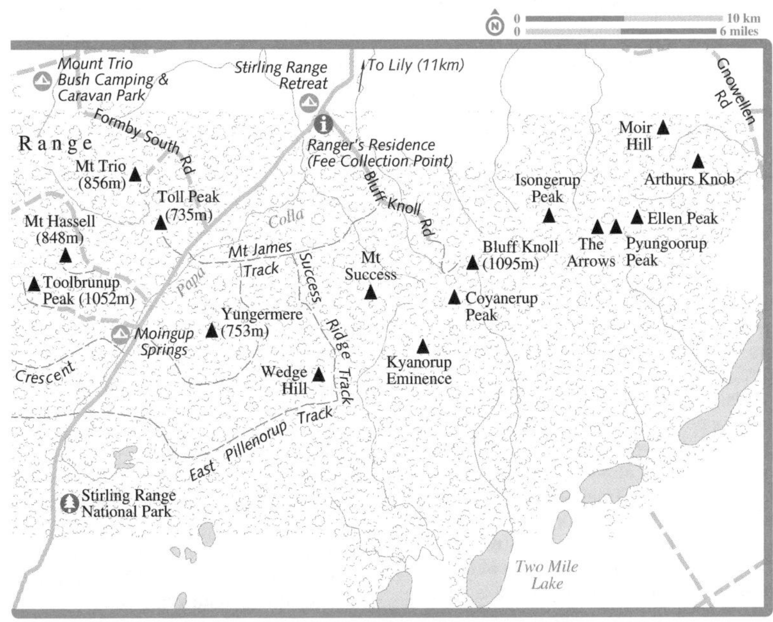

a backpackers' lodge to self-contained, rammed-earth cabins at this dusty site.

Moingup Springs CAMPGROUND $
(Chester Pass Rd; site per adult/child $7/2) DEC's only campground within the park; no showers or electricity.

Bremer Bay

POP 250

Edged with brilliant white sand and translucent green waters, this fishing and holiday hamlet, 61km from the South Coast Hwy, is a sleepy nook where life is lived gazing out to sea. While you're at it, you might spot southern right whales, which from July to November turn the bay into a cetacean maternity ward.

The **visitor centre** (☎9837 4171; www.bremerbay.com; Mary St; ⏲9am-5pm Mon-Fri; 📶) is in the shire library, which also has internet access (per 15 minutes $2.20).

Bremer Bay Beaches Resort & Tourist Park (☎9837 4290; www.bremerbaybeaches.com.au; Wellstead Rd; sites per 2 people $30, cabins from $98; 🏊) has shady campsites, a well-equipped campers' kitchen and a seasonal pizzeria. It's a 1.5km walk through the dunes to the beach.

Fitzgerald River National Park

Midway between Albany and Esperance, this gem of a national park (entry car/motorcycle $11/5) has been declared a Unesco Biosphere Reserve. Its 3300 sq km contains half of the orchid species in WA (more than 80, 70 of which occur nowhere else), 22 mammal species, 200 species of birds and 1700 species of plants (20% of WA's described species). It's also the blossoming ground of the royal hakea *(Hakea victoria)* and qualup bell *(Pimelia physodes)* flowers. Wildflowers are most abundant in spring, but flowers – especially the hardy proteas – bloom throughout the year.

Walkers will discover beautiful coastline, sand plains, rugged coastal hills (known as 'the Barrens') and deep, wide river valleys. In season, you'll almost certainly see whales and their calves from the shore at **Point Ann**, where there's a lookout and a heritage walk that follows a short stretch of the 1164km **No 2 rabbit-proof fence** (built between 1904 and 1960). Short walks are also accessible at **East Mt Barren** (three hours) and **West Mt Barren** (two hours). For information on wilderness walks check with the **DEC rangers** Jerramungup (☎9835 5043; Quiss Rd); Bremer Bay (☎9837 1022; Murray Rd); East Mount Barren (☎9838 3060; Hamersley Dr).

Although the park is one of the areas in southern WA least affected by the dieback fungus (a killer of native trees), precautions are in place to ensure it remains so; respect the 'no entry – dieback' signs, and clean your shoes before each walk.

The three main 2WD entry points to the park are from the South Coast Hwy (Quiss Rd and Pabelup Dr), Hopetoun (Hamersley Dr) and Bremer Bay (along Swamp and Murray Rds). This last is the prettiest route, winding through acres of flowering shrubs. All roads are gravel, and likely to be impassable after rain, so check locally before you set out.

Sleeping

Quaalup Homestead CAMPGROUND $
(☎9837 4124; www.whalesandwildflowers.com.au; Quaalup Rd; sites per person from $10, r from $85) Completely isolated and totally magical, this 1858 homestead is secluded deep within the southern reaches of the park. Electricity is by way of solar panels, so leave the plug-in toys behind and forget about mobile phone coverage. Sleeping options range from a bush campsite with gas BBQs to a set of cosy units and chalets scattered around the grounds. Quaalup Rd is reached from Pabelup Dr.

DEC campsites CAMPGROUND $
(site per adult/child $7/2) Of DEC's five national-park campsites only St Mary Inlet (near Point Ann) can be reached by 2WD. The two at Hamersley Inlet and the others at Whale Bone Beach, Quoin Head and Fitzgerald Inlet can only be reached by 4WD or on foot.

Hopetoun

POP 590

Once as sleepy as Bremer Bay, Hopetoun has nearly doubled in size in recent years due to the opening of a nickel mine. The beauty of the beaches hasn't changed but there are now a few more eating options and the local pub fills up with young workers in dusty overalls. From the jetty at the end of the main drag (Veal St) there are wonderful watery views. Beside it is a child-friendly beach with a swimming pontoon.

The old train route between Ravensthorpe and Hopetoun is now a **heritage walking track**. To the west of town, separating it from Fitzgerald River National Park, is the almost landlocked **Culham Inlet** (great for fishing – especially for black bream). To the east is the scenic but in parts extremely rough **Southern Ocean East Drive**, heading to beaches with campsites at **Mason Bay** and **Starvation Bay**. If you're in a 2WD, don't be tempted to head to Esperance this way; if you'd prefer not to double back to the highway at Ravensthorpe, take Jerdacuttup road (past the airport) instead.

The world's longest fence – the 1833km-long **No 1 rabbit-proof fence** – enters the sea at Starvation Bay; it starts at Eighty Mile Beach on the Indian Ocean, north of Port Hedland. The fence was built during the height of the rabbit plague between 1901 and 1907. However, the bunnies beat the fence-builders to the west side so it wasn't as effective a barrier as hoped.

Sleeping & Eating

Hopetoun Motel & Chalet Village MOTEL $$

(☎9838 3219; www.hopetounmotel.com.au; 458 Veal St; r around $130; wifi) A very nice rammed-earth complex with comfy beds and quality linen.

Toun Beach Cafe CAFE $

(19 Veal St; breakfast & lunch $12-17, dinner $20-30; ⏰breakfast & lunch daily, dinner Tue-Sat) Sit upstairs for excellent breakfasts and water views at this cool-looking cafe. The simple dinner menu offers a step up from the pub. You'll find tourist brochures in the foyer.

Deck CAFE $

(Veal St; ⏰10.30am-4.30pm Sep-May) A welcome addition to the Hopetoun summer scene, making it hard to resist a daily ice cream. Check out their book of travellers' tips.

Esperance

POP 9600

Esperance sits in solitary splendour on the Bay of Isles, a seascape of aquamarine waters fringed with squeaky white beaches. There's no need to fight for space here, as the town's isolation all but guarantees it. Yet Esperance has its share of devotees who will bundle up the kids for the mammoth pilgrimage from Perth, just to plug into the low-key, community-oriented vibe. In Kalgoorlie, nobody would question the wisdom of driving 390km to this, their nearest beach. For travellers taking the coastal route across the continent, it's the last sizable town before hitting the Nullarbor wilderness.

Some of Australia's most picture-perfect beaches can be found in the even more remote national parks to the town's southeast. Out in the bay, the pristine environment of the Recherche Archipelago can be wild and windy, or turn on a calmly charming show; its 105 islands are home to colonies of fur seals, penguins and a variety of sea birds.

History

Esperance's indigenous name, Kepa Kurl (water boomerang), refers to the shape of the bay. Archaeological finds on Middle Island suggest that it was occupied before the last Ice Age, when it was still part of the mainland.

Esperance received its current name in 1792 when the *Recherche* and *l'Espérance* sailed through the archipelago and into the bay to shelter from a storm. In the 1820s and 1830s the Recharge Archipelago was home to Black Jack Anderson – Australia's only pirate. From his base on Middle Island he raided ships and kept a harem of Aboriginal women, whose husbands he had killed. He was eventually murdered in his sleep by one of his own men.

Although the first settlers came in 1863, it wasn't until the gold rush of the 1890s that the town really became established as a port. When the gold fever subsided, Esperance went into a state of suspended animation until after WWII.

WORTH A TRIP

STOKES NATIONAL PARK

Pretty **Stokes National Park** (per car/motorcycle $11/5), 90km west of Esperance, is set around Stokes Inlet, known for its long beaches and rocky headlands. The park has small patches of low forest but most of its 107 sq km is covered in scrub and coastal heath, sheltering kangaroos and plenty of birds. You might also spot seals if you're lucky. It's a popular spot for anglers and there's a bush **campground** (sites per adult/child $7/2), which has the distinct advantage of being 2WD accessible.

In the 1950s it was discovered that adding missing trace elements to the soil around Esperance restored its fertility. The town has since rapidly become an agricultural centre and it continues to rely on the waterfront to export grain and minerals from the region's farms and mines.

Sights & Activities

Great Ocean Drive SCENIC DRIVE
Many of Esperance's most dramatic sights can be seen on this well-signposted 40km loop. Starting from the waterfront it heads southwest along the breathtaking stretch of coast that includes a series of popular surfing and swimming spots, including **Blue Haven Beach** and **Twilight Cove**. Stop to enjoy the rollers breaking against the cliffs from **Observatory Point** and the lookout on **Wireless Hill**. A turn-off leads to the **wind farm**, which supplies about 23% of Esperance's electricity. There's a walking track among the turbines that is quite surreal when it's windy – and it often is.

The route then turns back and passes by the **Pink Lake**, or should that be the-lake-formerly-known-as-pink. Salt-tolerant algae once provided an unmistakeable rosy tint, but a storm a few years back flushed it out.

Esperance Museum MUSEUM
(cnr James & Dempster Sts; adult/child $6/2; ⏲1.30-4.30pm) This is one of those zany regional museums where glass cabinets are randomly crammed with collections of sea shells, frog ornaments, tennis rackets and bed pans. It's absolutely charming, even if most of the displays wouldn't look amiss in a junk shop. Bigger items include boats, a train carriage and the remains of the USA's spacecraft *Skylab*, which made its fiery re-entry at Balladonia, east of Esperance, in 1979.

Museum Village HISTORIC BUILDINGS
The museum consists of galleries and cafes occupying various restored heritage buildings; markets are held here on Sunday mornings. Aboriginal-run **Kepa Kurl Art Gallery** (www.kepakurl.com.au; cnr Dempster & Kemp Sts; ⏲10am-4pm Mon, Wed & Fri, 10am-1pm Tue & Thu, 9am-1pm Sun) has reasonably priced works by local and Central Desert artists.

Lake Warden Wetland System LAKES
Esperance is surrounded by extensive wetlands, which include seven large lakes and over 90 smaller ones. The 7.2km return **Kepwari Wetland Trail** (off Fisheries Rd) takes in **Lake Wheatfield** and **Woody Lake**, with boardwalks, interpretive displays and good birdwatching. **Lake Monjimup**, 14km to the northwest along the South Coast Hwy, is divided by Telegraph Rd into a conservation area (to the west) and a recreation area (to the east). The conservation side has boardwalks over inky black water where it's hard to see where the paperbark trees end and their mirror image begins. The much more orderly recreation side has themed banksia, hakea and grevillea gardens, a hedge maze and great grassy areas for throwing a ball around.

Cannery Arts Centre GALLERY
(1018 Norseman Rd; gold coin donation; ⏲10am-4pm Mon-Fri) Has artists studios, interesting exhibitions and a shop selling local artwork. For more local art, pick up the *Esperance Art Trail* brochure, listing 14 stops.

FREE **Ralph Bower Adventureland Park** PLAYGROUND
(Taylor St Jetty) Popular children's playground with a miniature train (rides $2; ⏲10am-4.30pm Sat & Sun May-Sep, daily Oct-Apr).

Tours

Mackenzie's Island Cruises CRUISE
(☎08-9071 5757; www.woodyisland.com.au; 71 The Esplanade; ⏲daily late Sep-May) Mackenzie's tours Esperance Bay and Woody Island in a power catamaran (half-/full day $88/139), getting close to fur seals, sea lions, Cape Barren geese and (with luck) dolphins. In January it operates a Woody Island ferry (adult/child return $51/22).

Kepa Kurl Eco Cultural Discovery Tours INDIGENOUS
(☎9072 1688; www.kepakurl.com.au; Museum Village) Explore the country from an Aboriginal perspective: visit rock art and waterholes, sample bush food and hear ancient stories (adult/child $115/80; minimum four).

Eco-Discovery Tours 4WD
(☎0407 737 261; www.esperancetours.com.au) Runs 4WD tours along the sand to Cape Le Grand National Park (half-/full day $95/165, minimum two/four) and two-hour circuits of the Great Ocean Drive (adult/child $55/40).

Esperance Diving & Fishing DIVING, FISHING
(☎9071 5111; www.esperancedivingandfishing.com.au; 72 The Esplanade) Takes you wreck-

diving on the *Sanko Harvest* (two-tank dive including all gear $235) or charter fishing throughout the archipelago.

Sleeping

TOP CHOICE **Esperance B&B by the Sea** B&B $$
(☎9071 5640; www.esperancebb.com; 34 Stewart St; s/d $110/150) This beachhouse has a private guest wing and the views from the deck overlooking Blue Haven Beach are breathtaking, especially at sunset. It's just a stroll from the ocean and a five-minute drive from Dempster St.

Clearwater Motel Apartments MOTEL $$
(☎9071 3587; www.clearwatermotel.com.au; 1a William St; s $110, d $140-195; ❄) The bright and spacious rooms and apartments here have balconies and are fully self-contained, and there's a well-equipped shared barbecue area. It's just a short walk from both waterfront and town.

Woody Island Eco-Stays CAMPGROUND $
(☎9071 5757; www.woodyisland.com.au; sites per person $16, on-site tents $33-60, huts $96-145; ⏱late Sep–Apr) It's not every day you get to stay in an A-class nature reserve. Choose between leafy campsites (very close together) or canvas-sided bush huts, a few of which have a private deck and their own lighting. Power is mostly solar, and rainwater supplies the island – both are highly valued.

Island View Esperance APARTMENTS $$$
(☎9072 0044; www.esperanceapartments.com.au; 14-15 The Esplanade; apt from $200) It's easy living in these architect-designed and tastefully furnished one- to three-bedroom apartments, some with floor-to-ceiling windows overlooking the waterfront. The kitchens have all the mod cons, and there's a spacious living area.

Driftwood Apartments APARTMENTS $$
(☎0428 716 677; www.driftwoodapartments.com.au; 69 The Esplanade; apt from $125; ❄) Each of these seven smart blue and yellow apartments, right across from the waterfront, has its own BBQ and outdoor table setting. The two-storey, two-bedroom units have decks and a bit more privacy.

Blue Waters Lodge YHA HOSTEL $
(☎9071 1040; www.yha.com.au; 299 Goldfields Rd; dm/s/d $27/45/67) On the beachfront about 1.5km from the town centre, this rambling place feels a little institutional but the management are friendly and it looks out over a tidy lawn to the water. Hire bikes to cycle the waterfront.

Jetty Resort MOTEL $$
(☎9071 3333; www.thejettyresort.com.au; 1 The Esplanade; r $125-195; @≋) You can't miss this white balconied building as you drive along the beachfront. There's a variety of rooms from rather ordinary ones in an older block to the better ones with the balconies. All have access to the pool and barbecue, and there's a day spa and cars for hire.

Goldie's Place APARTMENT $
(☎9071 2879; www.goldiesplaceesperance.com.au; 51 Goldfields Rd; apt from $90) The young owners have two spotless and sizeable apartments in different locations – the bigger one below their house.

Eating

Taylor Street Jetty CAFE $$
(Taylor St Jetty; lunch $13-19, dinner $24-32; ⏱breakfast & lunch Wed-Mon, dinner Thu-Mon; 📶) This attractive, sprawling cafe by the jetty serves cafe fare, tapas, seafood and salads. Locals hang out at the tables on the grass or read on the covered terrace; wi-fi is free with an order of more than $10; and it's a child-friendly zone.

Onshore Cafe CAFE $
(105 Dempster St; mains $7-17; ⏱breakfast & lunch Mon-Sat) A homewares-store-cum-cafe in a breezy modern space next to the cinema, this place serves light lunches, as well as excellent coffee, croissant and cake.

Ocean Blues CAFE $$
(19 The Esplanade; mains $22-34; ⏱closed Sun dinner & Mon) Wander in sandy-footed and order some simple lunch (burgers, salads, sandwiches, wraps) from this unpretentious eatery. Dinners are more adventurous, representing good value for the price.

Entertainment

Fenwick 3 Cinemas CINEMA
(☎9072 1355; www.ausaf.com.au; 105 Dempster St) Shows a good mix of blockbusters and arty movies.

Information

DEC (☎9083 2100; 92 Dempster St) Has information on the national parks in the Esperance region.

Visitor Centre (☎9083 1555; www.visitesperance.com; cnr Kemp & Dempster Sts; ⏱9am-5pm Mon-Fri, 9am-2pm Sat, 9am-noon Sun)

Getting There & Away

AIR Esperance Airport (EPR; Coolgardie-Esperance Hwy) is 18km north of the town centre. **Skywest** (☎1300 660 088; www.skywest.com.au) has one to three flights per day to and from Perth (1¾ hours).

BUS **Transwa** (☎1300 662 205; www.transwa.wa.gov.au) services stop at the visitor centre. These include:

» GE1 to/from Perth ($83, 10¼ hours, thrice weekly);

» GE2 to/from Perth ($83, 10 hours), Mundaring ($81, 9¼ hours), York ($74, 8½ hours) and Hyden ($51, five hours) thrice weekly;

» GE3 to/from Kalgoorlie ($53, five hours, thrice weekly), Coolgardie ($51, 4¾ hours, weekly) and Norseman ($29, 2¼ hours, thrice weekly);

» GE4 to/from Albany ($62, 6½ hours, twice weekly).

Getting Around

There are plenty of **taxis** (☎9071 1782) in Esperance. For car rentals try **Avis** (☎9071 3998; www.avis.com.au; 63 The Esplanade) or **Budget** (☎9071 2775; www.budget.com.au); both have airport offices. **Hollywood Car Hire** (☎9071 3144) is the local car-rental mob.

Around Esperance

Cape Le Grand National Park NATIONAL PARK

An easy day tour from Esperance, **Cape Le Grand National Park** (entry per car/motorcycle $11/5) starts 60km to the east of town and boasts spectacular coastal scenery, turquoise water, dazzling talcum-powder-soft beaches and excellent walking tracks. It offers good fishing, swimming and **camping** (sites per adult/child $9/2) at **Lucky Bay** and **Le Grand Beach**, and day-use facilities at gorgeous **Hellfire Bay**. Make the effort to climb **Frenchman Peak** (a steep 3km return, allow two hours), as the views from the top and through the 'eye', especially during the late afternoon, are superb.

Rossiter Bay is where the British and Aboriginal duo Edward John Eyre and Wylie fortuitously met the French whaling ship *Mississippi,* in the course of their epic 1841 overland crossing, and spent two weeks resting onboard. The 15km **Le Grand Coastal Trail** links the bays; you can do shorter stretches between beaches.

Just outside the eastern edge of the park, old-fashioned **Orleans Bay Caravan Park** (☎9075 0033; orleansbay@bigpond.com; sites per 2 people/chalets from $20/80) is a shady, child-friendly place to stay, 2km from gorgeous **Wharton Beach**.

Cape Arid National Park NATIONAL PARK

Further east, at the start of the Great Australian Bight and on the fringes of the Nullarbor Plain, is **Cape Arid National Park** (per car/motorcycle $11/5). The park is rugged and isolated, with good bushwalking, great beaches, campsites and more of that crazy squeaky sand.

Whales (in season), seals and Cape Barren geese are seen regularly here. Most of the park is 4WD-accessible only, although the Thomas River Rd, which leads to the shire **campsite** (sites per adult/child $7/2), is accessible to all vehicles. For the hardy, there is a tough walk to the top of **Tower Peak** on Mt Ragged (3km return, three hours), where the world's most primitive species of ant was found thriving in 1930.

FREE **Peak Charles National Park** NATIONAL PARK

There are no charges to visit or camp at this granite wilderness area, 130km north of Esperance. There are only basic facilities provided (long-drop toilets); you'll need to be completely self-sufficient here.

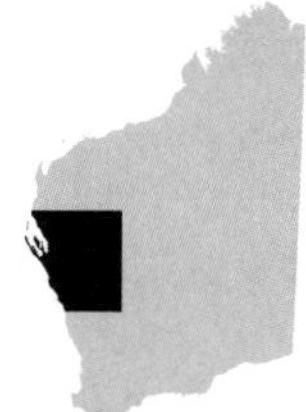

Monkey Mia & the Central West

Includes »

Best Places to Eat

» Saltdish (p166)
» Old Pearler Restaurant (p173)
» Yallibiddi Café (p176)
» Bentwood Olive Grove (p166)
» Provincial (p166)

Best Places to Stay

» Gnaraloo Station (p177)
» Weelaway (p166)
» Ocean West (p166)
» Fish & Whistle (p176)
» Bentwood Olive Grove (p166)

Why Go?

The pristine coastline and sheltered turquoise waters of Malgana country draws tourists and marine life from around the world. Aside from the famous dolphins of Monkey Mia, the submerged sea-grass meadows of World Heritage area Shark Bay play host to dugongs, rays, sharks and turtles, while on land rare marsupials take refuge in remote national parks. Limestone cliffs, red sand and salt lakes litter the stark interior.

Further south among the Nhanda, the gorges of Kalbarri invite adventurers to explore their depths, while above, wildflowers carpet the plains and seabirds wheel away from the battered cliffs as whales migrate slowly southwards.

Veggies are ripening in Carnarvon as anglers and board riders check the tides, and wind-surfers are waiting for the 'Doctor' (strong afternoon sea breeze) to blow. In Geraldton, the only decision to make is whether to have that second macchiato before a brisk walk along the foreshore.

When to Go

Monkey Mia

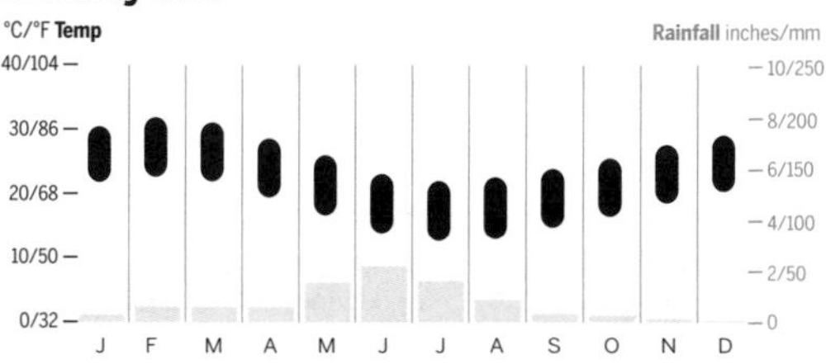

June & August The winter swells pump the breaks off Gnaraloo Station.

August & September Kalbarri lays a carpet of wildflowers.

November–February Windsurfers clutch their sails from Geraldton to Carnarvon.

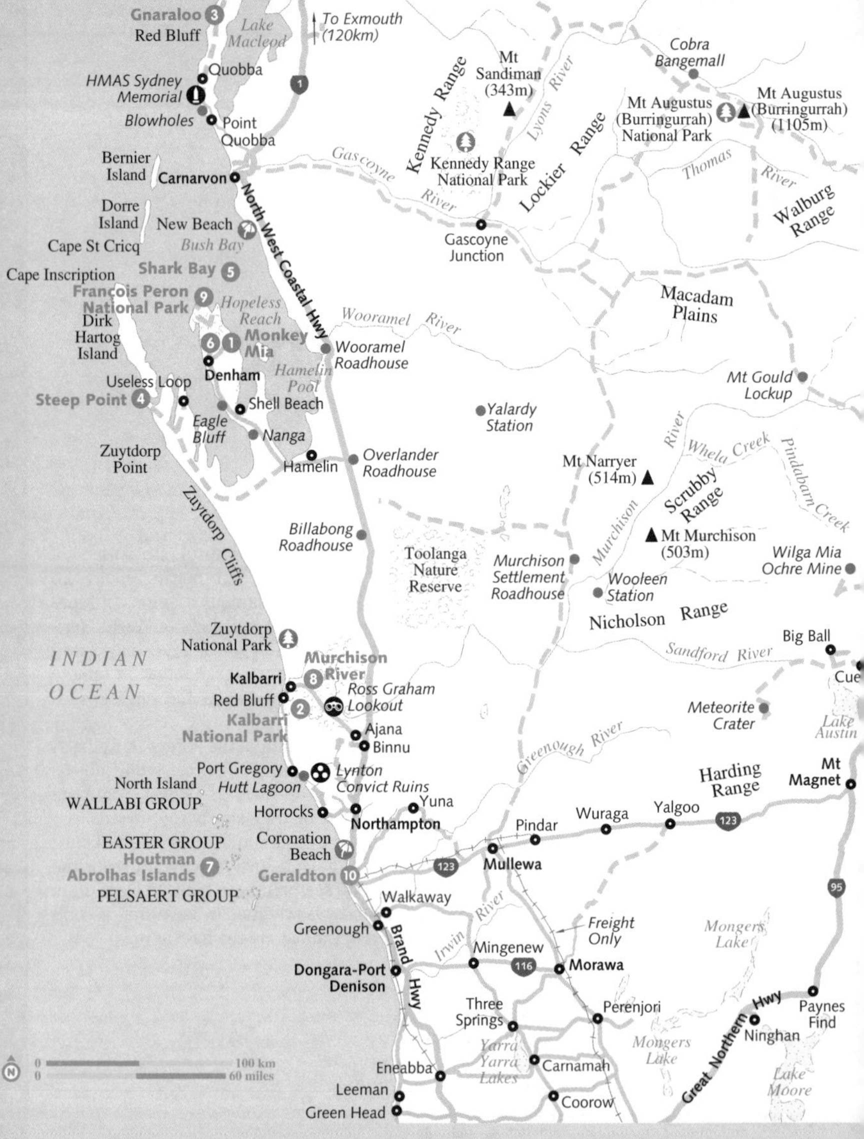

Monkey Mia & the Central West Highlights

1. Watch the wild dolphins feed at **Monkey Mia** (p174)
2. Canoe the deep gorges of **Kalbarri National Park** (p168)
3. Surf the wild Tombstones break at **Gnaraloo** (p177)
4. Drive out to the Australian mainland's most westerly tip, **Steep Point** (p174)
5. Sail out and look for dugongs in **Shark Bay** (p174)
6. Immerse yourself in **Malgana culture** (p174) on a Wula Guda Nyinda tour at Monkey Mia
7. Dive on ancient shipwrecks at the **Houtman Abrolhos Islands** (p167)
8. Horse ride along the mighty **Murchison River** (p170)
9. Spot marine life from a coastal walk in the **François Peron National Park** (p173)
10. Soak up some coffee and culture at **Geraldton's** (p164) museums, galleries and cafes

Getting There & Around

AIR

Skywest (☎1300 660 088; www.skywest.com.au) Flies regularly to Geraldton.

Skippers (☎1300 729 924; www.skippers.com.au) Services Kalbarri, Geraldton, Shark Bay and Carnarvon.

BUS

Greyhound (☎1300 473 946; www.greyhound.com.au) Runs services three times weekly between Broome and Perth along the coast.

Transwa (☎1300 662 205; www.transwa.wa.gov.au) Runs regular buses between Perth and Kalbarri, Geraldton & Dongara along the Brand Hwy (Rte 1).

BATAVIA COAST

The formidable coastline from Dongara-Port Denison to Kalbarri has a rich history, littered with shipwrecks that date from the first European contact. Today the coast provides a rich bounty, as modern shipping fleets make the most of a lucrative crayfish industry.

Dongara-Port Denison

POP 4000

Pretty little Dongara and Port Denison, twin seaside towns 359km from Perth, are known for their beautiful beaches, historic buildings and laid-back atmosphere. Port Denison has most of the beaches and accommodation, while Dongara's main street, shaded by century-old figs, has the banks, and internet and food options.

Sights & Activities

You can find the *Walk Dongara Denison* brochure at **The Holiday Shop** (33 Moreton Tce, Dongara) – the visitor centre no longer distributes it. There are 11 historic or nature-based outings to choose from, as well as the **Irwin River Nature Trail**, on which you might spot birds, such as black swans, pelicans or cormorants.

Interesting historic buildings include the restored **Russ Cottage** (Point Leander Dr; adult/child $2.50/0.50; ⌚10am-noon Sun), built in the late 1860s, which has a kitchen floor made from compacted anthills; and the sandstone **Royal Steam Flour Mill** (Brand Hwy), which is not open to the public. In the old police station, the cells of the **Irwin District Museum** (☎9927 1404; admission $2.50; ⌚10am-noon Mon-Sat) hold informative historical displays.

Denison Beach Marina brims with boats that haul crayfish, the towns' livelihood, while the **Fisherman's Lookout Obelisk** at Port Denison makes an excellent sunset viewpoint.

Sleeping & Eating

Note that public and school holidays attract a surcharge.

There's a supermarket, cafes and takeaways on Moreton Tce and a good bakery on Waldeck St in Dongara, while the **Port Store** (52 Point Leander Dr) in Port Denison has most necessities.

TOP CHOICE **Priory Lodge** BOUTIQUE HOTEL $$
(☎9927 1090; www.prioryhotel.com.au; 11 St Dominics Rd, Dongara; r from $70-130; mains $19-28; ❄≋ᯤ) There's a touch of *Picnic at Hanging Rock* about this leafy former nunnery and ladies college. It features charming period furniture, polished floorboards, black-and-white photos, and wide verandahs. There's live music and pizza on weekends, Sunday roasts, and steaks every night.

Dongara Tourist Park CARAVAN PARK $
(☎9927 1210; www.dongaratouristpark.com.au; 8 George St, Port Denison; unpowered/powered sites $22/28, cabins 1-bed/2-bed $95/130; ❄ᯤ) The best camping option has shaded, spacious sites behind South Beach. The two-bed cabins on the hill have great views, and there's a lush pergola for dining outdoors.

Port Denison Holiday Units APARTMENTS $$
(☎9927 1104; www.portdenisonholidayunits.com.au; 14 Carnarvon St, Port Denison; d $110-120; ❄ᯤ) These spotless, spacious, self-catering units are just a block from the beach; some have marina views.

Dongara Hotel Motel MOTEL & RESTAURANT $$
(☎9927 1023; www.dongaramotel.com.au; 12 Moreton Tce, Dongara; d $130, mains $18-38; ⌚breakfast, lunch & dinner; ❄≋ᯤ) Since it hired some classy Vietnamese chefs, the Dongara is serving up the best food in town, with an emphasis on fresh seafood, and a good selection of Southeast Asian staples like *mie goreng* and phàt thai. The motel rooms are adequate if not flash.

Little Starfish CAFE $$
(☎0448 344 215; White Tops Rd, Port Denison; mains $10-30; ⌚8am-4pm Wed-Mon) Hidden away in the South Beach car park, this funky snack shack does nice things with seafood.

Information

Moreton Tce has several banks with ATMs.

Telecentre (☎9927 2111; 11 Moreton Tce; ⊙9am-4pm Mon-Fri; @)

The Holiday Shop (☎9927 1900; 33 Moreton Tce, Dongara) Good for general info, the *Walk Dongara Denison* brochure and bus tickets.

Visitor centre (☎9927 1404; www.irwin.wa.gov.au; 9 Waldeck St; ⊙9am-5pm Mon-Fri, to noon Sat)

Getting There & Around

Dongara-Port Denison is accessible via the Brand Hwy, Indian Ocean Dr or Midlands Rd (Rte 116).

Greyhound has services to Broome ($330, 29 hours, Monday, Wednesday and Friday) and Perth ($55, six hours, Wednesday, Friday and Sunday). Transwa runs daily to Perth ($50, six hours) and Geraldton ($13, one hour). Buses arrive/depart from the visitor centre.

Geraldton

POP 37,500

Capital of the midwest, and surrounded by excellent beaches, Gero's a place on the move. The largest town between Perth and Darwin has huge wheat handling and fishing industries that make it independent of the fickle tourist dollar, and seasonal workers flood the town during crayfish season. There is a slick new (albeit empty) marina and stunning foreshore area, as well as a strong art and culture scene, some fine-dining cafes and restaurants, good local music and superb windsurfing.

Sights & Activities

Western Australian Museum MUSEUM
(☎9921 5080; www.museum.wa.gov.au; 1 Museum Pl; donation; ⊙9.30am-4pm) This excellent museum has intelligent multimedia displays on the area's natural, cultural and Indigenous

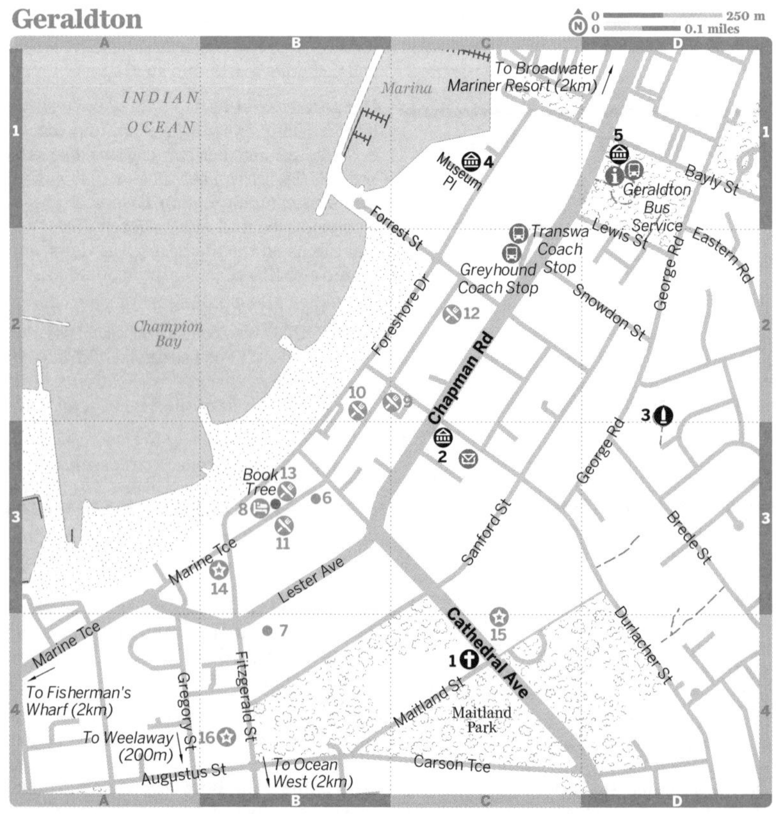

history. The Shipwreck Gallery documents the tragic story of the *Batavia*, while video footage reveals the sunken HMAS *Sydney II*. On Sundays at 2pm you can sail in the longboat moored behind the museum.

Cathedral of St Francis Xavier CHURCH
(Cathedral Ave; tours $5; ⏲tours 10am Mon, Wed & Fri) The elaborate cathedral is the finest example of the architectural achievements of the multiskilled Monsignor John Hawes. Its most striking features include imposing twin towers with arched openings; a central dome; Romanesque columns; and boldly striped walls.

FREE **Geraldton Regional Art Gallery** ART GALLERY
(☎9964 7170; 24 Chapman Rd; ⏲10am-4pm Tue-Sat, from 1pm Sun) This gallery has an excellent permanent collection, including paintings by Norman Lindsay and Elizabeth Durack, provocative contemporary work and engaging exhibitions.

Yamaji Art INDIGENOUS CRAFTS
(☎9965 3440; Bill Sewell Complex, Chapman Rd; ⏲varied, call first) If you manage to find it open, you can purchase Yamatji arts, bowls, didgeridoo and music.

Old Geraldton Gaol Craft Centre HISTORIC BUILDING
(☎9921 1614; Bill Sewell Complex, Chapman Rd; admission free; ⏲10am-4pm Mon-Sat) The crafts are secondary to the gloomy cells that housed prisoners from 1858 to 1986, and the historic documents that detail their grim circumstances.

Commanding the hill overlooking Geraldton is the **HMAS Sydney II Memorial**, which commemorates the 1941 loss of the ship and its 645 men after a skirmish with the German raider *Kormoran*. There are free daily tours at 10.30am.

Geraldton has great **cycle paths**, including the 10km-long coastal route from **Tarcoola Beach** to Chapman River. Grab the excellent *Active Travel Cycling and Walking* brochure from the visitors centre and check your bike hire options.

Geraldton is surrounded by spectacular **beaches** perfect for swimming, surfing, wind- and kite-surfing. You can hire (or buy used) equipment from **G-Spot Xtreme** (☎9965 5577; www.gspotxtreme.com.au; 241a Lester Ave; windsurfer/kite-surfer/kayak $100/50/70) and they'll also hook you up with instructors.

Discover the region's aquatic splendour with **Batavia Coast Dive Academy** (☎9921 4229; www.bcda.com.au; 153 Marine Tce; local dive with/without equipment $140/100), which offers open-water courses (full PADI $600) and a range of diving trips, including three-day chartered trips to the Abrolhos ($900 per person).

The **Blessing of the Fleet** (www.gfcblessing.com; Fisherman's Wharf; $5), mixing religion, boats, pageantry and rock'n'roll in a carnival atmosphere, is normally held on the last weekend in October.

There's free wi-fi along the foreshore.

Sleeping

Accommodation in Geraldton hasn't kept pace with the rest of change, and quite a few

Geraldton

Sights
1 Cathedral of St Francis Xavier C4
2 Geraldton Regional Art Gallery C3
3 HMAS Sydney II Memorial D2
Old Geraldton Gaol Craft Centre ... (see 5)
4 Western Australian Museum C1
5 Yamaji Art D1

Activities, Courses & Tours
6 Batavia Coast Dive Academy B3
7 G-Spot Xtreme B4

Sleeping
8 Foreshore Backpackers B3
Freemason's Hotel .... (see 9)

Eating
9 Freemasons Hotel C2
10 Go Health Lunch Bar B2
11 Provincial B3
12 Saltdish C2
13 Topolinis Caffe B3

Entertainment
14 Orana Cinemas B3
15 Queens Park Theatre C4
16 Up B4

WORTH A TRIP

GREENOUGH

Located 24km south of Geraldton, the rural area of historic Greenough makes a pleasant overnight alternative. Sights such as the **Central Greenough Historical Settlement** (Brand Hwy, Rte 1; adult/child $6/3; ⌚9am-5pm), with its handful of 19th-century buildings, and the **Pioneer Museum** (www.greenough-pioneer-museum.com; Phillips Rd; adult/child $4.50/free; ⌚9.30am-3.30pm) detail early settler life and offer a chance to stretch the legs, although the area's main attractions are its excellent food and lodgings.

Bentwood Olive Grove (☎9926 1196; www.bentwood.com.au; Brand Hwy; d $100, mains $28-31; ⌚lunch Thu-Sun May-Nov;) has a wonderful cafe that serves up gourmet lunches and decadent desserts, and a beautiful stone cabin that sleeps six. There are lovely gardens in which to wander around, and WWOOFers (Willing Workers on Organic Farms) are welcome. Try the spinach, feta & pine-nut tart or the exquisite grilled salmon.

You can almost picture horse-drawn coaches pulling up to the **Hampton Arms Inn** (☎9926 1057; www.hamptonarms.com.au; Company Rd; s/d $75/95, mains $12-32; ⌚Tue-Sun), built in 1863. It features period bedrooms (some with fireplaces), a cluttered bookshop crammed with rare titles, a formal dining room and a cosy, well-stocked bar.

While away the days swimming and fishing at **Double Beach Holiday Park** (☎9921 5845; www.doublebeach.com.au; 4 Hull St, Cape Burney; unpowered/powered sites $23/28, cabins $80-120), with its quiet, shady sites and great BBQ pergola. It's located behind the dunes at the mouth of the Greenough River.

The Transwa daily service to Geraldton will drop you on the Brand Hwy.

stalwarts are in need of an update. Expect price hikes for school and public holidays.

TOP CHOICE **Weelaway** B&B $$
(☎9965 5232; www.weelaway.com.au; 104 Gregory St; r $130-140;) Weelaway offers exquisitely decorated rooms in a heritage listed house dating from 1862. There are formal lounge rooms, shady, wide verandahs, and a well-stocked library, and it's all within walking distance of the CBD.

TOP CHOICE **Ocean West** APARTMENTS $$
(☎9921 1047; www.oceanwest.com.au; 1 Hadda Way; 1-/3-bedroom from $125/170;) Don't let the 60s brick put you off; these fully self-contained units have all been tastefully renovated, making them one of the best deals in town. The wildly beautiful Back Beach is just across the road.

Foreshore Backpackers HOSTEL $
(☎9921 3275; 172 Marine Tce; dm/s/d $25/40/60; @) Shambolic, rambling, multistoreyed, and oozing character, this central hostel is full of hidden nooks, lounges, sunny balconies and world-weary travellers. It's the best place to swap information and stories, and get information about jobs.

Sunset Beach Holiday Park CARAVAN PARK $
(☎9938 1655; http://sunset-beach-holiday-park.wa.big4.com.au; Bosley St; powered sites $33, cabins $85-110) About 6km north of the CBD, Sunset Beach has roomy, shaded sites just a few steps from a lovely beach.

Broadwater Mariner Resort RESORT $$$
(☎1800 181 480; www.mariner.broadwaters.com.au; 298 Chapman Rd; studio/1-/2-bedroom from $175/228/277;) This resort offers spotless, tastefully appointed rooms with a corporate vibe, across from the excellent St Georges Beach.

Eating

Geraldton has great food options, including takeaways, coffee lounges, bakeries and supermarkets.

TOP CHOICE **Saltdish** CAFE $$
(☎9964 6030; 35 Marine Tce; breakfast $6-18, lunch $13-26; ⌚7.30am-2.30pm Mon-Sat) The hippest cafe in town does innovative, contemporary brekkies and light lunches, industrial strength coffee, and screens films in its courtyard during summer evenings. Try the baked eggs or curry-spiced squid. BYO available (customers can bring alcohol they've purchased elsewhere).

Provincial MODERN AUSTRALIAN $$
(☎9964 1887; www.theprovincial.com.au; 167 Marine Tce; breakfast $7-20, mains $16-28; ⌚7am-late) The much-loved Bella Vista has moved a few doors up and morphed into a stencil-art-decorated wine bar that serves Mediterranean-Oz-fusion dishes such as Wa-

gyu burgers, stuffed eggplants, home-made pasta (think angel hair with crabmeat) and wood-fired pizzas.

Go Health Lunch Bar CAFE $

(☎9965 5200; 122 Marine Tce; light meals around $9; 8.30-3pm Mon-Fri, to 1pm Sat; @) Vegetarians can rejoice at the choice of fresh juices and smoothies, excellent espresso, healthy burritos, lentil burgers, focaccias and other light meals from this popular lunch bar in the middle of the mall.

Topolinis Caffe ITALIAN $$

(☎9964 5866; 158 Marine Tce; mains $23-38; 8.30am-late) This home-style licensed bistro is perfect for an afternoon coffee and cake, a preshow bite, or just a relaxed family feed. The $34 dinner-and-movie deal (Sunday to Thursday) and Monday half-price pasta are popular.

Freemasons Hotel PUB $$

(☎9964 3457; www.freemasonshotel.com.au; cnr Marine Tce & Durlacher St; dm/d $40/90, meals $16-32; 11am-late) Try the meals cooked on sizzling stone slabs for a taste sensation at this beautiful old pub. They also have a small number of budget rooms.

☆ Entertainment

Freemasons is a favourite drinking spot, with regular live music and occasional DJs and dance nights.

Orana Cinemas CINEMA

(☎9965 0568; www.oranacinemas.com.au; cnr Marine Tce & Fitzgerald St; tickets $15) Head here for the latest flicks.

Queens Park Theatre THEATRE

(☎9956 6662; cnr Cathedral Ave & Maitland St) Stages theatre, comedy, concerts and films.

Up NIGHTCLUB

(☎9921 1400; 60 Fitzgerald St; Thu-Sat) Three bars including a large clubbers' dance floor, late-night pool room and an outdoor chill patio.

Information

There are several banks with ATMs along Marine Tce.

Batavia Tickets (☎9964 8881; www.bataviatickets.com.au; old railway station) Sells tickets for the long-distance buses that depart outside.

Book Tree (176 Marine Tce; 9.30am-4.30pm Mon-Fri) Scour the floor-to-ceiling shelves of preloved books for some on-the-road reading.

Geraldton Regional Hospital (☎9956 2222; Shenton St; 24hr) Emergency facilities.

Gero.com.au (www.gero.com.au) Excellent online resource for local gigs, dining, gossip.

Jam Great little free monthly booklet detailing what's on.

Sun City Books & Internet Corner (☎9964 7258; 49 Marine Tce; 9am-5pm Mon-Fri, to

HOUTMAN ABROLHOS ISLANDS

Better known as 'the Abrolhos', this archipelago of 122 coral islands, 60km off the coast of Geraldton, is home to some amazing wildlife, including sea lions, green turtles, carpet pythons, over 90 seabird species and the Tammar wallaby. Much of the flora is rare, endemic and protected, and the surrounding reefs offer great diving thanks to the warm Leeuwin Current, which allows tropical species such *Acropora* (staghorn) coral to flourish further south than normal.

These gnarly reefs have claimed many ships over the years, including the ill-fated *Batavia* (1629), and *Hadda* (1877), and you can dive on the wreck sites. The general public can't stay overnight, but a number of Geraldton operators offer day trips on which you can bushwalk, picnic, dive, snorkel, surf or fish. Pick up the handy *Houtman Abrolhos Islands Visitors Guide* from Geraldton's visitors centre.

Recommended operators:

Shine Aviation Services SCENIC FLIGHTS

(☎9923 3600; www.shineaviation.com.au; 90min/half-/full-day tours $175/180/240)

Geraldton Air Charters SCENIC FLIGHTS

(☎9923 3434; www.geraldtonaircharter.com.au; 90min/half-/full-day tours $185/220/240)

Oceania Dive DIVING

(☎99212420; www.oceaniadive.com.au) Popular 3-/4-/5-day fishing, diving, surfing and snorkelling trips that fill quickly – at roughly $300 per day.

1pm Sat; @) Lots of terminals and a decent selection of books.

Visitor centre (☎9921 3999; www.geraldtontourist.com.au; Bill Sewell Complex, Chapman Rd; ⏲9am-5pm Mon-Fri, 10am-4pm Sat & Sun) One of the best around, with lots of great info sheets and helpful staff who'll book accommodation, tours and transport.

Getting There & Around

SkyWest flies daily to Perth, and regularly to Carnarvon, Monkey Mia, Exmouth and Karratha.

Greyhound buses run three times weekly to Perth ($60, six hours) from the old railway station, and north along the coast to Carnarvon ($100, six hours) and Broome ($324, 28 hours). Transwa has services to Perth daily ($58, six hours) and three times weekly to Kalbarri ($26, 2½ hours). There's also a twice-weekly service to Meekathara ($68, seven hours). **Transgeraldton** (☎9923 2225; www.buswest.com.au) operates eight routes to local suburbs (all-day ticket $4). Taxis can be called on ☎131 008.

Kalbarri

POP 2000

Magnificent red sandstone cliffs end abruptly, falling prey to the Indian Ocean's slow war of attrition. The beautiful Murchison River snakes through tall, steep gorges before ending treacherously at Gantheaume Bay. Wildflowers line paths frequented by kangaroos, emus and thorny devils, while whales breach just offshore, and rare orchids struggle in the rocky ground. To the north, the towering line of the limestone Zuytdorp cliffs remains aloof, pristine and remote.

Kalbarri is surrounded by stunning nature, and there's great surfing, swimming, fishing, bushwalking, horse riding and canoeing both in town and in Kalbarri National Park. While the vibe is mostly low key, school holidays see Kalbarri stretched to the limit.

Sights & Activities

KALBARRI NATIONAL PARK

With its magnificent river red gums and Tumblagooda sandstone, the rugged **Kalbarri National Park** (per car $11), contains almost 2000 sq km of wild bushland, stunning river gorges and savagely eroded coastal cliffs. There's abundant wildlife, including 200 species of birds, and spectacular wildflowers between July and November.

A string of lookouts dot the impressive coast south of town and the easy **Bigurda Trail** (8km one-way) follows the cliff tops between **Natural Bridge** and **Eagle Gorge**; from July to November you may spot migrating whales. Closer to town are **Pot Alley**, **Rainbow Valley**, **Mushroom Rock** and **Red Bluff**, the last accessible via a walking trail from Kalbarri (5.5km one-way).

The river gorges are east of Kalbarri, 11km down Ajana Kalbarri Rd to the turn-off, and then 20km unsealed to a T-intersection. Turn left for lookouts over **The Loop** and the superb **Nature's Window** (1km return). Bring lots of water for the unshaded **Loop Trail** (8km return). Turning right at the T leads to **Z-Bend** with a breathtaking lookout (1.2km return) or you can continue steeply down to the gorge bottom (2.6km return). Head back to the highway and a further 24km before turning off to **Hawk's Head**, where there are great views and picnic tables, and **Ross Graham** lookout where you can access the river. It's possible to **hike** 38km from Ross Graham to The Loop in a demanding four-day epic, but be warned, there are no marked trails and several river crossings.

OTHER ATTRACTIONS

FREE **Pelican Feeding** WILDLIFE
(☎9937 1104; Grey St; ⏲8.45am) Kalbarri's most popular attraction.

Kalbarri Wildflower Centre NATURE RESERVE
(☎9937 1229; off Ajana Kalbarri Rd; adult/child $5/2; ⏲9am-1pm Wed-Mon Jun-Oct) Stroll 1.8km along a labelled **wildflower trail**, or take a **guided tour** ($10; ⏲10am).

Kalbarri Boat Hire CANOEING
(☎9937 1245; www.kalbarriboathire.com; Grey St; kayak/canoe/surf cat/powerboat per hr $15/15/45/50) Located on the foreshore, this place hires out various aquatic transports. They also run four-hour breakfast and lunch canoe trips down the Murchison (adult/child $65/45).

Kalbarri has a network of cycle paths along the foreshore, and you can ride out to **Blue Holes** for snorkelling, **Jakes Point** for its surf and fishing, and **Red Bluff Beach**, 5.5km away. Any of the lookouts along the coast are perfect for watching the sunset.

Tours

This is just a selection of tours; the visitor centre has a full list and also takes bookings.

Kalbarri Abseil ABSEILING
(☎9937 1618; www.abseilaustralia.com.au; half-/full-day tours $80/135 Apr-Nov, half-day $65

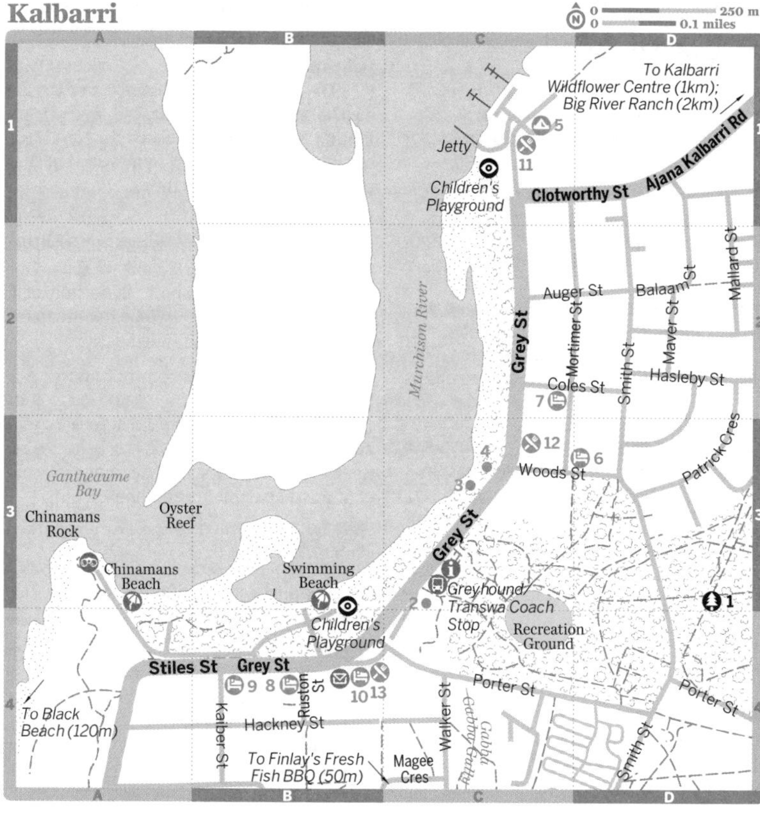

Kalbarri

Sights

1 Kalbarri National Park D3

Activities, Courses & Tours

2 Kalbarri Air Charter C3
3 Kalbarri Boat Hire C3
4 Pelican Feeding C3

Sleeping

5 Anchorage Caravan Park C1
6 Kalbarri Backpackers D3
7 Kalbarri Reef Villas C2
8 Murchison View Apartments B4
9 Pelican Shore Villas B4
Pelican's Nest .... (see 6)
10 Ray White Kalbarri Accommodation Service B4

Eating

11 Gorges Café C1
12 Grass Tree C3
13 Restaurant Upstairs B4

Dec-Mar) Get vertical amid the gorges of Kalbarri National Park. Fine for beginners.

Kalbarri Adventure Tours CANOEING
(☎9937 1677; www.kalbarritours.com.au; adult/child $90/70) Combine canoeing, bushwalking and swimming around the park's Z-Bend/Loop area.

Kalbarri Air Charter SCENIC FLIGHTS
(☎9937 1130; www.kalbarriaircharter.com.au; 62 Grey St; flights $59-285) Offers 20-minute scenic flights over the coastal cliffs, and longer flights over gorges, the Zuytdorp cliffs and the Abrolhos Islands.

DON'T MISS

BIG RIVER RANCH

Take a horse swimming at **Big River Ranch** (☎9937 1214; www.bigriverranch.net; off Ajana Kalbarri Rd; camp sites per person $10, powered sites $30, dm/d $20/60; trail rides 60/90/120min $55/70/90;) 2km east of Kalbarri on the Ajana Kalbarri Rd. Trail rides of varying lengths (including overnight) should suit most riders, and will allow you to explore Murchison River country. Accommodation includes grassy tent sites, van and camper spaces (some powered), and rustic bunkhouse rooms.

Kalbarri Sandboarding SANDBOARDING
(☎9937 2377; www.sandboardingaustralia.com.au; adult/child $80/70) Muck around on sand dunes, then go for a snorkel on these fun half-day tours.

Kalbarri Wilderness Cruises CRUISES
(☎9937 2259; www.kalbarricruises.com.au; cruises adult/child $40/28) Runs popular two-hour licensed river cruises that explore nature along the Murchison.

Sleeping

There's a lot of choice but avoid school holidays, when prices skyrocket. The visitor centre is your friend.

Murchison View Apartments APARTMENTS $$
(☎9937 1096; www.kalbarrimurchisonviewapartments.com.au; cnr Grey & Ruston Sts; 2-bedroom units from $140;) These spacious, fully self-contained apartments with balconies are great value; right opposite the waterfront.

Anchorage Caravan Park CARAVAN PARK $
(☎9937 1181; www.kalbarrianchorage.com.au; cnr Anchorage Lane & Grey St; powered sites $34, cabins with/without bathroom $100/70;) The best option for campers, Anchorage has roomy, nicely shaded sites that overlook the river mouth.

Kalbarri Backpackers HOSTEL $
(☎9937 1430; www.yha.com.au; cnr Woods & Mortimer Sts; dm/d $29/77; @) This nice, shady hostel with a decent pool and BBQ is one block back from the beach. Bike hire is $20 per day.

Pelican Shore Villas APARTMENTS $$$
(☎9937 1708; www.pelicanshorevillas.com.au; cnr Grey & Kaiber Sts; villas $133-204;) These beautiful manicured town-houses have all the mod cons, and the best view in town.

Pelican's Nest APARTMENTS $$
(☎9937 1430; www.pelicansnestkalbarri.com.au; 45-47 Mortimer Street; d $100-140; @) Adjoining Kalbarri Backpackers, the Nest has a selection of neat rooms (some with kitchenettes), and excellent facilities.

Kalbarri Reef Villas APARTMENTS $$
(☎9937 1165; www.reefvillas.com.au; cnr Coles & Mortimer Sts; units $130-180;) One block behind the foreshore, these fully self-contained two-storey, two-bedroom apartments face onto a palm-filled garden.

Ray White Kalbarri Accommodation Service RENTAL HOUSES $-$$$
(☎9937 1700; www.kalbarriaccommodation.com.au; Kalbarri Arcade, 44 Grey St; holiday houses per week $500-1700) Has a wide range of self-contained apartments and houses.

Eating

There are supermarkets and takeaways at the shopping centres, and bistros at the taverns.

TOP CHOICE **Gorges Café** CAFE $$
(☎9937 1200; Marina Complex, Grey St; meals $6-23; ⏰7.30am-4pm Wed-Mon, to 2pm Sat & Sun) Ask at this airy cafe for its Morning Cure and you won't be disappointed; it does wonderful breakfasts and lunches, just opposite the jetty.

Grass Tree MODERN AUSTRALIAN $$
(☎9937 2288; www.thegrasstree.com.au; 94-96 Grey St; mains $15-$33; ⏰noon-late Fri-Tue) With a great surf view and an exciting, innovative menu, there's no better place for lunch. A nice chilled wine washes down twice-cooked pork belly or smoked chicken and chickpea salad.

Restaurant Upstairs MODERN AUSTRALIAN $$$
(☎9937 1033; 1st fl, Porter St; mains $20-45; ⏰6pm-late Fri-Wed) The menu at this fine-dining establishment features local seafood, Asian fusion and outback faves like kangaroo and crocodile.

Finlay's Fresh Fish BBQ SEAFOOD $$
(☎9937 1260; 24 Magee Cres; mains $15-30; ⏰5.30-8.30pm Tue-Sun) You'll either love it or hate it, but you'll certainly always remember your no-frills BBQ fish dinner at this Kalbarri institution, where the huge portions of fish come with lashings of (usually, but not always) tongue-in-cheek abuse.

Information

There are ATMs at the shopping centres on Grey and Porter Sts.

Kalbarri Café (☎9937 1045; Porter St; ⌚8.30am-7pm; @) For internet.

Kalbarri Community Resource Centre (☎9937 1933; Hackney St; ⌚9am-3pm, Mon-Fri; @) Fax and internet.

Traveller's Book Exchange (☎9937 2676; ⌚9am-5pm Mon-Fri, to noon Sat; @) Internet and secondhand books.

Visitor centre (☎1800 639 468; www.kalbarri.org.au; Grey St; ⌚9am-5pm) Has lots of info on the national park and activities around town, and can book accommodation and tours. There's internet at the library next door.

Getting There & Around

Skippers flies to Perth via Monkey Mia four times weekly.

Getting to/from Perth ($72, 10 hours) and Geraldton ($26, 2½ hours) by bus is easiest with Transwa. Heading to/from points further north you'll need Greyhound, which stops at Binnu, 77km away on the highway. Arrange a **shuttle** (☎0419 371 888; $40) to meet/drop you. From Binnu you can reach Overlander Roadhouse (for Monkey Mia, $50, two hours), Coral Bay ($100 eight hours), Broome ($300, 26 hours) and Perth ($100, eight hours).

Kalbarri Auto Centre (☎9937 1290) rents 4WDs and sedans from $60 per day, while **BicycleWA** (☎9937 1105; 8 Porter St; half-/full-day $10/20), inside Kalbarri Palms Resort, hires cycles. Both bikes and scooters can be hired from **Kalbarri Air Charter** (☎9937 1130; 62 Grey St; bikes half-/full-day $10/20, scooters half-/full-day $45/85).

SHARK BAY

The World Heritage–listed area of Shark Bay, stretching from Kalbarri to Carnarvon, consists of more than 1500km of spectacular coastline, containing turquoise lagoons, barren finger-like peninsulas, hidden bays, white-sand beaches, towering limestone cliffs and numerous islands. It's the westernmost part of the Australian mainland, and one of WA's most biologically rich habitats, with an array of plant and animal life found nowhere else on earth. Lush beds of seagrass and sheltered bays nourish dugongs, sea turtles, humpback whales, dolphins, stingrays, sharks and other aquatic life. On land, Shark Bay's biodiversity has benefited from Project Eden, an ambitious ecosystem regeneration program that has sought to eradicate feral animals and reintroduce endemic species. Shark Bay is also home to the amazing stromatolites of Hamelin Pool.

The Malgana, Nhanda and Inggarda peoples originally inhabited the area, and visitors can take Indigenous cultural tours to learn about 'country'. Shark Bay played host to early European explorers and many geographical names display this legacy. In 1616, Dutch explorer Dirk Hartog nailed a pewter dinner plate (now in Amsterdam's Rijksmuseum) to a post on the island that now bears his name, WA's largest.

Getting There & Away

Shark Bay airport is located between Denham and Monkey Mia. Skippers fly to Perth four times weekly. Flights from Perth go via Kalbarri.

The closest Greyhound approach is the Overlander Roadhouse, 128km away on the North West Coastal Hwy. **Shark Bay Car Hire** (☎0427 483 032; www.carhire.net.au; shuttle $65, car/4WD hire per day $40/185) runs a connecting shuttle (book ahead!).

Overlander Roadhouse to Denham

Twenty-nine kilometres along Shark Bay Rd from the Overlander Roadhouse is the turn-off for **Hamelin Pool** (not nearby Hamelin Station!), a marine reserve that contains the world's best-known colony of **stromatolites**.

HORROCKS & PORT GREGORY

The tiny seaside villages of Horrocks and Port Gregory, 92km and 68km south of Kalbarri, respectively, are as quiet as they come. Horrocks, the smaller, prettier of the two, has several accommodation options including the laid-back **Horrocks Beach Caravan Park** (☎9934 3039; www.horrocksbeachcaravanpark.com.au; sites $24-32, cabins $65-88) right behind the dunes, and the nearby, bargain **Beachside Cottages** (☎9934 3031; d $75-85). Port Gregory, on the far side of the mysterious Pink Lakes, and with a fringing reef, is great for fishing and snorkelling. **Port Gregory Caravan Park** (☎9935 1052; www.portgregory.com; powered sites $29, cabins $90-100) is your best choice.

FREE CAMPING!

Just as most shires in the country are shutting down free camp sites, Shark Bay shire offers a choice of four. **Goulet Bluff**, **Whalebone**, **Fowlers Camp** and **Eagle Bluff** are all coastal camp sites 20km to 40km south of Denham in the area known as South Peron. To camp here, you must first obtain a (free!) permit from the **Shark Bay visitor centre** (p173). While this is easily arranged via phone (if yours has any reception), in practice it's better to scope the sites first, then get the permit from Denham. There are no facilities and a one-night limit applies to the whole area.

These coral-like formations consist of cyanobacteria almost identical to organisms that existed 3.5 billion years ago, and, through their use of photosynthesis, are considered largely responsible for creating our current atmosphere, paving the way for more complex life. There's an excellent boardwalk with information panels, best seen at low tide.

The nearby 1884 **Telegraph Office** (admission $5.50; ⊙check at shop) houses a fascinating museum containing possibly the only living stromatolites in captivity. The **Postmasters Residence** is also the office for the tiny **Hamelin Pool Caravan Park** (☎9942 5905; unpowered/powered sites $22/25) and serves Devonshire teas, pies and ice creams.

Along the road you would have passed the turn-off for **Hamelin Station** (☎9948 5145; www.hamelinstationstay.com.au; campsites $20, s/d/f $65/95/125) which has lovely rooms in converted shearers' quarters, a brand new kitchen and spotless ablutions block. There's great bird life at the nearby waterhole.

As Shark Bay Rd swings north, you'll pass the turn-off for **Useless Loop** (a closed salt-mining town) and **Steep Point**, the Australian mainland's most westerly tip (see p174).

The dusty former sheep station **Nanga Bay Resort** (☎9948 3992; www.nangabayresort.com.au; unpowered/powered sites $25/30, donga/motel/hut/villa $50/165/180/250; ❄≋) has a range of accommodation, and the Fishermens Huts, which sleep four to six people, have good views, though some of the other options are a little depressing.

Inside the vermin-proof fence, and 55km from Hamelin turnoff, is the road to deserted **Shell Beach**, where tiny cockle shells, densely compacted over time, were once quarried as building material for places like the Old Pearler Restaurant in Denham.

You'll pass turn-offs to free campsites before reaching **Eagle Bluff**, which has clifftop views overlooking an azure sea. You may spot turtles, sharks or manta rays.

Denham

POP 1500

Beautiful, laid-back Denham, with its aquamarine sea and palm-fringed beachfront, makes a great base for trips to the surrounding Shark Bay Marine Park, nearby François Peron and Dirk Hartog Island National Parks, and Monkey Mia, 26km away.

Australia's westernmost town originated as a pearling base, and the streets were once paved with pearl shell. Knight Tce, the now-tarmac main drag, has everything you need.

Sights & Activities

Shark Bay World Heritage Discovery Centre MUSEUM
(☎9948 1590; www.sharkbayinterpretivecentre.com.au; 53 Knight Tce; adult/child $11/6; ⊙9am-6pm) One of WA's best museums has displays on Shark Bay's ecosystem, its Indigenous people, and early explorers and settlers.

Ocean Park AQUARIUM
(☎9948 1765; www.oceanpark.com.au; Shark Bay Rd; adult/child $17/12; ⊙9am-5pm) Superbly located on a headland just before town, this family-run aquaculture farm features an artificial lagoon where you can take a 45-minute guided tour to observe feeding sharks, turtles, stingrays and fish. The licensed cafe has sensational views, and it also conducts full-day 4WD tours with bushwalks and snorkelling to François Peron ($180) and Steep Point ($350).

Little Lagoon, 4km from town, is a pleasant picnic spot with tables and barbecues; you can walk, drive or cycle there. Don't be surprised if an emu wanders by.

Tours

Aussie Off Road Tours 4WD
(☎0429 929 175; www.aussieoffroadtours.com.au) Culture and history feature strongly in these excellent Indigenous-owned and operated tours, including twilight wildlife ($90), full-day François Peron National Park ($189), overnight camping in François Peron ($300) and overnight to Steep Point ($390).

Shark Bay Scenic Flights SCENIC FLIGHTS
(☎9948 1773; www.sharkbayair.com.au) Offers various scenic flights, including 15-minute Monkey Mia flyovers ($55), 40-minute trips over Steep Point and the Zuytdorp Cliffs ($150) and one-way charters to/from the Overlander Roadhouse ($120).

Shark Bay Coaches & Tours SIGHTSEEING
(☎9948 1081; www.sbcoaches.com; bus/quad bike $80/80) Half-day bus tours to all key sights, and two hour quad-bike expeditions to various locations.

Capricorn Sea Kayaking KAYAKING
(☎0427 485 123; www.capricornseakayaking.com.au; 7 days $1495) This Perth-based outfit offers several seven-day sea-kayaking trips that it runs in Shark Bay between May and September.

Sleeping & Eating

Denham has accommodation for all budgets, and some places offer long-stay discounts and/or school-holiday surcharges. There's a supermarket, bakery, cafes and takeaways on Knight Tce.

Bay Lodge HOSTEL $
(☎9948 1278; www.baylodge.info; 113 Knight Tce; dm/d from $26/68; @≋) Every room at this YHA hostel has its own en suite, kitchenette and TV/DVD. Ideally located across from the beach, it also has a great pool, a larger common kitchen, and a shuttle bus to Monkey Mia.

Denham Seaside Tourist Village CARAVAN PARK $
(☎1300 133 733; www.sharkbayfun.com; Knight Tce; unpowered/powered/en-suite sites $29/34/42, cabins $80, 1-/2-bedroom chalets $120/130; ❄) This lovely, shady park on the water's edge is the best in town, and you can even borrow a drill for your tent pegs. Cover up at night against the bloodsucking mosquitoes; ring first if arriving after 6pm.

Oceanside Village CABINS $$
(☎1800 680 600; www.oceanside.com.au; 117 Knight Tce; cabins $130-185; ❄≋) These neat self-catering cottages with sunny balconies are perfectly located directly opposite the beach.

Tradewinds APARTMENTS $$
(☎1800 816 160; www.tradewindsdenham.com.au; Knight Tce; units $140-160; ❄) Spacious, fully self-contained, modern units right across from the beach.

TOP CHOICE **Old Pearler Restaurant** SEAFOOD $$$
(☎9948 1373; 71 Knight Tce; meals $26-48; ⊙dinner Mon-Sat) Built from shell bricks, this atmospheric nautical haven does fantastic seafood. The exceptional platter features local red emperor, whiting, cray, prawns and squid – it's all grilled, not fried.

Sunset Mura Mura Cafe CAFE $$
(☎9948 1047; Knight Tce; lunch $14-20; ⊙8am-8.30pm, to 6pm Tue & Wed;) Bright and cheerful, the Sunset does great brekkies, lunch wraps, calzones and burgers, and for those campers sick of cooking, great takeaway home-cooked meals are ready for reheating.

Shark Bay Bakery BAKERY $
(☎9948 1442; Knight Tce; ⊙8am-5pm Mon-Fri, 8am-2pm Sat) Nicely located between the ocean and the laundromat, this bakery's home-made muesli and yoghurt hits the spot while your clothes go round.

Information

There are ATMs at Heritage Resort and Shark Bay Hotel.

Community Resource Centre (☎9948 1787; 67 Knight Tce; @) Internet, faxes and CD/DVD burning.

Department of Environment & Conservation (☎9948 1208; www.dec.gov.au; 89 Knight Tce; ⊙8am-5pm Mon-Fri) Park passes, information and camping permits.

Post office (Knight Tce; ⊙8am-5pm Mon-Fri, 8am-1pm Sat, 9am-noon Sun; @) Has a pharmacy and internet access.

Shark Bay Home Page (www.sharkbay.org.au) Great information, interactive maps and downloadable permits.

Shark Bay Visitors Centre (☎9948 1590; www.sharkbaywa.com.au; 53 Knight Tce; ⊙9am-6pm) Located in the Discovery Centre foyer; has good parks info, and accommodation and tour bookings. Issues free bush-camping permits for South Peron.

François Peron National Park

Covering the whole peninsula north of Denham is an area of low scrub, salt lakes and red sandy dunes, home to the rare bilby, mallee fowl and woma python. There's a scattering of rough **camp sites** (per person $7) alongside brilliant white beaches, all accessible via 4WD (deflate tyres to 20psi). Don't miss the fantastic **Wanamalu Trail** (3km return), which follows the cliff-top between

WAY OUT WEST IN EDEL LAND

The Australian mainland's westernmost tip is **Steep Point**, just below **Dirk Hartog Island**. It's a wild, wind-scarred, barren cliff top with a beauty born of desolation and remoteness. The **Zuytdorp Cliffs** stretch away to the south, the limestone peppered with blowholes, while leeward, bays with white sandy beaches provide sheltered camp sites. The entire area is known as **Edel Land National Park**. Anglers have been coming here for years to game fish off the towering cliffs, but few tourists make the 140km rough drive down a dead-end road.

Access to the area is via Useless Loop Rd, and is controlled by **Department of Environment & Conservation** (DEC; ☎9948 3993; entry permit per vehicle $11, camping per person $7). There is a ranger station at Shelter Bay, with camping nearby; at Steep Point (rocky and exposed); and at False Entrance to the south. Sites are strictly limited and must be booked in advance. You'll need a high-clearance 4WD as the road deteriorates past the Useless Loop turn-off (approximately 100km from Shark Bay Rd). Tyres should be deflated to 20psi. Ensure you bring ample water and enough fuel to return to the Overlander Roadhouse (185km) or Denham (230km). During winter, a barge runs from Shelter Bay to Dirk Hartog Island (bookings essential). The excellent www.sharkbay.org.au has all the details and downloadable permits. Hire-car companies will not insure for this road, though (expensive) tours can be arranged from Denham. The drive is pure adventure; Steep Point is probably more easily reached by boat, but then that's not the Point, is it?

Cape Peron and Skipjack Point, from where you can spot marine life in the crystal waters below. Those with 2WD can enter only as far as the old **Peron Homestead** where there's a short 'lifestyle' walk around the shearing sheds, and an artesian bore hot tub to soak in. Park entry is $11 per vehicle. Tours start around $180 from Denham or Monkey Mia, but if there's a group of you, consider hiring your own 4WD from Denham for the same price.

Monkey Mia

Watching the wild dolphins turning up for a feed each morning in the shallow waters of **Monkey Mia** (adult/child/family $8/3/15), 26km northeast of Denham, is a highlight of every traveller's trip to the region. Don't be put off by the resort vibe – once you see these beautiful, intelligent mammals up close you'll forget about everything else. Watch the way they herd fish upside down, trying to trap them against the surface. The pier makes a good vantage point. The first feed is around 7.45am, but you'll see them arrive earlier, and hang around after the session, as the dolphins commonly come a second, and sometimes even a third time.

The **Monkey Mia Visitors Centre** (☎9948 1366; ⏲8am-4pm) dispenses information, books tours and has a good range of publications.

You can **volunteer** to work full time with the dolphins for between four and 14 days – it's popular, so apply several months in advance and specify availability dates. Contact the **volunteer coordinator** (☎9948 1366; monkeymiavolunteers@westnet.com.au).

Tours

Wula Guda Nyinda Aboriginal Cultural Tours INDIGENOUS CULTURE
(☎0429 708 847; www.wulaguda.com.au; adult/child $40/20) Local Aboriginal guide Darren 'Capes' Capewell leads excellent bushwalks where he teaches you 'how to let the bush talk to you'. You'll learn some local Malgana language, and identify bushtucker and indigenous medicine. The evening 'Didgeridoo Dreaming' walks are magical. There's also a 'Saltwater Dreaming' kayak tour (three hours, adult/child $90/50).

Aristocat II CRUISES
(☎1800 030 427; www.monkey-mia.net; 2½hr tours $75) Cruise in comfort on this large catamaran, and you might see dugongs, dolphins and loggerhead turtles. You'll also stop off at the **Blue Lagoon Pearl Farm**.

Wildsights ADVENTURE TOURS
(☎1800 241 481; www.monkeymiawildsights.com.au) Offers similar cruises on the smaller *Shotover* catamaran (2½ hours $69), where you're closer to the action. It also does a full-day 4WD trip to François Peron National Park ($189), and there's a discount if you book both trips.

Sleeping & Eating

Monkey Mia is a resort and not a town, so eating and sleeping options are limited to the Monkey Mia Dolphin Resort. Self-catering is a good option.

Monkey Mia Dolphin Resort RESORT $$$
(☎1800 653 611; www.monkeymia.com.au; camp site per person $15, van sites back/beach $37/50, dm/d $29/89, garden units $238, beachfront villas $320; ) Although the location is stunning, trying to cater for all markets, including campers, backpackers, package and top-end tourists, is never a great idea. The staff are friendly, and the backpacker 'shared en suites' are good value, but the same can't be said of the top-end rooms. This place gets seriously crowded and at times sounds like a continuous party. The restaurant has sensational water views but bland, overpriced meals, while the backpacker bar has cheaper food and liquoured-up backpackers.

Getting There & Away

There is no public transport to Monkey Mia from Denham. If you stay at Bay Lodge in Denham, you can use their shuttle but it only runs alternate days. Your other options are hiring a car or bicycle.

GASCOYNE COAST

This wild, rugged, largely unpopulated coastline stretches from Shark Bay to Ningaloo, with excellent fishing, and waves that bring surfers from around the world. Subtropical Carnarvon, the region's hub, is an important fruit-and-vegetable-growing district, and farms are always looking for seasonal workers. The 760km Gascoyne River, WA's longest, is responsible for all that lushness, though it flows underground for most of the year. Inland, the distances are huge, the temperatures are high, you'll find the ancient eroded rocks of the Kennedy Range, as well as massive Mt Augustus (Burringurrah).

Carnarvon

POP 6900

At the mouth of the Gascoyne River, fertile Carnarvon, with its fruit and vegetable plantations and thriving fishing industry, makes a pleasant stopover between Denham and Exmouth. This friendly, vibrant town has quirky attractions, a range of decent accommodation, well-stocked supermarkets and some great food. The tree-lined CBD exudes a tropical feel, and the palm-fringed waterfront is a relaxing place to amble. The long picking season from March to January ensures plenty of seasonal work.

Sights & Activities

Established jointly with NASA in 1966, the **OTC Dish** (Mahoney Ave) at the edge of town tracked Gemini and Apollo space missions, as well as Halley's Comet, before closing in 1987. There are plans to establish a NASA museum, though at present you can just

DIRK HARTOG ISLAND NATIONAL PARK

The slim, wind-raked island, which runs parallel to the Peron Peninsula, once attracted Dutch, British and French explorers (who left pewter plates nailed to posts as calling cards), but in recent years its visitors have been mostly fisherfolk and sheep. Now with the pastoral lease terminated, WA's largest island has become a national park; Department of Environment & Conservation (DEC) plans to create an endangered-species sanctuary. While the island's western coast is dominated by the same exposed Zuytdorp Cliffs and low vegetation that stretch from Steep Point to Kalbarri, basic **camp sites** (per person $11) are scattered around the sheltered eastern and northern shores. There's a number of important historical sites, and visiting the island still requires expedition planning.

The last leaseholders, the Wardle family, offer full-board accommodation in their **Dirk Hartog Island Lodge** (☎9948 1211; www.dirkhartogisland.com; full board per person $290; Mar-Oct; 📶), an atmospheric, century-old, limestone-converted shearers' quarters, with a gourmet restaurant and bar. All meals are included but return transfers (by plane or boat) from Denham are an additional $190 per person. The lodge also operates a **barge** (per person return $55; ⌚Mar-Oct) to the island from Steep Point, and this is the best way to access the island and the coastal camp sites. Bookings for both the barge and camp sites should be made months in advance. Denham DEC, the Lodge and www.sharkbay.org.au are the best sources of information.

wander around. The first landing has a fine view over the town.

Carnarvon's luxuriant plantations along North and South River Rds provide a large proportion of WA's fruit and veg. The **Gascoyne Food Trail** brochure from the visitor centre lists which ones you can visit. **Bumbak's** (449 North River Rd; tours $6.50; ⏲shop 9am-4pm Mon-Fri Apr-Jan, tours 10am Mon-Fri Apr-Oct) offers tours and sells a variety of fresh and dried fruit, preserves, honey and yummy home-made ice cream. Check out the delicious produce at the **Gascoyne Arts, Crafts & Growers Market** (Civic Centre car park; ⏲8-11.30am Sat May-Oct).

You can walk or ride 2.5km along the old tramway to the **Heritage Precinct** on Babbage Island, once the city's port. The striking **One Mile Jetty** (admission tram/walking $7/4; ⏲9am-4.30pm) provides great fishing and views; you can either walk or take a vintage tram to the end. Don't miss the view from the top of the creaky water tower in the nearby **Railway Station Museum** (⏲9am-5pm).

Gwoonwardu Mia (☎9941 1989; www.gahcc.com.au; 146 Robinson St; ⏲10am-3pm Mon-Fri) is a stunning building that depicts a cyclone, and represents the five local Aboriginal-language groups. It also houses a cultural centre, art gallery and hospitality-training cafe (Yallibiddi Café; p176).

The last weekend of October sees the town taken over by desert riders competing in the gruelling 511km **Gascoyne Dash** (Gassy Dash; www.gasdash.com).

The palm-lined **walking path** along the side of the Fascine (the body of water at the end of Robinson St) is a pleasant place for a wander, especially at sunset; **windsurfing** is popular at Pelican Point.

Tours

Tour operators turn over quickly in Carnarvon, so check with the visitor centre for availability.

Outback Coast Safaris 4WD
(☎9941 3448; www.outbackcoastsafaris.com.au; 1-/3-day tours $90/$390) Offers a full-day tour to the Kennedy Range, or a three-day camping trip to Mt Augustus. Also available for coastal charters.

Sleeping

Most accommodation, including numerous caravan parks, is spread out along the 5km feeder road from the highway. Try to arrive before 6pm.

TOP CHOICE **Fish & Whistle** HOSTEL $
(☎9941 1704; 35 Robinson St; dm/s/motel $25/45/99; ❄@📶🏊) Travellers love this big, breezy backpackers with its wide verandahs, bunk-free rooms, enormous communal spaces, excellent kitchen and happy vibe. There are air-con motel rooms out back, a pool and barbie area, and discounts for longer stays. The owners can help guests find seasonal jobs, and provide transport to work every day ($25 per week).

Coral Coast Tourist Park CARAVAN PARK $
(☎9941 1438; www.coralcoasttouristpark.com.au; 108 Robinson St; unpowered/powered sites $28/30, cabins $60-155; ❄🏊) This pleasant, shady park, with tropical pool and grassy sites, is the closest to the town centre. There's a variety of well-appointed cabins, a decent camp kitchen, and bicycles for hire.

Carnarvon Central Apartments APARTMENTS $$
(☎9941 1317; www.carnarvonholidays.com; 120 Robinson St; 2-bedroom apt $115; ❄) These neatly maintained, fully self-contained apartments are popular with business travellers.

Gateway Motel MOTEL $$
(☎9941 1532; www.thegatewaymotel.com; 309 Robinson St; d/units $115/156; ❄📶🏊) Basic motel rooms are complemented by larger apartments with cooking facilities. The bistro has themed buffet nights including pasta Mondays ($26), Chinese Wednesdays ($30) and not-to-be-missed seafood Fridays and Saturdays ($35).

Capricorn Holiday Park CARAVAN PARK $
(☎9941 8153; www.capricornholidaypark.com.au; 1042 North West Coastal Hwy, just past junction; unpowered/powered sites $30/32, cabins $120; ❄📶🏊) Out on the highway, this peaceful, friendly park has lots of shade, a covered pool, and lovely bougainvillea.

Eating

With all that great produce, there's some fine dining to be found in Carnarvon. Knight Tce also has a supermarket, takeaways and some early-opening cafes.

Yallibiddi Café INDIGENOUS FUSION $$
(☎9941 3127; 146 Robinson St; mains $15-30; ⏲9am-3pm Mon-Fri) Inside Gwoonwardu Mia, this training cafe produces mouth-watering blends of bushtucker and contemporary cuisine. Try the excellent bush tapas with

smoked kangaroo, emu and lemon-myrtle chicken or the Thai kangaroo salad. The students progress from here to the fine-dining Yallibiddi in Francis St.

Waters Edge MODERN AUSTRALIAN **$$$**
(☎9941 1181; www.thecarnarvon.com.au; 121 Olivia Tce; mains $22-40; s/d $65/80; ⊙dinner Wed-Mon, lunch Fri-Sun; ❄) Tuck into some seared scallops with *nuoc cham* (Vietnamese dipping sauce), Tuscan pork belly, or local snapper pie out the back of the Carnarvon Hotel. They also have clean, basic rooms.

Sheridans Café CAFE **$$**
(☎9941 3482; Robinson St; mains $14-30; ⊙8am-5pm Mon-Sat) Funky music accompanies a funky menu that includes laksa, chilli mussels and banana splits.

Hacienda Crab Shack SEAFOOD **$$**
(☎9941 4078; small boat harbour; price varies by weight; ⊙9am-4pm, shorter hrs Sun) Got an Esky? Then fill it full of freshly steamed crabs, prawns, mussels, shucked oysters and fish fillets from this fishmonger.

Information

There's a post office on Camel Lane and ATMs on Robinson St.

Books & Stuff (Robinson St; ⊙10am-4pm Mon-Sat) An eclectic collection of new, old and local books, with a nice 'reading' courtyard. BYO coffee.

Visitor centre (☎9941 1146; www.carnarvon.org.au; Civic Centre, 21 Robinson St; ⊙9am-5pm Mon-Fri, 9am-noon Sat & Sun; @) Very helpful with information, maps, local books and produce. Look for *Carnarvon & Apollo* (Dench & Gregg) that details the town's NASA connection.

Getting There & Around

Skippers fly daily to Perth, and twice weekly to Geraldton.

Greyhound buses head to Perth ($162, 13 hours), Broome ($272, 21 hours) and Exmouth ($160, five hours) three times per week, and stop at the visitor centre.

Gascoyne Wholesalers (☎9941 2638; 322 Robinson St; scooters $30), opposite Gwoonwardu Mia, has scooters.

Point Quobba to Gnarraloo Bay

While the North West Coast Hwy heads inland, the coast north of Carnarvon is wild, windswept and desolate; a favourite haunt of surfers and fisherfolk. Not many make it this far, but those who do are rewarded by huge winter swells, high summer temperatures, relentless winds, amazing marine life, breath-snapping scenery and some truly magical experiences.

Turn down Blowholes Rd, 12km after the Gascoyne bridge, then proceed 49km along the sealed road to the coast. The **blowholes**, where waves spray out of limestone chimneys, are just left of the T-intersection. **Point Quobba**, 1km further south, has beach shacks, excellent fishing and some gritty camp sites (a fee is payable), and not much else.

Heading right from the T onto dirt, after 8km you'll come across a lonely little cairn staring out to sea, commemorating HMAS *Sydney II*. Two kilometres further is **Quobba Station** (☎9948 5098; www.quobba.com.au; unpowered/powered sites $10/12, cabin per person $30-55) with plenty of rustic accommodation, a small store and legendary fishing.

Still on Quobba, but 60km north of the homestead, is **Red Bluff** (☎9948 5001; www.quobba.com.au; unpowered sites per person $12, shack per person from $20, bungalow/safari retreat $170/$345), a spectacular headland with a wicked surf break, excellent fishing and the southern boundary of the Ningaloo Marine Park (p187). Accommodation comes in all forms, from exposed camp sites and palm shelters, to exclusive upmarket tents with balconies and killer views.

The jewel, however, is at the end of the road around 150km from Carnarvon; **Gnaraloo Station** (☎9942 5927; www.gnaraloo.com; unpowered site per person $20, cabin d $130-210; 📶). Surfers from around the world come every winter to ride the notorious **Tombstones**, while summer brings turtle monitoring and windsurfers trying to catch the Carnarvon Doctor, the strong afternoon sea breeze. There's excellent snorkelling close to shore and the coastline north from **Gnarraloo Bay** is eye-burningly pristine. You can stay in rough camp sites next to the beach at **3-mile**, or there's a range of options up at the homestead, the nicest being stone cabins with uninterrupted ocean views – great for spotting migrating whales (between June and November) and sea eagles. Gnaraloo is always looking for willing workers, and there's such a nice vibe happening that many folk come for a night and end up staying months. Who could blame them!

Coral Coast & the Pilbara

Includes »

Best Places to Eat

» Nikki's (p191)

» Whalers (p185)

» Zephyrs (p198)

» Ningaloo Health (p185)

» Moby's Kitchen (p192)

Best Places to Stay

» Ningaloo Club (p182)

» Crossing Pool (p192)

» Samson Beach Chalets (p192)

» Ningaloo Lodge (p185)

» Ningaloo Lighthouse Caravan Park (p187)

Why Go?

Lapping the edge of the Indian Ocean, the turquoise waters of the Coral Coast nurture a unique marine paradise – one of the few places you can swim with the world's largest fish, the gentle whale shark. Fringed by World Heritage–nominated Ningaloo Reef, the deserted beaches and crystal-clear lagoons play host to myriad other sea life including humpback whales, manta rays and loggerhead turtles. Development is thankfully low-key, and towns few and far between.

The Coral Coast is also Western Australia's adventure playground. The clean beaches and shallow lagoons are ideal for swimming and snorkelling while surfers can enjoy close reef breaks and big winter swells. There's world-class diving and fishing, excellent seafood and superb sunsets.

Inland, the huge, rusty chunk of iron ore known as the Pilbara hides another gem, the sublime Karijini National Park, where deep gorges, hidden pools and desolate peaks entice many a walker.

When to Go

Exmouth

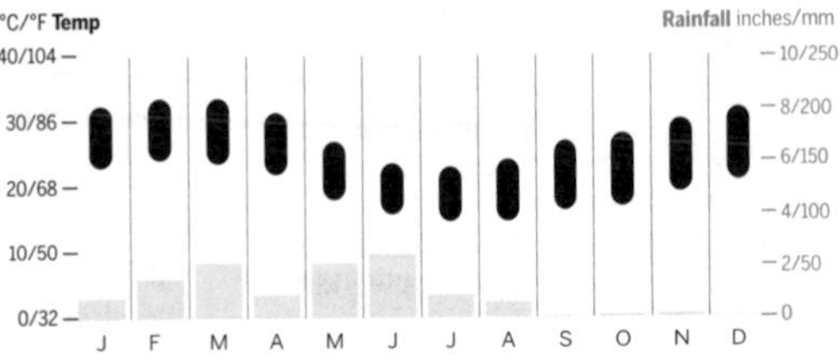

April–July Whale shark season – don't miss the swim of a lifetime.

September & October Karijini's gorges warm up and wildflowers blanket the ranges.

November–March Ningaloo is full of turtle love, eggs and hatchlings.

Getting There & Around

AIR

The following airlines service the Coral Coast and the Pilbara:

Airnorth (☎1800 627 474; www.airnorth.com.au)

Golden Eagle (☎9172 1777; www.goldeneagleairlines.com)

Qantas (☎13 13 13; www.qantas.com.au)

Skywest (☎1300 660 088; www.skywest.com.au)

Strategic (☎135 320; wwwflystrategic.com)

Virgin Blue (☎13 67 89; www.virginblue.com.au)

BUS

Greyhound (☎1300 473 946; www.greyhound.com.au) runs three times weekly between Broome and Perth along the coast.

Integrity (☎1800 226 339; www.integritycoachlines.com.au) runs weekly between Perth and Port Hedland via the inland Great Northern Hwy.

CORAL COAST

The Coral Coast extends from Coral Bay to Onslow shadowing the spectacular Ningaloo Marine Park – arguably WA's most precious natural attraction. Remote beaches, bays, lagoons and islands run along the coast while the jagged limestone peaks and gorges of Cape Range National Park rise out of the otherwise flat, arid expanse of North West Cape.

Coral Bay

POP 190

The tiny seaside village of Coral Bay lies just north of the Tropic of Capricorn and its beautiful location and good facilities make it one of the easiest places to access the exquisite Ningaloo Marine Park. The town consists of just one street and a sweeping white-sand beach on **Bills Bay** where you can swim and snorkel close to shore. It's also a great base for outer-reef activities like scuba diving, fishing and whale watching (June to November) and tourists flock here in the winter months to swim with whale sharks (April to July) and manta rays (May to November).

Keep to the southern end of the bay when swimming as the northern end (Skeleton Bay) is a breeding ground for reef sharks. You can hire snorkel gear, kayaks and glass-bottom canoes on the beach. There's also great snorkelling at **Purdy Point**, 500m south along the coast. Not surprisingly, the lookout above the beach car park provides excellent sunset panoramas. The town is chockers from April to October.

There are ATMs at the shopping centre and the Peoples Park grocer, and internet access at some of the tour outlets and Fins Cafe.

Fish-feeding occurs on the beach at 3.30pm everyday.

Tours

Popular tours from Coral Bay include swimming with whale sharks, spotting marine life (whales, dolphins, dugongs, turtles and manta rays), coral viewing from glass-bottom boats, and quad-bike trips. Tour operators have offices in the shopping centre and caravan parks.

Coral Bay Adventures WILDLIFE
(☎9942 5955; www.coralbayadventures.com) This excellent company offers half and full-day trips of wildlife watching ($85/190), swimming with whale sharks ($390) or manta rays ($165), whale watching ($110) and coral viewing on a glass-bottom boat (one/two hours $33/46). It can also provide free snorkel hire for the length of your stay.

Ningaloo Reef Dive DIVING
(☎9942 5824; www.ningalooreefdive.com) This PADI and eco-certified dive crew offers snorkelling with whale sharks ($365, from late March to June), reef dives ($160) and a full range of dive courses (from $380).

Ningaloo Kayak Adventures KAYAKING
(☎9948 5034; www.ningalookayakadventures.com; tours $40-60) On the main beach. It offers two- and three-hour kayak tours with stops for snorkelling. You can also hire a glass-bottom canoe ($25 per hour), wetsuit and snorkelling gear ($15 per day).

Coral Coast Tours 4WD
(☎9948 5052; www.coralcoasttours.com; half-day adult/child $135/78, full-day $185/124) Go exploring and wildlife spotting along the rugged coastal tracks through Warroora Station. Or if it's windy, take a Blo Kart (sand yacht) out onto a nearby salt lake ($50 per hour). Airport transfers from $75.

Sail Ningaloo SAILING
(☎9942 5869; www.sailningaloo.com.au; 3-day tours from $1550; Apr-Oct) The fully cashed-up can select from a number of multi-day reef sailing cruises onboard the catamaran *Shore Thing*.

Coral Coast & the Pilbara Highlights

1 Swim with 'gentle giant' whale sharks in **Ningaloo Marine Park** (p187)

2 Snorkel over marine life at **Turquoise Bay** (p189), in Ningaloo Marine Park

3 Descend into the 'centre of the earth' on an adventure tour in **Karijini National Park** (p193)

4 Scuba dive off the **Navy Pier** at Point Murat, one of the world's finest shore-dives (p187)

5 Watch the annual humpback whale migration at **North West Cape** (p187)

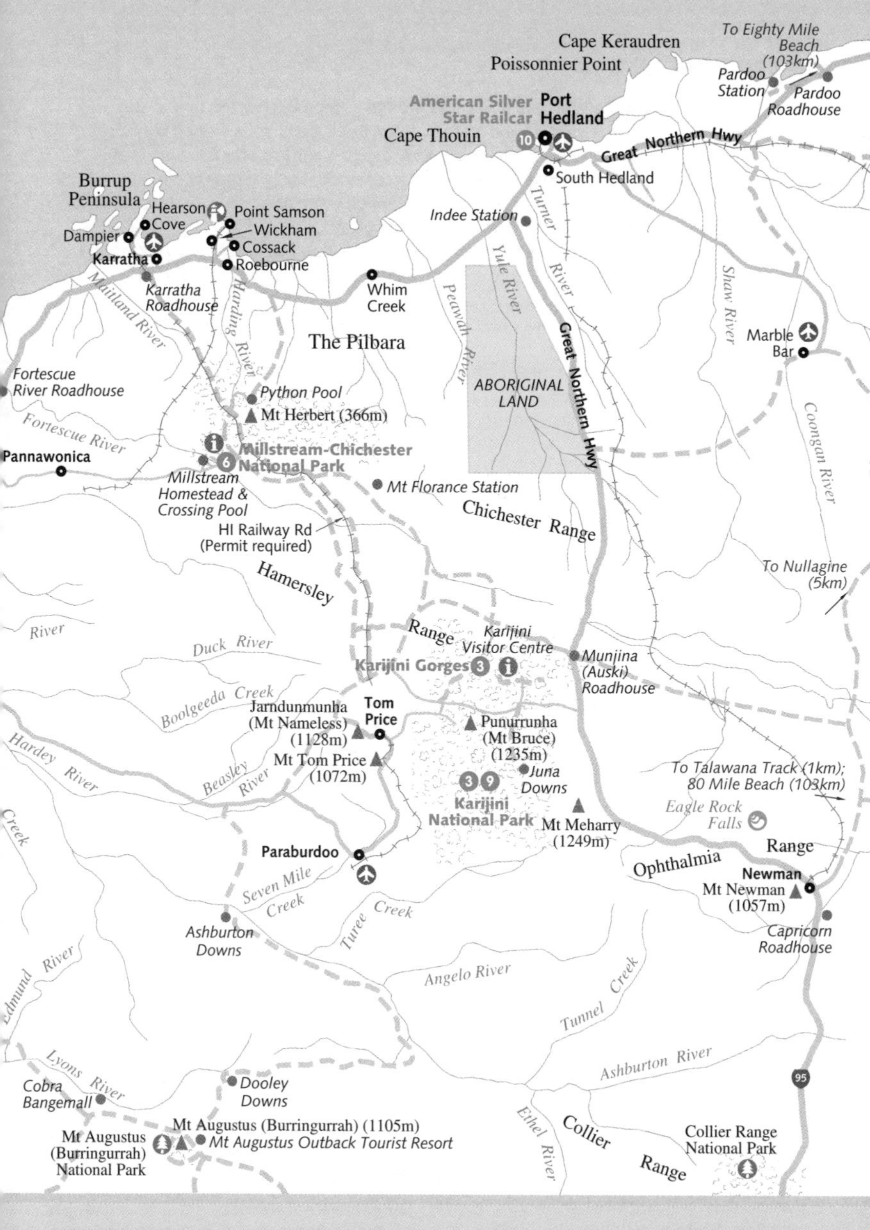

6 Cool off in an idyllic waterhole at **Millstream-Chichester National Park** (p192)

7 Track turtles on remote beaches and become a certified 'turtle guide' at the **Jurabi Turtle Centre** (p186)

8 Spot rare black-flanked rock wallabies on a cruise into stunning **Yardie Creek Gorge** (p190)

9 Engage in a spot of peak bagging on the state's **highest peaks** (p194)

10 Enjoy a real coffee in the lounge of a 1930s **American Silver Star Railcar** (p198)

STATION STAYS

If you're sick of cramped caravan parks and want to escape the hordes, or just stay somewhere a little more relaxed and off the beaten track, consider a station stay. Scattered around the Coral Coast are a number of sheep and cattle stations (some former, some still working) that offer varying styles of accommodation – it may be an exquisite slice of empty coast, or a dusty spot in the home paddock, a basic room in the shearers' quarters or a fully self-contained, air-conditioned cottage.

Don't expect top-notch facilities; in fact, a lot of sites don't have any at all. Power and water are at a premium, so the more self-sufficient you are, the more you will enjoy your stay – remember, you're getting away from it all. What you will find is loads of wildlife, stars you've never seen before, oodles of space, some fair dinkum outback and an insight into station life.

Some stations offer wilderness camping away from the main homestead (usually by the coast) and you'll need a 4WD for access and a chemical toilet (i.e. a van). These places tend to cater for fisher-types with boats and grey nomads who stay by the week.

Some stations only offer accommodation during the peak season (April to October).

Warroora (9942 5920; www.warroora.com; camping per day/week $7.50/37.50, r per person $30, cottage $130) Offers wilderness camp sites along the coast and cheap rooms in the shearers' quarters as well as a self-contained cottage and homestead. It's 47km north of Minilya.

Bullara (9942 5938; www.bullara-station.com.au; Burkett Rd, camping $11, tw/d $90/120; Apr-Oct) Has four queen and two twin share rooms in renovated shearers' quarters, unpowered camping and communal kitchen (BYO food). Also runs half-day station tours ($110). It's 70km north of Coral Bay.

Giralia (9942 5937; www.giralia.net.au; Burkett Rd; camping per person $10, budget s/d $60/70, 4-person cottage $140, homestead r $260;) Well set-up for travellers with a bush camping area (some powered sites) and kitchen, budget rooms with share bathroom, a family cottage and air-conditioned homestead rooms with breakfast and dinner included. The coast is 40 minutes away by 4WD. Meals and liquor available. It's 110km north of Coral Bay.

Sleeping & Eating

Avoid school holidays and book well ahead for peak season (April to October). Holiday houses can be rented online from www.coralbay.org. Prices start from $1000 per week.

TOP CHOICE **Ningaloo Club** HOSTEL $
(9948 5100; www.ningalooclub.com; dm $27-29, d with/without bathroom $120/95;) Clean and friendly, this excellent hostel located opposite Bayview is a great place to meet people, and boasts a central pool, well-equipped kitchen, bar, lounge and games area. It also sells Greyhound tickets (the coach stops outside) and books discounted tours.

Peoples Park Caravan Village CARAVAN PARK $$
(9942 5933; www.peoplesparkcoralbay.com; unpowered sites $32, powered sites $36-44, cabins 1-/2-bedroom $220/235, hilltop villas $265;) This excellent caravan park offers grassy, shaded sites and a variety of fully self-contained cabins. Friendly staff keep the modern amenities and spacious camp kitchen spotless, and it's the only place with freshwater showers. The hilltop villas have superb views and internet is available at nearby Fins Cafe.

Fins Cafe INTERNATIONAL $$
(9942 5900; Peoples Park; mains dinner $28-36; breakfast, lunch & dinner;) Book ahead for dinner at this intimate, outdoor BYO with its ever-changing blackboard menu showcasing local seafood, Asian-style curries and Mediterranean/Oz fusion dishes.

Ningaloo Reef Resort RESORT $$$
(1800 795 522; www.ningalooreefresort.com.au; d/apt from $199/273, penthouse $375;) Among palms just above the beach, this resort has a combination of well-appointed motel-style rooms and larger apartments, with garden or ocean views. It's also the local pub, with happy hours (Tuesdays and Fridays) and live music Thursdays attracting

a crowd. **Shades restaurant** (mains $15-35) delivers predictable fare.

Reef Cafe ITALIAN $$
(☎9942 5882; Bayview; mains $21-36; ⏰6pm-late) While this licensed family-friendly bistro features seafood and steaks, most people come for its pizzas and gelato.

The shopping centre **bakery** (⏰6.30am-5.30pm) is the best option for early risers and vegetarians with its muesli and salad rolls. The nearby supermarket has higher prices than either Carnarvon or Exmouth.

Getting There & Away

Coral Bay is 1144km north of Perth and 118km south of Exmouth, off the Minilya–Exmouth Rd.

Skywest flies into Exmouth's Learmonth Airport, 118km to the north; most Coral Bay resorts can arrange a private shuttle on request.

Greyhound coaches stop thrice weekly on the Perth/Broome run. There's a connection to/from Exmouth requiring a bus change at Giralia around midnight.

Exmouth

POP 2500

Exmouth began life during WWII as a US submarine base, though it didn't flourish until the 1960s with the establishment of the Very Low Frequency (VLF) communications facility at North West Cape. Fishing (especially prawns) and oil and gas exploration took off at the same time and both these industries are still thriving (you can see the flare of gas platforms from Vlamingh Head at night).

Tourism, a mere trickle in the '80s after the protection of pristine Ningaloo Reef, now accounts for the bulk of all visitors, reaching flood proportions during the April to October peak season. Don't let that put you off, as this modern, laid-back town makes a perfect base to explore nearby Ningaloo Marine and Cape Range National Parks. Alternatively, just wash away the dust and relax, restock, repair and reconnect with civilisation after a long road trip. The town is full of wildlife and emus commonly walk down the street, 'roos lounge around in the shade, lizards amble across the highway and corellas, galahs and ringnecks screech and swoop through the trees.

Exmouth is at the western end of the Pilbara's 'cyclone alley', and in 1999 Cyclone Vance caused widespread devastation, reaching wind speeds of 267km/h.

As you enter Exmouth, you'll pass the corporate wasteland of the new marina whose development stalled during the 2009 global financial crisis. It will be interesting to see whether 'New Broome' becomes a reality.

Sights & Activities

Ningaloo Kite & Board WINDSURFUNG, KITEBOARDING
(☎9949 2770; 16 Nimitz St) In summer, windsurfing and kiteboarding are popular, and Ningaloo Kite & Board knows the best locations, and can also arrange lessons.

Exmouth is flat, hot and sprawling with most of the attractions outside town and no public transport. A set of cycle paths ring the town and continue out to the **Harold E Holt Naval Base** (HEH) where you can follow the road to **Bundegi Beach** (14km). Watch out for dingos. Bikes can be hired from **Exmouth Minigolf** (☎9949 4644; www.exmouthminigolf.com.au; Murat Rd; per day $20; ⏰9am-8pm).

Twitchers might find waders and waterbirds around the **sewerage works** and emus and birds of prey at the **golf course** (both off Willersdorf Rd).

Turtle volunteering is popular from November to January (see the boxed text, p186).

Town Beach, 1km east, is popular with locals, though swimmers and anglers usually head north and surfers go to the western cape. Likewise, snorkellers and divers head to **Ningaloo Marine Park** or the **Muiron Islands**, which have some excellent sites like the **Cod Hole**. Try to find the informative Department for Environment and Conservation (DEC) book *Dive and Snorkel Sites in Western Australia*. Several dive shops in town offer PADI courses.

Tours

Adventure tours from Exmouth include swimming with whale sharks, wildlife spotting, diving, sea kayaking, fishing and surf charters, and coral viewing from glass-bottom boats. Some companies only operate during peak season (late April to mid-October). Check conditions carefully regarding 'no sighting' policies and cancellations.

Outside the whale shark season, tours focus on manta rays. You need to be a capable snorkeller to get the most out of these experiences. It's normally 30% cheaper if you

Exmouth

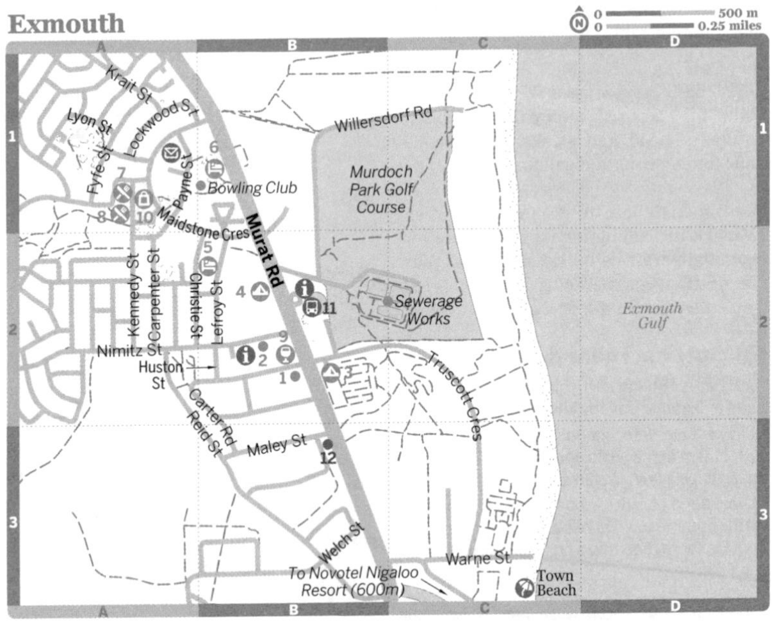

Exmouth

Activities, Courses & Tours
1 Exmouth Minigolf B2
2 Ningaloo Kite & Board B2

Sleeping
3 Exmouth Cape Holiday Park B2
Exmouth Holiday Accommodation/Ray White .... (see 10)
4 Exmouth Ningaloo Caravan & Holiday Resort B2
5 Ningaloo Lodge B2
6 Potshot Hotel Resort B1

Eating
7 Ningaloo Health A1
Pinocchio .... (see 4)
8 Whalers Restaurant A1

Drinking
9 Grace's Tavern B2

Shopping
10 Exmouth Shopping Centre A1

Transport
11 Greyhound Coach Stop B2
12 Tours 'N' Travel B3

don't swim. Below is just a selection of operators – see the visitor centre for a full list.

Capricorn Kayak Tours KAYAKING
(☎0427 485 123; www.capricornseakayaking.com.au; half-/1-/2-/5-day tour $79/149/595/1495 Apr-Oct) Capricorn offers single- and multi-day kayaking and snorkelling tours along the lagoons of Ningaloo Reef.

Kings Ningaloo Reef Tours WILDLIFE
(☎9949 1764; www.kingsningalooreeftours.com.au; snorkel/observer $375/260) Longtime player Kings still gets rave reviews for its whale shark tours. It's renowned for staying out longer than everyone else, and has a 'next available tour' no-sighting policy.

Ningaloo Ecology Cruises BOAT CRUISE
(☎9949 2255; www.ningalootreasures.com.au; 1/2.5hr $40/60) Has one-hour glass-bottom boat trips (April to October), and longer 2½-hour trips (all year) including snorkelling. Tours leave from Tantabiddi and there's a free transfer from town.

Ningaloo Whaleshark-N-Dive DIVING
(☎1800 224 060; www.ningaloowhalesharkndive.com.au) Offers dive tours to Lighthouse Bay on the west coast, and longer liveaboard tours to the Muiron (three-day) and Montebello Islands (seven-day).

Montebello Island Safaris BOAT CRUISE
(☎0419 091 670; www.montebello.com.au; Apr-Oct) Has a permanent houseboat moored at the Montebello Islands where you can dive, snorkel, surf and fish to your heart's content on a six-night tour.

Sleeping

Accommodation is limited; book ahead, especially for the peak season (April to October).

TOP CHOICE **Ningaloo Lodge** GUESTHOUSE $$
(☎1800 880 949; www.ningaloolodge.com.au; Lefroy St; d $125;) These clean, tastefully appointed motel rooms are the best deal in town with a modern communal kitchen, barbecue, shady pool and free wi-fi all within walking distance of either pub.

Exmouth Ningaloo Caravan & Holiday Resort CARAVAN PARK $
(☎9949 2377; www.exmouthresort.com; Murat Rd; unpowered/powered sites $33/39, dm/d $28/77, chalets $160-200;) Across from the visitor centre, this relaxed, spacious park has grassy sites, self-contained chalets, four-bed dorms, an on-site restaurant and even a pet section. If you're tenting, this is your best bet.

Exmouth Cape Holiday Park CARAVAN PARK $
(☎1800 621 101; www.aspenparks.com.au; cnr Truscott Cres & Murat Rd; unpowered/powered/en suite sites $30/45/72, dm/d $30/95, cabin d $120-277;) The Cape offers van sites with their own en suites, as well as four-bed dorms, budget twins and a host of different cabin options. There's a good camp kitchen, though the few unpowered tent sites are rather cramped.

Potshot Hotel Resort RESORT $$
(☎9949 1200; www.potshotresort.com; Murat Rd; dm/d $28/65, motel d $98, studio $179, apt from $205;) A town-within-a-town, this bustling resort has seven-bed dorms, standard motel rooms, luxury Osprey apartments and several bars, catering for all comers.

Novotel Ningaloo Resort RESORT $$$
(☎9949 0000; www.novotelningaloo.com.au; Madaffari Dr; d/apt from $275/355;) In the marina, the Novotel Ningaloo is at the pointy end of sophistication (and expense) in Exmouth. The tastefully designed rooms are spacious, well equipped and all include balconies.

Exmouth Holiday Accommodation/Ray White RENTAL HOUSE $$$
(☎9949 1144; www.exmouthholidays.com.au; 3 Kennedy St; holiday houses per week from $700;) Ray White has a wide range of weekly rentals, from fibro shacks to double-storey mansions.

Eating & Drinking

TOP CHOICE **Whalers Restaurant** SEAFOOD $$
(☎9949 2416; www.whalersrestaurant.com.au; 5 Kennedy St; mains lunch $7-24, dinner $27-40; 9am-2pm & 6pm-late) Delicious Creole-influenced seafood is the star attraction at this Exmouth institution. Sit back on the leafy verandah and share a seafood tasting plate with soft-shell crab and local prawns, or try the signature New Orleans gumbo. Non-fishheads can hook into chargrilled kangaroo or Mexican fajitas. The lunch menu is more bistro-like.

Ningaloo Health CAFE $
(☎9949 1400; www.ningaloohealth.com.au; 3A Kennedy St; mains $8-18; 7.30am-4pm;) Breakfasts start with a bang at this tiny cafe – try the chilli eggs on blue vein toast with jalapenos, or a bowl of Vietnamese *pho* (beef-and-rice-noodle soup). The less brave can dive into a berry pancake stack, bircher muesli or a detox juice. NH also does light lunches, salads, smoothies, takeaway picnic hampers (great for a day trip to Cape Range National Park) and the best coffee around.

Mantaray's Bar & Brasserie INTERNATIONAL $$$
(☎9949 0000; Madaffari Dr; mains lunch $16-23, dinner $39-45; lunch & dinner;) Novotel Ningaloo's in-house restaurant is the perfect place for a long, lazy waterside lunch with local, quality ingredients, affordable dishes and the best view in town.

Pinocchio ITALIAN $$
(☎9949 2577; Murat Rd; mains $16-35; 6pm-late) Located inside the Exmouth Ningaloo Caravan Park, this licensed alfresco *ristorante* is popular with locals and travellers alike. Families are well catered for, there's a pleasant deck by the pool, and the tasty pasta and pizza servings are huge.

Grace's Tavern (☎9949 1000; Murat Rd; dinner) and **Potshot Hotel** (☎9949 1200; Murat Rd; dinner) are your drinking options and

NINGA TURTLE GUIDES

For those with time, one of the most satisfying things you can do on the Coral Coast is to volunteer for a turtle-monitoring project. Getting up close to these magnificent creatures, knowing that you're actively taking part in their conservation, is truly rewarding. Both Exmouth and Port Hedland run organised volunteer programs each turtle season (November to February).

Exmouth volunteers need to commit to a five-week period and be prepared to spend most of that time at a remote base. Days start at sunrise with five hours work collecting data on turtle nesting, habitat and predation, then the rest of the day is free to enjoy the surroundings. Volunteers pay $1000, which covers all equipment, meals, transport from Exmouth and insurance. Accommodation is usually in tents or swags at a Department for Environment and Conservation (DEC) research station or remote beach. Registration opens in September each year. See the excellent **Ningaloo Turtle Program** (NTP; www.ningalooturtles.org.au) website for more information.

If you enjoy interaction of the human kind, consider NTP's turtle guide program. You will need to complete at least the first module ($172) of the TAFE formal training course, Turtle Tour Guiding, before commencing at the **Jurabi Turtle Centre** (JCT) and this course gains credits towards a Certificate III in Tourism. The JCT plays an important role in minimising the disturbance to nesting turtles and hatchlings by educating tourists and supervising interaction during the breeding period.

Port Hedland volunteers should register in August for **Pendoley Environmental's** (www.penv.com.au) tagging program, which works alongside the oil and gas industry at sites like Barrow Island. Typical placements are for 16 days with all expenses covered, there's a strict selection process and you'll be working mostly at night with minimal free time. The environmental group **Care for Hedland** (kellyhowlett35@hotmail.com) also runs volunteer monitoring programs, and training sessions kick off in November.

both serve decent pub meals. Grace's also does curries and will home-deliver.

There's a supermarket, bakery and several takeaways at **Exmouth Shopping Centre** (Maidstone Cres).

Shopping

The **Exmouth Shopping Centre** (Maidstone Cres) has a couple of dive shops, a gift shop and a surf and camping store.

Exmouth Fish Co SEAFOOD
(☎9949 2565; Murat Rd, Learmonth; ⏰8am-4pm) If you want to take some of that sensational seafood home with you, check out the Exmouth Fish Co near the airport, where you can purchase vacuum-sealed local prawn and fish packs.

Information

Department for Environment and Conservation (DEC; ☎9947 8000; www.dec.wa.gov.au; 20 Nimitz St; ⏰8am-5pm Mon-Fri) Supplies maps and brochures for Ningaloo and Cape Range, including excellent wildlife guides. Can advise on turtle volunteering.

Exmouth Hospital (☎9949 1011; Lyon St)

Library (☎9949 1462; 22 Maidstone Cres; ⏰9am-4pm, until noon Sat, closed lunch & all day Fri & Sun; @) Internet and fax access.

Money (Maidstone Cres) Bank, ATM.

Police (Maidstone Cres)

Post office (Maidstone Cres)

Tours 'N' Travel (☎9949 4457; www.ningalootours-travel.com.au; cnr Murat Rd & Maley St; ⏰8.30am-7pm; @) Internet and secondhand books.

Visitor centre (☎1800 287 328; www.exmouthwa.com.au; Murat Rd; ⏰9am-5pm Mon-Fri, until 1pm Sat & Sun; @) Useful information about Exmouth and the national parks, books tours, tickets and accommodation.

Getting There & Away

Exmouth's Learmonth Airport is 37km south of town. Skywest flies to Perth daily, and weekly to Karratha (Monday), Shark Bay/Monkey Mia (Saturday) and Broome (April to October).

Buses stop at the visitor centre. Greyhound runs a shuttle out to the Giralia turn-off to connect with the thrice-weekly Perth/Broome service (Perth $250, 18 hours; Broome $300, 19 hours; Coral Bay $100, two hours).

Red Earth Safaris (☎1800 501 968; www.redearthsafaris.com.au) Offers a weekly Perth express departing Exmouth 7am Sunday (one-way $200, 30 hours).

Getting Around

Airport Shuttle Bus (☎9949 4623; $20) Meets all flights; reservations are required when heading to the airport.

Allens (☎9949 2403; rear 24 Nimitz St) Cars start at $45 per day with 150 free kilometres while Budget, Avis and Europcar also have agents.

Exmouth Boat & Kayak Hire (☎0438 230 269; www.exmouthboathire.com) Tinnies (small dinghies) or something larger (including a guide!) can be hired from $100 per day.

Exmouth Camper Hire (☎9949 4050; www.exmouthcamperhire.com.au; 16 Nimitz St) Rents vans (from $100 per day) with everything you need to spend time in Cape Range, including solar panels.

Tours 'N' Travel (☎9949 4457; www.ningaloo-tours-travel.com.au; cnr Murat Rd & Maley St) Has scooters from $44 per day.

Around Exmouth

Heading north past HEH, the **VLF antenna array** dominates the cape's northern tip, and was once the tallest structure in the southern hemisphere.

Keep straight at the Yardie Creek turn-off for **Bundegi Beach**, 14km north of Exmouth, where clear, sheltered waters provide pleasant swimming and good fishing.

There's great diving at nearby **Bundegi Reef**, but even better slightly north under the **Navy Pier** at Point Murat (named for Napoleon's brother-in-law by French explorers). Rated one of the world's best shore dives, there's an eye-melting array of marine life including nudibranchs, scorpion fish, moray eels and reef sharks. As it's on defence territory, you'll need to join a tour.

Turn back onto Yardie Creek Rd and head west for the best beaches. Take the first right, signposted **'Mildura Wreck'** to the end to see the 1907 cattle ship that ran aground on the reef. Along the way are turn-offs, which lead to the ruggedly beautiful **Surfers Beach** (Dunes), with grassy dunes and great waves for experienced surfers.

Ideally located just south of Surfers Beach, **Ningaloo Lighthouse Caravan Park** (☎9949 1478; www.ningaloolighthouse.com; Yardie Creek Rd; unpowered/powered sites $29/35, cabins $95, bungalows $125, lighthouse/lookout chalets $150/245; ❄≋) has superb chalets with fantastic views and shady sites for mere mortals.

It's hard to miss the hilltop **Vlamingh Head Lighthouse**, built in 1912 – where spectacular views of the entire cape make it a great place for whale spotting and watching sunsets.

Nearby is the excellent **Jurabi Turtle Centre**. Visit by day to read about the turtle lifecycle, and obtain the DEC pamphlet *Marine Turtles in Ningaloo Marine Park*. Return at night to observe nesting turtles and hatchlings (November to March), remembering to keep the correct distance and never to shine a light or camera flash directly at any animal. Those people who have more time can volunteer to become a 'turtle tracker'. Check **Ningaloo Turtle Program** (www.ningalooturtles.org.au) to obtain more information.

Fantastic beaches continue down the western side of the cape such as clothing-optional **Mauritius Beach**, 21km from Exmouth, and the snorkelling favourites of **Lakeside** (54km), **Turquoise Bay** (65km) and **Oyster Stacks** (69km).

The entrance to **Cape Range National Park** (per car $11) is at 40km and camp sites are allocated here (when open). At 53km you'll find the **Milyering visitor centre** (☎9949 2808; Yardie Creek Rd; ⏲9am-3.45pm), which serves Ningaloo Marine Park and Cape Range National Park. You can buy tickets here for the Yardie Creek cruise, hire snorkelling gear ($10), and experienced 4WD-ers can check road conditions for the rough coastal track continuing south to Coral Bay.

Ningaloo Marine Park

Recently extended and World Heritage-nominated, the Ningaloo Marine Park now protects the full 300km length of the exquisite Ningaloo Reef, from Bundegi Reef on the eastern tip of the peninsula to Red Bluff on Quobba Station far to the south.

Ningaloo is Australia's largest fringing reef, in places only 100m offshore, and it's this accessibility, and the fact that it's home to a staggering array of **marine life** that makes it so popular. Sharks, manta rays, humpback whales, turtles, dugongs and dolphins complement more than 500 species of fish.

North West Cape

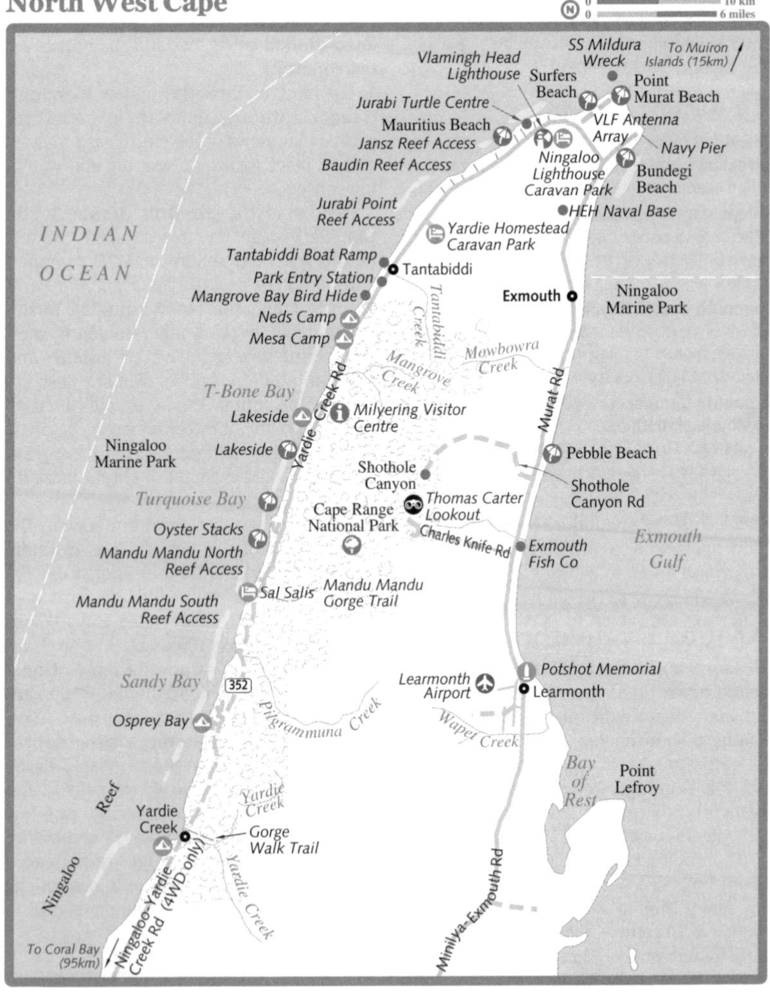

There's excellent marine activity to enjoy year-round:

November to March Turtles – three species nestle and hatch in the sands.

March and April Coral spawning – an amazing event seven to nine days after the full moon.

April to July Whale sharks arrive for the coral spawning.

May to November Manta rays are present all year round; their numbers increase dramatically over winter and spring.

June to November Humpback whales – breed in the warm tropics then head back south to feed in the Antarctic.

Over 220 species of hard **coral** have been recorded in Ningaloo, ranging from bulbous brain corals found on bommies, to delicate branching staghorns and the slow-growing massive coral. While less colourful than soft corals (which are normally found in deeper water on the outer reef), the hard corals have amazing formations. Spawning, where branches of hermaphroditic coral simultaneously eject eggs and sperm into the water, occurs after full and new moons between

February and May, but the major frenzy usually happens six to 10 days after the March and April full moons.

It's this spawning that attracts the park's biggest drawcard, the solitary speckled **whale shark** *(Rhiniodon typus)*. Ningaloo is one of the few places in the world where these gentle giants arrive like clockwork each year to feed on plankton and small fish, making it a mecca for marine biologists and visitors alike. The largest fish in the world, the whale shark can weigh up to 21 tonnes, although most weigh between 13 and 15 tonnes, and reach up to 18m long. They can live for 70 years.

To learn more about the inhabitants, track down a copy of the DEC's *The Marine Life of Ningaloo Marine Park & Coral Bay*.

Activities

Most travellers visit Ningaloo Marine Park to **snorkel**. Stop at **Milyering visitor centre** (☎9949 2808; Yardie Creek Rd; ⏲9am-3.45pm) for maps and information on the best spots and conditions. Check its tide chart and know your limits, as the currents can be dangerous. The shop next to the park office sells and rents snorkelling equipment ($10 per day, $15 overnight).

The best (and hence most popular) snorkelling spots:

Lakeside Walk 500m south along the beach from the car park then snorkel out with the current before returning close to your original point.

Oyster Stacks These spectacular bommies are just metres offshore, but you need a tide of at least 1.2m and sharp rocks make entry/exit difficult. If you tire, don't stand on the bommies, look for some sand.

Turquoise Bay Everyone's favourite. Walk 300m south along the beach, swim out for about 40m and float face down – the current will carry you over coral bommies and abundant sea life. Get out before the sandy point then run back along the beach and start all over! Don't miss the exit point or the current will carry you out through the gap in the reef. Can be overcrowded in peak season.

Lighthouse Bay SCUBA DIVING
There's great scuba diving at Lighthouse Bay at sites like the Labyrinth and Blizzard Ridge. Check out the DEC book *Dive and Snorkel Sites in Western Australia* for other ideas.

Tours

See Tours under Exmouth (p183) and Coral Bay (p179).

Cape Range National Park

The rugged 510-sq-km **Cape Range National Park** (per car $11) comprises a third of the North West Cape peninsula and is rich in wildlife, including the rare black-flanked rock wallaby, five different types of bat and over 200 species of birds. Spectacular deep canyons and eroded red limestone gorges cut dramatically into the range, before emptying out onto the arid coastal dunes and turquoise waters of Ningaloo Reef.

The main park access is via Yardie Creek Rd. Several areas in the east are accessible from unsealed roads off Minilya–Exmouth Rd, south of the town. At present there is no public through route across the range. **Milyering visitor centre** (☎9949 2808; Yardie Creek Rd; ⏲9am-3.45pm) has a comprehensive display of the area's natural and cultural history, and great maps and publications.

SURFING THE CAPE

The big swells arrive on the North West Cape between July and October. **Dunes** (Surfers Beach) has a popular reef break accessible from the first car park. **Lighthouse Bombie**, a couple of kilometres south, is further out and a bit more challenging. Beginners should continue south down the cape to **Wobiri Access** where the waves are gentler and surf classes are sometimes held.

Serious surfers should consider getting a few mates together for a boat charter to the outer reef and the **Muiron Islands**, where there are countless breaks and no one to ride them. You can camp on **South Muiron** with a permit from Exmouth DEC. Your charter fee should include all meals, accommodation (onboard or camping) and fishing and snorkelling gear. Charters may be arranged from both Exmouth and Coral Bay, but check with the Exmouth visitor centre first, as the owner may have just sailed off for the Mentawais. You could try **Ningaloo Fusion Charters** (☎0438 993 284; www.ningaloofusioncharters.com).

CAPE RANGE/ NINGALOO CAMP SITES

Try to check out the different camp site areas a day before if possible. Neds Camp and Osprey are the largest camping grounds with 15 sites each, and North T-Bone and North Mandu are the smallest with three. Milyering visitor centre also has a photo list showing the different beaches. During peak season there's normally a camp host residing at each site.

Sights & Activities

On the east coast, 23km south of Exmouth, the scenic and at times incredible, **Charles Knife Rd** climbs dramatically above the **canyon** of the same name. The road follows the knife-edge ridge up through rickety corners and you'll need frequent stops to take in the breathtaking views. Further along, there's a turn-off on a rough track to **Thomas Carter lookout** where (in the winter months) you can walk the 8km **Badjirrajirra loop trail** through spinifex and rocky gullies. There's no shade or water up here.

Don't miss the beautiful **Shothole Canyon** (the turn-off is 16km south of Exmouth), with its colourful walls. You drive along its base to a pretty picnic area with plenty of exploration options.

On the west coast, look for migratory birds at the **Mangrove Bay Bird Hide**, 8km from the entrance station. **Mandu Mandu Gorge** (3km return) is a pleasant but dry walk from a car park 20km south of the Milyering visitor centre.

Much nicer is the walk to **Yardie Creek Gorge** (2km return) with its permanent water, sheer cliffs and excellent views. You can take the relaxing one-hour **Yardie Creek Cruise** (9949 2808; adult/child $25/12; 11am daily) up the short, sheer gorge to spot rare black-flanked rock wallabies.

Only experienced 4WD-ers should contemplate the hazardous Yardie Creek crossing (low tide only!), and the dodgy costal track that continues south through Ningaloo Station to Coral Bay. Check for the latest road conditions with the Milyering visitor centre.

Sleeping

There are sandy, compact **camp sites** (per person $7) along the coast within the park. Facilities and shade are minimal, but most have toilets. Sites are limited and allocated upon arrival at the entrance station (not the visitor centre!) – ask for a generator-free site if you're after quiet. Currently it's not possible to book in advance, though this may change as long entrance station queues (appearing hours before opening in peak season) are common.

Yardie Homestead Caravan Park CARAVAN PARK $
(9949 1389; www.yardie.com.au; Yardie Creek Rd; unpowered/powered sites $26/30, d $75, cabin $110, chalet $180;) Located just outside the park boundary, this former sheep station caters mainly for anglers, though travellers are also welcome and there are some nice grassy tent sites. There's a range of cabins (most require a security bond) plus a pool, shop and camp kitchen.

Sal Salis LUXURY WILDERNESS $$$
(1300 790 561; www.salsalis.com; South Mandu entrance; wilderness tent s/d $1095/1460; Mar-Dec) Want to watch that flaming crimson Indian Ocean sunset from between 500-threadcount pure cotton sheets? Pass the Chablis! For those who want their camp without the cramp, there's a minimum two-night stay, three gourmet meals a day, a free bar (!) and the same things to do as the couple over the dune in the pop-up camper.

THE PILBARA

Miners swarm like ants over the high, eroded ranges of the interior while ore trains snake down to the plains, spewing their riches onto ships at a string of busy ports stretching from Dampier to Port Hedland. Fifty per cent larger than Germany, but with only one person per 12 sq km, this is a land of big temperatures, big machinery, big risks and big distances.

But hidden in the arid spinifex wilderness are two beautiful gems – the Karijini and Millstream-Chichester National Parks, home to spectacular gorges, amazing waterfalls, deep tranquil pools and abundant wildlife.

Dampier to Roebourne

Most travellers skip this mining services section of the coast as there's not much to see, unless you like huge industrial facilities.

Accommodation is ludicrously overpriced and almost impossible to find thanks to the resources boom and the flood of FI-FO (fly in, fly out) workers. House prices and rents are among the highest in the country, and huge suburbs of donga (small, transportable buildings) are springing up on town outskirts to handle the overflow. However, the area has good transport, well-stocked supermarkets and useful repair shops.

DAMPIER

Dampier is the region's main port. Spread around King Bay, it overlooks the 42 pristine islands of the **Dampier Archipelago**, and supports a wealth of marine life in its coral waters, but heavy industry has blighted Dampier's shores. The nearby **Burrup Peninsula** contains possibly the greatest number of rock art petroglyphs on the planet, but is under threat from continued industrial expansion (see www.burrup.org.au). The most accessible are at **Deep Gorge** near **Hearson Cove** where you can also view Staircase to the Moon; you'll need a 4WD for the rest of the peninsula.

Sleeping

Dampier Transit Caravan Park CARAVAN PARK $

(☎9183 1109; The Esplanade; unpowered/powered sites $18/22) Has a handful of grassy sites overlooking the water.

KARRATHA

Most travellers bank, restock, repair stuff and get out of town before their wallet ignites.

From behind the visitor centre, the **Jaburara Heritage Trail** (3.5km one-way) takes visitors through significant traditional sites and details the displacement and eventual extinction of the Jaburara people. Bring plenty of water and start early.

Sleeping & Eating

Accommodation prospects are dire in Karratha; try to stay at beautiful Point Samson instead. Otherwise, search online for last-minute deals.

Pilbara Holiday Park CARAVAN PARK $$

(☎9185 1855; www.aspenparks.com.au; Rosemary Rd; powered sites $50, motel/studio d $220/210; ❄@≋) Neat, well run with good facilities, though tent sites are expensive.

All Seasons Karratha HOTEL $$$

(☎9185 1155; www.accorhotels.com.au; Searipple Rd; d from $258; ❄@≋) This hotel has pleasant rooms with data ports (15 minutes free), three bars, a pool and bistro.

Karratha Sushi Bar SUSHI $

(☎9183 8789; Balmoral Rd; ⏲10am-9pm daily) For something different, try the excellent sushi here.

The shopping centre has most things you'll need including ATMs, takeaway food and supermarkets. The JavaVan coffee, in the visitor centre car park, is the best in town.

Information

Karratha visitor centre (☎9144 4600; www.pilbaracoast.com; Karratha Rd; ⏲9am-5pm Mon-Fri, 10am-1pm Sat & Sun, shorter hours Nov-Apr; @) Has good local info, supplies Hamersley Iron (HI) road permits, books tours, and may be able to find you a room.

Getting There & Away

Karratha is exceptionally well connected. Virgin Blue and Qantas both fly daily to Perth, while Qantas also offers weekly direct flights to most other capitals. Skywest flies to Perth four times a week, and Exmouth on Mondays. Airnorth flies to Broome (Tuesday and Friday) with a Darwin connection, and Port Hedland (Tuesday).

Greyhound coaches run to Perth ($214, 23 hours, Tuesday, Thursday and Saturday) and Port Hedland ($34, three hours, Tuesday, Thursday and Saturday). Buses depart Perth (Monday,

WORTH A TRIP

PASS THE SALT

When you're 122km up a dead-end road off a highway 264km from the nearest town, and your principle industry is salt mining, it's little wonder you don't get many visitors. But those who make it to Onslow are rewarded by one of the nicest restaurants on the coast, the excellent **Nikki's** (☎9184 6121; First Ave; mains $32-45; ⏲6.30pm-late), whose open verandah overlooks the beautiful **Sunrise Beach**. Make sure you book, as it would be a pity to miss the signature grilled barramundi in laksa sauce, the five spice chilli squid or pan-seared scallops. Enjoy some fine West Australian wine, watch the Staircase to the Moon from the deck, then return to your tent at the laid-back, aptly named **Ocean View Caravan Park** (☎9184 6053; Second Ave; unpowered/powered sites $30/35, cabins $80).

Wednesday and Friday) and Port Hedland (Tuesday, Thursday and Saturday).

ROEBOURNE

Roebourne, 40km east of Karratha, is the oldest Pilbara town still in existence (1866) and home to a large Aboriginal community. It has some excellent old buildings, including the **visitor centre** (☎9182 1060; Queen St; ⏰9am-4pm Mon-Fri, 9am-3pm Sat & Sun, shorter hours Nov-Apr) housed in the Old Gaol, which is also a **museum** (admission by donation). Don't miss the mineral display in the courtyard.

Roebourne also has a thriving Indigenous art scene, and you'll pass the odd gallery on the highway. See www.roebourneart.com.au for more details.

COSSACK

The scenic ghost town of Cossack, at the mouth of the Harding River, was previously the district's main port, but was usurped by Point Samson and then eventually abandoned. Many of the historic bluestone buildings date from the late 1800s and there's a 6km **Heritage Trail** around the town that links all the major sites (pick up the brochure from Roebourne visitor centre). Attractions include the self-guided **Social History Museum** (adult/child $2/1; ⏰9am-4pm), celebrating the town's zenith. The pioneer **cemetery** has a tiny Japanese section dating from when Cossack was WA's first major pearl-fishing town. Follow the road past the cemetery to **Reader Head Lookout** with great views over the river mouth. You can see the Staircase to the Moon from here.

Sleeping

Cossack Budget Accommodation GUESTHOUSE $
(☎9182 1190; d with/without air-con $85/65; ❄) Has clean rooms in the atmospheric old police barracks. Bring your own food as there are no restaurants.

POINT SAMSON

Point Samson is a small, industrial-free seaside village, home to great seafood and clean beaches, which make it the nicest place to stay in the area. There's good **snorkelling** off Point Samson, and the picturesque curved beach of Honeymoon Cove.

Sleeping & Eating

Samson Beach Chalets CHALETS $$$
(☎9187 0202; www.samsonbeach.com.au; Samson Rd; chalets $220-440; ❄📶🏊) Offers beautifully appointed, self-contained one- and two-bedroom chalets just a short walk from the beach. There's a shady pool, free wi-fi and in-house movies.

Samson Beach Caravan Park CARAVAN PARK $
(☎9187 1414; Samson Rd; powered sites $37) A tiny park in lovely, leafy surrounds, close to the water and tavern. Bookings are essential in school holidays.

Moby's Kitchen SEAFOOD $
(☎9187 1435; mains $11-30; ⏰11am-2pm & 5-8.30pm Mon-Fri, 11am-8.30pm Sat & Sun) Does great seafood at honest prices on a shady deck overlooking the ocean.

Millstream-Chichester National Park

The tranquil waterholes of the Fortescue River form cool, lush oases in the midst of arid, spinifex-covered plateaus and basalt ranges. Lying between Karijini and the coast, the **Millstream** pools are the perfect place to break a trip. Lovely **Crossing Pool** with palms, pelicans, picnic tables and gas barbecues is an idyllic camp site, though some may prefer the larger **Milliyanha Campground** with its camp kitchen and close access to the visitor centre. The **Murlamunyjunha Trail** (7km, two hours return) links both areas and features interpretive plaques explaining the use of native plants by the park's traditional owners, the Yindjibarndi. Camp sites are $7 per person.

Once the station homestead, the unmanned **visitor centre** (☎9184 5144; ⏰8am-4pm) now details the park's history, ecology and Yindjibarndi culture. Lilies and shady palms ring the nearby **Jirndarwurrunha Pool** which has strong cultural significance to the Yindjibarndi – please don't swim here.

Millstream-Chichester is one of the most important Indigenous cultural sites in WA. Unlike Karijini, where the gorges were avoided, Millstream was a focal point for surrounding tribes, and a lifeblood in dry times, sustaining a wide variety of animals and bushtucker. **Nhangganggunha** (Deep Reach Pool; 🏊) is believed to be the resting place of the Warlu, the creation serpent, and is being developed into the main day use area.

In the park's north are the stunning breakaways and eroded mesas of the **Chichester Range**. If you didn't come from Roebourne, then don't miss the amazing panorama from the top of **Mt Herbert** (10 minutes from the car park). You can continue walking to **McKenzie Spring** (4.5km, one hour return). Lower down the range, **Python Pool** is worth a look, though check for algal bloom before diving in; it's linked to Mt Herbert by the **Chichester Range Camel Trail** (16km, six hours return). **Snake Creek campground** is another kilometre downhill.

Tom Price

POP 4500

Driving into Tom Price, you'd be forgiven for thinking that a tiny piece of Frodo's Shire has been dumped into the heart of Mordor – it's a green, manicured oasis surrounded by burnt and broken hills of rust red ironstone.

Most travellers stop briefly while passing through to nearby Karijini National Park, for internet, fuel, supermarket plundering and **Hamersley Iron** (HI) road permits. There's little reason to stay overnight, even if you could find a room.

Tom Price is WA's highest town at 747m above sea level. **Jarndunmunha** (Mt Nameless; 1128m) – 'place of rock wallabies' in Guruma – is 3km west of Tom Price and you can drive to the top in a 4WD or walk from the bottom (three hours return) for views over the town and surrounding mines.

If you like big holes, the visitor centre's 90-minute **mine tour** (adult/child $28/15; ⌚10am daily Apr-Oct) takes you into the massive bowels of the huge open-cut pit.

Stay on the asphalt if coming from Nanutarra, as the unsealed Paraburdoo bypass is a notorious tyre-eater.

Sleeping & Eating

Tom Price Tourist Park TOURIST PARK $
(☎9189 1515; Mt Nameless Rd; unpowered/powered sites $30/37, dm $37, d $107, cabins d $155-185; ❄≋) Has decent facilities but it's 2km from town and normally full of workers.

Tom Price Hotel Motel MOTEL $$
(☎9189 1101; budget s $105, motel standard/deluxe d $170/191; ❄) With clean rooms, but is almost always booked out. The bistro (mains $16 to $38) is the best place to eat in town and is open from breakfast.

There are several takeaways and a supermarket across the road from the library.

Information

Library (Central Rd; ⌚10am-varies; @) Next door to the visitor centre, has reliable, speedy internet. ATMs are across the road.

Visitor centre (☎9188 1112; www.tompricewa.com.au; Central Rd; ⌚8.30am-5pm Mon-Fri, until 12.30pm Sat & Sun, shorter hours Nov-Apr) Can supply HI road permits, advise on conditions, and book tours.

Karijini National Park

Arguably one of WA's most magnificent destinations, **Karijini National Park** (per car $11) reveals itself slowly, like a shy rock wallaby. Riven and ragged ranges, upthrust and twisted by nature, glow like molten lava in the setting sun. Wedge-tailed eagles soar above grey-green spinifex while goannas shelter under stunted mulga. Kangaroos and wildflowers dot the plains, which end

DEATH OF A HERO

On the afternoon of 1 April 2004, two separate incidents occurred in the Karijini gorges that required rescue services. Both involved tourists who had fallen in areas beyond the warning signs, one from the bottom of Weano Gorge and the other in Hancock Gorge beyond Kermits Pool. By the time the emergency services arrived from Tom Price and Newman, it was almost dark. The first tourist was located at Junction Pool, placed in a stretcher and hauled up through the gates at Oxers Lookout around midnight.

There were reports of rain in the surrounding area. The second rescue was more complex as the injured tourist's location had been misreported. Six rescue workers, including SES volunteer Jim Regan from Newman, were in Hancock Gorge at the time. At 4am a huge wall of water came rushing through the gorge and washed four of the six, plus the injured tourist (now in a stretcher) away. After sunrise on 2 April, three of the four, plus the tourist were located safe near the bottom of the gorge and subsequently rescued, though it would be another day before police divers found the body of Jim Regan. His memorial is at Oxers Lookout.

Karijini National Park

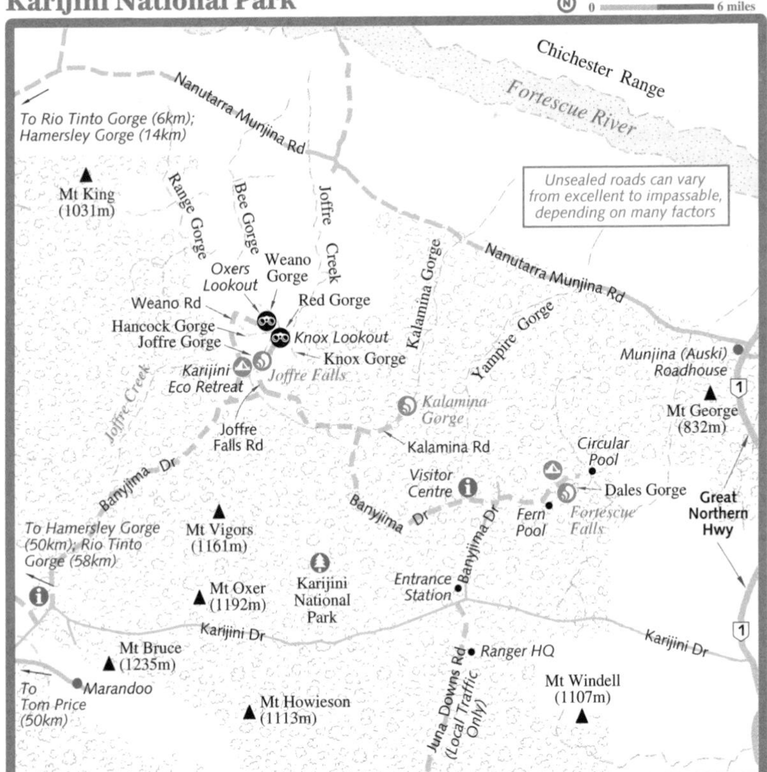

abruptly at deep, dark incisions. The sound of distant water tinkles invitingly up from the chasms.

While the breathtaking gorges, with their plunging waterfalls, cool, deep pools and smooth, sculptured channels are Karijini's most popular drawcard, there are many other attractions. The park is home to a wide variety of fauna and flora, with an estimated 800 different plant species, including some 50 varieties of wattle (acacia). You'll see dragon lizards scurrying over rocks, hear the odd dingo and perhaps catch a glimpse of an endangered Olive Python lurking on the far side of a pool. The park is also home to WA's three highest peaks (Mt Meharry, Mt Bruce and Mt Frederick).

Banyjima Dr, the park's main thoroughfare, connects with Karijini Dr at two entrance stations. The eastern access is sealed to the visitor centre and Dales Gorge, while the rest of the park is unsealed. Take extra care on all unsealed sections, as tourist rollovers are far too common. Avoid driving at night.

Choose walks wisely, dress appropriately and never enter a restricted area (the Eco Retreat keeps an 'Idiots List') without a certified guide. Avoid the gorges during and after rain, as flash flooding does occur.

Sights & Activities

Entering Banyjima Dr from the east, it's 19km to scenic **Dales Gorge**, where there's a camping ground. A short, sharp descent leads to **Fortescue Falls**, behind which a leafy stroll upstream reveals the beautiful **Fern Pool**; head downstream from Fortescue Falls to picturesque **Circular Pool**; ascend to **Three Ways Lookout** and return along the cliff top.

Wide **Kalamina Gorge**, 24km from the visitor centre, is the easiest gorge to enter and suitable for families – there's a small tranquil pool and falls. Joffre Falls Rd, 11km from the Kalamina turn, leads to stunning **Knox Gorge**, passing the lookout over the spectacular **Joffre Falls**. Knox Gorge has several nice swimming holes, fringed by native figs, while in **Joffre Gorge** the icy pools are perennially shaded.

Weano Rd junction is 32km from the visitor centre, and the **Eco Retreat** is nearby. The final 13km to the breathtaking **Oxers Lookout** can be rough, but it's worth it for the magnificent views of the junction of Red, Weano, Joffre and Hancock Gorges some 130m below.

A steep descent into **Hancock Gorge** (partly on ladders) will bring you first to the sunny **Amphitheatre**, then along the slippery **spider walk** to the sublime **Kermits Pool**. On the other side of the car park, a rough track winds down to the surreal **Handrail Pool** in the bowels of **Weano Gorge**. Swimming in these pools is a magical experience, but obey all signs and don't even think about entering a restricted area (see the boxed text, p193).

Hamersley Gorge GORGE WALKING

Away in Karijini's northwest corner, off Nanutarra-Wittenoom Rd, this makes a pleasant stopover if you're heading north to Karratha. Idyllic swimming holes and a waterfall lie only minutes from the car park.

Punurrunha WALKING, CLIMBING

Gorged out? Then go and get some altitude on WA's second-highest mountain (Mt Bruce; 1235m; 9km return trip), a superb

WORTH A TRIP

JOURNEY TO THE CENTRE OF THE EARTH *STEVE WATERS*

The instructor sits down in the water slide, gives me the thumbs up, pushes off, then disappears. I hear a splash echo from below. He's done this a thousand times. I've haven't done it once, and I'm next.

We're in the depths of Karijini's Knox Gorge. It's 35°C 'upstairs' in the park, but the water in the gorge is freezing, and while we're all in summer wetsuits, everybody's shivering, waiting their turn. The day started early when our guides, Dan and Pete, kitted us out with wetsuits, gorge slippers, harnesses, helmets and inner tubes. A short, sunny stroll down from Knox Lookout brought our small group to a pool ringed by native figs, where we practised paddling. A quick 'jump test' off a 2m rock to check we won't 'choke' at the first obstacle (the one I'm staring at), and we were off into the restricted zone, with the gorge shrinking rapidly to a single body width.

I sit down, give the thumbs up, and push off, and over the 4m drop into the plunge pool. An involuntary scream and I'm underwater. It's scary and exhilarating and I'd love to do it again, but once over the edge, there's no way back. Soon we're all down, and floating in the Styx-like water, and Dan sets up the 8m abseil into the next pool. Light falls in narrow shafts as sheer walls tower above us.

After abseiling we swim the pool, climb over a rock and through a crack, and then suddenly we're out of Knox and into the sun at the bottom of Red Gorge. We haul up onto a nearby 'beach', warm our bodies on the hot rocks, and eat some energy food.

Soon we're off again, this time for a sunny, relaxed paddle along the tranquil pools of Red Gorge. We pass the entrance to Weano Gorge, a 40m-high waterfall, on the way to our lunch spot at Junction Pool, 130m below Oxers Lookout. As we munch sandwiches, we watch a rock wallaby bounding about halfway up the vertical face, seemingly oblivious to the sheer drop only centimetres away.

Joffre Gorge leads off darkly to the south but we head into Hancock Gorge, and a tight, steep, slippery climb beside a cascade leading through The Centre of the Earth to Garden Pool. Sublime, and sobering, Regans Pool is next and as Pete lays in the rope for the steep, slippery climb above the pool, the rest of us float silently, lost in our thoughts (see boxed text, p193).

The climb is the last hurdle as we ascend steeply, doubly clipped into the anchor rope. A short traverse and we're back into the regular universe at Kermits Pool, and our final swim. The Spider Walk holds no challenge and soon we're through the sunny Amphitheatre and up the exit ladders to the car park. We've been out all day, and it's been one action-packed, adrenalin-charged adventure.

CHRISTMAS & COCOS (KEELING) ISLANDS

Christmas Island

POP 1600

Tropical Christmas Island (CI) may be an Australian territory, but its closest neighbour is Java, Indonesia, 360km to the north; Perth lies 2600km to the southeast. A rugged limestone mountain, CI was settled in 1888 to mine phosphate – still the main economic activity. Its people are a mix of Chinese, Malays and European-Australians, a blend reflected in the island's food, languages, customs and religions.

In spite of mining activity, 63% of the island remains protected by CI National Park. Tall rainforest covers the plateau, and a series of limestone cliffs and terraces attract endemic nesting sea birds, including the gorgeous golden bosun and rare Abbott's booby. A network of trails run through the park, and it's possible to camp at Dolly Beach with a permit from **Parks Australia** (☎9164 8755; www.environment.gov.au). CI is famous for the spectacular annual movement in November/December of millions of red land crabs marching from the forest down to the coast to breed, covering everything in sight. Marine life is also dramatic, with bright corals and fish on the fringing reefs attracting snorkellers in the dry season, and divers throughout the year. A sea swell can bring decent surf during the wet season (roughly December to March) and there's a surf shop on the island.

Christmas Island visitor centre (☎9164 8382; www.christmas.net.au) can coordinate accommodation, diving, fishing and car hire. Its excellent website has links for package tours, local businesses and detailed island information.

Accommodation includes backpackers, self-contained units, motel-style rooms or resort-style suites ranging from $50 to $395 per night. There are several restaurants serving Chinese, Malay and Mod Oz cuisine.

Christmas Island has achieved notoriety in recent years as a processing centre for asylum seekers arriving by boat from Indonesia, and as recently as December 2010 witnessed mass drownings after one of these boats broke up on the cliffs during a storm.

Cocos (Keeling) Islands

POP 650

Some 900km further west (2750km from Perth) are the Cocos (Keeling) Islands (CKI), a necklace of 27 low-lying islands around a blue lagoon that inspired Charles Darwin's theory of coral atoll formation. CKI was settled by John Clunies-Ross in 1826 and his family remained in control of the islands and their Malay workers until 1978, when CKI became part of Australia's Indian Ocean territories. Today about 550 Malays and 100 European-Australians live on Home and West Islands. It's a very low-key place in which to walk, snorkel, dive, fish, windsurf and relax. While most people come on a package, you can visit independently, and camping is allowed at Scout Park on West Island, and on Direction and South Islands. You will need to bring all your own gear. Check out the island-information website: www.cocos-tourism.cc which has a list of accommodation. Divers should visit www.cocosdive.com.

Getting There & Away

Virgin Blue (☎13 67 89; www.virginblue.com.au) flies from Perth to both islands, at least twice a week. Prices start at around $460 for either island, and from $200 between the two. There's also a return charter flight on Fridays from Kuala Lumpur to Christmas Island, which must be booked with **Island Explorer Holidays** (☎1300 884 855; www.islandexplorer.com.au). Australian visa requirements apply, and Australians should bring their passports.

ridge walk with fantastic views all the way to the summit. Start early, make sure you carry lots of water and allow five hours. The access road is located off Karijini Dr opposite the western end of Banyjima Dr.

Tours

The only way to appreciate fully the magical quality of Karijini's gorges is to take an accredited adventure tour through the restricted areas.

TOP CHOICE **West Oz Active Adventure Tours** ADVENTURE
(☎0438 913 713; www.westozactive.com.au; Karijini Eco Retreat; $225-245; ⌚Apr-Oct) Offers action-packed trips through gorges to Junction Pool below Oxers Lookout, and combines hiking, swimming, floating on inner tubes, climbing, sliding off waterfalls and abseiling. All equipment (including harness, lunch and wetsuit) is supplied and once into the restricted areas, you won't see another soul.

Lestok Tours BUS
(☎9188 1112; www.lestoktours.com.au; $145) Runs full-day bus outings to Karijini from Tom Price.

Sleeping & Eating

Dales Gorge camping CAMPGROUND $
(site per adult/child $7/2) Though somewhat dusty, the large DEC camping ground at Dales Gorge offers shady, spacious sites with nearby toilets and picnic tables. Forget tent pegs though, you'll be using rocks as anchors.

Karijini Eco Retreat RESORT $$$
(☎9425 5591; www.karijiniecoretreat.com.au; camp site $29, Eco Tent d high/low season $289/145) This 100% Indigenous-owned retreat is a model for sustainable tourism. Grill your own mains ($30) at the open bar and restaurant. Campers get hot showers and the same rocks as the DEC camping ground. Things are cheaper in summer when the retreat winds down and the restaurant (but not the bar!) closes.

Information

Visitor centre (☎9189 8121; Banyjima Dr; ⌚9am-4pm Apr-Oct, from 10am Nov-Mar) Indigenous-managed with excellent interpretive displays highlighting Banyjima culture and park wildlife, good maps and walks information, a public phone and really great air-con.

Getting There & Away

There's no public transport. The closest airports are the mining towns of Paraburdoo (101km southwest) and Newman (201km southeast).

Integrity coaches stop at Munjina (Auski) on Thursdays (northbound) and Fridays (southbound). Munjina is the best place to wait for a lift.

Port Hedland

POP 16,000

Port Hedland ain't the prettiest place. Ringed by railway yards, iron-ore stockpiles, salt mountains, furnaces and a massive deep-water port, the average tourist might instinctively floor the accelerator. Yet Hedland is not just another bland prefab Pilbara town. With a heritage spanning over 115 years it's been battered by cyclones, plundered by pearlers, bombed by the Japanese and hosted royalty.

Of course, iron ore has played a huge part in the town's current fortunes, and ore from the mines of Newman is exported from the docks at a greater tonnage than any other Australian port. Port Hedland is riding the resources boom and this pushes up prices and squeezes accommodation options, yet it's also sparked a renaissance.

There's a vibrancy around town as old pubs are renovated, the art and cafe scene (real coffee!) is expanding, fine dining is flourishing, cocktail and tapas bars are sprouting and cycle paths are spreading along the foreshore. Just don't mind the red dust.

Sights & Activities

Collect the excellent *Port Hedland Cultural & Heritage Sites* brochure from the visitor centre and take a self-guided tour around the CBD, or hire one of their bicycles and meander along the **Richardson St Bike Path** to a cold beer at the **Yacht Club** (Sutherland St).

Between November and February **flatback turtles** nest on nearby beaches. Check at the visitor centre for volunteer options (see also p186).

Courthouse Gallery ART GALLERY
(☎9173 1064; www.courthousegallery.com.au; 16 Edgar St; ⌚9am-4pm Mon-Fri, until 2pm Sat & Sun) Supports local contemporary and Indigenous art with frequent exhibitions.

Marapikurrinya Park PARK
Watch ridiculously large tankers from this park at the end of Wedge St – see the visitor centre for shipping times. After dark, from the park's **Finucane Lookout** you can stare into the eye of Sauron (actually BHP Billiton's Hot Briquetted Iron plant on Finucane Island).

Pretty Pool POOL
This is a popular fishing and picnicking spot (beware of stonefish), 7km east of the town centre. Nearby Goode St is handy to observe Port Hedland's **Staircase to the Moon** (see the boxed text, p205) from March to October.

Tours

BHP Billiton IRON ORE
(adult/child $26/20; ⌚9.30am Mon, Wed & Fri) The popular iron-ore plant tour departs from the visitor centre.

Sleeping & Eating

Like most mining towns, finding a room in Hedland isn't easy or cheap. If you haven't booked well ahead, the visitor centre may be able to help.

TOP CHOICE **Zephyrs** CAFE $
(☎0411 143 663; lunch $10-15, tapas $8-15; ⏱10am-5pm Tue-Thu, until late Fri & Sat, until 2pm Sun) Possibly the coolest cafe in the Pilbara, this 1930s American Silver Star railcar sits next to the Courthouse Gallery and serves excellent coffee, cakes and light lunches in the original observation lounge. Tapas are available Friday and Saturday evenings.

Cooke Point Caravan Park CARAVAN PARK $$
(☎9173 1271; www.aspenparks.com.au; cnr Athol & Taylor Sts; powered sites $50, d without bathroom $140, motel/unit d $220-280;) You might be able to snag a dusty van or tent site here, but the other options are usually full. There's a nice view over the mangroves near Pretty Pool and the amenities are well maintained.

Esplanade Hotel RESORT $$$
(☎9173 2783; www.theesplanadeporthedland.com.au; 2-4 Anderson St; d $360; @) Previously one of the roughest pubs in Port Hedland, the 'Nade is now an exclusive 4.5-star resort with fully clothed staff, sumptuous doubles, fine dining (mains $32 to $45) and sophisticated tapas cocktail nights held high in the Crows Nest turret.

Port Hedland Yacht Club LICENSED CLUB $
(☎9173 3398; Sutherland St; ⏱Thu-Sun) Locals loved the old tin 'Yachtie' for its cheap drinks, great Thai kitchen and water views. At the time of research a swish new replacement was being built next door, so expect prices to rise accordingly.

There are supermarkets, cafes and takeaways at both the **Boulevard** (cnr Wilson & McGregor Sts) and **South Hedland** (Throssell Rd) shopping centres.

Information

There are ATMs along Wedge St and in the **Boulevard shopping centre** (cnr Wilson & McGregor Sts). Internet is available at the visitor centre, the **library** (Dempster St) and the **Seafarers Centre** (cnr Wedge & Wilson Sts).

Hospital (☎9158 1666; Sutherland St)

Visitor centre (☎9173 1711; www.phvc.com.au; 13 Wedge St; ⏱9am-4pm Mon-Fri, 10am-2pm Sat; @) This very helpful centre hires bicycles ($24 per half-day), sells bus tickets and can arrange iron-ore plant tours, turtle monitoring (November to February) and tickets on the Pilbara mail run.

Getting There & Away

Virgin Blue and Qantas both fly to Perth daily, and Qantas also goes direct to Melbourne (Tuesday). Skywest offers handy Bali flights (Saturday and Sunday), plus Broome (Sunday) and Perth (Sunday). Airnorth flies to Broome (Tuesday and Friday) with a Darwin connection, and Karratha (Friday). Golden Eagle Airlines fly to Broome (Monday to Thursday) and on Tuesday to Newman on the Pilbara mail run. Strategic has weekly flights to Bali (Tuesday) and Brisbane (Wednesday).

Greyhound coaches run to Perth ($258, 26 hours, Tuesday, Thursday and Saturday) and Broome ($87, eight hours, Tuesday, Thursday and Saturday). Buses depart Perth (Monday, Wednesday and Friday) and Broome (Tuesday, Thursday and Saturday). Integrity departs Perth Wednesday using the quicker ($232, 22 hours) inland route via Newman, returning Friday. Both depart from the visitor centre and South Hedland's shopping centre.

Getting Around

The airport is 13km from town; **Airport Shuttle Service** (☎9173 4554; $22) meets every flight while **Hedland Taxis** (☎9172 1010) charges around $33. **Hedland Bus Lines** (☎9172 1394) runs limited weekday services between Port Hedland and Cooke Point (via the visitor centre) and on to South Hedland ($3.50). **McLaren Hire** (☎9140 2200; www.mclarenhire.com.au) offers a large range of rental 4WDs.

Broome & Around

Includes »

Best Places to Eat

- PumpHouse (p219)
- The Aarli (p208)
- Parry Creek Farm (p219)
- Jila Gallery (p214)
- Mornington Wilderness Camp (p215)

Best Places to Sleep

- Beaches of Broome (p206)
- Middle Lagoon (p212)
- Bali Hai Resort & Spa (p206)
- Home Valley Station (p215)
- Parry Creek Farm (p219)

Why Go?

Swashbuckling Broome, sandwiched between desert and sea like Rothko meeting Cezanne, and with a vibrancy of purpose, creativity and disdain for formality, conjures a world that's somehow intangible, yet deeply alluring. People flock here chasing a dream, yet they find a reality like nowhere else. And that's why it's so appealing. It's also home to one of Australia's most iconic attractions, the sublime Cable Beach.

Aboriginal culture runs deep across the region, from the distant Kimberley gorges where ancient Wandjina and Gwion Gwion stand vigil over sacred waterholes, to the welcoming communities of the Dampier Peninsula.

The Kimberley is Australia's last frontier, a wild land of remote, spectacular scenery spread over large distances with a severe climate, sparse population and minimal infrastructure. Unnoticed for many years, it's now the focus for increasing numbers of adventurers willing to explore its vast spinifex plains, towering waterfalls, deep gorges and refreshing pools.

When to Go

Broome

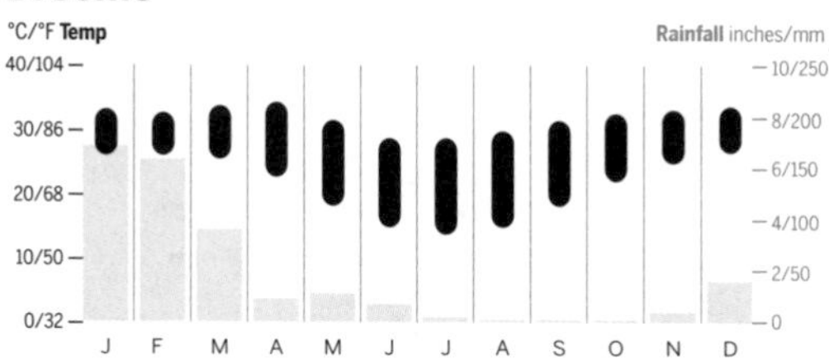

April The best time for a Kimberley flyover – Mitchell and King George Falls are booming!

May Enjoy Broome while it's still green before the masses arrive.

September & October As tourists leave, nature comes out – turtles and migrating birds.

Broome & Around Highlights

1. Take a camel ride at sunset along Broome's **Cable Beach** (p202)
2. Learn about traditional culture with Aboriginal communities on the pristine **Dampier Peninsula** (p211)
3. Tackle the notorious **Gibb River Road** in a 4WD adventure (p214)
4. Fly over the amazing waterfalls of **Mitchell** and **King George Falls** after the Wet (p216)
5. Ride the wild **Horizontal Waterfalls** (boxed text, p213)
6. Sit back with a cold drink and enjoy the **Staircase to the Moon** (boxed text, p206)
7. Canoe the mighty **Ord River** in a three-day self-guided epic (p218)
8. Immerse yourself in Indigenous art at **Aboriginal art cooperatives** (p210)
9. Cruise spectacular **Geikie Gorge** (p217)
10. Visit untouched **James Price Point** while you still can (p212)

0 100 km
0 60 miles

TIMOR SEA

Cape Londonderry
Cape Bougainville
Napier Broome Bay
Faraway Bay
Honeymoon Bay
4 King George Falls
KALUMBURU ABORIGINAL LAND
Cape Voltaire
Admiralty Gulf
Port Warrender
Kalumburu
Cape St Lambert
Walsh Point
Bigge Island
Joseph Bonaparte Gulf
King George River
Surveyor's Pool
Kimberley Coastal Camp
OOMBULGURRI ABORIGINAL LAND
ABORIGINAL LAND
Mitchell Plateau
Munurru
Drysdale River National Park
Cambridge Gulf
Mitchell Falls 4
Mitchell River National Park
Berkeley River
King Edward River
Kalumburu Rd
Carson River
Mitchell River
Mt Trafalgar (390m)
Prince Regent Nature Reserve
King Cascades
Prince Regent River
Cockburn Ranges
Wyndham
Parry Lagoons Nature Reserve
Ord River
Miner's Pool
Drysdale River
Drysdale River Station
Gibb River
Home Valley Station
Emma Gorge Resort
Mirima National Park
Kununurra
Ellenbrae Station
Emma Gorge
King River
Ord River 7
Argyle Homestead
Chamberlain Gorge
El Questro Wilderness Park
Zebedee Springs
The Kimberley
Synnot Range
Lake Argyle Tourist Village
Lake Argyle
Durack River
Chamberlain River
Mt Elizabeth Station
Barnett River Gorge
Mt Barnett Roadhouse & Manning River Gorge
Gibb River Rd
Durack Range
Argyle Diamond Mine
Galvans Gorge
Bell Gorge
Adcock Gorge
Wilson River
Lennard River Gorge
Hann River
Adcock River
Warmun (Turkey Creek)
Ord River
Iminitji Store
Bedford Downs
Mt Ord (937m)
ABORIGINAL LAND
Purnululu National Park
King Leopold Range
Fitzroy River
Mornington Wilderness Camp
NT
Lennard River
Tunnel Creek National Park
Ord River
Leopold River
Leopold Downs
Oscar Range
O'Donnell River
9 Geikie Gorge
Mueller Range
Elvire River
Halls Creek
Duncan Rd
Fitzroy Crossing
China Wall
Mt Amhurst
Old Halls Creek
Margaret River
Jubilee Downs
Palm Springs
Mimbi Caves
Sawpit Gorge
Ranges
Yiyilli
Kundat Djaru
Sturt Creek
Christmas Creek
Larrawa Station
Christmas Creek
Tanami Rd
Wolfe Creek Meteorite Crater
To Canning Stock Route; Billiluna (40km)

Getting There & Around

AIR

The following airlines service Broome and the Kimberley:

Airnorth (☎1800 627 474; www.airnorth.com.au)

Golden Eagle (☎9172 1777; www.goldeneagleairlines.com)

Qantas (☎13 13 13; www.qantas.com.au)

Skywest (☎1300 660 088; www.skywest.com.au)

Strategic (☎135 320; wwwflystrategic.com)

Virgin Blue (☎13 67 89; www.virginblue.com.au)

BUS

Greyhound (☎1300 473 946; www.greyhound.com.au) runs three times weekly Broome–Perth and daily Broome–Darwin.

BROOME REGION

Broome sits on the far western edge of the Kimberley, at the base of the pristine Dampier Peninsula, surrounded by the aquamarine waters of the Indian Ocean and the fractal-like creeks and mudflats of Roebuck Bay. It's a good 2000km from the closest capital city.

Port Hedland to Broome

The Big Empty stretches from Port Hedland to Broome, as the highway skirts the edge of the Great Sandy Desert. It's 609km of willie-willies and dust and not much else. There are only two roadhouses, Pardoo (148km) and Sandfire (288km), so keep the tank full. The coast, wild and unspoilt, is never far away.

Sleeping

The following places are all packed from May to September.

Eighty Mile Beach Caravan Park CARAVAN PARK $

(☎9176 5941; www.eightymilebeach.com.au; unpowered/powered sites $30/34, dongas s/d $45/55, cabin $170) Around 250km from Port Hedland, this shady, laid-back park backs onto a beautiful white-sand beach with great fishing, and nesting turtles (November to March).

Port Smith Caravan Park CARAVAN PARK $

(☎9192 4983; www.portsmithcaravanpark.com.au; unpowered/powered sites $24/30, dongas s/d $60/70, cabin $165) There's loads of wildlife at this park on a tidal lagoon, 487km from Port Hedland.

Barn Hill Station STATION $

(☎9192 4975; www.barnhill.com.au; unpowered $20, powered sites $24-28, cabins d $75) Barn Hill, 490km from Port Hedland, is a working cattle station with its own 'mini-pinnacles'.

Broome

POP 16,000

Occupying the narrow spit of red pindan separating the mangroves of Roebuck Bay from the aquamarine Indian Ocean, Broome has always relied on nature for its fortunes. Its early days as a pearling centre saw Japanese, Chinese and Malays joining local Aboriginals in open-water diving, where many drowned, caught the bends or were taken by sharks. Broome's cemeteries are a silent remember of this harsher time. Today, Broome still exports pearls around the world, produced on modern sea farms.

Tourists flock here during the Dry (April to October), with romantic notions of camels, beaches and sunsets. Magnificent sure, but there's a lot more to Broome than Cable Beach and tourists are sometimes surprised when they scratch the surface and find red pindan just below.

Broome's centre is Chinatown, on the shores of Roebuck Bay, while Cable Beach and its resorts are 6km west on the Indian Ocean. The airport stretches between the two. The port and Gantheaume Point are 7km south.

The Dry's a great time to find casual work, in hospitality or out on the pearl farms. In the Wet, it feels like you're inside a warm moist glove, and while many places close, others offer amazingly good deals as prices plummet.

Each evening, the whole town pauses, collective drinks in mid-air, while the sun melts back into the sea.

Sights & Activities

CABLE BEACH AREA

Cable Beach BEACH

(Map p203) Cable Beach, 6km west of Broome, is one of Australia's most iconic beaches, with turquoise waters and beautiful, white sand curving away to the sunset. Clothing is optional north of the rocks, while south, walking trails lead through the red dunes of **Minyirr Park**, a spiritual place for the Rubibi people. The visitor centre

Broome

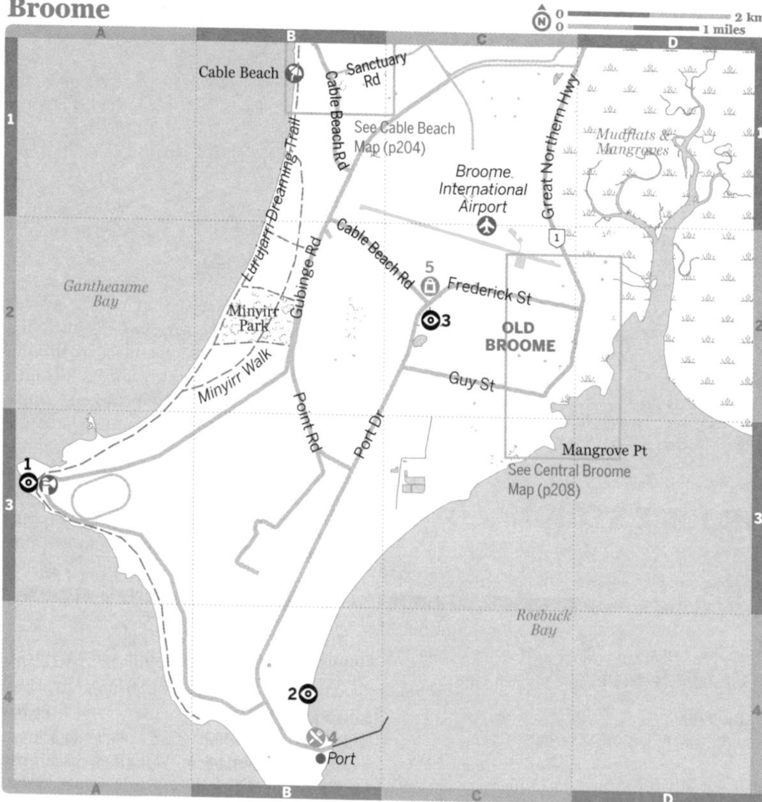

has a map, or go with an **Indigenous guide** (☎9194 0150). Cable Beach is synonymous with camels, and an evening ride along the sand is a highlight for many visitors.

Gantheaume Point LANDMARK
(Map p203) In the dying sun, red eroded cliffs turn scarlet at this peaceful lookout 7km south of Broome. Nearby lies one of the world's most varied collections of **dinosaur footprints**, thought to be 135 million years old, and difficult to find except at very low tides.

Malcolm Douglas Crocodile Park ZOO
(Map p204; ☎9192 1489; www.malcolmdouglas.com.au;.cnr Cable Beach & Sanctuary Rd; adult/child/family $30/25/70; ⏱10am-5pm Mon-Fri, from 2pm Sat & Sun) Australia's original crocodile hunter matured into a passionate conservationist. Visit during **feeding time** (Dry/Wet 3/4pm). See also the Malcolm Douglas Wilderness Wildlife Park outside Broome (p211).

Broome

Sights

1 Gantheaume Point & Dinosaur Prints A3
2 Hovercraft Tours B4
3 Japanese, Chinese & Muslim Cemeteries C2

Eating

4 Wharf Restaurant B4

Shopping

5 Kimberley Camping & Outback Supplies C2

Lurujarri Dreaming Trail INDIGENOUS TOUR
(Map p203; ☎9192 2959; www.environskimberley.org.au/lurujarri/lht_home.htm) This 50km trail follows the coast north from Gantheaume Pt to Minari. The Goolarabooloo-Millibinyarri Indigenous Corporation runs several guided

Cable Beach

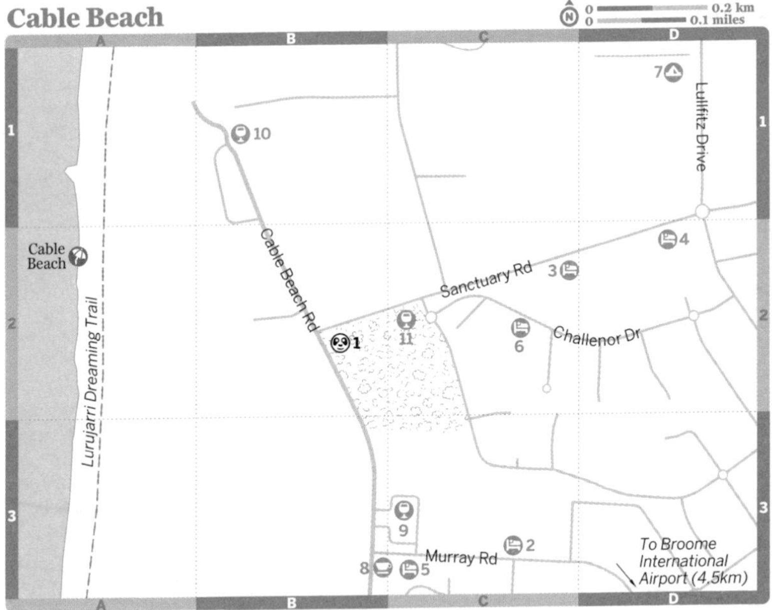

Cable Beach

Sights

1 Malcolm Douglas Crocodile Park........B2

Sleeping

2 Bali Hai Resort & Spa........C3
3 Beaches of Broome........C2
4 Cable Beach Backpackers........D2
5 Palm Grove Holiday Resort........C3
6 Seashells Resort........C2
7 Tarangau Caravan Park........D1

Eating

8 Cable Beach General Store........B3

Drinking

9 Diver's Tavern........C3
10 Sunset Bar & Grill........B1
11 ZeeBar........C2

trips lasting one to two weeks, between May and June each year, staying at traditional camp sites.

CHINATOWN AREA

Chinatown LANDMARK
(Map p207) Few Chinese remain in Broome's historical and commercial heart, though tin shanties are still visible lining Carnarvon St, Short St, Dampier Tce and Napier Tce.

Sun Pictures CINEMA
(Map p207; ☎9192 3738; www.sunpictures.com.au; 27 Carnarvon St; adult/child/family $16.50/11.50/55) Slink back in a canvas deckchair in the world's oldest operating picture gardens and enjoy the latest movies. The history of the Sun building is the history of Broome itself – don't miss the informative **History Tours** ($5; ⏰10.30am & 1pm Mon-Fri).

Pearl Luggers HISTORIC BOATS
(Map p207; ☎9192 2059; www.pearlluggers.com.au; 31 Dampier Tce; admission free, 1hr tour adult/child/family $20/10/50) Offers guided tours covering Broome's tragic pearling past. It's free to look over the boats.

Broome Museum MUSEUM
(Map p207; ☎9192 2075; www.broomemuseum.org.au; 67 Robinson St (enter Saville St); adult/child $5/1; ⏰10am-4pm Mon-Fri, until 1pm Sat & Sun, until 1pm Wet) Has interesting exhibits documenting the town's pearling history and Japanese bombing during WWII.

Cemeteries HISTORICAL
A number of cemeteries testify to the multicultural makeup of Broome society, the most striking being the **Japanese Cemetery** (Map p203) on Frederick St with 919

graves (mostly pearl divers) while **Chinese and Muslim cemeteries** are nearby. There's a small **pioneer cemetery** (Map p207) by Town Beach, overlooking the bay.

Town Beach BEACH
(Map p207) Tiny Town Beach is fine for a dip, just ensure it's not stinger season.

Port BEACH
(Map p203) Has a pleasant sandy beach and good fishing from the jetty. You might even see whales, turtles or dolphins.

Tours

Camels

It's a feisty business but at last count there were three camel-tour operators running at Cable Beach offering similar trips.

Broome Camel Safaris CAMELS
(☎0419 916 101; www.broomecamelsafaris.com.au; 30min afternoon ride $25, 1hr sunset ride adult/child $60/40) Alison, the only female camel-tour operator in Broome, offers afternoon and evening trips.

Red Sun Camels CAMELS
(☎1800 18 44 88; www.redsuncamels.com.au; 40min morning ride adult/child $30/20, 1hr sunset ride $50/35) Red Sun runs both morning and sunset tours, with a shorter trip at 4pm (30 minutes $20).

Ships of the Desert CAMELS
(☎0419 954 022; www.shipsofthedesert.com.au; 40min morning ride adult/child $25/20, 1hr sunset ride $50/30) The original camel tour company offers morning and sunset trips, and a shorter afternoon option (30 minutes $25).

Not-Camels

Broome Trike Tours HARLEYS
(☎0407 575 237; www.broometriketours.com.au; town/tasting tours $90/165) Bush tucker, Harleys and mango wine – only in Broome.

Kujurta Buru INDIGENOUS CULTURE
(☎9192 1662; www.kujurtaburu.com.au; adult/child half-day $77/39) Nagula half-day tours explore Yawuru culture and country, including spear throwing and bush tucker tasting.

Broome Adventure Company KAYAKING
(☎1300 665 888; www.broomeadventure.com.au; 3/4hr kayak tour $70/90) These eco-certified coastal kayaking trips running all year include pick-up from your accommodation.

Astro Tours ASTRONOMY
(☎0417 949 958; www.astrotours.net; adult/child $75/45) Fascinating after-dark two-hour stargazing tours, held just outside Broome. Price includes taxi transfers, or self-drive and save $10.

Hovercraft Tours HOVERCRAFT
(☎9193 5025; www.broomehovercraft.com.au; 1hr tour adult/child $105/75, sunset/flying boat tours $150/95) Skim over tidal flats to visit historical sights, including, on very low tides, the wrecks of flying boats sunk during WWII.

Willie Pearl Lugger Cruises BOAT CRUISE
(☎0428 919 781; www.williecruises.com.au; adult/child $120/60) Sunset sailing cruises on a traditional pearl lugger may spot whales, dolphins and turtles (July to September).

Broome Sightseeing Tours CITY
(☎9192 0000; www.broomesightseeingtours.com.au; adult/child $50/25) These two-hour tours cram in all the main sights and include a free beer tasting at Matso's Brewery. An extra $13 buys you the one-hour **Pearl Luggers** tour immediately afterwards.

Festivals & Events

Dates (and festivals!) vary from year to year. Check with the visitor centre or the community website (www.broome.wa.au).

Staircase to the Moon MOON
(⏲Mar-Oct) Three magical nights each month at full moon.

STAIRCASE TO THE MOON

The reflections of a rising full moon, rippling over low-tide exposed mudflats, create the optical illusion of a golden stairway leading to the moon. Between March and October, full moons see Broome buzzing with everyone eager to see the spectacle. At Town Beach there's a lively evening market with food stalls and people bring their foldup chairs, although the small headland at the end of Hamersley St has a better view. While Roebuck Bay parties like nowhere else, this phenomenon happens across the Kimberley and Pilbara coasts, in fact, anywhere with some east-facing mudflats. Other good viewing spots are One Arm Point at Cape Leveque, Cooke Point in Port Hedland, Sunrise Beach at Onslow, Hearson Cove near Dampier and the lookout at Cossack. Most visitor centres publish the dates on their websites.

Gimme Fest INDIGENOUS MUSIC
(www.goolarri.com; May) Showcasing the best of Indigenous music.

Kullari NAIDOC Week INDIGENOUS CULTURE
(www.goolarri.com; late Jun–mid-Jul) Celebration of Aboriginal and Torres Strait Islander culture.

Environs Annual Art Auction ART
(www.environskimberley.org.au; Jul) Annual environment fundraiser auctioning work by local and Indigenous Kimberley artists.

Broome Race Round HORSE RACING
(www.broometurfclub.com.au; Jul/Aug) Kimberley Cup, Ladies Day and Broome Cup are when locals and tourists frock up.

Opera Under the Stars OPERA
(www.operaunderthestars.com.au; Aug) One night only at the Cable Beach Amphitheatre.

Worn Art FASHION
(www.theatrekimberley.org.au; Aug) A fabulous spectacle of fashion, performance, music and dance.

Shinju Matsuri Festival of the Pearl PEARL
(www.shinjumatsuri.com.au; Aug/Sep) Broome's homage to the pearl includes seven to 10 days of parades, food, concerts, fireworks and dragon boat races.

Mango Festival MANGO
(Nov) A celebration of the fruit in all its forms.

Sleeping

Accommodation is plentiful, but either book ahead or be flexible. Prices plummet in the Wet.

TOP CHOICE **Beaches of Broome** HOSTEL $$
(Map p204; ☎1300 881 031; www.beachesofbroome.com.au; 4 Sanctuary Rd, Cable Beach; dm $32-45, motel d $140-180; ❄@📶🏊) Broome's newest budget accommodation is more resort than hostel. Shady common areas, a poolside bar and a modern self-catering kitchen complement spotless, air-conditioned rooms. Dorms come in a variety of sizes, and the motel rooms are beautifully appointed. Scooter hire available.

Bali Hai Resort & Spa SPA RESORT $$$
(Map p204; ☎9191 3100; www.balihairesort.com; 6 Murray Rd, Cable Beach; d $368-498; ❄📶🏊) Lush and tranquil, this beautiful small resort has gorgeously decorated studios, each with individual outside dining areas and open-roofed bathrooms. The emphasis is on relaxation, and the on-site spa offers a range of exotic therapies to achieve it – try the 120-minute 'Passion of the Pearl'. The off-season prices are a bargain.

Tarangau Caravan Park CARAVAN PARK $
(Map p204; ☎9193 5084; www.tarangaucaravanpark.com; 16 Millington Rd; unpowered/powered sites $30/36) A quiet alternative to often noisy Cable Beach caravan parks, Tarangau is a laid-back spot with pleasant grassy sites 1km from the beach.

Kimberley Klub HOSTEL $
(Map p207; ☎9192 3233; www.kimberleyklub.com; 62 Frederick St; dm $26-31, d/apt $125/160; ❄@📶🏊) This big, laid-back tropical backpackers is a great place to meet other travellers. Features include poolside bar, games room, massive kitchen, an excellent noticeboard and organised activities most nights.

Palm Grove Holiday Resort RESORT $$
(Map p204; ☎9192 3336; www.palmgrove.com.au; cnr Cable Beach & Murray Rds; unpowered/powered sites $34/41, studio d $180, 2-bed units $195; ❄@🏊) Right behind Cable Beach, this park offers a good mix of comfy air-con cabins and shady powered camp sites. There's a great camp kitchen and lovely swimming pool, but the unpowered sites cop full sun.

Eco Beach LUXURY WILDERNESS $$$
(☎9193 8015; www.ecobeach.com.au; Thangoo Station, Great Northern Hwy; safari tent/villa d from $225/345; ❄🏊) This award-winning luxury ecoresort is set on secluded coastline 120km southwest of Broome. There's a choice of safari tents or villas, a top-notch restaurant and a host of tours and activities. They also support WWOOFers (Willing Workers on Organic Farms) and a seasonal turtle-monitoring program in partnership with **Conservation Volunteers Australia** (www.conservationvolunteers.com.au; 6 days from $1000; ⏱Nov-Jan). From Broome, you can reach the resort by catamaran ($60), shuttle bus ($30), helicopter ($270) or your own vehicle.

Seashells Resort APARTMENTS $$$
(Map p204; ☎1800 800 850; www.seashells.com.au; 4 Challenor Dr; 1-/2-/3-bedroom apt $295/360/425; ❄📶🏊) A short walk to Cable Beach, these spacious apartments, all with verandahs and fully equipped kitchens offer great value for groups. The largest holds six, and there's pleasant landscaped gardens, barbecues and pool.

Roebuck Bay Caravan Park CARAVAN PARK $
(Map p207; ☎9192 1366; 91 Walcott St; unpowered/powered sites d $28/35, on-site vans d $90)

Right next to Town Beach, this shady park has good facilities, including a communal kitchen and barbecue area.

Cable Beach Backpackers HOSTEL $
(Map p204; ☎1800 655 011; www.cablebeachbackpackers.com; 12 Sanctuary Rd; dm $24-29, d $75;) Within splashing distance of Cable Beach, this relaxed place has a lush tropical courtyard, swimming pool, big communal kitchen and bar.

Eating

Be prepared for 'Broome Prices' (exorbitant), 'Broome Time' (when it should be open but it's closed) and surcharges: credit cards, public holidays, weekends. Service can fluctuate wildly as most staff are just passing through. Most places close in the Wet. Businesses need to make enough during the Dry to survive the Wet, when most places close or keep shorter hours.

The back lanes of Chinatown, especially around **Johnny Chi Lane**, have cheap weekday lunch options. All pubs and resorts have in-house restaurants, and some, like JC's Kitchen at the Roey (see p209) are great value, while at others, you're simply paying for the view.

Self-caterers can enjoy well-stocked supermarkets and bakeries at Paspaley and Boulevard Shopping Centres.

TOP CHOICE **The Aarli** TAPAS $$
(Map p207; ☎9192 5529; 2/6 Hamersley St, cnr Frederick; tapas & mains $11-20, pizzas $18-20; ⊙8am-late daily Dry;) Meaning 'fish' in Bardi, the Aarli is cooking up some of the most inventive and tasty titbits in Broome. The Med-Asian fusion tapas are excellent with a cold beer or chilled wine, and the pizzas are simple and scrumptious, but, really, you want to share the signature baked whole fish ($45), because it is superb.

Azuki JAPANESE $$
(Map p207; ☎9193 7211; 1/15 Napier Tce; sushi $8-10, mains $15-34; ⊙lunch & dinner Mon-Fri, dinner Sat Dry;) Enjoy the exquisite subtlety of authentic Japanese cuisine at this tiny BYO – from the takeaway thick, fresh sushi rolls to wonderfully tasty bento boxes.

Wharf Restaurant SEAFOOD $$$
(Map p203; ☎9192 5800; Port of Pearls House, Port Dr; mains $20-40; ⊙10am-10pm) Settle back for a long, lazy seafood lunch with waterside ambience and the chance of a whale sighting. OK, it's pricey and the service can be hit or miss, but the wine's cold and the chilli blue swimmer crab is sensational. Just wait until after 2pm before ordering oysters.

noodlefish ASIAN FUSION $$
(Map p207; ☎9192 1697; 6 Hamersley St, cnr Frederick St; mains $25-33; ⊙6-9pm Tue-Sat) This quirky alfresco BYO is doing fantastic contemporary Asian dishes using classic Kimberley ingredients. While the accent is on seafood, there's plenty to please all palates. Get there early, because you can't book and they'll only take cash.

Cable Beach General Store CAFE $
(Map p204; ☎9192 5572; cnr Cable Beach & Murray Rds; ⊙6.30am-7.30pm daily; @) Cable Beach unplugged – a typical Aussie corner shop with coffee, pancakes, barra burgers, pies and internet, and no hidden charges. You can even play a round of **mini-golf** (adult/child/family $6/5/20).

Town Beach Cafe CAFE $$
(Map p207; ☎9193 5585; Robinson St; breakfast $10-17, lunch $16-24; ⊙7.30am-2pm Tue-Sun, dinner Fri & Sat) With a great view over Roebuck Bay, the alfresco tables of the Town are an ideal spot for an early brekkie. The caramelised banana pancakes are divine.

Yuen Wing ASIAN GROCERY $
(Map p207; 19 Carnarvon St) Your best bet for spices, noodles and all things Asian.

Drinking & Entertainment

Check the gig guide on www.broome.wa.au.

Tides Garden Bar RESORT
(Map p207; ☎9192 1303; www.mangrovehotel.com.au; 47 Carnarvon St) The Mangrove Resort's casual outdoor bar is just the place for a few early evening beverages while contemplating Roebuck Bay. There's good bistro meals, half-price oysters between 5.30pm and 6.30pm, and live music towards the end of the week, including touring big names. You don't need to move to watch the Staircase to the Moon.

Sunset Bar & Grill RESORT
(Map p204; ☎9192 0470; Cable Beach Club Resort, Cable Beach Rd) Arrive around 4.45pm, grab a front-row seat, order a drink and watch the show – backpackers, package tourists, locals, camels and a blistering Indian Ocean sunset tinged by imported coconut palms.

Roebuck Bay Hotel PUB
(Map p207; ☎9192 1221; www.roebuckbayhotel.com.au; 45 Dampier Tce; ⊙noon-late) The 'Roey'

Central Broome

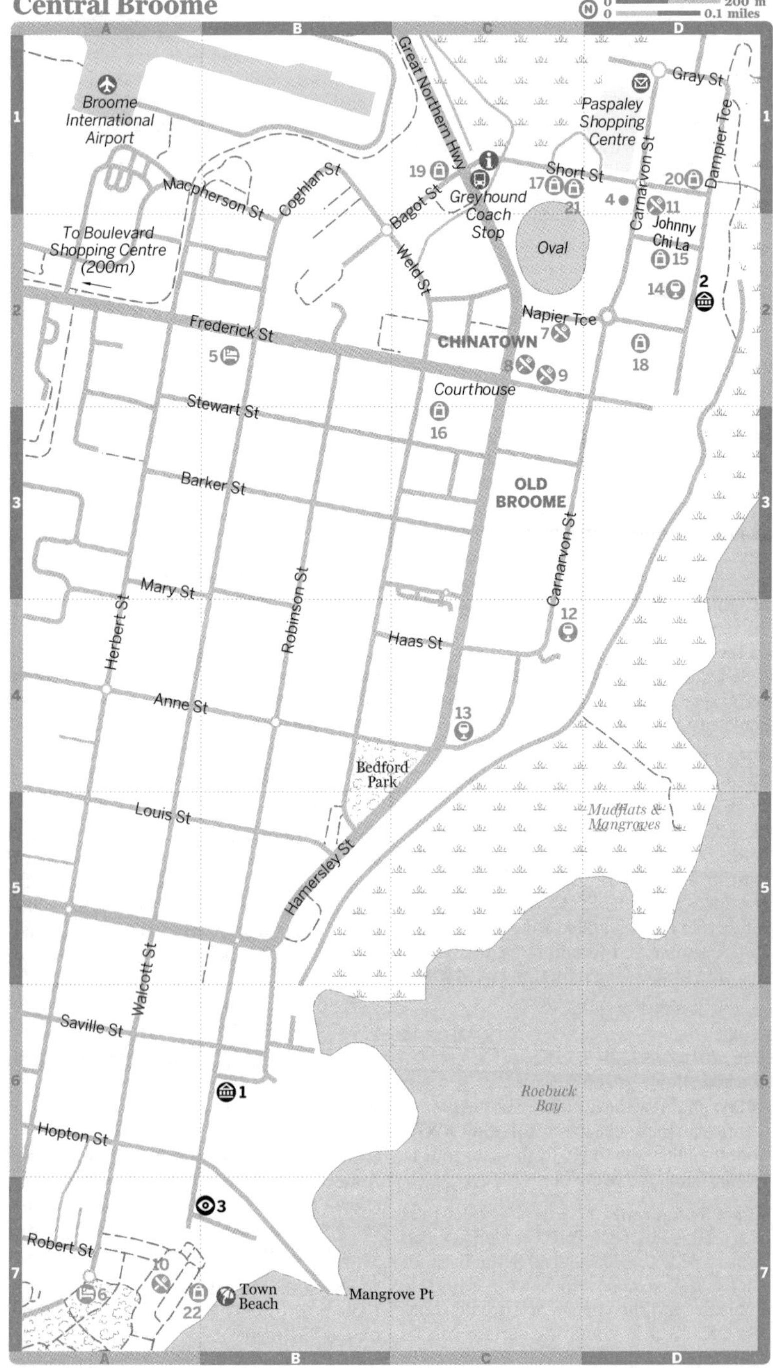

Central Broome

Sights
1 Broome Museum ... B6
2 Pearl Luggers ... D2
3 Pioneer Cemetery ... B7

Activities, Courses & Tours
4 Sun Pictures ... D1

Sleeping
5 Kimberley Klub ... B2
6 Roebuck Bay Caravan Park ... A7

Eating
7 Azuki ... C2
8 noodlefish ... C2
9 The Aarli ... C2
10 Town Beach Cafe ... A7
11 Yuen Wing ... D1

Drinking
12 Tides Garden Bar ... C4
13 Matso's Broome Brewery ... C4
14 Roebuck Bay Hotel ... D2

Shopping
15 Broome Beads and Fine Jewellery ... D2
16 Courthouse Markets ... C3
17 Gecko Gallery ... C1
18 Kimberley Bookshop ... D2
19 Magabala Books ... C1
20 Paspaley Pearls ... D1
21 Short St Gallery ... C1
22 Town Beach Markets ... A7

is a Broome institution with different bars offering sports, live music, DJs and cocktails until the wee hours of the morning. It also does a range of accommodation and has a great kitchen.

Matso's Broome Brewery PUB
(Map p207; ☎9193 5811; 60 Hamersley St; ⏰music 3-6pm Sun) Get a Smokey Bishop into you at this casual backpackers pub and kick back to live music on the verandah. Bring something for the sandflies.

Diver's Tavern LIVE MUSIC
(Map p204; ☎9193 6066; Cable Beach Rd) Don't miss the popular Wednesday jams and Sunday Session.

ZeeBar COCKTAIL BAR
(Map p204; ☎9193 6511; www.zeebar.com.au; 4 Sanctuary Rd; ⏰6pm-late) This stylish bar and bistro near Cable Beach mixes up tasty cocktails, great tapas and DJs. Tuesday is trivia night.

Shopping

The galleries and jewellers on Short St and Dampier Tce are full of extraordinary Indigenous art from the Kimberley and milky treasures from the deep.

Gecko Gallery INDIGENOUS ART
(Map p207; ☎9192 8909; www.geckogallery.com.au; 9 Short St; ⏰10am-6pm Mon-Fri, 10am-2pm Sat & Sun, shorter hours during the Wet) The ever-helpful Belinda Cornish specialises in East Kimberley and Western Desert art, including canvasses, prints and etchings.

Short St Gallery INDIGENOUS ART
(Map p207; ☎9192 2658; www.shortstgallery.com.au; 7 Short St; ⏰10am-5pm Mon-Fri, 10am-2pm Sat) Regular exhibitions highlight Indigenous art from across the country.

Paspaley Pearls PEARLS
(Map p207; ☎9192 2203; www.paspaleypearls.com; 2 Short St) Started Australia's first cultured pearl farm 420km north of Broome at Kuri Bay in the 1950s.

Broome Beads and Fine Jewellery BEADS
(Map p207; ☎9192 5223; www.broomebeads.com.au; 4 Johnny Chi Lane) Haven't found any jewellery you like? Then make your own with beads from here.

Kimberley Camping & Outback Supplies OUTDOOR GEAR
(Map p203; ☎9193 5909; www.kimberleycamping.com.au; cnr Frederick St & Cable Beach Rd) Camp ovens, jaffle irons and everything else you need for a successful expedition.

Kimberley Bookshop BOOKSTORE
(☎9192 1944; 4 Napier Tce; ⏰9am-5pm Mon-Fri, 9am-2pm Sat) Stocks an extensive range of books on Broome and the Kimberley.

Magabala Books BOOKSTORE
(☎9192 1991; www.magabala.com; 1 Bagot St; ⏰9am-4.30pm Mon-Fri) Indigenous publishers with selection of novels, social history, biographies and children's literature.

Courthouse Markets MARKET
(Map p207; Hamersley St; ⏰mornings Sat, additional Sun Apr-Oct) Get your local arts, crafts and general hippy gear here.

KIMBERLEY ART COOPERATIVES

The art of the Kimberley is like no other Indigenous art in Australia. Encompassing the powerful and strongly guarded Wandjina, the prolific and puzzling Gwion Gwion (Bradshaw) images, bright tropical coastal colours, subtle and sombre ochres of the bush and the abundance when desert meets river, every work sings a story about country.

To experience it firsthand, visit some of these Aboriginal-owned cooperatives; most are accessible by 2WD:

Mowanjum Art & Culture Centre (☎9191 1008; www.mowanjumarts.com; Gibb River Rd, Derby; ⏲9am-5pm daily, closed Sat & Sun Wet) Just 4km along the Gibb River Rd, is this impressive new building and gallery representing artists renowned for their Wandjina and Gwion Gwion images.

Waringarri Aboriginal Arts Centre (☎9168 2212; www.waringarriarts.com.au; 16 Speargrass Rd, Kununurra; ⏲8.30am-4.30pm Mon-Fri) This excellent gallery-cum-studio hosts local artists working with ochres in a unique abstract style. They also represent artists from Kalumburu.

Warmun Arts (☎9168 7496; www.warmunart.com; Great Northern Hwy, Warmun; ⏲9am-4.30pm Mon-Fri) Between Kununurra and Halls Creek, Warmun artists use ochres to explore Gija identity. Phone first for a verbal permit, or visit the Halls Creek visitor centre.

Laarri Gallery (☎9191 7195; yiyilischool@activ8.net.au; Yiyili; ⏲8am-4pm school days) This tiny not-for-profit gallery in the back of the community school has interesting contemporary-style art detailing local history. It's 120km west of Halls Creek and 5km from the Great Northern Hwy. Phone ahead.

Yaruman Artists Centre (☎9168 8208; Kundat Djaru) Sitting on the edge of the Tanami, 162km from Halls Creek, Yaruman's acrylic works feature the many local soaks (waterholes). The weekly mail run from Kununurra stops here (Ringer Soak).

Warlayirti Artists Centre (☎9168 8960; www.balgoart.org.au; Balgo; ⏲9am-5pm) This centre 255km down the Tanami Track is a conduit for artists around the area and features bright acrylic dot-style as well as lithographs and glass. Phone first to arrange an entry permit.

ℹ Information

There are ATMs on Carnarvon, Hamersley and Short Sts, and Napier Tce.

For noticeboards to buy, sell, and search for lifts try the hostels, **Fongs** (29 Saville St) and **Yuen Wing** (19 Carnarvon St).

Internet Access

Broome Community Resource Centre (☎9193 7153; 40 Dampier Tce; per hr $5; ⏲9am-5pm Mon-Fri, until noon Sat; @) Professional internet with cheap printing, laptops are OK.

Cable Beach General Store (☎9192 5572; cnr Cable Beach Rd & Murray Rd; internet per hr $6; ⏲6.30am-7.30pm daily; @)

Galactica DMZ Internet Café (☎9192 5897; 4/2 Hamersley St; per hr $5; ⏲10am-8pm; @) Many terminals, skype, webcams, CD/DVD burning, gaming, laptops are OK. Upstairs behind McDonald's.

Internet Resources

Broome Community Website (www.broome.wa.au) Gig guide/what's on.

Events in the Kimberley (www.eventsinthekimberley.com.au)

Kimberley Tourism Association (www.kimberleytourism.com)

Post

Post office (Map p207; Paspaley shopping centre)

Medical & Emergency Services

Broome District Hospital (☎9192 9222; 28 Robinson St; ⏲24hr)

Permits

Department of Indigenous Affairs (DIA; ☎1300 651 077; www.dia.wa.gov.au) Apply online for free permits to visit Aboriginal communities. Three-day processing time.

Tourist Information

Broome Visitor Centre (Map p207; ☎1800 883 777; www.broomevisitorcentre.com.au; Male Oval, Hamersley St; ⏲8.30am-5pm Mon-Fri, until 4pm Sat & Sun, shorter hours Dec-Mar) On the roundabout entering town, with great info, road conditions, Staircase to the Moon and tide times. It can book transport, accommodation and tours, both local and to the Dampier Peninsula.

Travel Agencies

Travelworld (☎9193 7233; Boulevard Shopping Centre) Has helpful, professional staff who can organise most flights.

 Getting There & Away

Virgin Blue and Qantas fly daily to Perth and Qantas also has a direct Sunday flight to/from Melbourne. Airnorth flies daily to Darwin (except Saturday) and Kununurra, and Tuesday/Friday to Karratha and Port Hedland. Skywest flies daily to Perth, and to Darwin and Exmouth during April to October. It also has a handy weekly connection to Bali (via Port Hedland). Golden Eagle flies to Fitzroy Crossing, Halls Creek and Port Hedland four times weekly.

Greyhound buses leave the visitor centre daily for Darwin, and Tuesday, Thursday and Saturday for Perth.

 Getting Around

Town Bus Service (☎9193 6585; www.broomebus.com.au; adult/child $3.50/1.50, day pass $10) links Chinatown with Cable Beach every hour (7.10am to 6.23pm year-round), plus half-hourly (8.40am to 6.40pm) from May to mid-October. Under 16s ride free with an adult; timetables from the visitor centre.

All major rental car companies are represented though no one offers unlimited kilometres. Local operator **Broome Broome** (☎9192 2210; www.broomebroome.com.au) offers cars (from $63 per day), 4WD ($153) and scooters ($35). **Britz** (☎9192 2647; www.britz.com; 10 Livingston St) hires campervans and 4WD Toyota Land Cruisers (from $176 per day) – essential for Gibb River Rd.

Broome Cycles (☎Chinatown 9192 1871, Cable Beach 0409 192 289; www.broomecycles.com.au; $50 deposit) rents bicycles for $24/84 per day/week. For taxis phone **Broome Taxis** (☎9192 1133) or **Chinatown Taxis** (☎1800 811 772).

Around Broome

Malcolm Douglas Wilderness Wildlife Park — ZOO

(☎9193 6580; www.malcolmdouglas.com.au; Great Northern Hwy; adult/child/family $35/20/90; ⏲10am-5pm Apr-Nov, from 2pm Sat & Sun) Visitors enter through the jaws of a giant crocodile to this 30-hectare wildlife park, established by Malcolm Douglas as an animal refuge 16km northeast of Broome. The park is home to dozens of crocs (feedings 3pm), as well as kangaroos, cassowaries, emus, dingos, jabirus and numerous birds.

Broome Bird Observatory — NATURE RESERVE

(☎9193 5600; www.broomebirdobservatory.com; Crab Creek Rd; admission by donation; camp sites per person $14, dongas s/d $50/75, chalet $160; ⏲8am-5pm) On Roebuck Bay, 25km from Broome, this amazing bird observatory is a vital staging post for hundreds of migratory species, some travelling over 12,000km. Tours range from an excellent two-hour walk ($75) to a five-day all-inclusive course ($1090). Self-guided trails, accommodation, and binoculars are available. The dirt access road can close during the Wet.

Dampier Peninsula

The red pindan of the Dampier Peninsula ends abruptly above deserted beaches or mangrove bays, while turquoise waters lap, and sunsets turn ancient cliffs to molten crimson. This is country; home to Indigenous settlements of the Ngumbarl, Jabirr Jabirr, Nyul Nyul, Nimanburu, Bardi, Jawi and Goolarabooloo peoples.

Access is by 4WD, along the largely unsealed 215km-long Cape Leveque Rd. Visiting Aboriginal communities requires both a DIA permit and one from the community, payable at the office on arrival. Communities can close suddenly, so always book ahead from the Broome Visitor Centre and grab the booklet *Ardi – Dampier Peninsula Travellers Guide* (www.ardi.com.au) for $3. You should be self-sufficient, though limited supplies are available.

On Cape Leveque Rd, turn left after 14km onto Manari Rd, and head north along the spectacular coast. There are **bush camping sites** (no facilities) at Barred Creek, Quandong Point, James Price Point and Coulomb Point, where there is a **nature reserve**. Conventional vehicles should make it to **James Price Point**, whose pristine future is threatened by plans to construct a huge LNG facility there. The Goolarabooloo and Jabirr Jabirr peoples are protesting the decision. At the time of research, the outcome was unclear.

Back on Cape Leveque Rd, it's 110km to **Beagle Bay** (☎9192 4913), notable for the extraordinarily beautiful mother-of-pearl altar at Beagle Bay church, built by Pallottine monks in 1918. There's no accommodation, but fuel is available (weekdays only). Contact the office on arrival.

TOP CHOICE **Middle Lagoon** (☎9192 4002; www.middlelagoon.com.au; unpowered/powered sites per person $15/20, beach shelter d $50, cabins d $150-250), 180km from Broome and surrounded by empty beaches, is superb for swimming, snorkelling, fishing and doing nothing. There's plenty of shade and birdlife, and the cabins are great value, though the access road is terrible. The **Whale Song Cafe** at nearby Munget does light meals.

Between Middle Lagoon and Cape Leveque, **Lombadina** (☎9192 4936; entry per car $10; s/d $75/140, cabin 4-person $180-260), 200km from Broome, is a beautiful tree-fringed village with fishing (from $175), whale watching ($220), mudcrabbing ($88), kayaking ($77) and Indigenous 'footprint' tours ($35). There are lodge-style rooms and self-contained cabins, but no camping. Fuel is available weekdays.

Nearby, tiny **Chile Creek** (☎9192 4141; www.chilecreek.com; entry per car $10; sites per person $16.50, bush bungalows $100, safari tents 4-person $185), 7km from Lombadina down a disintegrating track, offers basic bush camp sites, and modern en suite safari tents and renovated bungalows, all just a short stroll to a lovely beach. Go mudcrabbing with Roma, and she'll show you her famous chilli crab recipe.

Cape Leveque is spectacular, with gorgeous beaches and stunning red cliffs. Ecotourism award-winner **Kooljaman** (☎9192 4970; www.kooljaman.com.au; entry per car $10; unpowered/powered sites d $36/41, dome tents $60, cabins with/without bathroom d $165/140, safari tents d $260; wi-fi) offers grassy camp sites, driftwood beach shelters, hilltop safari tents with superb views, and stuffy budget domes. There's a minimum two-night stay, and the place is packed from June to October. The BYO **restaurant** (mains $26-50; ⊙Apr-Oct) opens for lunch and dinner, or you can order 'bush butler' (BBQ pack) service.

If you prefer less bling, there are a couple of outstations offering camp sites between Cape Leveque and One Arm Point. **Goombading** (☎0457 138 027; unpowered/powered sites per person $15/20), with a fantastic water view, is very relaxed, and hosts Unja and Jenny are keen to share Bardi culture, and offer spear-making, fishing and crabbing tours.

You can't camp at **Ardiyooloon** (One Arm Point; $10 entry) but you can visit this neat community with a well-stocked store, fuel, a barramundi hatchery and great fishing and swimming with views of the Buccaneer Archipelago.

A handful of other outstations offer camping, fishing and crabbing opportunities.

Chomley's Tours (☎9192 6195; www.chomleystours.com.au; 1-/2-/3-/4-day tour $245/470/675/660) offers one- to four-day tours of the peninsula, some with mudcrabbing and kayaking, as well as one-way transfers ($180).

Kujurta Buru (☎9192 1662; www.kujurtaburu.com.au) provides transport Sunday, Tuesday and Thursday from Broome to Beagle Bay ($75) and Lombadina, Kooljaman and Ardiyooloon (all $120) returning the same day.

THE KIMBERLEY

Derby

POP 5000

Late at night while Derby sleeps, the boabs cut loose and wander around town, marauding mobs flailing their many limbs in battle against an army of giant, killer crocs emerging from the encircling mudflats... If only.

There are crocs hiding in the mangroves, but you're more likely to see birds, over 200 different varieties, while the boabs are firmly rooted along the two main parallel drags, Loch and Clarendon Sts. Derby, sitting on King Sound, is the departure point for tours to the Horizontal Waterfalls and Buccaneer Archipelago, and the western terminus of the Gibb River Rd (GRR). It's also the West Kimberley's administrative centre, and the refugee detention facility at nearby RAAF Curtin brings in hordes of contractors.

Sights & Activities

The visitor centre's excellent town map lists every conceivable attraction.

Wharefinger Museum MUSEUM
(admission by donation) Grab the key from the visitor centre and have a peek inside the nearby museum, with its atmospheric shipping and aviation displays.

Jetty LANDMARK
Check out King Sound's colossal 11.5m tides from the circular jetty, 1km north of town, a popular fishing, crabbing, birdspotting and staring-into-the-distance haunt. Yep, there's crocs in the mangroves.

Old Derby Gaol HISTORICAL BUILDING
(Loch St) Along with the **Boab Prison Tree** (7km south), this old gaol is a sad reminder of man's inhumanity to man.

Bird Hide BIRD-WATCHING

There's a bird hide in the wetlands (aka sewerage ponds) at the end of Conway St.

Joonjoo Botanical Trail WALKING

This 2.3km trail, opposite the GRR turn-off, has neat interpretive displays from the local Nyikina people.

Tours

The Horizontal Waterfalls are Derby's top draw and most cruises also include the natural splendours of remote King Sound and the Buccaneer Archipelago. There are many operators to choose from (see the visitor centre for a full list). Most tours only operate during peak season.

One Tide Charters CRUISES

(☎9193 1358; www.onetide.com; 5/8/12 days) Offers eco-certified all-inclusive multiday 'sea safaris' with overnight camping on remote beaches, a ride through the Horizontal Waterfalls, mudcrabbing, fishing and freshwater swimming on exotic islands.

Horizontal Falls Adventure Tours SCENIC FLIGHT

(☎9192 2885; www.horizontalfalls.com.au; fly-cruise-fly tour Derby/Broome $690/790) Flights to Horizontal Falls including a speedboat ride through the falls. Has overnight and cruise options with partner, Kimberley Extreme.

Bush Flight SCENIC FLIGHT

(☎9193 2680; www.bushflight.com.au; 90/120/150min flights $250/340/425) To Horizontal Waterfalls, you can look but not touch.

West Kimberley Tours CAMPING

(☎9193 1550; www.westkimberleytours.com.au) Half/full day tours around town ($60/75). There's a Windjana Gorge and Tunnel Creek day trip ($135), and two- to seven-day Kimberley camping tours ($198 per day).

Festivals & Events

Boab Festival MUSIC, CULTURAL

(www.derbyboabfestival.org.au; Jul) Derby goes off with concerts, sports (including mud footy), races (horse and mudcrab varieties), poetry readings, art exhibitions and street parades.

Sleeping & Eating

Any decent accommodation is normally full of contract workers. If you're heading to/from the Gibb, consider stopping at Birdwood Station (20km) instead.

There are several takeaways and cafes along Loch and Clarendon Sts.

TOP CHOICE **Desert Rose** B&B $$

(☎9193 2813; 4 Marmion St; d $198;) The best sleep in town is worth booking ahead for; spacious, individually styled rooms with a nice shady pool, leadlight windows and a sumptuous breakfast. Host Anne is a font of local information.

TOP CHOICE **Jila Gallery** ITALIAN $$

(☎9193 2560; 18 Clarendon St; mains $20-30; ⏰7am-2pm & 6pm-late Tue-Fri, 6pm-late Sat) Enjoy the best coffee and cake within light years while perusing an eclectic mixture of contemporary and Indigenous art. This friendly gallery-cum-trattoria also does

DON'T MISS

HORIZONTAL WATERFALLS

One of the most intriguing features of the Kimberley coastline is the phenomenon known as 'Horizontal Waterfalls'. Despite the name, the falls are simply tides gushing through narrow coastal gorges in the Buccaneer Archipelago, north of Derby. What creates such a spectacle are the huge tides, often varying up to 11m. The water flow reaches an astonishing 30 knots as it's forced through two narrow gaps 20m and 10m wide – resulting in a 'waterfall' reaching 4m in height.

Many tours leave Derby (and some from Broome) each Dry, by either air, sea or a combination of both. It's become de rigueur to 'ride' the tide change through the gorge on a high-powered speedboat, at best risky, and accidents have occurred. Scenic flights are the quickest and cheapest option, and some seaplanes will land and transfer passengers to a waiting speedboat for the adrenalin hit. If you prefer to be stirred, not shaken, then consider seeing the falls as part of a longer cruise through the archipelago. Book tours at Derby and Broome visitor centres.

alfresco pizza, pasta and signature Italian dishes.

Kimberley Entrance Caravan Park CARAVAN PARK $
(☎9193 1055; www.kimberleyentrancecaravanpark.com; 2 Rowan St; unpowered/powered sites $28/33) You'll always find room here, though not all sites are shaded. There's a nice outdoor area with tables, although expect lots of insects this close to the mudflats.

Boab Inn PUB $$
(☎9191 1044; www.derbyboabinn.com; Loch St; d $220; lunch $10-20, dinner $24-32; ❄@) Excellent counter meals and free wi-fi make this the lunch stop of choice. The motel-style rooms are clean, comfortable and normally booked out.

Information

The supermarket and ATMs are on Loch and Clarendon Sts.

Derby visitor centre (☎1800 621 426; www.derbytourism.com.au; 2 Clarendon St; ⌚8.30am-4.30pm Mon-Fri, 9am-noon Sat year-round, 9am-noon Sun Apr-Sep) A mandatory stop, has super helpful advice on road conditions, accommodation, bus tickets and tour bookings.

Library (Clarendon St; ⌚closed Sun; @) Internet, first five minutes free.

Post office (Loch St)

Getting There & Away

Strategic flies to Perth four times a week.

As well, the visitor centre sells tickets for the weekly mail run ($395) flights that stop at remote stations – there's a northern and southern loop, and you can use this flight to get into/out of the Gibb.

Greyhound buses to Darwin ($325, 24 hours) and Broome ($65, two hours) stop at the visitor centre.

Gibb River Road

Cutting a brown swathe through the scorched heart of the Kimberley, the legendary **Gibb River Road** ('the Gibb' or GRR) provides one of Australia's wildest outback experiences. Stretching some 660km between Derby and Kununurra, the largely unpaved GRR is an endless sea of red dirt, big open skies and dramatic terrain. Rough, sometimes deeply corrugated, side roads lead to remote gorges, shady pools, distant waterfalls and million acre cattle stations. Rain can close the road anytime and permanently during the Wet. This is true wilderness with minimal services so good planning and self-sufficiency are essential.

Several stations offer overnight accommodation from mid-April to late October and advance bookings are essential during the peak period of June to August. Hema Map's *Kimberley Atlas & Guide* provides the best coverage while visitor centres sell *The Gibb River & Kalumburu Road Guide* ($5).

For just a sniff of outback adventure, try the 'tourist loop' along the GRR from Derby onto Fairfield Leopold Downs Rd to **Windjana Gorge** and **Tunnel Creek** then exit onto the Great Northern Hwy near Fitzroy Crossing.

A high-clearance 4WD (eg Toyota Land Cruiser) is mandatory, with two spare tyres, tools, emergency water (20L minimum) and several days' food in case of breakdown. Britz in Broome is a reputable hire outfit (see p211). Fuel is limited and expensive, most mobile phones won't work, and temperatures can be life-threatening. Broome and Kununurra are best for supplies.

The wheel-less can jump on an organised tour, or fly in on the **mail run** from Derby.

Tours

Western Xposure 4WD
(☎9414 8423; www.westernxposure.com.au; 7-day $1445) Runs seven-day and longer camping trips through the GRR.

Kimberley Wild Expeditions 4WD
(☎1300 738 870; www.kimberleywild.com.au) Consistent award winner. Tours range from one/two-day Broome ($139) to nine-day GRR ($1995).

Kimberley Adventure Tours 4WD
(☎1800 083 368; www.kimberleyadventures.com.au) Runs between Broome and Darwin including the GRR and Purnululu National Park ($1650, nine days).

Information

Good internet resources are www.gibbriverroad.net and www.kimberleyaustralia.com. Also try the shire websites and the Derby and Kununurra visitor centre sites.

For maps, buy the Hema *Kimberley Atlas & Guide* ($30) or *Regional Map – The Kimberley* ($10).

Department of Environment & Conservation (DEC; www.dec.wa.gov.au) Park permits, camping fees, info. A Holiday Pass ($40) works out cheaper if visiting more than three parks in one month.

Mainroads Western Australia (MRWA; ☎138 138; www.mainroads.wa.gov.au; ⌚24hr) Highway conditions.

Shire of Derby/West Kimberley (☎9191 0999; www.sdwk.wa.gov.au) For condition of side roads.

Shire of Wyndham/East Kimberley (☎9161 1002; www.thelastfrontier.com.au) Kalumburu/Mitchell Falls road conditions.

DERBY TO WYNDHAM/KUNUNURRA

The first 100-odd kilometres of the GRR from Derby are sealed.

The 2000-hectare **Birdwood Downs Station** (☎9191 1275; www.birdwooddowns.com; camping $12.50, savannah huts per person incl breakfast & dinner $130) offers rustic savannah huts, dusty camping and a pleasant 'village green' with butterflies. WWOOFers are welcome and it's also the **Kimberley School of Horsemanship**, with lessons, riding camps and trail rides (two-hour sunset ride $99).

Just after Inglis Gap is the turn-off (50km rough) to the remote **Mt Hart Wilderness Lodge** (☎9191 4645; www.mthart.com.au; camp site per person $15; r per person incl dinner & breakfast $290; ⌚Dry) with grassy camp sites, pleasant gorges, swimming and fishing holes. Seven kilometres past the Mt Hart turn-off brings you to the narrow **Lennard River Gorge** (3km return walk).

March Fly Glen, at the 204km mark, despite its name, is a pleasant, shady picnic area ringed by pandanus. Don't miss stunning **Bell Gorge**, 29km down a rough track, with a picturesque waterfall and popular plunge pool; you can camp at **Silent Grove** (adult/child $11/2). Refuel (diesel only) and grab an ice cream at **Imintji Store** (☎9191 7471; ⌚7am-4.30pm, shorter hours in Wet), your last chance for supplies. Next door is **Over the Range Repairs** (☎9191 7887) where Neville is your best, if not only, hope of mechanical salvation on the whole Gibb.

Part of the Australian Wildlife Conservancy, the superb **Mornington Wilderness Camp** (☎9191 7406; www.awc.org.au; entry fee $25; camp site per adult/child $18/8, safari tents incl full board s/d $295/500; ⌚Dry) is as remote as it gets, lying on the Fitzroy River, a very rough, incredibly scenic 95km drive south of the Gibb's 247km mark. Nearly 400,000 hectares are devoted to conserving the Kimberley's endangered fauna and there's excellent canoeing, birdwatching and bushwalking. Choose from shady camp sites or spacious, raised tents with verandahs. The bar and restaurant offer picnic hampers and the best cheese platter this side of Margaret River.

Beautiful **Galvans Gorge** with waterfall, swimming hole, rock wallabies and Wandjina art is the most accessible of all gorges, less than 1km from the road. **Mt Barnett Roadhouse** (☎9191 7007), at the 300km point, has the least reliable opening hours and most expensive fuel on the GRR. The dusty camp site at **Manning River Gorge** (per person $13), 7km behind the roadhouse, is often full with travellers waiting for fuel. At least there's a good swimming hole.

Further up the Gibb (338km mark) is the turn-off to **Mt Elizabeth Station** (☎9191 4644; www.mountelizabethstation.com; camp sites per person $14, s/d incl breakfast & dinner $170/340; ⌚Dry), one of the few remaining private leaseholders in the Kimberley. Peter Lacy's 200,000-hectare property is a good base for exploration to nearby gorges, waterfalls and Indigenous rock art. Wallabies frequent the camp site, and the home-style, three-course dinners ($35) hit the spot.

At 406km you reach the Kalumburu turn-off. Head right on the GRR, and pull into atmospheric **Ellenbrae Station** (☎9161 4325; camp sites per person $15, bungalows d $150) for fresh scones and quirky bungalows. The GRR continues through spectacular country, crossing the mighty Durack River and, at 579km, there are panoramic views of the Cockburn Ranges, Cambridge Gulf and Pentecost River.

The privations of the Gibb are left behind after pulling into amazing **Home Valley Station** (☎9161 4322; www.homevalley.com.au; camp sites adult/child $16/5, eco tents sleeping 4 $190, homestead d from $240; ❄@📶🏊), an Indigenous hospitality training resort with a superb range of luxurious accommodation. There are excellent grassy camp sites and motel-style rooms, a fantastic open bistro, tyre repairs and activities including swimming, fishing and cattle mustering.

At 589km cross the infamous **Pentecost River** – take care as water levels are unpredictable and saltwater crocs lurk nearby. Slightly further is 400,000-hectare **El Questro Wilderness Park** (☎9169 1777; www.elquestro.com.au; 7-day park permit $17.50; ⌚Dry), a vast former cattle station with scenic gorges (Amelia, El Questro) and Zebedee thermal springs. Boat tours explore **Chamberlain Gorge** (adult/child $54/27; ⌚3pm); you can hire your own ($95). The shady, riverside camp sites at **El Questro Station**

WORTH A TRIP

MITCHELL FALLS & DRYSDALE RIVER

In the Dry, Kalumburu Rd is easily navigable as far as **Drysdale River Station** (9161 4326; www.drysdaleriver.com.au; camp sites $9-14, d $130; 8am-5pm), 59km from the Gibb River Rd (GRR), where there's fuel, meals and accommodation, and you can check ongoing conditions. Scenic flights to Mitchell Falls operate April to September (from $325).

The **Ngauwudu** (Mitchell Plateau) turn-off is 160km from the GRR, and within 6km a deep rocky ford crosses the **King Edward River**, formidable early in the season. Another 2km brings the **Munurru Campground** (adult/child $7/2) with excellent nearby rock art. From the Kalumburu Rd it's a rough 87km, past lookouts and forests of *livistona* palms to the camping ground at **Mitchell River National Park** (entry per vehicle $11, camping adult/child $7/2).

Leave early if walking to **Punamii-unpuu** (Mitchell Falls; 8.6km return). The easy trail meanders through spinifex, woodlands and gorge country, dotted with Wandjina and Gwion Gwion rock art sites, secluded waterholes, lizards, wallabies and brolga. The falls are stunning, whether trickling in the Dry, or raging in the Wet (when only visible from the air). You can swim in the long pool above the falls, but swimming in the lower pools is strictly forbidden because of their cultural importance to the Wunambal people. Most people will complete the walk in three hours.

Township (camp sites per person $15, bungalows d $325;) are good value. There's also an outdoor bar and upmarket **steakhouse** (mains $18-36).

Ten kilometres along the GRR is El Questro's **Emma Gorge Resort** (safari cabins d $270; Dry;), where a 40-minute walk reaches a sublime terminal plunge pool and waterfall, one of the prettiest in the whole Kimberley. The resort has an open-air bar and restaurant, though the non-air-con cabins are stuffy and overpriced.

At 630km you cross King River and at 647km you finally hit bitumen – turn left for Wyndham (48km) and right to Kununurra (53km).

Devonian Reef National Parks

Three national parks with three stunning gorges were once part of a western 'great barrier reef' in the Devonian era, 350 million years ago. Windjana Gorge and Tunnel Creek National Parks are accessed via Fairfield Leopold Downs Rd (linking the Great Northern Hwy with Gibb River Rd), while Geikie Gorge National Park is just northeastof Fitzroy Crossing.

In **Windjana Gorge National Park** (per car $11), the walls of beautiful **Windjana Gorge** soar 100m above the Lennard River, which surges in the Wet, but is a series of pools in the Dry. Scores of freshwater crocodiles lurk along the banks. Bring plenty of water for the 7km return walk from the **camping ground** (per person $10).

Tunnel Creek (per car $11, no camping), famous as the hideout of rebel Jandamarra, is a 750m-long passage, 3m to 15m wide, created by the creek cutting through a spur of the Napier Range. In the Dry, you can walk the full length by wading partly through knee-deep water. Watch out for bats and take a strong torch. There are Aboriginal paintings at either end.

The magnificent **Geikie Gorge** is 22km north of Fitzroy Crossing and the best way to experience it and spot wildlife is on a **DEC boat tour** (9191 5121; 1hr tour adult/child $28/5; 8am & 3pm May-Oct, additional trips in peak season). The self-guided trails are sandy and hot. Another excellent option is taking a cultural cruise with a local Bunuba guide from **Darngku Heritage Tours** (0417 907 609; www.darngku.com.au; culture & cruise 2hr adult/child $65/55, 3hr $80/65).

Wyndham

POP 900

A gold-rush town fallen on leaner times, Wyndham is scenically nestled between rugged hills and the Cambridge Gulf, some 100km northwest of Kununurra. Sunsets are superb from the spectacular **Five Rivers Lookout** on Mt Bastion (325m) overlooking the King, Pentecost, Durack, Forrest and Ord Rivers entering Cambridge Gulf.

A giant 20m croc greets visitors entering town, but you can see the real thing at **Wyndham Crocodile Farm** (☎9161 1124; Barytes Rd; adult/child $17/10; ⏰10am-2pm Mar-Nov, to noon Dec-Feb) out past the port (5km). Feeding time is 11am. The port precinct also contains a small **museum** (⏰10am-3pm daily Dry) and the **Wyndham Town Hotel** (☎9161 1202; O'Donnell St; d $130; meals $15-35; ❄) with its legendary meals and overpriced rooms.

In town, **Five Rivers Cafe** (☎9161 2271; Great Northern Hwy; ⏰8am-5pm Mon-Fri) serves up great coffee, breakfasts and barra burgers, while laid-back **Wyndham Caravan Park** (☎9161 1064; Baker St, Three Mile; unpowered/powered sites $25/30, dongas s/d $50/70; 🏊) offers grassy, shady camp sites.

Greyhound drops passengers 56km away at the Victoria Hwy junction. Internet is available at the **Telecentre** (26 Koojarra Rd; ⏰8am-4pm Mon-Fri; @) and Tuesday's mail run flight will get you to Kununurra. Call for a **taxi** (☎0418 950 434).

Kununurra

POP 6000

Kununurra is a relaxed town in the midst of an oasis of lush farmland and tropical fruit plantations, thanks to the Ord River irrigation scheme. With good transport and communications, excellent services and well-stocked supermarkets, it's every traveller's favourite slice of civilisation between Broome and Darwin.

Kununurra is also the departure point for most of the tours in the East Kimberley, and with all that fruit, there's plenty of seasonal work. Note there's a 90-minute time difference with the Northern Territory (NT).

Sights & Activities

Across the highway from the township, **Lily Creek Lagoon** is a mini-wetlands with amazing birdlife, boating and freshwater crocs. **Lake Kununurra** (Diversion Dam) has pleasant picnic spots and great fishing. Groups could consider hiring their own 'barbie' boat from **Kununurra Self Drive Hire Boats** (☎0409 291 959; Lakeside Resort; per hr from $88).

Self-guided two/three-day **canoe** trips run from Lake Argyle along the scenic **Ord River** to Kununurra, overnighting at designated riverside camp sites. Canoes, camping equipment and transport are provided while you supply your own food and sleeping bag. You can choose to paddle the whole way back, or bail out along the way. **Go Wild** (☎1300 663 369; www.gowild.com.au; 3 days $180) offers early bail-out options or extra days to their eco-certified standard three-day trip. **Big Waters** (☎1800 650 580; www.bigwaters.com.au; 3 days $175) offers a similar three-day tour.

Mirima National Park NATIONAL PARK

(per car $11) A stunning area of rugged sedimentary formations like a mini-Bungle Bungles. The eroded gorges of Hidden Valley are home to brittle red peaks, spinifex, boab trees and abundant wildlife. The **Wuttuwutubin Trail** (500m return) leads through a narrow gorge to a lookout, whereas the slightly longer **Didbagirring Trail** (1km return) climbs steeply up loose scree to a vantage point overlooking the park. Early morning or dusk are your best chances of seeing wildlife.

Kununurra Historical Society Museum MUSEUM

(Coolibah Dr) The small historical museum has an interesting exhibit on the wartime crash of an A20-62 Wirraway and subsequent recovery mission. It's opposite the Country Club exit.

Kelly's Knob VIEWPOINT

A favourite sunset viewpoint on the town's northern fringe,

DON'T MISS

PARRY LAGOONS NATURE RESERVE

This beautiful RAMSAR-listed wetland, 15km from Wyndham, teems in the Wet with migratory birds arriving from as far away as Siberia. There's a bird-hide and boardwalk at **Marlgu Billabong** (4WD) and an excellent view from **Telegraph Hill**. Back on the highway, steep steps lead down to the **Grotto**, a deep, peaceful pool in a small gorge, perfect for a quiet dip.

Parry Creek Farm (☎9161 1139; www.parrycreekfarm.com.au; unpowered/powered sites $29/34, r $110, cabins $210; ❄🏊), surrounded by the nature reserve, is a lovely place to stay, with its own billabong and hordes of bird and animal life. Comfy rooms and air-con cabins are connected by a raised boardwalk around the billabong for easy bird spotting. The licensed cafe serves excellent baked barramundi and other gourmet offerings.

Purnululu National Park

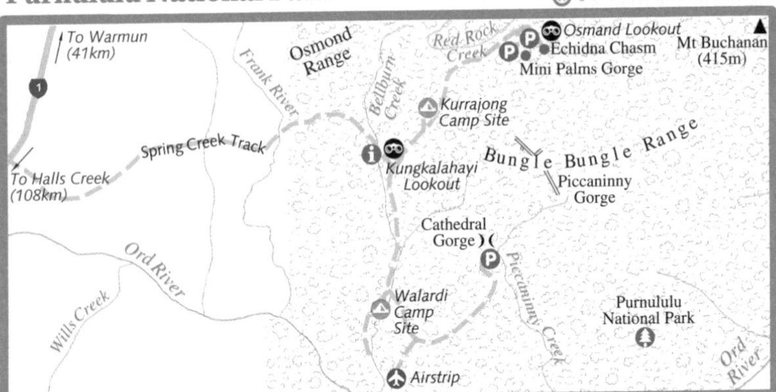

Tours

Alligator Airways SCENIC FLIGHTS
(☎1800 632 533; www.alligatorairways.com.au) Scenic flights to the Bungle Bungles (adult/child $295/195) and the Kimberleys ($695).

Go Wild ABSEILING
(☎1300 663 369; www.gowild.com.au) Apart from self-guided canoe trips, these guys also offer caving ($180), abseiling (from $150) and bushwalking (from $40) tours.

Kununurra Cruises CRUISES
(☎9168 1718; www.thebbqboat.com.au; adult/child $95/45) Popular sunset 'BBQ Dinner' cruises on Lily Creek Lagoon and the Ord River. BYO drinks.

Shoal Air SCENIC FLIGHTS
(☎9169 3554; www.shoalair.com.au) Has various flights around Bungles, Cambridge Gulf, Kalumburu and the majestic Mitchell and King George Falls.

Sleeping

There's a great variety of accommodation to choose from, and remember, the more it costs, the more discount you'll get in the Wet. Watch out for mozzies if you're camping near the lake.

Hidden Valley Caravan Park CARAVAN PARK $
(☎9168 1790; Weaber Plains Rd; unpowered/powered sites $30/34, cabin d $125; @ 🛜 🏊) Under the looming crags of Mirima National Park, this excellent little park has nice grassy sites and is popular with seasonal workers. The self-contained cabins are good value. Bike hire is available (half/full day $15/25).

Kimberley Croc Backpackers HOSTEL $
(☎1300 136 702; www.kimberleycroc.com.au; 120 Konkerberry Dr; dm $24-30, d $90-110; ❄ @ 🛜 🏊) This slick, modern YHA close to the action has a large pool and barbecue area and excellent kitchen facilities. They also run the nearby **Kimberley Croc Lodge** for seasonal workers, where a bed in a five-share unit (own en suite, TV and bar fridge) will cost you $145 per week.

Lakeview Apartments APARTMENTS $$$
(☎9168 0000; www.lakeviewapartments.net; 224 Victoria Hwy; 1-/2-/3-bedroom apt $230/280/380; ❄ 🛜 🏊) These spacious, self-contained apartments that are located across from Lily Creek Lagoon have all mod cons, fully equipped kitchens, free wi-fi and cable. There's a weekendminimum two-night stay.

Lakeside Resort CARAVAN PARK $$
(☎9169 1092; www.lakeside.com.au; Casuarina Way; unpowered/powered sites $30/34, self-catering studio d $185, motel d $205; ❄ @ 🏊) At the edge of Lily Creek Lagoon, there's a good range of accommodation set within leafy grounds.

Kununurra Backpackers HOSTEL $
(☎1800 641 998; www.kununurrabackpackers.com.au; 22 Nutwood Cres; dm $23-25, d $60-65; ❄ @ 🛜 🏊) There's a nice, leafy garden and large shared kitchen in this friendly hostel popular with seasonal workers.

Kimberley Grande HOTEL $$$
(☎9166 5600; www.thekimberleygrande.com.au; Victoria Hwy; d/with spa $200/355; ❄ 🏊) Large, sumptuous rooms at Kununurra's most exclusive hotel overlook the lap pool or open onto the garden. The on-site bistro does a selection of steaks and seafood ($25 to $50).

Eating

The big resorts all have restaurants offering similar fine-dining experiences. There are two well-stocked supermarkets and several takeaways. Most places keep shorter hours during the Wet.

TOP CHOICE **PumpHouse** MODERN AUSTRALIAN $$$
(9169 3222; www.ordpumphouse.com.au; Lakeview Dr; lunch $16-24, dinner $30-40; 11.30am-late Tue-Fri, from 8am Sat & Sun; wi-fi) Idyllically situated on Lake Kununurra, the PumpHouse's innovative dishes feature fine produce – try the rump with blue cheese and pine nuts, or the oven-baked pork fillet wrapped in speck. Watch the catfish swarm should a morsel (accidentally of course!) slip off the verandah. There's also an excellent wine list and free wi-fi.

Wild Mango CAFE $
(9169 2810; 20 Messmate Way; breakfast $8-12, lunch $6-13; 7.30am-5pm daily, shorter hours Sat & Sun; wi-fi) The hippest, healthiest feed in town with curry wraps, mouth-watering pancakes, chai smoothies, real coffee, gelato and free wi-fi. The entrance is in Konkerberry Dr.

Kimberley Cafe CAFE $
(9169 2574; 4 Papuana St; breakfast $5-22, lunch $7-17; 8.30am-4pm Mon-Fri, until 1pm Sat) All-day breakfasts are popular here and lunches consist of salads, burgers, thick homemade sausage rolls, and a pretty good souvlaki.

Gulliver's Tavern PUB FARE $$
(9168 1666; 196 Cottontree Ave; mains $12-34) GT's serves all the usual counter meals and some spicy Asian ring-ins, out back in its popular beer garden.

Shopping

Zebra Rock Gallery DESIGN
(9168 1114; www.zebrarock.biz; Packsaddle Rd; admission by donation; 8am-5pm) On the Ord

PURNULULU NATIONAL PARK & BUNGLE BUNGLE RANGE

Looking like a packet of half-melted Jaffas, the World Heritage **Purnululu National Park** (per car $11; Apr-Dec) is home to the incredible ochre and black striped 'beehive' domes of the Bungle Bungle Range.

The distinctive rounded rock towers are made of sandstone and conglomerates moulded by rainfall over millions of years. Their stripes are the result of oxidised iron compounds and algae. To the local Kidja people, *purnululu* means sandstone, with Bungle Bungle possibly a corruption of 'bundle bundle', a common grass. Whitefellas only 'discovered' the range during the mid-1980s.

Over 3000 sq km of ancient country contains a wide array of wildlife, including over 130 bird species. **Kungkalahayi Lookout** has a fine view of the range. Look for tiny bats high on the walls above palm-fringed **Echidna Chasm** (one hour return) in the north, but it's the southern area comprising aptly named **Cathedral Gorge** (45 minutes return) that's most inspiring. Remote and pristine **Piccaninny Gorge** is best experienced as a 30km overnight round trip; check with the parks' visitor centre for details. The restricted gorges in the northern part of the park can only be seen from the air.

Rangers are based here April to December and the park is closed outside this time. You'll need a high clearance 4WD for the 52km twisting, rough road from the highway to the visitor centre near Three Ways junction; allow 2½ hours. There are five deep creek crossings, and the turn-off is 53km south of Warmun. **Kurrajong Camp Site** (Apr-Sep only) and **Walardi Camp Site** (Apr-Dec) have fresh water and toilets (per person $11).

Tours

Most Kimberley tour operators include Purnululu in multi-day tours. See the Kununurra Tours section for tours operating from Kununurra. You can also pick up tours at Warmun Roadhouse and Halls Creek. Helicopters will get you closer than fixed-wing flights.

East Kimberley Tours SIGHTSEEING
(9168 2213; www.eastkimberleytours.com.au; tours from $315) Has a wide range of tours from both Kununurra and Warmun.

Sling Air HELICOPTER FLIGHTS
(1800 095 500; www.slingair.com.au; 18/30/48min flights $215/325/525) Runs helicopter flights from the Bellburn airstrip in the park.

OUTBACK MAIL RUNS

Delivering the mail in the outback is a serious business, and even more so in the Kimberley where roads can be closed for months on end. Weekly mail flights depart both Derby and Kununurra to service far-flung stations, and if there's a spare seat, tourists can tag along. This provides a fascinating look into station life, and a bird's-eye view of the surrounding country. While most opt for the full round-trip, these flights are particularly useful to those without wheels who'd like to access a particular (or several) station(s). Seats are limited, and station passengers hold preference over sightseers. You can book tickets at the visitor centres; prices listed are round-trip – individual stations will be cheaper. Similar mail runs operate in the Pilbara from Newman and Port Hedland.

Derby Northern Loop ($395; ⊙Fri) Services the western Gibb including Mt Hart, Mt Barnett, Mt Elisabeth and Mornington.

Derby Southern Loop ($395; ⊙Mon) Includes Dampier Downs, Fitzroy Crossing and Beefwood Park.

Kununurra Northern Loop ($360; ⊙Tue) Services the eastern Gibb including Wyndham, Home Valley, Ellenbrae, Drysdale River, Mitchell Plateau, Kalumburu and Oombulgurri.

Kununurra Southern Loop A ($470; ⊙Wed) Heads down the Tanami via Halls Creek, Billaluna, Balgo and Mulan.

Kununurra Southern Loop B ($365; ⊙Thu) This sees few passengers, so getting bumped is rare – Birrindudu, Ringer Soak, Flora Valley and Nicholson.

River 14km from Kununurra, produces jewellery and sculptures from the unique zebra siltstone found around Lake Argyle. The leafy grounds and small tearoom are a pleasant place to relax. Kids can feed the fish.

Bush Camp Surplus OUTDOOR GEAR
(☎9168 1476; cnr Papuana St & Konkerberry Dr) The best camping gear between Broome and Darwin.

Artlandish INDIGENOUS ART
(☎9168 1881; www.aboriginal-art-australia.com; cnr Papuana St & Konkerberry Dr; ⊙9am-4.30pm Mon-Fri, to 1pm Sat) Has a great range of Kimberley ochres as well as acrylics from the Western Desert.

Lovell Gallery ART
(☎9168 1781; www.lovellgallery.com.au; 144 Konkerberry Dr; ⊙9am-5pm daily, shorter hours in Wet) Check out the 16m-long *Beyond the Beehives* mural and the psychedelic boabs.

Kununurra Markets MARKET
(Whitegum Park; ⊙8am-noon Sat Dry) Opposite the visitor centre. Stalls feature local crafts and produce.

Information

DEC office (☎9168 0200; Konkerberry Dr) For park permits.

District hospital (☎9168 1522; 96 Coolibah Dr; ⊙24hr) Emergency facilities.

Kununurra Telecentre (☎9169 1868; Coolibah Dr; ⊙8am-6pm Mon-Fri, 9am-1pm Sat; @) Internet, flash-drives, printing.

Library (☎9169 1227; Mangaloo St; ⊙8am until various, closed Sun; @)

Travel World (☎9168 1888) In the shopping mall. Can book tours, airline and bus tickets, and luxury wilderness accommodation.

Visitor centre (☎9168 1177; www.kununurratourism.com; Coolibah Dr; ⊙8am-5pm daily Apr-Oct, shorter hours Nov-Mar) Check here for information on tours, seasonal work and road conditions.

Getting There & Around

Airnorth flies to Broome and Darwin daily, and to Perth on Saturdays. Skywest flies to Broome (Monday, Wednesday and Friday) with a connection to Perth.

Greyhound has daily buses to Darwin ($188, 12 hours) and Broome ($215, 13 hours) continuing to Perth (Tuesday, Thursday and Saturday only) that stop at the 24-hour BP roadhouse on Messmate Way. Destinations include Halls Creek ($78, four hours), Fitzroy Crossing ($165, seven hours), Derby ($193, 10 hours) and Katherine ($118, eight hours).

Avis (☎9168 1999), **Budget** (☎9168 2033) and **Thrifty** (☎1800 626 515) rental cars are all available.

Call for a **taxi** (13 10 08).

Understand Perth & West Coast Australia

›

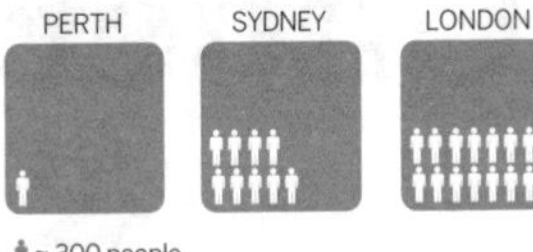

Perth & the West Coast Today

The Lay of the Land

Mining money has officially stamped Western Australia (WA) with wealth. Despite its small population (2.3 million), the state has been the strongest economic performer in the country for the last few years. The average family's income is higher than those over east – to the tune of a carton of beer per week. This may not sound like much, but it does translate into brand-new oversized homes, squeaky-shiny boats plonked casually on front lawns, and a population noted for its confidence and brash energy.

This frontier land has been built on mining money, and today many major iron-ore mines get into the ground only with substantial Chinese investment. Gargantuan projects such as Gorgon Gas are tapping into natural gas estimated at $500 billion, employing thousands of workers. For the Australian economy, these are very big biscuits.

Still a Tough Nanny?

Law and order remain key political and social concerns. Premier Colin Barnett, who took power from Labor to form a coalition government following a hung parliament in the 2008 state election, waged his Liberal Party campaign on a strong 'tough on crime' platform. Laws considered heavy-handed by some, such as $500 fines for not wearing a seatbelt, and strident anti-graffiti legislation, have contributed to WA's image as a nanny state.

Despite this pejorative moniker, other policy areas have been upheld as exemplars of forward-thinking. Perth's rail system is heralded as one of the best in the country. However, most people live in car-dependent suburbs – they need to drive in order to access public transport, then have to fight for a parking space at the train station. This problem is exacerbated each time a new suburb is built, and today Perth's sprawling suburbs have bled out into one mega-city.

Faux Pas

» Championing daylight savings. The state voted it down in a referendum in 2009.

» Asking for a pot, half-pint or schooner at the bar. It's a middie.

» Talking about how wonderful it is in the eastern states. No one's interested.

Top Films

Rabbit-Proof Fence (2002), directed by Phillip Noyce

Japanese Story (2003), directed by Sue Brooks

Last Train to Freo (2006), directed by Jeremy Sims

Gallipoli (1981), directed by Peter Weir

Top Books

Everything by Tim Winton, especially *Cloudstreet* (1991) and *The Turning* (2006)

Sand (2010), John Kinsella and Robert Drewe

Tales from Outer Suburbia (2008), Shaun Tan

Benang (1999), Kim Scott

belief systems

(% of population)

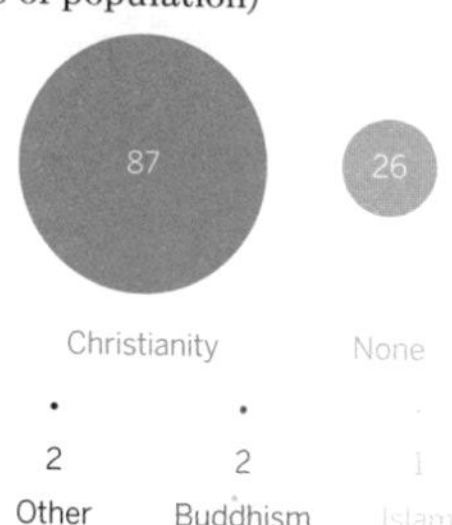

if Perth were 100 people

65 would be born in Australia
11 would be born in the UK
3 would be born in New Zealand
21 would be born elsewhere

New Deals Brokered

As in other parts of Australia, Aboriginal communities in WA struggle on, many mired in disadvantage, and a form of unspoken segregation between white Australians and Aboriginal Australians appears to exist. Divisions persist, but the search for petroleum and gas has brought mining companies and Aboriginal groups to the negotiating table in deals brokered – both successfully and unsuccessfully – for mining companies to set up shop on traditional Aboriginal lands. Whether the Barnett government should press on with a gas precinct at James Price Point, the Kimberley, has been highly contentious.

Ken Wyatt of the Liberal Party made political history in the 2010 federal election when he became the first Australian Aboriginal person to be elected to the House of Representatives. Wyatt's mother was one of the stolen generations (see p228).

Today the West Australian spirit remains nothing if not fiercely independent – not too far a cry from the referendum in 1933, when the state successfully voted for secession. (The British said no.) West Australians continue to cherish 'the lifestyle': a life lived outdoors by the beach and the barbecue, and overlaid with a relaxed yet confident tone. And with flights from Perth to Bali cheaper than those to Sydney, West Australians seem to have less need than ever to invest themselves in the goings-on of the rest of the country. Welcome to Boom Town.

Australian Football League: A WA Primer

WA has two teams in the AFL: the Fremantle Dockers and the West Coast Eagles. The Dockers (also just 'Freo') were born in 1995, and enjoy a working-class, underdog image. West Coast, founded in 1986, has three premierships – the last in 2006.

What is a CUB?

A cashed-up bogan (CUB) is a newly minted member of the working class. He puffs his chest out just as much as a regular bogan, but sports a fluoro-coloured $80,000 ute and keeps a few jet skis in the double garage.

Useful Terms

» **FI-FO:** Fly-In, Fly-Out workers on the mines; also 'Fit In Or F*** Off', which may be emblazoned on a T-shirt.

» **CUB:** Cashed-Up Bogan.

» **Golden triangle:** Perth's rich, white, western suburbs, which form a triangle along the beach and up along the Swan River.

History

Michael Cathcart

Michael Cathcart presents history programs on ABC TV, is also a broadcaster on ABC Radio National and teaches history at the Australian Centre, University of Melbourne.

The story of Western Australia's history is one of hardship, boom, bust, and boom again. Human history started some 40,000 years ago, when the first people are thought to have arrived – although some argue this could have occurred as long as 65,000 years ago.

Dirk Hartog is considered the first European explorer to land on the shores of WA (as a record of his journey he displayed a pewter plate on an island in Shark Bay in 1616, now known as Dirk Hartog Island).

The British set up a military base in Albany, in the south of the state, in 1826. Perth was then founded in 1829, when Captain James Stirling declared all surrounding land property of King George IV.

In 1829, immigrants led by Stirling arrived in the territory of the Noongar people, sparking controversy between the two groups. Conflict with the indigenous population continued, notably in the Battle of Pinjarra (1834), when some 25 Aborigines and one European were killed.

Western Australia began its economic transformation with the discovery of gold in the 1880s and the inception of the nickel boom in the early 1960s, albeit thwarted by the two world wars and the Depression. Riches from the mines at Mt Newman, Tom Price and Kalgoorlie, among several others, dovetailed into the economic bubble of the 1980s, which burst when WA Inc (as the dealings among select businessmen and state politicians came to be known) was discovered to have lost $600 million in public money. Ever enterprising, it was not long, however, before the state was soon back on its feet, enjoying untrammelled economic mining growth and development by 2010.

TIMELINE

40,000 years ago

First humans arrive on the shores of Australia.

1616

Dutch explorer Dirk Hartog lands on an island in Shark Bay, marking his visit with a pewter plate on which he inscribed a record of his visit.

1697

De Vlamingh replaces Hartog's plate with his own.

First Arrivals

People first arrived on the northern shores of Australia at least 40,000 years ago. As they began building shelters, cooking food and telling each other tales, they left behind signs of their activities. They left layers of carbon – the residue of their ancient fires – deep in the soil. Piles of shells and fishbones mark the places where these people hunted and ate. And on rock walls across WA they left paintings and etchings, some thousands of years old, which tell their stories of the Dreaming, that spiritual dimension where the earth and its people were created, and the law was laid down.

Contrary to popular belief, these Aboriginal people, especially those who lived in the north, were not entirely isolated from the rest of the world. Until 6000 years ago, they were able to travel and trade across a bridge of land that connected Australia to New Guinea. Even after white occupation, the Aborigines of the northern coasts regularly hosted Macassan fishermen from Sulawesi, with whom they traded and socialised.

When European sailors first stumbled on the coast of 'Terra Australis', the entire continent was occupied by hundreds of Aboriginal groups, living in their own territories and maintaining their own distinctive languages and traditions. The fertile Swan Valley around Perth, for example, is the customary homeland of about a dozen groups of Noongar people, each speaking a distinctive dialect.

The prehistory of Australia is filled with tantalising mysteries. In the Kimberley, scholars and amateur sleuths are fascinated by the so-called Bradshaw paintings. These enigmatic and mystical stick figures are thousands of years old. Because they look nothing like the artwork of any other Aboriginal group, the identity of the culture that created them is the subject of fierce debate.

Meanwhile there are historians who claim the Aborigines' first contact with the wider world occurred when a Chinese admiral, Zheng He, visited Australia in the 15th century. Others say that Portuguese navigators mapped the continent in the 16th century.

SPARSE POPULATION

Today Western Australia, the largest state in the country, is also the most sparsely populated, being home to less than 10% of the population.

Early Dutch Exploration

These are intriguing theories. But most authorities believe that the first man to travel any great distance to Aboriginal Australia was Dutchman Willem Janszoon. In 1606, Janszoon sailed the speedy little ship *Duyfken* out of the Dutch settlement at Batavia (modern Jakarta) to scout for the Dutch East India Company, and found Cape York, at Australia's northern extremity, which he thought was an extension of New Guinea.

Ten years later, another Dutch ship, the *Eendracht,* rode the mighty trade winds across the Atlantic, bound for the 'spice islands' of modern

1629

Debauchery, rape and murder break out while the *Batavia* is shipwrecked at the Houtman Abrolhos Islands. All crew but two are subsequently executed at senior merchant Francisco Pelsaert's behest.

1826

The British army establishes a military post in Albany, on the southern coast.

1829

Led by Captain James Stirling, a boatload of free immigrants land in the territory of the Noongar people.

1829

Governor Stirling declares all surrounding Aboriginal lands to be the property of King George IV. Perth is founded.

Indonesia. But the captain, Dirk Hartog, misjudged his position, and stumbled onto the island (near Gladstone) that now bears his name. Hartog inscribed the details of his visit onto a pewter plate and nailed it to a post. In 1697, the island was visited by a second Dutch explorer, Willem Hesselsz de Vlamingh, who swapped Hartog's plate for one of his own.

Many of the first ships to bring convicts to WA were whalers. Human cargo would be unloaded and then the ships continued whaling.

Other Dutch mariners were not so lucky. Several ships were wrecked on the uncharted western coast. The most infamous of these is the *Batavia*. After the ship foundered in the waters off modern Geraldton in 1629, the captain, Francisco Pelsaert, sailed a boat to the Dutch East India Company's base at Batavia. While his back was turned, some demented crewmen unleashed a nightmare of debauchery, rape and murder on the men, women and children who had been on the ship. When Pelsaert returned with a rescue vessel, he executed the murderers, sparing only two youths whom he marooned on the beach of the continent they knew as New Holland.

The Dutch were businessmen, scouring the world for commodities. Nothing they saw on the dry coasts of this so-called 'New Holland' convinced them that the land or its native people offered any promise of profit. When Dutch navigator Abel Tasman charted the western and southern coasts of Australia in 1644, he was mapping not a commercial opportunity but a maritime hazard.

In Came the British

By the early 19th century, it was clear that the Dutch had no inclination to settle WA. Meanwhile, the British were growing alarmed by the activities of the French in the region. So on Christmas Day 1826, the British army warned them off by establishing a lonely military outpost at Albany, on the strategically important southwestern tip of the country.

The founding of Perth is most famously depicted in George Pitt Morison's painting, *The Foundation of Perth* (1829). It is often erroneously credited as an authentic record of the ceremony rather than a historical reconstruction.

The Founding of Perth

The challenge to Aboriginal supremacy in the west began in 1829, when a boatload of immigrants arrived with all their possessions in the territory of the Noongar people. These trespassers were led by Captain James Stirling – a swashbuckling and entrepreneurial naval officer – who had investigated the coastal region two years earlier. Stirling had convinced British authorities to appoint him governor of the new settlement, and promptly declared all the surrounding Aboriginal lands to be the property of King George IV. Such was the foundation of Perth.

Frontier Conflict

As a cluster of shops, houses and hotels rose on the banks of the Swan River, settlers established sheep and cattle runs in the surrounding country. This led to conflict with the Aborigines, following a pattern which

1834

The Battle of Pinjarra occurs after Stirling leads a punitive expedition against the Noongar. It is thought that 25 Aborigines are shot, with Stirling's camp suffering one fatality.

1840–41

An Aboriginal man called Wylie and explorer Edward Eyre make a staggering journey across the Nullarbor Plain to Albany.

1850

Shiploads of male convicts start to arrive in Fremantle. They go on to build key historical buildings such as Fremantle prison, Government House and Perth Town Hall.

1860s

With no democracy, a network of city merchants and squatters exercises control over the colony.

was tragically common throughout the Australian colonies. The Aborigines speared sheep and cattle, sometimes for food, sometimes as an act of defiance. In the reprisals which resulted, people on both sides were killed, and by 1832 it was clear the Aborigines were organising a violent resistance. Governor Stirling declared that he would retaliate with such 'acts of decisive severity as will appal them as people for a time and reduce their tribe to weakness'.

In October 1834 Stirling showed he was a man of his word. He led a punitive expedition against the Noongar, who were under the leadership of the warrior Calyute. In the Battle of Pinjarra, the Governor's forces shot, according to one report, around 25 Aborigines and suffered one fatality themselves. This display of official terror had the desired effect. The Noongar ended their resistance and the violence of the frontier moved further out.

The Deployment of Convicts

Aboriginal resistance was not the only threat to the survival of this most isolated outpost of the British Empire. The arid countryside, the loneliness and the cost of transport also took their toll. When tough men of capital could make a fortune in the east, there were few good reasons to struggle against the frustrations of the west, and most of the early settlers left. Two decades on, there were just 5000 Europeans holding out on the western edge of the continent. Some of the capitalists who had stayed began to rethink their aversion to using cheap prison labour.

In 1850 – just as the practice of sending British convicts to eastern Australia ended – shiploads of male convicts started to arrive in Fremantle harbour.

Exploration & Gold

Meanwhile, several explorers undertook journeys into the remote Aboriginal territories, drawn in by dreams of mighty rivers and rolling plains of grass 'further out'. Mostly their thirsty ordeals ended in disappointment. But the pastoralists did expand through much of the southwestern corner of WA, while others took up runs on the rivers of the northwest and in the Kimberley.

Perhaps the most staggering journey of exploration was undertaken by an Aboriginal man called Wylie and the explorer Edward Eyre, who travelled from South Australia, across the vast, dry Nullarbor Plain, to Albany.

By the 1880s, the entire European population of this sleepy western third of Australia was not much more than 40,000 people. In the absence of democracy, a network of city merchants and large squatters exercised political and economic control over the colony.

FREMANTLE ARTS CENTRE

Built by convicts, the Fremantle Arts Centre was once a lunatic asylum and then a poorhouse, or 'women's home'. Today this Gothic building is a thriving arts centre well worth a visit.

1880s–90s

Gold changes everything. The first discoveries are in the Kimberley and the Pilbara, followed by massive finds in Coolgardie and Kalgoorlie.

1890

The state's first trade unions are formed by three men. Unions exert a substantial influence for the following century.

» Fremantle Arts Centre

The great agent of change was gold. The first discoveries were made in the 1880s in the Kimberley and Pilbara, followed by huge finds in the 1890s at Coolgardie and Kalgoorlie, in hot, dry country 600km inland from Perth. So many people were lured by the promise of gold that the population of the colony doubled and redoubled in a single decade. But the easy gold was soon exhausted, and most independent prospectors gave way to mining companies that had the capital to sink deep shafts.

The Great Pipeline to Kalgoorlie

The year 1890 also saw the introduction of representative government, a full generation after democracy had arrived in the east. The first elected premier was a tough, capable bushman named John Forrest, who borrowed courageously in order to finance vast public works to encourage immigrants and private investors. He was blessed with the services of a brilliant civil engineer, CY O'Connor. O'Connor oversaw the improvement of the Fremantle harbour, and built and ran the state's rail system. But O'Connor's greatest feat was the construction of a system of steam-powered pumping stations along a mighty pipeline to drive water uphill, from Mundaring Weir near Perth to the thirsty goldfields around distant Kalgoorlie.

By the time Forrest opened the pipeline, O'Connor was dead. His political enemies had defamed him in the press and in parliament, falsely accusing him of incompetence and corruption. On 10 March 1902, O'Connor rode into the surf near Fremantle and shot himself. Today, the site of his anguish is commemorated by a haunting statue of him on horseback, which rises out of the waves at South Beach.

Ironically, just as the water began to flow, the mining industry went into decline. But the 'Golden Pipeline' continues to supply water to the mining city of Kalgoorlie where gold is once again being mined, on a Herculean scale unimaginable a century ago. Today you can visit the No 1 Pump Station at Mundaring Weir and follow the Golden Pipeline Heritage Trail as a motorist from Perth to Kalgoorlie, where you can visit the rather astonishing Super Pit.

The Stolen Generations

At the turn of the century, the lives of many Aborigines became more wretched. The colony's 1893 Education Act empowered the parents of white schoolchildren to bar any Aboriginal child from attending their school, and it was not long before Aborigines were completely excluded from state-run classrooms. The following decade, the government embarked on a policy of removing so-called 'half-caste' children from their parents, placing them with white families or in government institutions. The objective of the policy was explicit. Full-blood Aborigines were to

1890

Representative government is formed. Bushman John Forrest is the first elected premier.

1893

Inception of the Education Act, which allows white parents to bar Aboriginal children from schools. What follows is a policy of removal of 'half-caste' children from their parents.

1901

Western Australia and the other colonies are federated to form the nation of Australia.

1902

Following false accusations of incompetence and corruption, CY O'Connor, engineer of the great pipeline from Perth to Kalgoorlie, takes his own life at a Fremantle beach.

be segregated in the belief that they were doomed to extinction, while half-caste children were expected to marry whites, thereby breeding the Aborigines out of existence. These policies inflicted great suffering and sadness on the many Aborigines who were recognised in the 1990s as 'the stolen generations'.

Wars & the Depression

On 1 January 1901, WA and the other colonies federated to form the nation of Australia. This was not a declaration of independence. This new Australia was a dominion within the British Empire. It was as citizens of the Empire that thousands of Australian men volunteered to fight in the Australian Imperial Force when WWI broke out in 1914. They fought in Turkey, Sinai and in Europe – notably on the Somme. Over 200,000 of them were killed or wounded over the terrible four years of the war. Today, in cities and towns across the state, you will see war memorials that commemorate their service.

Though mining, for the time being, had ceased to be an economic force, farmers were developing the lucrative West Australian wheat belt, which they cultivated with the horse-drawn stump-jump plough, one of the icons of Australian frontier farming. At the same time, a growing demand for wool, beef and the expansion of dairying added to the state's economic growth.

Nevertheless, many people were struggling to earn a living – especially those ex-soldiers who were unable to shake off the horrors they had endured in the trenches. In 1929, the lives of these 'battlers' grew even more miserable when the cold winds of the Great Depression blew through the towns and farms of the state. So alienated did West Australians feel from the centres of power and politics in the east that, in 1933, two-thirds of them voted to secede from the rest of Australia. Although the decision was never enacted, it expressed a profound sense of isolation from the east which is still a major factor in the culture and attitudes of the state today.

In 1939, Australians were once again fighting a war alongside the British, this time against Hitler in WWII. But the military situation changed radically in December 1941 when the Japanese bombed the American Fleet at Hawaii's Pearl Harbor. The Japanese swept through Southeast Asia and, within weeks, were threatening Australia. Over the next two years they bombed several towns in the north of the state, including Broome, which was almost abandoned.

It was not the British but the Americans who came to Australia's aid. As thousands of Australian soldiers were taken prisoner and suffered in the torturous Japanese prisoner-of-war camps, West Australians opened their arms to US servicemen. Fremantle was transformed into an Allied

Kim Scott's *Benang* (1999), which won the Miles Franklin Award in 2000, is a confronting but rewarding read about the assimilation policies of the 20th century and the devastating effect they had on Aboriginal Australia.

BENANG

1914
Over 200,000 are killed or wounded in WWI.

1933
Two-thirds of the voting population votes to secede from the rest of the country. Although never enacted, secession remains topical.

1939
WWII begins. Several towns in WA's north, including Broome, are bombed during the war. Fremantle is turned into an Allied naval base, and a US submarine-refuelling base is established at Exmouth.

1963
Development of the gargantuan Ord River Irrigation Scheme to fertilise the desert.

WESTERN AUSTRALIA IN BLACK & WHITE

Like other Aboriginal Australians in the rest of the country, the 70,000 or so who live in Western Australia (WA) are the state's most disadvantaged group. Many live in deplorable conditions; outbreaks of preventable diseases are common, and infant mortality rates are higher than in many developing countries.

The issue of racial relations in WA is a problematic one, and racial intolerance is still evident in many parts of the state. Especially (but not exclusively) in the remote northwest, a form of unofficial apartheid appears to exist, and travellers are bound to be confronted by it.

naval base for operations in the Indian Ocean, while a US submarine-refuelling base was established at Exmouth. In New Guinea and the Pacific, Americans and Australians fought together until the tide of war eventually turned in their favour.

Postwar Prosperity

When the war ended, the story of modern WA began to unfold. Under the banner of 'Postwar Reconstruction', the federal government set about transforming Australia with a policy of assisted immigration, designed to populate Australia more densely as a defence against the 'hordes' of Asia. Many members of this new workforce found jobs in the mines, where men and machines turned over thousands of tonnes of earth in search of the precious lode. On city stock exchanges, the names of such West Australian mines as Tom Price, Mt Newman and Goldsworthy became symbols of development, modernisation and wealth. Now, rather than being a wasteland that history had forgotten, the West was becoming synonymous with ambition, and a new spirit of capitalist pioneering. As union membership flourished, labour and capital entered into a pact to turn the country to profit. In the Kimberley, the government built the gigantic Ord River Irrigation Scheme, which boasted that it could bring fertility to the desert – and which convinced many West Australians that engineering and not the environment contained the secret of life.

Largely set in Western Australia, *Gallipoli* (1981, directed by Peter Weir, screenplay by David Williamson) is an iconic Australian movie exploring naivety, social pressure to enlist and, ultimately, the utter futility of this campaign.

There was so much country, it hardly seemed to matter that salt was starting to poison country in the wheat belt or that mines scoured the land. In 1952, the British exploded their first nuclear bomb on the state's Montebello Islands. And, when opponents of the test alleged that nuclear clouds were drifting over Australia, the government scoffed. The land was big and the government wanted a strong, nuclear-armed ally to protect Australia in the Cold War world.

1980s

The state becomes known as WA Inc, a reference to its image as a giant corporation intent on speculation and profit.

1983

'Bondie' (Alan Bond) funds the racing yacht *Australia II*, which wins the America's Cup with its secret winged keel. Bond is later jailed for corporate fraud.

1990s

Aboriginal rock art, featuring distinctive stick-like images, is found in the Kimberley. Known as the Bradshaw paintings, these could be among the earliest figurative paintings ever executed.

» Bradshaw paintings

This spirit of reckless capitalism reached its climax in the 1980s when the state became known as 'WA Inc' – a reference to the state in operation as a giant corporation in which government, business and unions had lost sight of any value other than speculation and profit. The embodiment of this brash spirit was an English migrant named Alan Bond, who became a multimillionaire.

Once bankrupt and convicted of corporate fraud, Alan Bond's wealth was estimated at $265 million by *Business Review Weekly* in 2008.

The State Today

Today the population of the entire state is just 2.3 million people – about half of whom have come from overseas. Fewer than 70,000 of these are Aborigines. In 1993, the federal government recognised that Aborigines with an ongoing association with their traditional lands were the rightful owners, unless those lands had been sold to someone else.

1990s
The stolen generations are formally recognised.

1995
The Fremantle Dockers join the Australian Football League.

1998
One of Australia's most infamous trade union battles is waged in Fremantle between the Maritime Union and Patrick Corporation (a stevedore company).

2000s
Unparalleled economic growth due to the mining boom.

The Environment

Tim Flannery
Tim Flannery is a scientist, explorer and writer. He has written several award-winning books including *The Future Eaters*, *Throwim Way Leg* and *The Weather Makers*.

The first naturalists to investigate Australia were astonished by what they found. Here the swans were black – to Europeans this was a metaphor for the impossible – while mammals such as the platypus and echidna were discovered to lay eggs. It really was an upside-down world, where many of the larger animals hopped, where each year the trees shed their bark rather than their leaves and where the 'pears' were made of wood.

It's worthwhile understanding the basics about how nature operates in Australia. This is important because there's nowhere like Australia, and once you have an insight into its origins and natural rhythms, you will appreciate the place so much more.

The Land

Its Sleepy Soil

There are two big factors that go a long way towards explaining nature in Australia: its soils and its climate. Both are unique. Australian soils are the more subtle and difficult to notice of the two, but they have been fundamental in shaping life here. On the other continents, in recent geological times processes such as volcanism, mountain building and glacial activity have been busy creating new soil. Just think of the glacier-derived soils of North America, north Asia and Europe. They feed the world today, and were made by glaciers grinding up rock of differing chemical composition over the last two million years. The rich soils of India and parts of South America were made by rivers eroding mountains, while Java in Indonesia owes its extraordinary richness to volcanoes.

Mt Augustus (1106m), on the central west coast, is the largest rock in the world, twice the size and three times as old as Uluru in the Northern Territory.

All of these soil-forming processes have been almost absent from Australia in more recent times. Only volcanoes have made a contribution, and they cover less than 2% of the continent's land area. In fact, for the last 90 million years, beginning deep in the age of dinosaurs, Australia has been geologically comatose. It was too flat, warm and dry to attract glaciers, its crust too ancient and thick to be punctured by volcanoes or folded into mountains. Look at Uluru and Kata Tjuta (the Olgas). They are the stumps of mountains that 350 million years ago were the height of the Andes. Yet for hundreds of millions of years they've been nothing but nubs.

Under such conditions no new soil is created and the old soil is leached of all its goodness by the rain, and is blown and washed away. Even if just 30cm of rain falls each year, that adds up to a column of water 30 million kilometres high passing through the soil over 100 million years, and that can do a great deal of leaching. Almost all of Australia's mountain ranges are more than 90 million years old, so you will see a lot of sand here,

GOING CAMPING? HERE'S THE OVERVIEW *REBECCA CHAU*

Stretching out under the night's sky is perhaps the best way to experience Western Australia's big-ticket natural attractions. Most parks are managed by the Department of Environment & Conservation (DEC), which has offices throughout the state. Camping is allowed in designated areas of specific parks (around $14 per night for two people). The DEC produces informative brochures on the major national parks and nature reserves, as well as reams of other literature and maps. To be assured of a camp site during peak periods, park rangers recommend turning up early in the morning (with a smile), when sites are being vacated, to secure a spot.

You will also need a park pass. If you will be visiting multiple parks, the DEC Holiday Pass is an economical option, as about $40 (per vehicle) will buy you unlimited access to parks for four weeks. If you're taking it a bit slower, the Annual All Parks Pass ($80) grants you unlimited entry to most parks (check the fine print) across the state for a year. Passes are available on the DEC website (www.dec.wa.gov.au), visitor centres and park entrances.

and a lot of country where the rocky 'bones' of the land are sticking up through the soil. It is an old, infertile landscape, and life in Australia has been adapting to these conditions for aeons.

Enter El Niño

Australia's misfortune in respect to soils is echoed in its climate. In most parts of the world outside the wet tropics, life responds to the rhythm of the seasons – summer to winter, or wet to dry. Most of Australia experiences seasons – sometimes very severe ones – yet life does not respond solely to them. This can clearly be seen by the fact that although there's plenty of snow and cold country in Australia, there are almost no trees that shed their leaves in winter, nor do any Australian animals hibernate. Instead there is a far more potent climatic force that Australian life must obey: El Niño.

The cycle of flood and drought that El Niño brings to Australia is profound. The rivers – even the mighty Murray River, the nation's largest, which runs through the southeast – can be kilometres wide one year, while you can literally step over its flow the next. This is the power of El Niño, and its effect, when combined with Australia's poor soils, manifests itself compellingly. As you might expect from this, relatively few of Australia's birds are seasonal breeders, and few migrate. Instead, they breed when the rain comes, and a large percentage are nomads, following the rain across the breadth of the continent.

Wildlife

Australia's plants and animals are just about the closest things to alien life you are likely to encounter on earth. That's because Australia has been isolated from the other continents for a very long time – at least 45 million years. The other habitable continents have been able to exchange various species at different times because they've been linked by land bridges. Just 15,000 years ago it was possible to walk from the southern tip of Africa right through Asia and the Americas to Tierra del Fuego. Not Australia, however. Its birds, mammals, reptiles and plants have taken their own separate and very different evolutionary journey, and the result today is the world's most distinct – and one of its most diverse – natural realms.

Tim Flannery's *The Future Eaters* is a highly readable overview of evolution in Australasia, covering the last 120 million years of history, with thoughts on how the environment has shaped Australasia's human cultures.

The Secrets of the Marsupials

Australia is, of course, famous as the home of the kangaroo and other marsupials. Unless you visit a wildlife park, such creatures are not easy to see as most are nocturnal. Their lifestyles, however, are exquisitely attuned to Australia's harsh conditions. Have you ever wondered why kangaroos, alone among the world's larger mammals, hop? It turns out that hopping is the most efficient way of getting about at medium speeds. This is because the energy of the bounce is stored in the tendons of the legs – much like in a pogo stick – while the intestines bounce up and down like a piston, emptying and filling the lungs without needing to activate the chest muscles. When travelling long distances to find meagre feed, such efficiency is a must.

Marsupials are so efficient that they need to eat a fifth less food than equivalent-sized placental mammals (everything from bats to rats, whales and ourselves). But some marsupials have taken energy efficiency much further. If you visit a wildlife park or zoo you might notice that far-away look in a koala's eyes. It seems as if nobody is home – and this is near the truth. Several years ago biologists announced that koalas are the only living creatures that have brains that don't fit their skulls. Instead they have a shrivelled walnut of a brain that rattles around in a fluid-filled cranium. Other researchers have contested this finding, however, pointing out that the brains of the koalas examined for the study may have shrunk because these organs are so soft. Whether soft-brained or empty-headed, there is no doubt that the koala is not the Einstein of the animal world, and we now believe that it has sacrificed its brain to energy efficiency. Brains cost a lot to run – our brains typically weigh 2% of our bodyweight, but use 20% of the energy we consume. Koalas eat gum leaves, which are so toxic that they use 20% of their energy just detoxifying this food. This leaves little energy for the brain, and living in the tree tops where there are so few predators means that they can get by with few wits at all.

The peculiar constraints of the Australian environment have not made everything dumb. The koala's nearest relative, the wombat (of which there are three species), has a large brain for a marsupial. These creatures live in complex burrows and can weigh up to 35kg, making them the largest herbivorous burrowers on Earth. Because their burrows are effectively air-conditioned, they have the neat trick of turning down their metabolic activity when they are in residence. One physiologist who studied their thyroid hormones found that biological activity ceased to such an extent in sleeping wombats that, from a hormonal point of view, they appeared to be dead! Wombats can remain underground for a week at a time, and can get by on just a third of the food needed by a sheep of equivalent size. One day, perhaps, efficiency-minded farmers will keep wombats instead of sheep. At the moment, however, that isn't possible, for the largest of the wombat species, the northern hairy-nose, is one of the world's rarest creatures, with only around 100 surviving in a remote nature reserve in central Queensland.

One of the more common marsupials you might catch a glimpse of in the national parks around Australia's major cities is the species of antechinus, or marsupial mouse. These nocturnal, rat-sized creatures lead an extraordinary life. The males live for just 11 months, the first 10 of which consist of a concentrated burst of eating and growing. And like teenagers, the day comes when their minds turn to sex, which then becomes an obsession. As they embark on their quest for females they forget to eat and sleep. Instead they gather in logs and woo passing females by serenading them with squeaks. By the end of August – just two weeks after they reach 'puberty' – every single male is dead, exhausted by sex and by carrying around swollen testes. This extraordinary life history may also have evolved in response to Australia's trying environmental conditions. It seems likely that if the males survived mating, they would compete with the females as they tried to find enough food to feed their growing

NUMBATS

Keep your eyes peeled for the banded anteater, also known as the numbat. Tiny, light-footed and incredibly shy, the numbat is a solitary creature who will venture outside its neatly delineated territory only to find a mate. Singular dietary requirement: termites.

young. Basically, antechinus dads are disposable. They do better for antechinus posterity if they go down in a testosterone-fuelled blaze of glory.

If you are very lucky, you might see a honey possum. This tiny marsupial is an enigma. Somehow it gets all of its dietary requirements from nectar and pollen, and in the southwest there are always enough flowers around for it to survive. No one, though, knows why the males need sperm larger even than those of the blue whale, or why their testes are so massive. Were humans as well endowed, men would be walking around with the equivalent of a 4kg bag of potatoes between their legs!

So challenging are the conditions in Australia that its birds have developed some extraordinary habits. The kookaburras, magpies and blue wrens you are likely to see – to name just a few – have developed a breeding system called 'helpers at the nest'. The helpers are the young adult birds of previous breedings, which stay with their parents to help bring up the new chicks. Just why they should do this was a mystery until it was realised that conditions in Australia can be so harsh that more than two adult birds are needed to feed the nestlings. This pattern of breeding is very rare in places like Asia, Europe and North America, but it is common in a wide array of Australian birds.

Field Guide to the Birds of Australia is full colour, splendidly detailed, accessible and portable. This endlessly fascinating reference, Pizzey and Knight's claim to fame, is in its 8th edition.

Specialist Plants

Australia's plants can be irresistibly fascinating. If you happen to be in the Perth area in spring, it's well worth taking a wildflower tour. The best flowers grow on the arid and monotonous sand plains, and the blaze of colour produced by the kangaroo paws, banksias and similar native plants can be dizzying. The sheer variety of flowers is amazing, with 4000 species crowded into the southwestern corner of the continent. This diversity of prolific flowering plants has long puzzled botanists. Again, Australia's poor soils seem to be the cause. The sand plain is about the poorest soil in Australia – almost pure quartz. This prevents any one fast-growing species from dominating. Instead, thousands of specialist plant species have learned to find a narrow niche, and so coexist. Some live at the foot of the metre-high sand dunes, some on top, some on an east-facing slope, some on the west and so on. Their flowers need to be striking in order to attract pollinators, for nutrients are so lacking in this sandy location that insects like bees are rare.

Whale, shark, or fish? Head to Ningaloo Reef around April to June to swim alongside the many-metres-long, remarkably docile whale sharks.

If you do get to walk the wildflower regions of the southwest, keep your eyes open for the sundews. Australia is the centre of diversity for

TOP WESTERN AUSTRALIA WILDFLOWER SPOTS
REBECCA CHAU

Some starting points:

» Kings Park, Perth (see p55). Especially the Botanic Garden, with its 2000 or so species.

» Fitzgerald River National Park, between Albany and Esperance on the south coast (see p156).

» Porongurup National Park, north of Albany (see p153). Doubles as a low-key wine region.

» Stirling Range National Park, also north of Albany (see p154). Also a wonderful hiking and camping area.

» Mullewa, in the central Midlands (see p111). The annual wildflower show blooms in August.

» Kalbarri National Park, on the Batavia Coast (see p168).

» Wongan Hills and Morawa, in the central Midlands (see p111).

these beautiful, carnivorous plants. They've given up on the soil supplying their nutritional needs and have turned instead to trapping insects with sweet globs of moisture on their leaves, and digesting them to obtain nitrogen and phosphorus.

The Environmental Story

The European colonisation of Australia, commencing in 1788, heralded a period of catastrophic environmental upheaval, with the result that Australians today are struggling with some of the most severe environmental problems to be found anywhere. It may seem strange that a population of just 22 million, living in a continent the size of the USA minus Alaska, could inflict such damage on its environment, but Australia's long isolation, its fragile soils and difficult climate have made it particularly vulnerable to human-induced change.

Environmental Battles Waged, and Continued

» 1970s: environmentalists took on and defeated the Albany whaling industry.

» 1980s: clashes with loggers over the old-growth, jarrah, karri and wandoo forests in the southwest.

» 2000s: Ningaloo Reef saved from development of a $200-million-dollar marina resort.

» Today: controversy over a planned major gas refinery at the Kimberley's James Price Point.

Damage to Australia's environment has been inflicted in several ways, the most important being the introduction of pest species, destruction of forests, overstocking rangelands, inappropriate agriculture and interference with water flows. Beginning with the escape of domestic cats into the Australian bush shortly after 1788, a plethora of vermin, from foxes to wild camels and cane toads, have run wild in Australia, causing extinctions in the native fauna. One out of every 10 native mammals living in Australia prior to European colonisation is now extinct, and many more are highly endangered. Extinctions have also affected native plants, birds and amphibians.

The destruction of forests has also had a profound effect. Most of Australia's rainforests have suffered clearing, while conservationists fight with loggers over the fate of the last unprotected stands of 'old growth'. Many Australian rangelands have been chronically overstocked for more than a century, the result being extreme vulnerability of both soils and rural economies to Australia's drought and flood cycle, as well as extinction of many native species. The development of agriculture has involved land clearance and the provision of irrigation, and here again the effect has been profound. Clearing of the diverse and spectacular plant communities of the Western Australian wheat belt began just a century ago, yet today up to one-third of that country is degraded by salination of the soils. Between 70kg and 120kg of salt lies below every square metre of the region, and clearing of native vegetation has allowed water to penetrate deep into the soil, dissolving the salt crystals and carrying brine towards the surface.

In terms of financial value, just 1.5% of Australia's land surface provides over 95% of agricultural yield, and much of this land lies in the irrigated regions of the Murray-Darling Basin. This is Australia's agricultural heartland, yet it too is under severe threat from salting of soils and rivers. Irrigation water penetrates into the sediments laid down in an ancient sea, carrying salt into the catchments and fields.

In *The Weather Makers*, Tim Flannery argues lucidly and passionately for the immediate need to address the implications of a global climate change that is damaging all life on earth and endangering our very survival. An accessible read.

Despite the enormity of the biological crisis engulfing Australia, governments and the community have been slow to respond. It was in the 1980s that coordinated action began to take place, but not until the 1990s that major steps were taken. The establishment of Landcare (www.landcareaustralia.com.au), an organisation enabling people to effectively address local environmental issues, and the expenditure of over $2 billion through the federal government initiative Caring for Our Country (www.nrm.gov.au) have been important national initiatives. Yet so difficult are some of the issues the nation faces that, as yet, little has been achieved in terms of halting the destructive processes. Individuals are also banding together to help. Groups such as the Bush Heritage Australia (www.bushheritage.org.au) and the Australian Wildlife Conservancy (AWC; www.

NINGALOO'S CLOSE SCRAPE *REBECCA CHAU*

Some locals still sport 'Save Ningaloo' bumper stickers on their cars. No one seems to pay much attention to the faded stickers these days, but they're a reminder of one of the most high-profile and fiercely contested environmental campaigns the state has seen. 'Save Ningaloo', with its thousands of protestors, successfully blocked development of a massive marina resort (slated for 2003) on a loggerhead turtle nesting ground. Ningaloo, comprising 280km of coral reef, and species such as manta rays, whale sharks, dugongs, humpbacks and turtles, is one of the last healthy major reef systems in the world.

australianwildlife.org) allow people to donate funds and time to the conservation of native species. Some such groups have been spectacularly successful; the AWC, for example, already manages many endangered species over its 2.5-million-hectare holdings.

So severe are Australia's problems that it will take a revolution before they can be overcome, for sustainable practices need to be implemented in every arena of life – from farms to suburbs and city centres. Renewable energy, sustainable agriculture and water use lie at the heart of these changes, and Australians are only now developing the road map to sustainability that they so desperately need if they are to have a long-term future on the continent.

For detailed direction on where and how to surround yourself in wildflowers, see the Wildflower Society of Western Australia's website (www.members.ozemail.com.au/~wildflowers).

Local Produce & Wine

What You'll Find Today

Truth is, regional produce and local wines are the highlights here, and restaurants tend to be slightly more expensive than what you might expect. Slow-paced, outdoor eating is what Western Australia (WA) does best, and for this you should wind your way into the wine regions of Margaret River, the Porongurups, Denmark and the Swan Valley – in these areas nestle some of the state's best restaurants and winery-restaurants. Select spots up north – Broome, Kununurra, Exmouth – remain underrated, and Geraldton has an emerging fine dining scene.

Regional produce to snuffle up into your stomach in the manner of a truffle-hunting dog includes marron (small freshwater crayfish unique to the southwest), crayfish (rock lobster, from up north), McHenry Hohnen beef (Margaret River) and barramundi (the Kimberley). Importantly, some of WA's best produce can be picked up at a supermarket, roadhouse or pub: Browne's iced coffee and yoghurts, Harvey Fresh products (orange juice is its gold standard) and chilli mussels, the state's low-key, low-fuss dish.

The food scene is, of course, most active in Perth. Having strived – and, in some cases, foundered – throughout the last two decades in their attempt to keep up with dining standards internationally and over east, WA restaurants have now settled into their own skin a little more. Chefs embrace and quietly celebrate the region's produce, which is of an excel-

Best for Vegetarians

» **Perth restaurants:** Annalakshmi, Juicy Beetroot, Chutney Mary's

» **Perth/Fremantle grocery:** Kakulas Bros and Kakulas Sisters

» **Up north:** You're on your own

TOP COOKBOOKS TO COLLECT

» *Wine and Food* by Kate Lamont. Winemaker and chef Kate Lamont unpretentiously matches food with wine – chapters are helpfully organised into champagne, light whites, robust whites, dessert wines etc. Lamont has eponymous cellar doors, wineries and restaurants in the Swan Valley, Margaret River and Perth.

» *Whole Food* by Jude Blereau. A straightforward cookbook devoted to unprocessed food. Blereau has been promoting whole food in Perth for the last two decades or so.

» *Degustation* by Alain Fabrègues. Perhaps more a memento of your travels than a working cookbook, this mini-shrine to French degustation is produced by the chef at the Loose Box, a dining destination in Mundaring that has long enjoyed an excellent reputation.

» *Must Eat* by Russell Blaikie. A nicely done French-style working cookbook that prises out the best of the region's produce – Cone Bay barramundi, Mt Barker chicken, Jarrahdene free-range pork. Must is a well-regarded wine bar and restaurant in Mt Lawley, Perth.

ESSENTIAL CELLAR DOOR STOPS

Aside from the founding five (see p240), a second set of wineries remain standouts:

» **Devil's Lair** Small, cosy, stylish cellar door with top-of-the-line Chardonnay and Cabernet. Check out the Fifth Leg series as well.

» **Happs** Extensive, impressive range of wines (including the Three Hills range). And pottery.

» **Howard Park** Brilliant Cabernet and Shiraz, and a wide range of styles and prices. It also makes the MadFish range.

» **Pierro** Powerful Chardonnay and Sauvignon Blanc. The reds are not as impressive.

» **Voyager Estate** (p133) Great wines across the board, and an elegant cellar door and restaurant.

» **Xanadu** (p133) Broad range, decent cellar door and restaurant.

lent standard, crafting interpretations with Manjimup truffles, Mt Barker chicken and Shark Bay scallops. Spots in the city (Balthazar, Greenhouse), Mt Lawley (Must Winebar, Jackson's) and Shenton Park (Star Anise) are leading top-end nooks. In Fremantle, most of the best cluster around the city centre, with select secrets in North Fremantle (Harvest) and down on Fishing Boat Harbour (Little Creatures, Mussel Bar).

Across the state, food becomes patchier, and you can pay too much by anyone's standards for a middling pasta or burger in smaller towns as well as in Perth. Generally, the best value can be found at the top end, and then down the bottom (Asian eateries in Northbridge, and farmers markets). If you're willing to do a little research, you will still have a wonderful time at the table.

Then There's Beer

The state's leading exponents of working-class beer are Emu Bitter ('EB'; quite bitter) and Swan Draught (less tart than EB). Neither claims to have a complicated taste, and you should knock back at least one of these coldies while you're here.

Top boutique beers include Little Creatures Pale Ale (along with the light Rogers, Bright Ale and the refreshing Pilsner), Fat Yak, and the beers at Duckstein, in the Swan Valley. Little Creatures in Fremantle is also a big, laid-back dining destination in its own right.

Up north, boutique beers as well as EB and Swan are surprisingly difficult to find. Instead Carlton, XXXX and Tooheys dominate.

Australian beer has a higher alcohol content than British or American beers. Standard beer is around 5% alcohol (midstrength is around 3.5%; light, 2% to 3%).

Wine & the Cellar Door

Wine is a big deal here. Although the leading wine-producing region, Margaret River, produces only 3% of Australia's grapes (suggesting the place is small-fry), it actually accounts for over 20% of the country's premium wines. It seems that Margaret River, the first place to roll off any local's tongue when the topic of wine, food and the good life comes up, has always had one eye fixed firmly on quality.

The first wineries began to put down roots in the southwest in the 1960s. Vasse Felix, today a thriving winery, cellar door and restaurant, is the notable early player. Although the Australian wine industry enjoyed a sustained period of growth from the '60s to the 2000s, by 2005 and 2006 it found itself in a state of oversupply. But because the southwest has always focused on low-yield, quality output, it hasn't felt the bite as keenly

DINING OUT

Tipping is not required in WA.

BYO – Bring Your Own beer or wine to the restaurant – is a widely accepted and budget-friendly practice.

as other regions in the country. And Margaret River has been buoyed by reliable rain; 2007 to 2009 were very good vintages.

There is one winery that specialises in mass volume: Houghton Wines, founded in 1836 in the Swan Valley. You'll see the White Classic on tables everywhere, and it's pretty good value. But to many locals Houghton is a cheap wine, and so the winery has had trouble selling some of its other more upmarket wines such as its 2009 Rieslings and the Wisdom range, which are worth it.

Aside from the Swan Valley and Margaret River, key winery regions in the state are the Great Southern (Frankland, the Porongurups, Denmark, Mt Barker), Pemberton, and the Peel and Geographe regions. Together with Margaret River these uphold WA's reputation as a world-class producer of a wide variety of table wines, both red and white.

Five Underrated Wineries

» Arlewood

» Ashbrook

» Harewood

» Heydon Estate

» Juniper Estate

Margaret River

WA's best wineries are firmly planted in Margaret River, 250km (3½ hours' drive) southwest of Perth. Here the climate is defined by the wind from the ocean that cools the area, producing Margaret River's distinctive, quality wines that are elegant, ripe and rich.

Margaret River also produces a lot of wine using a blend of Semillon and Sauvignon Blanc grapes. These very popular fruity wines are not Margaret River's very best, but they are often the most affordable. Cape Mentelle, Cullen Wines and Lenton Brae all make particularly exotic examples.

Best Margaret River Winery Restaurants

» Cullen Wines

» Knee Deep in Margaret River (the draw here is really the food)

» Leeuwin Estate

» Vasse Felix

Swan Valley

The Swan Valley may once have aspired to take on Margaret River. These days, though, it's given up the game, and the Swan Valley's true merit lies in its proximity to Perth and its small clutch of winery-restaurants – not the wines per se. It's hotter up here than down south, so the long-and-lazy outdoor dining opportunities are better, and you can take the boat from Perth along the Swan River to Sandalford Winery.

Houghton Wines is the area's best winery, and the Houghton Classic White, a blend of white-wine grapes that drinks like a mix of tropical, zesty fruits, is the Swan Valley's most distinguished and ubiquitous wine. Others of note include Lamont Wines and Sandalford. Best for lunch are Riverbank Estate and Lamont's (albeit tapas only).

Peel & Geographe Regions

This area stretches south of Perth, in the direction (but short) of Margaret River, from Rockingham to Donnybrook. Because the Peel region

MARGARET RIVER'S FOUNDING FIVE

Five top wineries comprise the cornerstone of Margaret River, and they're just as strong today as they were 20 years ago.

» **Cape Mentelle** Makes consistently excellent Cabernet Sauvignon and a wonderful example of Sauvignon Blanc Semillon.

» **Cullen Wines** (p129) Still in the family, it produces a superb Chardonnay and an excellent Cabernet Merlot.

» **Leeuwin Estate** (p133) A brilliant estate: excellent wines, a stylish cellar door and a highly regarded restaurant. Put Chardonnay on the map with one of the best in Australia – the Art Series.

» **Moss Wood** Makes a heady Semillon, a notable Cabernet Sauvignon and a surprising Pinot Noir.

» **Vasse Felix** (p128) Very good all-round, must-see winery.

starts about 70km south of Perth, it's often hot, dry and rugged. Much like the Swan Valley, wine here is not generally considered of great significance. Millbrook Winery, relatively close to Perth, is excellent for lunch, with a big, wraparound verandah from which you can survey the vines.

Further south, in the slightly cooler Geographe region, you'll find a large selection of wineries of varying quality, and most people are here for one thing: Capel Vale. This winery has a 30-year history of winemaking excellence, particularly with Chardonnay, Shiraz and, more recently, Merlot. Willow Bridge Estate also produces a large number of well-priced wines; the whites attract attention.

Wine for Dudes (www.winefordudes.com) has excellent wine tours led by a winemaker – not that anyone thought wine wasn't for dudes.

Great Southern & Pemberton

The Great Southern region will never challenge Margaret River's preeminence among wine-touring regions – Margaret River is so spectacularly beautiful – but it nevertheless produces good-quality wines. Wine tourism here is not as developed, and that can be a good thing. Shiraz, Cabernet Sauvignon, Riesling and Sauvignon Blanc do especially well down here.

The region stretches from the southeast town of Frankland, further southeast to Albany, and then west again to Denmark. Mt Barker, smackbang in the middle, is 350km southeast of Perth. The Great Southern's wines are full of flavour and power, but they won't blow your head off. They have a sense of elegance – try the peppery Shirazes.

In Frankland, Alkoomi is still a family-run business, and produces both a great Cabernet Sauvignon and Riesling. Ferngrove produces an honest Chardonnay, an excellent Shiraz and a brilliant Cabernet Sauvignon-Shiraz blend called 'the Stirlings'. Finally, Frankland Estate is one of the key wineries that has helped revitalise Riesling.

The Wine Industry Association of Western Australia (www.winewa.asn.au) runs wine courses for consumers and the industry.

There are more wineries southwest of Frankland, in Mt Barker, and among the nearby Porongurup range. Riesling and Shiraz are consistently great performers here; also try the lean, long-flavoured Cabernet Sauvignon. Two of the best are Forest Hill (try its Cabernet Sauvignon) and Plantagenet Wines, the area's best winery. Chardonnays, Rieslings and reds are the types to seek out here.

Further south, in Denmark and Albany, you'll find some of the most esteemed wine names in Australia: Howard Park, which also has a post at Margaret River; West Cape Howe; and Wignall's Wines. Howard Park, the standout of the area, has superb Cabernet Sauvignon, Riesling and Chardonnay. West Cape Howe is a straightforward winery that's excellent value, and Wignall's Wines is noted for its Pinot Noir.

For information and tasting notes about Western Australian wines, and to shop online for reds and whites, visit www.mrwines.com.

If you travel east of Margaret River in the direction of the Great Southern wine region, about halfway between the two you'll hit the Pemberton–Manjimup area (280km due south of Perth). Pemberton is a beautiful, undulating area that's home to vast numbers of the area's famous karri trees, and its cool-ish climate produces cooler wine styles – Pinot Noir, Merlot and Chardonnay in particular. Excellent producers in Pemberton are Salitage Wines and Smithbrook Wines. Salitage is a large, stylish winery with all the bells and whistles – and the wines to back it up. Try one of the winery tours. Smithbrook Wines is probably the best in this area. Excellent Merlot.

Boom, Boom, Boom: Mining Life Today

If you fly into Perth, it will hit you straightaway: young people here have money. Gone is the old social order of toiling through an apprenticeship, siphoning off a portion of the pay packet for a deposit on a house in 10 years' time. Gone are the days of laboured double-major university degrees – primers for a life of white-collar modesty – as the one-and-only way to get ahead. Gone, too, is the rite of passage once observed among fit young men: a summer's work on the mines. Today, for a significant proportion of the West Australian population, working on the mines is day-to-day life.

Many of those who aren't out on the mines – who remain in metropolitan areas, primarily Perth – have had their lives changed by the mining boom, most apparently through their bank balance. Labour shortages in metropolitan areas (since so many have flown to the mines) have driven wages up, particularly for tradespeople. The mining peak of 2008 saw groups of brand-new, $80,000 utes clustered around building sites in Perth, and owned by young tradies barely out of their apprenticeships. To those flying overhead, these brightly coloured utes must look like toy beetles, insects marking out the path to wealth.

From the Ground Up

Western Australia (WA) is a frontier land built on mining money. Once a quieter part of the country focused on wheat, meat and wool, the state's fortunes were transformed by the discovery of gold in Coolgardie (1892) and Kalgoorlie (1893). Gold-mining reached fever pitch in the 1930s, with a revival in the mid-1980s. Today gold-mining is still going strong, and in Kalgoorlie you can visit the Super Pit, an open-pit gold mine the size of 35 football fields sunk 360m into the ground.

But iron ore is today's multi-billion-dollar blockbuster industry. Karara mine in the mid-west, for example, sits on $100 billion worth of iron ore at 2010 market prices. All this magnetite dug up out of the ground, later to become iron ore, is expected to generate $3 billion per year in export revenue for the next 30 years. Most of it will go to China.

Foreign investment is big business. Although this has raised the eyebrows of some Australians more accustomed to exercising command over their own land, now almost every new petroleum or gas project is foreign-owned or has a foreign partner (Chinese, but also Japanese and Singaporean, among others), and the same pattern is emerging in iron ore and coal. Consider that in iron-ore mining, for example, about $1 billion must be made available upfront just to develop the extraction machinery. Australia simply doesn't have that kind of money.

Life in the Wet Mess

The demonstrable signs of wealth are stamped in pockets across the state. In Perth, this is most notable in the western suburbs that line the beach and select positions along the Swan River: gardens manicured to an inch of their life and Mercedes aplenty. However, the original source of all this affluence remains outside most travellers' field of view. A Pilbara gold-mining town like Telfer, considered the most remote town in WA, is one example of a mine that economically and socially influences life elsewhere but which most locals – and visitors – never see.

Life in Telfer is altogether different to that on the coast. It is less a traditional country town – main street, two quiet pubs, a community hall – and more a gargantuan mine and its attendant camp, purpose-built for its hundreds of workers. Mining companies have in fact dismantled and rebuilt the town a few times in Telfer's history. In the mid-1990s, it was discovered to be cheaper to fly the entire workforce in and out of Telfer rather than permanently put up the men on-site. Those flown in would work for a sustained period of time (say, four weeks), then have a week or two off back home in Perth or over east. This enabled mining companies to recruit from a broader, more skilled labour force, since all too many workers were unwilling to commit themselves long-term to a massively isolated gold mine. And so the 'fly-in, fly-out' (FI-FO) work culture was born.

Cashed-up Bogans, a documentary by local filmmaker Jules Duncan, explores the lives of working-class West Australians and their new-found lifestyle based on big spending and hard partying.

CASHED-UP BOGANS

FI-FO life is perhaps no more apparent than in Karratha, once a sleepy, nondescript country town, now infamous for its bulging FI-FO population, expensive food and severe accommodation shortages. Woodside has set up camp here, exploring for gas off the north coast. Camp was set up so speedily, in fact, that there wasn't time to build brick-and-tile homes before work began. So today in Karratha, bolted on to the original small town centre, are a number of suburbs comprised of 'dongas' – makeshift, moveable, one-man accommodation units. A typical donga in Gap Ridge, the main suburb, has a single bed, TV, shower and toilet carved into a shipping-container-like box-home. Meals are taken in the wet mess, much like a mess hall.

Places like Gap Ridge are home to an almost entirely young, moneyed, male population, and this is creating a pattern of influx and change that in Karratha is echoed in other mining towns across the state. Many labourers are away from home and family, and have considerable funds to sink into beer and good times. Locals in Karratha, for example, have become increasingly vocal in their criticism that an entire FI-FO population parties in their town without regard for the community.

The FI-FO lifestyle ('work hard, play hard' is a closely held slogan) is also evident in Perth where, on any given weeknight, whichever bar or pub happens to be open late is packed to the gills with hard-partying men. Despite regular – in some cases, daily – breathalysing on many mine sites, the culture of drinking remains big. Many have mastered the technique of taking in 10 beers after work and blowing zero the next morning. Some on the mines posit that the popularity of recreational drugs in WA is attributable to the speed with which they can be flushed through the system. Marijuana lingers for an inconveniently long time, and random drugs tests are par for the course on-site.

All these social shifts have not gone unnoticed by politicians, including Premier Colin Barnett. One initiative intended to quell discontent is 'Royalties for Regions' – a policy of putting money back into regional areas like Karratha, which have not seen proper new infrastructure despite the boom. The cost and logistics of, say, putting in a new shopping centre is prohibitive; construction workers would need to be flown in and, in any case, wages would need to compete with those of Woodside. With young, unskilled labourers earning $150,000 per annum in mining, Karratha is probably not getting a new shopping mall anytime soon.

You're in or You're Out

Aboriginal Australian employment is very low within the mining industry. Some argue that training programs for Aboriginal Australians, attempts to settle Australia's most disadvantaged into the Western working life, have not proved effective. Many observe that the gap is widening between the resource-boom-driven 'haves' and 'have-nots', the latter struggling on with high rent, high cost of living, and a pervasive sense of not having been invited to the party they weren't planning to attend anyway.

Boomtown 2050, by landscape architect Richard Weller, is a nicely packaged book about how a rapidly growing town like Perth could be developed – sustainably.

Mining magnate Andrew 'Twiggy' Forrest, in 2010 labelled Australia's richest man by *Forbes*, also a former stockbroker with an interest in alpacas, has boldly promised support for 50,000 jobs for Aboriginal Australians. This government-backed program is also one of the most high-profile attempts by a key mining figure to not only change employment patterns but speak frankly about the lack of opportunity afforded to Aboriginal communities across the state. Just how the 50,000 jobs will be effectively taken up in the long term is yet to be determined, and that will be the tricky bit.

Survival Guide

Directory A–Z

Accommodation

The full gamut of options is available in Western Australia (WA), from camping grounds to high-end hotels. Perth's accommodation is generally more expensive than the rest of the state, although popular regions such as Margaret River, Broome, the Coral Coast and the Pilbara mining towns come very close. For the sake of simplicity, we've used the same price rating throughout the state.

In most areas you'll find seasonal price variations. Over summer (December to February) and at other peak times, particularly school and public holidays, prices are at their highest. Outside these times discounts and lower walk-in rates can be found. One exception is the far north, where the wet season (November to March) is the low season and prices can drop by as much as 50%. Low-season prices are quoted in this guidebook except for the Coral Coast & the Pilbara and Broome & Around chapters, as few travellers visit in the low/wet season.

Accommodation in the Pilbara can be hard to find, due to the fly-in, fly-out mining phenomena. Camping is often the best option.

B&Bs

Bed and breakfast (B&B) options include everything from rooms in a heritage building to a simple bedroom in a family home. A full cooked breakfast is not the norm. Tariffs for couples are typically in the $150 to $250 bracket, but can be much higher for exclusive properties. For online information, try www.australianbedandbreakfast.com.au, www.babs.com.au or www.ozbedandbreakfast.com.

BOOK YOUR STAY ONLINE

For more accommodation reviews by Lonely Planet authors, check out hotels.lonelyplanet.com/Perth and West Coast Australia. You'll find independent reviews, as well as recommendations on the best places to stay. Best of all, you can book online.

Camping & Caravan Parks

For many travellers, touring with a tent or campervan is the consummate WA experience. In the outback and up north you often won't even need a tent, and nights spent around a campfire under the stars are unforgettable. Check with visitor centres before heading out on long drives to confirm where there are free roadside stops. Many of these have been phased out in the shires immediately north of Perth but they become more frequent the further you are from the metropolis.

Designated camp sites in national parks cost $7/2 per adult/child with no or basic facilities other than a place to pitch your tent. For sites with showers (including unpowered caravan sites) the price is $9/2. Note that you will also need to pay entrance fees for many national parks, but only on the day you enter the park. If you're exploring several parks, it makes sense to pick up a four-week national park holiday pass ($40).

Commercial holiday parks are found all over the state. Prices range between $20 and $40 for a two-person site, with unpowered tent sites at the lower end of the scale and powered caravan sites at the top end. Lots of caravan parks are phasing out unpowered sites because they make less money from them – and everyone charges their electronic gadgets up in the camp kitchens. Most holiday parks offer units, which can range from simple cabins sharing the communal toilet block to flash self-contained, beachside chalets and apartments. In many beach towns these are the most upmarket accommodation options on offer.

Pick up a copy of the free, annually updated guide to *Caravanning, Camping and Motorhoming in WA*, available at visitor centres around the state, or visit the website www.caravanwa.com.au.

Dongas

Commonly found in the outback, especially in mining towns, the donga sits somewhere between a shed and a cabin. It's basically a prefab tin room (usually air-conditioned) with a single bed, TV and small fridge. You'll sometimes see them listed on a tariff sheet as 'budget room'. There are 'donga suburbs' springing up on the outskirts of towns and roadhouses all over the Pilbara.

Farmstays & Station Stays

For a true outback experience, some of the state's farms and stations offer a rural getaway. The Gascoyne and Pilbara areas are popular spots for station stays. At some you can kick back and watch other people raise a sweat, while others require you to pull your weight. Most accommodation is very comfortable – in the main homestead (B&B-style, many providing dinner on request) or in self-contained cottages on the property. Other farms provide budget options in outbuildings or former shearers' quarters – providing you an opportunity to wear that Akubra hat without looking silly. See www.towncountryaccommodationwa.com.au for options.

Hostels

Hostels are a highly social and very economical fixture of the WA accommodation scene. Many offer internet access, swimming pools, bars, weekly barbecues and free transport. Prices for dorm beds range from $23 to $35, while private rooms can be had for $60 to $85; the better ones have their own en suite bathrooms. Staff can often help in securing seasonal work.

For peace and quiet, avoid the party places and stay in the smaller hostels where often the owner is also the manager. Some hostels have become permanent addresses for contract workers, which tends to change the atmosphere, often for the worse. Wherever possible we've omitted these from the book.

A **Youth Hostel Association** (YHA; www.yha.com.au) or **Hostelling International** (HI; www.hihostels.com) annual membership (in Australia $42) gives a 10% discount at participating hostels. You can sign up at the first YHA you stay in, or collect 10 stamps for full-price nights stayed in YHAs for free membership.

VIP Backpackers (www.vipbackpackers.com) also offers membership-based discounts in participating WA hostels. For $43 you'll receive a 12-month membership, with discounts on accommodation and some transport, tours and activities. You can join online, at VIP hostels or at larger agencies dealing in backpacker travel.

Hotels & Motels

Outside of Perth there are few traditional full-service hotels. Along the coast, the bigger properties tend to be resort-style, with separate guest chalets or cottages, or they offer self-contained apartments. Rates vary widely from day to day, depending on the availability of rooms, length of stay, special events and the season; generally the earlier and longer your booking, the cheaper it will be.

Motels vary widely in quality (some seem stuck in a 1970s time warp, and not in a good way) but many are reasonably modern and comfortable. In rural areas it pays to book ahead as motels can often be booked out by government workers or tour groups.

Pubs

Pubs (from the term 'public house') in Australia are often called hotels – and they do often have accommodation. In country towns, pubs are

PRACTICALITIES

» Leaf through the *West Australian* or the national *Australian* broadsheet from Monday to Saturday, and the *Sunday Times* on Sunday.

» Switch on the box to watch the ad-free ABC, the government-sponsored and multicultural SBS, or the commercial TV stations Seven, Nine and Ten.

» Tune in to ABC on the radio – pick a program and frequency from www.abc.net.au/radio.

» DVDs sold in Australia can be watched on players accepting region 4 DVDs (the same as Mexico, South America, Central America, New Zealand, the Pacific and the Caribbean). The USA and Canada are region 1 countries, and Europe and Japan are region 2.

» For weights and measures, the metric system is used.

» Smoking is banned from public transport, airplanes, cars carrying children, between the flags at patrolled beaches, within 10m of a playground and government buildings. It's also banned within bars and clubs but permitted in alfresco or courtyard areas.

SLEEPING PRICE RANGES

» $ – up to $100 per night for the cheapest double room

» $$ – cheapest double $100 to $200

» $$$ – cheapest double over $200

GST REFUNDS

The Goods and Services Tax (GST) is a flat 10% tax on all goods and services with the exception of basic food items (milk, bread, fruits and vegetables etc). By law the tax is included in the quoted or shelf prices, so all prices in this book are GST-inclusive.

If you purchase goods with a minimum value of $300 from any one supplier (on the same invoice) no more than 30 days before you leave Australia, you are entitled under the Tourist Refund Scheme (TRS) to a refund of any GST paid. The scheme only applies to goods you take with you as hand luggage or wear onto the plane or ship. You can collect your refund at the airport up to 30 minutes before departure. At Perth airport, the refund counter is just after passport control. For more information, contact the **Australian Customs Service** (☎1300 363 263; www.customs.gov.au).

invariably found in the town centre and are often the grandest buildings in town, as they were generally built during boom times. In tourist areas some have been restored but generally the rooms to rent remain old-fashioned, with a long, creaky amble down the hall to the bathroom. You can sometimes rent a single room at a country pub for not much more than a hostel dorm, and you'll be in the social heart of the town to boot. But if you're a light sleeper, never book a room above the bar.

Some pubs have separate motel-style accommodation at the back of the hotel as well. Few have a separate reception area – just ask in the bar if there are rooms available.

Rental Accommodation

The ubiquitous holiday flat resembles a motel unit but has cooking and often laundry facilities. It can come with two or more bedrooms and is often rented on a weekly basis – prices per night are higher for shorter stays.

The other alternative in major cities is to take out a serviced apartment. **Number Six** (www.numbersix.com.au) has a range of apartments in great locations around Perth, Fremantle and Margaret River.

If you're interested in a shared flat or house for a long-term stay, delve into the classified advertisements sections of the daily newspapers; Wednesday and Saturday are usually the best days. Noticeboards in universities, hostels, bookshops and cafes are also good to check out.

If it's self-contained accommodation you're after, many of the places reviewed in this book will fit the bill. Check out the listings flagged with 'cottages', 'chalets', 'apartments' or even 'caravan parks' and you'll find a hefty selection to choose between.

Business Hours

Reviews in our On the Road chapters don't list opening hours unless they differ substantially from the following:

Banks 9.30am-4pm Mon-Thu, 9.30am-5pm Fri, some open Sat am

Restaurants Breakfast 8-10.30am, lunch noon-3pm, dinner 6-9pm

Shops 9am-5pm Mon-Fri, 9am-noon or 5pm Sat, late-night shopping until 9pm Thu or Fri; Sun trading is not common

Customs Regulations

For comprehensive information on customs regulations, contact the **Australian Customs Service** (☎02-6275 6666; www.customs.gov.au).

On arrival, declare all goods of animal or plant origin. Authorities are keen to protect Australia's unique environment and agricultural industries by preventing weeds, pests or diseases getting into the country. Luggage is screened or X-rayed – if you fail to declare quarantine items on arrival and are caught, you risk an on-the-spot fine of over $200 or even prosecution and imprisonment. For more information on quarantine regulations contact the **Australian Quarantine and Inspection Service** (AQIS; ☎02-6272 3933; www.aqis.gov.au).

Duty-free allowances:

Alcohol – 2.25L

Cigarettes – 250

Other goods – up to $900 value; or items for personal use that you will be taking with you when you leave

SCHOOL HOLIDAYS

The Christmas season is part of the summer school holidays (mid-December to late January), when transport and accommodation are often booked out, and there are long, restless queues at tourist attractions. There are three shorter school holiday periods during the year that change slightly from year to year. Generally, they fall in mid-April, mid-July and late September to mid-October.

Discount Cards

Carrying a student card entitles you to a wide variety of discounts throughout WA. The most common card is the **International Student Identity Card** (ISIC; www.isic.org), which is issued to full-time students aged 12 years and over, and gives the bearer discounts on accommodation, transport and admission to some attractions. It's available from student unions, hostelling organisations and some travel agencies; for more information, see the website of the **International Student Travel Confederation** (ISTC; www.istc.org).

The ISTC is also the body behind the International Youth Travel Card (IYTC or Go25), which is issued to people who are between 12 and 26 years of age and not full-time students, and gives equivalent benefits to the ISIC. A similar ISTC brainchild is the International Teacher Identity Card (ITIC), available to teaching professionals.

Embassies & Consulates

The principal diplomatic representations to Australia are in Canberra, but many countries are represented in Perth by consular staff. Look in the *Yellow Pages* directory for a more complete listing.

It's important to realise what your own embassy – the embassy of the country of which you are a citizen – can and can't do to help you if you get into trouble. Generally speaking, it won't be much help in emergencies if the trouble you're in is even remotely your own fault. Remember that while in Australia you are bound by Australian laws. Your embassy will not be sympathetic if you end up in jail after committing a crime locally, even if such actions are legal in your own country.

Canada (Map p52; ☎08-9322 7930; www.canadainternational.gc.ca; 3rd fl, 267 St Georges Tce, Perth)

France (Map p56; ☎08-6263 4455; www.ambafrance-au.org; Ste 14, 44 Kings Park Rd, West Perth)

Germany (Map p52; ☎08-9221 2941; www.canberra.diplo.de; Level 18, Exchange Plaza, 2 The Esplanade)

Ireland (☎08-9385 8247; www.embassyofireland.au.com) Ireland has an honorary consul in Perth but not a physical office.

Netherlands (Map p56; ☎08-9486 1579; www.netherlands.org.au; 1139 Hay St, West Perth)

New Zealand (☎02-6270 4211; www.nzembassy.com; Commonwealth Ave, Canberra)

UK (Map p52; ☎08-9224 4700; www.fco.gov.uk; Level 26, Allendale Sq, 77 St Georges Tce, Perth)

USA (Map p52; ☎08-9202 1224; http://perth.usconsulate.gov; 4th fl, 16 St Georges Tce, Perth)

Electricity

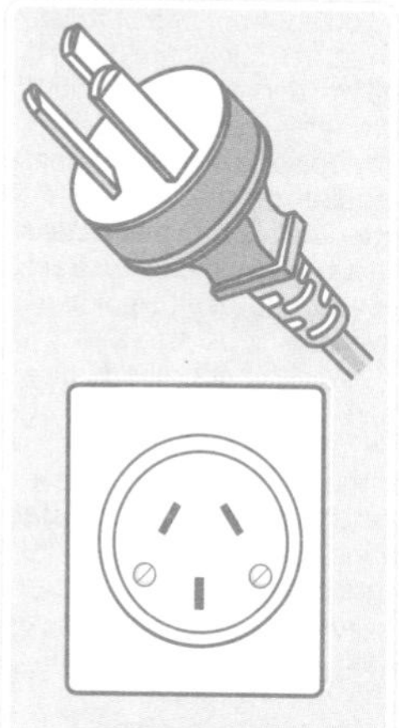

Gay & Lesbian Travellers

In general Australians are open-minded about homosexuality and, in WA, gays and lesbians are protected by anti-discrimination legislation and share an equal age of consent with heterosexuals (16 years).

That said, Perth has the state's only gay and lesbian venues (see p61) and its scene (centred around Northbridge) pales in comparison with the likes of Sydney or Melbourne. It's unlikely that you'll experience any problems during your stay, although the further away from the main centres you go, the more likely you are to run into overt homophobia.

Useful resources:

Gay & Lesbian Community Service of WA (☎08-9420 7201; www.glcs.org.au; 2 Delhi St, West Perth) Information and counselling line.

Gay & Lesbian Tourism Australia (GALTA; www.galta.com.au) Has a handful of WA members offering accommodation and tours.

Q Pages (www.qpages.com.au) Gay and lesbian business directory and what's on listings.

Health

Australia is a remarkably healthy country in which to travel, considering that such a large portion of it lies in the tropics. Tropical diseases such as malaria and yellow fever are unknown, diseases of insanitation such as cholera and typhoid are unheard of, and, thanks to Australia's isolation and quarantine standards, even some animal diseases such as rabies and foot-and-mouth disease have yet to be recorded.

Few travellers should experience anything worse than an upset stomach or a bad hangover – and if you do fall ill, the standard of hospitals and health care is high.

Before You Go

Since most vaccines don't produce immunity until at least two weeks after they're given, visit a physician four to eight weeks before departure. Ask your doctor for an International Certificate of Vaccination (otherwise known as the yellow booklet), which will list all the vaccinations you've received. This is mandatory for countries that require proof of yellow-fever vaccination upon entry (this vaccination is sometimes required in Australia), but it's a good idea to carry it wherever you travel.

Bring medications in their original, clearly labelled, containers. A signed and dated letter from your physician describing your medical conditions and medications, including generic names, is also a good idea. If carrying syringes or needles, be sure to have a physician's letter documenting their medical necessity.

Insurance

If your health insurance doesn't cover you for medical expenses abroad, consider getting extra insurance – check www.lonelyplanet.com for more information. Find out in advance if your insurance plan will make payments directly to providers or reimburse you later for overseas health expenditures.

REQUIRED VACCINATIONS

Proof of yellow-fever vaccination is required only from travellers entering Australia within six days of having stayed overnight or longer in a yellow-fever infected country. For a full list of these countries visit the websites of the **World Health Organization** (www.who.int/ith) or that of the **Centers for Disease Control & Prevention** (www.cdc.gov/travel).

Availability & Cost of Health Care

Health insurance is essential for all travellers. While health care in Australia is of a high standard and not overly expensive by international standards, considerable costs can build up and repatriation is extremely expensive.

Australia's health-care system is a mixture of privately run medical clinics and hospitals alongside a government-funded system of public hospitals. The Medicare system covers Australian residents for some health-care costs. Visitors from countries with which Australia has a reciprocal health-care agreement (New Zealand, the UK, the Netherlands, Sweden, Finland, Norway, Italy, Malta and Ireland) are eligible for benefits to the extent specified under the Medicare program. If you are from one of these countries check the details before departure. In general the agreements provide for any episode of ill health that requires prompt medical attention. For further details visit www.medicareaustralia.gov.au/yourhealth/going_overseas/vtta.htm.

Over-the-counter medications are widely available at privately owned pharmacies throughout Australia. These include painkillers, antihistamines for allergies and skincare products.

You may find that medications that are readily available over the counter in some countries are only available in Australia by prescription. These include the oral contraceptive pill, most medications for asthma and all antibiotics. If you take medication on a regular basis bring an adequate supply and ensure you have details of the generic name, as brand names may differ between countries.

Infectious Diseases

Bat Lyssavirus

This disease is related to rabies and some deaths have occurred after bites. The risk is greatest for animal handlers and vets. Rabies vaccine is effective, but the risk to travellers is very low.

Dengue Fever

Also known as 'breakbone fever', because of the severe muscular pains that accompany the fever, this viral disease is spread by a species of mosquito that feeds primarily during the day. Most people recover in a few days but more severe forms of the disease can occur, particularly in residents who are exposed to another strain of the virus (there are four types) in a subsequent season.

Giardiasis

Giardiasis is widespread in the waterways around Australia. Drinking untreated water from streams and lakes is not recommended. Water filters, and boiling or treating water with iodine, are effective in preventing the disease. Symptoms consist of intermittent bad-smelling diarrhoea, abdominal bloating and wind. Effective treatment is available (tinidazole or metronidazole).

Meningococcal Disease

This disease occurs worldwide and is a risk with prolonged, dormitory-style accommodation. A vaccine exists for some types of this disease, namely meningococcal A, C, Y and W. No vaccine is presently available for the viral type of meningitis.

Ross River Fever

The Ross River virus is widespread throughout Australia and is spread by mosquitoes living in marshy areas. In addition to fever the disease causes headache, joint and muscular pains and a rash, before resolving after five to seven days.

Sexually Transmitted Diseases

STDs occur at rates similar to most other Western countries. Always use a condom with any new sexual partner. Condoms are readily available in chemists and through vending machines in many public places including toilets.

Viral Encephalitis

Also known as Murray Valley encephalitis virus, this is spread by mosquitoes and is most common in northern Australia, especially during the wet season (November to April). This potentially serious disease is normally accompanied by headache, muscle pains and light insensitivity. Residual neurological damage can occur and no specific treatment is available. However, the risk to most travellers is low.

TAP WATER & OTHER WATER SOURCES

Tap water is universally safe in WA. Increasing numbers of streams, rivers and lakes, however, are being contaminated by bugs that cause diarrhoea, making water purification essential. The simplest way of purifying water is to boil it thoroughly. Consider purchasing a water filter; it's very important when buying a filter to read the specifications, so that you know exactly what it removes from the water and what it doesn't. Simple filtering will not remove all dangerous organisms, so if you cannot boil water it should be treated chemically. Chlorine tablets will kill many pathogens, but not some parasites like giardia and amoebic cysts. Iodine is more effective in purifying water and is available in tablet form. Follow the directions carefully and remember that too much iodine can be harmful.

Environmental Hazards

Heat Exhaustion & Heatstroke

Heat exhaustion occurs when fluid intake does not keep up with fluid loss. Symptoms include dizziness, fainting, fatigue, nausea or vomiting. On observation the skin is usually pale, cool and clammy. Treatment consists of rest in a cool, shady place and fluid replacement with water or diluted sports drinks.

Heatstroke is a severe form of heat illness that occurs after fluid depletion or extreme heat challenge from heavy exercise. This is a true medical emergency: heating of the brain leads to disorientation, hallucinations and seizures. Prevention is by maintaining an adequate fluid intake to ensure the continued passage of clear and copious urine, especially during physical exertion.

Hypothermia

Hypothermia is a significant risk especially during the winter months in southern parts of Australia. Early signs include the inability to perform fine movements (such as doing up buttons), shivering and a bad case of the 'umbles' (fumbles, mumbles, grumbles, stumbles). The key elements of treatment include changing the environment to one where heat loss is minimised, changing out of any wet clothing, adding dry clothes with windproof and waterproof layers, adding insulation and providing fuel (water and carbohydrate) to allow shivering, which builds the internal temperature. In severe hypothermia, shivering actually stops – this is a medical emergency requiring rapid evacuation in addition to the above measures.

Marine Animals

Marine spikes, such as those found on sea urchins, stonefish, scorpion fish, catfish and stingrays, can cause severe local pain. If this occurs, immediately immerse the affected area in hot water (as hot as can be tolerated). Keep topping up with hot water until the pain subsides and medical care can be reached. The stonefish is found only in tropical Australia; antivenin is available.

Marine stings from jellyfish such as box jellyfish also occur in Australia's tropical waters, particularly during the wet season (November to April). If you are stung, first aid consists of washing the skin with vinegar to prevent further discharge of remaining stinging cells, followed by rapid transfer to a hospital; antivenin is widely available.

Snakes

Australian snakes have a fearful reputation that is justified in terms of the potency of their venom, but unjustified in terms of the actual risk to travellers and locals. They are endowed with only small fangs, making it easy to prevent bites to the lower limbs (where 80% of bites occur) by wearing protective clothing (such as gaiters) around the ankles when bushwalking. The bite marks are small and preventing the spread of toxic venom can be achieved by applying pressure to the wound and immobilising the area with a splint or sling before seeking medical attention. Application of an elastic bandage (you can improvise with a T-shirt) wrapped firmly, but not tightly enough to cut off the circulation, around the entire limb – along with immobilisation – is a life-saving first-aid measure.

Spiders

Redback spiders are found throughout Australia. Bites cause increasing pain at the site followed by profuse sweating and generalised symptoms. First aid includes application of ice or cold packs to the bite and transfer to hospital.

White-tailed (brown recluse) spider bites may cause an ulcer that is very difficult to heal. Clean the wound thoroughly and seek medical assistance.

Insurance

Don't underestimate the importance of a good travel insurance policy that covers theft, loss and medical problems – nothing will ruin your holiday plans quicker than an accident or having that brand-new digital camera stolen.

Some policies specifically exclude designated 'dangerous activities' such as scuba diving, parasailing, bungee jumping, motorcycling, skiing and even bushwalking. If you plan on doing any of these things, make sure the policy you choose fully covers you for your activity of choice. Check that the policy covers ambulances and emergency medical evacuations by air.

For information on insurance matters relating to cars that are bought or rented, see p263. Worldwide travel insurance is available at www.lonelyplanet.com/travel_services. You can buy, extend or claim online at any time – even if you're already on the road.

Internet Access

Generally in WA, if you are prepared to pay you will be able to get online. You will find internet cafes located in cities, sizable towns and pretty much anywhere else that travellers congregate across WA. In addition, you will find that many backpacker hostels offer connections and in smaller towns Community Resource Centres (also called telecentres) offer the fastest internet access. The cost ranges from under $4 an hour in the William St strip in Perth to $10 an hour in locations that are more remote. The average is about $6 an hour, usually with a minimum of 10 minutes' access.

The best bets for free wi-fi connections are public libraries, some of the better local cafes, and branches of some of the big American fast-food and coffee chains. Places marked with our wi-fi symbol (📶) within the On the Road chapters have either free or charged wi-fi connections available.

Legal Matters

Most travellers will have no contact with the police or legal system, unless they break the rules of the road while driving. There is a significant police presence around most population centres and they have the power to stop your car and see your licence (you're required to carry it), check your vehicle for roadworthiness and insist that you take a breath test for alcohol.

First-time offenders who are caught possessing small amounts of illegal drugs are likely to receive a fine rather than go to jail, but a conviction may affect your visa status. Note that if you remain in Australia after your visa expires, you will officially be classified as an 'overstayer' and could face detention and expulsion, and be prevented from returning to Australia for a period of up to three years.

Maps

When you arrive in a new town, the local tourist information office will probably have a serviceable street map. For more detailed maps, try the **Royal Automobile Club of WA** (RACWA; www.rac.com.au), which has a stack of road maps available (including free downloadable route maps).

Gregory's and UBD both produce Perth street directories that are useful for a long stay. *Roads & Tracks WA* is an excellent reference if you're travelling extensively through the state – especially off the beaten track. **Hema Maps** (www.hemamaps.com.au) are the best for the north, especially the dirt roads. UBD publishes a handy *South West & Great Southern* book, with regional and town maps.

Landgate (www.landgate.wa.gov.au) produces a variety of mapping products that cover the whole state, including a range of topographical maps that are good for bushwalking.

Money

In this book all prices are given in Australian dollars, unless otherwise stated.

ATMs

Bank branches are found throughout the state, most with 24-hour ATMs attached. Today, even in the smallest town you'll find an ATM – probably tucked away in the local pub. Most ATMs accept cards from other banks and are linked to international networks.

Cash

The Australian dollar is made up of 100 cents; there are 5c, 10c, 20c, 50c, $1 and $2 coins, and $5, $10, $20, $50 and $100 notes. Although the smallest coin in circulation is 5c, prices are sometimes still marked in single cents and then rounded to the nearest 5c when you come to pay.

There are no notable restrictions on importing or exporting travellers cheques. Cash amounts equal to or in excess of the equivalent of A$10,000 (in any currency) must be declared on arrival or departure.

Changing foreign currency or travellers cheques is usually no problem at banks throughout WA or at licensed moneychangers such as Thomas Cook or Amex in the major cities.

Credit & Debit Cards

Visa and MasterCard are widely accepted for everything from a hostel bed or a restaurant meal to an adventure tour, and a credit card is pretty much essential (in lieu of a large deposit) for car hire. With debit cards, any card connected to the international banking network (Cirrus, Maestro, Plus and Eurocard) will work. Charge cards such as Diners Club and Amex are not as widely accepted.

Eftpos has been embraced by many Australian businesses, even in the most remote parts of the state.

Travellers Cheques

With the ease of electronic means of payment, travellers cheques have fallen out of fashion. Still, Amex, Thomas Cook and other well-known international brands are easily exchanged and are commission-free when exchanged at their bureaux; however, local banks charge hefty fees (around $7) for the same service.

Photography

Australians are keen adopters of technology and all your requirements for digital photography and video can be met in WA. However, if you need memory cards, batteries or DV tapes, purchase them in the larger cities and towns as they're cheaper and more readily available than in the remote areas. Most photo labs have self-service machines that allow you to make your own prints and burn CDs and DVDs of your images and, of course, they still stock and develop film for those keeping it old-school.

Public Holidays

New Year's Day 1 January
Australia Day 26 January
Labour Day First Monday in March
Easter (Good Friday & Easter Monday) March/April
Anzac Day 25 April
Foundation Day First Monday in June
Queen's Birthday Last Monday in September
Christmas Day 25 December
Boxing Day 26 December

Safe Travel

Animal Hazards

Australia is home to some seriously dangerous creatures and critters. On land there are poisonous snakes and spiders, while in the sea the deadly box jellyfish awaits and the theme tune from *Jaws* plays constantly as white pointer sharks cruise up and down the coast. Just so you're not safe anywhere, the saltwater crocodile spans both. However, in reality you're unlikely to see many of these creatures in the wild, much less be attacked by one – you are far more likely to suffer the consequences of downing too many beers, getting seriously sunburnt or trying not to hit that kangaroo in your car headlights when driving at dusk.

Box Jellyfish

There have been fatal encounters between swimmers and these large jellyfish on the northern coast. Also known as the sea wasp or 'stinger', their venomous tentacles can grow up to 3m long. You can be stung anytime, but November to March is when you should stay out of the water unless you're wearing a 'stinger suit', available from sporting shops in the stinger zone.

For information on treating box jellyfish stings, see p251.

Crocodiles

Up in the northwest of WA, saltwater crocodiles can be a real danger. As well as living around the coast they are found in estuaries, creeks and rivers, sometimes a long way inland. Observe safety signs or ask locals whether an inviting waterhole or river is croc-free before plunging in – these precautions have been fatally ignored in the past, with the last fatality in 1987 and an attack in 2006.

Insects

For four to six months of the year you'll have to cope with those two banes of the Australian outdoors: the fly and the mosquito (or 'mozzie'). Flies are more prevalent in the outback and to counter them the humble fly net is effective, though never glamorous. Repellents such as Aerogard and Rid may also help to deter the little bastards, but don't count on it.

Mozzies are a problem in summer, especially near wetlands in tropical areas, and some species are carriers of viral infections (see p250). Try to keep your arms and legs covered after sunset and slap on that repellent.

One favourite little pest in the northern coastal areas is the biting midge (often called a sandfly). These cheeky little bloodsuckers can make a meal of you without you noticing for several hours – when you start itching. While locals can infuriatingly appear immune, it's almost a rite of passage for those heading north to be covered in bites – until you learn to cover up at dusk.

Ticks and leeches are also common. For protection, wear loose-fitting clothing with long sleeves. You can apply 30% DEET on exposed skin, repeated every three to four hours, and impregnate clothing with permethrin (which kills insects but is safe to humans).

Sharks

In 2010 there were at least three major shark attacks in WA, one fatal, and all at reasonably popular surfing and swimming spots. Be aware that when you are in the water you are in the shark's domain and while this isn't great comfort, statistically you have a far greater chance of being struck by lightning.

Snakes

There are many venomous snakes in the Australian bush, the most common being the brown and tiger snakes. Unless you're interfering with one, or have the misfortune to stand on one, it's extremely unlikely that you'll be bitten. The golden rule if you see a snake is to do as the Beatles do and 'let it be'.

For information on treating snake bites, see p251.

Spiders

The redback is the most common poisonous spider in WA. It's small and black with a distinctive red stripe on its body; for bites, apply ice and seek medical attention. The white-tailed spider is a long, thin, black spider with a white tail, and has a fierce bite that can lead to local inflammation and ulceration. Hospitals have antivenin on hand for all common snake and spider bites, but it helps to know what it was that bit you.

A BIT OF PERSPECTIVE

There's approximately one shark-attack fatality per year in Australia, and a similar number of croc-attack deaths. Every now and then the number increases slightly, but usually because people have become complacent about impinging on these creatures' territories. Blue-ringed octopus deaths are even rarer – only two in the last century – and there's only ever been one confirmed death from a cone shell. Jellyfish do better, disposing of about two people each year. However, you're still over 100 times more likely to drown than be killed by one of these creatures.

On land, snakes kill one or two people per year (about the same as bee stings, or less than one-thousandth of those killed on the roads). There hasn't been a recorded death from a tick bite for over 50 years, nor from spider bites in the last 20.

Other Hazards

Bushfires

Bushfires are a regular occurrence in WA and in hot, dry and windy weather, be extremely careful with any naked flame – cigarette butts thrown out of car windows have started many a fire. On a total fire ban day it's forbidden even to use a camping stove in the open.

Bushwalkers should seek local advice before setting out. When a total fire ban is in place, delay your trip until the weather improves. If you're out in the bush and you see smoke, even a long distance away, take heed – bushfires move fast and change direction with the wind. Go to the nearest open space, downhill if possible. A forested ridge, on the other hand, is the most dangerous place to be.

Crime

Western Australia is a relatively safe place to visit but you should still take reasonable precautions. Don't leave hotel rooms or cars unlocked, and don't leave your valuables unattended or visible through a car window.

In recent years, there has been a spate of glassings (stabbings with broken glass) at Perth venues. If you see trouble brewing it's best to walk away. Take due caution on the streets after dark, especially around hot spots such as Northbridge. There have also been reports of drugged drinks in Perth pubs and clubs. Authorities advise women to refuse drinks offered by strangers in bars and to drink bottled alcohol rather than that from a glass. See p257 for more precautions.

Driving

Australian drivers are generally a courteous bunch, but rural 'petrolheads', inner-city speedsters and drink drivers can pose risks. Potential dangers on the open road include wildlife, such as kangaroos (mainly at dusk and dawn); fatigue, caused by travelling long distances without the necessary breaks; and excessive speed. Driving on dirt roads can also be tricky for the uninitiated. For more information on these and other potential dangers, see p264.

Hypothermia

More bushwalkers actually die of cold than in bushfires.

Even in summer, temperatures can drop below freezing at night and the weather can change very quickly. Exposure in even moderately cool temperatures can sometimes result in hypothermia. For more information on hypothermia and how to minimise its risk, see p251.

Outback Travel

If you're keen to explore outback WA, it's important not to embark on your trip without careful planning and preparation. Travellers regularly encounter difficulties in the harsh outback conditions, and trips occasionally prove fatal. For tips and advice on travelling in the outback, see p262.

Swimming

Popular beaches are patrolled by surf life-savers and flags mark off patrolled areas. Even so, WA's surf beaches can be dangerous places to swim if you aren't used to the often-heavy surf. Undertows (or 'rips') are the main problem. If you find yourself being carried out by a rip, just keep afloat; don't panic or try to swim against the rip, which will exhaust you. In most cases the current will stop within a couple of hundred metres of the shore and you can then swim parallel to the shore for a short way to get out of the rip and swim back to land.

On the south coast, freak 'king waves' from the Southern Ocean can sometimes break on the shore with little or no warning, dragging people out to sea. In populated areas there are warning signs; in other areas be extremely careful.

People have been paralysed by diving into waves in shallow water and hitting a sandbar; check the depth of the water before you leap.

Telephone

The two main telecommunications companies are **Telstra** (www.telstra.com.au) and **Optus** (www.optus.com.au). Both are also major players in the mobile (cell) market, along with **Vodafone** (www.vodafone.com.au), **Virgin** (www.virginmobile.com.au), **AAPT** (www.aapt.com.au) and **3** (www.three.com.au).

Local calls from private land lines cost 15c to 30c while local calls from public phones cost 50c; both allow for unlimited talk time. Calls to mobile phones attract higher rates and are timed.

Although the whole of WA shares a single area code (08), once you call outside of the immediate area or town, it is likely you are making a long-distance call. STD calls (no, not something you need to see a doctor about, it stands for Subscriber Trunk Dialling – a long-distance call within Australia) can be made from virtually any public phone and are cheaper during off-peak hours, generally between 7pm and 7am.

A wide range of phonecards is available in WA. Phonecards can be purchased at newsagents and post offices for a fixed dollar value (usually $10, $20, $30 etc) and can be used with any public or private phone by dialling a toll-free access number and then the PIN number on the card. Call rates vary, so shop around. Some public phones also accept credit cards.

Mobile Phones

Australia's GSM and 3G mobile networks service more than 90% of the population but leave vast tracts of the country uncovered, including much of inland WA. Perth and the larger centres get good reception, but outside these centres it's haphazard or nonexistent, especially in the north.

Australia's digital network is compatible with GSM 900 and 1800 (used in Europe), but is generally not compatible with the USA or Japanese systems. It's easy to get connected short term, as the main service providers all offer prepaid mobile services.

Phone Codes

☎0011 – International calling prefix (the equivalent of 00 in most other countries).

☎61 – Country code for Australia.

☎08 – Area code for all of WA. If calling from overseas, drop the initial zero.

☎04 – All numbers starting with 04 (such as 0410, 0412) are mobile phone numbers. If calling from overseas, drop the initial zero.

☎190 – Usually recorded information calls, charged at anything from 35c to $5 or more per minute (more from mobiles and payphones).

☎1800 – Toll-free numbers; can be called free of charge from anywhere in the country, though they may not be accessible from certain areas or from mobile phones.

☎1800-REVERSE (738 3773) or 12 550 – Dial to make a reverse-charge (collect) call from any public or private phone.

☎13 or 1300 – Charged at the rate of a local call. The numbers can usually be dialled Australia-wide, but may be applicable only to a specific state or STD district.

Note: Telephone numbers beginning with ☎1800, ☎13 or ☎1300 cannot be dialled from outside Australia.

Time

Australia is divided into three time zones: the Western Standard Time zone (GMT/UTC plus eight hours) covers most of WA; Central Standard Time (plus 9½ hours) covers the Northern Territory, South Australia and parts of WA's Central Desert and Nullarbor regions near the border; and Eastern Standard Time (plus 10 hours) covers Tasmania,

Victoria, New South Wales, the Australian Capital Territory and Queensland. So when it's noon in Perth, it's 1.30pm in Darwin and Adelaide, and 2pm in Sydney or Melbourne.

Daylight saving time – where clocks are put forward an hour – operates in most other states during the warmer months (October to March), but not in WA.

Tourist Information

For general statewide information, try the WA Visitor Centre (p75) in Perth, which will quickly bury you knee-deep in brochures, booklets, maps and leaflets on places all over the state.

Elsewhere, information is available from local tourist offices (listed throughout the book). In most cases they are excellent, with friendly staff (often volunteers) providing invaluable local knowledge such as local road and weather conditions.

Travellers with Disabilities

Disability awareness in WA is pretty high and getting higher. Legislation requires that new accommodation meets accessibility standards, and discrimination by tourism operators is illegal. Many of the state's key attractions provide access for those with limited mobility and an increasing number have also begun addressing the needs of visitors with visual or aural impairments; contact attractions in advance to confirm the facilities. Useful contacts include:

Association for the Blind of WA (☎08-9311 8202; www.abwa.asn.au)

Easy Access Australia (www.easyaccessaustralia.com.au) Bruce Cameron's guidebook is available from bookshops and provides details on easily accessible transport, accommodation and attraction options.

National Information Communication & Awareness Network (Nican; ☎TTY 02-6241 1220, TTY 1800 806 769; www.nican.com.au) An Australia-wide directory providing information on access issues, accessible accommodation, sporting and recreational activities, transport and specialist tour operators.

National Public Toilet Map (www.toiletmap.gov.au) The comprehensive website lists over 2300 public and private toilets, including those with wheelchair access.

People with Disabilities WA (PWdWA; ☎1800 193 331, 9485 8900; www.pwdwa.org) Its excellent website has extensive information on WA's major disability service providers.

Tourism WA (www.westernaustralia.com) Its website highlights all accessible listings (accommodation, restaurants, tours etc) with an icon.

WA Deaf Society (☎08-9441 2677, TTY 9441 2655; www.wadeaf.org.au)

Visas

All visitors to Australia need a visa – only New Zealand nationals are exempt, and even they receive a 'special category' visa on arrival. Visa application forms are available from Australian diplomatic missions overseas, travel agents or the website of the **Department of Immigration & Citizenship** (☎13 18 81; www.immi.gov.au).

eVisitor

Many European passport holders are eligible for an eVisitor, which is free and allows visitors to stay in Australia for up to three months. eVisitors must be applied for online and they are electronically stored and linked to individual passport numbers, so no stamp in your passport is required. It's advisable to apply at least 14 days prior to the proposed date of travel to Australia. Applications are made on the Department of Immigration & Citizenship website.

Electronic Travel Authority (ETA)

An ETA allows visitors to enter Australia anytime within a 12-month period and stay for up to three months at a time. Travellers from qualifying countries can get an ETA through any International Air Transport Association (IATA)–registered travel agent or overseas airline. They make the application for you when you buy a ticket and issue the ETA, which replaces the usual visa stamped in your passport – it's common practice for travel agents to charge a fee for issuing an ETA (in the vicinity of US$25). This system is available to passport holders of some 33 countries, including all of the European countries that are eligible for eVisitor.

The eight countries that are eligible for ETA but not eVisitor can make their application online at www.eta.immi.gov.au, where a $20 fee will apply. Those countries are Brunei, Canada, Hong Kong, Japan, Malaysia, Singapore, South Korea and the USA.

Tourist Visas

Short-term tourist visas have largely been replaced by the eVisitor and ETA. However, if you are from a country not covered by either, or you want to stay longer than three months, you'll need to apply for a visa. Tourist visas cost $105 and allow single or multiple entry for stays of three, six or 12 months and are valid for use within 12 months of issue.

Visa Extensions

Visitors are allowed a maximum stay of 12 months, including extensions. Visa extensions are made through the Department of Immigration & Citizenship and it's best to apply at least two or three weeks before your visa expires. The $255 application fee is nonrefundable, even if your application is rejected.

Work & Holiday Visas (462)

Nationals from Bangladesh, Chile, Indonesia, Iran, Malaysia, Thailand, Turkey and the USA between the ages of 18 and 30 can apply for a Work and Holiday visa prior to entry to Australia. It allows the holder to enter Australia within three months of issue, stay for up to 12 months, leave and re-enter Australia any number of times within that 12 months, undertake temporary employment to supplement a trip, and study for up to four months. The application fee is also $235.

Working Holiday Maker (WHM) Visas (417)

Young (aged 18 to 30) visitors from Belgium, Canada, Cyprus, Denmark, Estonia, Finland, France, Germany, Hong Kong, Ireland, Italy, Japan, Korea, Malta, the Netherlands, Norway, Sweden, Taiwan and the UK are eligible for a WHM visa, which allows you to visit for up to one year and gain casual employment.

The emphasis of this visa is on casual and not full-time employment, so you're only supposed to work for any one employer for a maximum of six months. A first WHM visa must be obtained prior to entry to Australia and can be applied for at Australian diplomatic missions abroad or online (www.immi.gov.au/visitors/working-holiday). You can't change to a WHM visa once you're in Australia.

You can apply for this visa up to a year in advance, which is worthwhile as there's a limit on the number issued each year. Conditions include having a return air ticket or sufficient funds for a return or onward fare, and an application fee of $235 is charged. For details of what sort of work is available, see Seasonal Work, p257.

Visitors who have worked as a seasonal worker in regional Australia for a minimum of three months while on their first WHM are eligible to apply for a second WHM while still in Australia. 'Regional Australia' encompasses the vast majority of the country, excepting major cities; the definition of 'seasonal work' is a little more specific. The Department of Immigration & Citizenship has good information. Tourism Australia also has a helpful website – www.work.australia.com.

Women Travellers

WA is generally a safe place for women travellers, although the usual sensible precautions apply here. It's best to avoid walking alone late at night in any of the major cities and towns. If you're out on the town, keep enough money aside for a taxi home. The same applies to outback and rural towns with unlit, semi-deserted streets between you and your temporary home. Lone women should also be wary of staying in basic pub accommodation unless it appears safe and well managed.

Lone female hitchers are really tempting fate – hitching with a male companion is safer.

Work

If you come to Australia on a tourist visa then you're not allowed to work for pay – working for approved volunteer organisations in exchange for board is OK. If you're caught breaching your visa conditions, you can be expelled from the country and placed on a banned list for up to three years.

Equipped with a WHM visa, you can begin to sniff out the possibilities for temporary employment. Casual work can often be found during peak season at the major tourist centres.

Seasonal Work

WA is in a labour shortage and a wealth of opportunities exist for travellers (both Australian and foreign) for paid work year-round.

In Perth, plenty of temporary work is available in tourism and hospitality, administration, IT, nursing, childcare, factories and labouring. Outside of Perth, travellers can easily get jobs in tourism and hospitality, plus a variety of seasonal work. Some places have specialised needs, such as Broome where there is lucrative work in pearling, on farms and boats.

INDUSTRY	TIME	REGION(S)
grapes	Feb-Mar	Denmark, Margaret River, Mt Barker, Manjimup
apples/pears	Feb-Apr	Donnybrook, Manjimup
prawn trawlers	Mar-Jun	Carnarvon
bananas	Apr-Dec	Kununurra
bananas	year-round	Carnarvon
vegies	May-Nov	Kununurra, Carnarvon
tourism	May-Dec	Kununurra
flowers	Sep-Nov	Midlands
lobsters	Nov-May	Esperance

Information

Backpacker accommodation, magazines and newspapers are good resources for local work opportunities. When you hit the road, check out noticeboards at hostels, internet cafes, supermarkets and telecentres.

Useful websites:

Australian Jobsearch (www.jobsearch.gov.au) Government site offering a job database.

Career One (www.careerone.com.au) General employment site, good for metropolitan areas.

Centrelink (www.centrelink.gov.au) The Australian government employment service has information and advice on looking for work, training and assistance.

Face2Face Fundraising (www.face2facefundraising.com.au) Fundraising jobs for charities and not-for-profits.

Gumtree (http://perth.gumtree.com.au) Great classified site with jobs, accommodation and items for sale.

Harvest Trail (http://jobsearch.gov.au/HarvestTrail) Specialised recruitment search for the agricultural industry, including a 'crop list' detailing what you can pick and pack, when and where.

Job Shop (www.thejobshop.com.au) WA-based recruitment agency specialising in jobs for WA as well as the Northern Territory.

MyCareer (www.mycareer.com.au) General employment site, good for metropolitan areas.

Seek (www.seek.com.au) General employment site, good for metropolitan areas.

Travellers at Work (www.taw.com.au) Excellent site for working travellers in Australia.

West Australian (www.thewest.com.au) WA's main newspaper advertises jobs online.

Volunteering

Lonely Planet's *Volunteer: A Traveller's Guide to Making a Difference Around the World* provides useful information about volunteering. Organisations that take on volunteers include the following:

Conservation Volunteers Australia (CVA; ☎1800 032 501, 03-5330 2600; www.conservationvolunteers.com.au) A nonprofit organisation focusing on practical conservation projects such as tree planting, walking-track construction, and flora and fauna surveys. It's an excellent way to get involved with conservation-minded people and visit some interesting areas of the country. Most projects are either for a weekend or a week and all food, transport and accommodation is supplied in return for a contribution to help cover costs ($40 per day, $208 per week).

Department of Environment & Conservation (DEC; www.dec.wa.gov.au) You'll find current and future opportunities at national parks all over WA listed on the website (click on the Community & Education tab and then Volunteer Programs). Opportunities vary enormously, from turtle tagging at Ningaloo Marine Park to feral animal control at Shark Bay. Travellers rave about their experience working with the dolphins at Monkey Mia, a program that always needs volunteer assistance (contact: alison.true@dec.wa.gov.au).

Willing Workers on Organic Farms (WWOOF; ☎03-5155 0218; www.wwoof.com.au) The idea is that you work four to six hours each day on a farm in return for bed and board, often in a family home. Almost all places have a minimum stay of two nights. As the name states, the farms are supposed to be organic (including permaculture and biodynamic growing), but that isn't always so. Some places aren't even farms – you might help out at a pottery or do the books at a seed wholesaler. Whether participants in the scheme have a farm or just a vegie patch, most are concerned to some extent with alternative lifestyles. You can join online by ordering the WWOOF listings book ($60). If you need these posted overseas, add another $5.

Other useful organisations include:

Earthwatch Institute (☎03-9682 6828; www.earthwatch.org) Offers volunteer 'expeditions' that focus on conservation and wildlife.

Go Volunteer (www.govolunteer.com.au) National website listing volunteer opportunities.

i-to-i (www.i-to-i.com) Conservation-based volunteer holidays in Australia.

Responsible Travel (www.responsibletravel.com) Volunteer travel opportunities.

STA (www.statravel.com.au) Click on 'Experiences' on its website and go to the volunteer link.

Transitions Abroad (www.transitionsabroad.com) Listings of volunteer opportunities, plus articles.

Volunteering Australia (www.volunteeringaustralia.org) Support, advice and volunteer training.

Transport

GETTING THERE & AWAY

Unless you're coming by land from other states in Australia, chances are you'll be touching down in Perth. Western Australia's (WA's) capital is considerably closer to Southeast Asia than it is to Australia's east coast – it's further from Sydney than it is from Jakarta.

Flights, tours and rail tickets can be booked online at www.lonelyplanet.com/bookings.

Entering the Country

Disembarkation in Australia is generally a very straightforward affair, with only the usual customs declarations. However, recent global instability has resulted in conspicuously increased security in Australian airports, both in domestic and international terminals, and you may find that customs procedures are now a little more time-consuming.

Air

Airports & Airlines

The east coast of Australia is the most common gateway for international travellers, although if you're coming from Europe, Asia or Africa you'll find it much more convenient, not to mention quicker, to fly directly to **Perth Airport** (code PER; ☎08-9478 8888; www.perthairport.com). Port Hedland has international flights to/from Bali, while Port Hedland and Broome both welcome interstate flights. If you do choose to fly to the east coast first, it's usually possible to book a connecting flight that will wing you across the country with little delay.

AIRLINES FLYING TO & FROM WA

All flights listed here are to Perth, unless otherwise specified, and all phone numbers are for dialling from within Australia. For flights within the state, see each destination's transport section in the On The Road chapters.

Air Asia (code D7; ☎1300 760 330; www.airasia.com) Budget flights from Kuala Lumpur and Denpasar (Bali).

Air Mauritius (code MK; ☎1300 332 077; www.airmauritius.com) Flies from Mauritius.

Air New Zealand (code NZ; ☎13 24 76; www.airnz.com.au) Flies from Auckland.

Airnorth (code TL; ☎1800 627 474; www.airnorth.com.au) Flies between Broome and Darwin.

Cathay Pacific (code CX; ☎13 17 47; www.cathaypacific.com) Flies from Hong Kong.

Emirates (code EK; ☎1300 303 777; www.emirates.com) Flies from Dubai.

Garuda Indonesia (code GA; ☎08-9214 5101; www.garuda-indonesia.com) Flies from Denpasar and Jakarta.

Jetstar (code JQ; ☎13 15 38; www.jetstar.com) Runs cheapies from Sydney, Melbourne, Brisbane and the Gold Coast. International routes include Jakarta and Denpasar.

Malaysia Airlines (code MH; ☎13 26 27, 08-9263 7043; www.malaysiaairlines.com) Flies from Kuala Lumpur and Kota Kinabalu.

Qantas (code QF; ☎13 13 13; www.qantas.com.au) Direct international flights from Hong Kong and Tokyo. Flies between Perth and all other Australian state capitals, as well as Cairns, Alice Springs and Uluru (Ayers Rock). Also flies from Kalgoorlie to Adelaide and from Broome to Sydney and Melbourne.

Royal Brunei Airlines (code BI; ☎08-9321 8757; www.bruneiair.com) Flies from Bandar Seri Begawan.

Singapore Airlines (code SQ; ☎13 10 11; www.singaporeair.com.au) Flies from Singapore.

Skywest (code XR; ☎1300 660 088; www.skywest.com.au) Flies from Darwin to Broome.

South African Airways (code SA; ☎1300 435 972; www.flysaa.com) Flies from Johannesburg.

Strategic Airlines (code VC; ☎13 53 20; www.flystrategic.

com.au) Flies from Brisbane to Port Hedland and from Denpasar to both Perth and Port Hedland.

Thai Airways International (code TG; ☎1300 651 960; www.thaiairways.com) Flies from Bangkok.

Tiger Airways (code TR; ☎03-9335 3033; www.tigerairways.com) Cheap flights from Melbourne and Singapore.

Virgin Blue (code DJ; ☎13 67 89; www.virginblue.com.au) Flies to Perth from the other Australian state capitals, except Canberra; and from Adelaide to Broome. Sister airline Pacific Blue heads to Denpasar and Phuket.

Tickets

Automated online ticket sales work well if you're planning a simple one-way or return trip on specified dates, but are no substitute for a travel agent with the low-down on specials deals, strategies for avoiding stopovers and other useful advice.

Paying by credit card offers some protection if you end up dealing with a rogue fly-by-night agency, as most card issuers provide refunds if you can prove you didn't get what you paid for. Even better, buy a ticket from a bonded agent, such as one covered by the **Air Travel Organiser's Licence** (ATOL; www.atol.org.uk) scheme in the UK. If you have doubts about the service provider, at the very least call the airline and confirm that your booking has been made.

Round-the-world tickets can be a good option for getting to Australia, and Perth is an easy inclusion on these tickets.

Land

WA's main population centres are isolated from the rest of Australia, and interstate travel entails a major sojourn. The nearest state capital to Perth is Adelaide, 2560km away by the shortest road route. To Melbourne it's at least 3280km, Darwin is around 4040km and Sydney 3940km. In spite of the vast distances, you can still drive across the Nullarbor Plain from the eastern states to Perth and then up the Indian Ocean coast and through the Kimberley to Darwin on sealed roads – if you dare.

Bus

The only interstate bus is the daily **Greyhound** (☎1300 473 946; www.greyhound.com.au) service between Darwin and Broome ($335, 23½ hours), via Kununurra, Fitzroy Crossing and Derby. See p261 for more information on Greyhound bus passes and deals.

Car, Motorcycle & Bicycle

No matter which way you look at it and where you're coming from, driving to Perth from any other state is a *very* long journey. But if you've got your own wheels and companions to share the driving and the fuel costs, it's certainly the best way to see the country. Be aware that there are strict quarantine restrictions when crossing the border, so scoff your fruit and vegetables or throw them out before you get there.

See p262 for details of road rules, driving conditions and information on buying and renting vehicles.

Hitching

Hitching is never entirely safe – we don't recommend it. Hitching to or from WA across the Nullarbor is definitely not advisable, as waits of several days are not uncommon.

People looking for travelling companions for the long car journeys to WA from Sydney, Melbourne, Adelaide or Darwin frequently leave notices on boards in hostels and backpacker accommodation.

Train

The only interstate rail link is the famous Indian Pacific, run by **Great Southern Railway** (☎08-8213 4592; www.trainways.com.au), which travels 4352km to Perth from Kalgoorlie (10 hours), Adelaide (two days), Broken Hill (2¼ days) and Sydney (three days). From Port Augusta to Kalgoorlie the seemingly endless crossing of the virtually uninhabited centre takes well over 24 hours, including the 'long straight' on the Nullarbor – at 478km this is

CLIMATE CHANGE & TRAVEL

Every form of transport that relies on carbon-based fuel generates CO_2, the main cause of human-induced climate change. Modern travel is dependent on aeroplanes, which might use less fuel per kilometre per person than most cars but travel much greater distances. The altitude at which aircraft emit gases (including CO_2) and particles also contributes to their climate change impact. Many websites offer 'carbon calculators' that allow people to estimate the carbon emissions generated by their journey and, for those who wish to do so, to offset the impact of the greenhouse gases emitted with contributions to portfolios of climate-friendly initiatives throughout the world. Lonely Planet offsets the carbon footprint of all staff and author travel.

the longest straight stretch of train line in the world. You can take 'whistle-stop' tours of some towns on the way.

One-way adult fares for the full journey are $716 (reclining seat), $1402 (sleeper cabin) and $2008 ('gold service', including meals). Substantial discounts are available off the seat-only price for backpackers, students, children and pensioners.

Cars can be transported between Perth and Sydney or Adelaide. This makes a very good option for those not wishing to drive across the Nullarbor Plain in both directions.

GETTING AROUND

Travelling widely around WA is time-consuming as the distances between key towns are vast (especially in the north).

Air

Unless you have unlimited time and an unlimited thirst for driving, you should consider a flight at some point. There are regular special fares and advance-purchase deals are generally the cheapest.

Airlines Flying Within WA

Airnorth (code TL; ☎1800 627 474; www.airnorth.com.au) Routes include Perth–Kununurra, Karratha–Port Hedland, Karratha–Broome, Port Hedland–Broome and Broome–Kununurra.

Cobham (code NC; ☎1800 105 503; www.cobham.com.au) Flies between Perth and Kambalda.

Golden Eagle (☎08-9172 1777; www.goldeneagleairlines.com) Flies from Broome to Port Hedland, Fitzroy Crossing and Halls Creek.

Qantas (code QF; ☎13 13 13; www.qantas.com.au) Flies Perth to Kalgoorlie, Paraburdoo, Newman, Karratha, Port Hedland and Broome.

Skippers Aviation (code JW; ☎1300 729 924; www.skippers.com.au) Flies three routes in both directions: Perth–Leonora–Laverton, Perth–Wiluna–Leinster, Perth–Mt Magnet–Meekatharra, Perth–Carnarvon, Perth–Geraldton–Carnarvon and Perth–Kalbarri–Monkey Mia

Skywest (code XR; ☎1300 660 088; www.skywest.com.au) The main regional operator; flies to Perth, Albany, Esperance, Kalgoorlie, Geraldton, Exmouth, Karratha, Broome and Kununurra.

Strategic Airlines (code VC; ☎13 53 20; www.flystrategic.com.au) Flies between Perth and Derby.

Virgin Blue (code DJ; ☎13 67 89; www.virginblue.com.au) Flies from Perth to Albany, Esperance, Geraldton, Exmouth, Newman, Karratha, Port Hedland, Christmas Island, Cocos (Keeling) Islands and Broome; and from Broome to Exmouth. Many of these are code-shared with Skywest.

Bicycle

Bicycle helmets are compulsory in WA (and all other states and territories of Australia), as are white front lights and red rear lights for riding at night.

If you're coming specifically to cycle, it makes sense to bring your own bike. Check with your airline for costs and the degree of dismantling/packing required. Within WA you can load your bike onto a bus to skip the boring bits of the country – and we've seen some cyclists in some very unlikely places in WA. Check with bus companies about how the bike needs to be secured, and book ahead to ensure that you and your bike can travel on the same vehicle.

Suffering dehydration is a very real risk in WA and can be life-threatening. It can get very hot in summer, and you should take things slowly until you're used to the heat. Cycling in 35°C-plus temperatures is bearable if you wear a hat and plenty of sunscreen, and drink *lots* of water.

Outback travel needs to be planned thoroughly, with the availability of drinking water the main concern – those isolated water sources (bores, tanks, creeks and the like) shown on your map may be dry or undrinkable, so you can't always depend on them. Also make sure you've got the necessary spare parts and bike-repair knowledge. Check with locals (start at the visitor centres) if you're heading into remote areas, and always let someone know where you're headed before setting off.

Useful contacts for information on touring around WA, including suggested routes, road conditions and cycling maps:

Bicycle Transportation Alliance (☎08-9420 7210; www.btawa.org.au)

Bikes for Australia (www.bfa.asn.au)

Cycle Touring Association of WA (www.ctawa.asn.au)

Bus

WA's bus network could hardly be called comprehensive, but it offers access to substantially more destinations than the railways. All long-distance buses are modern and well equipped with air-con, toilets and videos.

Main Companies

Greyhound (☎1300 473 946; www.greyhound.com.au) If you're heading north of Geraldton, Greyhound is the main provider. It has services from Perth to Broome via Geraldton, Carnarvon, Karratha and Port Hedland; and from Broome to Darwin, via the Great Northern Highway. Multiday passes allow you to take your time along the route.

Integrity Coach Lines (☎1800 226 339; www.integritycoachlines.com.au) Weekly buses between Perth and Port Hedland.

South West Coach Lines (☎08-9261 7600; www.veoliatransportwa.com.au) Runs services from Perth to all the major towns in the southwest; this is your best choice for the Margaret River wine region.

Transwa (☎1300 662 205; www.transwa.wa.gov.au) The state government's transport service, operating mainly in the southern half of the state. Main routes include Perth–Augusta, Perth–Pemberton, Perth–Albany (three different routes), Perth–Esperance (two routes), Albany–Esperance, Kalgoorlie–Esperance, Perth–Geraldton (three routes) and Geraldton–Meekatharra.

Car & Motorcycle

There is no doubt that travelling by vehicle is the best option in WA, as it gives you the freedom to explore off the beaten track. With several people travelling together, costs can be contained and, provided that you don't have any major mechanical problems, there are many benefits.

Motorcycles are another popular way of getting around. The climate is good for bikes for much of the year, and the many small trails from the road into the bush lead to perfect spots to spend the night. Bringing your own motorcycle into Australia will entail an expensive shipping exercise, valid registration in the country of origin and a Carnet de Passages en Douanes. This is an internationally recognised customs document that allows the holder to import their vehicle without paying customs duty or taxes. To get one, apply to a motoring organisation/association in your home country. You'll also need a rider's licence and a helmet. A fuel range of 350km will cover fuel stops up the centre and on Hwy 1 around the continent. The long, open roads are really made for large-capacity machines above 750cc, which Australians prefer once they outgrow their 250cc learner restrictions.

The **Royal Automobile Club** (RAC; ☎13 17 03; www.rac.com.au) has lots of useful advice on state-wide motoring, including road safety, local regulations and buying/selling a car. It also offers car insurance to its members, and membership can get you discounts on car rentals and some motel accommodation.

Driving Licence

You can use your own home country's driving licence in WA for up to three months, as long as it carries your photo for identification and is in English. Alternatively, arrange an International Driving Permit (IDP) from your home country's automobile association and carry it along with your licence.

Fuel

Fuel (predominantly unleaded and diesel) is available from service stations sporting the well-known international brand names. liquefied petroleum gas (LPG) is not always stocked at more remote roadhouses – if your car runs on gas it's safer to have dual fuel capacity.

Prices vary wildly in WA, even between stations in Perth. At the time of research we saw unleaded petrol (ULP) being sold for anything between $1.14/L and $1.23/L. By the time you get to Margaret River you're unlikely to find anything less than $1.30/L, while in the more remote areas expect to pay from $1.45/L to $1.70/L. Fuel prices are a major topic of discussion in WA, with the high prices having a significant effect on tourism in the outback. For up-to-date fuel prices across WA, visit the government fuel-watch website (www.fuelwatch.wa.gov.au).

Distances between fill-ups can be long in the outback but there are only a handful of tracks where you'll require a long-range fuel tank or need to use jerry cans. However, if you are doing some back-road explorations, always calculate your fuel consumption, plan accordingly and always carry a spare jerry can or two. Keep in mind that most small-town service stations are only open from 6am to 7pm and roadhouses aren't always open 24 hours. On main roads there'll be a small town or roadhouse roughly every 150km to 200km or so.

Hire

Competition between car-rental companies in Australia is fierce, so rates tend to be variable and lots of special deals come and go. The main thing to remember when assessing your options is distance – if you want to travel widely, you need to weigh up the price difference between an unlimited kilometres deal and one that offers a set number of kilometres free with a fee per kilometre over that set number.

As well as the big firms, there are numerous local firms. These are almost always cheaper than the big operators – sometimes half the price – but cheap car hire often comes with restrictions on how far you can take the vehicle away from the rental centre.

The big firms sometimes offer one-way rentals, but there are a variety of limitations, including a substantial drop-off fee. Ask plenty of questions about this before deciding on one company over another. There are sometimes good deals for taking a car or campervan from Broome, for example, back to Perth.

You must be at least 21 years old to hire from most firms – if you're under 25 you may only be able to hire a small car or have to pay a surcharge. It's cheaper if you rent for a week or more and there are often low-season and weekend discounts. Credit cards are the usual payment method.

Renting a 4WD enables you to safely tackle routes off the beaten track and get out to some of the natural wonders that most travellers miss in a conventional vehicle. Always check the insurance conditions carefully, especially the excess, as they can be onerous. Even for a 4WD, the insurance offered by most companies does not cover damage caused when travelling 'off-road', which basically means anything that is not a maintained bitumen or dirt road.

Major companies all have offices or agents in Perth and larger centres.

Avis (☎13 63 33; www.avis.com.au)

Backpacker Campervan & Car Rentals (☎1800 670 232; www.backpackercampervans.com)

Backpacker Car Rentals (☎08-9430 8869; www.backpackercarrentals.com.au) Cheap local agency, starting from $110 per week.

Bayswater Car Rental (☎08-9325 1000; www.bayswatercarrental.com.au) Excellent local company with four branches in Perth and Fremantle.

Britz Rentals (☎1800 331 454; www.britz.com) Hires fully equipped 4WDs fitted out as campervans, which are commonplace on northern roads. Britz has offices in all the state capitals, as well as Perth and Broome, so one-way rentals are possible.

Budget (☎1300 362 848; www.budget.com.au)

Campabout Oz (☎08-9477 2121; www.campaboutoz.com.au) Campervans, 4WDs and motorbikes.

Hertz (☎13 30 39; www.hertz.com.au)

Thrifty (☎1300 367 227; www.thrifty.com.au)

Wicked Campers (☎1800 246 869; www.wickedcampers.com.au) Notable for the lurid colour schemes of their vehicles.

Insurance

In Australia, third-party personal injury insurance is always included in the vehicle registration cost. This ensures that every registered vehicle carries at least minimum insurance. You'd be wise to extend that minimum to at least third-party property insurance as well – minor collisions with other vehicles can be surprisingly expensive.

When it comes to hire cars, it pays to know exactly what your liability is in the event of an accident. Rather than risk paying out thousands of dollars if you do have an accident, you can take out your own comprehensive insurance on the car, or (the usual option) pay an additional daily amount to the rental company for an 'insurance excess reduction' policy. This brings the amount of excess you must pay in the event of an accident down from between $2000 and $5000 to a few hundred dollars.

Be aware that if you're travelling on dirt roads you may not be covered by insurance. Also, most companies' insurance won't cover the cost of damage to glass (including the windscreen) or tyres. Always read the small print.

4WD DRIVING TIPS

We don't need to see more 4WDs on tow trucks; the victims of a dirt-road rollover, a poorly judged river crossing, or coming to grief when meeting the native fauna on the road. Here are some tips to help keep you from riding upfront in a tow truck:

» Before heading off-road, check the road conditions at www.mainroads.wa.gov.au.

» Recheck road conditions at each visitor centre you come across – they can change quickly.

» Let people know where you're going, what route you're taking and how long you'll be gone.

» Don't drive at night: it's safer to finish in the mid-afternoon to avoid wildlife.

» Avoid sudden changes in direction – 4WDs have a much higher centre of gravity than cars.

» On sand tracks, reduce tyre pressure to 140kpa (20psi) and don't forget to reinflate your tyres once you're back on the tarmac.

» When driving on corrugated tracks, note that while there is a 'sweet spot' speed where you feel the corrugations less, it's often too fast to negotiate a corner – and rollovers often happen because of this.

» When crossing rivers and creeks, always walk across first to check the depth – unless you're in saltwater crocodile territory, of course!

Purchase

If you're planning a stay of several months that involves lots of driving, buying a second-hand car will be much cheaper than renting. But remember that reliability is all-important. Breaking down in the outback is very inconvenient (and potentially dangerous) – the nearest mechanic can be a very expensive tow-truck ride away!

You'll probably get any car cheaper by buying privately through the newspaper (try Saturday's *West Australian*) rather than through a car dealer. Buying through a dealer does have the advantage of some sort of guarantee, but this is not much use if you're buying a car in Perth for a trip to Broome.

When you come to buy or sell a car, there are local regulations to be complied with. In WA a car has to have a compulsory safety check and obtain a Road Worthiness Certificate (RWC) before it can be registered in the new owner's name – usually the seller will indicate whether the car already has a RWC. Stamp duty has to be paid when you buy a car; as this is based on the purchase price, it's not unknown for the buyer and the seller to agree privately to understate the price.

To avoid buying a lemon, you might consider forking out some extra money for a vehicle appraisal before purchase. The **RAC** (☎13 17 03; www.rac.com.au) offers this kind of check in Perth and other large WA centres for around $169/185 for members/nonmembers; it also offers extensive advice on buying and selling cars on its website.

The beginning of winter (June) is a good time to start looking for a used motorbike. Local newspapers and the bike-related press have classified advertisement sections.

Fremantle has a number of second-hand car yards, including a cluster in North Fremantle on the Stirling Hwy, while in Perth there's the **Traveller's Auto Barn** (☎1800 674 374; www.travellers-autobarn.com.au; 365 Newcastle St, Northbridge).

Road Conditions

This huge state is not crisscrossed by multilane highways; there's not enough traffic and the distances are simply too great to justify them. All the main routes are well surfaced and have two lanes, but you don't have to get very far off the beaten track to find yourself on unsealed roads. Anybody who sets out to see the state in reasonable detail will have to expect to do some dirt-road travelling. A 2WD car can cope with the major ones, but if you want to do some serious exploration, you'd better plan on having a 4WD.

Driving on unsealed roads requires special care – a car will perform differently when braking and turning on dirt. Under no circumstances should you exceed 80km/h on dirt roads; if you go faster you will not have enough time to respond to a sharp turn, stock on the road, or an unmarked gate or cattle grid. So take it easy and take time to see the sights.

It's important to note that when it rains, some roads flood. Flooding is a real problem up north because of cyclonic storms. Exercise extreme caution at wet times, especially at the frequent yellow 'Floodway' signs. If you come to a stretch of water and you're not sure of the depth or what could lie beneath it, pull up at the side of the road and walk through it (excluding known saltwater crocodile areas, such as the Pentecost River crossing on the Gibb River Rd!). Even on major highways, if it has been raining you can sometimes be driving through 30cm or more of water for hundreds of metres at a time.

Mainroads (☎13 81 38; www.mainroads.wa.gov.au) provides statewide road-condition reports, updated daily (and more frequently if necessary).

Road Hazards

Travelling by car within WA means sometimes having to pass road trains. These articulated trucks and their loads (consisting of two or more trailers) can be up to 53.5m long, 2.5m wide and travel at around 100km/h. Overtaking them is tricky – once you commit to passing there's no going back. Exercise caution and pick your time, but don't get timid mid-manoeuvre. Also, remember that it is much harder for the truck driver to control their giant-sized vehicle than it is for you to control your car.

One thing you have to adjust to in WA is the enormous distances, which can lead to dangerous levels of driver fatigue. Stop and rest every two hours or so – do some exercise, change drivers or have a coffee. The major routes have rest areas and many roadhouses offer free coffee for drivers; ask for maps from the RAC that indicate rest stops.

Cattle, emus and kangaroos are common hazards on country roads, and a collision is likely to kill the animal and cause serious damage to your vehicle. Kangaroos are most active around dawn and dusk, and they travel in groups. If at all possible you should plan your travel to avoid these times of the day. If you see one hopping across the road in front of you, slow right down – its friends are probably just behind it.

It's important to keep a safe distance behind the vehicle in front, in case it hits an animal or has to slow down suddenly. If an animal runs out in front of you, brake if you can, but don't swerve unless it is safe to do so. You're likely to survive a collision with an emu better than a collision with a tree or another vehicle.

Road Rules

Driving in WA holds few surprises, other than those that hop out in front of your vehicle. Cars are driven on the left-hand side of the road (as they are in the rest of Australia). An important road rule is 'give way to the right' – if an intersection is unmarked, you must give way to vehicles entering the intersection from your right.

The speed limit in urban areas is generally 60km/h, unless signposted otherwise. The state speed limit is 110km/h, applicable to all roads in non-built-up areas, unless otherwise indicated. The police have radar speed traps and speed cameras and are very fond of using them in carefully hidden locations.

Oncoming drivers who flash their lights at you may be giving you a warning of a speed camera ahead – or they may be telling you that your headlights are not on. Whatever the circumstance, it's polite to wave back if someone does this. Try not to get caught flashing your lights yourself, since it's illegal.

Seat belts are compulsory – you'll be fined if you don't use them. Children must be strapped into an approved safety seat. Talking on a hand-held mobile phone while driving is illegal.

Drink-driving is a serious problem in WA, especially in country areas. Random breath tests are used in an effort to reduce the road toll. If you're caught driving with a blood-alcohol level of more than 0.05%, be prepared for a hefty fine, a court appearance and the loss of your licence.

Local Transport

Perth has an efficient, fully integrated public transport system called **Transperth** (☎13 62 13; www.transperth.wa.gov.au) that covers public buses, trains and ferries in a large area that reaches south to include Fremantle, Rockingham and Mandurah. Some of the larger regional centres, such as Bunbury, Busselton and Albany, have limited local bus services.

Taxis are available in most of the larger towns, where locals are reliant on them as a means of beating the booze buses and police patrols.

Tours

If you don't feel like travelling solo or you crave a hassle-free holiday where everything is organised for you, there are dozens of tours throughout WA to suit all tastes and budgets. The hop-on hop-off bus options are a particularly popular way for travellers to get around in a fun, relaxed atmosphere. Some adventure tours include serious 4WD safaris, taking travellers to places that they simply couldn't get to on their own without large amounts of expensive equipment.

The WA Visitor Centre (p75) in Perth has a wide selection of brochures and suggestions for tours all over the state. The tours listed here are only a selection of what's available (see the Tour sections in the On the Road chapters for more extensive lists of local tours). Prices given are rates per person in twin share; there's usually an extra supplement for single accommodation. Students and YHA members often get a discount.

AAT Kings Australian Tours (☎1300 228 546; www.aatkings.com.au) A long-established and professional outfit offering a wide range of fully escorted bus trips and 4WD adventures. At the time of writing they offered 17 tours in WA, ranging from a five-day Perth to Monkey Mia trip ($1610) to a 20-day Perth to Darwin 'West Coast Adventure' ($7550).

Active Safaris (☎1800 068 886; www.activesafaris.com.au) Adventure tour company running small-group 4WD safaris leaving from Perth, Exmouth and Broome. They range from a day trip from Perth to the Pinnacles ($149) to a 24-day Perth to Darwin and Kakadu safari ($3968).

Australian Adventure Travel (☎1800 621 625; www.safaris.net.au) Offers 4WD bus tours from Perth, Exmouth, Broome and Kununurra, ranging from a one-day Perth to Pinnacles trip ($165) to a 14-day Kimberley Explorer tour ($3495), departing from Broome.

Planet Perth Tours (☎08-8132 8294; www.planettours.com.au) Fast-paced budget minibus tours departing from Perth and heading to popular spots such as the southwest ($375, three days), Monkey Mia ($435, four days), Coral Bay ($490, four days) and Broome ($1125, nine days).

Red Earth Safaris (☎08-9279 9011; www.redearthsafaris.com.au) Operates a six-day Perth to Exmouth minibus tour ($685) with a two-day return trip ($200).

Western Xposure (☎08-9414 8423; www.westernxposure.com.au) Popular operator running safari trucks with a big selection of tours, including a 14-day Perth to Broome itinerary ($1845).

Train

The state's internal rail network, operated by **Transwa** (☎1300 662 205; www.transwa.wa.gov.au), is limited to the *Prospector* (Perth to Kalgoorlie); the *AvonLink* (Perth to Northam); and the *Australind* (Perth to Bunbury). Transperth's local train network reaches as far south as Mandurah.

behind the scenes

SEND US YOUR FEEDBACK

We love to hear from travellers – your comments keep us on our toes and help make our books better. Our well-travelled team reads every word on what you loved or loathed about this book. Although we cannot reply individually to postal submissions, we always guarantee that your feedback goes straight to the appropriate authors, in time for the next edition. Each person who sends us information is thanked in the next edition – and the most useful submissions are rewarded with a free book.

Visit **lonelyplanet.com/contact** to submit your updates and suggestions or to ask for help. Our award-winning website also features inspirational travel stories, news and discussions.

Note: We may edit, reproduce and incorporate your comments in Lonely Planet products such as guidebooks, websites and digital products, so let us know if you don't want your comments reproduced or your name acknowledged. For a copy of our privacy policy visit lonelyplanet.com/privacy.

OUR READERS

Many thanks to the travellers who used the last edition and wrote to us with helpful hints, useful advice and interesting anecdotes:

Patricia Aylward, Ron Bailey, Mika Bogerd, Helga Campbell-Waite, Lesley Carnogursky, Stephanie Carpenter, Kaung Chiau Lew, Emanuele Diamanti, Chris Edwards, Mick Garton, John Haggett, Andrew Hunt, Britta Janssen, Alex Jasper, Emma Jones, Bradley Jordan, Mieke Julicher, Jane Laudrup, Michael Levene, Derek Lycke, Tracey Marsich, Anders Ohman, Petra O'Neill, Dan Osborn, Philippe Rivoal, Tom Roberts, Julie Ross, Jean-Marc Ryckebusch, Simone Sala, Salina, Charlie Schultz, Mandy Smrcek, Ina Stenzel, Amelia Twiss

AUTHOR THANKS

Peter Dragicevich

To all the people I met on the road who were so gracious with their time and advice – particularly the staff at the visitor centres – thanks so much. A big thank you to Chris Oughton and Carol Adams for your hospitality, and to Igor Mihajlovic for all the tips and for showing me such a good time. Best wishes to all my uncles, aunties and cousins on the Erceg side – it was great to meet you all and I look forward to doing so again.

Rebecca Chau

Thanks: Ben Basell, Christina Chau, Craig Comrie, Simon Davis, Peter Dragicevich, Matt Forbes, Cameron Haskell, Rob Hildebrand, Maryanne Netto, Matt Trevenen, Steve Waters.

Steve Waters

Thanks to Neville, Phil and Darren, Gibb tyre repairers extraordinaire, Tim and Barry at Mt House for the same, Kimberly and your mum for the Priscilla moment, Gary and Kerry for wine and conversation, Jane and Lachie at Bidgemia for the avgas, Paul and Colleen for dinner and hospitality, Trace and Heath, Brodie, Abbidene, Meika and Kaeghan for curries and sorbets, Roz and Megan for caretaking, Sian for support and last but not least Captain Bartos for El Kimbo.

ACKNOWLEDGMENTS

Climate map data adapted from Peel MC, Finlayson BL & McMahon TA (2007) 'Updated World Map of the Köppen-Geiger Climate Classification', *Hydrology and Earth System Sciences*, 11, 163344.

Cover photograph: William Bay National Park, Western Australia, Orien Harvey / Lonely Planet Images ©

Many of the images in this guide are available for licensing from Lonely Planet Images: www.lonelyplanetimages.com.

THIS BOOK

This is the 6th incarnation of Lonely Planet's Western Australia guide. The 1st edition was written in 1995 by one intrepid author, Jeff Williams. Jeff also wrote the 2nd edition. Research on the 3rd edition was led by Sally Webb; the 4th by Susie Ashworth; and Terry Carter and Lara Dunston wrote the 5th edition, assisted by Rebecca Chau and Virginia Jealous. Peter Dragicevich was the coordinating author on this edition, joined by coauthors Rebecca Chau and Steve Waters. Tim Flannery wrote the Environment chapter and Michael Cathcart wrote the History chapter, with additions and updates in both chapters added by Rebecca Chau.

Commissioning Editor Maryanne Netto

Coordinating Editors Katie O'Connell, Alison Ridgway

Coordinating Cartographer Peter Shields

Coordinating Layout Designer Nicholas Colicchia

Managing Editor Liz Heynes

Managing Cartographer David Connolly

Managing Layout Designers Jane Hart, Celia Wood

Assisting Editors Alice Barker, Trent Holden, Gabrielle Innes, Evan Jones, Anne Mulvaney, Kristin Odijk, Jeanette Wall

Assisting Cartographers Anita Banh, Katalin Dadi-Racz, Valentina Kremenchutskaya, Andy Rojas, Tom Webster

Cover Research Naomi Parker

Internal Image Research Rebecca Skinner

Thanks to Sasha Baskett, Helen Christinis, Laura Jane, Yvonne Kirk, Lisa Knights, Anna Metcalfe, Wayne Murphy, Susan Paterson, Julie Sheridan, Laura Stansfeld, Juan Winata

index

000 Map pages
000 Photo pages

I

J

K

L

M

N

000 Map pages
000 Photo pages

V

W

Y

Z

how to use this book

These symbols will help you find the listings you want:

- Sights
- Activities
- Courses
- Tours
- Festivals & Events
- Sleeping
- Eating
- Drinking
- Entertainment
- Shopping
- Information/ Transport

These symbols give you the vital information for each listing:

- Telephone Numbers
- Opening Hours
- Parking
- Nonsmoking
- Air-Conditioning
- Internet Access
- Wi-Fi Access
- Swimming Pool
- Vegetarian Selection
- English-Language Menu
- Family-Friendly
- Pet-Friendly
- Bus
- Ferry
- Metro
- Subway
- London Tube
- Tram
- Train

Reviews are organised by author preference.

Look out for these icons:

TOP CHOICE Our author's recommendation

FREE No payment required

A green or sustainable option

Our authors have nominated these places as demonstrating a strong commitment to sustainability – for example by supporting local communities and producers, operating in an environmentally friendly way, or supporting conservation projects.

Map Legend

Sights

- Beach
- Buddhist
- Castle
- Christian
- Hindu
- Islamic
- Jewish
- Monument
- Museum/Gallery
- Ruin
- Winery/Vineyard
- Zoo
- Other Sight

Activities, Courses & Tours

- Diving/Snorkelling
- Canoeing/Kayaking
- Skiing
- Surfing
- Swimming/Pool
- Walking
- Windsurfing
- Other Activity/ Course/Tour

Sleeping

- Sleeping
- Camping

Eating

- Eating

Drinking

- Drinking
- Cafe

Entertainment

- Entertainment

Shopping

- Shopping

Information

- Post Office
- Tourist Information

Transport

- Airport
- Border Crossing
- Bus
- Cable Car/ Funicular
- Cycling
- Ferry
- Metro
- Monorail
- Parking
- S-Bahn
- Taxi
- Train/Railway
- Tram
- Tube Station
- U-Bahn
- Other Transport

Routes

- Tollway
- Freeway
- Primary
- Secondary
- Tertiary
- Lane
- Unsealed Road
- Plaza/Mall
- Steps
- Tunnel
- Pedestrian Overpass
- Walking Tour
- Walking Tour Detour
- Path

Boundaries

- International
- State/Province
- Disputed
- Regional/Suburb
- Marine Park
- Cliff
- Wall

Population

- Capital (National)
- Capital (State/Province)
- City/Large Town
- Town/Village

Geographic

- Hut/Shelter
- Lighthouse
- Lookout
- Mountain/Volcano
- Oasis
- Park
- Pass
- Picnic Area
- Waterfall

Hydrography

- River/Creek
- Intermittent River
- Swamp/Mangrove
- Reef
- Canal
- Water
- Dry/Salt/ Intermittent Lake
- Glacier

Areas

- Beach/Desert
- Cemetery (Christian)
- Cemetery (Other)
- Park/Forest
- Sportsground
- Sight (Building)
- Top Sight (Building)

Contributing Authors

Dr Tim Flannery wrote the Environment chapter. Tim is a scientist, explorer and writer. He has written several award-winning books including *The Future Eaters*, *Throwim Way Leg* and *The Weather Makers*. He lives in Sydney where he is a professor in the faculty of science at Macquarie University.

Dr Michael Cathcart wrote the History chapter. Michael teaches history at the Australian Centre, the University of Melbourne. He is well known as a broadcaster on ABC Radio National and has presented history programs on ABC TV. His most recent book is *The Water Dreamers* (2009), a history of how water shaped the history of Australia.

OUR STORY

A beat-up old car, a few dollars in the pocket and a sense of adventure. In 1972 that's all Tony and Maureen Wheeler needed for the trip of a lifetime – across Europe and Asia overland to Australia. It took several months, and at the end – broke but inspired – they sat at their kitchen table writing and stapling together their first travel guide, *Across Asia on the Cheap*. Within a week they'd sold 1500 copies. Lonely Planet was born.

Today, Lonely Planet has offices in Melbourne, London and Oakland, with more than 600 staff and writers. We share Tony's belief that 'a great guidebook should do three things: inform, educate and amuse'.

OUR WRITERS

Peter Dragicevich

Coordinating Author, Perth & Fremantle, Around Perth, Margaret River & the Southwest, South Coast If his great-grandfather Jure Dragicevich hadn't died in mysterious circumstances beneath a train in Kalgoorlie in 1913, Peter may have been born Western Australian. Instead, the family continued on to New Zealand, where Peter lived until his newspaper career took him to Australia in the late 1990s. He's subsequently worked on more than 20 Lonely Planet titles, including *Sydney* and *East Coast Australia*. Co-authoring *Perth & West Coast Australia* takes him one step closer to his goal of circumnavigating the continent, one book at a time. It also provided an opportunity to visit his great-grandfather's grave in a dusty corner of Kalgoorlie cemetery, connect with cousins in Perth, Wellard and Albany, and ponder once again the great waves of immigration that led people from far-flung corners of the globe to this vast, unrelenting land.

Read more about Peter at:
lonelyplanet.com/members/peterdragicevich

Rebecca Chau

Rebecca first started learning about Western Australia quite a while ago: back in the 80s, when she started school in Albany, in the south of the state. After growing up in this land crinkled by beaches and coveted by whales, she moved to Perth, and later became a commissioning editor for Lonely Planet in Melbourne. Also an author on the previous edition of this guide, she heads back to WA a couple of times a year. Perth's City Beach is her favourite pocket of sand and sea.

Steve Waters

Around Perth, Monkey Mia & the Central Coast, Coral Bay & the Pilbara, Broome & Around

Steve's first big trip through WA in a battered Torana included sleeping in the Pinnacles car park, cooking up fresh fish over a camp stove and trying to traverse the Kimberley during the Wet. On subsequent visits he chased the state's extremities in Karijini and Edel Land, and slept in the Pinnacles car park. This trip covered 17,600kms, five blown tyres, four lost hats, three pairs of wrecked sunglasses and a close shave with an emu as he traversed the coast from Kalumburu to Cervantes and everywhere in between. Steve's also authored the West Sumatra chapter of Lonely Planet's *Indonesia*, and while not on the road, can be found in LP's Melbourne office playing with databases.

Published by Lonely Planet Publications Pty Ltd
ABN 36 005 607 983
6th edition – July 2011
ISBN 978 1 74179 046 7

10 9 8 7 6 5 4 3 2 1
Printed in China